T. Patrick O'Neill
7 Erie Manor Lane
Henrietta, NY 14467
(716) 334-5913

FACES OF AMERICA

A History of the United States

ROLAND M. SMITH ★ EUGENE D. LEVY ★ MARTHA H. BROWN

HARPER & ROW, PUBLISHERS, INC.
New York   Philadelphia   San Francisco   London
1817

ABOUT THE AUTHORS

ROLAND M. SMITH

Dr. Roland Smith has taught junior and senior high school and has served as a consultant to a number of public school districts and Catholic diocesan school systems as well as to the Pennsylvania Department of Education. He is the author of many articles and a recipient of numerous awards and fellowships, including a Ford Foundation Faculty Research Grant and a Social Science Research Council Grant. For several years a professor of history at Carnegie-Mellon University, he is currently Associate Provost of Academic Affairs and Executive Director of the Office of Academic Affairs.

EUGENE D. LEVY

Dr. Eugene Levy is author of the biography *James Weldon Johnson: Black Leader, Black Voice* and co-author of a high school text of readings on ethnicity in American history and of a college text of readings in American history. Dr. Levy is currently Associate Professor of History, the Director of Undergraduate Studies in History, and Chairperson, University Affirmative Action Committee at Carnegie-Mellon University. He is also consultant to the Undergraduate History Program at Morgan State University.

MARTHA H. BROWN

Dr. Martha Brown has taught social studies on the elementary and junior high school levels. At Central Michigan University, where she is Associate Professor of History, she teaches courses in Women in America and Development of Black Culture, among others, and is Chairperson of the Black Culture Committee. She has received numerous honors including a Ford Foundation Fellowship for Ethnic Studies and a National Endowment for the Humanities Research Grant.

Maps by General Cartography, Inc.

Charts and Graphs by Felix Cooper

Art for Section Openers by Jerry Pinkney

Printed in the United States of America   828384RRD98765432

ISBN-0397-40260-0

ABOUT THE COVER What does the title *Faces of America* mean to you? Does it mean people? places? events? ideals? Start at the top left corner of the back cover: 1. Jefferson Memorial; 2. San Francisco's Chinatown; 3. French Quarter of New Orleans; 4. Northwest Coast totem pole; 5. Fishermen's Memorial, Glouces- ter, Massachusetts; 6. Pioneers Monument, Minneapolis; 7. Mount Rushmore showing George Washington, Thomas Jefferson, Theodore Roosevelt, Abraham Lincoln; 8. Independence Hall; 9. Arches National Park, Utah; 10. Booker T. Washington, *Lifting the Veil of Ignorance*, Tuskegee Institute, Alabama; 11. Sacajawea, Bismarck, North Dakota; 12. mission, Taos, New Mexico; 13. Paul Revere and Old North Church, Boston; 14. Washington Monument seen through the columns of the Lincoln Memorial; 15. Statue of Liberty. What other faces of our nation's history can you think of?

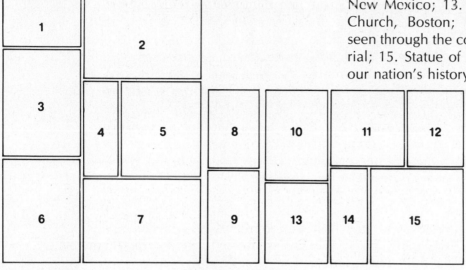

ABOUT THE SECTION OPENER *Faces of America* is divided into six sections paralleling the major time periods of our nation's history: Section I, Exploring and Colonizing; Section II, Building a New Nation; Section III, The Nation Comes of Age; Section IV, Nation in Conflict; Section V, Big Business and World Power; Section VI, Modern America. To help you identify the themes of the sections and some of the important people, we have designed a special section opener. As you begin Section I, you will see that only the top left corner is in color. As you move from one time period to the next, you will find another section in color until the entire picture is filled in.

TO THE READER

We, the authors of *Faces of America*, wrote this program because as teachers we could not find a text that did what we believed a United States history text should do. We wanted a text that would help students understand our nation's rich heritage and, at the same time, develop certain skills. In response to this need, we decided to write *Faces of America: A History of the United States*. We set three closely related goals that our text should help you, as students of U.S. history, reach.

The first goal of *Faces of America* is to tell the colorful story of our past. As historians, we enjoy studying the past and relating it to the present and the future. The way of life of the first Americans, the years of European exploration, and the events leading to the American Revolution are interesting and exciting to us. We hope that you, too, will find these stories and the later events presented in *Faces of America* informative and enjoyable. Further, we hope that as you read you will become aware of some of the ways that the past affects the present and the future.

The second goal of *Faces of America* is to make you aware of the many different peoples who have built our country. The American people have come from many backgrounds and have brought with them their languages, customs, traditions, and values. These are now part of our country. For almost 500 years, Native Americans, Europeans, Africans, Latin Americans, Asians, and Middle Easterners have lived and worked together. Unfortunately, they sometimes have fought one another as well. But this, too, is a part of our history. We believe that knowledge of the many cultures that make up the U.S. will help you to a greater understanding and appreciation of all the peoples who have contributed to our nation's development.

Finally, we hope *Faces of America* will help you to develop a wide range of skills. Social studies skills; reading, communication, and study skills; interaction skills; and thinking skills are all valuable tools that you can learn and practice by using *Faces of America*. By seeing how people of the past responded to life situations, you can gain insights into your own life decisions. By learning how to find and use information for decision making, you will be better able to make your own choices for your future and the future of your country.

We, the authors, believe *Faces of America* will lead you to master our three goals. We believe that the text will help you develop your interest in social studies, increase your understanding of yourself and others, and help you become responsible citizens. We also hope that you will enjoy reading *Faces of America* as much as we enjoyed writing it.

ROLAND M. SMITH • EUGENE D. LEVY • MARTHA H. BROWN

CONTENTS

SKILLS

TIME LINES

MAPS

CHARTS AND GRAPHS

TABLES

HOW TO USE THIS BOOK

The authors and editors of *Faces of America* wanted to create a book that would be interesting and enjoyable to read as well as easy for you, the student, to follow. As a result, they designed a number of special features to explain what each chapter is about, to make skill material easy to find, and to help you recognize important ideas. The illustrations on these two pages are examples of these features. Each briefly describes the feature and how it will help you. This book also includes the Declaration of Independence and the Constitution, on blue-tabbed pages for easy reference. Photo essays show you the art and culture of various historical periods. Military history is explained through map and picture essays. Charts and graphs appear throughout to explain social, political, and economic ideas. The many tables provide short, clear summaries of events. The Glossary lists the Social Studies Vocabulary in alphabetical order. Tables of Presidents and Vice-Presidents and important information about the states are also included.

LOOKING AHEAD

This chapter describes Spanish life in what is now the U.S. from the early 1600s to the Revolutionary War. You will learn how the Spanish lived, worked, played, and educated their children. After you study this chapter, you will be able to:

- locate the Spanish on a map of what is now the U.S.
- describe mission life.
- explain how the people of the towns and farms depended on each other.
- identify the four social classes among the Spanish in the Southwest.
- ★ describe a secondary source.

Social Studies Vocabulary

secondary source   creole   mestizo

Words and Terms

adobe   plaza   formal education

LOOKING BACK

1. Use the map to locate and list the boundaries in the 1700s of Spanish territory in what is now the U.S.
2. Write a paragraph describing life at a Spanish mission for a Native American. You will be making generalizations when you write your answer, because there were probably exceptions to this general pattern.
3. How did each of the following depend on the other two groups: **a.** craftworkers? **b.** merchants? **c.** farmers?
4. List the four social classes of Spanish America and who made up each class. As you learned on page 137, devices can help you recall information. Make up a device to help you recall the names of these four social classes.
★ 5. **a.** Define a secondary source. **b.** How is it different from a primary source?

Each chapter begins with Looking Ahead. The first part summarizes the main ideas of the chapter. The second part lists objectives, or goals, to achieve by studying the chapter and answering the questions in Looking Back. If you will notice, the questions in Looking Back ask about the material in the objectives and are in the same order as the objectives. If you answer the questions correctly, you will have learned what is important in the chapter. The blue star next to an objective shows that the chapter is teaching a particular skill. Under the objectives are listed Social Studies Vocabulary and important People, Places, Events, and Words and Terms. By reading Looking Ahead before you read the chapter, you will discover the important items to look for and remember as you read.

Faces of America helps you build skills with maps, charts, graphs, tables, cartoons, paintings, and photographs. It also builds skills in reading, studying, writing, and speaking about social studies material. Wherever the authors want to tell you about a particular skill, they use a skill section. Each skill section is marked by blue rules and stars.

★ The map Frontier in 1790 shows **population density.** This is the average number of people living in a given area. The map above shows the average number of people per square mile in the newly formed United States and its territories. The areas of highest population density are usually cities and large towns. **1.** In 1790, which areas—coastal plains, Appalachians, Piedmont, and so on—of the U.S. had the largest populations? **2.** What factors do you think caused this? **3.** Which areas were the least settled? **4.** What factors do you think caused this? **5.** Where was the frontier located in 1790?

BUILDING MAP SKILLS

UNIT III THE AMERICAN REVOLUTION

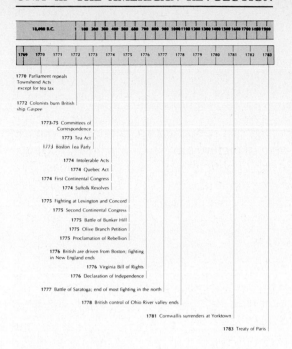

1770 Parliament repeals
Townshend Acts
except for tea tax

1772 Colonists burn British
ship Gaspee

1773-75 Committees of
Correspondence

1773 Tea Act

1773 Boston Tea Party

1774 Intolerable Acts

1774 Quebec Act

1774 First Continental Congress

1774 Suffolk Resolves

1775 Fighting at Lexington and Concord

1775 Second Continental Congress

1775 Battle of Bunker Hill

1775 Olive Branch Petition

1775 Proclamation of Rebellion

1776 British are driven from Boston; fighting
in New England ends

1776 Virginia Bill of Rights

1776 Declaration of Independence

1777 Battle of Saratoga; end of most fighting in the north

1778 British control of Ohio River valley ends

1781 Cornwallis surrenders at Yorktown

1783 Treaty of Paris

ernments in the world. A **constitutional government** is one in which law limits the power of the government. Many people in the 1780s did not believe a government built on such a constitution would last.

BASIC PRINCIPLES

Almost 200 years have passed since the writing of the Constitution. In these years, Americans have come to see that the Constitution is based on four principles. These are federalism, the separation of powers, the rights of individuals, and the adaptability of the Constitution to meet the needs of the times.

principle (PRIN-suh-puhl): basic rule

Each unit begins with a time line to show not only important events but also the amount of time it took for the events to happen. For this reason, the time line has two bars. The top bar shows the length of time that people have been living in what is now the United States. The second bar is the amount of time it took for the events in the unit to happen. Sometimes the second bar shows 100 years and sometimes as few as 15. By comparing the time lines of various units, you will be able to see how quickly or slowly change has taken place.

The Social Studies Vocabulary are words you should know as you study American history. The first time you meet such a term it is in dark type and is defined in the text. The words in the margin are called Vocabulary Builders. They are words you might not know but will probably read or hear in daily life. They are defined in the margin. Phonetic pronunciations are used with these and other words throughout the text to help you learn to say difficult words. A key to the pronunciation system is given on page 709.

PRACTICING YOUR SKILLS

What If . . . You have just read about the natural environment colonists found in New Mexico and in the Southern colonies. **What if** the climate and geography of New Mexico had been more like the natural environment of the Southern colonies? What effects might that have had on the economy, population, and growth of New Mexico?

Discussing Most people would agree with the authors' view that the early colonies had great social mobility. Did they really? Was social mobility limited in the English colonies by religion and education, if not by wealth?

Mapping, Researching, Writing
1. In Life in America: The Land, you read about land use and used a land use map of the U.S. Reread Chapter 3 of this unit and then draw a land use map showing the economic activities of each British colony. Be sure your map has a legend.
2. Today, many U.S. cities have some of the same or similar problems that colonial cities had. For example, cars have replaced coaches, but traffic jams still happen. Scan the section Growth of Towns and Cities in Chapter 3 and list the problems that existed. Read a daily newspaper or a weekly newsmagazine for articles about the problems of modern cities. Are the problems of modern cities the same as or different than those of colonial cities? Answer in a paragraph.
3. Research folk art in the colonies and make a bulletin board display of colonial folk art similar to the art on pages 176-177.

★ **Building Study Skills** Activity 2 above asks you to scan a section in the text. **Scanning** means to look over a piece of reading matter very quickly to find particular information. You use this skill when you look for a name in the telephone book, a chapter in a table of contents, or a topic in an index. Here are some tips to help you scan effectively.

- Let your eyes run rapidly down the page. Look for clues like capital letters, proper names, numerals, and key words.
- Keep in mind what you are searching for. Your objective is not to understand every word but to look for certain words.

At the end of each unit, the Practicing Your Skills page provides suggestions for reports, debates, discussions, and other activities to expand your understanding of the unit: The section called Exploring suggests activities based on your own state's or community's role in the history you have just studied. A bibliography for the unit as well as tips and activities for study, communication, or writing skills are also given on each Practicing Your Skills page.

HOW TO READ YOUR TEXTBOOK

Faces of America: A History of the United States has a new approach to studying the American people and their history. In this book, you will learn skills that can make you a better student and a better citizen. Mastering these skills can help you learn and use information more effectively. Before you begin to read your textbook, we want to give you a five-step method to develop your study skills. It is called the SQ3R method. The letters stand for *Skim, Question, Read, Recite, Review.* As you follow the SQ3R method, you will discover that remembering what you read is easier.

SKIM

Before you begin a reading assignment, first skim it. This means look quickly through it. Doing this will give you an idea of what the material is about. *Faces of America* is organized to help you with this step. Each chapter contains the following highlights for skimming:

- *Looking Ahead.* This section at the beginning of each chapter summarizes the main ideas and lists the objectives, or goals, for reading the chapter. Skim the list to help you decide what is important in the chapter.

- *Vocabulary, Places, People, Events,* and *Terms.* Skim these lists for a preview of what is to come. Notice the setting of a chapter and who is in it. Identify the words that are unfamiliar to you.

- *Headings.* This book has two types of headings. Headings in capital letters are similar to topics in an outline. Headings in both capital and small letters are similar to subtopics in an outline. The title of the outline is the chapter title. Skim the headings of each chapter before you begin reading. This will give you a structure, or framework, for reading and understanding.

- *Looking Back.* These review questions at the end of each chapter relate back to the list of objectives at the beginning of the chapter. Use the questions as a check on yourself. Skim them to see how well you did in deciding what was important.

- *Graphics.* Pictures, maps, charts, graphs, and tables are presented throughout the book. Look at them briefly to get a mental picture of the people, events, and things that will be important in the chapter.

QUESTION   After you have skimmed the chapter, ask yourself questions based on each heading. This will help you decide what facts to look for when you read. For example, take the first heading on page 7 and turn it into a question: What will I learn about the population? We suggest that when you first practice the SQ3R method, you actually write out your questions. Also ask yourself if you understand all the *Social Studies Vocabulary* in the list. If there are any words you do not know, look them up in the glossary before you begin to read.

READ   Read one section of the text at a time. Look for the answer to the question that you wrote for that heading.

RECITE   Recite the answers to your questions aloud. Also make notes on the answers. Your spoken answers and the notes you make on them should come from memory. The notes should be brief. They should be only the main points for each topic and subtopic.

REVIEW   Review the chapter. Read over the main points once again. You can use the *Looking Back* section as a guide. If you cannot answer any of your own questions or any of the *Looking Back* questions, reread the sections of the chapter that explain those points. Then answer the questions for those sections again.

You can use the SQ3R method with any textbook you have. Just look for special features like *Looking Ahead* and then adjust the skimming step to the textbook.

LIFE IN AMERICA

The variety of the U.S. can be seen in these three pictures: New York City, falls on the Yellowstone River, and a farm in Montana.

The People

LOOKING AHEAD

We Americans are really many different groups of people who share certain beliefs and a common history. We also share a common future. After you study Life in America: The People, you will be able to:

- explain how U.S. population has grown.
- ★ read and gather data from pictures about some ways we Americans are the same and some ways we are different.

Social Studies Vocabulary

immigrant	census	traditions
culture	data	democracy

You may have heard or read that the United States is a nation of immigrants. **Immigrants** (IM-uh-gruhnts) are people who have come here from other countries to live. You may also have heard us called a multicultural nation, a nation of many cultures. A **culture** is all the tools and objects that people make and use, their ways of eating and dressing, and their everyday activities. Culture also includes language, religious beliefs, customs, values, and folklore. Art, music, and literature are also included.

People of many cultures—Native American, European, African, Latin American, Asian, and Middle Eastern—have lived and worked here for almost 500 years. Unfortunately, we have sometimes fought one another, but this, too, is part of our history.

POPULATION

A nation's population can grow in two ways. One is through natural increase. This occurs when the number of people born during a period is greater than the number that die. Another way is through immigration. From 1820 to 1980 about 49 million people came to the U.S. from Europe, Asia, Africa, Latin America, and the Middle East. The mixing and blending of these people is a major theme of our history and of this text.

Today, the U.S. numbers more than 220 million people. This makes it the fourth largest country in the world. Only the People's Republic of China, India, and the Soviet Union have more people. The table on page 10 shows how much our population has grown since 1790.

Top: A Navajo woman helps a young patient with his studies. Older people are valuable sources of knowledge and help to others.

Center, left: This man is an architect. He designs and supervises the construction of houses, factories, and other buildings.

Center, right: These Japanese Americans are performing in a Cherry Blossom Festival. This festival is also celebrated in Japan.

Bottom: Tug-of-war is an age-old test of strength. At one time, it was an event in the Olympics.

★ BUILDING PICTURE SKILLS

Look at the pictures on pages 8 and 9. They show some of the ways we Americans are the same and some ways we are different. Study each picture carefully. Look at the details. **1.** How are the people dressed? **2.** Are the clothes similar to ones you wear? **3.** How do the uniforms worn by the Japanese American students differ from those worn by your school band? **4.** What are the people doing In these pictures? **5.** Are the activities the same as things you or people that you know do? **6.** Are the activities diffent? **7.** In a wedding in your culture do the bride and groom eat special food or do a special dance?

Top: More and more women are doing jobs that once only men did. This woman is repairing phone lines.

Center: With the help of sign language, this deaf student is learning algebra. There are over 1,500 different signs.

Bottom: Religion plays an important part in many cultures. Here a Mexican American wedding party leaves their church after the ceremony.

POPULATION OF THE UNITED STATES, 1790-2000

Year	Population
1790	3,929,000
1800	5,308,000
1840	17,069,000
1880	50,156,000
1920	105,711,000
1960	179,323,000
1980	226,505,000
2000	260,378,000

Source: U.S. Bureau of the Census

prediction
(prih-DIK-shuhn):
guess about
the future

The figure for the year 2000 is the Census Bureau's prediction of our population by then. Every ten years the Bureau takes a **census** (SEN-suhs). It counts the population and also takes **data,** or information, on age, sex, jobs, and so on.

DIFFERENCES AND SIMILARITIES

adapt (uh-DAPT):
to change to fit

Your first American ancestors may have come here many thousands of years ago by walking across the land bridge that once linked Alaska to Asia. Or they may have come recently by ship or plane. Whenever and however they came, they had to learn to adapt to the life they found in America. This often meant giving up old beliefs and ways of doing things to learn new ways. Most often, our ancestors had to learn a new language and a new way of earning a living. Many had to learn to take part in government for the first time.

But the groups that make up our nation did not give up all their traditions. **Traditions** (truh-DISH-uhns) are the customs, practices, and ways of doing things that are handed down from one generation to the next. Today, our country is a mix of religions, music, dance, art, literature, foods, and celebrations from all over the world.

generation
(jen-uh-RAY-shuhn):
a group of people
born around the
same time

While we Americans differ in some ways from one another, we do share some beliefs and ideals. For example, we believe in a **democracy** (dih-MAHK-ruh-see) — government in which citizens rule either directly or through elected representatives. We believe that all Americans have the right to live happy, healthy, useful lives. We believe that both citizens and the government should respect this right.

LOOKING BACK

1. Explain how each of the following has led to an increase in U.S. population: **a.** natural increase. **b.** immigration.
★ 2. Use the pictures on pages 8 and 9 to help you answer the following: **a.** What are some ways in which we Americans differ from one another? **b.** What are some of the ways we are the same?

The Land

LOOKING AHEAD

The natural environment has greatly influenced the history of the U.S. In Life in America: The Land, you will read about the natural regions of the U.S., their climates, natural resources, and land use. After you study this material, you will be able to:

★ read and gather data from different types of maps.
● list and explain the factors that influence climate.
● explain the importance of a water supply.
● explain the importance of conserving our natural resources.
★ describe the relationship between natural resources and land use by using maps.
★ define word meaning from the use of a word.

Social Studies Vocabulary

natural environment	basin	natural resources map
geography	plateau	land use map
political map	natural regions map	conservation
scale	climate	nonrenewable resource
natural region	latitude	economy
physical feature	natural resource	raw material
plain	legend	context clue

Places

natural regions of the U.S.

The natural environment is one of the factors that shape a nation's history. **Natural environment** includes all the natural influences and conditions that affect a group's development. Studying geography is one way to learn about the natural environment. **Geography** includes the earth's physical features, political and natural divisions, natural resources, climate, peoples, land use, industries, and products.

factor (FAK-tuhr): reason; something that causes a result

BUILDING MAP SKILLS

The map on page 12 is a **political map.** It shows the states and their capitals. Maps, like pictures, are much smaller than the real things they show. But on a map you can find true size by using the scale. **Scale** tells you the number of kilometers or miles on the earth that are represented by each centimeter or inch on the map. Each map is drawn to its own scale. To use the scale, measure the distance between two points on the map. Then compare your measurement with the scale. **1.** If you live in one of the 48 continental states, find the distance between your state capital and Washington, D.C. **2.** If you live in Alaska, find the distance between Juneau and the farthest northern point in Alaska. **3.** If you live in Hawaii, find the distance between Honolulu and the southern tip of Hawaii Island.

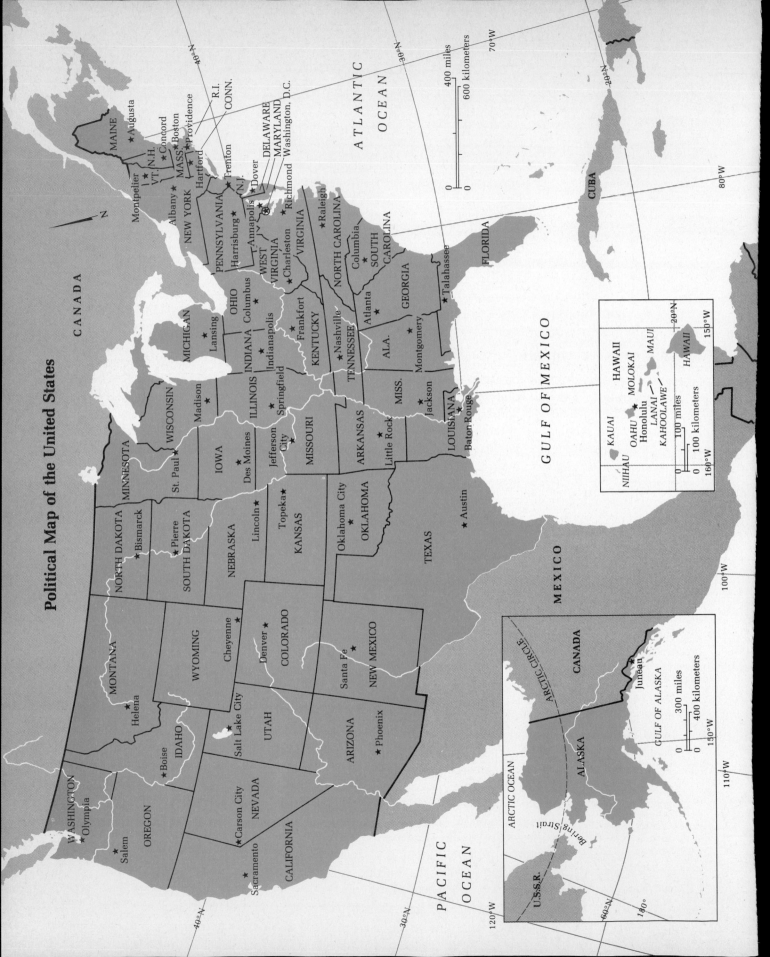

Political Map of the United States

N

CANADA

WASHINGTON ★ Olympia
★ Salem
OREGON
★ Sacramento
CALIFORNIA

MONTANA ★ Helena
IDAHO ★ Boise
★ Carson City **NEVADA**
★ Salt Lake City
UTAH
ARIZONA ★ Phoenix

WYOMING
★ Cheyenne
★ Denver
COLORADO
★ Santa Fe
NEW MEXICO

NORTH DAKOTA ★ Bismarck
SOUTH DAKOTA ★ Pierre
★ Lincoln **NEBRASKA**
★ Topeka
KANSAS
OKLAHOMA ★ Oklahoma City
TEXAS ★ Austin

MINNESOTA
★ St. Paul
IOWA ★ Des Moines
MISSOURI ★ Jefferson City
ARKANSAS ★ Little Rock
LOUISIANA ★ Baton Rouge

WISCONSIN ★ Madison
MICHIGAN ★ Lansing
ILLINOIS ★ Springfield
INDIANA ★ Indianapolis
OHIO ★ Columbus
KENTUCKY ★ Frankfort
TENNESSEE ★ Nashville
MISS. ★ Jackson
ALA. ★ Montgomery

MAINE ★ Augusta
★ Montpelier
VT. **N.H.** ★ Concord
★ Albany ★ Boston **MASS.**
NEW YORK ★ Providence R.I.
PENNSYLVANIA CONN.
★ Harrisburg Hartford
WEST Trenton **N.J.**
VIRGINIA ★ Annapolis **DELAWARE**
★ Charleston Dover **MARYLAND**
VIRGINIA Richmond ★ Washington, D.C.
NORTH CAROLINA ★ Raleigh
★ Columbia
SOUTH CAROLINA
GEORGIA ★ Atlanta
FLORIDA ★ Talahassee

ATLANTIC OCEAN

PACIFIC OCEAN

MEXICO

GULF OF MEXICO

CUBA

40° N
30° N
120° W
110° W
100° W
80° W
70° W
30° N
40° N

400 miles
600 kilometers

HAWAII
NIIHAU
KAUAI
OAHU MOLOKAI
Honolulu ★ LANAI MAUI
KAHOOLAWE
HAWAII
22° N
160° W 150° W
100 miles
100 kilometers

ALASKA
ARCTIC OCEAN
U.S.S.R.
Bering Strait
ARCTIC CIRCLE
CANADA
★ Juneau
GULF OF ALASKA
300 miles
400 kilometers
150° W
140°
60° N
120° W

Natural Regions of the United States

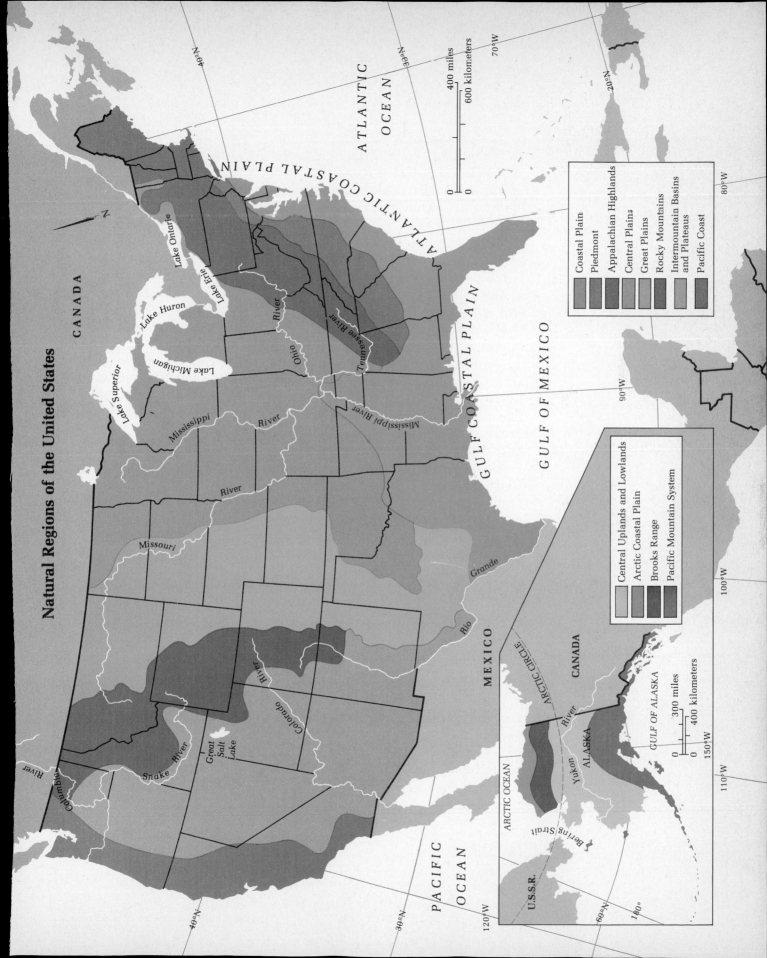

CANADA

ATLANTIC OCEAN

PACIFIC OCEAN

GULF OF MEXICO

MEXICO

Lake Superior
Lake Michigan
Lake Huron
Lake Ontario
Lake Erie

Mississippi River
Missouri River
Ohio River
Tennessee River
Mississippi River

Columbia River
Snake River
Colorado River
Great Salt Lake
Rio Grande

ATLANTIC COASTAL PLAIN
GULF COASTAL PLAIN

N

Coastal Plain
Piedmont
Appalachian Highlands
Central Plains
Great Plains
Rocky Mountains
Intermountain Basins and Plateaus
Pacific Coast

400 miles
600 kilometers

Central Uplands and Lowlands
Arctic Coastal Plain
Brooks Range
Pacific Mountain System

ARCTIC OCEAN
ARCTIC CIRCLE
U.S.S.R.
Bering Strait
ALASKA
Yukon River
CANADA
GULF OF ALASKA

300 miles
400 kilometers

180°
150°W
120°W
110°W
100°W
90°W
80°W
70°W

20°N
30°N
40°N

60°N

NATURAL REGIONS

Some geographers group land according to **natural regions.** These are areas in which at least one physical feature exists throughout. **Physical features** include valleys, mountains, rivers, lakes, and so on. The 48 continental states form eight natural regions.

The first is along the coast from Texas to New England and is called the Coastal Plain. A **plain** is flat land. Sometimes geographers further divide the Coastal Plain into the Gulf Coastal Plain and the Atlantic Coastal Plain.

Inland from the Atlantic section is the Piedmont (PEED-mahnt), an area of low mountains. Between the Plain and the Piedmont lies the fall line. Rapids and waterfalls form there where rivers from the mountains drop to the lower land of the Plain. West of the Piedmont and running into Maine are the Appalachian (ap-uh-LAY-chuhn) Highlands. These are slightly higher mountains than those of the Piedmont.

The middle of the country divides into the Central Plains and the Great Plains. West of the Plains from Mexico to Canada are the Rocky Mountains. Beyond them lies the region of Intermountain Basins and Plateaus. A **basin** is a bowl-shaped hollow in the land, and a **plateau** is a large area of raised, flat land. Some of the region is desert. The Pacific Coast region, which is mostly mountains and plains, is next.

Alaska has four natural regions. The Pacific Mountains lie along its southern coast. Next comes the region of Central Uplands and Lowlands. Hills and wide, swamplike river valleys are the main features of this region. North of it is the Brooks Range, the Alaskan part of the Rockies. The northernmost region is the Arctic Coastal Plain.

Most of the 132 islands of Hawaii are coral and sand, or rock. They are really the tops of mountains that rose long ago from the sea. The eight main islands have some plateaus and plains and are where most of the people live.

Each of the natural regions of the U.S. has a different climate and different natural resources. Together, these factors shape the various types of land use possible.

BUILDING MAP SKILLS

Locate your state on the political map and then on the **natural regions map** on page 13. **1.** In what natural region is your state? **2.** Is it in more than one region? **3.** Describe the main physical feature of each. **4.** Are neighboring states in the same region or regions as your state? If not, in what regions are they?

CLIMATE

The general weather conditions of a region are called **climate.** Many factors work together to produce it. **Latitude,** the distance north or

south of the equator, is the most important. Latitude is measured in degrees with the equator as zero. The degrees increase as we move north or south of the equator. Land close to the equator is hotter and more humid than land farther away.

The 48 continental states are in the middle latitudes, from 30° to 50° north of the equator. These areas generally have warm summers and cool or cold winters. Rainfall is plentiful and occurs year-round. The northern parts of the Coastal Plain, Piedmont, Appalachians, Central Plains, and the Great Plains generally have this type of climate. The southern parts of these regions generally have longer, hotter, more humid summers while winters are shorter and milder. This is because of the lower latitudes.

Hawaii, which is located at about 20° north latitude, is generally hot and humid year-round. Alaska is the other extreme. Located between 60° and 70° north latitude, it is generally cold. Precipitation occurs year-round but not in large amounts.

These are general weather patterns, but there are exceptions. Elevation (el-uh-VAY-shuhn)—the height of land above sea level—as well as wind direction and distance from mountains and water are also factors. For example, the higher the elevation is, the colder the temperature. Also, the more likely it is that precipitation will be snow. At middle elevations, precipitation is usually rain. Lowlands around mountains are generally dry.

Mountains also act as barriers to precipitation. The Rockies, for example, keep precipitation from the Great Plains. Most of the precipitation on the Great Plains comes from winds that blow south from Canada or north from the Gulf of Mexico. However, the farther an area is from mountains the less effect mountains have on weather.

The weather on the Plains can be extreme. Cattle can freeze to death in blizzards or die from lack of water and grass in the hot rainless summers.

precipitation
(prih-sip-uh-TAY-shuhn): rain, sleet, snow, hail

Top: Recreation is one of the nation's biggest businesses. The Appalachians provide many areas for hiking and skiing. This hiker is walking along the Appalachian National Scenic Trail, which extends from Georgia to Maine.

Left: This hydroelectric plant is built on the fall line in Virginia. The falling water turns the engines that produce electricity. The fall line is formed where the rivers of the Piedmont fall to the Coastal Plain.

Bottom: Oranges grow well in California's mild climate. Southern California often receives less than 30 centimeters (12 inches) of rain a year so irrigation is necessary. Notice how the coastal plain gives way to mountains.

Top: Mt. McKinley, the highest mountain in North America, lies within the Pacific Mountain region of Alaska. Some of Alaska's best farmland is found in this region.

Left: The region of the Intermountain Basins and Plateaus is not suited for much farming, but it is rich in mineral resources. This power plant burns coal.

Right: Because much of Hawaii is covered by rocks and a thin layer of topsoil, little of the land can be farmed. Hawaiians depend heavily for their income on the three million tourists a year who visit the state.

17

moderate
(MAHD-uhr-it):
even; not too much
or too little

The distance of an area from water—either an ocean or a large lake—can also make a difference in temperature and precipitation. Far inland from a body of water, summers are very hot and dry, and winters are very cold. This is the kind of climate the Intermountain Basins and Plateaus region has. The Great Lakes, on the other hand, keep the temperatures of the land near them moderate. They also provide most of the water that falls as rain.

Wind direction also makes a difference. The Pacific Coast, for example, has a milder, rainier climate than the Atlantic Coastal Plain. This is because the Pacific Coast is east of an ocean. In the northern hemisphere, winds blow from west to east. Winds blowing in from the Pacific Ocean over the Pacific Coast bring with them the cooler temperatures and moisture of the ocean.

How does all this relate to our country's history? Here is one example. Spain and California are at about the same latitude and both are east of an ocean. When the Spanish settled in California, they found a climate similar to their homeland's. They did not have to adapt their clothes, homes, or crops.

NATURAL RESOURCES AND LAND USE

Natural resources are all the things that are found naturally on or in land and water including fish, animals, soil, forests, and minerals. Air and water are also natural resources. Natural resources greatly influence land use. For example, farming depends a great deal on soil quality and water supply.

Water and Its Many Uses

Underground streams as well as rivers and lakes are sources of water for drinking and for irrigation. The water from rivers and lakes is also used in manufacturing, in producing electricity, for transportation, and for recreation. Most of our major cities are near rivers. Rivers are also the locations of dams, which give electric power for both home and industry. Dams also form reservoirs that can be used for swimming, boating, and fishing. Reservoirs also supply water to nearby communities. Major U.S. dams include Hoover Dam on the Colorado River between Nevada and Arizona and Grand Coulee (KOO-lee) Dam on the Columbia River in Washington. The Tennessee River and its branches have 50 dams. Power companies built some and the federal government built others to improve life in the Tennessee Valley.

Although we may sometimes forget, oceans are also natural resources. The Continental Shelf, a strip of shallow ocean floor along the coasts, is a major source of fish. In the future, oceans may also become the source of our fresh water. If efforts to protect our present supply of fresh water fail, we could run out. Removing the salt from sea water could give us a new supply. Some countries are already using fresh water produced in this way for irrigation and in homes and industry.

irrigation (ir-uh-GAY-shuhn): providing farmland with water

A **legend** is a list that explains the symbols on the map. It is the key to reading and understanding a map. By matching the colors or symbols on the map with the colors or symbols in the legend, you will be able to read the map. **Activity:** Besides soil and water, what other major resources does your state have? To find out, read the **natural resources map** on page 20 by matching the symbols to the legend.

BUILDING MAP SKILLS

Soil and Farming and Grazing

Soil quality and yearly precipitation are important in deciding if land can be used for farming and grazing. An area also has to have a long enough growing season—enough frost-free days. But people are also a factor. For example, if the soil is rich but there is little summer rain, farmers can use irrigation from rivers or underground water supplies to turn the land into farms. Where land is poor but water is available, the use of fertilizers can make the land productive.

Much of the soil of the Atlantic Coastal Plain is sandy and infertile. Where the soil is good, farmers grow vegetables and raise dairy herds. The Dairy Belt begins in the Atlantic Coastal Plain and stretches into the Central and Great Plains. The Gulf Coastal Plain is much better for farming. Soybeans, cotton, and corn are the chief crops grown there.

In parts of the Piedmont, the soil and climate—precipitation and the growing season—are ideal for soybeans and corn. The Piedmont

infertile (in-FER-tuhl): unable to make plants grow

Natural Resources of the United States

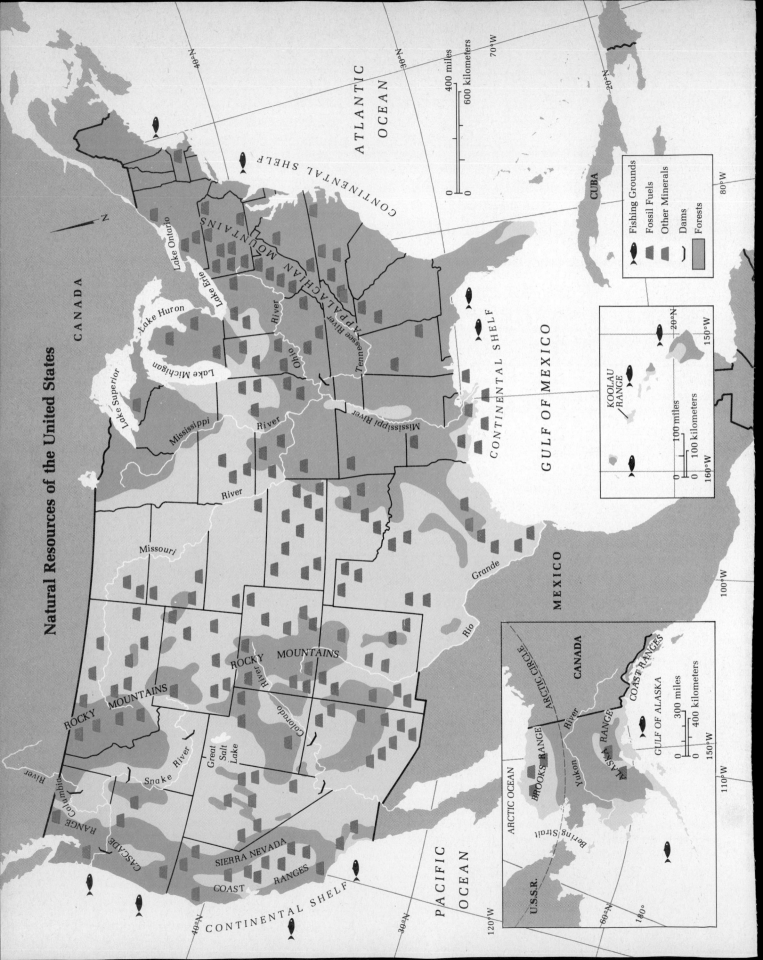

CANADA

ATLANTIC OCEAN

CONTINENTAL SHELF

Lake Superior
Lake Huron
Lake Michigan
Lake Ontario
Lake Erie

APPALACHIAN MOUNTAINS

Mississippi
River

Missouri
River

Ohio River

Tennessee River

Mississippi River

ROCKY MOUNTAINS

ROCKY MOUNTAINS

ROCKY MOUNTAINS

Colorado River

Snake River

Great Salt Lake

Columbia River

CASCADE RANGE

SIERRA NEVADA

COAST RANGES

PACIFIC OCEAN

CONTINENTAL SHELF

CONTINENTAL SHELF

GULF OF MEXICO

MEXICO

CUBA

Rio Grande

400 miles
600 kilometers

Legend
🐟	Fishing Grounds
▰	Fossil Fuels
▰	Other Minerals
)	Dams
▰	Forests

Inset (Hawaii)
KOOLAU RANGE
100 miles
100 kilometers
20°N
150°W
160°W

Inset (Alaska)
ARCTIC OCEAN
ARCTIC CIRCLE
BROOKS RANGE
CANADA
Yukon River
ALASKA RANGE
COAST RANGES
GULF OF ALASKA
Bering Strait
U.S.S.R.
300 miles
400 kilometers
150°W
110°W
60°N
180°

70°W
80°W
100°W
110°W
120°W
20°N
30°N
40°N
50°N

Land Use of the United States

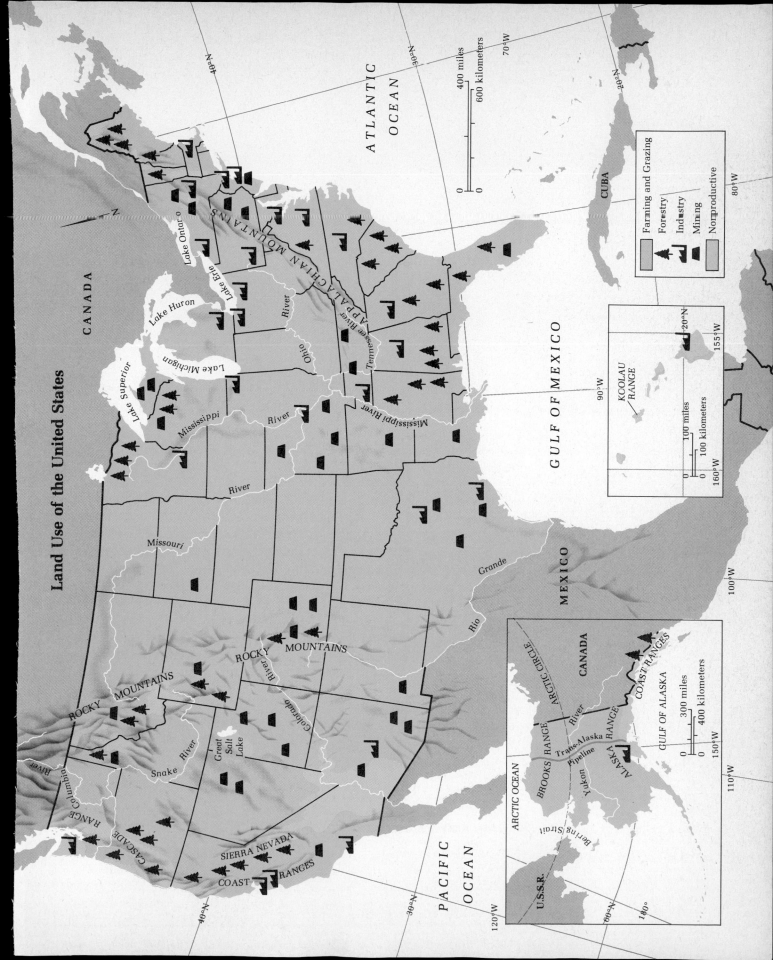

ATLANTIC OCEAN

PACIFIC OCEAN

GULF OF MEXICO

CANADA

MEXICO

CUBA

Lake Superior

Lake Michigan

Lake Huron

Lake Erie

Lake Ontario

APPALACHIAN MOUNTAINS

Tennessee River

Ohio River

Mississippi River

Missouri River

Snake River

Columbia River

Colorado River

Rio Grande

Great Salt Lake

ROCKY MOUNTAINS

ROCKY MOUNTAINS

SIERRA NEVADA

COAST RANGES

CASCADE RANGE

KOOLAU RANGE

155°W
160°W
20°N

100 miles
100 kilometers

0

90°W

70°W
80°W

30°N

40°N

N

400 miles
600 kilometers

0
0

Legend

- Farming and Grazing
- Forestry
- Industry
- Mining
- Nonproductive

Alaska inset

ARCTIC OCEAN

U.S.S.R.

CANADA

ARCTIC CIRCLE

BROOKS RANGE

Yukon River

Trans-Alaska Pipeline

ALASKA RANGE

COAST RANGES

GULF OF ALASKA

Bering Strait

180°
150°W
110°W
100°W
120°W

60°N

300 miles
400 kilometers

0
0

These students are conserving our natural resources by recycling aluminum cans and planting trees. What other things can we do to save renewable and nonrenewable resources?

in general is suited to farming and dairy herding. In the Appalachians, the river valleys are very fertile, but the soil in the rest of the region is thin and sandy.

Much of our farming is done in the Central and Great Plains. Parts of the these regions are known as the Corn and Wheat belts. Soybeans and hay are also grown there. The soil in the Intermountain Basins and Plateaus region is poor. But farmers can raise some crops with irrigation from reservoirs. Along the Pacific Coast, the soil is very fertile, and river irrigation is widely used.

In Alaska, people do some farming and dairy herding in the Pacific Mountain region. In the Central Uplands and Lowlands and the Arctic Coastal Plain, hunting and reindeer herding are common. Most of Hawaii is rocky, so only about ten percent of the land is farmed.

BUILDING MAP SKILLS

Look at the **land use map** on page 21 and then at the natural resources map. **1.** What are the major uses of land in your state? **2.** Do natural resources determine land use in any way? **3.** How? Give examples. **4.** What other factors can you think of that might affect land use?

Forests and Forestry

Forests provide wood and wood products, recreation areas, underground water supplies, and homes for animals. Once, more than half the 48 continental states were forests. But they were cut down by settlers clearing land for farms and towns. Today, conservation is needed to prevent more loss. **Conservation** (kahn-suhr-VAY-shuhn) is the protection of natural resources. Our national forests are protected and re-seeded by the U.S. Forest Service. The Forest Service also advises people on the best use of privately owned forests.

Fossil Fuels

Forests are renewable. They can be reseeded. But the U.S. depends on many natural resources that cannot be replaced. Among these **nonrenewable** (nahn-rih-NOO-uh-buhl) **resources,** as they are called, are fossil (FAHS-uhl) fuels. These are energy sources that are taken from the ground, such as petroleum (puh-TROH-lee-uhm) — crude oil — natural gas, and coal.

We have become so dependent on oil that our nation's economy would stop without it. An **economy** (ih-KAHN-uh-mee) is a system for making, distributing, and using goods, and providing services. At one time, the U.S. produced enough oil to meet its needs. But in recent years, production has not kept up with use. We now depend on foreign oil to make up the difference. Among the products made from oil are gasoline, heating oil, kerosene, plastics, and detergents. Natural gas — often found with oil deposits — is used mainly for cooking and heating.

Although oil is important, coal is our chief source of energy. Sixty-eight percent of the coal mined in the U.S. is burned to produce electricity. In the future, the sun and other sources may replace coal as our chief energy source, but this is a long way off. In the form of coke, coal is also a raw material in the production of steel and chemicals. **Raw materials** are materials used in the manufacture of other goods.

A folk song says:
"This land is your land
This land is my land
From California to the
    New York island
From the redwood forests
    to the Gulf Stream
    waters;
This land was made for
    you and me."
This introduction is
meant to share our land
and people with you.

Minerals and Mining

Minerals are also nonrenewable resources. Some minerals that are important to our economy are iron ore and copper. In the 1970s, the U.S. used an average of 126 million metric tons (128 million long tons) of iron ore a year. Iron is used in the manufacture of many goods including steel. Practically everything we wear or use is made by iron or steel machines. One way to conserve iron is to recycle scrap steel. Energy in the form of coal is also saved with this method.

Industry

Industry depends on several factors besides natural resources. One is a food supply for workers. Another is a transportation system. Raw materials and food must be shipped in, and finished goods must be shipped out.

Today, the U.S. is the world's leading industrial country, and California is our leading industrial state. In terms of dollar value, California produces more goods than any other state. Among its products are planes, computers and TVs. New York, Ohio, Illinois, Michigan, and Pennsylvania are the next five important manufacturing states, but this may change. Since the 1960s, industries have been moving from these states to the Sun Belt—the southern third of the U.S. Good climate and improved transportation have attracted industry and people to this region.

Houston, Texas, is one of the fastest growing cities in the Sun Belt. It is a major port, business center, and oil-refining area.

BUILDING VOCABULARY SKILLS

Although we have defined many words in the text or in the margin, you will probably come across some words that are unfamiliar. Using context clues can help you discover the meaning of these words. **Context clues** can be other words in the sentence or paragraph that suggest the word's meaning, how the word is used in the sentence, where it comes in the sentence. **Activity:** See if you can discover the meaning of the following from context clues: **factors,** page 14; **barrier,** page 15; **fertile,** page 22.

LOOKING BACK

★ 1. Using the maps, describe your state by major physical features, general climate, major natural resources, and major land use.

2. **a.** List five factors that influence climate. **b.** Choose one and explain how it affects climate.

3. Describe how water affects the following: **a.** farming. **b.** industry. **c.** recreation.

4. Why conserve: **a.** water? **b.** forests? **c.** fossil fuels?

★ 5. Describe how the natural environment influences one type of land use found in your state. As the basis of your description, use the relationship of physical features, climate, or natural resources to land use. Use the maps to help you.

★ 6. **a.** What are context clues? **b.** How can they help in reading?

24

PRACTICING YOUR SKILLS

What If . . .   The South has ideal soil, climate, and water resources for farming. During the colonial period, small Southern farms were growing into large plantations. To make money, owners discovered they needed large amounts of cheap labor. They found their supply by importing Africans as slaves. **What if** the climate and soil of the South had been similar to that of New England? How might our history have been different?

Building Communication Skills   As students, you often take part in formal **discussion** of topics like the one above. Outside school, too, you take part in discussions at home and with friends. Here are a few tips to help you be an effective participant.

- Be prepared. Read your assignment so that you have something to contribute.
- Be open-minded. Have your own ideas, but do not have your mind made up.
- Be willing to share your ideas and opinions.
- Listen carefully when others are speaking.
- Respect the ideas of others. Everyone has a right to an opinion.
- Do not make disagreements personal. It is all right to disagree with another's ideas, but not with the person.
- Be clear in expressing your ideas.

Activity: Discuss why you think it is, or is not, important to conserve natural resources. What would conservation mean to the way you live?

Mapping, Researching
1. Keep a record of the TV weather or collect the weather map from the daily newspaper for a week. Using this data make a weather map that shows the development of a weather system.
2. List three jobs that depend on good weather reporting.
3. Investigate one renewable energy source: solar, wind, wood, or geothermal. List its advantages and disadvantages.

Exploring
1. Look at the restaurant listings in the yellow pages of your local phone book. Write down all the ethnic groups that seem to be represented—Chinese, Polish, Greek, and so on. Ethnic groups are groups that share the same traditions. Does your community seem to be made up of a number of ethnic groups?
2. Look in the phone book to see if there is a recycling center in your community. If so, what does it recycle? Make posters to advertise the center in your school and community. If your community does not have a recycling center, consider setting one up at school. What kinds of things should you consider before beginning?

Reading   Adams, James T. *Album of American History,* 6 vols. New York: Scribner, 1969.
Espenshade, Edward, Jr. and Joel Morrison, eds. *Goodes World Atlas*. 15th ed. Chicago: Rand McNally, 1977. Paperback.
Hirsch, S. Carl. *Guardians of Tomorrow: Pioneers in Ecology*. New York: Viking, 1971. From Thoreau to Rachael Carson.
Keating, Bern. *Mighty Mississippi*. Washington, D.C.: National Geographic Society, 1971. Physical, economic, and cultural factors.
Sedeen, Margaret, ed. *National Geographic Picture Atlas of Our Fifty States*. Washington, D.C.: National Geographic Society, 1978. Text as well as many maps.
Wood, Frances and Dorothy. *America, Land of Wonders*. New York: Dodd, Meade, 1973. Includes geological history of each natural region.

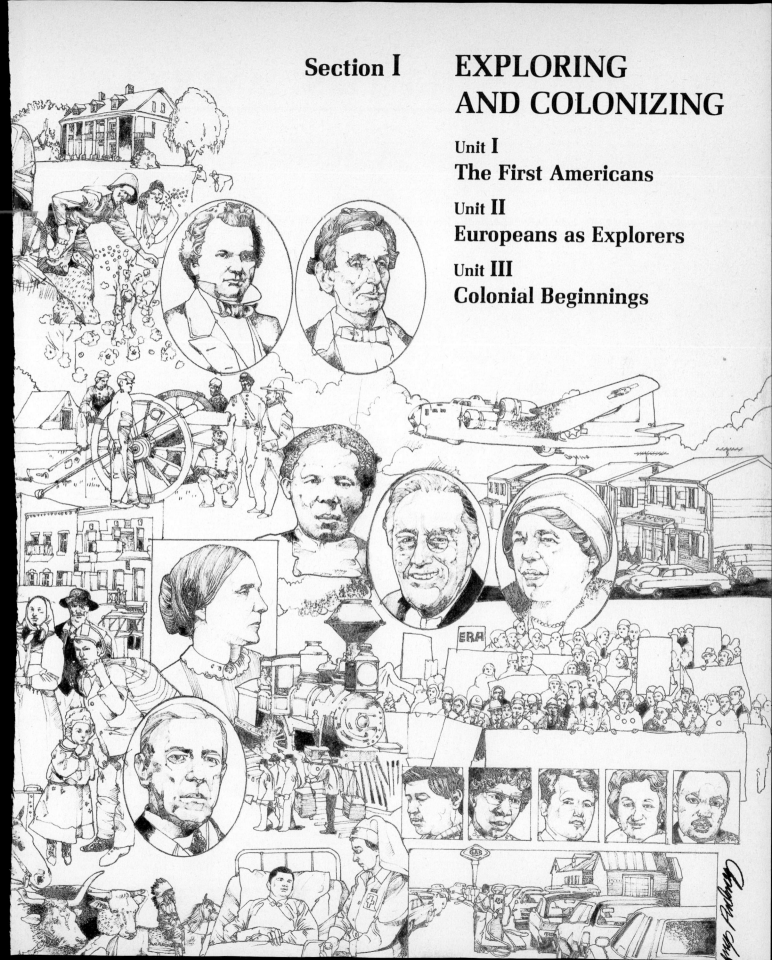

Section I

EXPLORING AND COLONIZING

Unit **I**
The First Americans

Unit **II**
Europeans as Explorers

Unit **III**
Colonial Beginnings

THE FIRST AMERICANS

	18,000 B.C.	8000 B.C.	2500 B.C.	1000 B.C.	1	500	1000	1500

*c. **35,000** First peoples come from Asia

c. **18,000** First evidence of big-game hunting as a way of life

c. **8000** Food gathering begins

c. **2500** Farming begins

c. **1000** B.C. -200 A.D. Adena mound culture

c. **100** B.C.-700 A.D. Hopewell mound culture builds on Adena

c. **100** B.C.-1200s A.D. Mogollon culture in Southwest

c. **1-1400s** Hohokam culture in Southwest

c. **100-1540** Anasazi culture in Southwest

c. **500-1600s** Mississippian culture builds on earlier mound cultures

c. **500** Local cultures develop in California

c. **1000-1600** Woodlands culture develops

1540 Spanish arrive in Southwest

1500s-1700s Native Americans obtain horses

1500s Iroquois form League of Five Nations

1722 Iroquois form Six Nations

*c. abbreviation for circa (SER-kuh) meaning *around*, with dates

Chapter 1

Beginnings

LOOKING AHEAD

This chapter is about when, how, and why the first people came to the Americas. It also describes the methods archaeologists use to learn about early groups. One topic archaeologists study is how the first Americans adapted to their environment. After you study this chapter, you will be able to:

- describe the movement of the first people into the Americas.
- explain how archaeologists use material remains to learn about earlier times.
- explain why the first Americans changed from big-game hunting to farming.
- ★ read a time line to follow the sequence of events from big-game hunting to farming.
- explain the changes that result from having a steady food supply.

Social Studies Vocabulary

archaeologist	artifact	time line
B.C.	radiocarbon dating	sequence of events
prehistoric	dendrochronology	trade
material remains	domesticate	culture region

Places

Bering Strait

Words and Terms

linguist	language family	dig	free time

This scraper was made from the shinbone of a caribou, a large deer. Archaeologists believe that the tool is around 27,000 years old.

The first people probably arrived in the Americas at least 35,000 years ago. But it might have been as much as 50,000 or even 100,000 years ago. **Archaeologists** (ahr-kee-AHL-uh-jists), scientists who study past cultures, are not certain when, how, or why these people came. However, archaeologists generally agree that people came from Siberia some time before 10,000 B.C. (before Christ). They came across the land bridge that connected Siberia and Alaska. After 8000 B.C., melting ice from the last ice age flooded the land bridge. Today, this area is known as the Bering Strait (BAIR-ing STRAYT).

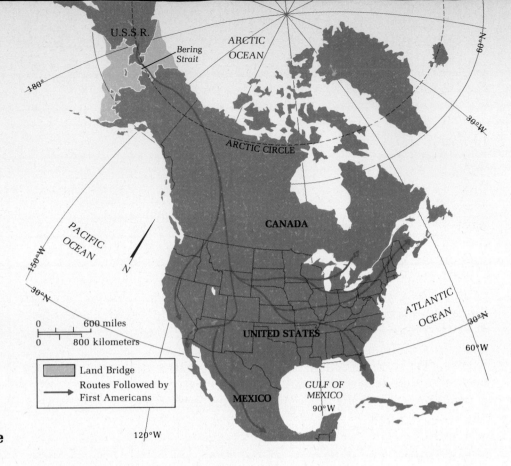

Over the Land Bridge

WHY THE FIRST PEOPLE CAME

Archaeologists believe that these first people were big-game hunters. They ate elephant-like animals called mammoths, and also buffalo, camels, and horses. As the game moved across Siberia, the hunters and their families followed. When the animals passed over the land bridge, so did the hunters.

The movement into the Americas happened slowly. Probably thousands of years passed from the time the first groups began moving eastward and their descendants arrived in Alaska. More centuries passed as these groups moved through the Americas. As temperatures rose and the last ice age ended, the ice sheets covering much of North America slowly melted. A few ice-free paths were formed through the Rockies. The game wandered along them looking for food and the hunters followed. They came down through western Canada, east and south across what is now the U.S., south into Mexico, and on into South America. Archaeologists believe that by 7000 B.C. people had reached the tip of South America.

People probably came in family groups. A group might hunt in one general area for generations. In time, part of the group would decide to move on. The wanderers might meet a group that had settled in an area and join camps. Or the earlier group might be forced out.

As groups separated, many languages and cultures developed. Linguists (LING-gwists), people who study language, estimate that before Columbus 12 language families and over 200 languages had de-

descendant
(dih-SEN-duhnt): member of a later generation

veloped in what is now the U.S. A language family is one in which all the languages come from the same source and are similar.

LEARNING ABOUT EARLY LIFE

To learn about **prehistoric** (pree-his-TOR-ik) people, those who lived before history was recorded, archaeologists study **material remains.** These are **artifacts** (AHR-tuh-fakts)—any objects that people have made—as well as bones, plants, rocks, and soil from a dig. Although archaeologists may spend years at a dig, they spend even more time in the laboratory analyzing and dating what they find.

analyze (AN-uh-lyz): to study carefully

Artifacts such as pottery and cloth can show archaeologists what people knew about making pottery, painting, and weaving. These items can sometimes tell about a group's religious beliefs, too. Tools, weapons, and ornaments—or lack of them—can show whether a group were hunters, farmers, traders, or a little of all three. From boards, stones, or bricks, archaeologists can piece together a picture of the kind of shelter a group had.

Besides artifacts, other material remains can tell archaeologists much about early people. Rocks and soil samples show climate and soil fertility. These can help archaeologists explain why a group did, or did not, farm. By studying human bones, archaeologists can determine the size and shape of earlier people. They can tell how healthful their diets were. By studying animal bones, archaeologists can tell the types of animals used for food and the weapons that killed them.

Dating Remains

Besides learning what artifacts were for or what people ate, archaeologists try to find out when a group lived. They do this by dating, or

This dig and others like it at Chaco Canyon National Park, New Mexico, are helping archaeologists learn about the way of life of the Anasazi.

deciding the age of, remains. There are several methods of dating remains that archaeologists can use.

One is **radiocarbon dating,** also called carbon-14 dating. It measures the amount of carbon-14 left in wood, bone, and other things that were once alive. Carbon-14 builds up in all things while they are living. When they die, it decays at a known rate. Unfortunately, radiocarbon dating is only accurate for objects newer than the 1200s B.C.

Another dating method is **dendrochronology** (den-droh-kruh-NAHL-uh-jee), or tree-ring dating. Each ring in a tree trunk counts as one year. Dendrochronology is correct to the year. But it can be used only in areas where trees grow to great ages. Where archaeologists can use both tree-ring and carbon-14 datings, they can narrow dates to within a few hundred years. When thousands of years are involved, this is very useful.

decay (dih-KAY): to lose radioactive strength

Spearpoints

In 1926, George McJunkin, a cowboy, found a spearpoint in the ribs of a bison, or buffalo, skeleton in New Mexico. That particular species had died out at least 10,000 years before. This was the first evidence that people were in the Americas at the same time as ice-age animals. Until this find, archaeologists had only thought it possible. They called the spearpoint shape Folsom (FOHL-suhm) after a nearby town. Since 1926, Folsom points have been found throughout the U.S. and in Mexico and Canada. Most of the Folsom points date to between 9000 and 8000 B.C.

species (SPEE-sheez): group that has characteristics in common

In the 1930s, archaeologists uncovered even older spearpoints in Colorado. These were named Clovis (KLOH-vis) points and dated to about 10,000 to 9000 B.C. Less well-shaped points called Sandia (san-DEE-uh) have also been dug up in North America. These may date to 18,000 B.C., but archaeologists are unsure. They do not have enough material remains to test.

Archaeologists can tell by the shape of a spearpoint the period to which it belongs—Folsom, Clovis, Sandia, or some other. But to find more accurate dates, carbon-14 tests must be made on objects, such as wood, charcoal, and cloth, that contain carbon-14. Stone spearpoints do not contain it.

Scientists use charcoal from campsites to help them determine when spearpoints, such as this Clovis point, were made and used.

HOW THE FIRST PEOPLE LIVED

As people became separated, they moved into different environments. Although each group had to adapt to its own environment, most groups went through the same stages of development. For example, a change in food production was always marked by a change in tools. The stages took place at different times in different places and not every group passed through each stage. Where changes occurred, they took place over hundreds of years. As a result, stages always overlapped.

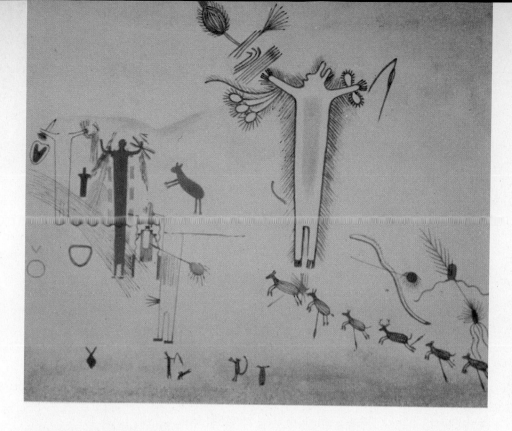

What can you learn about the life of Plains Native Americans from this 1,000-year-old Texas cave painting?

Big-Game Hunting

The first people in the Americas were hunters who used large bones and stones as tools and weapons. These were rough objects, because the hunters did not know how to sharpen the edges into points. In the next stage, from about 18,000 to 8000 B.C., hunters learned to sharpen and shape their tools. For this reason, the Clovis point is better shaped than the Sandia point. The Folsom point is smaller and sharper than either. Hunters also made scrapers and knives.

From Hunting to Gathering

After about 8500 B.C., ice-age animals gradually died out. The end of these animals may have come because of climate changes or from overkilling. As big-game hunting ended, people turned to food gathering. They found and ate wild grains, nuts, roots, and berries. Instead of spearpoints, people needed tools for grinding. It is important to remember that food gathering did not begin all at once in any area. People may have been eating plants along with meat by 15,000 B.C.

From Gathering to Farming

As people began to eat more plants, they found that some plants grew better than others. They learned that they could get more food by gathering and planting seeds from these plants. They **domesticated** (duh-MES-tuh-kayt-uhd) wild plants—began to plant and harvest plants. But as you will read, farming developed differently in different regions, and not all regions were suited to it.

33

WORKING WITH TIME LINES

The following is a time line of important dates for different stages in Native American development. A **time line** is an arrangement of events or **sequence of events** with their dates in the order in which they occurred. This time line is based on archaeologists' dating of artifacts. It shows, for example, the date of the first evidence that has been found of big-game hunting in North America. Notice how stages overlap among the areas. Remember, too, that stages overlapped within areas.

Read the time line to answer the following questions: **1.** How many years passed between the first evidence of big-game hunting in North America and evidence of big-game hunting in the Northwest? **2.** Which were the first and last areas to begin food gathering? **3.** How many years passed between the time the first and last areas began food gathering? **4.** When did farming begin in the Woodlands? **5.** How many years was this before the spread of farming to the Plains?

B.C.

c. 18,000	Evidence of big-game hunting in North America: Sandia points in Southwest
c. 10,000	Big-game hunting in California
c. 9500	Big-game hunting in the Great Basin
c. 9000	Big-game hunting in Woodlands, on Plains
c. 8500	Big game begin dying out
c. 8000	Food gathering appears in Woodlands Big-game hunting on Plateau
c. 7000	Food-gathering Desert culture appears in Great Basin Food gathering spreads to Southwest (Desert culture influence)
c. 6000-5000	Food gathering spreads through Intermountain Basins and Plateaus (Desert culture influence)
c. 6000	Big-game hunting in Northwest
c. 5000	Food gathering in California (Desert culture influence) Food gathering or hunting and gathering on the Plains
c. 2500-2000	Farming spreads to Southwest (Mexican influence)
c. 1000	Farming spreads to Woodlands (Mexican influence) Fishing in Northwest
c. 500	Farming spreads to eastern and northern Plains (Woodlands influence)

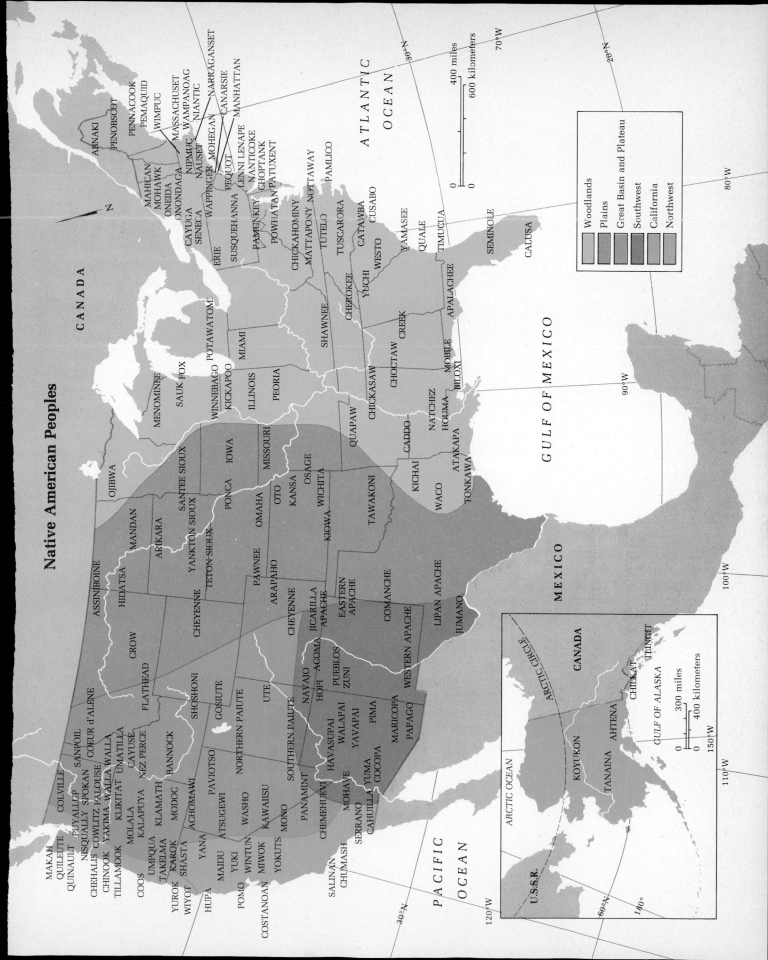

Native American Peoples

Some Native Americans wove baskets so tightly they could hold water. This basket comes from the Paiute of Nevada.

A STEADY FOOD SUPPLY

When food gatherers turned to farming, they were sure of having enough food for the first time. As a result, their lives changed greatly. First, population increased. Second, villages sprang up because people did not have to move around in search of food. Third, the number and type of artifacts increased. People could have more belongings since they did not have to carry them around. They also had more time to make things such as baskets and pottery. Fourth, trade developed to exchange extra goods with other groups. **Trade** is the buying, selling, or exchanging of goods and services. Fifth, people had more free time—time free from getting food. They used this free time to make goods and develop more elaborate social and religious groups than they had had.

These changes took place to some degree even if a group continued to hunt, gather, or fish for some of its food. In certain regions, farming never developed. But where a people developed a steady supply of enough food, some or all of these changes occurred. In the remainder of the unit, you will be reading about how these changes affected Native Americans.

CULTURE REGIONS AND GEOGRAPHY

A **culture region** is an area in which people of different groups adapt to their surroundings in similar ways. In this unit, you will be studying about these culture regions: Woodlands, Plains, Great Basin, Plateau, Southwest, California, and Northwest Coast. They are about the same divisions as the natural regions you read about in Life in America: The Land. This is because geography played so great a part in the development of the various cultures. Physical features, climate, and natural resources shaped the way the first Americans saw themselves and their world.

LOOKING BACK

1. **a.** Why did the first people cross the land bridge? **b.** How did groups become separated? **c.** Use the map to identify the directions of the major paths these people took.
2. What can archaeologists learn about early people by studying material remains?
3. Why did the first Americans go from: **a.** big-game hunting to food gathering? **b.** food gathering to farming?
★ 4. Use the time line on page 34 to answer these questions. What is the date of the first evidence of each of the following in each culture region: **a.** big-game hunting? **b.** food gathering? **c.** farming? **d.** fishing?
5. What five changes occur in a culture when people develop a steady food supply?

Chapter 2   Woodlands Peoples

LOOKING AHEAD

This chapter is about the different cultures that developed, spread, and disappeared in the Woodlands. It describes the importance of farming to their development. You will also read about how cultures build on one another. After you study this chapter, you will be able to:

- describe how farming influenced the mound-building cultures of the Woodlands.
- describe how each mound culture built on the one before it.
- ★ find the main ideas and supporting details to describe Iroquois government.

Social Studies Vocabulary

a people	government	league
class	clan	role
A.D.	council	main idea
division of labor	nation	supporting detail

People

Adena	Hopewell	Mississippian	Iroquois

Places

Woodlands culture region

Words and Terms

earthworks	city-state

Archaeologists have given the term *Woodlands* to the cultures that grew up in the eastern half of the U.S. When these cultures were developing, forests covered much more of the land than they do today. The peoples who settled there had to adapt to a forest environment.

When we use the term **a people** in this unit, we mean all the persons who belong to the same culture. Remember, though, that each culture region is made up of many cultures and many peoples. They share certain similarities, but they also have differences.

This broken piece is all that is left of an Iroquois comb. What can you learn from it about Iroquois designs, handicrafts, and personal appearance?

MOUND CULTURES

Farming spread into the Woodlands around 1000 B.C. The idea probably came from Mexico through the Mississippi Valley. Not all Wood-

This Adenan artifact, called the serpent mound, is just one of thousands found in the eastern U.S. According to the map on the opposite page, in which states might Adenan artifacts be found? Where were the other mound cultures?

lands groups turned to farming. Where there was plenty of game, fish, and wild plants, people were less likely to farm. Even many of those who farmed also hunted and fished. This way of life continued until the Europeans came.

As groups became more dependent on farming, their cultures changed. On page 36, you read about the five changes that take place when people have a steady food supply. These changes happen slowly. The mound builders of the Woodlands are a good example of how cultures gradually change as a steady food supply develops.

Adena

The first mound culture was the Adena (uh-DEE-nuh). It rose in the Ohio River valley some time around 1000 B.C. Archaeologists are not sure how much farming the Adenans (uh-DEE-nuhnz) did. They may have harvested wild plants rather than farmed.

ceremonies
(SER-uh-moh-neez):
celebrations

Adenans are called mound builders because of their burial mounds. The mounds were probably used for religious ceremonies as well as graves. The earliest mounds were low piles of dirt. By the end of the culture, the mounds were huge and surrounded by large, round earthworks. Earthworks are piles of dirt built for defense.

It must have taken thousands of workers to carry the tons of dirt needed to build the mounds. This fact makes archaeologists believe the Adenans had a class system. **Class** is the grouping of people according to social and economic rank. The Adenans must have had some form of ruler to get them to work together.

Through trade or the movement of people, Adenan influence spread through the northeast. However, by about 200 A.D. (after Christ), the Adenans had disappeared and archaeologists do not know why. The Hopewell culture took their place.

Hopewell

The first traces of Hopewell culture date to about 100 B.C. in the Ohio River valley. Archaeologists have been able to put together a good picture of Hopewell culture. Although corn, squash, and beans were raised, hunting and fishing were as, or even more, important than farming. The Hopewellians (hohp-WEL-ee-uhns) adopted the class system of the Adenans and developed it further. They had both a ruling class and a priest class. A **division of labor** also existed. People were trained to use different skills. Only certain people did certain jobs. Artist and trader were two of the jobs.

Hopewellians may have been the first traders north of Mexico. Their trade network stretched from the Rockies to the Atlantic and from the Great Lakes to the Gulf coast. But between 500 and 700 A.D., Hopewell culture began to fade. Archaeologists think it was because of a decline in trade.

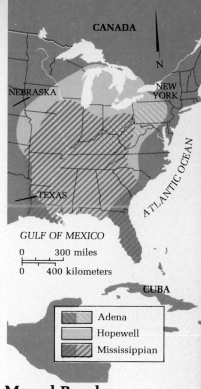

Mound Peoples

Mississippian

The third mound-building culture was the Mississippian. It began between 500 and 700 A.D. in the Mississippi Valley. The development of the Mississippian culture shows what occurs when farming becomes the chief source of food.

The people came to depend on corn as their main crop. It needed very fertile soil so the first Mississippian centers developed along rivers. There, yearly flooding left rich soil along the banks. In time, the growing population may not have been able to raise enough food from the land around the first centers. Between 700 and 1600, the people began moving west, south, and southeast. They followed the major river valleys.

In its early stages, Mississippian culture followed Hopewellian patterns. But differences soon arose. Centers became much larger. Besides burial mounds, the centers contained markets, homes, and workshops. There were often one or more giant temple mounds within the walls. Division of labor existed as it had in the Hopewellian culture, but it was more developed. Besides farmers, artists, and traders, archaeologists have found evidence of upper classes, a warrior class, and slaves.

The religious and government systems were one. **Government** is a formal way of exercising power over others. Each center and its villages and farms were the heart of a city-state ruled by priests. Besides local territory, a city-state might rule distant settlements. The Mississippians, unlike the Hopewellians, seem to have spread their influence by war.

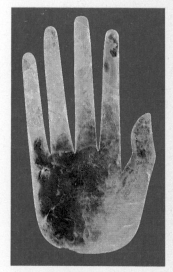

This ornament of mica, a mineral that can be broken into thin strips, was found in a Hopewell mound. Mica was one of the chief trade goods of the Hopewellians.

Mississippian culture began to fade in the 1500s. The northern centers disappeared—possibly because the soil wore out. The people moved either to the plains or the forests. In either case, they had to adapt their ways to a new environment. The southern centers continued into the 1600s. Europeans who explored what are now the states of Louisiana, Mississippi, Florida, Georgia, Alabama, North Carolina, and Tennessee, met some of the last of the mound builders—Natchez (NACH-ez), Chickasaw (CHIK-uh-saw), Choctaw (CHAHK-taw), and Cherokee (CHER-uh-kee).

OTHER CULTURES

Between 1000 and 1600 A.D., the peoples of the northeastern Woodlands were developing their own ways of doing things. In general, these groups combined hunting and farming. Those who lived along rivers and coasts fished, too. Most groups lived in villages or towns. Some built their villages like forts because of frequent wars.

Often villages contained several clans. A **clan** is a group of people that claims to be descended from the same person. Villages were governed by **councils** (KOWN-suhls), groups of people who make laws. Council members from all the villages within a nation would sometimes meet. During this period, groups with similar cultures—customs, traditions, language, and so on—came to think of themselves as **nations.**

Iroquois: Government

Iroquoian (ir-uh-KWOI-uhn) is the name of a Native American language family. Five Iroquoian-speaking nations—the Mohawk, Oneida (oh-NY-duh), Cayuga (kay-OO-guh), Onondaga (ahn-uhn-DAW-guh), and Seneca (SEN-uh-kuh)—lived in what is now northern New York State. In the late 1500s, they joined in a league called the Five Nations. A **league** (LEEG) is a union of several peoples, groups, or nations to promote common interests. About 1722, after being pushed out of North Carolina by colonists, the Tuscarora (tuhs-kuh-ROR-uh) moved north and joined the league. Then it became known as the Six Nations.

The Iroquois (IR-uh-kwoi) had a highly developed government system. Women had powerful roles in this system. A **role** is the part a person has in a group. The older women in a village chose the men who represented the clans on councils. Each Iroquois village had a council and so did each nation. The council for a nation decided only that nation's business. The Council of the League did not interfere in affairs within member nations. However, it did govern affairs among member nations. It also handled matters with other Native American peoples. It was this council, for example, that declared war. Each nation had one vote on the Council of the League. But decisions had to be agreed on by all members. The main purpose of the league was to

A Calusa of southern Florida carved and painted this deer head in the 1400s.

The Ojibwa, called Chippewa by Europeans, fished for much of their food. This painting shows a camp at their summer fishing grounds at Sault Ste. Marie in what is now Michigan.

keep the Iroquois from fighting each other. But there was another goal. Chiefs of the Seneca spoke about it in the late 1700s:

> Many nations lived in this country. But they had no wisdom. They warred together. The Six Nations were powerful and forced them to make peace. They kept their lands. They lived under the protection of the Six Nations, as brothers of their fathers. They were men and when at peace had the right to live upon the earth.

A **main idea** is the key point of a paragraph, section, or chapter. Sometimes a main idea is directly stated as a sentence. To help you test whether a sentence states the main idea, look for **supporting details.** These are details that back up this idea. Being able to locate main ideas and supporting details will help you decide what is or is not important to remember about a topic as you study. Look at the section on Iroquois government. **1.** What is the stated main idea of the second paragraph? **2.** Two of the supporting details for the second paragraph are: Each village had a council; so did each nation. Find another supporting detail.

BUILDING READING SKILLS

LOOKING BACK

1. List any of the five changes that occurred in each of the following cultures because of a steady food supply: **a.** Adena. **b.** Hopewellian. **c.** Mississipian.
2. Give one example of how Hopewell culture built on Adenan culture.
3. **a.** According to the text, what kind of government did the Iroquois have? **b.** List two details that describe it.

Chapter 3   **Plains Nations**

LOOKING AHEAD

This chapter describes how the environment affected the development of two different cultures on the Plains. One was a hunting culture; the other mixed hunting with farming. You will also read how outside forces, such as the horse, changed the cultures. After you study this chapter, you will be able to:

★ show how the horse changed Plains cultures.
● list the chief features of the Plains hunting culture.
★ describe how the Mandan and Teton Sioux adapted to the horse.

Social Studies Vocabulary

society   culture trait   cause and effect

People

Mandan   Teton Sioux

Places

Plains culture region

Words and Terms

nomadic hunting
band

The Plains culture region covers about one-third of the U.S. The earliest people on the Plains were big-game hunters. Between 5000 and 2500 B.C., gathering or hunting and gathering spread across the Plains. On the southern Plains, this way of life continued into the 1800s A.D. The environment there was not suited to farming. But on the northern and eastern Plains, climate, soil, and water resources were better. Some time after 500 B.C., gathering gave way to farming, though hunting remained important. Knowledge of farming may have spread onto the Plains from the Woodlands.

FARMING AND HUNTING

Around 800 A.D., a real farming economy was developing on the northern and eastern Plains. Permanent villages were growing up along rivers and streams. Women were farming beans, squash, corn,

and sunflowers. Men continued to hunt, but hunting was less important than it had been. The hunters moved after the buffalo on foot
because they had no horses.

Horses

In the north and east, this farming and hunting way of life continued
into the 1700s. By then, almost every nation on the Plains had horses.
The first horses had come with the Spanish to the Southwest in the
1500s. From time to time horses escaped and were caught by Native
Americans. Native Americans also raided each other's villages and
European settlements for horses. In some parts of the Plains, horses
became a valuable trade good.

With horses, Native Americans could follow buffalo herds for long
distances. The final kill was swift and easy. Buffalo became more important for food and clothing. Some farming and hunting nations,
such as the Cheyenne (shy-AN) and Sioux (SOO), gave up farming for
buffalo hunting.

Mandan: Farmers and Traders

Not all Plains peoples turned entirely to hunting when they got
horses. The Mandan (MAN-dan), for example, continued to farm

**Karl Bodmer, a Swiss
artist traveling
in the U.S., painted this
Mandan village in 1833.
Four years later most
of the Mandan nation was
dead from smallpox
spread by white traders.**

Babies were placed in cradleboards, such as this one from the Comanche, to free their mothers for other work.

advisor: person who gives an opinion about what should be done

along the Missouri River in what is now North Dakota. But they also became traders to their neighbors who hunted on horseback. The Mandan traded vegetables and tobacco for buffalo meat and hides. When Europeans came, the Mandan added guns, axes, knives, beads, and cloth to their trade goods.

The Mandan had clans like the Woodlands peoples, but they also had societies. A **society** (suh-SY-uh-tee) is like a club. It is a group of people who share certain interests. The Mandan had social and warrior-soldier societies, which both women and men could join. Women had their own societies, too, like the Enemy Women's Society. It held victory dances after raids. Each society had its own duties and ceremonies. The Dog Society, for example, was made up of warriors. These warriors took part in real raids, but they also played out their roles in ceremonies.

HUNTING

While northern and eastern peoples farmed and hunted, other groups on the Plains hunted buffalo, deer, and elk on foot and gathered wild foods such as berries and nuts. With the coming of horses and, later, of guns, life changed dramatically for these peoples. Buffalo meat became their chief source of food. The hides of the buffalo were used to make clothes and tipi (TEE-pee) covers. Little was left to waste. By the end of the 1700s, nomadic hunting—moving in search of food— was the usual way of life for Native Americans on the southern Plains.

Before then, only men went on hunts, but now whole villages went. The peoples abandoned dirt homes and lived in tipis year-round. These could be taken down quickly and easily moved to new camps. Because everything a person owned had to be carried, containers had to be unbreakable. Leather pouches became the only way to carry goods. Artwork had to be done on hides and tent covers that could be rolled up. Porcupine quill embroidery and beadwork on clothes became the main forms of decoration.

As more people got horses, they moved onto the Plains. Some people came only to hunt and then rode back to their homes. Others came to stay. Those with horses and guns forced out those without them. Wars were frequent but were usually a series of short raids. Warriors did not kill their enemies but struck them with a stick. This was called counting coup (KOO) and was considered braver than killing.

Unlike the Woodlands peoples, Plains hunters had little government. Nations were divided by bands, groups of families that lived and traveled together. Among some peoples, bands were organized by clans. When a nation came together for a council or a hunt, each band camped in its own circle or semicircle. Chiefs were selected because of bravery or wisdom, but they were only advisors. Councils of leading warriors really made the decisions, which were based on agreement. Male and female societies were also important to the hunters' social and governmental lives.

Teton Sioux: Once Farmers

By the mid-1700s, the Teton (TEE-tuhn) Sioux had been forced from Minnesota onto the plains of North and South Dakota. They were pushed out by the Ojibwa (OH-jib-way) and Cree (KREE), who had been armed by French and British trappers. Because life on the Plains was centered on horses, the Teton Sioux gradually exchanged their farming and hunting culture for a hunting one. The societies, festivals, and other culture traits of the Plains hunters became theirs. A **culture trait** is a characteristic shared by members of the same culture. For example, horses became the Teton Sioux's most valuable property.

Below is a Teton Sioux song that was made up by Swift Dog when he gave a captured horse to his sister. Music was an important part of Native American life during this time. There were songs for societies, religious songs, lullabies, and songs to tease friends and enemies. Warriors also made up songs to honor an event like this raid. Anyone could make up a song. There were no official songwriters.

Swift Dog said: "When the railroad first passed through the Black Hills we went on the warpath as far as the end of the road. We went through Shell River. I do not remember what tribe we went after, but I think it was the Omaha." Swift Dog captured a horse which he gave to his sister with the following song.

Sister, I Bring You a Horse
Older Sister, come out. Horses
I bring. Come out.
One you may have.

Because they moved so often, Plains Native Americans painted their pictures on hides that could be rolled up for easy carrying. This buffalo robe shows a Mandan battle.

BUILDING READING SKILLS

You have just read how the coming of the horse brought changes to the Plains peoples. This relationship between two events is called **cause and effect. 1.** Try to answer the question: What changes came about because of the horse? Replace *changes* with *effects* and replace *came about* with *were caused.* Using the words *cause* and *effect* in a question is a way to see if the question is asking for a cause-and-effect relationship. **2.** Is the question above asking for a cause and an effect?

LOOKING BACK

1. Generally speaking, what effects did the horse have on: **a.** farming and hunting peoples? **b.** hunting peoples?
2. Based on data under the heading Hunting, list five traits of the Plains culture.
3. **a.** What change did the Mandans make in their way of life because of the horse? **b.** How did the horse change the life of the Teton Sioux?

Chapter 4   Basin and Plateau Peoples

LOOKING AHEAD

This chapter is about the differences and similarities between the Basin and Plateau cultures. The original cultures were directly influenced by the environment. With the coming of the horse, changes occurred. After you study this chapter, you will be able to:

- describe the development of the Desert culture in the Great Basin and Plateau.
- identify the spread of Plains traits to the Shoshoni as an example of cultural diffusion.
- describe changes the horse made among the Nez Perce.
- ★ compare and contrast the Basin and Plateau cultures.

Social Studies Vocabulary

extended family   cultural diffusion
custom   compare and contrast

People

Desert culture   Shoshoni   Nez Perce

Places

Great Basin culture region   Plateau culture region

Two separate cultures developed within the Intermountain Basins and Plateaus. One grew in the Great Basin where the climate is dry, and water, plants, and animals are scarce. Much of the land is desert and salt flats. A salt flat is caused when a lake or pond dries up, leaving only the salt. The Plateau has valleys, mountains, and rivers. In parts, the land is rocky and infertile, but the rivers are rich with fish.

Neither area developed farming. In the Basin, the people remained hunters, gatherers, and fishers. In the Plateau, fishing was much better, and the people also traded. But the groups were never sure of a steady food supply. Archaeologists have not found any groups in either region similar to the mound builders.

DESERT CULTURE

The first peoples of the Great Basin and the Plateau were big-game hunters. Sometime around 7000 B.C., a food-gathering and small-game-hunting culture developed in the Great Basin. Archaeologists call it the Desert culture.

The people ate seeds, berries, roots, rabbits, and mountain sheep. They fished wherever there were lakes and rivers. To fit their new way of life, the Desert people developed food-grinding tools and baskets. They needed tools, for example, to crush the seeds and the baskets to hold the food they gathered.

About 6000 to 5000 B.C., people of the Desert culture began moving into the Plateau. They were escaping a drying out of the climate in the Great Basin. The Desert people mixed with the groups already in the Plateau and their influence changed the way of life in the Plateau. In time, the Plateau peoples turned more and more to food gathering. They, too, began to use food-grinding tools and baskets like those of the Desert people.

Around 2500 B.C., the climate began to cool off, and people moved back into the Basin. As a result of this separation, different Basin and Plateau cultures developed.

BASIN CULTURE

In the Basin, the Desert culture continued with little change until the Europeans came in the 1800s. The people remained hunters and gatherers. They traveled in small bands that were usually extended families. An **extended family** includes father, mother, unmarried and married children and their families, grandparents, uncles, aunts, and cousins. During the warmer seasons, a family would move from place to place looking for food. During the winter, several families would settle together in one village. Each village had a leader, but there was no real government.

Around 1700, horses appeared in the eastern and northern Basin. The animals were probably traded from Southwest Native Americans. Where horses were used, the Basin culture became like that of the Plains hunters. In other areas, the Desert culture continued.

Shoshoni: Hunter-gatherers Turned Hunters

The Shoshoni (shoh-SHOH-nee) lived in the northern part of the Great Basin but roamed from the Wyoming Rockies to eastern Oregon. They were among the earliest Basin peoples to have horses and to move onto the Plains to hunt buffalo. In time, they borrowed the clothing, weapons, and war customs of the Plains hunters. A **custom** is a way of doing something or of acting. For example, the Shoshoni gave up their bark- or grass-covered homes for tipis. Their feasts and ceremonies became similar to those of the Plains peoples. This is an example of **cultural diffusion** (dih-FYOO-zhuhn), the spread of culture from one group to another.

Among most early Native Americans, dancing was important. People danced for religious and for ceremonial reasons as well as for fun. Below is a description of a Shoshoni dance for fun. It was recorded at the Shoshoni reservation at Wind River, Wyoming.

Plains Native Americans used their paintings to record important events in a man's or nation's history. This painting is from the Shoshoni. How is it similar to the Mandan buffalo robe?

Only men took part in the dance. They wore cloths painted black and white that covered them from waist to thighs. The men painted themselves all over with black dots. Each carried a bow and blunt arrows. The women or other nondancers split sticks and put a bead or other small object in the split. These were placed in front of the dancers. The men danced up to the sticks, then pretended to run away in fear. At times they would rush at the audience and pretend to shoot them. Finally, the dancers grabbed up the sticks. Then men from the audience would throw water at them. The dancers would then run away a short distance and begin the dance again.

What can archaeologists learn from this 3,000-year-old duck decoy about how Basin peoples obtained food? The decoy was found in Lovelock Cave, Nevada.

PLATEAU CULTURE

After the climate changed around 2500 B.C., the Plateau region became cooler. Fish reappeared, and fishing became important. New kinds of artifacts began to appear. Stone tools and carvings, burial mounds, and copper objects, among other things, came into use. They seem to have been brought by a people from the Northwest. The Plateau culture developed from a slow blending of the new and the old.

During the winter, Plateau peoples settled in villages along river valleys. In summer, they traveled to the mountains where they collected roots and berries and hunted. By about 1000 A.D., the Plateau groups had developed a government system that made them different from the Basin peoples. Villages had their own leaders who were usually chosen because of talent and ability. But in some villages, leaders ruled because they were descended from earlier leaders. When several bands joined for a hunt or for war, the leaders of each band chose new leaders for the whole group.

Outside Influences

After about 1300, trade with Pacific Coast peoples brought new influences to western parts of the plateau. For example, some western Plateau peoples began building their houses of mats and boards and weaving their clothes of bark the way Northwest peoples did.

The eastern Plateau groups were more influenced by the Plains. During the early 1700s, they started to use horses. Although they continued to fish, the eastern Plateau people also hunted buffalo. Some hunts lasted several years. Along with buffalo hides and meat, the hunters brought back Plains culture traits.

Nez Perce: Fishers Turned Hunter-traders

The Nez Perce (NEZ PERS) lived in the Columbia and Snake river valleys in what is now Oregon, Idaho, and Washington. Before the horse, they lived mainly by salmon fishing. At first, the Nez Perce had little use for horses because they did little hunting. But the horses did well in the plateau. The few small herds grew rapidly, and the Nez

As the Nez Perce moved onto the Plains, they adopted much of the culture of the Plains, such as beadwork.

Perce became skilled horse breeders and traders. Some of the horses were Appaloosas (ap-uh-LOO-suhz)—brown horses with a large white patch with black spots on their rumps. These horses became important as trade goods.

In time, the Nez Perce became skilled riders. The following is from the diary of an Army officer who went to a Nez Perce council in 1855.

Thursday, May 31—This evening we went, as usual, to the Nez Perce camp. There was a footrace but the great events of the evening were the horseraces. Each of the peoples here has a large number of horses. So wherever the people are, the prairies about them are covered with these animals. They roam at large until wanted by their masters. Part of these come from the wild horses of the prairies. Some, from the marks with which they are branded, show that they have been stolen from the Spanish in Upper Mexico.

Living as the people do on horseback, racing forms one of their greatest amusements. They will ride for miles, often having bets depending on the result. On this occasion we saw nearly thirty start at once and dash over the plain like the winds, sweeping round in a circle of several miles.

Because of their skill in horse breeding and riding, the Nez Perce turned more and more to hunting. Like the Shoshoni, they adopted much of the Plains hunting culture.

BUILDING READING SKILLS

When you **compare and contrast** two or more things, you look for the ways they are the same and the ways they are different. **1.** How is the Plateau culture the same as the Basin culture? **2.** How is it different?

To help you answer these questions, make two tables. Title one Basin Culture and one Plateau Culture. Under each, list the characteristics of the culture after 2500 B.C. Use as headings: Economy; Outside influences; Changes that occurred. See how many things are the same and how many are different.

LOOKING BACK

1. **a.** Describe the Desert culture that developed in the Great Basin. **b.** Why did it spread to the Plateau?
2. List two culture traits that spread from the Plains to the Shoshoni.
3. What changes did the horse bring to the Nez Perce?
★ 4. Compare and contrast the Basin and Plateau cultures after 2500 B.C. by writing one statement about their similarities and one about their differences. Include in your statement the economy, outside influences, and any changes that occurred because of outside influences.

Chapter 5   Southwest Cultures

LOOKING AHEAD

This chapter describes the development of three cultures in the Southwest. They all began in the Cochise culture, but environment and outside influences caused each to develop differently. After you study this chapter, you will be able to:

- compare and contrast the ways the Southwest cultures dealt with lack of water.
- ★ state the order in which the Southwest cultures rose and declined.
- describe the effects that the Mogollon, Hohokam, and Anasazi cultures had on one another.

Social Studies Vocabulary

acculturation   chronology

People

Zuni

Places

Southwest culture region

This Navajo sand painting shows white cornstalks and yellow pollen on a background of black earth. Why was corn important to the peoples of the Southwest?

The Southwest culture region is one of mountains, canyons, valleys, and desert. There are several rivers but little rainfall. Yet this region produced farming cultures.

COCHISE CULTURE

As you read in Chapter 1, the Southwest is where the first Sandia, Clovis, and Folsom points were found. By around 7000 B.C., big-game animals were dying out and the Desert culture was spreading into the area. As you may recall from the last chapter, the Desert culture began in the Great Basin and was based on food gathering. Archaeologists call the Desert culture in the Southwest the Cochise (koh-CHEES) culture. For several thousand years, the people of the Southwest also were food gatherers.

Between 2500 and 2000 B.C., corn appeared in the region. It probably came from Mexico through trade. The change to farming was slow, and farming as a way of life did not take hold until about 500 B.C.

Early Southwest Peoples

THREE ENVIRONMENTS—THREE CULTURES

Three cultures developed out of the Cochise: the Mogollon (moh-guh-YOHN), Hohokam (hoh-HOH-kuhm), and Anasazi (ah-nuh-SAH-zee). Although many of their early culture traits were like those of the Cochise, each culture developed differently. For example, each had to adapt to its own environment. Each was influenced by outside forces, though their reactions to these forces were different. As you read about the three, look for differences and similarities. Also look for cause-and-effect relationships.

Mogollon

The Mogollon culture appeared around 100 B.C. in the mountains of Arizona, New Mexico, and northern Mexico. In the beginning, the people were mainly gatherers. During the next 200 years, they learned to grow corn and beans without irrigation. In this area, the rains come in spring and midsummer. The Mogollon discovered that by building small stone dams on hillsides they could slow the runoff of rain. This allowed water to soak into the ground so crops could grow. The Mogollon also learned to plant near rivers and streams. There, occasional flooding watered their crops.

Between 1050 and 1200 A.D., influences from the Anasazi people began to appear in Mogollon culture. For example, the Mogollon stopped building round, dirt pit houses. Instead, they built large stone apartment houses as the Anasazi did. Sometime in the 1200s, the Mogollon culture disappeared. It had taken on so many Anasazi culture traits that it became part of Anasazi culture.

Hohokam

Archaeologists believe that the Hohokam culture began around 2,000 years ago. By about 600 A.D., the Hohokam had learned to build irrigation canals. Their canal systems were large and widespread. One system, for example, covered 240 kilometers (150 miles). Because they could direct river water wherever they wanted, the Hohokam slowly settled across central and southern Arizona.

Beginning around 900, Anasazi culture traits appeared among the Hohokam. Archaeologists believe these were brought by Anasazi moving peacefully into the area. What is most important about the coming of the Anasazi is what happened to the Hohokam. Like the Mogollon, they began to use Anasazi ideas. For example, the Hohokam also replaced their one-room dirt pit houses with one-story stone houses of many rooms.

During the 1400s, Hohokam culture faded away. Archaeologists do not know why. Nor are they sure what happened to the people. Some archaeologists believe the modern Pima (PEE-ma) and Papago (PAP-uh-goh) are descendants of the Hohokam.

This mountain sheep is really a bowl used for grinding. It was carved from volcanic ash about 800 A.D. and is from the Hohokam people.

Through trade or invasion the Hohokam were influenced by the Maya of Mexico. Among the traits they adapted was the building of earthen pyramids similar to this stone one of the Maya.

Anasazi

Anasazi culture began in the area where the four corners of Arizona, New Mexico, Colorado, and Utah meet. Archaeologists believe people were in the region around 2,000 years ago. These people were hunters and gatherers who also farmed corn and squash. Some archaeologists believe the corn came from the Woodlands. Around this time, some Woodlands people were moving west from the Mississippi Valley.

Sometime around 100 A.D., the Anasazi began to depend more and more on farming. Like the Mogollon, they depended on spring and midsummer rains and occasional flooding for irrigation. The Anasazi settled in villages and built pit houses. Archaeologists believe they borrowed this house style from the Mogollon. By 1100, the Anasazi had developed their own house style. They were building large stone apartment buildings of several stories with many rooms.

As settlements grew, religious, social, and political organizations developed. Their religion centered on nature and farming. Rain and good harvests were the themes of their ceremonies and dances. The ruling council for each settlement was taken from the male religious societies of the community. Religion, social groups, and government were all connected. Unlike the Mississippians, though, the Anasazi were peaceful. They did not force their rule on others.

As you have read, Anasazi influences began to move outward after 700. They spread not through war but through acculturation. **Acculturation** (uh-kuhl-chuh-RAY-shuhn) is a culture's taking of some culture traits from another culture with which it has contact over a long period. Each culture may influence the other, but one usually dominates. The change in house styles is an example.

dominate (DOM-uh-nayt): to have power over

By the late 1200s, the Anasazi were leaving their cliff dwellings. Archaeologists are not sure why, but they give several reasons. Tree-ring dating shows a drought, or long period without rain, in the area from 1276 to 1299. It is also possible that there was a widespread outbreak of disease. Nomadic peoples such as the Apache (uh-PACH-ee) may have moved into the area, forcing the Anasazi out. People may also have left settlements because of arguments between clans.

The Anasazi built new settlements in other areas and continued their old ways. But in 1450 they left many of these, too. When the Spanish arrived in 1540, they found people only in the Rio Grande (REE-oh GRAND) valley in New Mexico, at Acoma (AK-oh-muh) and Zuni (ZOON-yee) in New Mexico, and at Hopi (HOH-pee) in Arizona. The Spanish called the Anasazi villages *pueblos* (PWEB-lohs), meaning towns in Spanish. The Spanish also called the people *Pueblos*, and the name has lasted.

Zuni: A Pueblo People

The first Europeans the Zuni met were searching for the Seven Cities of Cibola (SEE-boh-luh). These cities were supposed to be built of gold and filled with jewels. Instead, the Spanish found stone villages whose people were able to grow corn in the desert. Corn was the chief food of the Pueblos and the basis of their religious and social lives. Below is a Zuni prayer asking for a good harvest. To the Zuni, the earth was like a mother and the sun was their father. As you read this, think of the different stages of growth—planting, watering, growing.

When spring comes,
All the different kinds of corn,
We shall lay to rest in the ground.
With their earth mother's living waters,
They will be made into new beings.
Coming out standing into the daylight
Of their sun father,
Calling for rain,

Anasazi cliff dwellings can be seen in many parts of the Southwest and in Colorado and Utah. This one is in Mesa Verde National Park, Colorado. Name some advantages and some disadvantages to cliff dwelling.

To all sides they will stretch out their hands.
Then from wherever the rain makers stay quietly
They will send forth their misty breath;
Their massed clouds filled with water will come out to sit down with us;
With outstretched hands of water they will embrace the corn—
Desiring that it should be so,
I send forth my prayers.

A modern Hopi artist painted this ceremony. The masked dancers represent Kachinas, or Hopi spirits, who dance and pray for good crops. They also punish bad children. The striped dancers are clowns.

In Chapter 1 of this unit, you learned that a time line shows the order or sequence in which events occurred. **Chronology** (kruh-NAHL-uh-jee) is another word for sequence of events. You can read a time line to find the sequence of events, but you can also discover chronology by reading text. Look through this chapter to find the order in which the Southwest cultures rose and declined. **1.** List the information, including the dates, in chronological order. **2.** Did any of the cultures overlap? **3.** By how many years?

BUILDING CHRONOLOGICAL SKILLS

LOOKING BACK

1. How did each of the following solve the problem of lack of water: **a.** the Mogollon? **b.** the Hohokam? **c.** the Anasazi?
★ 2. List in chronological order the rise and decline of the Southwest cultures. Include dates.
3. Describe how one of the Southwest cultures reacted to the others. **a.** Did it borrow culture traits from the others? **b.** As a result, did it change many of its own?

Chapter 6

Early Californians

LOOKING AHEAD

This chapter is about the peoples of California and their environment. You will see how the environment shaped their culture and how they used the environment to their advantage. After you study this chapter, you will be able to:

- describe how the physical features of California led to different languages.
- show how the early Californians used the environment.
- ★ pick out generalizations about the effects of free time on Californians.

Social Studies Vocabulary

myths   values   generalization

People

Pomo

Places

California culture region

varied (VAIR-eed): having many differences

At one time, the present state of California had the largest population of Native Americans north of Mexico. It was also the most varied. The environment these peoples had adapted to ranged from forests to deserts. Most of it, though, was mild in climate and rich in natural resources.

EARLIEST PEOPLES

By about 5000 B.C., big game had disappeared and the people were food gatherers. By then, the Desert culture had spread into California from the Great Basin. Its influence lasted for several thousand years. Besides food gathering, the people did some hunting, fishing, and shellfish gathering. Along the southern coast, they caught and ate sea animals such as dolphins. The population slowly grew.

MANY GROUPS, MANY LANGUAGES

Early Californians carved animal figures to ask the spirits for help in getting food. Someone made this whale to ask for a good hunt.

Around 500 A.D. and for the next thousand years, a number of cultures developed. Archaeologists think that 105 different groups — from 275,000 to 350,000 people — were living in the region when the Spanish began to colonize in 1769. So many groups had developed because of the physical features of the region. The many river valleys and mountains kept the people separated. Because of this separation, differences in language also arose. In this small area, 5 of the 12 Native American language families of the U.S. were spoken.

ACORN GATHERERS

Even though the region's physical features were different, the climate and natural resources were similar. Because of this, some common culture traits developed. The use of acorns for food was one. Another was an increase in free time.

The early Californians never farmed. Their environment provided them with plenty of food. They had fish, shellfish, sea animals, elk, deer, rabbits, birds, and many kinds of nuts, berries, and roots to eat. The most important food of most Californians, though, was acorns. Acorns could be stored for long periods and then ground into flour for mush or bread. The acorn became as important to early Californians as the buffalo was to Plains peoples.

Free Time

Generally, in plant-gathering cultures, people have to spend much of their time searching for food. Free time—time free from getting food—is something only farming peoples enjoy. But because they did not have to search for food, the Californians had free time, too. This meant they had time not just to make useful items such as baskets but also to decorate them. They had time to give to developing government and social and religious groups.

Because they were so separated, Californians did not have large government units. Each group, which may have been no more than a few hundred people, had its own leader. This person managed the group's affairs but was generally advised by a council. Some villages were organized by clans. Others were organized according to territory. To these people, clan membership was less important than where they lived.

This Pomo woman is weaving a bowl. Among Native Americans who did not have pottery, baskets were used as bowls, dishes, and even cooking pots.

How is this Pomo baby carrier similar to and different from the Plains cradleboard?

Both men and women had societies. Some societies were religious. Some were organizations that prepared young people for their jobs in life. For example, among the Pomo (POH-moh) who lived north of what is now San Francisco, young men paid to join a society of workers and be trained by them. One of the most important skills was basketmaking. The Pomo developed it into an art.

Pomo: Basket Makers

The Californians, like other Native American groups, had a rich collection of tales and myths. **Myths** (MITHS) often explain a group's beliefs. Among the Pomo and other Californians, older men and women used tales and myths to teach children their group's values. **Values** are those qualities a person or group considers important. Below is part of a Pomo myth about obedience.

> While the chief, named Wolf, went out to the mountains, the people were turned into animals for being disobedient. The chief's son alone remained. After that, when his father went out to hunt, the boy would cry. He was lonely. The chief began taking the boy along. But he told the boy, "When I find a deer, I will go toward it to shoot it, but you must look down. Don't look at me. If you do, I shall be turned into a deer and so will you." After a while, they saw a deer in the shade of a tree. The father went toward the deer, but the boy looked at him. Both were immediately turned into deer.

BUILDING READING SKILLS

A **generalization** (jen-uhr-uhl-uh-ZAY-shuhn) is a conclusion that is reached after gathering and analyzing data. It pulls together the common themes and ideas behind a number of examples and specific facts. For example, when archaeologists say that Californians based their economy on acorn gathering, they are making a general statement, or a generalization. Archaeologists analyzed many groups of early Californians and found that most depended more on acorns for food than on any other plant or on game. **1.** Find one generalization archaeologists make about the effect of free time on early Californians. **2.** How do you think they came to this generalization?

LOOKING BACK

1. How did California's physical features cause a variety of languages to develop?
2. **a.** What were two culture traits that early Californians had in common?   **b.** What part did the environment play in the development of each?
3. Read the material under the heading Free Time. Pick out two generalizations about free time's effect on early Californians.

Chapter 7   Northwest Coast Peoples

LOOKING AHEAD

This chapter is about the later fishing and trading groups of the Northwest Coast. Archaeologists know little about the earliest groups. Like the Californians, the later peoples did not farm. Yet they were able to develop complex societies. After you study this chapter, you will be able to:

- state and explain the main reason archaeologists find it difficult to study the Northwest Coast peoples.
- describe the environment's influence on these peoples.
- pick out a generalization about the potlatch.
- ★ classify data about Northwest Coast peoples.

Social Studies Vocabulary

craft   status
surplus   classify

People

Tlingit

Places

Northwest Coast culture region

Words and Terms

potlatch   totem pole

Totem poles represent figures from a clan's history. This totem pole from Alaska shows a raven and a man holding two salmon.

The people of the Northwest Coast were little influenced by other culture regions. The sea was the chief factor that affected their development. It gave them their food and their wealth. The Northwest Coast peoples were the wealthiest Native Americans north of Mexico.

EARLIEST PEOPLE

There is some evidence that big-game hunters roamed the Northwest Coast more than 8,000 years ago. Material remains show that by 1000 B.C. people who fished and hunted sea animals were in the area. During the next 2,000 years, fishing became the way of life along the coast. The people did some hunting and plant gathering, but they ate mostly fish and sea animals, such as porpoises (POR-puh-suhz), sea lions, and whales.

Archaeologists' Problem

The early Northwest Coast people are difficult for archaeologists to study. For one thing, the groups used materials, such as wood, that decay. In addition, the groups lived in an area of heavy rainfall. Moisture causes wood to rot quickly. Peoples who made pottery, like the Southwest Native Americans, left behind many more clues about their lives. From pottery, for example, archaeologists can tell time periods for cultures. Pottery also indicates changes in the development of a people's skills.

Because of a lack of such clues, knowledge of the Northwest Coast between about 1000 B.C. and 1200 A.D. is limited. Archaeologists have had more success in learning about the groups since then. What you will be reading is a general description of the later peoples.

FISHING

As you read in Chapter 2 of this unit, farming usually provides people with a steady food supply and free time. With this extra time, people develop organizations and crafts. A **craft** is work, such as carpentry, that requires skill with the hands.

abundant:
more than enough

Abundant fishing provided the Northwest Coast peoples with a steady food supply. Once they learned to preserve fish by smoking and drying it, they could create surpluses. A **surplus** (SER-pluhs) is more than is needed. In a surplus economy, Northwest Coast peoples had time for things other than just getting food.

Society

One result of free time and plenty of food was the development of a class system. The Northwest Coast peoples placed great emphasis on a man's **status** (STAY-tuhs), or social position. A woman's status was not considered. A man was ranked higher or lower than other men according to his place in the family. The closer he was in direct line of descent from the clan's founding ancestor, the higher his status.

The highest rank was that of chief. The chief was usually the oldest man in the clan. His younger brothers were next in importance, according to age. Younger brothers took over as leaders as older ones died. The lowest ranking were the most distant relatives. Below them were the slaves, who had been bought, traded, or taken in war.

Status was so important to Northwest Coast peoples that it became the reason for giving parties. The party was called a potlatch (PAHT-latch), which means to give. A man held a potlatch to give relatives more important rights and privileges. During the ceremony, the host would give away his property—canoes, blankets, even slaves. The more wealth a man gave away, the higher his status. The potlatch was supposed to show a man's or family's wealth and also confirm it.

Fishing was the chief way Northwest Coast peoples obtained food. This painting shows salmon fishing along the Colville River in what is now Washington. What other groups fished for food?

Potlatch guests were both witnesses and proof. Their coming and accepting gifts was supposed to show agreement with the host's idea of his importance.

Arts and Crafts

The use of wood by the Northwest Coast peoples is another example of how the environment influenced them. Cedar forests grew throughout the region. The peoples used the trees to make houses, canoes, tools, and household goods. The inner bark was woven into clothing. The rough outer bark was made into mats. The roots were used for cord and rope. These were used in fishing and in making household goods. Some peoples wove blankets from cedar bark and the hair of mountain goats.

In some areas of the Northwest Coast, houses had elaborately carved door posts and poles. The carvings—some of which are called totem (TOH-tuhm) poles—identified the family and clan who lived there and told their history. Masks, headdresses, and statues were also carved from wood. Some people made wooden boxes and rattles.

Tlingit: Fishers and Traders

The Tlingit (TLING-uht) were fishers and traders who lived in Alaska's Pacific Mountain region. Because of their abundant food supply, they developed division of labor. Only certain people did certain jobs. Tlingits were wood carvers, blanket weavers, silversmiths, or blacksmiths. Jobs were divided along family lines. For example, if a family had a talent for weaving blankets, it made blankets only. Within Tlingit families, customs and skill also decided the job of each

Blanket weaving was a valuable skill among Northwest Coast peoples. In this painting of a Salish dwelling, one woman spins dog and goat hair into yarn while another weaves.

member. Some people provided food while others worked at crafts.

This specialization encouraged trade. Each family in a village had to trade its specialty with other families for the things it needed. Tlingit people in one area might have different skills and resources than people in other areas. The communities would trade with each other for goods the way families did. Some of the trade goods were Chilkat (CHIL-kat) blankets, woven from cedar bark and the hair of mountain goats. Blanket designs represented different animals.

BUILDING READING SKILLS

To **classify** data means to arrange it into a system according to topics. In this chapter, you learned that the later Northwest Coast peoples shared certain culture traits. **1.** Make a table using the following terms as headings: Fishing; Arts and Crafts. Read the chapter again. Select the artifacts that were used in fishing and those that were part of the arts and crafts. List the data in the correct columns. **2.** Did you find that some data belonged under both headings?

LOOKING BACK

1. **a.** What is the main idea of paragraph 1 of the section Archaeologists' Problem? **b.** What are the supporting details?
2. What influence did the following have on the culture of the Northwest Coast peoples: **a.** the sea? **b.** the forests?
3. Pick out a generalization that explains the purpose of a potlatch.
4. Based on this chapter, select two topics you could use to classify data about the Northwest Coast peoples.

PRACTICING YOUR SKILLS

What If . . .   By the 1800s, the Plains peoples depended on horses. **What if** the Spanish had not brought horses with them? Would the life of the Plains peoples have changed anyway once they met Europeans? What culture traits, if any, would have changed?

Discussing   Many of the things in this unit on Native Americans may have been new to you. For example, you may have thought all Native Americans hunted buffalo from horseback. Pick out two or three things that surprised you. Discuss them with the class. Compare how you and your classmates viewed Native Americans before and after reading this material. Think about the following: Do you have a different picture of Native Americans now? Why do you think you saw them the way you did? Considering this unit, did you have a realistic picture?

Building Writing Skills   In Chapter 2 of this unit, you read about the importance of being able to locate main ideas and supporting details in your reading. When you write, you have main ideas and supporting details, too. But in writing, these are called topic sentences and supporting details. The **topic sentence** states what you will discuss and is often the first sentence when you are writing a paragraph. When you are reporting on something that you have read about, the main idea can become your topic sentence. Supporting details of the reading can be rearranged into details that support your topic sentence.
Activity: In 1754, Benjamin Franklin drew up a plan to unite the colonies. Called the Albany Plan of Union, it was based on the Iroquois League. Research and write a paragraph on the major points of the plan.

Researching, Making a Time Line, Writing

1. Fifty-five million years ago a prehistoric horse known as Eohippus (ee-oh-HIP-uhs) roamed North America. Research the development and disappearance of prehistoric horses in North America. Use the data to make a time line showing the time span of each species.
2. A number of cliff dwellings are now under the care of the National Park Service. Research one such park and write a paragraph about how and when it was found or what archaeologists uncovered about it.

Exploring

1. If your town or city has a local museum or historical society, find out if it has any artifacts of Native Americans. Arrange for a visit. Take notes on the names of the peoples, where they lived, and what happened to them. Draw pictures of the artifacts for a bulletin board display. Note type of artifact, date, size, shape, and use of each.
2. Arrange with your teacher for a Native American festival. Bring in collections of Native American legends, myths, songs, dances, and artifacts or pictures.

Reading

Bierhorst, John. *A Cry from the Earth*. New York: Scholastic Book Service, 1978. Native American music.

———, ed. *In the Trail of the Wind: American Indian Poems and Ritual Orations*. New York: Dell, 1971. Paperback. An anthology.

Highwater, James C. *Many Smokes, Many Moons*. Philadelphia: Lippincott, 1978. Native American cultural traditions.

Jacobson, Daniel. *Indians of North America* Series, 3 vols. New York: Watts, 1977.

O'Dell, Scott. *Sing Down the Moon*. New York: Houghton, 1970. Fiction. A Navajo girl tells the story of her people.

Raphael, Ralph B. *The Book of American Indians*. New York: Arco, 1973.

UNIT II   EUROPEANS AS EXPLORERS

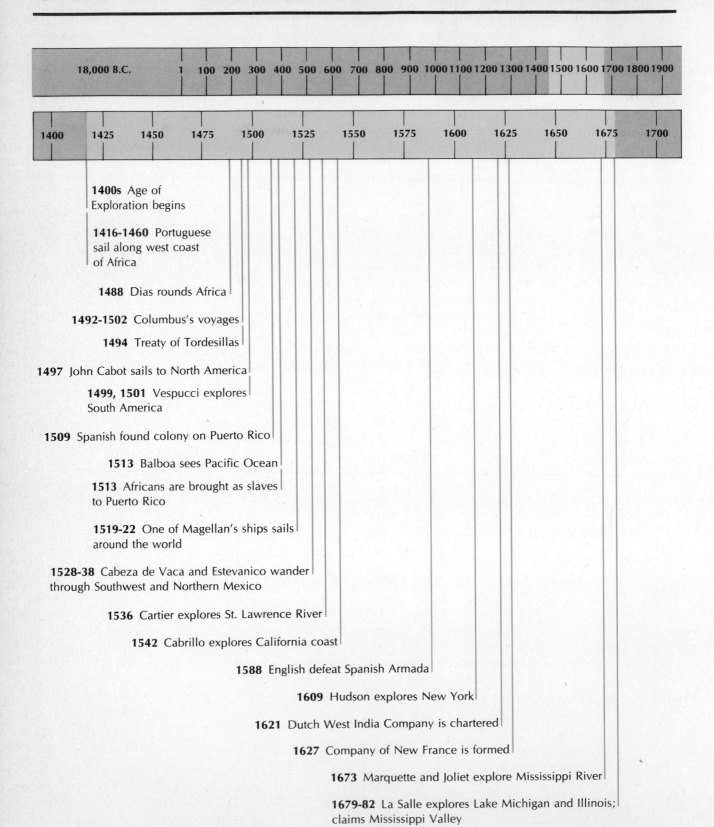

| 18,000 B.C. | 1 | 100 | 200 | 300 | 400 | 500 | 600 | 700 | 800 | 900 | 1000 | 1100 | 1200 | 1300 | 1400 | 1500 | 1600 | 1700 | 1800 | 1900 |

| 1400 | 1425 | 1450 | 1475 | 1500 | 1525 | 1550 | 1575 | 1600 | 1625 | 1650 | 1675 | 1700 |

1400s Age of
Exploration begins

1416-1460 Portuguese
sail along west coast
of Africa

1488 Dias rounds Africa

1492-1502 Columbus's voyages

1494 Treaty of Tordesillas

1497 John Cabot sails to North America

1499, 1501 Vespucci explores
South America

1509 Spanish found colony on Puerto Rico

1513 Balboa sees Pacific Ocean

1513 Africans are brought as slaves
to Puerto Rico

1519-22 One of Magellan's ships sails
around the world

1528-38 Cabeza de Vaca and Estevanico wander
through Southwest and Northern Mexico

1536 Cartier explores St. Lawrence River

1542 Cabrillo explores California coast

1588 English defeat Spanish Armada

1609 Hudson explores New York

1621 Dutch West India Company is chartered

1627 Company of New France is formed

1673 Marquette and Joliet explore Mississippi River

1679-82 La Salle explores Lake Michigan and Illinois;
claims Mississippi Valley

Chapter 1   Changes in Europe

LOOKING AHEAD

In Unit I, you read about what some of our ancestors were doing during the early history of the Americas. Many of our ancestors, though, came much later from Europe. This chapter discusses life in Europe from about 1000 to the 1500s A.D. It will help you understand the changes in Europe that led to overseas explorations. After you study this chapter, you will be able to:

- list the sequence of events that changed Europe between c. 1000 and the early 1500s.
- explain the effects of the crusades on European trade.
- state two reasons for the interest of Europeans in an all-water route to Asia.
- ★ list the effects of certain inventions on exploration.
- describe how the rise of nation states and the Reformation affected some Europeans.

Social Studies Vocabulary

profit   inference

People

crusaders   Johann Gutenberg   Martin Luther
Muslims   John Calvin   Henry VIII

Places

Holy Land   Asia
Middle East   Mediterranean Sea

Events

crusades   Reformation

While Mississippians were building city-states and the Anasazi were dry farming, Europeans also were forming governments and building religious and social groups. By the late 1400s, Europeans were eager to explore, trade with, and settle in distant lands. This Age of Exploration did not begin suddenly. A number of changes had to occur before people were ready to leave their homelands.

These changes began around 1000 A.D. For several hundred years before that, most Europeans lived on manors. Manors were like large farms and were owned by powerful nobles or high-ranking members of the Roman Catholic Church. At that time most Europeans were

Astrolabes such as this one helped early sailors find their way on the seas.

Christians and belonged to this Church. The manors were worked by men and women called serfs. They owed to their landowner most of what they grew or made. In return, a landowner protected his or her serfs during the many wars of the period.

Most Europeans knew little about the next manor, let alone the rest of the world. Because each manor was almost self-sufficient, there was little trade or travel between manors. Probably the biggest change to occur around 1000 was the increase in trade. An unlikely factor that helped bring about this increase was a series of religious wars, called the crusades (kroo-SAYDS).

self-sufficient
(SELF-suh-FISH-uhnt):
able to take care of
all one's own needs

THE CRUSADES

The first crusade was called in 1096 by the pope, the head of the Roman Catholic Church. He asked European Christians to stop fighting one another and fight to open the Holy Land. This is Jerusalem (juh-ROO-suhl-uhm) and the area around it in the Middle East. Most of the events of the Bible happened there.

Muslims had taken control of the area in the 600s and refused to let Christians visit it. Muslims (MUHZ-luhms) are followers of Islam (IS-luhm), a religion that began in the Middle East in the 600s. It is based on the teachings of Muhammed (mu-HAM-uhd), who believed that God or Allah (AL-uh) spoke to him and told him to spread His message. By about 700, Muslims had gained control of much of the Middle East and North Africa.

The crusades lasted about 200 years. Although many died on both sides, the crusades did not open the Holy Land. But they encouraged in Europeans an interest in Asia and Asian goods.

INCREASING TRADE

The Italian ships that carried crusaders to the Middle East returned filled with perfumes, medicines, sugar, spices, silks, and jewels. Europeans came to value and depend on many of these goods, especially spices. There was no refrigeration then and food spoiled quickly. Spices covered the taste of spoiled meat. The demand grew for Eastern goods, and Italian merchants took advantage of this.

Before the crusades, Muslims had controlled trade in the eastern Mediterranean (med-uh-tuh-RAY-nee-uhn). By the 1200s, Italian merchants had set up their own trading bases in Middle Eastern ports. In these ports, they made contact with Muslim traders who carried goods between Asia and the Middle East. It was a long, difficult trip over mountains and across deserts.

Before trade goods reached European markets, they passed through the hands of many merchants. Each time an item changed hands, the seller charged enough to make a profit. A **profit** is the money remain-

Before the invention of the printing press, all books, maps and charts had to be copied by hand. Why were errors possible? Could errors in a map be dangerous?

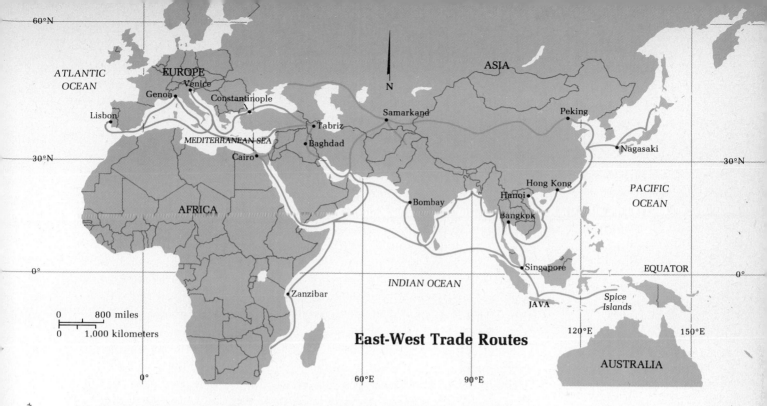

East-West Trade Routes

ing after all expenses are paid. By the time goods reached London or Paris, their prices were many times the original cost.

By the 1400s, Europeans along the Atlantic coast began to look for cheaper and faster routes to these Asian goods. They wanted to cut out all merchants along the way and also to break the hold of Italians and Muslims on this trade. European merchants saw great profits for themselves if they could find an all-water route to Asia.

INVENTIONS

Certain changes in European shipbuilding and sailing equipment encouraged the interest of the merchants. During the 1400s, Europeans began to design larger, faster, safer, and more maneuverable ships. For the first time, their ships could sail more directly into the wind. This was done by using triangular-shaped sails. These sails could be turned more than square sails so they caught the wind better. Navigational (nav-uh-GAY-shuhn-uhl) or sailing aids were also developed. Compasses and astrolabes (AS-truh-laybs) that found direction and position at sea were invented.

Another development that boosted the confidence of Europeans as they took to the seas was the use of guns and gunpowder. Gunpowder was introduced into Europe from China, and guns may have come from the Arabs around 1250.

Although it may seem strange, the invention of the printing press also encouraged European interest in exploration. About 1454, Johann Gutenberg (GOOT-uhn-berg) began to use movable type for printing. For the first time, many copies of books, maps, charts, and

maneuverable
(muh-NOO-vruh-buhl):
manageable; easy
to steer

other printed material could be made quickly. Before then, such things had to be copied by hand, and one copy could take weeks or even months to make. Books were rare and belonged only to the wealthy. As books became more plentiful after the mid-1400s, more people learned to read. They began to develop an interest in other places and people.

BUILDING READING SKILLS

Sometimes a cause-and-effect relationship is fully explained. Both the cause and the effect are actually stated. This is the kind of cause-and-effect relationship you learned about on page 46. Often, though, all or part of a cause or of an effect is only suggested. You have to make an inference about one or the other. This means you have to analyze and evaluate the given data to reach a conclusion. An **inference** (IN-fuhr-uhns) is a statement that interprets or explains the meaning of facts. It is not a fact but is based on facts.

You have just read about four inventions that affected exploration. With each one, the cause of the change—the invention—is described. But its effect on exploration is only suggested. Read the section again. Think about the effects of the inventions. **1.** How would being able to sail into the wind make sailing more useful? **2.** How would being able to find direction at sea affect exploration? **3.** How might guns and gunpowder affect it? **4.** How might printing a book about another land make people want to explore?

Marco Polo, an Italian trader, traveled through Asia in the 1200s. Here he is shown at the court of Kublai Khan, ruler of China. Polo's *Description of the World* encouraged Europeans to seek the riches of Asia.

RISE OF NATION STATES

The growth of trade brought with it the end of manors. Serfs moved to the fast-growing towns and cities and took up crafts as tailors, shoemakers, weavers, and spinners, among other jobs. A new class developed between the upper-class nobles and church leaders and the lower-class serfs. This was the middle class of craftworkers and merchants.

By the early 1500s, nation states had developed in parts of Portugal, Spain, and France. Before this, power in these areas had been divided among many nobles. With the end of manors and the growth of towns, some of the stronger nobles seized power. They unified large areas and brought the lesser nobles under their power. To increase their wealth and power, many of these new kings and queens paid for voyages of exploration. The monarchs hoped the voyages would do three things: increase trade; bring new lands and people under their control; convert people to Christianity.

convert (kuhn-VERT): to change from one belief to another

THE REFORMATION

The last great event that changed Europe at this time was the Reformation (ref-uhr-MAY-shuhn). In the early 1500s, Martin Luther in Germany, John Calvin in Switzerland, and King Henry VIII of England broke away from the Roman Catholic Church. They protested some of its teachings and its power. These breaks with the Church began a movement known as the Protestant Reformation. Protestants thought of themselves as reforming or making the Church better.

Because of the Reformation, each monarch decided which religion the people in his or her nation would follow. Some monarchs remained Catholics. Others became Protestants. Those people who refused to accept the decision of their monarchs were persecuted. Wars broke out. Over the next several hundred years, many Europeans left their homelands looking for peace and religious freedom. Thousands came to the Americas.

persecute: to treat badly; to punish

LOOKING BACK

1. In How to Read Your Textbook, you learned how to skim. Skim this chapter to list in chronological order the events that changed Europe between c. 1000 and the early 1500s.
2. What was the effect of the crusades on European trade?
3. Why were Europeans along the Atlantic coast interested in an all-water route to Asia in the 1400s?
★ 4. **a.** List the inventions that encouraged exploration. **b.** How did each affect exploration?
5. Why did the Reformation cause some Europeans to leave their homelands?

Chapter 2   Age of Exploration

LOOKING AHEAD

This chapter describes the early European explorations of the world. You will learn how Europeans found the Americas accidently. You will also begin to see what European attitudes were toward Native Americans. After you study this chapter, you will be able to:

- compare Henry the Navigator's reasons for encouraging exploration and those of other monarchs.
- list the sequence of voyages that led to finding an all-water route to Asia.
- classify data about explorations.
- ★ read a table to learn about explorations.
- ★ read a historical map to see Columbus's four voyages.

Social Studies Vocabulary

legend	table
colony	historical map

People

Vikings	Bartholomeu Dias	Isabella
Bjarni Herulfsson	Vasco da Gama	Arawak
Leif Ericson	Christopher Columbus	
Henry the Navigator	Ferdinand	

Places

Scandinavia	Portugal	Spain
Vinland	Cape of Good Hope	Watlings Island

Words and Terms

saga	academy

The many changes you read about in the last chapter led to the European Age of Exploration. Mapping and settling the Americas was one result of these explorations. But the Europeans of the 1400s may not have been the first to visit America.

EARLIEST EXPLORERS

Vikings (VY-kings) may have sailed to North America as early as the 900s A.D. Vikings were traders and warriors who lived in Scandinavia (skan-duh-NAY-vee-uh)—Denmark, Sweden, Norway, and Iceland.

They were also expert sailors. While other Europeans feared sailing out of the sight of land, Vikings sailed as far as Greenland.

There are several Viking sagas (SAH-guhs) or stories about their visits to North America. The sagas were not written down until the 1100s or 1200s and later Europeans thought they were legends. **Legends** are stories that may or may not be true and that are passed from one generation to the next. Some historians, however, are beginning to believe the sagas are true.

One saga tells of Bjarni Herulfsson (bee-YAR-nee HAR-yuhlf-suhn) who in 986 sailed from Iceland for Greenland. A storm arose and blew his ship off course. For days he and his crew sailed on in the fog without knowing their direction. When the fog lifted, they saw before them a flat, wooded land, not the ice-covered mountains of Greenland. Herulfsson did not go ashore, but scholars believe he saw what we know as Cape Cod, Massachusetts.

Around 1000, Leif Ericson (LAYV ER-ik-suhn), another Viking, may have set out to find the lands Herulfsson had seen. The sagas tell of Ericson's landing at Newfoundland (NOO-fuhnd-land). He then sailed south to a land the Vikings called Vinland (VIN-land) because of its grape vines. Some historians believe Ericson landed in what is today Massachusetts.

According to the sagas, attempts at settlement failed, and the Vikings gave up interest in the West. Several hundred years passed before exploration of the Americas began again. Then, it was not Vikings that came, but other Europeans sailing under Portuguese and Spanish flags.

This painting by Jan Vermeer of a mapmaker dates to 1669. Early mapmakers used sailors' records as sources for their maps.

Columbus takes leave of Isabella and Ferdinand for his trip to find Asia. This 1590 woodcut was made by cutting the design on a wood block, inking the block, and pressing it on paper.

PORTUGUESE BEGINNINGS

Portugal had become a strong nation state in the early 1400s under King John I. One of his sons, Prince Henry, wanted to learn more about the lands and sea routes south of Portugal. Although he was not a sailor, he is known as Henry the Navigator because of his great interest in exploration.

Henry encouraged explorations for several reasons. He had heard stories of gold and of a Christian kingdom south of the Sahara (suh-HAIR-uh) in Africa. He wanted to find both. The Christian kingdom could help him take the Holy Land from the Muslims. It could also act as a base for spreading Christianity in Africa. In addition, Henry thought an all-water route to Asia could be found by way of Africa. He was looking for a way that Portugal could trade directly with India. This would greatly increase Portugal's wealth and power.

Henry realized that the success of his plans depended on two things. His sailors had to have better ships and better knowledge of geography and of navigation. Henry set up an academy (uh-KAD-uh-mee), or school, to study these things. He brought to it geographers, mapmakers, astronomers, and mathematicians as teachers. As students, he sent sea captains and shipbuilders. They studied navigational methods, maps, and charts; designed better ships; and discussed possible explorations. Because of Henry's academy, Portugal in the 1400s knew more about sailing and geography than any other European nation.

astronomer
(uhs-TRAHN-uh-muhr):
one who studies the stars, planets, and other heavenly bodies

Trips into the Unknown

Henry's students put into practice on the seas what they learned at the academy. Through the years, Henry sent his captains farther and farther south along the west coast of Africa. Wherever they landed, they made contact with Africans and set up trading forts.

By the time Henry died in 1460, his captains had explored as far as modern Sierra Leone (see-ER-uh lee-OHN). After Henry's death, Portugal continued the search. In 1488, Bartholomeu Dias (DEE-ahs) rounded the Cape of Good Hope, but his frightened crew forced him to turn back. In 1498, Vasco da Gama (duh GAH-muh) rounded the Cape and sailed to India. On his return, he sold his cargo of spices and silks for 60 times the cost of the trip.

With such huge profits to be made, the Portuguese started regular trips to Asia. They began taking business away from the Mediterranean, and soon Portugal was a center for trade goods from the East.

CHRISTOPHER COLUMBUS

Not everyone believed that Africa held the fastest and cheapest way to Asia. Christopher Columbus, an Italian sailor and mapmaker, believed the Portuguese should be sailing west. Many Europeans in the 1400s believed the earth was flat, but some, especially scholars, were convinced it was round. Columbus held this view. He believed that if he sailed west, he would eventually reach the East. He also thought that nothing lay between Europe and Asia.

In 1484, Columbus went to John II of Portugal with his idea. He wanted the king to finance a voyage westward across the Atlantic to Asia. King John's advisors disagreed with Columbus. They believed a water route lay by way of Africa. This was before Dias and da Gama showed that there was no waterway through it.

finance (fuh-NANS): to pay for

Support from Spain

After Portugal refused him help, Columbus took his plan to other European monarchs. Finally, in 1492. Ferdinand and Isabella of Spain agreed to finance his expedition. They gave him the authority to claim for Spain any non-Christian lands he might reach. This authority was the basis for later Spanish claims in the Americas.

Columbus set sail on August 3, 1492. His three ships—the *Nina*, the *Pinta*, and the *Santa Maria*—had a crew of 90 men and boys. During the 70-day trip, some frightened sailors aboard the *Santa Maria* staged a mutiny. But it was quickly put down.

Before dawn on the morning of October 12, a lookout on the *Pinta* saw land. The land—now called Watlings (WAHT-lingz) Island—is in the Bahamas (buh-HAH-muhz) in the Caribbean (kar-uh-BEE-uhn). At daylight the crew saw people whom Columbus described in this way:

expedition (eks-puh-DISH-shuhn): trip taken for a special reason

mutiny (MYOOT-uhn-ee): revolt against authority

I knew that they were a people who could be more easily converted to our holy faith by love than by force. We gave some of them red caps and

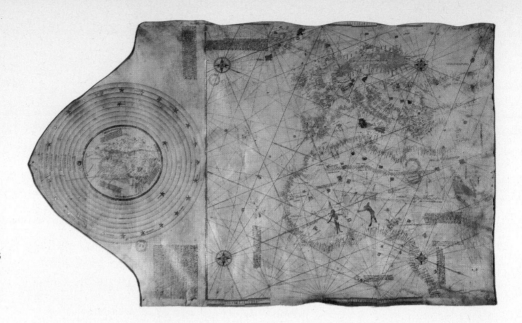

Columbus drew this map of Europe and Africa about 1492. Compare his map with a modern map of the same area. How different are they?

glass beads to put round their necks. We gave them many other things of little value which gave them great pleasure. These gifts made them so much our friends that it was a marvel to see. Afterwards, swimming and bringing us parrots, cotton threads, darts, many other things, they came to the ship's boats.

Carrying the Spanish flag, Columbus went ashore and named the island San Salvador (san SAL-vuh-dor), or Holy Savior, in honor of Jesus. Columbus thought he had reached the Indies, the name Europeans gave to Asia. Columbus was so convinced of this that he called the people *Indians*. He ignored the fact that they called themselves *Arawak* (AR-uh-wahk).

Other Voyages

Columbus made three more westward voyages. On each trip, he took along men to found colonies. A **colony** is a group of people sent to another land to set up a permanent settlement. The people remain citizens of the parent country.

During the second voyage in 1493, Columbus claimed various islands in the Caribbean for Spain. On his third voyage, he sailed as far as the mouth of the Orinoco (or-uh-NOH-koh) River in what is today Venezuela (ven-uh-zuh-WAY-luh). This was the first time Europeans saw the South American continent.

The fourth voyage brought Columbus to Central America. He reached what are today the nations of Honduras (hahn-DUR-uhs), Nicaragua (nik-uh-RAH-gwuh), Costa Rica, and Panama. Columbus returned to Spain for the last time in 1504. Everywhere he had gone in the Americas Columbus had found people, plants, and wildlife that were unknown in Asia. But he died in 1506 still convinced that he had reached the Indies.

THE SEARCH FOR A WATER ROUTE TO ASIA

Explorer	Date	Objective*	Gained Objective: Yes or No	Other Outcomes
Explorers sailing for Henry the Navigator	1416-1460	To search the west coast of Africa for gold, a Christian kingdom, and a route to Asia	In part	Explored and charted islands in Atlantic west of Europe and about one-fourth of West African coast
Bartholomeu Dias	1488	To reach India by sea	No	Proved water passage to east coast of Africa existed
Vasco da Gama	1497-1499	To reach India by sea	Yes	Made Portugal center for trade goods from Asia
Christopher Columbus	1492	To reach Asia by sailing west	No	First known European to reach the Americas; saw the Bahamas, Cuba, Haiti; started colony on Haiti
	1493	To reach Asia	No	Found colony on Haiti destroyed; started first permanent European colony in the Americas at Isabela (Dominican Republic); explored and claimed Guadeloupe, Jamaica, Puerto Rico; explored island of Marie Galante
	1498	To reach Asia	No	Reached Trinidad and mainland of South America at Orinoco River, Venezuela
	1502	To reach Asia	No	Reached Martinique in Lesser Antilles and Honduras, Nicaragua, Costa Rica, and Panama in Central America

*objective (uhb-JEK-tiv): goal; purpose; motive

A **table** arranges data in rows and columns according to topics. There are many kinds of tables. You read a numerical table in Life in America: The People. The table above shows categories of ideas. It takes all the people, dates, places, and objectives from the chapter and classifies them according to five topics. Each column lists only one topic. Wherever columns cross, there is related information. **1.** What was the objective of Bartholomeu Dias? **2.** Did he gain it? **3.** What were other outcomes of his voyage?

BUILDING SKILLS WITH TABLES

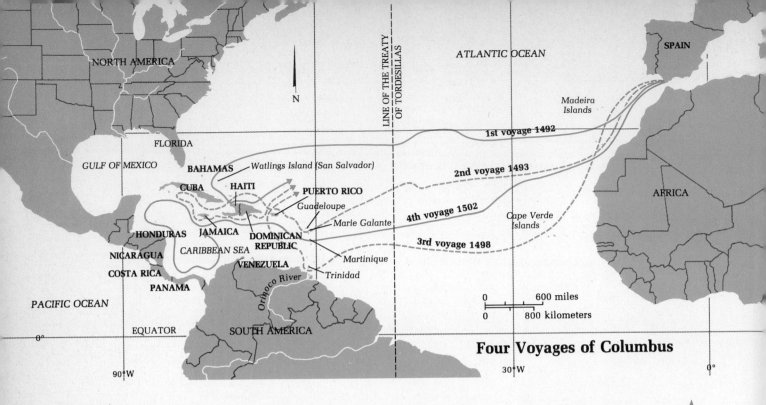

Four Voyages of Columbus

BUILDING MAP SKILLS

There are many types of maps. In Life in America: The Land, you worked with maps that showed political boundaries, natural regions, natural resources, and land use. Most of the maps in this textbook show historical data. This **historical map** shows the four voyages of Columbus. To help you locate this information, we have given you modern political boundaries in gray. Most historical maps only show you what the boundaries of countries were when the historical event took place. However, we think it is easier to understand the information if you can find familiar places and names. **1.** List the modern names of the areas Columbus landed on. **2.** List the areas that he sailed past.

LOOKING BACK

1. Reread page 72. Were Henry's reasons for exploring Africa the same as or different from reasons of others at the time?
2. How far along the African coast had the Portugese sailed by: **a.** 1460? **b.** 1488? **c.** 1498?
3. Using the table of explorations, answer the following questions: **a.** When did explorers for Henry the Navigator sail? **b.** What was their objective? **c.** What was Columbus's objective on each voyage? **d.** Make a table classifying explorations according to the country that financed them. Use these topics: Explorer; Nation Sailed For; Lands Found.
4. Using the historical map of Columbus's voyages, find: **a.** the modern U.S. state he came closest to. **b.** the greatest distance he traveled.

Chapter 3   Spanish in the Americas

LOOKING AHEAD

Columbus's voyages created great interest in the lands west of the Atlantic Ocean. This Chapter will tell you about other Spanish voyages of exploration and their goals. You will also learn how Spain and Portugal divided the lands and peoples between them. After you study this chapter, you will be able to:

- tell how America was named.
- describe the importance of the voyages of Vespucci, Balboa, and Magellan.
- identify the purposes of the Line of Demarcation and the Treaty of Tordesillas.
- ★ explain the major reason for the Spanish search for Cibola.
- read a table to explain the objectives of the early Spanish in the Americas.

Social Studies Vocabularly

isthmus	longitude	treaty	empire

People

Amerigo Vespucci	Cortes	Estevanico
Magellan	Aztecs	Fray Marcos de Niza
Balboa	Calusa	de Soto
Ponce de Leon	Narvaez	Coronado
Cordoba	Apalachee	
Maya	Cabeza de Vaca	

Places

Isthmus of Panama	Mexico	Seven Cities of Cibola
Puerto Rico	Florida	

Words and Terms

Line of Demarcation	Treaty of Tordesillas

Although Columbus believed he had found the Indies, it soon became clear that he had not. Between 1499 and 1501, Amerigo Vespucci (ves-POO-chee), an Italian merchant and explorer, sailed with Spanish and Portuguese expeditions along the coast of South America as far as modern Uruguay (YUR-uh-gway). In a long letter about his voyages, he told of a "new world" between Europe and Asia.

Vespucci was accidently responsible for the name *America*. His letter was published and a German geographer read it. When the geographer published a map of the world in 1507, he named the so-called "new world" *America* in honor of Vespucci.

In 1513, Vasco Nunez de Balboa (bal-BOH-uh), looking for gold, traveled across the Isthmus of Panama. An **isthmus** (IS-muhs) is a narrow strip of land that joins two larger areas. Instead of finding gold, Balboa became the first European to see the Pacific Ocean from the Americas. Other explorers then began to look for a sea route to the Pacific and on to India.

Knowledge of the true size of the globe came several years later. In 1519, the Portuguese navigator Ferdinand Magellan (muh-JEL-uhn) set out with five ships and a crew of 287 to find a way around South America to Asia. After crossing the Pacific, Magellan was killed in the Philippines (FIL-uh-peenz). Only one ship and 18 crew members returned, but the voyage added to European knowledge of the world.

NEW LANDS DIVIDED

Even before Vespucci's letter and these other voyages, the Spanish wanted to protect their claims to the new lands. They were especially worried about the Portuguese. In 1493, the Spanish asked the pope's help. Most Europeans still recognized the authority of the pope.

Pope Alexander VI drew a line through the Atlantic Ocean from north to south at about 38 degrees west longitude. **Longitude** (LAHN-juh-tood) is the distance of earth east or west of 0° at Greenwich, England. This is called the Line of Demarcation (dee-mahr-KAY-shuhn). All lands that lay west of the line could be explored and claimed by Spain. All lands east of the line could be explored and claimed by Portugal. All the people in these lands were to belong to the European nation that claimed their region. The Portuguese were not happy with the placement of the line. In 1494 by the Treaty of Tordesillas (tord-uh-SEE-yuhs), they had it moved about ten degrees farther west. A **treaty** is an agreement between nations.

SPANISH OBJECTIVES

Many Spanish soon followed Columbus across the Atlantic. Wealthy nobles who wanted more wealth and people who wanted to become rich came. Adventurers looking for excitement as well as gold led them. The Spanish monarchs encouraged them all because they wanted to add land and people to their rule.

Missionaries were also sent to convert the peoples of the Americas to Christianity. The Spanish were convinced that their religion was the one true faith. This is one reason they forced their religion on Native Americans. The Spanish, however, also believed that if Native Americans followed the religion of Spain, they would accept Spanish rule more easily. The Spanish wanted to teach more than their religion to Native Americans. They wanted to replace Native Ameri-

can customs and traditions with the Spanish way of life. It is not unusual for one culture group to think its ways better than all others.

At first, the Spanish built settlements only on the islands in the Caribbean. From these they explored north, west, and south.

San Juan in the late 1600s was a busy port. According to the map on page 81, which explorer landed on Puerto Rico?

Puerto Rico

One of the early settlements was made on Puerto Rico. The Arawak called it Borinquen (boh-reeng-KAYN), but the Spanish renamed it Puerto Rico. In 1508, Juan Ponce de Leon (PAHNS duh LEE-uhn) found gold on the island and the following year a colony was started. The Spanish forced the Arawak to work Spanish mines and plantations on land that had once been theirs. Diseases, terrible working conditions, and harsh punishment finally killed the Arawak. In 1513, their places were taken by Africans.

In 1521, a settlement was made near present-day San Juan. This settlement became a leading outpost of the Spanish in the Americas. Treasure ships stopped there for supplies before continuing their trip from Mexico to Spain.

The Maya

One of the first places the Spanish explored on the mainland was Mexico. There they did not meet any of the Native Americans you read about in the unit The First Americans. They met other groups, some of whom were ancestors of modern Mexican Americans.

In 1517, Francisco Fernandez de Cordoba (KOR-doh-bah) sailed from Cuba to Mexico. He was looking for people to use as slaves in Cuba. What he found were remains of the Mayan (MAH-yuhn) culture. This culture was at its height from 300 to 900 A.D. Its influence and power spread from Mexico into Guatemala (gwah-tuh-MAH-luh), Honduras, Belize (be-LEEZ), and El Salvador (el SAL-vuh-dor). For unknown reasons, Mayan culture began to decline around 900.

There are many unanswered questions about the Maya because the Spanish destroyed their art, manuscripts, temples, and homes. In their eagerness to spread Christianity, the Spanish destroyed all evidence of non-Christian worship. From what evidence archaeologists can find, they know the Mayan economy was based on farming with some trade. There was a class of priest-scholars who were probably the rulers. Science and art were highly developed. By the 600s, the Mayan calendar was more accurate than the one Europeans used in the 1500s.

The Aztec Empire

In 1519, Hernando Cortes (kor-TEZ) left Cuba for Mexico. He was supposed to explore, but Cortes was more interested in gold. When he landed, he found the Aztec (AZ-tek) empire. An **empire** is a large territory or group of states ruled by a single government.

The Aztecs had once lived in northern Mexico, but by 1325 A.D. they had moved into the area around what is now Mexico City. By conquering their neighbors, they had built a rich, powerful empire. It had a complex government and social system. At the top were priests and nobles. Next came farmers, traders, and craftworkers. At the bottom were slaves—usually conquered peoples.

Within two years, the Spanish had seized the empire. The Aztecs far outnumbered them, but the Spanish had three advantages. They had guns and gunpowder and help from some of the conquered peoples. In addition, the Spanish had the advantage of horses, which the Aztecs had never seen.

Florida

The Spanish also explored northward from Central America. In 1513, Ponce de Leon sailed from Puerto Rico to Florida. The Spanish named Florida what are now the states of Florida and parts of Georgia, Alabama, and Mississippi. Besides gold, Ponce de Leon was looking for a fountain of youth whose waters would keep him young. He found nothing but was convinced there was gold in Florida. In 1521, he returned to set up a colony. Missionaries came with him to convert the Calusa (kuh-LOO-suh) who lived around Tampa Bay where the explorer landed. Because of Spanish cruelty to them, the Calusa struck back. Ponce de Leon was wounded and later died. The survivors fled to Cuba.

In 1528, Panfilo de Narvaez (nahr-VAH-ais) tried again to start a colony in Florida. However, the climate, diseases, and conflict with the Apalachee (ap-uh-LACH-ee) over land discouraged the settlers. They set sail for Mexico, but a storm destroyed their ships. Only four people survived.

The four, including Alvar Nunez Cabeza de Vaca (Kah-BAYT-sah duh VAHK-ah), spent the next eight years wandering through what is now the southwestern U.S. and northern Mexico, looking for other Span-

This picture was drawn by someone living at the time Cortes conquered Mexico. It shows part of his expedition which had Native Americans, blacks, and Malinche, a guide and interpreter.

The Spanish in the Americas

LINE OF THE TREATY OF TORDESILLAS

ATLANTIC OCEAN

40°N
30°N
20°N
10°N
60°W

PUERTO RICO

DOMINICAN REPUBLIC

CUBA

FLORIDA

CARIBBEAN SEA

70°W

PANAMA

80°W

SOUTH AMERICA

EQUATOR

CANADA

Ohio River

SOUTH CAROLINA

GEORGIA

TENNESSEE

Tennessee River

ALA.

MISS.

Mississippi River

Missouri River

ARK.

Mississippi River

LOUISIANA

GULF OF MEXICO

KANSAS

OKLAHOMA

Arkansas R.

COLORADO

Colorado River

NEW MEXICO

TEXAS

Rio Grande

MEXICO

ARIZONA

PACIFIC OCEAN

N

600 miles
800 kilometers
0

90°W
100°W
110°W

0°
10°N
20°N
30°N
40°N

Ponce de Leon
Balboa
Narvaez
Cabeza de Vaca and Estevanico
De Soto
Coronado

EARLY EXPLORATIONS OF THE AMERICAS

Explorer	Date	Objective	Gained Objective: Yes or No	Other Outcomes
Amerigo Vespucci	1499-1500	To find an all-water route to Asia	No	Explored northern coast of South America and part of Caribbean
	1501	To find an all-water route to Asia	No	Explored east coast of South America south to Uruguay; first to describe America as "new world"; realized Columbus had not reached the Indies
Juan Ponce de Leon	1508	To explore new lands	Yes	Explored and conquered Puerto Rico; discovered gold on the island
	1513	To search for gold and the fountain of youth	No	Reached and explored east and west coasts of Florida
	1521	To explore and colonize Florida	No	Wounded and died
Vasco Nunez de Balboa	1513	To find a rich country near a great sea	In part	Claimed the Pacific Ocean for Spain; proved that Columbus had not reached Asia
Francisco Fernandez de Cordoba	1517	To take Native Americans as slaves for the Spanish in Cuba	No	Found remains of Mayan culture
Hernando Cortes	1519-1521	To explore Mexico and look for gold	Yes	Conquered the Aztec empire
Ferdinand Magellan	1519-1522	To reach Asia by sailing west	Yes	Magellan died in the Philippines, but one of his ships continued journey and became first to sail around the world; true size of globe known as a result of the voyage
Panfilo de Narvaez	1528	To start a colony in Florida	No	Explored Florida and northern coast of Gulf of Mexico; shipwrecked on route to Mexico
Alvar Nunez Cabeza de Vaca and Estevanico	1528-1538	To start a colony in Florida as part of Narvaez expedition	No	Shipwrecked on Texas coast; traveled by foot to Mexico; among first Europeans to see what is now Texas

Explorer	Date	Objective	Gained Objective: Yes or No	Other Outcomes
Estevanico and Fray Marcos de Niza	1539	To find the Seven Cities of Cibola	No	Explored Arizona and parts of western New Mexico; Estevanico killed; Fray Marcos returned to Mexico, told of faraway city of silver
Hernando de Soto	1539-1542	To find the Seven Cities of Cibola	No	Reached and crossed Mississippi River; explored parts of what are now Florida, Georgia, Carolina, Tennessee, Alabama, Mississippi, Arkansas, Louisiana
Francisco Vasquez de Coronado	1540-1542	To find the Seven Cities of Cibola	No	Found Pueblos; gave Spain knowledge of North American inland—parts of what are now New Mexico, Texas, Arizona

ish. Cabeza de Vaca kept a journal or written record of events. Below are a few paragraphs from Cabeza de Vaca's journal. In them, he describes what took place when he and his three companions came to a Native American village. Historians believe that the village was located in what is now the present state of Texas.

> At nightfall we came to a village. The people looked at us in surprise and fear. When they grew accustomed to our appearance, they felt our faces and then their own, comparing. [The beards of the Spanish probably puzzled the people.]
>
> We stayed there overnight. In the morning they brought us their sick, asking our blessing. They shared with us what they had to eat. They did this with kindness and goodwill, gladly giving up some of their food to give us some. We remained here several days.

Seven Cities of Cibola

In their wanderings, the four met many Native Americans. Some told of great cities of wealth somewhere to the north. Some of the people told these stories just to entertain their guests. Others told them as tricks to convince the Spanish to move on.

The four finally reached Mexico City in 1538. Their story of the Seven Cities of Cibola, as they were called, excited many Spanish. In 1539, Estevanico (es-tay-vahn-EE-koh), an African who had been a slave of one of the survivors of the Narvaez expedition, and Fray Marcos de Niza (day NEE-sah) set out to find Cibola. Estevanico was killed, but Fray Marcos returned to Mexico. He said that before he turned back, he had seen a city of silver far away. Historians believe he saw a distant pueblo with the sun shining on it.

Hernando de Soto (dih SOH-toh) continued the search. He landed with 600 soldiers at Tampa Bay, Florida, and marched north and then west. In 1541, he and his expedition became the first Europeans to cross the Mississippi River. De Soto died of a fever in 1542. What was left of his expedition returned to Mexico.

In 1540, Francisco Vasquez de Coronado (kor-uh-NAH-doh) explored parts of what are now New Mexico, Texas, Oklahoma, Kansas, and Arizona looking for Cibola. He found buffalo, grazing land, and Native Americans, as you read in the unit The First Americans, but not Cibola. In 1542, his discouraged group returned to Mexico City.

The information these explorers gathered would be valuable in the later settlement of the Southwest. For the time being though, the Spanish had lost interest in the land north of Mexico. The failures of de Soto and Coronado along with the opening of Mexican mines centered Spanish attention on Mexico.

BUILDING READING SKILLS

Although the main idea is sometimes stated, more often you have to infer it. You have to decide for yourself the key point of a paragraph, section, or chapter from the information given. You can collect data in four steps to make this inference.

- Read the heading and the section carefully. What is the topic of the section? The main idea will relate to this topic.
- Review the people the section is about. Who were they?
- Review the action of the section. What, if anything, did the people do?
- Put your thoughts about the section together in a sentence. This is the main idea.

In doing the second and third steps you may also be inferring some of the supporting details for the main idea. **Activity:** Answer each of the steps above to find the main idea of the Seven Cities of Cibola.

LOOKING BACK

1. How was America named?
2. How did Magellan's voyage build on those of Vespucci and Balboa?
3. **a.** Why did the Spanish ask for the Line of Demarcation? **b.** What did the Portuguese ask for in the Treaty of Tordesillas?
4. **a.** What is the main idea of the section Seven Cities of Cibola? **b.** What details support this idea?
5. Use the table to help you answer this question and question **6.** What was each of the following looking for: **a.** Balboa? **b.** Cordoba? **c.** Cortes? **d.** Ponce de Leon? **e.** Estevanico? **f.** de Soto? **g.** Coronado?
6. Did each accomplish what he set out to do?

Chapter 4   Northwest Passage

LOOKING AHEAD

In this chapter, you will learn why the French, Spanish, English, and Dutch became interested in exploring North America. You will read about their voyages and the claims that resulted from them. After you study this chapter you will be able to:

- explain why Europeans were looking for a Northwest Passage to Asia.
- list the areas of the U.S. that explorers claimed for France, Spain, England, and the Netherlands.
- read a table to compare the objectives and the outcomes of the explorers.
- ★ recognize continuity and change of purpose in French, English, and Dutch explorations.

Social Studies Vocabulary

charter   colonization   continuity and change

People

Verrazano	John Cabot	Marquette
Cartier	Drake	Joliet
Cabrillo	Hudson	La Salle
Vizcaino	Champlain	Raleigh

Places

St. Lawrence River	Quebec	New Orleans
California	Mississippi River	Hudson River
Great Lakes	valley	valley

Words and Terms

Armada   Company of New France
Northwest Passage   Dutch West India Company
Dutch East India Company

John White, an early visitor to the Americas, recorded what he saw in drawings. This one shows a pineapple, one of the many new foods that Europeans found and took back to Europe or to their colonies in Africa.

Although Spain and Portugal had a head start in exploring the Americas, other European nations soon followed. Once their explorers realized that Columbus had not found Asia, they set a new goal. They started looking for an all-water route through the Americas. Their explorers soon decided that this route would have to be through North America. This hoped-for waterway became known as the Northwest Passage.

EXPLORERS FOR FRANCE

In the early 1500s, France became interested in the Americas. In 1524, the French king sent Giovanni de Verrazano (ver-ra-TSA-noh) to look for the Northwest Passage. Verrazano sailed along the North American coast from Cape Fear, North Carolina, to Newfoundland. In his report to the king, he gave Europeans their first description of this part of the Americas.

In 1534 and again in 1536, Jacques Cartier (kahr-tee-AY) explored the St. Lawrence River for France. He met Hurons (HYUR-uhnz) who told him of a country of gold and diamonds to the west. This tale so interested the French they sent Cartier back in 1541. He sailed far up the river and started a colony near present-day Quebec (kwih-BEK). It lasted only two years. Cold weather, no gold or silver, and the refusal of the League of the Iroquois to give up their land sent the French home. Because the French were fighting in Europe, they showed little interest in North America until the early 1600s. But Cartier's explorations laid the basis for French claims to the St. Lawrence.

THE SPANISH SEARCH

This detail from an illustrated map shows Cartier founding Quebec. Look at the maps on pages 81 and 90. What areas appear to have been explored for both France and Spain?

The Spanish also joined the search for an all-water route to Asia. In 1542, Juan Rodriguez Cabrillo (ka-BREE-yoh) and his crew probably became the first Europeans to explore the coast of California. They sailed north from Mexico and landed at what is now San Diego (san dee-AY-goh) Bay. Cabrillo claimed all the land for Spain.

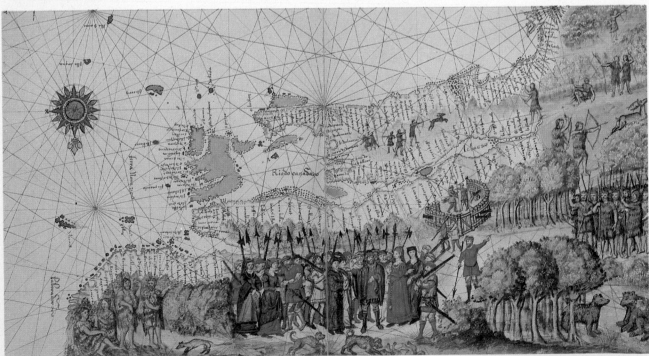

For many years after Cabrillo's expedition, the Spanish did not explore California further. Cabrillo had not found gold, silver, or a water route through North America. The mines in Mexico and the riches of the Philippines were of more interest to the Spanish.

In the late 1500s, though, the Spanish again explored the coast. They were looking for a place to set up a warning station. Pirates hiding along the Pacific Coast were raiding treasure ships returning from the Philippines. Sebastian Vizcaino (veez-kah-EE-noh), a wealthy merchant, led several explorations to California. In 1596 and again in 1602, he set out to map the coast and look for pearls, gold, and silver. After the station was set up at a place Vizcaino named Monterey (mahn-tuh-RAY), the Spanish again lost interest in California.

ENGLAND'S INTEREST

One of the first nations to follow Columbus to America was England. In 1497 and 1498, the English king financed voyages by John Cabot (KA-buht). Cabot explored the coast from Newfoundland possibly as far south as Chesapeake (CHES-uh-peek) Bay. He was the first European to see the North American mainland. His son, Sebastian, explored North America in the early 1500s while looking for the Northwest Passage.

The exploration of the Cabots laid the basis for England's later claims in North America. England, however, did not immediately follow up the work of the Cabots. The English were more interested in the profits from the known routes to Asian trade.

Drake's Voyage

By the mid-1500s England had a strong navy and was raiding Spanish ships and settlements in the Americas. Sir Francis Drake, one of England's most daring pirates, decided to go after the treasure ships in the Pacific. He was also looking for the Northwest Passage.

In 1577, he sailed with five ships down the east coast of South America, through what became the Strait of Magellan, and up the west coast. He went as far north as what is now the modern U.S.-Canada border and turned back only because of the cold. Drake stopped near present-day San Francisco and claimed the area for England. He then turned westward and reached home three years after he had set sail. His trip showed that if there was a northwest passage, it was farther north than what is now Vancouver (van-KOO-vuhr), Canada.

A Sea Power

Soon after Drake's voyage, an event happened that gave England an advantage in settling the Americas. In an eight-day battle in 1588, the English defeated the Spanish navy, known as the Armada (ar-MAH-duh). With two-thirds of the Armada destroyed, England gained an easy sea route to the Americas. English ships no longer had to head straight out across the Atlantic. They could sail south along the coast of Europe for a distance before heading west. The winds and ocean currents farther south are better for ocean travel than those near England. Once free of the Spanish, England became a major sea power.

DUTCH IN NORTH AMERICA

The Dutch also became interested in the Northwest Passage. In 1609, the Dutch East India Company hired Henry Hudson to search for the water route. Hudson explored along the east coast of North America and sailed into what is now New York Harbor and up the river that was named for him. At what is now Albany, he met and traded with Iroquois for furs.

CHANGES IN THINKING

Cartier, Hudson, and other explorers failed to find the Northwest Passage. But Europeans gradually stopped looking at North America as a barrier to the riches of Asia. Explorers told of the abundance of fish, trees, and fur-bearing animals. Soon settling North America became more important than looking for a way through it.

New France

One of the first Europeans to see the value of North America was Samuel de Champlain (sham-PLAYN). While searching for the Northwest Passage, he explored Canada from the St. Lawrence to Lake Huron — part of the Great Lakes. He founded the successful settlement of Quebec in 1608 and later set up trading posts to trade for furs with Native Americans.

In 1627, the Company of New France was formed to encourage settlement. Laws in New France were very strict and all colonists had to be Roman Catholic. Few settlers came to New France until 1663 when the French government took control of the colony. Even then the population of New France remained small, about 3,200 people. The colony included eastern Canada and parts of the northeastern and Great Lakes areas of the present U.S.

French land claims increased greatly in the next few years. In 1673, Jacques Marquette (mahr-KET), a missionary, and Louis Joliet (joh-lih-ET), a fur trader, explored the Mississippi River. They represented France's two interests in North America. Marquette wanted to convert the Native Americans and Joliet wanted to trade for furs with them. From 1679 to 1682, Robert Cavalier, Sieur de La Salle (luh SAL) continued the exploration of the interior. In 1682, he and his expedition floated down the Mississippi River in canoes to the Gulf of Mexico.

interior (in-TIR-ee-uhr): inland

According to this engraving, Quebec was a good-sized town by the early 1700s. What was the basis of its wealth?

He claimed for France all the lands that were watered by the Mississippi or by any stream or river flowing into it. He named the land *Louisiana* in honor of his king.

Between 1700 and 1724, the French set up a line of forts from the Great Lakes to the Gulf of Mexico. These were used as fur trading posts and as a barrier to English and Spanish settlement. In 1718, the French founded New Orleans at the mouth of the Mississippi. It soon became the center of the French fur trade in North America.

Dutch Colonization

Because of Hudson's explorations, the Dutch claimed the entire area now called the Hudson River valley. Dutch expeditions also explored Long Island in New York and Delaware Bay in New Jersey. They set up fur trading posts wherever they went.

In 1621, the Dutch West India Company was given a charter by the Dutch government. A **charter** is a grant by a government of rights and privileges. This charter allowed the company to control all Dutch trade in Africa and the Americas. Although trade was the company's main interest, it soon began bringing Dutch settlers to the Americas.

privilege (PRIV-uh-lij): special favor; advantage

Attempts at English Settlement

By the late 1500s, the English began to show an interest in **colonization** (kahl-uh-nuh-ZAY-shuhn). This is the building of permanent settlements in another country. The settlers remain citizens of the parent

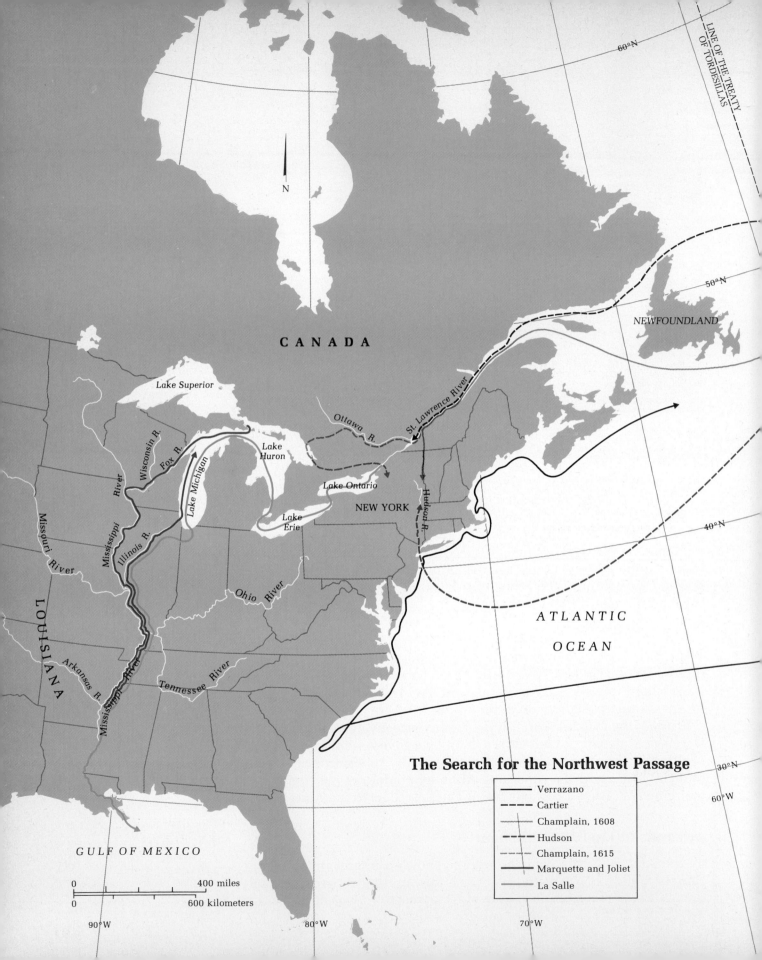

LINE OF THE TREATY OF TORDESILLAS

60°N

50°N

NEWFOUNDLAND

C A N A D A

Lake Superior

Ottawa R.

St. Lawrence River

Wisconsin R.

Fox R.

Lake Huron

River

Lake Michigan

Missouri River

Mississippi River

Illinois R.

Lake Ontario

Lake Erie

NEW YORK

Hudson R.

40°N

LOUISIANA

Ohio River

ATLANTIC

OCEAN

Arkansas R.

Tennessee River

Mississippi River

30°N

60°W

The Search for the Northwest Passage

———	Verrazano
– – –	Cartier
———	Champlain, 1608
— — —	Hudson
–·–·–	Champlain, 1615
———	Marquette and Joliet
———	La Salle

GULF OF MEXICO

0   400 miles

0   600 kilometers

N

90°W

80°W

70°W

THE SEARCH FOR A NORTHWEST PASSAGE

Explorer	Date	Objective	Gained Objective: Yes or No	Other Outcomes
Giovanni de Verrazano	1524	To find Northwest Passage for France	No	Explored North American coast from North Carolina to Newfoundland, including New York Bay; gave Europeans first idea of this part of North America
Jacques Cartier	1534 and 1536	To find Northwest Passage for France	No	Explored Labrador and St. Lawrence River; claimed it for France
Juan Rodriguez Cabrillo	1542	To find Northwest Passage for Spain	No	Explored California coast; claimed it for Spain
Francis Drake	1577-1580	To raid Spanish colonies in Peru and Chile	Yes	Explored west coast of North America to Vancouver; showed that if Northwest Passage existed, it was north of Vancouver; claimed area around San Francisco for England; sailed around the world
Samuel de Champlain	1608 and 1615	To find Northwest Passage for France	No	Explored St. Lawrence, northern New York, Great Lakes; founded Quebec
Henry Hudson	1609	To find Northwest Passage for the Netherlands	No	Explored Hudson River north to Albany; basis for the Netherlands' claims to land
Jacques Marquette and Louis Joliet	1673	To find Northwest Passage for France	No	Explored Mississippi Valley from Great Lakes to Arkansas
Robert Cavalier, Sieur de La Salle	1679-1682	To find Northwest Passage for France	No	Explored Lake Michigan and Illinois region; explored Mississippi River to Gulf of Mexico; claimed vast region of Louisiana for France

This is White's drawing of a type of banana found in the Caribbean.

country. In 1583, a settlement was attempted in Newfoundland, but the colonists were so unhappy they returned home.

The following year, Sir Walter Raleigh (RAW-lee) financed a settlement on Roanoke (ROH-uh-nohk) Island, in what is now North Carolina. Queen Elizabeth I had given him a larger area of land along the Atlantic north of Florida. He named the entire colony *Virginia* in her honor. The settlers spent their time looking for gold and fighting among themselves. They returned to England within the year.

In 1587, a second group arrived on Roanoke Island. They soon ran out of supplies and John White, the governor, returned to England for more. England was at war with Spain at the time and White's ship was forced into service. It was three years before he could return. When he did, the men, women, and children he had left behind were gone. The only clue was the word *CROATAN* (kroh-uh-TAN) carved on a tree. It was the name of another island. Bad weather forced White to give up his search and no trace has ever been found of the Lost Colony, as it is called.

BUILDING CHRONOLOGICAL SKILLS

Recognizing **continuity and change** is an important social studies skill. Related events happening one after another is called **continuity** (kahn-tuh-NOO-uh-tee). Continuity can be seen in an unbroken series of events or in a series of events with the same purpose. Often in history continuity actually leads to change. There may be a continuous or connected series of events that gradually builds to change.

Consider the early explorations described in this chapter. **1.** What was the continuity of purpose behind them? Now review the last three sections about the French, Dutch, and English. **2.** What changes do you see in their interest in North America? In answering these questions, you will be inferring information. An inference question does not always use the word *infer*.

LOOKING BACK

1. Why were Europeans looking for a Northwest Passage to Asia?
2. What areas of North America were claimed because of the work of the following explorers: **a.** Cartier? **b.** Hudson? **c.** La Salle? **d.** Raleigh?
3. What countries did each of the above represent?
4. Use the table to help you answer this question and question **5.** How successful were the following in accomplishing their objectives? **a.** Verrazano? **b.** Cartier? **c.** Cabrillo? **d.** Champlain? **e.** Hudson? **f.** Marquette and Joliet? **g.** La Salle?
5. What extra benefits did each of the above gain?
★ 6. What was the continuity of objectives, or similar purpose, for the early explorations described in this chapter?
★ 7. What change can you see in the reasons behind the later efforts of: **a.** the French? **b.** the Dutch? **c.** the English?

PRACTICING YOUR SKILLS

What If . . .   **What if** Christopher Columbus had accepted the idea that the world was flat? Would someone else have decided to explore westward? Would it have been much later before anyone did?

Building Thinking Skills

In the **What If** activities, you are doing what is called **predicting alternative futures.** You are being asked to change your way of looking at a situation and to come up with possible different endings. This ability to change your thinking — to be flexible — will be very important to you in the future. According to futurists, life will be very different by the year 2000. **Futurists** (FYOO-chuhr-ists) are people who study the future.

Columbus was good at viewing different possibilities. He looked at what was known about the geography of the world and decided there was another way to reach Asia by ship. He was right and he was wrong. But his prediction changed world history. How were the following also flexible in their thinking: **1.** Prince Henry? **2.** Vespucci? **3.** Champlain?

Discussing

Why do you think Europeans renamed land, rivers, and mountains when these already had names given them by Native Americans? Europeans even renamed Native American groups. What does this tell you about Europeans' view of themselves and of Native Americans?

Researching, Writing, Making a Time Line

1. Research and write a short description of Francisco Pizarro's (pih-ZAHR-oh) conquest of the Inca empire in Latin America. Include what he was looking for and why the Inca thought he could be useful to them.
2. Research and write a paragraph about the life of a serf on a European manor. Be sure to include a topic sentence and supporting details.
3. Combine the data from all the tables in this unit into one time line. List the dates of each explorer and what he did. Use the time line to discuss the length of time it took to understand that Columbus had not found a "new world" and then how long it took to decide to settle the new land.

Exploring

1. According to this unit, do you live in an area that European explorers visited? If so, look in an atlas for the names of towns, mountains, or rivers that show Europeans explored and claimed the land. For example, if you live in Louisiana, find French or Spanish place names. List at least five names.
2. If you live in a city or town with a Spanish, French, English, or Dutch name, look in the library or historical society for a local history. Write a paragraph describing when your community was founded, by whom, and why.

Reading

Buehr, Walter, *The Spanish Conquistadores.* New York: St. Martin, 1976.

Hale, John R. *Age of Exploration.* Morristown, New Jersey: Silver Burdett, 1966. A pictorial history.

Holbrook, Sabra. *The French Founders of North America and Their Heritage.* New York: Atheneum, 1976.

Humble, Richard. *The Explorers.* Morristown, New Jersey: Silver Burdett, 1978. Maps and pictures of the routes of early explorers.

Langdon-Davies, John. *Columbus and the Discovery of America.* New York: Viking, 1972.

Parish, Helen. *Estebanico.* New York: Viking, 1974.

Wernick, Robert. *The Vikings.* Morristown, New Jersey: Silver Burdett, 1979.

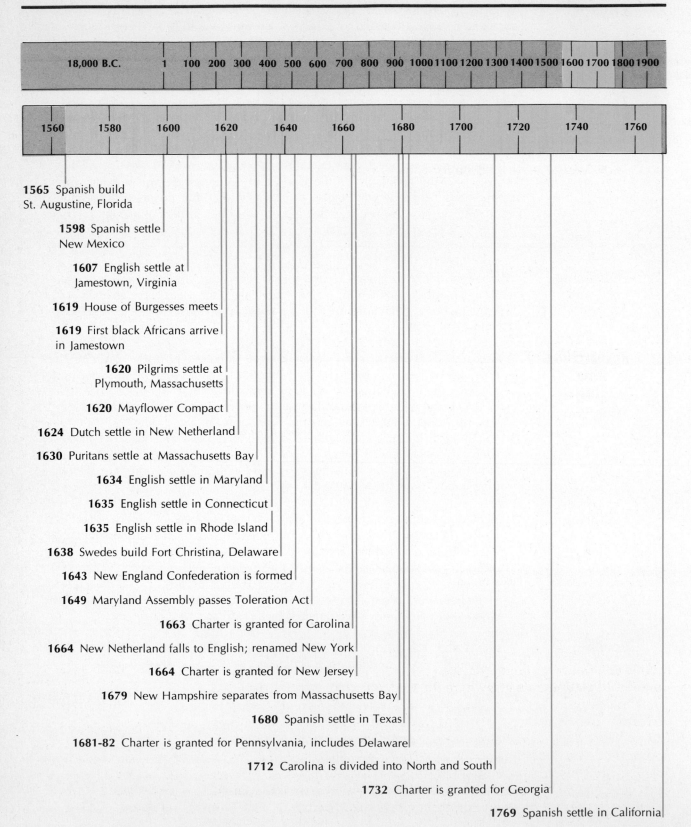

| 18,000 B.C. | 1 | 100 | 200 | 300 | 400 | 500 | 600 | 700 | 800 | 900 | 1000 | 1100 | 1200 | 1300 | 1400 | 1500 | 1600 | 1700 | 1800 | 1900 |

| 1560 | 1580 | 1600 | 1620 | 1640 | 1660 | 1680 | 1700 | 1720 | 1740 | 1760 |

1565 Spanish build St. Augustine, Florida

1598 Spanish settle New Mexico

1607 English settle at Jamestown, Virginia

1619 House of Burgesses meets

1619 First black Africans arrive in Jamestown

1620 Pilgrims settle at Plymouth, Massachusetts

1620 Mayflower Compact

1624 Dutch settle in New Netherland

1630 Puritans settle at Massachusetts Bay

1634 English settle in Maryland

1635 English settle in Connecticut

1635 English settle in Rhode Island

1638 Swedes build Fort Christina, Delaware

1643 New England Confederation is formed

1649 Maryland Assembly passes Toleration Act

1663 Charter is granted for Carolina

1664 New Netherland falls to English; renamed New York

1664 Charter is granted for New Jersey

1679 New Hampshire separates from Massachusetts Bay

1680 Spanish settle in Texas

1681-82 Charter is granted for Pennsylvania, includes Delaware

1712 Carolina is divided into North and South

1732 Charter is granted for Georgia

1769 Spanish settle in California

Chapter 1   New Spain

LOOKING AHEAD

This chapter is about the beginnings of Spanish settlements on the mainland of what is now the U.S. Between 1500 and the late 1700s, the Spanish built settlements in Florida, the southwestern part of the present U.S., Texas, and California. After you study this chapter, you will be able to:

- describe the purpose for Spanish missions in Florida.
- ★ describe and identify a primary source.
- list the reasons for so few Spanish in Texas.
- explain Spain's interest in California.
- identify the main problem in governing New Spain.

Social Studies Vocabulary

primary source   land grant

People

Menendez de Aviles   Pope
Onate   Serra

Places

Viceroyalty of New   St. Augustine   Texas
   Spain   New Mexico   San Antonio
Mexico City   Rio Grande Valley   California
Florida   Santa Fe   San Diego

Words and Terms

viceroy   presidio   hacienda
civilian   Council for the Indies   mission

As you may recall from the unit Europeans as Explorers, Spain's attempts at colonizing Florida in the early 1500s failed. But Spain went on to build settlements elsewhere. In 1535, Mexico, Central America, the islands in the Caribbean, and the southern part of what is now the U.S. from the Pacific to the Atlantic became the Viceroyalty of New Spain. Viceroyalty (vys-ROY-uhl-tee) was the name given to Spanish colonies in the Americas. The viceroyalties were governed by officials called viceroys. The capital of New Spain, Mexico City, was built on the ruins of the Aztec capital. From Mexico City, the Spanish ruled their North American empire for over 300 years.

The Spanish took Aztec golden ornaments such as this snake, melted them down, and shipped the gold to Spain to pay for more expeditions.

An artist's view of
St. Augustine in 1670
shows blacks being used
as slaves. Founded in
1565, St. Augustine
is one of the oldest
cities in the U.S.

FLORIDA

Because Spain was using most of its resources in Central and South America, it had little time or interest for Florida. As you may recall, the Spanish had not found any gold or silver there. To the Spanish, the climate was hot and uncomfortable. But most important perhaps was the fact that the Native Americans were willing to fight for their land. In the beginning, there were enough of them and so few Spanish that the Native Americans were successful against European guns.

But outside influences soon changed Spain's view of Florida. In 1564, the French built a fort near present-day Jacksonville, Florida. To protect its interests, Spain sent Don Pedro Menendez de Aviles (muh-NEN-duhs day ahv-uh-LAYS) to force the French out. In 1565, he built a fort to the south of the French and named it St. Augustine (AW-guhs-teen). From this base, the Spanish attacked the French and drove them from Florida.

Missions and Presidios

Florida, in the 1600s and 1700s, attracted few civilians (suh-VIL-yuhns)—people who were neither missionaries nor soldiers. To hold Florida, the Spanish set up a series of presidios and missions. Presidio (prih-SEED-ee-oh) is the Spanish word for fort. Missions were villages built for Native Americans and under the authority of a priest. They were set up to teach Christianity and the Spanish way of life to Native Americans. All the labor needed to run the missions was provided by Native Americans. For protection, the priests often built their missions near presidios.

By forcing many Native Americans to live in missions, the Spanish greatly strengthened their hold over their territory. As you may recall from the unit Europeans as Explorers, the Spanish believed that their culture was better than any other. The Spanish were determined that

Native Americans would accept Spanish ways. With presidios for support, the missions became the tool for this forced acculturation.

During the 1600s, missionaries moved west to the Apalachicola (ap-uh-lach-ih-KOH-luh) River and along the coast as far north as what is today South Carolina. At the height of their importance, there were 40 missions in the region. In time, the missions were weakened by attacks from other Europeans and by Native Americans angered by Spanish cruelty. During the 1600s, the French often joined with the Creek and Timucua (tim-uh-KOO-uh) against the Spanish. Many times, missionaries had to leave their posts until help came. From time to time, new missionaries arrived to reoccupy old missions or to set up new ones. The greatest threat to the Spanish, though, was the English settling of Charles Town, South Carolina, in 1670. You will read about this in Chapter 5 of this unit.

cruelty (KROO-uhl-tee): harsh treatment toward others that causes them pain or suffering

NEW MEXICO

Spain's disappointment with the Southwest after Coronado's expedition was so great that the Spanish did not explore it again for 40 years. But as time went by, the dream of fame and fortune in the Southwest grew. In the 1580s and 1590s, the Spanish sent several expeditions into the land Coronado had explored. They were still looking for gold, silver, pearls, and people to convert to Christianity.

The First Settlement

In 1598, the first group of Spanish colonists moved into the Southwest. They were led by Don Juan de Onate (oh-NYAH-tay), the son of an explorer. The groups went north along the upper Rio Grande, the river that is now part of the boundary between the U.S. and Mexico. The colonists numbered about 400 and came from all classes. Like the U.S. pioneers of the 1800s, they were looking for a better life.

Onate claimed the upper Rio Grande Valley for Spain and called it New Mexico. It included parts of the present states of Arizona, Colorado, Texas, Nebraska, Oklahoma, and New Mexico. In 1610, Santa Fe, in the northern part of the modern state of New Mexico, became the capital.

Missionaries accompanied the colonists and set up missions among the Pueblos. As you may recall from the unit The First Americans, the Pueblos were descended from the Anasazi. At the time of Coronado's expedition in 1540, the Pueblos numbered more than 16,000 in 80 settlements. In the 1600s, most missionary work was done among the Pueblos in southern and central New Mexico. Later missions spread into what is modern Arizona. There they were the chief form of settlement until the early 1700s.

Onate's group met little opposition from the Pueblos. They were not a warlike people, but they would fight to defend their homes. At Acoma, a Spanish colonist was killed in an argument and Onate

opposition (ahp-uh-ZISH-uhn): action against

burned the pueblo as punishment. The people in the other pueblos agreed to live under Spanish rule. However, they did not forget what the Spanish had done.

Some of the colonists hunted for gold and silver rather than farm. When they found nothing, they became discontented. One group tried to leave, and Onate had them caught and punished. In 1601, on his return from exploring, Onate found that most of the colonists had gone back to Mexico.

These colonists complained about Onate and about life in New Mexico. The missionaries complained about the Spanish treatment of the Pueblos. The following is part of letter by Fray Juan de Escalona (es-kay-LOH-nah) to the viceroy:

commit (kuh-MIT): to do

> The first and greatest difficulty, from which have sprung all the evils and the ruin of this land, is that this conquest was given to a man like Don Juan de Onate. Soon after he came here, his people began to commit many crimes against the Native Americans. The Spanish robbed them of the corn they had gathered for themselves. Here corn is God. The people have nothing else with which to support themselves.
>
> The governor did not want to plant a community plot to feed his people, though we priests urged him to. The Native Americans agreed to it so that their food would not be taken. This effort was of no use. The people have to provide everything. The whole land has been reduced to such need that the people drop dead from starvation. Your lordship must not believe that the Native Americans part willingly with their corn, or the blankets with which they cover themselves. This stealing is done by threats and force of arms, the soldiers burning some of the houses and killing the people. This was the cause of the Acoma war.

resign (rih-ZYN): to quit

Because of the complaints, Onate resigned as governor of New Mexico in 1607.

WORKING WITH SOURCES

The paragraphs you have just read are from a translation of a letter written in Spanish in the early 1600s. Its writer, Fray Juan de Escalona, actually lived among the Pueblos and the Spanish during Onate's rule. Fray de Escalona's original letter is a primary source. A **primary source** is a first-hand or eyewitness account of an event. It may be a letter, diary, journal, speech, document, autobiography, law, painting, drawing, cartoon, photograph, poster, song, poem, legend, myth, or folktale, among other things. A primary source may also be an artifact, for example, a building, coin, stamp, pottery, basket, or weapon. Much of the illustration in this textbook is primary source material. **Activity:** The paragraphs translated from Cabeza de Vaca's journal in Chapter 3 of the unit Europeans as Explorers are also a primary source. Look through the unit and see if you can find another primary source.

The Spanish built missions to teach Native Americans Christianity and Spanish culture. The missions were a way to keep Native Americans under Spanish control. Here a priest baptizes a Native American.

Pueblo Revolt of 1680

After suffering almost 100 years of Spanish cruelty and forced labor, the Pueblos revolted in 1680. Pope (poh-PAY), one of their leaders, was able to unite the different pueblos. The people attacked every Spanish town, ranch, and mission. They attacked the capital, Santa Fe, and cut off its food and water supplies. The Spanish fled.

In 1692, a Spanish military expedition reclaimed New Mexico. After 12 years, Santa Fe was again a Spanish city. It had been captured without bloodshed, but the Spanish met fierce fighting at other pueblos. Not until the summer of 1696 were all former Spanish settlements retaken.

Slow Growth

Although colonists returned after the Pueblo revolt, New Mexico grew slowly. Spain offered land grants to its wealthy citizens, but few were accepted. A **land grant** is land given away by a government. Life in New Mexico was difficult. The climate was hot and dry, and good farmland was found only in small patches. Because water was in such short supply, early settlements were located near the central Rio Grande and its tributaries. For these reasons, New Mexico became a colony of widely scattered towns rather than large cities.

Colonists in New Mexico farmed, raised cattle, mined for gold and silver, and traded. Most of the trade was carried on with Mexico. The chief trade goods of New Mexico were woolen blankets, candles, salt, strings of chili peppers, and buffalo skins. None of these earned much money for the New Mexicans. Most of their needs had to be supplied from Mexico City over difficult and dangerous routes. As a result, the goods were expensive, and most colonists remained poor.

tributary (TRIB-yuh-ter-ee): small stream that flows into a larger stream, river, or other body of water

In 1610, the Spanish made Santa Fe the capital of their New Mexico territory. Why were the Spanish slow to settle this area?

By the late 1700s, a yearly caravan to Mexico began to serve New Mexico. Each November, it started at the northernmost river towns. At each stop along the way south, it picked up wagons loaded with trade goods. These goods were sold or traded for things from Mexico, South America, Europe, Asia, and the Philippines.

TEXAS

In their search for gold and silver, Coronado and de Soto traveled across what is now Texas. Because they failed to find any riches, the Spanish ignored Texas until the 1680s. At that time, the explorations of La Salle along the Gulf Coast drew Spanish attention to Texas. In 1682, the first two missions were built near what is now El Paso.

While missions were the main Spanish way of settling Texas, they were not the only way. Presidios and, later, towns were built. The Spanish founded a presidio and the mission of San Antonio de Valero (san ahn-TOH-nyoh day vah-LAY-roh), known as the Alamo, in 1718. Within 15 years, four more missions were built nearby. In 1731, 15 families settled at San Fernando de Bexar (SAN fuhr-NAN-doh day BAY-hahr). This settlement, along with the mission and presidio, became known as San Antonio. In 1773, it became the capital of Spanish-held Texas.

Throughout the 1700s, Texas never became more than an outpost of scattered Spanish settlements. Most of the colonists lived in south-central Texas where there was good farmland and friendly relations with the Native Americans. In other parts, the Apache, Comanche (kuh-MAN-chee), and Wichita (WICH-uh-taw), in order to keep their lands, fought the Spanish. Missions were never successful in subduing these peoples. In addition, the officials of New Spain felt their

subdue (suhb-DOO): to conquer

100

money could be better spent in Mexico than in Texas. They could not see that Texas could ever bring them much money.

CALIFORNIA

California was the last of Spain's colonization efforts in the Americas. More than 150 years passed between Cabrillo's exploration of California and settlement. Spain turned its attention to California only when other European nations showed an interest in it in the mid-1700s. To strengthen its claim to California, Spain began to colonize the area.

In 1769, the first presidio was built at San Diego, and Fray Junipero Serra (SER-uh) set up the first mission nearby. In all, 18 missions, 3 presidios, and 3 towns were started along the coast. Among these were San Francisco and Los Angeles. You will read more about California in the unit Manifest Destiny.

GOVERNMENT OF NEW SPAIN

Life in New Spain was ruled by people in Spain. A Council for the Indies wrote all the laws for the Viceroyalty. The council was appointed by the monarch to oversee things as small as the width of streets. To enforce the laws, officials were sent from Spain. Of these, the viceroy was the most important, but thousands of other officials were sent, too. From Mexico City, these officials governed Florida and Spanish lands north of the Rio Grande. The colonists themselves had no voice in electing these officials or in deciding how the colonies were to be governed.

oversee: to manage; to look after

There were many problems in governing a colony from so far away. The biggest problem was distance. It took months for letters describing laws to travel across the ocean. Because the council was so far away, it did not really know what conditions were like in the Americas. As a result, it was difficult for the council to write very effective or useful laws. Away from the settlements, laws were not easy to enforce. Wealthy landowners ruled their haciendas as they wished, regardless of the law. Haciendas (hah-see-EN-duhs) were large farms or ranches.

In the early 1700s, Fray Francisco Kino founded 24 missions in what is now Arizona and New Mexico. He helped the Pima raise cattle and new kinds of grain and vegetables.

LOOKING BACK

1. Why did the Spanish build missions in Florida?
★ 2. Why is Fray Juan de Escalona's letter considered a primary source?
3. Why was the settling of Texas so unsuccessful?
4. Why did the Spanish become interested in California?
5. State the main problem that the Spanish had in governing New Spain. Give two details to support your answer.

Chapter 2   Jamestown and Virginia

LOOKING AHEAD

This chapter describes Jamestown, England's first successful colony on the North American mainland. You will read about England's reasons for colonization and then about the actual settlement. You will also read about the relationship between colonists and Native Americans. Jamestown is important, too, because it had the first representative assembly in North America. After you study this chapter, you will be able to:

- compare and contrast the reasons for settling Jamestown with Spain's reasons for colonization.
- describe the change in relations between the colonists and the Powhatan.
- explain the continuity and change that led to the use of Africans as slaves in Virginia.
- describe how making Virginia a royal colony created an unequal division of power.

Social Studies Vocabulary

joint-stock company
indentured servant
slavery

representative assembly
royal colony

Places

Virginia

Jamestown

People

John Smith

Lord Delaware

John Rolfe

Words and Terms

Virginia Company
The Powhatan

tenant farmer
plantation

House of
Burgesses

Events

starving time

Bacon's Rebellion

This 1596 woodcut of a tobacco plant was used to advertise tobacco in Europe. Why was tobacco so important to the growth of the Southern colonies?

As you may recall from the unit Europeans as Explorers, trade increased greatly during the Age of Exploration. Merchants became wealthier and more important. Like modern businesspeople, they wanted to find new ways to invest their money. They were also looking for new places to sell their goods and for cheaper and better sources of raw materials.

John White drew this view of Jamestown in the early 1600s. Why was this location chosen for settlement?

REASONS FOR SETTLEMENT

Sir Walter Raleigh's failure to build a permanent settlement convinced English merchants of one thing. Financing colonization was too costly and too risky for one or two people. So some of them formed a **joint-stock company.** This is a company organized to raise money to finance an activity by selling shares in the company. The shareholders divide any profit among themselves. The joint-stock company was called the Virginia Company.

In April 1606, James I granted a charter to the company to colonize the coast of what is now North Carolina, Virginia, and Delaware. In the charter, he directed the company to:

- bring Christianity and European culture to the peoples;
- search for gold, silver, and copper;
- trade with the peoples they found;
- find a route through North America to China and India.

JAMESTOWN FOUNDED

On April 26, 1607, the first band of colonists—about 100 men and boys—arrived in Virginia. They explored the coast for two weeks until they found a suitable spot on a river for their town. They named both the town and the river for the king. The colonists chose this location because it could be easily defended in case the Native Americans were unfriendly. It was also hidden from the view of Spanish ships. But it was a poor choice for a settlement for other reasons. It was swampy and difficult to farm. The area was also full of disease-carrying mosquitoes.

In addition to these problems, the governing council that the Virginia Company had selected could not work together. Members quarreled with one another and the other colonists. Almost half the

103

Virginia Colony in 1660

colonists were from the English upper class and were not used to hard work. They wanted to spend their time searching for gold. Other settlers wanted everyone to work on basic jobs like plowing fields and planting crops. Unable to agree, the colonists did almost nothing. By fall 1607, more than half had died from disease and starvation. Had it not been for Native Americans who brought food, the remaining colonists would have died, too.

Because the governing council could not agree, Captain John Smith, one of the council, took charge. He told those who refused to work that they would not eat. Under Smith's leadership, the colonists cleared land and planted crops. More colonists came, and by 1609 the population numbered about 500 men and women.

In its early years, the colony's population never grew larger, and usually it was much smaller. Although new colonists came, the death rate from disease, lack of food, and war with the Native Americans was always high.

Colonists and the Powhatan

When the English settled at Jamestown, almost 50 small Native American nations lived in the Chesapeake Bay region. Powhatan (pow-uh-TAN), a local leader, had formed an empire of about 30 of these nations. This union has been called the Powhatan.

In the beginning, the Powhatan were helpful to the colonists. They showed the colonists how to grow new crops and brought them some food. By fall 1608, the colonists still were not growing enough to feed themselves. Smith tried to scare the Powhatan into supplying more food. He burned their villages and fields. The Powhatan fought back and decided to let the colonists starve.

In summer 1609, Smith returned to England because of an injury. No one else could get the colonists to work together. As a result, the colony went through a period known as the "starving time." Only one colonist in ten lived. Things became so bad that the survivors were ready to abandon Jamestown by the following year. The only thing that saved the colony was the arrival of 150 new colonists with supplies and a new governor, Lord Delaware. He reorganized the colony and began to rebuild it. He also adopted Smith's policy toward the Powhatan.

Under orders from the Virginia Company, Lord Delaware and later governors tried to weaken the Powhatan. The nations were to obey the governor rather than Powhatan. They were to bring food and furs to the English. The company hoped to force the Native Americans to work for the colonists as the Spanish had done. Like the Spanish, the company wanted Native Americans' lands.

The Powhatan resisted by attacking English settlements. The English answer was to burn Native American villages. Warfare between the two groups lasted through the 1600s. In 1607, Smith had estimated that 30,000 Native Americans lived near Jamestown. A count in 1667 showed only about 2,000 left.

Pocahontas, a Powhatan, was painted while visiting England in 1616 with her husband John Rolfe. She died of smallpox a year later.

This picture was printed in 1619 to attract settlers to Virginia. New colonists found that hunting and fishing were not just sports but necessary to live.

GROWTH OF THE COLONY

In 1618, the colony began to change. Six years earlier, John Rolfe had begun growing tobacco in Virginia. The first cargo was shipped to England in 1613. By 1619, tobacco was the colony's major product.

But if the colony were to make a profit, the Virginia Company needed to attract more people. At first, all land had been owned and worked in common. The company paid a person's passage in return for seven years of unpaid labor. After the seven years, a person would become a tenant farmer. Tenant farmers are people who live on and farm another's land. The rent for using the land is usually paid in crops. With this system, there was little incentive for the colonists to work hard. But the company thought that if people owned their own land, this would change.

incentive (in-SEN-tiv): reason; reward for doing something; thing that causes an action

After 1619, colonists who paid their own way received 40 hectares (100 acres) of land. Later, the company gave 20 hectares (50 acres) to anyone who paid another's way. In the beginning women were included in this plan. But soon women were being brought only as servants so they would marry quickly. The colony's leaders felt that families had more of an interest in making the colony succeed than single people did.

Workers

As Jamestown became successful, colonists spread along the James River and inland along other rivers and streams. Settlements called plantations were established and farmers began to raise tobacco on the fertile land. To grow tobacco, large amounts of land and labor are needed. Virginia in its early days had plenty of land — once the Native Americans were removed. But the supply of labor was a problem.

establish (es-TAB-lish): to set up

To get more workers, the planters started to hire **indentured** (in-DEN-chuhrd) **servants.** These were people who agreed to work without pay for a certain period — five or seven years — in exchange for

The first blacks to come to what is now the U.S. were indentured servants. How did the system change from indenture to slavery?

their passage to the colony. During the time of indenture, servants received food, clothing, and housing. They could not leave or marry until they had finished their contract. Those who disobeyed were punished. When the contract was finished, a servant received 20 hectares (50 acres) of land and enough supplies to start a farm.

As the demand for tobacco grew, the indenture system did not provide enough workers for the fields. What seemed like the answer to the problem began a chain of events that led to **slavery** (SLAYV-uhr-ee), the owning of people, in the English colonies.

The First Africans

In 1619, a Dutch ship sailed into Jamestown Harbor with a number of Africans aboard. Although their services were bought by planters, the 1623 census of the colony lists them as servants. Like European indentured servants, they worked for a certain period of years for food, clothing, and shelter. At the end of their contracts, they received land. This appears to be true until the 1650s.

But things were changing. By at least the 1640s, Africans were being forced to work longer and longer terms of service. By 1660, Virginia had made slavery legal for Africans. Over the next 100 years, Africans as slaves took the place of European indentured servants. By 1750, slaves made up almost half the population of Virginia.

House of Burgesses

As you read at the beginning of the chapter, the colony was first governed by a council of seven selected by the Virginia Company. The council seemed to spend more time arguing than making decisions and was replaced by a governor. He was named by the company.

In 1619, the governor called for a **representative** (rep-rih-ZEN-tuh-tiv) **assembly.** This is a group of people elected by their fellow citizens to make laws. Representative government was one of the rights the colonists had enjoyed as citizens in England. The assembly in Virginia was called the House of Burgesses (BER-jih-sez) and was the first lawmaking body in the English colonies. Two free men from each plantation were called to attend. The first meeting had 22 members.

A ROYAL COLONY

James I was angered that the men who controlled the Virginia Company wanted more power for the people and less for the monarch. In 1624, he made Virginia a royal colony. A **royal colony** was one whose governor and council were appointed by the monarch. The House of Burgesses was allowed to continue, but the governor had more power. This unequal division of power was to become a problem throughout the colonies until it finally exploded in the American Revolution.

Bacon's Rebellion

Bacon's Rebellion is just one example of the problem. By the late 1600s, colonists has spread along more of the coasts and farther inland. Jamestown had become the capital of a widespread colony. The descendants of the first colonists had the largest and best lands along the coast. Newcomers had to move into the wilderness. In order to build farms, they tried to push the Native Americans off the land. The Native Americans resisted and war resulted. The farmers demanded protection from the government at Jamestown.

rebellion: a fight against authority

The government was controlled by wealthy coastal planters, supported by the governor. They provided for their own defense and neglected the colonists farther inland. In 1676, Nathanial Bacon, a farmer, decided to act. He and his followers attacked the Native Americans without the governor's approval. Declared a rebel, Bacon turned on the governor and began seizing territory. The governor, William Berkeley (BERK-lee), was able to destroy the revolt.

neglect (nih-GLEKT): to pay little attention to

Some reforms did come about because of Bacon's Rebellion. One was the election of a new House of Burgesses. The governor had not called for an election in 15 years.

reform (rih-FORM): change for the better; improvement

LOOKING BACK

1. Reread Spain's reasons for colonization on pages 96 and 97. Compare and contrast those reasons with England's.
2. At first the Powhatan helped the colonists. What did the English, under Lord Delaware and later governors, do to change this relationship?
3. **a.** Describe the use of Africans as servants in Virginia.
   b. Through the years, how did this lead to a change in their role in society?
4. What problem arose when Virginia was made a royal colony?

Chapter 3   Pilgrims and Puritans

LOOKING AHEAD

This chapter tells the story of the Pilgrims who settled Plymouth Colony in New England. You will read about their relations with the Native Americans of the region. You will also read about the colonizing of Massachusetts Bay by Puritans. After you study this chapter, you will be able to:

- explain the conditions that made Puritans leave England.
- identify the importance of the Mayflower Compact.
- describe the relationship between church and state in Massachusetts Bay.
- explain the reasons for the expansion of English settlements beyond Massachusetts Bay Colony.
- identify material as a primary source.

Social Studies Vocabulary

politics	representative government
self-government	

People

Puritans	Wampanoag	William Bradford
Pilgrims	Massasoit	John Eliot
Samoset	Squanto	

Places

Plymouth colony	Massachusetts Bay Colony

Words and Terms

state religion	freemen
Mayflower Compact	General Court

Oliver Cromwell led the Puritans in a civil war against the English king, Charles I. The king was executed, and Cromwell made England into a Puritan state until his death in 1658.

To understand the English settlements at Plymouth and Massachusetts Bay, you need to understand the forces that drove the people to an unknown land far from England. Religion, politics, and the economy led them to take such a risk. **Politics** (PAHL-uh-tiks) is the activities and organizations through which people and groups seek power or control of government. Of the three factors, religion was the most important.

ENGLISH BACKGROUND

During the early 1600s, it was dangerous for Europeans to practice a religion other than the one approved by their governments. As you read in the unit Europeans as Explorers, King Henry VIII of England broke away from the Roman Catholic Church and started the Church of England or the Anglican (ANG-gluh-kuhn) Church. The Church of England became the official state religion, the one the government supported. Everyone had to belong to it. People found practicing other religions were severely punished.

Among such people were the Puritans. They felt that the Church of England had not gone far enough in shedding Roman Catholic practices. They wanted to stay within the Church of England but purify, or reform, it. Another group of Puritans, the Separatists (SEP-uh-ruh-tists), wanted to separate completely from the Church of England and form their own church. Both groups of Puritans were persecuted for their beliefs. Some were fined or sent to jail. Many fled.

English politics also caused Puritan unrest. Parliament (PAHR-luh-muhnt) is the English representative assembly that the House of Burgesses was modeled on. King James I, who ruled from 1603 to 1625, tried to govern without Parliament. Charles I, who became king in 1625, did not call Parliament into session from then until 1640. Both men believed that the monarch was above the law and any law-making body. They believed monarchs ruled because they were chosen by God. Conflict over this idea and over the kind of church that England should have broke out between the king and Parliament. During this time, many members of Parliament were Puritans.

Some Puritans also wanted to leave England because of its economic problems. Many large landowners found they could make more money raising sheep than by renting land to tenant farmers. When the farmers were forced off the land, they went to towns and cities, looking for work. But there were not enough jobs, and unemployment was high.

shed: to get rid of

THE PILGRIMS

In 1608, a group of Separatists had left England for Holland. There, all Christians were allowed religious freedom. As the years passed, the English grew unhappy in their adopted land. They had separated from the Church of England, but they did not wish to become Dutch by acculturation. This was happening. Their children, for example, were growing up speaking Dutch rather than English.

By 1619, the Pilgrims, or travellers, as they are called, had decided to leave Holland. They believed that America would give them a chance to keep their religion and their way of life. They received permission from the Virginia Company to settle north of Jamestown. To raise money to pay for their trip, they formed a joint-stock company with London merchants.

In September 1620, the Pilgrims set sail on the *Mayflower*. There were 102 passengers. Of these, only about half were Pilgrims. The rest were simply English people who hoped for a better life in America. The trip lasted 65 days. Many people became sick from the poor food

People discovered practicing a religion other than the one approved by their government might find themselves fined, imprisoned, or even burned alive.

109

and crowded conditions. After dropping anchor in what is modern Cape Cod Bay and exploring the area nearby, the Pilgrims settled at a spot they called Plymouth.

The Mayflower Compact

While still aboard the *Mayflower*, the Pilgrims wrote an agreement setting down rules of government. The Mayflower Compact, or agreement, is short, but it is the first of a series of documents written in America on self-government. **Self-government** is government of, by, and for the people.

> In the name of God, Amen. We whose names are underwritten, the loyal subjects of our respected ruling Lord King James, by the grace of God, of Great Britain, France, and Ireland, king, defender of the faith, etc.
>
> Having agreed for the glory of God and advancement of the Christian faith and honor of our king and country to a voyage to plant the first colony in the northern parts of Virginia, do seriously and together in the presence of God, and one another, combine ourselves together into a political body. We do this for our better ordering and preservation of the ends mentioned before. And for these reasons to enact and plan such just and equal laws, rules, acts, and offices, from time to time, as shall be thought best for the general good of the colony. Unto which we promise all due submission and obedience. In witness whereof we have hereunder signed our names at Cape Cod the 11th of November, in the reign of our ruling Lord King James of England, France, and Ireland the eighteenth, and of Scotland the fifty-fourth. Anno Domini 1620

enact (en-AKT): to make into a law

submission (suhb-MISH-uhn): giving in to another's control

In the Mayflower Compact, the Pilgrims declared their right to self-government. The right to vote, though, was given only to freemen. These were men who owned property and were members in good standing of the church. The General Court, a representative assembly of freemen, was set up. It set taxes, acted as a court, and made laws. It was the supreme authority in the colony. The day-to-day governing was handled by a governor, appointed by the General Court. The court also decided who would be given the title of freeman.

Plymouth Colony

temporary (TEM-puh-rer-ee): not lasting for a long time

The Pilgrims had little food during the winter of 1620-21. Many had only temporary shelters. By spring, almost half the colonists had died. Besides the problems of food and shelter, the Pilgrims at first feared the Native Americans of the region. In the beginning, the Native Americans watched the colonists from a distance. Finally, in March 1621, Samoset (SAM-oh-set), a member of the Pemaquid (PEM-uh-kwid) nation, walked into the village. He spoke in English of a disease that had killed many of his people. They had caught it from some English traders who had come to the area earlier. Several days later, Samoset returned with Massasoit (MAS-uh-soit), the

Plymouth Plantation has been restored, or returned to its original state, as a working village where visitors may see how colonists in 1624 lived and worked.

leader of the Wampanoag. In time, the Pilgrims and Massasoit made a treaty of friendship that lasted for over 40 years.

Samoset also brought with him Squanto (SKWAHN-toh). Squanto, a Patuxent (puh-TUKS-uhnt), had been kidnapped, sold into slavery in Spain, and escaped to England. He had made his way back to America in 1618 only to find most of his people dead. He remained in Plymouth, acting as a guide and interpreter. He showed the colonists how to raise corn and to gather wild foods. The Pilgrims were soon raising and using corn for food as the Native Americans did. This use of corn by the colonists is an example of cultural diffusion between the Wampanoag and the colonists.

interpreter (in-TER-pruh-tuhr): person who translates words into another language

Growth of Plymouth

Despite many problems, the colony grew under the leadership of Governor William Bradford. Many colonists died in the first years, but others came from England to take their places. By 1624, Plymouth had 124 people. By 1630, the number was nearly 300 and by 1637, 549. Almost all were farmers, though the colony did some fur trading with the Native Americans. At first, the people worked the land in common as the people in Jamestown had. But in 1623, the land was divided among families and the colony prospered. The colony, though, never became large, rich, or powerful.

prosper (PRAHS-puhr): to do well; to succeed

Plymouth Colony is important for three reasons, however. It was the first colony founded by people seeking religious freedom. Second, Plymouth was founded on the idea of self-government. Virginia had the House of Burgesses, but it had come 12 years after the colony was founded. Third, Plymouth Colony proved that people could live in the colder areas north of Virginia. Plymouth's success helped bring other Puritans to Massachusetts Bay. They founded several colonies that became more important and powerful than Plymouth. In 1691, Plymouth was made part of Massachusetts Bay.

Boston was settled in 1630. Two years later, it was made the capital of Massachusetts Bay. Who founded the colony?

MASSACHUSETTS BAY

In 1629, a group of Puritan leaders and English merchants formed a partnership to set up a colony north of Plymouth. This partnership was called the Massachusetts Bay Company. The objective of the new colony was to make money for the owners. Profits were to come from fishing, farming, and fur trading. Because of conditions in England, the Massachusetts Bay Company had no trouble finding colonists. By late summer 1630, over 1,000 Puritans had come to Massachusetts Bay. They settled first at a place they called Salem. Later, they built Boston, Charlestown, and Cambridge. Over 10,000 people settled in the colony during the 1630s.

Church and State

The charter of Massachusetts Bay Company really set up a business in which the shareholders governed the colony. At first, only the men who owned shares could vote. They were called freemen and elected a governor and council yearly. The three groups met four times each year to make the laws. These meetings, as in Plymouth, were called General Courts. However, the number of freemen was small, only 12 in 1630. After 1631, the rank of freeman was increased to include church members who were not shareholders.

In 1634, by action of the General Court, Massachusetts Bay gained a **representative government.** This is government in which lawmaking power is given by the people to those they elect. This is the kind of government Jamestown had after the House of Burgesses was set up. In Massachusetts Bay, the freemen of each town chose the representatives who went to the General Court.

The General Court governed the entire colony. Towns, however, elected local officials and governed themselves through town meetings. These were held as often as once a week. Landowners who were also church members were allowed to vote. People who did not own property could only give their opinions.

In spite of the colony's General Court and the town meeting, self-government during the early years of Massachusetts Bay was limited. Until about the 1660s, the right to vote and to hold public office belonged to Puritans only.

The Puritans wanted to model their government after ideas in the Bible. Because their ministers knew more about the Bible than anyone else, the people looked to them for guidance. Also, Puritan ministers decided who could or could not be a church member. Not every man who went to church was given the title of church member. Because only adult male church members were allowed to become freemen, only they could vote. In this way, the ministers controlled the opinions and policies of the government. For a time, church and state in Massachusetts Bay were one.

A Code of Laws

In 1641, the General Court passed the first code or set of laws in the English colonies, the Body of Liberties. Some of these laws were:

- No brutal, cruel, or harsh physical punishment will be allowed among us.
- All jurors will be selected by the freemen of their town.
- Any man who insults God, the Father, Son, or Holy Ghost, or curses God shall be put to death.
- Any person who murders another on purpose because of hatred or cruelty, not for self-defense or by accident, shall be put to death.
- No man shall be sentenced twice by a civil court for the same crime or offense.

Mission to the Native Americans

Like the Spanish and French, the English worked to convert the Native Americans in their colonies to Christianity. As you may recall from Chapter 2 of this unit, bringing Christianity to the Native Americans was one goal of the Virginia Company's charter. Some attempts were made in Jamestown and the Virginia Colony. However, more efforts were made in Massachusetts Bay.

John Eliot, a Puritan minister, worked among the Native Americans in Massachusetts Bay for almost 60 years. In 1651, he organized a village of Native Americans at Natick (NAY-tik). Within 25 years, he had 14 villages and several thousand converts. By 1663, he had translated the Bible into the Algonquian (al-GAHNG-kee-uhn) language of the people.

Like the Spanish, Eliot and the missionaries who followed him believed that the Native Americans should learn European ways of life as well as Christianity. The villages had schools where reading and writing in English and crafts were taught. Some Native Americans were trained to teach and preach among their people.

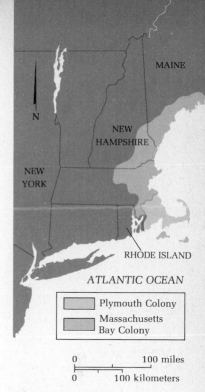

Plymouth and Massachusetts Bay Colonies in 1660

MAINE
NEW HAMPSHIRE
NEW YORK
RHODE ISLAND
ATLANTIC OCEAN

Plymouth Colony
Massachusetts Bay Colony

0   100 miles
0   100 kilometers

offense (uh-FENS): breaking a law, crime

John Eliot was a Puritan minister who worked among Native Americans in Massachusetts Bay in the 1600s. He taught them to read and write and translated the Bible into several Native American languages.

The colonists' desire for land, however, would touch even these peaceful villages in the 1670s. You will read about this in Metacom's War in the next chapter.

THE SPREAD OF SETTLEMENTS

In Europe during the early 1600s, land was scarce. There was little chance that anyone born without land would ever own any. A desire to own land became an important reason for Europeans to come to America. Those who settled in New Spain and those who came to the English colonies shared the same feelings.

As more and more Puritans came, the coast became filled with villages. People began to push inland, seeking land of their own and founding new settlements. This is similar to what happened in Virginia. Other settlements in what became known as New England were founded because Puritans refused to allow other religions in their towns. You will read about these colonies next.

LOOKING BACK

1. What conditions in England moved Puritans to come to America?
2. Why is the Mayflower Compact considered important to the development of government in the U.S.?
3. How did the Puritan religion affect government in: **a.** the General Court? **b.** towns of Massachusetts Bay?
4. Give two reasons for the expansion of settlements beyond Massachusetts Bay Colony.
5. **a.** Are the two readings in this chapter both primary sources? **b.** According to the description on page 98, what kind of primary source is each? **c.** How are the two sources different in their purposes?

Chapter 4   New England Expansion

LOOKING AHEAD

This chapter describes the colonies that developed as people spread out from Massachusetts Bay. You will read how the present states of Rhode Island, Connecticut, New Hampshire, and Maine were founded. You will also read about the relations between the colonies and the Native Americans of the region. After you study this chapter, you will be able to:

- describe the founding of Rhode Island.
- identify the importance of the Fundamental Orders of Connecticut.
- ★ make a generalization about Native American and English feelings about land.
- explain how New Hampshire and Maine were settled.
- describe the conflict between Massachusetts colonists and the royal government.

Social Studies Vocabulary

constitution	civil war
ally	confederation

People

Roger Williams	Thomas Hooker	Edmund Andros
Narraganset	John Davenport	
Anne Hutchinson	John Mason	
John Winthrop	James II	

Places

Rhode Island	New Hampshire
Connecticut	Maine

Words and Terms

New England Confederation

Events

Pequot War	Metacom's War

Many settlers arriving in Massachusetts Bay did not agree with the way the Puritans were governing the colony. These people either left the colony on their own or were forced to leave. They went into the wilderness of New England—the present states of Rhode Island, Connecticut, New Hampshire, and Maine—and built settlements. Vermont did not separate from New York and New Hampshire until 1777.

New England Colonies in 1700

MAINE

NEW HAMPSHIRE

NEW YORK

RHODE ISLAND

ATLANTIC OCEAN

0   100 miles

0   100 kilometers

RHODE ISLAND

In 1631, Roger Williams, a minister, arrived in Massachusetts Bay from England. Unlike the leaders of the colony, Williams believed that church and state should be separate. Neither should enforce the views of the other. Williams declared that only God knew for sure what the correct religion was. He argued that all people should have the right to worship as they pleased. He also said that the colonists could not take land from the Native Americans without paying for it. In 1635, the colony's leaders ordered Williams to leave.

Williams and some followers fled south. In time, they bought land from the Narraganset (nar-uh-GAN-set) and settled along Narragansett Bay in what is now Rhode Island. Williams called his small settlement Providence, for he had "a sense of God's merciful Providence in guiding me." Other settlements soon followed. One, Portsmouth, was founded by Anne Hutchinson.

In 1634, Hutchinson, her husband, and 10 children had arrived in Boston. Hutchinson was a deeply religious woman who preached in her home. Women were not allowed to be ministers and preach in churches. She attacked most Puritan ministers for preaching about church attendance, good behavior, and proper dress. She thought they should be talking about spiritual purity. Hutchinson gained a large following even though most ministers and government leaders were against her. Finally, in 1637, Governor John Winthrop called together a group to decide if she were a heretic (HER-uh-tik), one teaching false religion. Hutchinson and her followers were ordered to

Anne Hutchinson was tried as a heretic and forced to leave Massachusetts Bay. What was she accused of?

confess their errors. Most did, but Hutchinson refused. A year later, she and her family were expelled from Massachusetts Bay. They fled southward to the protection of William's settlement.

By 1643, there were four towns in the region we call Rhode Island. To protect themselves from being taken over by a larger colony, the leaders of the towns asked the monarch for a charter. It was granted in 1644. The charter allowed the towns to control their own affairs and guaranteed religious freedom. It also gave all adult males the right to vote. In 1663, a new charter limited political rights somewhat. It required an adult male to own property before he could vote, but the colonists continued to have self-government. The colony also remained a refuge for those fleeing religious persecution.

CONNECTICUT

By 1635, the English had moved south and west to settle along the Connecticut River. In 1636, Thomas Hooker, a minister from Cambridge, and over 100 followers settled around what is now Hartford. They had left Massachusetts Bay because they disagreed with its Puritan leaders. For example, they thought it wrong that people who were not church members were kept from voting.

In 1639, leaders from the new towns of Windsor and Wethersfield joined with those from Hartford to draw up the Fundamental Orders of Connecticut. This was the first constitution in the English colonies. A **constitution** (kahn-stuh-TOO-shuhn) is a set of basic laws and a plan of government. The orders based the government of the colony on the will of the people and not on that of a monarch. The orders gave Connecticut a governor, council, and a general court similar to

Thomas Hooker and his followers are on their way to found what will become the city of Hartford, Connecticut. Why did they leave Massachusetts Bay?

refuge (REF-yooj): shelter; safe or protected place

fundamental (fun-duh-MEN-tuhl): basic

117

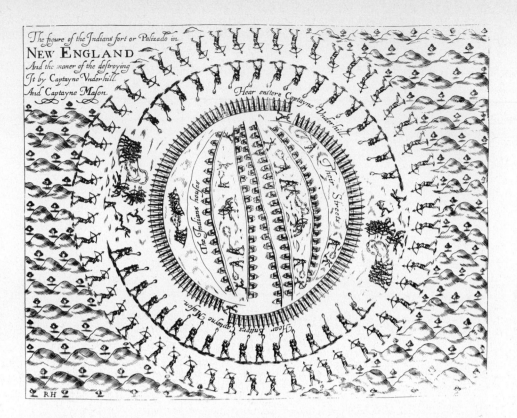

This drawing shows the destruction of a Pequot village in Connecticut by Puritan soldiers in 1637. More than 600 Pequot were killed.

Massachusetts Bay's. Unlike the Puritan colony, however, there was no religious requirement for voting.

New settlements continued to develop along Connecticut's south coast. In 1637, John Davenport and a group of Puritans from England established the town of New Haven. New Haven and Connecticut often argued over boundaries and over control of nearby lands. In 1662, Connecticut received a charter that extended its boundaries to include New Haven and other coastal towns. The charter for Connecticut states:

> We order, declare, and appoint, in this charter, for us, our heirs, and followers, that for the better ordering and managing of the business of the said company there shall be one governor, one deputy-governor, and twelve assistants. From time to time they will be elected out of the freemen of the said company in such manner and form as is expressed in this document. These officers shall apply themselves to take care of the general business, the land, the inheritable property to be granted, and the government of the people of it.

War with the Pequot

The spread of English settlements throughout New England soon spelled disaster for the Native Americans of the region. A Native American family needed several square kilometers of forest to support itself by hunting and fishing. When the English came, they cleared the forests for farms. This reduced the area in which Native Americans could roam freely. In clearing the land, the English also destroyed animal homes. Besides farming, the English also hunted and fished for some of their own food. This reduced the supply of food for Native Americans. It soon became clear that both Native Americans and English could not share the same land.

The English settlements in Connecticut were on the land of the Pequot (PEE-kwaht). The Pequot had moved into southern New England about 100 years before the English. They had conquered other peoples and become the strongest nation in the area. When the English tried to take their land, the Pequot fought back.

In May 1637, the English attacked the main Pequot settlement near the Mystic River in Connecticut. With their Narraganset and Mohegan (moh-HEE-guhn) allies, the English burned the fort and the village. An **ally** (AL-eye) is a person, group, or country united with another for common benefits. Those Pequot who were not killed were sold into slavery. This ended Native American resistance to English settlement in Connecticut.

resistance (rih-ZIS-tuhns): act of opposing

BUILDING READING SKILLS

In Chapter 6 of the unit The First Americans, you learned what a generalization is and how to recognize one. Now you are going to learn how to make generalizations. Data for making a generalization is not always stated directly. Sometimes only some or part of the data is suggested. To make a generalization about how Native Americans and English colonists felt about land, you may have to interpret—infer—their feelings from their actions.

Use the following steps:

- Reread the section War with the Pequot to find out how the Native Americans used the land.
- Reread the section to find out how English colonists used the land.

1. How did each use the land? **2.** Why were both groups unable or unwilling to share the same land? **3.** What does the use of the land tell you about how the Native Americans and the colonists felt about the land? **4.** Combine this data into a general statement about each group's feelings toward the land. Remember that this is a generalization. Not every member of both groups may have shared the group's feelings.

NEW HAMPSHIRE AND MAINE

Although the main paths of settlement went south and west from Massachusetts Bay, Puritans also pushed north toward French Canada. In the 1620s, John Mason and others were given land by the king for settlement. By 1630, the region that later became New Hampshire and Maine had a few groups of fishers and trappers. During the 1630s and 1640s, hundreds of settlers moved north. Some came directly from England and others came from Massachusetts Bay. All were looking for a better life.

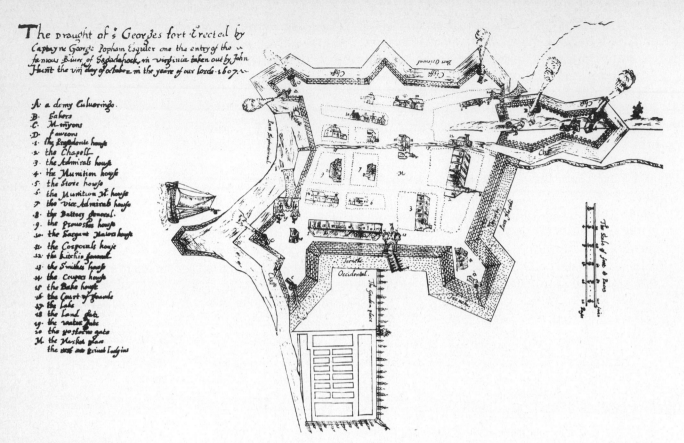

The draught of ye Georges fort Erected by Capbayne George Popham Esquier one the entry of the famous River of Sagadahock, in virginia taken out by John Hunt the viii day of october in the yeare of our lordes 1607.

A. a demy Culueringe.
B. Sakers
C. Minyons
D. fawcons
1. the Presidente house
2. the Chapell
3. the Admirals house
4. the Munition house
5. the Store house
6. the Munition Ye house
7. the Vice Admirals house
8. the Battery generall.
9. the Provosts house
10. the Sergeant Maiors house
11. the Corporals house
12. the kitchin generall
13. the Smithes house
14. the Coupers house
15. the Bake house
16. the Court of Guarde
17. the Lake
18. the Land Gate
19. the water Gate
20. the posterne gate
M. the Market place
the rest are private Lodgins

This is the plan for a fort to be built in Maine in 1607. Because of the hardships of colonial life and the cold, the settlers returned to England. The fort was never built.

By the 1650s, Massachusetts had extended its control over the entire area. In 1677, Maine was officially claimed by Massachusetts and became part of the Bay colony. Settlers in New Hampshire, however, were growing tired of being controlled from Boston. In 1679, an English court decided Massachusetts had no right to the area. The king granted New Hampshire a royal charter giving the colony a lawmaking council. However, the royal governors most often dominated the government.

NEW ENGLAND CONFEDERATION

For most of the period from 1642 to 1660, civil war raged in England between Puritans and supporters of the king. **Civil War** is war between parts of the same state or nation. From 1645 to 1660, the Puritans ruled England without a monarch. During this time, the American colonies were left to solve their own problems. The New England Confederation was one such attempt. A **confederation** (kuhn-fed-uhr-AY-shuhn) is a government system that results from the loose joining of states into a union. The states give up some, but not most, of their government powers.

In 1643, delegates from Connecticut, New Haven, Plymouth, and Massachusetts Bay met to draw up a constitution for the confederation. The purpose of the confederation was defense against French,

Dutch, and Native American attacks. The confederation settled a few arguments among the colonies over boundaries and raised money for common projects. Its real importance, however, lay in showing that the colonies could work together in matters of common interest. The New England Confederation planted the seeds of union.

Metacom's War

One of the problems that the New England Confederation had to deal with was Metacom's (met-uh-KAHM) War. Metacom, whom the English called King Philip, was the son of Massasoit. He had become the leader of the Wampanoag after his father's death in 1661. During this time, Metacom had seen the relationship between his people and the English worsen. The colonists violated more and more of the treaty of friendship agreed to in 1621 by Massasoit and the Pilgrims. In 1671, Metacom was forced to agree to a new treaty. According to it, the New England Confederation would make the rules for selling land to the colonists. The Native Americans had to obey.

In addition, the Native Americans over the years had become dependent on the colonists for such trade goods as iron tools, cooking pots, alcohol, and guns. By the mid-1600s, the various peoples were finding it harder and harder to trade for these goods. So many beaver had been killed for the fur trade that there were few beaver left to trap and sell. The Native Americans had nothing else to use for trade. They had no future that Metacom could see. He wanted to unite the Native Americans in New England to resist the English and get back their lands.

As Metacom was gaining allies, three Wampanoag were accused of murdering an English informant and were hanged in 1675. War broke out between the Native Americans and the English. The early successes of the Wampanoag brought group after group to fight by their sides—Wimpuc, Narraganset, and Mohegan. At the beginning of the war, the converts in Eliot's villages remained friendly to the colonists. You read about Eliot in Chapter 3 of this unit. The colonists, however, came to fear all Native Americans and treated them all cruelly, even the converts. As a result of the harsh treatment, the converts turned against the colonists.

By winter, the English settlements in the upper Connecticut Valley were in ruins. Colonists had fled to towns along the coast where they thought they would be safe. In winter 1676, the Native Americans began to weaken. Disease, lack of food, and lack of weapons—not a lack of courage—were defeating them. Metacom was killed and no one else was able to keep the different peoples together. By fall, the war was over.

Hundreds of Native Americans and colonists had been killed. Many towns and villages on both sides had been destroyed. It took years for the colonists to rebuild. Those Native Americans who survived and who did not move were forced to live under even stricter laws. Because of the fighting skill of the Native Americans in the war,

Metacom was chief of the Wampanoag. In 1675, he led a group of Native American allies against the English in order to get back their lands.

Masachusetts Bay Colony used the silver pine-tree shilling from 1652 until 1682, though England had forbidden the colonies to coin their own money.

the colonists feared them. Out of this fear, the colonists came to see Native Americans as savage. This view lasted for over 200 years.

ROYAL VERSUS POPULAR CONTROL

When the English civil war ended, the new king, Charles II, tightened royal control of the American colonies. English merchants had convinced the monarch that the colonies were becoming too independent. By selling goods to foreign countries against English law, New England traders were taking business away from English merchants. Massachusetts was the most disobedient of the colonies. It had been avoiding other laws from England as well. It coined its own money and its Puritan leaders refused religious freedom to members of the Church of England.

Charles decided to punish Massachusetts. In 1684, he took away the colony's charter and made Massachusetts a royal colony. Upon his death later that year, Charles's brother, the Duke of York, became King James II. James appointed Sir Edmund Andros (AN-druhs) governor of New England, New York, and New Jersey. Rhode Island and Connecticut were made royal colonies.

Andros quickly became unpopular with the colonists. He set taxes without consulting the colonial assemblies. Town meetings could be held only with his approval. He also enforced certain trade laws passed by Parliament that hurt colonial trade. You will read about these laws in the unit Becoming Americans.

The colonists were so angered that when the English removed James II in 1689 in the Glorious Revolution, the colonists arrested Andros. He was jailed and later returned to England. In 1691, Massachusetts received a new charter. The governor was to be appointed by the monarch, and all Protestants were to be allowed freedom of worship. Rhode Island and Connecticut regained their lost charters. But the colonists' struggles against royal control of their affairs would not end until the American Revolution.

LOOKING BACK

1. Why was Roger Williams expelled from Massachusetts Bay?
2. Why are the Fundamental Orders of Connecticut important in the history of American government?
★ 3. Support the following general statement or generalization: Native Americans and English colonists could not live in peace on the same land because their ways of life were so different. **a.** How did Native Americans use the land? **b.** How did the colonists use the land? **c.** What facts from your reading show that these two cultures did not live in peace?
4. Why were New Hampshire and Maine settled?
5. What factors caused: **a.** the king to make Massachusetts a royal colony? **b.** the colonists to arrest Andros?

Chapter 5   Southern Expansion

LOOKING AHEAD

This chapter describes the settling of the southern colonies of Maryland, Carolina, and Georgia. You will read about the reasons for settling the various colonies as well as the relations between the colonists and the Native Americans. After you study this chapter, you will be able to:

- compare and contrast the reasons for the colonization of Maryland, Carolina, and Georgia.
- ★ classify the reasons for the conflict that occurred between colonists in Maryland.
- list the sequence of events that led to the Tuscarora and Yamasee wars.

Social Studies Vocabulary

skilled worker   proprietary colony   labor force

People

Lord Baltimore   William Berkeley   James Oglethorpe
Leonard Calvert   John Colleton

Places

Maryland   Carolina   Georgia

Words and Terms

General Assembly   Toleration Act

Events

Tuscarora War   Yamasee War

Although Jamestown survived, no other colonies were begun in the South until the 1630s. It was a hundred years later before the fourth and final southern colony was founded. The three later colonies—Maryland, Carolina, and Georgia—were similar to Virginia in many ways. Each was based on farming and private ownership of land. Each in time came to have a representative assembly.

This seal of Carolina was adopted by the eight proprietors of the colony in the mid-1600s.

MARYLAND

Lord Baltimore, a Roman Catholic and a friend of the king, believed Catholics should have a place to live and worship as they pleased. In

This view of Baltimore was drawn by John Moale in 1752. The city was originally founded as a trading center for tobacco plantations in the Maryland colony.

1632, he asked Charles I for land to start a colony in America. The king gave Lord Baltimore four million hectares (ten million acres) on Chesapeake Bay. It was to be named *Mary Land* in honor of the queen, Henrietta Maria.

Plan for Settling

Besides giving people a safe place to worship, Lord Baltimore hoped to earn money from his colony. He needed colonists to plant and farm tobacco so he offered 40 hectares (100 acres) to people who paid their own way. Colonists who brought their families and servants received 20 hectares (50 acres) for each of these people. Anyone who paid the passage for five indentured servants received 400 hectares (1,000 acres). In return, colonists agreed to pay yearly rent for the land.

The first group of settlers sailed into Chesapeake Bay in March 1634. Leonard Calvert, Lord Baltimore's brother and Maryland's first governor, headed the expedition. The group chose a spot on Chesapeake Bay for their settlement and named it St. Mary's. Among the first settlers were over 200 skilled workers, servants, and farmhands as well as 17 gentlemen and their families. A **skilled worker** is a person whose work demands a special ability or training. The colonists planted crops soon after they arrived and before beginning other projects. In this way they avoided a starving time like Jamestown's.

Governing the Colony

Maryland was a **proprietary** (pruh-PRY-uh-ter-ee) **colony,** one whose charter granted ownership of all land to one person or group. Lord Baltimore's charter made him the only proprietor (pruh-PRY-uhtuhr), or owner, of Maryland. He had the complete power to govern and make laws for the colony. However, the charter required that he have the "advice and consent" of free adult males to the laws. A representative assembly like the House of Burgesses was set up in 1635. Later, Lord Baltimore agreed to allow the General Assembly, as it was called, to make the laws.

Conflict and Toleration

Most of the large landowners were Roman Catholic, while the small farmers and indentured servants were Protestant. From the beginning, Protestants far outnumbered Roman Catholics. The Roman Catholics, however, controlled the government because they were the wealthy landowners. They wanted Maryland to be a Catholic colony, with Catholic laws and officials. Protestants, because they were so many, thought they should control the government.

Lord Baltimore called for toleration between the two groups. Toleration (tahl-uhr-AY-shuhn) means allowing other people the freedom of their beliefs. In 1649, Lord Baltimore was able to force the General Assembly to pass the Toleration Act.

> Be it therefore ordered and enacted by the Lord Proprietor, with the advice and agreement of this Assembly, that no person or persons within this province, or the islands, harbors, or creeks belonging to it, who claims to believe in Jesus Christ shall be in any way troubled, disturbed, or discouraged for, or because of, his or her religion, nor in the free practice of it, nor in any way forced to the belief or practice of any other religion.

Lord Baltimore's wish had become law, but the conflicts continued as Catholics and Protestants argued over control of the colony.

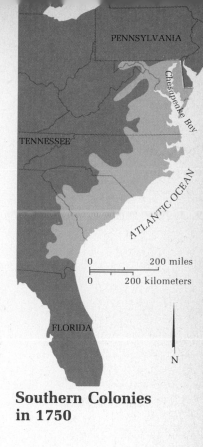

Southern Colonies in 1750

conflict (KAHN-flikt): fight; disagreement

In Chapter 7 of the unit The First Americans, you learned how to classify data. For that activity, all the data was actually given in the text. Sometimes, though, you may have to infer part of the data. You have to do that to classify reasons for the conflict among Maryland's colonists. **Activity:** Reread the section Conflict and Toleration. Classify reasons according to these categories: religious, political, economic.

BUILDING READING SKILLS

Slavery in Maryland

Besides Virginia, Maryland was one of the earliest southern colonies to employ slave labor. In the beginning, white indentured servants worked Maryland's tobacco plantations. In 1671, slaves were only about five percent of Maryland's population. But in the late 1600s, Charles II allowed the Royal African Company to sell slaves in the colonies. As a result, the number of slaves in Maryland increased rapidly. By 1700, slaves made up 20 percent of Maryland's population.

CAROLINA

The founders of Carolina had one purpose in mind for their colony. They wanted it to make money for them. In March 1663, eight Englishmen led by Sir William Berkeley and Sir John Colleton (KAHL-eh-tuhn), were given a charter for what are now the states of North and South Carolina and Georgia. The region was called Carolina in honor of King Charles II. As proprietors, the eight had complete authority over the colony. They planned to set up manors similar to those you read about in the unit Europeans as Explorers. People, however, wanted to own their own land and would not come to Carolina under these terms.

In 1666, the proprietors changed their plan in order to attract settlers. Any free person who came with family and servants would be given land to work and live on forever. For each man, woman, child, and male servant 40 hectares (100 acres) were given. Twenty hectares (50 acres) were given for each female servant and slave. In addition, indentured servants would be given land at the end of their contracts. Men would receive 40 hectares (100 acres) and women half that amount. Indentured servants made up most of the labor force until the early 1700s. Then planters began bringing in large numbers of Africans as slaves. A **labor force** is the number of people employed or able and willing to work.

Albemarle

The first settlement in Carolina was built just south of Virginia in the Albemarle (AL-buh-mahrl) Sound area. Most of the settlers came from Virginia. In 1664, the proprietors appointed a governor. The following year an elected assembly met for the first time. Life in Albemarle was much like the plantation system of Virginia and Maryland. By 1700, between 4,000 and 5,000 people lived in Albemarle.

In the early 1700s, slave labor replaced the work of indentured servants on the plantations of North and South Carolina.

Charles Town

The proprietors started a second settlement, Charles Town, in 1670 in the southern part of their land. This settlement was moved to a less swampy location in 1680. Rice grew well at the new spot and black and Native American slaves provided cheap labor. In time, large rice plantations developed around Charles Town. (Its name was changed to Charleston in 1783.)

As settlements spread out beyond the city, colonists began to trade in furs and deerskins with the Westo (WES-toh) and Creek. Charles Town soon became a trading center. In the colonial period, it was the only large city in the Southern colonies. By 1700, between 8,000 and 10,000 people lived there. They came mostly from Virginia, New England, Barbados (bahr-BAY-dohz) in the Caribbean, Scotland, France, and West Africa.

The proprietors appointed a governor and a council. There was also an elected assembly called the Commons House of Assembly. By 1693, it had gained the right to make laws.

Tuscarora and Yamasee

As in New England, Native Americans in the southern colonies came to depend on trade with the English. But contact with the colonists brought problems. In Carolina, colonists captured Native Americans and sold them as slaves in New England and the West Indies. The Tuscarora of northern Carolina wanted to stop this sale of their women and children as slaves. At first, the Tuscarora tried peaceful methods. They asked Pennsylvania to allow them to settle in that colony. The request was ignored.

ignore (ig-NOR): to pay no attention to

In 1711, the Tuscarora and several smaller groups, such as the Pamlico (PAM-luh-koh), attacked slave traders in northern Carolina. Slave traders from southern Carolina, hoping to capture Native Americans as slaves, helped their northern neighbors. The Tuscarora were defeated in 1713. Many had been killed or taken as slaves. Some moved north into what is now New York State.

In 1715, the Yamasee (YAH-muh-see) fought a larger war against the slave traders. Like the Tuscarora, the Yamasee had lost much of their land to the colonists. A 1707 Carolina law restricted them to a small part of their former lands, but a bigger problem was the slave traders. They raided Yamasee villages, and the Carolina government gave no protection to the Yamasee. So, in April 1715, the Yamasee gathered together 15 Native American peoples including the Creek, Choctaw, Cherokee, and Apalachee. Numbering about 30,000, they attacked slave traders living on the Carolina frontier.

former: earlier; having taken place in the past

Alarmed by the Native American resistance, other British* colonies sent help. By fall 1715, the Yamasee and Creeks had been defeated.

---

* In 1707, England and Scotland joined together as Great Britain. For events after this date, we will use the words *Great Britain* and *British* rather than *England* and *English*.

Those who were not killed or taken as slaves fled to Florida. The Yamasee War, as it is called, was the largest Native American revolt in the Southern colonies.

Royal Colonies

In 1712, Albemarle and Charles Town became the centers of the two colonies of North and South Carolina. In 1729, both became royal colonies. North Carolina had never been profitable for the proprietors and they had gladly sold it to the king ten years earlier. That same year, the people of South Carolina had revolted against the proprietors. The colonists were angered because the proprietors had not sent troops to fight in the Yamasee War. The proprietors had also attempted to gain more control of the colony's government.

GEORGIA

Georgia was the last of the southern colonies and the last of the 13 English colonies to be founded. This area had originally been part of the Carolina colony.

In 1732, the king granted a charter to a group of London businesspeople headed by James Oglethorpe (OH-guhl-thorp). They wanted to set up a colony for poor English people jailed for debts. The English government was interested in the colony because it wanted a buffer between South Carolina and the Spanish in Florida. The colony was expected to keep the Spanish from spreading north into English-held lands. The new colony was named *Georgia* in honor of King George II. In 1733, Oglethorpe founded the first settlement, Savannah.

buffer (BUF-uhr): something used to separate two or more areas

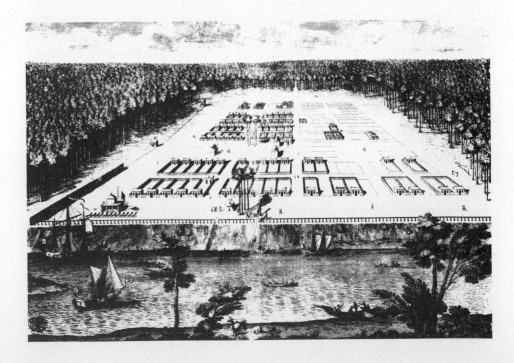

This town plan shows Savannah as it appeared in 1732. This was the first settlement in the Georgia colony.

James Oglethorpe took these Native Americans to London in 1734. This painting records their meeting with the owners of the Georgia colony.

Under the plan of settlement, each person received a 20-hectare (50-acre) farm, tools, and enough supplies for the first year. To encourage hard work, the managers forbade alcohol and slavery. They also forbade land sales without their permission. The system, however, did not work.

Only a few prisoners settled in the colony. Some of the other settlers were poor, but many were craftworkers or farmers from Germany, Scotland, Wales, and Ireland. They had come to make a better living, but the colony was not growing. Some Georgians asked permission to follow the example of the South Carolinians who worked slaves on large plantations. South Carolinians also took rum in trade with the West Indies. Oglethorpe and the other proprietors refused. Many colonists moved to South Carolina. In time, the proprietors had to agree to the colonists' terms. As a result, Georgia developed a plantation system much like that of South Carolina.

The proprietors were too busy to give much attention to the government of Georgia. In 1752, they turned Georgia over to the monarch. It was made a royal colony and given a governor, a council, and an elected assembly.

LOOKING BACK

1. Why was each of the following colonies founded: **a.** Maryland? **b.** Carolina? **c.** Georgia?
★ 2. Explain in a paragraph the reasons for the conflict between Catholics and Protestants in Maryland. (Consider religion, politics, and economics as possible factors.)
3. Describe in chronological order the reasons the Tuscarora and Yamasee went to war against the British colonists.

Chapter 6

Middle Colonies

LOOKING AHEAD

This chapter is about settlement of the Middle colonies—the present states of New York, New Jersey, Pennsylvania, and Delaware. The Dutch began European colonization of the region, followed by the Swedes and English. By 1644, the English controlled the east coast of North America from Maine to Carolina. You will also read about the relations between the Native Americans and the colonists in the Middle colonies. After you study this chapter, you will be able to:

- make a generalization about the treatment of Native Americans by the Dutch and by William Penn.
- describe the reasons the English wanted New Netherland.
- explain why the Quakers bought West Jersey.
- list William Penn's reasons for starting Pennsylvania.

Social Studies Vocabulary
legislature

People

Peter Minuit	Deborah Moody	Quakers
Manhattan	George Carteret	William Penn
Maria van Rensellaer	John Berkeley	Lenni Lenape

Places

New Netherland	New York	Delaware
New Amsterdam	New Jersey	Lower Counties
New Sweden	Pennsylvania	

Words and Terms

Dutch West India Company	patroon
	Holy Experiment

Between New England and Maryland, two European countries, the Netherlands and Sweden, started colonies. Because of the voyages of Henry Hudson and other explorers that you read about in the unit Europeans as Explorers, the Dutch claimed the land from the Hudson River to Delaware Bay. They called it New Netherland. The Swedes, though they did not explore the Americas, also wanted colonies. They planted a small settlement on the banks of the Delaware River. Neither colony was ever very strong. In the end, both were taken over by the English.

THE DUTCH IN NEW NETHERLAND

During summer 1624, Dutch colonists built three settlements in New Netherland: Nut Island, now called Governor's Island near modern New York City; Fort Nassau (NAS-aw) in what is now New Jersey; and Fort Orange at present-day Albany, New York. Two years later, the Dutch settled on Manhattan Island. Peter Minuit (MIHN-yoo-it), governor of New Netherland, bought the island from the Manhattan people for $24. This settlement was called New Amsterdam. New Netherland was really a series of trading posts owned by the Dutch West India Company. Like the joint-stock companies, this company was founded to carry on trade in the Americas.

The population of New Netherland grew slowly. For one thing, few people were needed to work at the trading posts. For another, the Netherlands offered political and religious freedom at home. Few Dutch had any incentive to leave their comfortable lives for the unknown in the Americas.

Even so, the Dutch West India Company needed colonists to grow food for the trading posts. To increase the population, the company started the patroon (puh-TROON), or landowner, system. Any person who brought 50 or more people to the Dutch colony would be given large amounts of land. Each patroon had authority over the people living on his or her land. A few patroonships were granted along the Hudson, Connecticut, and Delaware rivers. In general, they were not successful. Few people wanted to work another's land when they could get their own land in other colonies. As a result, the Dutch West India Company brought Africans as slaves to work the land. Although the patroonships did not grow, New Amsterdam by 1664 was a wealthy trading center.

The Dutch began to settle their colony of New Netherland in 1624. This is an early picture of the settlement at New Amsterdam. Why did the colony grow slowly?

One patroonship that did attract people was owned by Kiliaen van Rensellaer (vahn REN-suh-lahr) and, after his death, by his wife Maria. Another landowner was Lady Deborah Moody. In 1643, after fleeing religious persecution in Massachusetts Bay, she and some followers received permission from the Dutch to start a settlement. She bought land from the Canarsie (kuh-NAHR-see) and set up a community at Gravesend.

In contrast to the English colonies, New Netherland had no legislature or other form of representative government. A **legislature** (LEJ-is-lay-chuhr) is a group in government with the duty and power to make laws. As property of the trading company, New Netherland was ruled by a director-general, or governor, assisted by a small council. They made laws, set taxes, tried court cases, and waged war.

wage: to conduct; to direct against

Native American Resistance

From the voyage of Henry Hudson on, the Dutch were friendly with the Native Americans. Because New Netherland depended on the fur trade, friendship was to the colony's advantage. The Iroquois were the main suppliers of furs. However, as the Dutch expanded, Dutch-Native American relations worsened. As in other colonies, conflict broke out over colonists' dishonest trade practices and their taking of Native American lands.

Around New Amsterdam the conflict was severe. The Dutch demanded that the Native Americans obey Dutch laws. The Dutch tried to force obedience. They attacked the Wappinger (WAHP-pin-juhr) and several smaller groups. Although the Native Americans fought back, they were so divided that their defeat by the Dutch was certain. Because of differences in language and customs, the various peoples could not unite.

As happened in other colonies, Native Americans in time came to depend on European trade goods in order to live. Alcohol, given them

When the English took New Amsterdam, Peter Stuyvesant was governor. Here he leads the surrender of his fort to the English. What was the basis of their claim to New Netherland?

by the colonists, helped destroy their will and ability to fight back. Overall, the later change in the government of New Netherland from Dutch to English brought no difference in the relations between Europeans and Native Americans.

RISE AND FALL OF NEW SWEDEN

Like the Dutch, the Swedes were interested in the profits from the fur trade. In 1638, 50 Swedes settled Fort Christina, near the present city of Wilmington, Delaware. They bought the land from the Lenni Lenape (LE-nee luh-NAH-pee), or Delaware. In time, the Swedes built a highly profitable fur trade with the Susquehanna (suhs-kwuh-HAN-uh), or Conestoga, who lived and hunted around Delaware Bay.

Because living conditions in Sweden, as in the Netherlands, were good, New Sweden did not attract many colonists. To settle the colony, the Swedish government sent convicts and soldiers. By 1653, only 250 people had come to the colony. Many were Dutch or Finns rather than Swedes. The Swedes introduced the log cabin to the Americas.

The Swedes' act of planting a colony in Dutch territory angered the Dutch. But they did not move against the Swedes until the Swedes captured a Dutch fort. In revenge, the Dutch took Fort Christina in 1655. The fall of the fort ended New Sweden and established Dutch control in Delaware Bay.

NEW YORK

The fertile lands and profitable fur trade controlled by the Dutch attracted English attention. For many years, the English had argued that the area was really English because of John Cabot's voyages. In 1664, English ships captured New Amsterdam.

The English king, Charles II, gave his brother, the Duke of York, all the area known as New Netherland. The region became the royal colony of New York, and New Amsterdam became New York City. Like other English royal colonies, it was given a governor appointed by the monarch. In 1683, after increasing protests from the colonists, the king granted them a representative assembly. In 1685, the Duke of York became King James II. He did away with New York's assembly and the legislatures of other English colonies. As you may recall from Chapter 4 of this unit, James appointed Sir Edmund Andros as governor of New York, New Jersey, and New England. After the Glorious Revolution that removed James, Andros was sent back to England.

In 1691, under a new governor, New York's assembly again met. New York had a population of 32,000. Most were Dutch, but there were some English, Swedes, French, Portuguese, and Africans. With New York City as a growing trading center, the colony was well on its way to becoming wealthy.

New Netherland and New Sweden

Sir Edmund Andros was appointed governor of several colonies by King James II. Andros was against self-rule for the colonies. After James was overthrown, Andros was imprisoned by the people of Boston.

This watercolor shows the beginning of a settlement in New Jersey. Look at the maps in this unit. Why do you think most settlements were along the coast or on rivers?

concession (kuhn-SESH-uhn): something given up

NEW JERSEY

In June 1664, the Duke of York gave part of New Netherland to two friends, Sir George Carteret (KAHR-tuhr-et) and Lord John Berkeley. The land was named New Jersey and became a proprietary colony.

There were a few settlements in New Jersey. The Dutch had settled along the west bank of the Hudson River. Along the Delaware River were people from the former colony of New Sweden. To attract more colonists, the proprietors issued the Concessions and Agreements of the Proprietors of New Jersey. This document offered cheap land, religious freedom, and representative government.

In 1674, Lord Berkeley sold his share of the colony to Quakers. Quakers, or the Society of Friends, was an English religious group that disagreed with the Church of England. They believed that there was something of God in every person. Therefore, everyone was equal: men and women, blacks, Native Americans, all groups. Quakers also believed that killing was wrong. They refused to fight and stated that killing even as punishment for breaking the law was wrong. Some governments considered such ideas dangerous. For example, punishment for being a Quaker in England and Massachusetts Bay was severe.

By 1676, the Quakers had worked out an agreement with Berkeley's partner, Carteret. He was to keep East Jersey, where most of the colonists lived. This area was roughly the northern half of the colony. The Quakers were to have West Jersey to the south. Under Quaker control, West Jersey grew rapidly. Peace within the colony attracted colonists and new towns.

In 1682, Carteret sold East Jersey to a second group of Quakers that included William Penn. After 1700, East and West Jersey were united into the royal colony of New Jersey. Until 1738, New Jersey was ruled by the royal governor of New York.

PENNSYLVANIA

In 1680, William Penn asked Charles II for land in the Americas as payment for a loan Penn's father had given James I. The following year, Penn received a charter making him the only proprietor of a vast amount of land north of Maryland. The king suggested naming the colony *Penn-Sylvania* or *Penn's Woods*.

Penn set out to build a free, self-governing colony, with complete political and religious freedom. He said it was a Holy Experiment. He explained his ideas in a letter to settlers already living in the region. Following is part of that letter:

> I hope you will not be troubled at your change and the king's choice. You are not at the mercy of a governor that comes to make his fortune great. You will be governed by laws of your own making, and live as a free, and, if you will, serious and industrious people. I will not take the rights of any, or oppress his person. In short, whatever serious and reasonable men can reasonably desire for the security and improvement of their own happiness, I shall heartily agree to.

Penn had advertisements circulated throughout Europe inviting people to settle in Pennsylvania. Many people came to the colony seeking religious or political freedom. General offers of land attracted other colonists. Although land was plentiful, the plantation system and slavery did not develop in Pennsylvania. Most of the early colonists were Quakers who opposed slavery.

oppress (uh-PRESS): govern cruelly

circulate (SER-kyoo-layt): to send around; to give out

This painting by Benjamin West was done in the 1770s. It is his idea of how the signing of a treaty between the Lenni Lenape and William Penn looked in 1682. Many paintings of historical events are painted years later.

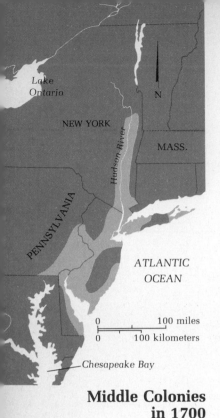

Middle Colonies in 1700

Penn as proprietor appointed the governor of the new colony. The colony's voters elected a council and a legislature, called the General Assembly. At first, all adult Christian males were allowed to vote. Later, property ownership was added as a requirement for voting.

Before he left England, Penn also sent a letter to the Lenni Lenape, the Native Americans who lived in the area. Penn expressed friendship and accepted Lenni Lenape ownership of the land. Before he arrived in the colony, he sent Quakers to buy the land from the Native Americans. After he arrived, he made several treaties with the Lenni Lenape to make sure he owned the land.

After Penn returned to England in 1706, peaceful relations with the Native Americans fell apart. As the colony grew, more colonists took land that belonged to the Lenni Lenape without paying them. Also, fur trading began between Native Americans and colonists. Trading brought conflict to Pennsylvania as it had to New York and the southern colonies.

DELAWARE

As you may recall, the first permanent settlement in what is now Delaware was Fort Christina built by the Swedes. It was lost to the Dutch in 1655 and to the English in 1664. When Penn was planning his colony, he wanted an outlet to the sea such as Delaware offered. In 1682, the Duke of York gave him Delaware. It was called the Lower Counties because it was downstream on the Delaware River from Philadelphia, the major city in Pennsylvania.

Under Penn's plan, Pennsylvania and Delaware were to have the same number of representatives in Pennsylvania's assembly. As settlement in Pennsylvania spread farther north and west, people in the Lower Counties feared that Pennsylvania would have many more representatives in the assembly. The needs of the Lower Counties would seem unimportant to them. As a result, the people of the Lower Counties asked for their own assembly. Penn agreed, and in 1704, this assembly met for the first time. But Pennsylvania's governors continued to rule the Lower Counties until the American Revolution.

LOOKING BACK

1. Based on their actions, how did each of the following feel about the Native Americans who lived in their colonies: **a.** early Dutch colonists? **b.** later Dutch colonists? **c.** William Penn? **d.** later Pennsylvania colonists? Remember: a question does not always use the phrase "make a generalization" even though that is what you are being asked to do. If you were asked to pull together common themes or ideas behind a number of examples, you are being asked to make a generalization.
2. Why did the English want New Netherland?
3. Why did the Quakers want to buy West Jersey?
4. List Penn's reasons for wanting to start Pennsylvania.

PRACTICING YOUR SKILLS

What If . . .   Spain made several unsuccessful attempts at colonizing Florida in the early 1500s. Spain showed little interest in North America again until the mid-1500s. **What if** Ponce de Leon, Narvaez, and de Soto had found gold and silver in Florida? How might this discovery have changed Spain's plans for exploring and colonizing the Americas? What might Spain have done about the English settlements of the early 1600s?

Discussing   Maryland, Rhode Island, and Pennsylvania were the first colonies to pass laws granting religious toleration. Discuss some of the reasons why these colonies passed such laws before the other colonies.

Writing, Making a Table

1. In this unit you have read how colonial governments differed from colony to colony. Some colonies were controlled more strictly from Europe than others. Write a paragraph comparing: **a.** the governments of the Spanish colonies and Massachusetts Bay.   **b.** the governments of New Netherland and Virginia.
2. On a separate sheet of paper make a table showing all 13 English colonies; the date each was founded; by whom; the type of government each had at its founding, and any changes in it. Use this table as a study guide.

Exploring   As you have read, colonies had different requirements for voting. In Massachusetts Bay, it was church membership. In other colonies, it was property ownership. Today, voting requirements are limited to age and residency—the time you have lived in an area. Find out the age and residency requirements for voting in your state. Are there any other limits on voting? Where would you register? Where would you vote?

Building Study Skills   Do you sometimes have trouble remembering the information you are supposed to be learning? These five tips can help you **recall** information:

- Pay attention when you read or listen. Really concentrate.
- Practice remembering. Repeat silently to yourself the information you want to remember.
- Repeat the information out loud. This is the Recite step of the SQ3R method.
- Ask yourself questions about the information.
- Invent a trick to remember the information. Make up a rhyme, silly sentence, or silly world.

Activity: What information in this unit can the following sentence help you remember? **R**aisins **p**ack **e**nergy. **Hint:** The first letter of each word stands for a reason for Puritan migration to the Americas.

Reading   Bennett, Lerone, Jr. *Before the Mayflower: A History of the Negro in America, 1619-1964*. Baltimore, Maryland: Penguin, 1966.

Hillbrand, Percie V. *Swedes in America*. Minneapolis, Minnesota: Lerner, 1966.

Hults, Dorothy. *New Amsterdam Days and Ways: The Dutch Settlers of New York*. New York: Harcourt, 1963.

Nabokov, Peter, ed. *Native American Testimony: An Anthology of Indian and White Relations/First Encounter to Dispossession*. New York: Crowell, 1978.

Rich, Louise Dickenson. *King Phillip's War, 1675-76: New England Indians Fight the Colonists*. New York: Watts, 1972.

States and the Nation Series, 50 vols. New York: Norton, 1976-80. Historical events of all 50 states.

Section II BUILDING A NEW NATION

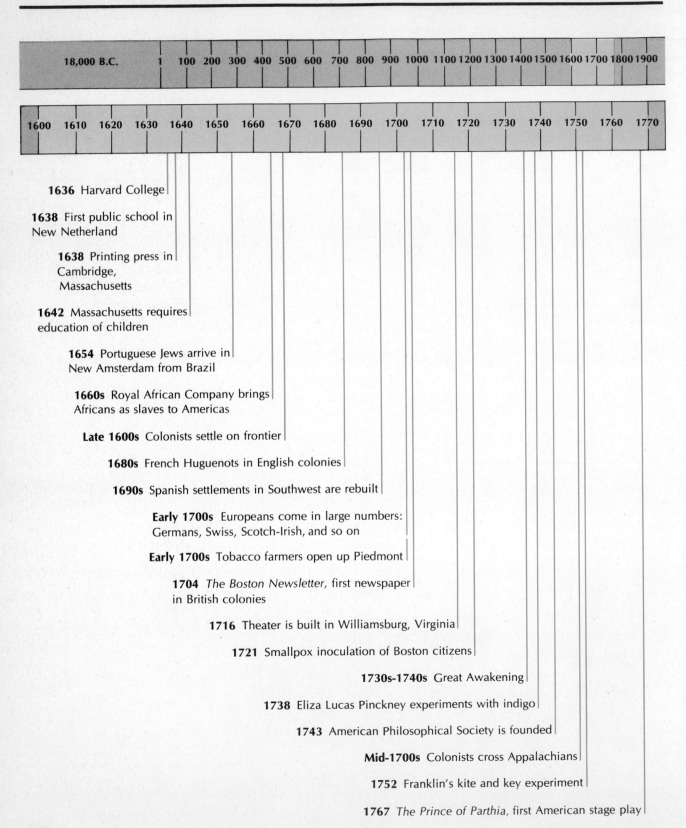

18,000 B.C.	1	100	200	300	400	500	600	700	800	900	1000	1100	1200	1300	1400	1500	1600	1700	1800	1900

1600	1610	1620	1630	1640	1650	1660	1670	1680	1690	1700	1710	1720	1730	1740	1750	1760	1770

1636 Harvard College

1638 First public school in New Netherland

1638 Printing press in Cambridge, Massachusetts

1642 Massachusetts requires education of children

1654 Portuguese Jews arrive in New Amsterdam from Brazil

1660s Royal African Company brings Africans as slaves to Americas

Late 1600s Colonists settle on frontier

1680s French Huguenots in English colonies

1690s Spanish settlements in Southwest are rebuilt

Early 1700s Europeans come in large numbers: Germans, Swiss, Scotch-Irish, and so on

Early 1700s Tobacco farmers open up Piedmont

1704 *The Boston Newsletter*, first newspaper in British colonies

1716 Theater is built in Williamsburg, Virginia

1721 Smallpox inoculation of Boston citizens

1730s-1740s Great Awakening

1738 Eliza Lucas Pinckney experiments with indigo

1743 American Philosophical Society is founded

Mid-1700s Colonists cross Appalachians

1752 Franklin's kite and key experiment

1767 *The Prince of Parthia*, first American stage play

Chapter 1

The Spanish

LOOKING AHEAD

This chapter describes Spanish life in what is now the U.S. from the early 1600s to the Revolutionary War. You will learn how the Spanish lived, worked, played, and educated their children. After you study this chapter, you will be able to:

- locate the Spanish on a map of what is now the U.S.
- describe mission life.
- explain how the people of the towns and farms depended on each other.
- identify the four social classes among the Spanish in the Southwest.
- ★ describe a secondary source.

Social Studies Vocabulary

secondary source   creole   mestizo

Words and Terms

adobe   plaza   formal education

In the last two units, you read about the Spanish conquest of the Americas. By the 1600s, other European nations began challenging Spanish claims in what is now the U.S. As a result, Spain began to replace explorers with soldiers, missionaries, and colonists.

Some European nations, such as England and the Netherlands, spread their influence in America mainly through settlements of colonists. Although Spain built some towns in what is now the U.S., its main ways of spreading Spanish culture were missions and presidios. There were many similarities among the towns, presidios, and missions of the Spanish colonies. We can piece together these similarities to make generalizations about Spanish life in what is now the U.S.

MISSION LIFE

The spiritual and physical center of the mission was the church. It was made of stone blocks or adobe (uh-DOH-bee), sun-dried bricks of mud. Near the church were houses for the missionaries and Native Americans, storerooms, a school, and craft shops. These were also made of adobe or stone. Often, all the buildings in the mission village were set around a square courtyard. Outside the village were the mission farms. Some missions also had ranches where cattle and horses were raised.

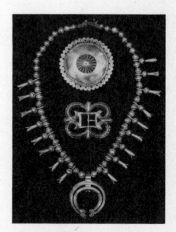

This silver necklace is Navajo and was made in New Mexico sometime before 1935. The design is called "squash blossom" and is still used by Navajo silversmiths.

Spanish Settlements

CANADA

Columbia R.

Snake R.

Missouri River

Mississippi River

Ohio River

Tennessee R.

San Francisco 1776

Monterey 1770

Los Angeles 1781

San Diego 1769

Colorado River

Gila River

Santa Fe 1609-10

El Paso 1680

Rio Grande

San Antonio 1718

Apalachicola River

St. Augustine 1565

ATLANTIC OCEAN

N

PACIFIC OCEAN

GULF OF MEXICO

Havana 1515

CUBA

SANTO DOMINGO

PUERTO RICO

San Juan 1508

Santo Domingo 1496

MEXICO

Mexico City 1521

0   400 miles

0   600 kilometers

Areas of Spanish Settlement

Viceroyalty of New Spain

The mission day began before dawn with religious services, followed by religion classes. Then the Native Americans began the work needed to run the missions. They raised crops, looked after the herds, and worked at crafts. The missionaries taught them pottery making, carpentry, weaving, blacksmithing, and soap and candle making. In the evening, the missionaries again taught religion and held services for the people. The children attended school at least twice a day. Religion was the main subject, but they also learned reading and writing in Spanish. The children were not taught their own language.

In 1745, Fray Padre Francisco Xavier Ortiz (AWR-tees) described the mission of San Antonio de Valero in Texas, which you may recall from the unit Colonial Beginnings:

The pueblo where the new converts lived had two rows of small huts built on either side of a water ditch. The huts were made of adobe bricks and were generally roofed with straw. The missionaries lived in a two-story structure of stone. It had three rooms on the second floor and offices and other rooms on the first. Next to it there was a large room where the women worked at the looms to make the cloth for their dresses. Next was a storage room for the mission corn and other grains.

The mission was well supplied with lands for raising crops and for pasturing livestock. All the land was irrigated by a large ditch which brought water from the river. All the products raised by the converts were used by them.

To cultivate the fields and carry on the other work, San Antonio de Valero had a blacksmith shop with all the tools necessary to repair and keep the farm equipment in working condition. There was also a carpenter shop with all its tools.

Mission Law

Spanish law was strictly enforced in the missions. The priests taught obedience as part of the religion lessons. In addition, there was usually a presidio nearby. Its soldiers could be called upon to catch and punish lawbreakers quickly. Because Native Americans were often forced into missions, runaways were a problem for the Spanish.

The Spanish had another method for keeping Native Americans under control. Occasionally, they allowed Native American leaders to keep their positions of power. The Spanish then used these leaders to keep their peoples obedient to Spanish authority.

DIFFERING OPINIONS

Historians differ on whether Spanish missions were good or bad for Native Americans. On one hand, the Spanish added new crops—sugar cane, wheat, apples, peaches, grapes—and farm animals—horses, oxen, mules, chickens, pigs, cows—to those the Native Americans had. The missions provided protection for their villages from neighboring peoples. The priests also tried to protect their villages from Spanish colonists and adventurers.

On the other hand, Native Americans were forced to give up their religions and ways of life. Native Americans were punished if found practicing their own ways. Also, Native Americans were forced to work to support the missions.

You have just read that historians have different opinions about whether Spanish missions were good or bad for Native Americans. These opinions were written long after mission life ended. Historians read 300-year-old sources and evaluated mission life based on them. Because historians' accounts are not eyewitness accounts, they are called secondary sources. A **secondary source** is second-hand information about an event, including comments and so on, from one who was not involved or even there. A secondary source may be an account from the same time as, or from a later time than, the event it describes. There are many kinds of secondary sources such as newspaper stories, magazine articles, editorials, and historian's interpreta-

WORKING WITH SOURCES

tions. A historian's interpretation is a secondary source based on a study of primary sources.

In Chapter 1 of the last unit, you learned that the letter written by Fray Juan de Escalona was a primary source. It was an eyewitness account of someone who lived in a mission. Your textbook, on the other hand, is a secondary source. Its authors have not lived through all of American history. But they have read primary sources and historians' interpretations and then written their own secondary source. However, some primary sources have been quoted in your textbook. **1.** What is the difference between a primary source and a secondary source? **2.** Find one primary and one secondary source in your textbook.

TOWNS AND FARMS

Towns developed slowly in Spanish Florida and California. While Florida attracted some colonists in the 1600s and 1700s, colonization of California did not begin until the late 1700s. The mission system spread Spanish influence in these two areas until colonists came. Since New Mexico had both missions and towns by the early 1700s, this section will focus on life there.

focus (FOH-kuhs): to give full attention to

Spanish officials wanted colonists to live in towns rather than on scattered farms so laws could be enforced more easily. Towns also offered greater protection in case of conflict with the Apache, Navajo, or other Native Americans of the region. Towns were built around a plaza (PLAH-zuh), or square. On one side was the church. Opposite it was the town's government building. Around the other two sides were one-story, adobe houses. Most had only two or three small rooms, though wealthier colonists had larger homes.

Craftworkers and merchants had their shops in or near their homes. They bartered (BAHR-tuhrd), or traded, with one another for the goods they needed. On Sundays, the plaza became a marketplace. Farmers traded their crops for the goods they needed from the merchants and craftworkers. The farmers, too, lived in towns and went out each day to their fields. The people also had orchards and common grazing lands scattered outside town.

In the beginning of New Mexico's settlement, there were a number of haciendas. These were usually far from towns. Life on a hacienda was similar to life on a manor in Europe before the Age of Exploration. The Pueblos provided the labor. Each hacienda produced most of the food and many of the other things it needed.

The Pueblo Revolt of 1680 drove the Spanish out of New Mexico, but by the 1690s, they had returned. By then, there were fewer Pueblos to work on the haciendas, and, as a result, fewer haciendas. In the 1700s, most farms were small. Raising cattle and sheep was the chief economic activity, though the colonists also grew grain, fruit, and vegetables.

Social Class and Family

In the Spanish Southwest, people who lived in towns and on farms were divided into four social classes. At the top were the **creoles** (KREE-ohlz) who were American-born descendants of colonists from Spain. They owned most of the farms and large businesses.

Below the creoles were the **mestizos** (mes-TEE-zohs) who were part Spanish and part Native American. Only Spanish and Native Americans could own land. Since mestizos were neither, they had to rent land. Their life was difficult. Most farm products mestizos raised had to be paid to their landowners as rent. Little was left to trade to merchants and craftworkers for supplies. Rather than live this way, some mestizos became craftworkers or owners of small businesses.

The Spanish expected the Native Americans to be the laborers in their settlements. Some worked for pay on haciendas, either as field hands or as craftworkers. Others owned their own small farms, craftshops, or small businesses.

The lowest class were the slaves. These were often Native Americans who broke Spanish law. They were taken from their people and made slaves to upper-class colonists. The Spanish also brought a few blacks from Mexico as slaves.

The colonists lived in extended families. As you may recall from the unit The First Americans, an extended family includes parents, children, grandchildren, and other relatives. The head of the family received complete obedience from the members of the household.

Education

Formal education—education in schools—was rare. When the colonies were newly settled, the more basic needs of food, shelter, and defense came first. Missionary priests provided some schooling for children of wealthier colonists. Daughters were taught only at home, but wealthy families often sent their sons to Mexico City to study.

A typical Spanish mission included a church, school, homes, and craft shops. The buildings were built around a courtyard and surrounded by thick walls for protection.

These Spanish American couples are dancing the fandango. The dancers stamp their feet, snap their fingers, and clap wooden finger cymbals called castanets.

The Spanish had founded a university there in 1551. Law, religion, mathematics, and engineering were among the subjects taught. Although the Spanish established several universities in the Americas during the 1500s, none were located in the present-day U.S. The population was too small.

By the late 1700s, a few schools had been set up in New Mexico. However, there were never enough teachers to keep them open on a regular basis.

Free Time

Much of the social life centered around religion. Weddings, baptisms, and funerals were times for meeting friends. Religious holidays were the cause of celebrations that often included horse racing, dancing, and bullfighting. Religious music was popular and the violin and guitar were favorite instruments. Hunting was also popular. Almost every week in the plazas, the colonists enjoyed folk dances such as the fandango (fan-DANG-goh). From time to time, traveling circuses and theater groups provided entertainment.

LOOKING BACK

1. Use the map to locate and list the boundaries in the 1700s of Spanish territory in what is now the U.S.
2. Write a paragraph describing life at a Spanish mission for a Native American. You will be making generalizations when you write your answer, because there were probably exceptions to this general pattern.
3. How did each of the following depend on the other two groups: **a.** craftworkers? **b.** merchants? **c.** farmers?
4. List the four social classes of Spanish America and who made up each class. As you learned on page 137, devices can help you recall information. Make up a device to help you recall the names of these four social classes.
★ 5. **a.** Define a secondary source. **b.** How is it different from a primary source?

146

Chapter 2   More People, More Land

LOOKING AHEAD

In the last unit, you read about the founding of the English colonies along the Atlantic Coast. These colonies grew steadily as more English as well as people from other countries arrived. As land along the coast was settled, colonists spread inland. Most of these people came by choice, but some were forced to come. After you study this chapter, you will be able to:

- classify the reasons why some Europeans chose to come to the English colonies.
- ★ read a bar graph to learn the white population of each colony.
- describe the sequence for buying and selling Africans in the Triangular Trade.
- describe why and how the frontier was settled.

Social Studies Vocabulary

frontier	statistical	monopoly
bar graph	unskilled worker	

People

Germans	Scotch-Irish	Huguenots
Pennsylvania	Welsh	Africans
Dutch	Jews	

Places

Tidewater	Great Valley	Great Wagon Road

Words and Terms

Royal African	Triangular Trade	seasoning
Company	Middle Passage	

As you may recall from the last unit, the population of the British colonies grew rapidly in the 1600s and 1700s. The population in 1770 was about ten times what it had been in 1690. Part of the growth was from natural increase. Part was from the large numbers of Europeans and Africans who came.

IMMIGRANTS BY CHOICE

In the 1600s, most settlers in the English colonies had been English. Only in the Middle colonies where Dutch, Swedes, and Finns had

Salzburgische Emigranten

Nichts, als das Evangelium
Vertreibt uns ins Exilium.
Verlaſſen wir das Vaterland,
So ſind wir doch in Gottes Hand.

German-speaking immigrants were the first non-English colonists to come in large numbers. Why did they come?

settled were there many colonists from other countries. Even with the arrival of thousands of non-English in the 1700s, New England remained mostly English. It was to the Middle and Southern colonies that Germans, Scotch-Irish, Welsh, and other groups came. Although required to work for a certain time, indentured servants made up a large number of the immigrants who came by choice.

Germans

Soon after Penn founded his colony, immigrants from what is now Germany settled near Philadelphia. German-speaking immigrants were the first non-English people to come to the colonies in large numbers. Long years of war had left much of Germany poor. Also, Roman Catholic rulers in parts of Germany were persecuting Protestants. In time, Pennsylvania received more German-speaking immigrants than any other colony. Cheap land, religious freedom, and reports from Germans already in Pennsylvania attracted them.

In the early 1700s, a group of Germans and German-speaking Swiss settled about 113 kilometers (70 miles) west of Philadelphia. They soon became known as Pennsylvania Dutch from the German word for *German, Deutsch* (DOICH). Most of the Pennsylvania Dutch were farmers. But some were craftworkers whose skills helped develop Pennsylvania's industry.

Scotch-Irish

In the 1500s, Elizabeth I of England encouraged Scottish families to move to Ireland. She wanted the Protestant Scots to help make a Protestant country of Catholic Ireland. In the early 1700s, problems in Ireland sent many descendants of the Scotch-Irish to the colonies.

Parliament had passed a law ending the sale of Irish cloth to England. The law protected English clothmakers at the expense of the Scotch-Irish. Most Scotch-Irish made their livings by raising sheep and making cloth. Most were tenant farmers. As had happened to Puritans in England, the Scotch-Irish were being pushed off the land as owners began raising livestock. In addition, the Scotch-Irish, who were Presbyterians (prez-buh-TIR-ee-uhnz), were taxed to support the Church of England. Yet, Presbyterians could not hold public office.

Some of the Scotch-Irish who came to America went to the frontier of the Southern colonies. The **frontier** is the boundary between settled lands and wilderness. In the late 1600s, it was the unsettled area west of the older coastal settlements. Other Scotch-Irish went into the Piedmont and Appalachian Mountains of New York and Pennsylvania. In America, the Scotch-Irish became farmers, weavers, and traders.

Bar graphs make it easy to compare statistical data at one period in time. **Statistical** (stuh-TIS-tuh-kuhl) means having to do with numerical facts. Look at the bar graph on this page. Notice the title. It tells you the information that is shown on the graph. This bar graph represents, in picture form, data about white population in the 13 colonies in 1750. It shows you the size of different colonies at the same time. The colonies are listed along the bottom of the graph. Read the names from left to right. The number information, or statistics, is given along the left-hand side. Read it from the bottom to the top of the graph. Notice that the higher the bar the more people the bar represents. **1.** Which colony had the largest white population? **2.** Which had the smallest? You may figure out exact numbers by placing a ruler from the number to the top of a bar.

BUILDING GRAPH SKILLS

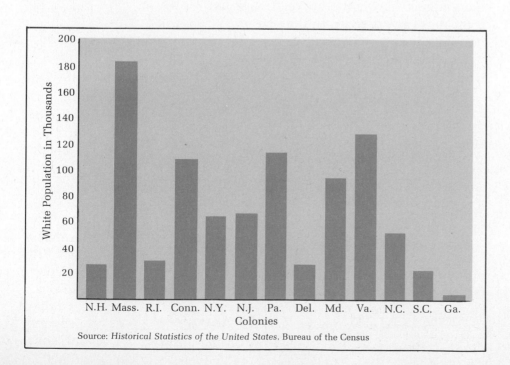

Source: *Historical Statistics of the United States.* Bureau of the Census

White Population of the 13 Colonies in 1750

Other Groups

Like the Germans and Scotch-Irish, the Welsh came to the colonies looking for a better life. The Welsh are from Wales, which became part of England in the 1530s. The first Welsh settlers in America were Quakers who came to escape religious persecution. In 1682, Penn gave them a large piece of land near Philadelphia for a Welsh state. By 1700, Welsh had settled several towns northwest of Philadelphia, but they were never able to start their country. Their lands remained an area of small farms within Pennsylvania.

In 1654, the first Jews to come to North America arrived in New Amsterdam. They were fleeing persecution in Portugal and Brazil. The Dutch and later the English gave them freedom and protection. By the time of the Revolutionary War, there were over 2,000 Jews in the colonies. They settled in large coastal towns such as Newport, Rhode Island; Philadelphia; Charles Town; and Savannah. Many entered craft and shipping businesses.

French Huguenots (HYOO-guh-nahts) came to the English colonies in the 1680s. Because they were Protestant, the Roman Catholic rulers of France were persecuting them. Many Huguenots were craftworkers or farmers. Many settled in Carolina. The colony's proprietors were trying to attract settlers to develop new crops in the colony.

AFRICANS IN CHAINS

During the 1500s, the Spanish and Portuguese were building large sugar plantations in the Caribbean and in Brazil. To be profitable, the plantations needed large supplies of cheap labor. In the Caribbean, the Spanish first tried Native Americans. However, most soon died from abuse and disease. In Brazil, there was no large Native American population for the Portuguese to use.

The Spanish and Portuguese began looking for another supply of labor. During the 1400s, as you may recall from the unit Europeans as

This ship's plan shows the crowding on a slave ship. Millions of blacks died from mistreatment and disease on the Middle Passage. With so many deaths, why did the slave trade last?

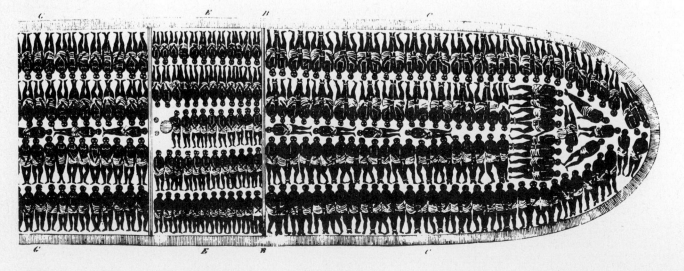

Explorers, the Portuguese were moving down the west coast of Africa. Wherever they stopped, they set up trading posts. Among the items they traded for were African slaves. They were used in Portugal and Spain as house servants, field hands, and unskilled workers. An **unskilled worker** is a person whose work does not demand a special skill or craft. The Portuguese soon realized that Africans could be used for the same work in the Americas.

Traders from other nations soon followed the lead of the Portuguese. As more colonies were founded in the Americas, the demand for slaves grew. Europeans began to take people in large numbers from Africa's western coast, especially from what are now the countries of Senegal (sen-ih-GAWL), Ghana (GAH-nuh), Congo (KAHNG-goh), Angola (ang-GOH-luh), Guinea (GIHN-ee), Benin (buh-NIHN), and Nigeria (ny-JIR-ee-uh).

In the 1660s, the English began to play a role in the slave trade. The English government gave the Royal African Company a monopoly on English trade in Africa. **Monopoly** (muh-NAHP-uhl-ee) means the complete control of a product or service. The company began bringing Africans to the West Indies and the North American colonies.

Because of the Royal African Company, it became cheaper for a colonist to buy a slave than the contract of an indentured servant. The number of slaves grew while the number of indentured servants declined. This increase in cheap labor was happening at the same time planters in the Southern colonies were developing tobacco, rice, and indigo plantations. Indigo (IN-duh-goh) is a plant used to make blue dye.

This bronze picture of a European soldier was made by a sculptor in Benin sometime between 1400 and 1600.

Triangular Trade

As the demand for slaves grew, the buying and selling of people became part of a regular trading pattern. Called the Triangular Trade, it joined Africa's west coast, the islands of the Caribbean, and the colonies of North America.

On each of the three parts of its voyage, a ship carried a different cargo. It set out for Africa from a colonial port loaded with rum, cloth, beads, guns, and other goods. Along Africa's west coast this cargo was traded for human beings. A black African woman might be traded for about 7.6 liters (about 2 gallons) of rum and five beads. A man might be worth seven guns, two cases of rum, and some cloth. The Africans then began the Middle Passage, the second part of the Triangular Trade route. This was the trip across the Atlantic.

On slave ships, Africans were forced into spaces that were sometimes no more than 45.6 centimeters (about 18 inches) high. Aboard ship, the Africans lived chained together for six to ten weeks. They were given little food or water. The air was foul. Occasionally, in good weather, they were taken on deck for fresh air.

Historians estimate that perhaps one third of the Africans died during the Middle Passage. Although the number of slaves arriving in the Americas was much less than the original cargo, slavers made large

This bronze figure was made in the Kingdom of Ife in the 1300s. Ife is now a modern city in Nigeria in West Africa.

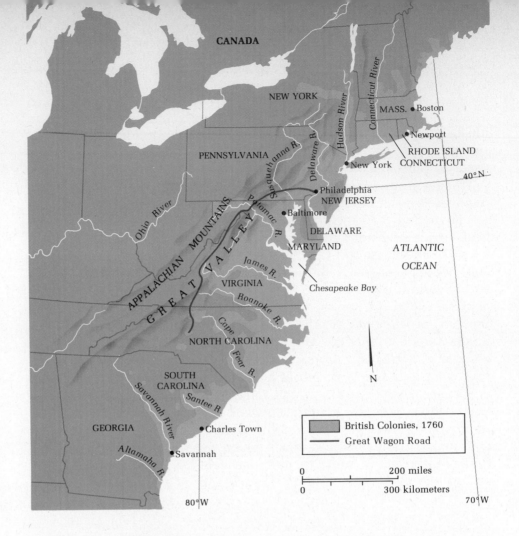

CANADA

NEW YORK

MASS. • Boston

• Newport

PENNSYLVANIA

RHODE ISLAND
CONNECTICUT

40° N.

• Philadelphia
NEW JERSEY

• New York

• Baltimore

DELAWARE

MARYLAND

ATLANTIC

OCEAN

APPALACHIAN MOUNTAINS

GREAT VALLEY

Ohio River

Susquehanna R.

Delaware R.

Hudson River

Connecticut River

Potomac R.

James R.

Chesapeake Bay

VIRGINIA

Roanoke R.

Cape Fear R.

NORTH CAROLINA

N

SOUTH
CAROLINA

Santee R.

Savannah River

☐ British Colonies, 1760
— Great Wagon Road

GEORGIA

• Charles Town

0   200 miles

Altamaha R.

• Savannah

0   300 kilometers

80° W

70° W

**Areas of British
Settlement in 1760**

profits. Many plantation owners were willing to buy Africans as slaves. For these reasons, the slave trade lasted into the 1800s.

In the 1750s, Olaudah Equiano (ek-wih-AH-noh), a ten-year-old boy, was captured on the West African coast and sold into slavery. Equiano later described the conditions on the slave ship:

> The first thing I saw when I arrived on the coast was the sea, and a slave ship. These filled me with astonishment, which soon turned into terror, when I was carried on board. I was immediately looked at by some of the crew to see if I were healthy. I was sure they were going to kill me. Their complexions, differing so much from ours, their long hair, and the language they spoke (which was very different from any I had ever heard) convinced me.
>
> At last, when the ship had got in all its cargo, we were all put under deck. The closeness of the place, the heat, and the number in the ship, which was so crowded that each had scarcely room to turn, almost suffocated us. This produced so much perspiration that the air soon became unfit for breathing. It brought on a sickness among the slaves, of which many died—falling victims to the greed of their purchasers.

The Middle Passage often ended on the islands of the Caribbean. Even slaves who were later taken to North America usually spent some time in the Caribbean. On Caribbean plantations, slaves worked long hours and were trained in the daily routine of plantation life. This was called seasoning. Buyers in North America preferred slaves who had been seasoned.

Survivors of the Middle Passage were exchanged for goods made in the Caribbean islands. The most important was molasses, which is made from sugar cane. On the third part of the trip, the molasses was taken to one of the colonies where it was made into rum. Some of the rum was exchanged for other trade goods. But most of it was used to buy more slaves on the next trip.

THE FRONTIER

Most people coming to the English colonies in the 1600s settled near the coast. By the 1700s, many colonists were pushing inland. In the north, they moved into the forests of northern New England, New York, and central Pennsylvania.

In the Southern colonies, they left the older settlements of the Tidewater for the frontier of the Piedmont. Tidewater was the name given to that part of the Atlantic Coastal Plain between New Jersey and Georgia. It extends 80 to 161 kilometers (50 to 100 miles) inland. West of it, the Piedmont gradually slopes into the Appalachians. By about 1775, colonists had settled the Piedmont and were pushing across the Appalachians.

Land and People

By the 1770s, there were about 250,000 people living on the frontier. This was out of a total population of 2,148,000 in the British colonies. Colonists moved onto the frontier for many reasons. Some people were attracted by the adventure of life on the frontier. Others wanted to live alone in a wilderness where laws were few. Hunters and trappers moved into the frontier as game along the coast was killed off. But the chief reason for settling the frontier was land. By 1700, as more people had come to the colonies, most of the good land near the coast had been taken. Newcomers who wanted land had to move inland. On the frontier, land was plentiful. Much of it was free.

Poor people and young people ready to go out on their own moved to the frontier. Indentured servants who ran off before their contracts were up disappeared into it. Runaway slaves did, too. Many of those who settled the frontier were American-born daughters and sons of earlier colonists. Many, though, were the new immigrants—Germans, Scotch-Irish, Welsh, and French.

Routes Inland

People moved into the frontier by several routes. Water routes were the easiest. In the northern colonies, people used the Connecticut,

Many families settled along water routes on the frontier. Why?

Hudson, Delaware, and Susquehanna rivers to go inland. In the South, the Potomac (puh-TOH-muhk), Shenandoah (shen-uhn-DOH-uh), Roanoke, and Santee (san-TEE) rivers connected the Tidewater to the frontier.

The best land routes were valleys and gaps between mountains. One of the most traveled land routes was through the Great Valley in the Piedmont. The Great Valley stretches south from Maryland between the Allegheny (al-uh-GAY-nih) and Blue Ridge mountains. From the north, the easiest way into the Great Valley was over the Great Wagon Road from Pennsylvania. The Great Wagon Road had been an Iroquois warrior path. The Iroquois used the path to trade or to war against nations in what became Virginia and the Carolinas.

LOOKING BACK

1. Why did each of the following groups come to the English colonies: **a.** Germans? **b.** Scotch-Irish? **c.** Welsh? **d.** Jews? **e.** Huguenots? **f.** Africans? Classify the data according to economic, religious, or political reasons or a combination of the three.

★ 2. Use the bar graph to answer the following questions. **a.** What is the purpose of a bar graph? **b.** Which colony had the smallest white population? **c.** Which had the largest? **d.** Which had the next largest white population?

3. Describe the three parts of the Triangular Trade route.

4. **a.** What was the main reason for the settlement of the frontier? **b.** Use the map in this chapter to describe one route used to reach the frontier.

Chapter 3

Economic Life

LOOKING AHEAD

This chapter describes how the people of the British colonies earned their livings. Many were farmers, but some were merchants or craftworkers. Others earned their living from the sea while a few worked in small industries. After you study this chapter, you will be able to:

★ identify the point of view of a slaveholder.
• describe how the economic life of the colonies was affected by the environment.
• identify the main economic activity in the Southern and Middle colonies and New England.
• list some problems of colonial cities.

Social Studies Vocabulary

cash crop   point of view   export
mixed farming   import

People

Eliza Lucas Pinckney   John Winthrop, Jr.

Places

Baltimore   Savannah   Philadelphia
Charles Town   Boston   Newport

Words and Terms

Bread Colonies

As the English colonies added land and people, each region—New England, Middle, and Southern—began to specialize in one or two economic activities. This specialization came about as the colonists adapted to the environment. New England came to be known for its fishing and foreign trade. In the Middle colonies, most people farmed though some trade was carried on. In the Southern colonies, farming was the most important activity.

FARMING

As each colony began, the first problem colonists faced was growing food. At first, they grew only enough to take care of their own needs. Later, as more land was cleared, they raised crops for sale. These

Since colonists had to make many of the things they used, many colonists became skilled in different crafts. This picture shows a carpenter at work.

155

Farming indigo for the blue dye that could be made from it became important to the economy of South Carolina. What other crops were important in Southern colonies in the 1700s?

crops, which are raised for profit rather than for the farmer's own use, are called **cash crops.** In the Southern colonies, raising cash crops became, and remained, the area's most important economic activity.

Planters and Farmers

Fertile soil, abundant rainfall, and a long growing season made it possible for southern colonists to raise tobacco, rice, and indigo. These crops were best grown on large farms, and the South had plenty of good farmland. It also had waterways for irrigation and transportation and good harbors at Baltimore, Charles Town, and Savannah.

As you may recall from the unit Colonial Beginnings, tobacco farming began at Jamestown. As the demand for tobacco increased, colonists spread out from Jamestown looking for land along the rivers. Water travel was easier than land travel and boats could load and unload goods right at a farm's dock. Virginians moved into the Albemarle region of what became North Carolina and then inland. Colonists in Maryland adopted a tobacco economy, too, and spread westward from St. Mary's. By the early 1700s, tobacco farmers were opening up land in the Piedmont. The Piedmont soon became a more important tobacco-producing area than the Tidewater. There, the soil had been worn out.

In South Carolina, rice became the most important cash crop, followed by indigo. Rice could be grown easily in the swamps along the coast. To start rice farming required a lot of money. As a result, there were few small rice farms.

From the earliest days of Charles Town, its settlers had tried to grow indigo on the land that was too dry for rice. In 1738, Eliza Lucas, later Pinckney, and her father settled on a plantation near Charles Town. She began experimenting with ways to grow indigo. Finally, in 1744, she succeeded. The crop became so popular that within three years South Carolina was selling 45,000 kilograms (100,000 pounds).

The most successful farmers built large farms called plantations. Here William Fitzhugh describes a Virginia plantation in the 1600s.

The plantation where I now live contains a thousand acres. At least 700 acres of it is rich forest, the remainder plantable land, without any waste either by marshes or great swamps. Upon it there are all necessary houses, ground and fencing, together with a choice crew of Negroes, most of them born in this country. The remainder are as likely as most born in Virginia. There are twenty-nine in all. My own dwelling house, furnished for a comfortable life, is a very good dwelling house with 13 rooms in it. It is furnished with brick chimneys, good cellars, a dairy, stable, barn, hen house, kitchen and all other conveniences and all new. There is a large orchard of about 2500 apple trees, a garden a hundred foot square, a yard with a good stock of cattle, hogs, horses, mares, sheep, and so on, and necessary servants for the supply and support of it. About a mile and a half distant is a good water grist mill that I find sufficient to feed my own family with wheat and Indian corn. The yearly crops of corn and tobacco together with the surplus of meat will amount annually to £60,000.

convenience (kuhn-VEEN-yuhns): something that makes life, work, and so on easier

BUILDING READING SKILLS

You have just read a primary source, an eyewitness description of a large plantation written by one who lived on that plantation. The author, William Fitzhugh, does not state his **point of view** about slavery. However, you can infer what he thinks from what he wrote. To make your inference, read the facts that Fitzhugh gives. Then put them together with things that you already know from this textbook and from other studies. **1.** What do you already know about the colony where Fitzhugh lived? **2.** What does the fact that he lived on a plantation tell you? **3.** Did the plantation depend on slave labor? **4.** What would you say was William Fitzhugh's viewpoint of slavery? **5.** What did you base your inference on?

These drawings show the steps in tobacco harvesting and selling around the early 1800s. After harvesting, the tobacco was dried, or cured, and then stored. After aging, the tobacco was inspected and sent to market.

This painting shows a farming community in Bethlehem, Pennsylvania, in 1757. What crops might have been grown on this farm?

Small farmers and their families provided for most of their own needs, too. However, they could not afford their own craftworkers. Sometimes when they needed special jobs done, they would rent craftworkers from a plantation. Unlike the planters, small farmers raised several crops, mainly vegetables and fruits. Sometimes the farmers sold a part of their crops, but mostly, they used all they grew.

Early colonial planters and small farmers used indentured servants. Bringing in an indentured servant allowed a farmer the right to more land. But in the late 1600s and throughout the 1700s, as you read in the last chapter, slave labor was becoming increasingly important to the southern economy. Planters grew to depend on slaves as they farmed more land. In South Carolina, for example, rice farming became successful only when large numbers of slaves were imported in the early 1700s. By 1760, there were more than 300,000 blacks as slaves in the British colonies. Almost 90 percent were in the South.

The Bread Colonies

The Middle colonies were too cold for warm-weather crops such as tobacco, rice, and indigo. Instead, farmers there raised wheat, oats, corn, vegetables, and fruit. Wheat soon became to the Middle colonies what tobacco was to Virginia—its most important cash crop. Because wheat is used to make bread, the Middle colonies became known as the Bread Colonies.

In the Middle colonies, farmers used a system of **mixed farming.** Instead of raising just one crop for sale, farmers raised several crops as well as livestock. In a one-crop economy like the Southern colonies had, if the crop failed, a farmer could be ruined. If one crop failed in mixed farming, there were still other crops as well as livestock a farmer could sell.

Farms in the Middle colonies varied in size. As you may recall from the unit Colonial Beginnings, the Dutch West India Company gave large farms in New Netherland to patroons. Many of these farms remained after the English took control. Some English also acquired large amounts of land. Some of these large landowners rented their land to tenant farmers. Others, both English and Dutch, used hired workers as well as slaves. Slavery was less popular in the Middle colonies than in the South because farms were small. Not as many workers were needed.

acquire (uh-KWYR): to get

Cheap, abundant land in Pennsylvania, New Jersey, and Delaware attracted many immigrants to these colonies. Most of the immigrants could afford about 40 hectares (100 acres). As a result, these three colonies became areas of small farms.

The Frontier

Although some hunting and trapping was done on the frontier, most of the land was turned into farms. But first, it had to be cleared. Great forests covered the eastern part of the U.S. Only 4 to 6 hectares (10 to 15 acres) was needed to grow enough crops to support a family. But it could take the family as long as four years of back-breaking work to clear the land.

The major crop of the frontier was corn, though many farmers also grew wheat, rye, barley, and oats. Farmers in the Piedmont of the Southern colonies grew tobacco. The early farm families ate almost everything they grew. Later, they were able to raise enough so they could sell the surplus.

New England

Most early colonists in New England were farmers. But unlike farmers in other colonies, they could only manage to grow enough to feed themselves. The climate was not suited to most crops. Much of the soil was rocky, sandy, or infertile.

In areas where the soil was better, farmers raised oats. Most of this crop was fed to livestock. Some of the livestock was sold in the Caribbean. Almost every house had an orchard and a vegetable garden. But because it was so difficult to earn a living by farming, many New Englanders turned to other jobs.

TRADE

The first trade in the colonies was with Native Americans. Colonists traded European-made goods, such as jewelry, guns, blankets, and iron pots, for furs and deerskins. The furs were sent to Europe to be made into hats and coats. Beaver was especially popular. Deerskins, too, were used to make clothing, boots, and shoes. This trade was the first way that colonists in Plymouth earned money. The fur trade was the main reason for establishing New Netherland, and much of South Carolina's early wealth came from this trade.

Merchants, Fishers, and Whalers

New Englanders also traded among themselves. In the 1630s, New England saw a steady stream of immigrants from England. Some had been merchants in London and became merchants in Massachusetts Bay, selling supplies to newcomers.

The 1640s brought few settlers from England, so the merchants turned to the Caribbean and Europe for new sources of trade. Besides dried codfish, they traded grain, pork, and beef. Because much of the land in the Caribbean was used for sugar plantations, little food was raised for local use. As a result, food imports carried on New England's ships became very important to these islands. **Imports** are goods brought into a country for sale. In return, New England merchants brought back wine, iron, salt, and molasses. By the early 1700s, some New England merchants were part of the Triangular Trade in slaves.

Fishing and whaling also led to trade. The English were fishing off the coast of Newfoundland long before they settled in the Americas. Soon after colonization began, the colonists began fishing those waters, too. By the mid-1600s, fish had become New England's most important export. **Exports** are goods sent to another country for sale. Whale oil, which was used for lighting, was also exported. Boston became the region's most important port. Fishing towns like Gloucester (GLAHS-tuhr) and Marblehead grew up along the coast of Massachusetts.

Farms and Trade Centers

Because the Southern colonies specialized in farming, few cities developed, except for ports. The port cities of Baltimore, Savannah, and Charles Town grew into important trading centers where farm produce was exchanged for manufactured goods. Many slaves also arrived through these ports.

In the Middle colonies, Philadelphia became an important trading center because of its excellent harbor. Farmers west and south of the city brought their goods to Philadelphia for export. Besides wheat and flour, Pennsylvania exported horses, pork, beans, and wax. The colony imported rum, sugar, molasses, silver, salt, wine, linen, and a few slaves.

In the unit Colonial Beginnings you learned that New Amsterdam began as a trading post. It had an ideal location for trade and one of

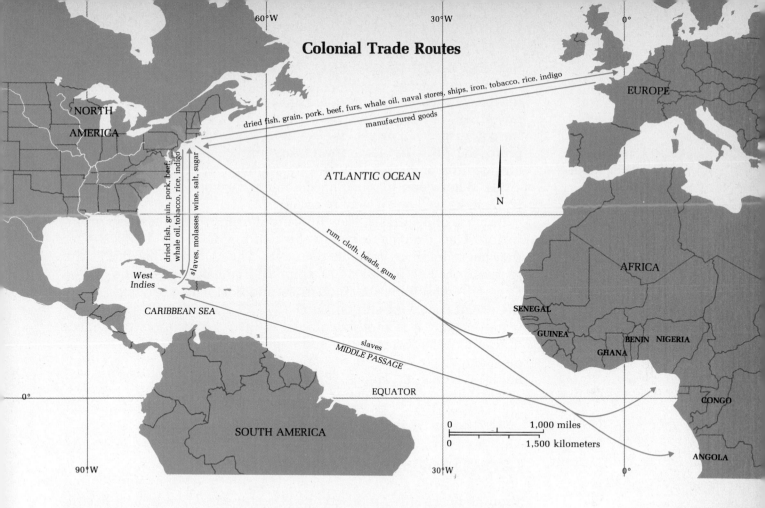

Colonial Trade Routes

dried fish, grain, pork, beef, furs, whale oil, naval stores, ships, iron, tobacco, rice, indigo

manufactured goods

NORTH AMERICA

ATLANTIC OCEAN

N

dried fish, grain, pork, beef, whale oil, tobacco, rice, indigo

slaves, molasses, wine, salt, sugar

West Indies

CARIBBEAN SEA

rum, cloth, beads, guns

AFRICA

EUROPE

SENEGAL

GUINEA

GHANA

BENIN NIGERIA

slaves
MIDDLE PASSAGE

EQUATOR

CONGO

SOUTH AMERICA

0   1,000 miles

0   1,500 kilometers

ANGOLA

the best harbors on the Atlantic coast. From New Amsterdam, the Hudson River formed a natural highway to the forests inland. These forests were rich in furs, especially beaver. The Dutch traded with the Iroquois for these furs.

After New Amsterdam became New York, the fur trade continued. By around 1710, though, the fur trade had declined because so many animals had been killed. New York then began to export wheat, flour, and naval stores. Naval stores are products, such as pitch, that are used in shipbuilding. Pitch was used to make ships watertight.

New Jersey had no big harbors, but it had many small ones. From these, merchants sent their goods to New York or Philadelphia. From either port, they were shipped to the Caribbean or Europe. The chief exports from New Jersey were beef, pork, wheat, and naval stores.

The Frontier

Merchants in small frontier towns collected farm products and furs from nearby areas and sent them to the port cities. In return, they received manufactured goods, such as iron pots, to sell to the pioneers. Towns in parts of the frontier that were settled first became places where later pioneers could buy supplies for the trip inland. Lancaster, Pennsylvania, for example, was founded about 1721. Within a few years it was selling supplies to travelers on the Great Wagon Road.

161

SHOPS, SHIPYARDS, AND MILLS

tannery (TAN-uhr-ee): place where animal hides are made into leather

Besides farming and trade, colonists had craft shops or worked with a few others in small industries. Some crafts and industries supplied the colonists' local needs. For example, many towns had grist mills to grind the local farmers' grain. Saw mills, tanneries, shoemakers, blacksmiths, and silversmiths were common in the larger towns and cities. When Penn planned his colony, for example, he wanted craft-workers as well as farmers to come.

Because of its forests, New England developed into a shipbuilding region. The colonists turned to shipbuilding in the mid-1600s when they began trading with other countries. The colonists also built ships to sell to the English. By 1700, shipbuilding had become one of New England's most important industries, and Boston had become its most important center for shipbuilding.

Iron making was another colonial industry. Most tools were made of iron, but they were heavy and expensive to import. New England had some deposits of iron ore, and in 1645, John Winthrop, Jr. started an iron works at Saugus (SAW-guhs), Massachusetts. Other iron works followed. Deposits of iron were also found in Pennsylvania and New Jersey.

GROWTH OF TOWNS AND CITIES

From the beginning, most colonists preferred to live in small settlements or towns. People from the same country or of the same religion built homes and farms near one another. Living together offered protection in a strange land. Also, business was easier when people lived close together.

Small towns developed in all the colonies but especially in New England. There, mountains and rocky soil limited places where people could live and farm. Although a few people in the Southern colonies could afford to build plantations, most people lived in towns. Small southern farmers also lived close to one another. On the frontier, the farms were far from one another and from the few towns that grew up for trade.

In the late 1600s and early 1700s, a few coastal towns developed into cities. The largest were Philadelphia, New York, Boston, Charles Town, and Newport. Their location near the Atlantic and their excellent harbors made them important trading centers. Merchants were attracted to these cities as were craftworkers, artists, doctors, lawyers, teachers, and unskilled workers.

Problems of Cities

As towns grew into cities, they developed problems. Traffic jams of stagecoaches, business carts, and private coaches were common.

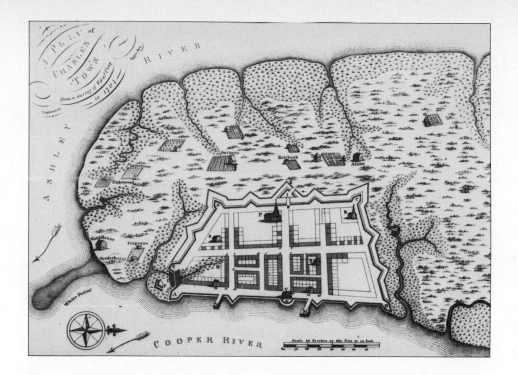

Even cities that were planned such as Charles Town had problems. What were the problems of colonial cities?

There were few rules to keep vehicles out of one another's way. Galloping horses were a danger to walkers and to the children who played in the streets.

The earliest city streets were dirt. Rain or snow turned them into rivers of mud. Later, streets were paved with bricks or stones. Even after they were paved, there were problems of trash in the streets. Because of this, disease spread rapidly. Disease was also spread through the water supply which came from springs and wells. It was not purified as it is today.

To correct these problems, colonial cities created police and fire departments. The cities also passed laws to keep streets clean and to direct traffic. Other city improvements included street lights, parks, and libraries. Colonists wanted their cities to be as much like those in Europe as possible.

LOOKING BACK

★ 1. **a.** What steps do you follow when you infer point of view? **b.** List three facts from Fitzhugh's description that led you to infer his point of view about slavery.
   2. How did the environment affect economic activities in: **a.** New England? **b.** Middle colonies? **c.** Southern colonies?
   3. Name the main economic activity in: **a.** New England. **b.** Middle colonies. **c.** Southern colonies. Give details that support your reason for each answer. Use the map to help you.
   4. List three problems of colonial cities.

Chapter 4   New Ways of Life

LOOKING AHEAD

This chapter describes the social classes, family life, education, and religions found in the British colonies. After you study this chapter, you will be able to:

- describe the class system in the colonies.
- read a bar graph to learn the size of the black population in the colonies.
- make a bar graph to determine the total population of the colonies.
- compare and contrast the roles of men, women, and children on farms and in towns.
- describe Penn's point of view about religious toleration.
- explain the reasons colleges with new courses of study began in the mid-1700s.
- use a secondary source to identify the effects of the Great Awakening on the colonists.

Social Studies Vocabulary

life-style	social mobility
society	nuclear family

People

Anne Catherine Hoof Green	Jonathan Edwards
George Whitefield	

Words and Terms

apprentice	dame school	evangelist

Events

Great Awakening

Colonial taverns were meeting places for friends to share a meal or play a game of cards. Often they were also inns where travelers could rent rooms.

The **life-style,** or way of life, that a group develops depends on many things. One is the environment. Another is the way people adapt to and use this environment. A third factor is the culture of the people—customs, beliefs, traditions, and so on. These three factors strongly influenced the life-style that developed in the British colonies. In the last chapter, you read about how the people adapted to the different environments in order to make their livings. In this chapter, you will read about the society these people created. **Society** in this sense means a group of people with a shared culture.

SOCIAL CLASSES

Europeans who came to the British colonies in the 1600s and 1700s became members of one of three social classes: upper, middle, or lower. In Europe, nobles were the upper class. In the colonies, the upper class was made up of wealthy landowners and merchants, high government officials, and clergy. Less than 5 percent of the colonists belonged to the upper class.

The middle class in the British colonies was made up of owners of small farms, craftworkers, shopkeepers, professional people—doctors, lawyers, teachers. This was the largest class.

The lower class were tenant farmers, servants, and unskilled workers. Indentured servants and free blacks also belonged to this class. The number of free blacks was small. Some were descendants of Africans who had come as indentured servants. Others had been set free by their owners. Slaves belonged to their own class, below all other classes in society.

The Frontier

In the early days on the frontier, there were few class differences. Everyone had to clear land and build homes and farms or stores. Success required skill and hard work, not money. However, as the frontier became more settled, some class differences appeared.

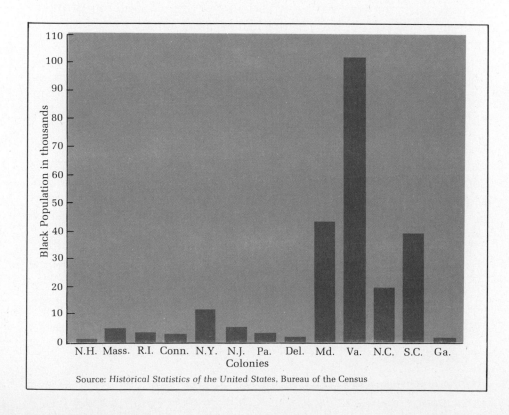

Source: *Historical Statistics of the United States*, Bureau of the Census

Black Population of the 13 Colonies in 1750

Some merchants became wealthy from trade, and successful farmers increased their landholdings. Also, as the frontier became settled, people from the upper classes moved inland. By the late 1700s, social classes on the frontier were the same as in eastern settlements.

Social Mobility

In Europe, most people remained in the class they were born into. If a person's parents were lower class, that person would most likely remain in the lower class. In the British and Spanish colonies, people had a chance for social mobility. **Social mobility** (moh-BIL-uh-tee) is the moving from one class to another. Besides being born into the upper or middle classes, colonists could move into them through skill and hard work. An indentured servant, for example, could buy land or learn a trade and become part of the middle class.

Land and opportunities were abundant in the colonies for those who came from Europe or had European ancestors. For blacks and Native Americans, it was different. Slaves were not allowed to own land or take advantage of opportunities for social mobility. Free blacks were, but they found it hard to enter the middle or upper classes. Free Native Americans were not part of colonial society. They remained through choice or force outside it. Europeans feared or respected them but did not view them as equals.

Slavery

Slaves—Africans and Native Americans—were considered property and were treated that way. Native American slaves were usually war captives taken in the Southern colonies. Many were kept there, but some were sold in other colonies or to the West Indies.

Most Africans who were brought to the colonies were sold in the South. New York, however, had many slaves. It was the largest importer of slaves north of Maryland. In Philadelphia and Boston, too, blacks made up 10 percent of the population by the mid-1700s.

In New York and the Southern colonies, most slaves worked as field hands on the plantations and large farms. A few blacks were cooks, maids, butlers, or other servants in the homes of their owners. Most slaves in New England and in the other Middle colonies were house servants or craftworkers. This was also true of the larger cities in the Southern colonies, such as Savannah and Charles Town.

Because plantations were self-sufficient, owners trained some slaves in blacksmithing, tanning, spinning, weaving, and similar crafts. Craftworkers had the greatest freedom to work and move about the plantations. Often, they were hired out for a time to other plantations or small farmers. Their owners received their pay.

Slave Protests

Although slaves were constantly watched, they found ways to protest their chains. They protested by working slowly or doing such a poor

Advertisements such as this one appeared regularly on posters and in newspapers in the 1700s.

Colonial women had many roles. They taught the children, cared for the sick, and clothed and fed their families. What jobs are the women in this picture doing?

job that they had to do the work over. They broke tools and took food, farm animals, and other items from their owners. And in spite of punishment, they ran away.

Runaways were hunted down by bloodhounds and recaptured. Owners used such punishments as whipping or cutting off part of a runaway's foot to keep slaves obedient. To gain their freedom, slaves sometimes turned to violence. One such slave uprising occurred in New York City in 1712. Twenty slaves set fire to a building and waited for white colonists to come. When they tried to put the fire out, the slaves killed them. The slaves attempted to run away but were captured, tortured, and killed. Colonists felt that by cruelly punishing the blacks, they could discourage future revolts. However, another slave revolt occurred in New York in 1741. This revolt led to the end of New York's slave trade and a rise in the number of white workers. Other blacks looked for a legal end to slavery. As early as 1766, slaves in Massachusetts asked the General Court for their freedom. Their requests were turned down.

FAMILY LIFE AMONG THE COLONISTS

Colonial families in the British colonies were large. Some were extended families that often included servants, workers, and slaves. Other families were nuclear. A **nuclear** (NOO-klee-uhr) **family** is made up of a parent or parents and one or more children. Colonial families of 10 or 12 children were common. Since most farms or businesses were family-run, children were needed as workers.

Farm Families

On the farm, everyone had a role. Men and boys worked the fields—sometimes with one or two indentured servants or slaves. Women and girls worked mostly in the house and in small vegetable and herb gardens nearby. They grew, preserved, and cooked the food. They made the family's clothing, candles, soap, and medicines. At planting and harvesting times, women and girls worked in the fields, too. Men and women who were too old to work in the fields or in the house cared for the younger children.

Outside of large towns where there were few doctors, women took care of the sick. Each housewife had her own favorite remedies. Some were made from wild plants and others came from her herb garden.

Townspeople

In the towns and cities, craftworkers and merchants could not be in their shops all the time. Often, their wives and children helped out. Women who worked in their husbands' or fathers' shops often learned their crafts. A silversmith, for example, might teach his wife or daughter the art of making silver plates, mugs, and candlesticks. If a husband died, his wife usually took over his business. For example, Anne Catherine Hoof Green became printer to Maryland after her husband's death. Daughters also took over businesses from fathers.

Free Time

The colonists brought with them the games and sports they had known in Europe. They played cricket and rugby. Cricket is similar to baseball. Rugby is like football. The colonists also bowled and played billiards (BIL-yuhrdz), a game similar to pool. Card games were popular, especially one called whist (WIST).

Music was another pastime that colonists brought with them from Europe. When they could find time, people entertained themselves or

These colonial riders are on a fox hunt. This sport was popular in Virginia and Maryland in the 1700s. What other sports were popular during this time?

This watercolor from the 1700s shows blacks entertaining themselves in the slave quarters. The dance and the instruments are believed to be from the Yoruba of western Africa.

family members by playing the violin and other instruments. Playing music for larger audiences began in the 1700s. People in some cities formed music societies to entertain themselves or to give concerts.

In the Southern colonies, because plantations and farms were widely scattered, visiting the neighbors usually took several days. Often such visits were the reasons for parties, hunts, and dances. For the less wealthy, barn raisings and quilting parties combined work with a chance to visit with friends. These two activities were popular throughout the colonies.

EDUCATION

Like the Spanish, the people in the British colonies spent most of the early years providing for food, shelter, and defense. Whenever possible, parents taught their children at home. This is how children on the frontier learned to read and write. Later, when life became more settled, schools were started.

Besides schools, children and even adults could receive an education by becoming apprentices. Apprentices (uh-PREN-tih-sez) were young people assigned to a craftworker to learn a skill. The apprentice learned a craft such as silversmithing or carpentry as well as how to read and write. In return, the apprentice helped in running the shop and in making items for sale. The apprentice usually lived with the craftworker's family.

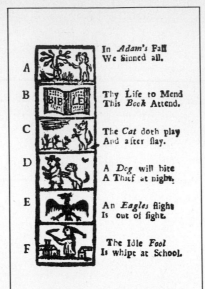

These are pages from *The New England Primer,* which was first printed in 1687. The book was designed to teach religion as well as reading and writing.

New England

Puritans believed that everyone should be able to read the Bible. In 1642, the General Court of Massachusetts passed the first education law in the colonies. It ordered parents to teach their children to read and to teach them a skill. In 1647, the General Court went further and required every town of 50 families to support a school. This first system of public education in the colonies taught reading, writing, arithmetic, and religion. By the 1670s, most colonies in New England had school laws.

One type of school that developed in New England was called the dame school. It was run by a woman in her home. Children received lessons in reading, writing, and arithmetic. Girls also learned knitting and embroidery—fancy stitch work. Some girls would earn their livings as adults doing this kind of work.

The first colleges in the colonies were set up in New England to train ministers. The early colleges taught Latin, Greek, mathematics, and science. Later, they trained the sons of the wealthy for other careers. Harvard, founded in 1636 in Cambridge, Massachusetts, was the first school of higher education in what is now the U.S.

Southern Colonies

tutor (TOO-tuhr): private teacher

Unlike New Englanders, Southern colonists lived far apart on plantations and farms. Because of the great distances, it was almost impossible to set up schools. Most education took place in the home with the parents as teachers. Children were taught the basics—reading, writing, and arithmetic. Children of wealthier parents had tutors. Some sons of wealthy planters were sent to England to study. Other young men attended the College of William and Mary, founded in Williamsburg, Virginia, in 1693. Some were sent to colleges in New England or the Middle colonies. No colleges in the colonies educated women.

Middle Colonies

The first public school in New Netherland began in 1638. In that year, the Dutch West India Company hired a teacher for the town's children. Most Dutch schools, though, were run by religious groups. Besides reading, writing, and arithmetic, religion was also taught. In New Jersey, religious groups and private individuals set up schools. In 1693, a public school system was founded.

Penn had planned a system of public education for Pennsylvania. Children were to be taught to read and write by age 12. However, many of the immigrant groups in the colony set up their own schools. As a result, it was difficult for Penn's system to work.

Some people believed that colleges should do more than train ministers or provide a general education for the sons of the wealthy. Benjamin Franklin was among those who argued that colleges should train men for special professions such as law and medicine. In the 1750s, two colleges were started that offered new fields of study: King's College, now Columbia University, and the College of Philadelphia, now the University of Pennsylvania.

RELIGION

As you may recall from the unit Colonial Beginnings, many people came to the British colonies seeking religious freedom. Although the Puritans wanted freedom for themselves, they refused it to others. During most of the 1600s, Puritans in Massachusetts Bay controlled both church and state. Many colonists left. Some established their own colonies. Others went to colonies that had religious toleration.

Rhode Island, Maryland, and Pennsylvania attracted many Europeans. At first, the largest group in Pennsylvania were Quakers. Later, Anglicans, Roman Catholics, Jews, Baptists, Congregationalists (kahng-gruh-GAY-shuhn-uhl-ists), and Lutherans also answered Penn's invitation to settle in the colony. In Virginia, North and South Carolina, and Georgia, the colonial governments supported the Anglican Church. People in those colonies were taxed to support the Anglican Church whether they wanted to or not.

Some colonists felt that religious toleration was having a bad effect. Religion seemed to be losing its importance in peoples' lives. To change this, the colonists turned to evangelists. Evangelists (ih-VAN-juh-lists) are preachers who stir up people's feelings for religion.

Because of the work of traveling evangelists, a new interest in religion swept the colonies in the 1730s and 1740s. It was called the Great Awakening. Ministers such as George Whitefield of England and Jonathan Edwards of Massachusetts led it. They traveled the colonies giving exciting sermons. Edwards believed that people did not fear God because God's punishments did not seem real. Edwards described hell so clearly that thousands repented in public for their sins. Whitefield's message was similar to Edwards'. People would be saved only if they returned to the strict rules of the Bible.

repent (ri-PENT): to feel sorry for something one has done

George Whitefield was one of the leading evangelists of the Great Awakening. What effects did the Great Awakening have on colonial life?

denounce
(dih-NOWNS):
to formally accuse;
to condemn

extent (eks-TENT):
the area over which
something extends

Three historians together viewed the Great Awakening 200 years after it ended and formed these opinions. As you may recall from Chapter 1 of this unit, their view is a secondary source. A revivalist is another word for evangelist.

The Great Awakening not only led to the division of existing congregations and the founding of new ones, but it also had a number of other results. Some of the revivalists denounced book learning. But others saw education as a means of furthering their own brand of religion. So they founded schools for the preparation of ministers. Many believed that revivalism, through its emphasis on righteous conduct, brought about an improvement in manners and morals. No doubt it did so, at least temporarily. To some extent, too, it aroused a spirit of humanitarianism, a concern for the physical as well as the spiritual welfare of the poor and oppressed. The widely preached doctrine of salvation for all—of equal opportunity to share in God's grace—encouraged the idea of equal rights to share also in the good things on earth. Thus, it stimulated feelings of democracy.

LOOKING BACK

1. Describe the social classes in the British colonies.
2. Use the bar graph in this chapter to answer the following questions: **a.** Which colony had the largest black population? **b.** Which colony had the smallest?
3. Use the bar graphs on pages 149 and 165 to make a bar graph showing the total population of the colonies in 1750.
4. What role did each of the following play on the farms and in the towns of the colonies: **a.** men? **b.** women? **c.** children?
5. What was Penn's point of view about religious toleration? You can infer this from his actions as stated on page 135.
6. Why did people want colleges to change their courses of study in the mid-1700s?
7. How did the Great Awakening affect: **a.** religion? **b.** education? **c.** politics?

Chapter 5   Cultural Life of the Colonies

LOOKING AHEAD

This chapter is about the cultural life of the Spanish Southwest and the English colonies from about 1600 to 1750. Most early art was folk art. Later, as the colonies became more settled, professional art, literature, and drama developed. People also became interested in science. After you study this chapter, you will be able to:

- ★ use pictures to learn about earlier ways of life.
- • explain why professional painters in the British colonies were able to support themselves by the mid-1700s.
- • describe the kinds of material that people in the British colonies read.
- • compare and contrast the development of the arts and sciences in the Spanish Southwest with the British colonies.

Social Studies Vocabulary

the arts   folk art   professional art

People

Gustavus Hesselius	Sarah Kemble Knight
John Smibert	Michael Wigglesworth
Joseph Blackburn	Anne Bradstreet
Benjamin West	Phillis Wheatley
John Singleton Copley	Cotton Mather
John Smith	Benjamin Franklin

Words and Terms

bulto   santo   inoculation

Events

Boston Newsletter   *The Prince of Parthia*

As you read in other chapters in this unit, life in both the Spanish and English colonies in the 1600s was difficult. In spite of the problems, colonists found time to do some painting and writing. In the 1700s, life was easier in the older coastal settlements of the British colonies. As a result, there was more time for **the arts**—painting, literature, drama, music—as well as for scientific interests.

However, life in the Spanish Southwest remained difficult. There was as little time for the arts in the 1700s as there had been in the 1600s. This was also true on the British frontier. However, the Spanish and the British shared a form of art—folk art.

This door fastener was made of wrought iron by a black in New Orleans. Wrought iron is a soft form of iron that can be easily worked into various shapes.

spouse (SPOWS): husband or wife

John Singleton Copley painted this portrait of Paul Revere, who was a silversmith. Before this portrait, people were not painted in work clothes, only in their dress clothes.

FOLK ART

Colonists of the 1500s and 1600s had little contact with the countries they had left. The colonists brought some tools and household goods with them, but most of what they needed to start a new life had to be found in the colonies. Repairing and replacing tools, making clothes, and finding food had to be done. Making things mainly for enjoyment, such as paintings, was rare.

However, art did exist. Most of it was **folk art,** or art made by the people, often by craftworkers. Folk art is usually made to be used. The art is less important than the object's use. A piece of furniture, a quilt, a piece of clothing or jewelry, or a decoration on a tool or dish may be considered folk art. Folk artists are usually self-taught.

In contrast, **professional,** or fine, **art** is created by specially trained artists. They are concerned with color, form, and line. They create their works to be looked at and enjoyed, not to be used. And their work is one of a kind. They want it to be original. Professional art was rare in the colonies, especially in the 1600s.

One of the best-known kinds of folk art is folk painting, which is done by ordinary people or craftworkers. Most folk painting was done for the artist's own enjoyment. Some of it, however, was done to earn money for the artist.

Portraits of wealthy merchants or farmers made up much of the folk painting done between 1600 and 1750. Some members of the middle and upper classes had portraits done of their spouses and children. Not enough colonists could afford to have their portraits painted to support the painters, however. Most colonial folk painters earned their livings by painting houses, barns, tavern and shop signs, and signs on wagons.

Among the Spanish

The folk art that developed in the Spanish Southwest was different from that of the British colonies. In the British colonies, Native Americans were forced to live away from European settlements. The colonists were not familiar with Native American arts and crafts. As a result, all folk art in the colonies was European.

In Spanish America, acculturation took place. Spanish and Native American cultures mixed—through force. The Spanish taught the Native Americans how to work with metals such as silver and tin. They also taught them how to carve stone and build with wood. The Native Americans brought to these skills their own designs and sense of color and form. The Native Americans were already skilled at weaving, pottery making, and basketmaking. As a result, the folk art of the Spanish Southwest is both Spanish and Native American.

As you have already read, the Roman Catholic Church played a large role in the cultural life of Spanish America. As a result, much of the folk art of the Spanish Southwest is related to religion. In the missions, Native Americans used their new crafts to build the mission churches. They and mestizo craftworkers also built the churches in the towns. Both were decorated with carved and painted statues of saints called bultos (BOOL-tohs) and santos (SAN-tohs).

Nonreligious examples of Spanish American folk art include the adobe house, carved furniture, pottery, jewelry, and baskets. For example, the Spanish taught the Native Americans to mix straw with the clay and bake it into bricks to strengthen their pueblos. On their cattle ranches, the Spanish built one-story adobe houses. The style developed into today's ranch-style house.

In the British Colonies

From the early 1600s to around 1750, folk art in the British colonies showed strong European influences. Furniture, dishes, and jewelry were copied from European examples. But by around 1700, folk art was beginning to look more American than European.

In the 1700s, two factors were influencing folk art. First, the American environment was different from the European environment. Household goods from Europe, such as pottery or fragile furniture was not strong enough for the rough frontier life. Stronger replacements had to be designed and made. Second, immigrants from countries other than England were coming to the colonies. With them came their ideas of art and their crafts. Some of the most colorful folk art was done by the Pennsylvania Dutch. Among their designs were the tulip, heart, and vine. All these ideas mixed together eventually.

The Africans who were brought to the Americas also brought their arts and skills with them. Pottery making, basket weaving, and wood carving were highly developed in West Africa. Colonists used the early African craftworkers to make goods for their farms and businesses. As time went by, slave owners also began training slaves in crafts. Large plantation owners, for example, had slaves who were furniture makers and leather workers.

Many of the earlier items looked like objects made in West Africa. Some carved walking canes, for example, had human or animal designs similar to those found in Africa. Some of these designs became part of colonial art. Many slaveowners, however, wanted to stamp out any traces of African culture. They destroyed or called sinful much of black folk art. They wanted blacks to forget Africa and accept their life as slaves. Slaveowners thought they were succeeding if blacks replaced African designs with European ones.

PROFESSIONAL ART

Not until the mid-1700s were professional artists able to make a living. By then, there were enough wealthy people who wanted paintings to decorate their homes and businesses. Some professional artists were immigrants. Gustavus Hesselius (he-SEE-lee-uhs) arrived from England in 1711 and John Smibert (SMY-buhrt) in 1729. In 1753, Joseph Blackburn settled in Boston after coming from England. These men all painted portraits.

Gustavus Hesselius, the most important portrait painter in the Middle colonies, painted Lapowinza of the Lenni Lenape for John Penn, one of William's sons.

A Pennsylvania craftworker carved and painted this chest around 1790. Notice the kinds of designs that the artist chose. Try to imagine what a colonial home was like and then consider why colonists decorated household goods and furniture. Who do you think might have owned a chest such as this?

This style of painting portraits in a home-like setting was popular in New England in the late 1700s. Hezekiah and Elizabeth Beardsley were painted with some of their possessions. What do their portraits tell you about their social class?

The pieces of art on these pages represent early American folk art. They are primary sources that can be used to learn more about the people who lived in the late 1600s and in the 1700s. By studying them carefully, you can learn how people lived and worked, how they worshiped, and what they did in their free time. **1.** Do you think Cynthia Burr lived in a rural or in an urban area? **2.** Why? **3.** Use the Beardsley portraits to describe the style of clothing worn in the late 1700s.

Spanish American folk artists painted pictures with religious themes. Where might a painting such as this one have been hung?

This drum was made by a black carver who decorated it with shapes and lines. The style is similar to African pieces. Compare and contrast the designs with those on the chest from Pennsylvania.

Young girls practiced their embroidery stitches by making samplers. Cynthia Burr completed this sampler in 1786. How old was she when she finished it?

By the mid-1700s, some American-born professional artists had become well known. One of the more famous was Benjamin West. He painted Penn's treaty with the Lenni Lenape and the death of General James Wolfe in the Battle of Quebec, which you will read about in the next unit. John Singleton Copley (KAHP-lee) was another American-born painter. Copley began his career in Boston as a student of Joseph Blackburn. Among Copley's subjects were Paul Revere and other wealthy Boston merchants.

LITERATURE

Just as there were few professional artists in colonial America, there were also few professional writers. Most literature was religious or was created in the course of daily life.

Spanish America

The Roman Catholic Church and the Spanish government in Mexico City kept tight control over what was read in Spanish America. They were afraid that ideas against the government or the church might enter the colonies. Most material printed in Spanish America came from Mexico City. In 1539, a printing press was set up there. Before anything could be published, permission from the government had to be obtained.

Spanish-American writers wrote mainly about religion. Another topic was their experiences in the Americas. You read one account by Cabeza de Vaca in the unit Colonial Beginnings. Most colonial au-

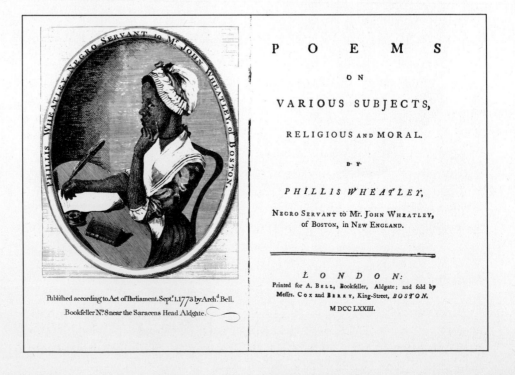

Phillis Wheatley was the first known black woman poet in the English colonies. Her first book of poems was published in 1773. What were popular forms of reading matter in the colonies?

178

thors were priests, soldiers, and a few educated settlers. Later Native American and mestizo writers recorded histories of their peoples.

The British Colonies

Historians use primary sources such as colonists' letters, diaries, and wills to learn what people were reading in the British colonies. Colonists' writings often mentioned popular books, articles, or papers. Colonists preferred books that gave advice for improving their lives and their work. Books on surgery, medicine, law, engineering, farming, and horse racing were especially popular. During the 1600s, religious books were widely read, especially among Puritans. Some of these books were the printed sermons of popular ministers. The sermons usually advised the colonists how to lead good lives.

Other literature by colonial authors included travel accounts, diaries, and histories. Some of the most popular travel accounts were written by Captain John Smith in the early 1600s and by Sarah Kemble Knight in the early 1700s. Important people such as William Bradford often kept journals or diaries.

The first printing press in the English colonies was established in Cambridge in 1638. The first newspaper in the colonies was the *Boston Newsletter* founded in 1704 by John Campbell. The first best seller was a volume of poetry, *Day of Doom*, by Michael Wigglesworth, printed in 1662. Anne Bradstreet, a poet, published *The Tenth Muse Lately Sprung Up in America* in 1650. Children had to memorize such poems because they were thought to teach morals.

We must not on the knee
Be always dandled,
Nor must we think to ride to Heaven
Upon a feather bed.

Michael Wigglesworth, *Meat out of the Eater*

dandle (DAN-duhl): to bounce up and down

A later colonial poet was Phillis Wheatley. She was born in what is now Senegal in West Africa about 1753 and brought as a slave to Boston in 1761. John Wheatley, a tailor, bought her as a servant. The Wheatleys taught Phillis to read and write and encouraged her to write. The following is from her poem *To the University of Cambridge*:

Improve your privileges while they stay:
Caress, redeem each moment, which with haste
Bears on its rapid wing eternal bliss.
Let hateful vice, so baneful to the soul,
Be still avoided with becoming care.

baneful (BAYN-fuhl): harmful; destructive

SCIENCE

During the 1600s, people in the English colonies had little time for science. In the 1700s, as settlements and free time increased, colonists' interest grew. Cities such as Boston and Philadelphia became centers of scientific discussion. Many ministers, doctors, and lawyers read books on science and performed experiments.

Cotton Mather, a Boston minister, was such a person. He argued in favor of the inoculation of Boston's citizens during a smallpox outbreak in 1721. Inoculation (in-ahk-yuh-LAY-shuhn) is the prevention of disease by injecting a mild form of it into a healthy person. This was a bold, new idea, and many people feared it. Science, however, has proven Mather right.

In Philadelphia, Benjamin Franklin experimented with electricity. His experiment with a kite and a key in 1752 is well known. Franklin helped found the American Philosophical Society in 1743. It was the first scientific society in the British colonies.

philosophical
(fil-uh-SAHF-uh-kuhl): dealing with the study of knowledge or truth

DRAMA

Drama in Spanish America, like literature and folk art, was usually religious. Plays were performed on church holidays by members of the community.

Puritans thought the theater was evil. When they gained power in England in the 1640s, they closed all theaters. In the colonies, the Puritans were able to keep theaters from being built in Massachusetts Bay. Newport, Rhode Island, was the only place in New England where plays were staged. In Pennsylvania, the Quakers also opposed drama. But in 1754, over Quaker protests, a traveling company was able to stage a play.

The first theater in the British colonies was built in Williamsburg, Virginia, in 1716. By 1750, theater was becoming popular entertainment. However, it was found mainly in larger towns and cities. New York and Philadelphia became leading theater centers. The first American play, *The Prince of Parthia* (PAHR-thih-uh), was staged in Philadelphia in 1767. It was written by Thomas Godfrey.

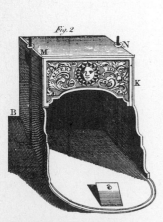

Benjamin Franklin designed this stove in 1754. It uses less wood and heats better than a fireplace.

LOOKING BACK

★ 1. Look at the pictures on pages 176-77. **a.** Describe the homes that some British colonists lived in. **b.** Name three ways folk artists decorated their pieces of art.

2. What was happening in the British colonies in the 1700s that made it possible for painters to support themselves by painting only pictures?

3. **a.** List the kinds of materials people read in the British colonies in the 1700s. **b.** What was the main purpose of their reading?

4. **a.** What made it possible for drama and an interest in science to develop in the British colonies in the 1700s? **b.** Why did these same artistic and scientific developments not happen in the Spanish Southwest? Remember the size of the population and pattern of settlement in the Spanish Southwest.

PRACTICING YOUR SKILLS

What If . . .   You have just read about the natural environment colonists found in New Mexico and in the Southern colonies. **What if** the climate and geography of New Mexico had been more like the natural environment of the Southern colonies? What effects might that have had on the economy, population, and growth of New Mexico?

Discussing   Most people would agree with the authors' view that the early colonies had great social mobility. Did they really? Was social mobility limited in the English colonies by religion and education, if not by wealth?

Mapping, Researching, Writing

1. In Life in America: The Land, you read about land use and used a land use map of the U.S. Reread Chapter 3 of this unit and then draw a land use map showing the economic activities of each British colony. Be sure your map has a legend.
2. Today, many U.S. cities have some of the same or similar problems that colonial cities had. For example, cars have replaced coaches, but traffic jams still happen. Scan the section Growth of Towns and Cities in Chapter 3 and list the problems that existed. Read a daily newspaper or a weekly newsmagazine for articles about the problems of modern cities. Are the problems of modern cities the same as or different than those of colonial cities? Answer in a paragraph.
3. Research folk art in the colonies and make a bulletin board display of colonial folk art similar to the art on pages 176-177.

Building Study Skills   Activity 2 above asks you to scan a section in the text. **Scanning** means to look over a piece of reading matter very quickly to find particular information. You use this skill when you look for a name in the telephone book, a chapter in a table of contents, or a topic in an index. Here are some tips to help you scan effectively.

- Let your eyes run rapidly down the page. Look for clues like capital letters, proper names, numerals, and key words.
- Keep in mind what you are searching for. Your objective is not to understand every word but to look for certain words.

Activity: Scan Chapter 1 for the occupations of colonists in the Spanish Southwest. Scan Chapter 4 for the various religious groups that came to the colonies.

Exploring   In Chapter 3 you read about the economic activities of the colonies. Some colonies or regions specialized in one or two activities—for example, fishing and whaling in New England and cash-crop farming in the South. Using reference materials in the library, find out what economic activities your area is noted for. Make a list of occupations that depend on these activities.

Reading

Brownlee, W. Elliot and Mary M. *Women in the American Economy: A Documentary History, 1675 to 1929.* New Haven: Yale University Press, 1976.

Colby, C. B. *Early American Crafts: Tools, Shops, and Products.* New York: Coward, 1967. Material culture.

Colonial Americans Series, 10 vols. New York: Watts, 1964-1976. Small industries and crafts of the colonial period.

Katz, William Loren. *Early America, 1492–1812.* New York: Watts, 1974. Treatment of minority groups from Columbus through early 1800s.

Lauber, Almon Wheeler. *Indian Slavery in the Colonial Times Within the Present Limits of the United States.* Williamstown, Massachusetts: Corner House, 1970.

Lomax, Alan. *Folk Songs of North America.* New York: Doubleday, 1975.

BECOMING AMERICANS

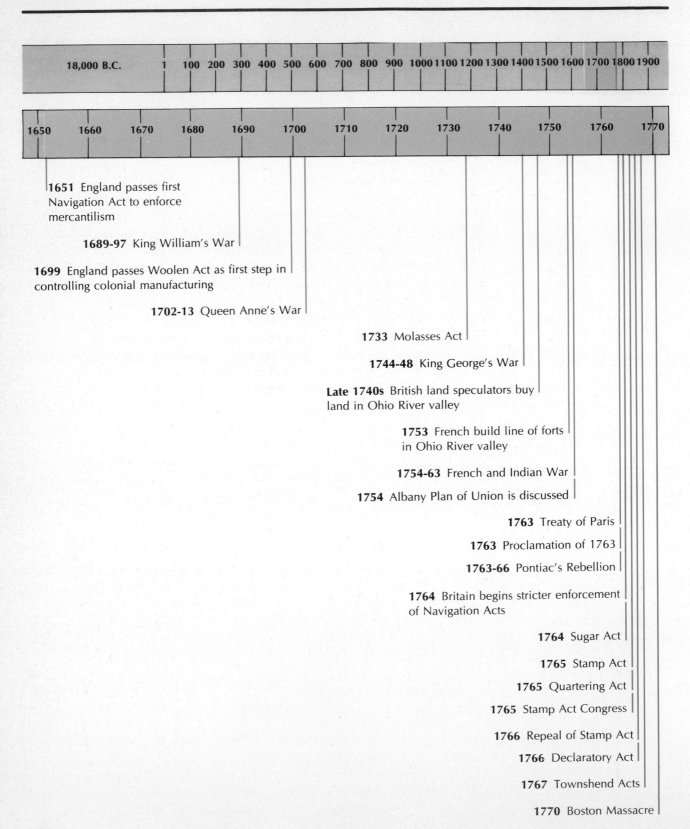

| 18,000 B.C. | 1 | 100 | 200 | 300 | 400 | 500 | 600 | 700 | 800 | 900 | 1000 | 1100 | 1200 | 1300 | 1400 | 1500 | 1600 | 1700 | 1800 | 1900 |

| 1650 | 1660 | 1670 | 1680 | 1690 | 1700 | 1710 | 1720 | 1730 | 1740 | 1750 | 1760 | 1770 |

1651 England passes first Navigation Act to enforce mercantilism

1689-97 King William's War

1699 England passes Woolen Act as first step in controlling colonial manufacturing

1702-13 Queen Anne's War

1733 Molasses Act

1744-48 King George's War

Late 1740s British land speculators buy land in Ohio River valley

1753 French build line of forts in Ohio River valley

1754-63 French and Indian War

1754 Albany Plan of Union is discussed

1763 Treaty of Paris

1763 Proclamation of 1763

1763-66 Pontiac's Rebellion

1764 Britain begins stricter enforcement of Navigation Acts

1764 Sugar Act

1765 Stamp Act

1765 Quartering Act

1765 Stamp Act Congress

1766 Repeal of Stamp Act

1766 Declaratory Act

1767 Townshend Acts

1770 Boston Massacre

Chapter 1   British Versus Colonial Control

LOOKING AHEAD

The American colonies were a source of great wealth for England and later Great Britain. To capture this wealth, the government had to exercise control over both colonial trade and colonial government. In this chapter, you will read how limits were put on trade. You will also learn how the colonies were governed. After you study this chapter, you will be able to:

- explain why the English government tried to restrict colonial trade and industry.
- ★ read a line graph to learn about tax revenue from the Navigation Acts.
- describe the advantages and disadvantages of the trade laws for the colonists.
- describe the English view of the purpose of its colonies.
- scan to classify the duties of the governor, the council, and the legislature.
- explain how colonial voting requirements changed.

Social Studies Vocabulary

mercantilism	customs duty	veto
balance of trade	petition	
line graph	bill of rights	

Words and Terms

Navigation Acts	Hat Act	Bill of Rights
enumerated goods	Iron Act	of 1689
Molasses Act	Magna Carta	Board of Trade
Woolen Act	Petition of Right	

Great Britain tried to control its American colonies in two ways. First, it passed laws to restrict colonial trade. Second, Great Britain sent its own officials to govern the colonies and force its laws on colonial legislatures. Both factors were important in the colonists' final decision to break away from Great Britain.

MERCANTILISM

From the beginning of exploration and colonization, European nations followed a policy known as mercantilism. **Mercantilism** (MER-kuhn-til-iz-uhm) is the economic theory or belief that colonies exist

On the British coat of arms, the lion stands for England, the unicorn for Scotland, the harp for Ireland. Note the similarity to Native American totem poles.

favorable: helpful; good

only to make the governing country richer. The colonies supply raw materials to the ruling country and may buy manufactured goods only from the ruling country. This establishes a favorable balance of trade for the ruling country.

Balance of trade is the difference in value between exports and imports. A favorable balance of trade means that the value of exports is higher than the value of imports. In order to keep a favorable trade balance, the ruling country had to prevent other countries from trading with its colonies. It also had to keep its colonies from gaining any power. This was done by controlling what the colonies made and sold, to whom they sold it, and how they shipped it.

For example, by law the English colonies could supply raw materials only to England. In return, the colonies could buy manufactured goods only from England. Since manufactured goods have a higher value than raw materials, the balance of trade would be favorable to England. The colonies, on the other hand, would have an unfavorable balance of trade.

The Navigation Acts

Beginning in 1651, the English Parliament passed a series of laws to enforce mercantilism. Some of these were known as Navigation Acts. The first one ordered that all goods shipped between England and its colonies had to be carried in English or colonial ships. The colonists had been using Dutch ships to carry their goods.

In 1660, another law listed goods that could be sent only to England or its colonies. These items were called enumerated (ih-NOO-muhr-ayt-uhd) goods. They included cotton, sugar, tobacco, and wood products. In time, such goods as rice and naval stores were added. The enumeration lists had two results. The English were sure of having needed goods, and the government was sure of collecting the revenue on the items.

revenue (REV-uh-noo): income, especially of a government, from taxes

In 1663, the English government went even further. It stated that all goods had to pass through England on their way to the colonies. Colonists could buy Dutch or Spanish goods, but the goods had to be shipped to England first. There, they were loaded onto English ships and sent to the colonies. In this way, England collected a tax on the goods. The costs to the colonists, however, were much greater than if the goods had come directly from the Dutch or Spanish.

Laws regulating trade continued to be made in the 1700s. For example, in 1733, plantation owners in the British West Indies persuaded Parliament to pass the Molasses Act. It placed a tax on sugar, rum, and molasses imported into the colonies from non-British colonies. British colonists had been buying these items from the French West Indies because the price was lower. The colonists had been smuggling the goods in without paying the tax. With the new tax and stricter enforcement of the laws, the French goods cost more than the British goods.

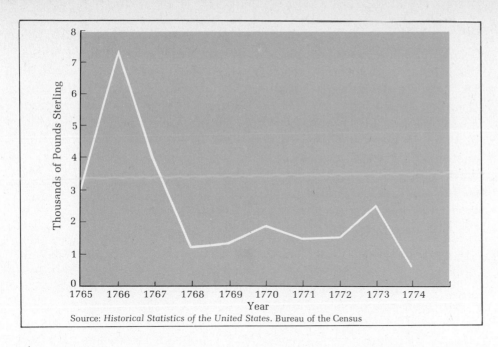

Source: *Historical Statistics of the United States,* Bureau of the Census

BUILDING GRAPH SKILLS

In the unit Life in Colonial America, you learned how to read a bar graph. A **line graph** is another way to show statistical data. It is an easy way to see quickly the differences in the sizes of similar items at different times. This line graph is about the tax revenue collected from 1765 to 1774 under the Navigation Acts. It counts the amount of taxes collected and then classifies it by years. The higher the line the more taxes collected. By using this kind of graph, you can see the differences in revenue over the ten years. **1.** Did taxes go up or down? **2.** Which year saw the greatest income? **3.** Which year saw the least income?

Two Views of the Trade Laws

The English government believed it had the right to regulate colonial trade. The trade laws it passed followed the policy of mercantilism. They were written to help English business. It was not their purpose to punish or rob the colonists.

The laws also helped some colonists. Colonial shipbuilders grew wealthy building ships for England and the other colonies. Colonial merchants and farmers prospered, too. For example, tobacco planters had a monopoly on the tobacco trade with England.

Some colonists, however, were angered by the trade laws. They did not agree with mercantilism. They did not want to be told where to sell their goods. They wanted to be able to sell them wherever they would get the best price. Some colonists began to feel that England was being run by selfish merchants.

Enforcement

England's colonial empire was worldwide. Because it was so large, the English had difficulty making people obey unpopular laws. In 1673, an act was passed that appointed customs officials in the colonies. These officials were to collect **customs duties,** or taxes on goods brought into each colony. But with such a long coastline, the colonists found it easy to smuggle goods. This was especially true when customs officials were paid by colonists to ignore the smuggling.

As you may recall from the unit Colonial Beginnings, Massachusetts lost its charter for a time because it disobeyed the trade laws. But few other attempts at enforcement were made. A report to the British government in 1766 stated:

> It was a matter of wonder to see what little care was taken to enforce the laws. The open breaking of the Acts of Trade and the disgraceful misuse of office which was common in most of the ports could not escape notice. The merchants had regularly undertaken those voyages which provided the greatest gain. They gave no further thought to their illegality than that the custom house must be silenced. The means for which was easily understood.

Restrictions on Colonial Industry

In 1699, Parliament took the first step to control colonial manufacturing. The English government did not want the colonies to make goods that could be made in England. English sheep raisers, manufacturers of woolen goods, and merchants who sold wool and woolen cloth were concerned about the growth of the colonial woolen industry. Some colonies were producing and using their own woolen goods and even exporting them to other colonies.

English merchants, manufacturers, and farmers asked Parliament for help. The result was the Woolen Act. Under this act, no raw wool, yarn, or wool cloth could be exported from one colony to another or to foreign countries. In this way, the English had a market in the colonies that did not produce wool.

Other laws followed the Woolen Act. In 1732, Parliament passed the Hat Act that forbade any colony from exporting beaver hats. It also limited the number of apprentices a hatmaker could have. In 1750, the Iron Act forbade the building of iron mills.

The effect of these laws on colonial industry was great. The laws forced the colonists to buy more of their goods from England. Often, these goods were sold to the colonists at higher prices than if the items had been made in the colonies.

GOVERNMENT OF THE COLONIES

Throughout the 1600s, as you may recall from the unit Colonial Beginnings, the colonists and the English government often disagreed

In the 1700s, colonial industries were starting to grow. These pictures show a cooper, or barrel maker, and a blacksmith. How did the British try to stop the colonists from selling the goods they made in place of British-made products?

about the governing of the colonies. This conflict occurred in almost every English colony in America and continued into the 1700s.

Rights of the English

The colonists felt that they were English subjects with the same rights as people living in England. Through the centuries, the English had been able to add to their rights even as their monarchs were gaining more power in Europe. These rights of the English were contained in several documents.

The first was the Magna Carta (MAG-nuh KAHRT-uh), or Great Charter. It was written in 1215. The Magna Carta established the right of the English to freedom from arrest without cause. Trial by a jury of one's peers, or equals, was also established. The Magna Carta also stated that no laws could be made without the consent of a council of nobles. Taxes could not be set except by consent of the nobles. The council grew into the English Parliament.

In 1628, the Petition of Right further limited the rights of the English monarchs. A **petition** (puh-TISH-uhn) is a request. The petition stated that the monarchs could not force people to provide food or housing for soldiers. Nor could the people be tried by a military court during peacetime. No English subject could be put in prison without a trial. The petition reinforced the right that no taxes could be set without the consent of Parliament.

The English Bill of Rights of 1689 again stated that the monarch could not tax the people without Parliament's consent. A **bill of rights** is a statement of the rights of individuals. According to this document, the monarch could not put aside a law without the consent of Parliament. The Bill of Rights gave the people the right to freedom of

Philadelphia's location on the Delaware River and near forests made it a center for shipbuilding. How did the Navigation Acts affect this colonial industry?

In 1734, Peter Zenger was accused of printing false statements in his newspaper about the governor of New York. Zenger was found innocent, and his trial was a major victory in the fight for freedom of the press.

speech and the right to petition. It also banned large fines as well as cruel and unusual punishments. This Bill of Rights greatly influenced the later writing of the Bill of Rights in the U.S. Constitution. You will read more about this in the unit A Plan of Government.

Control in the Colonies

Because of these rights, colonists expected to have some control over their government. They also expected to be taxed only by their elected representatives. As you read earlier in this chapter, the English government had a different viewpoint. Because of mercantilism, they believed the colonies were established to benefit England. Any right, such as self-government, came from England, and the colonists had only those rights England wished to give them.

As part of this policy, England set up a Board of Trade. It was to advise the monarch on colonial trade and government. The board recommended people as colonial officials and sent orders to colonial governors. The board also advised the monarch whether to accept or reject laws passed by colonial legislatures.

By the mid-1700s, there were three types of colonial government. New Hampshire, Massachusetts, New York, New Jersey, Virginia, North Carolina, South Carolina, and Georgia had all been made royal colonies. Proprietors continued to run Pennsylvania, Delaware, and Maryland. Connecticut and Rhode Island were allowed to remain self-governing. All three types had a governor and a legislature.

The Governor

As you may recall from the unit Colonial Beginnings, the main difference in the three forms of government was the way the governor was selected. In royal colonies, the monarch appointed the governor. In proprietary colonies, the proprietors, or owners, appointed him. In the third form—the most independent of the three—the voters elected the governor. The way the governor was chosen made a great difference in the amount of freedom each colony had.

Generally, the governor's job in a royal colony was to see that the legislatures passed laws that benefited Great Britain. At the same time, he was to oppose laws that were unfavorable. Governors in all colonies could veto any law passed by the legislatures. **Veto** (VEE-toh) means to reject or forbid a proposed law.

The Legislature

The governor and his advisors, the council, usually formed the upper house of the legislature. In most royal and proprietary colonies, council members were appointed by the monarch or proprietor. This was usually at the governor's suggestion. In Massachusetts, the upper house was chosen by the lower house. In Connecticut and Rhode Island, upper house members were elected by the colonists. In all colonies, the governor and council acted as the highest court. Judges for lower courts were appointed by the governor.

The lower house, often called the assembly, was made up of representatives elected by the colonists. This two-house system was similar to Parliament. Elections to the legislature were supposed to be held every two years. However, some royal governors, such as Berkeley of Virginia, refused to call elections for years.

The colonial legislatures were important. They passed many laws on local affairs. It was also in these legislatures that the rights of the colonists were protected. The legislatures had the right to set taxes and decide the salaries of the governors and judges. By refusing to pay the governor's salary, the legislatures found they could pass laws that displeased the governor. In order to be paid, the governor had to accept the laws.

Changes in Voting Requirements

The legislature was the place where colonists' rights were defended. The rules covering who could and could not vote for these lawmakers were important. In the early days of the colonies, religious and property requirements gave the right to vote to only a few men, as you may recall from the unit Colonial Beginnings. In parts of New England, only Puritans could vote. In the early royal colonies, voting was kept to members of the Anglican Church. In many colonies, Roman Catholics, Jews, Baptists, and Quakers could not vote.

Everywhere, a man had to own property in order to vote. Although women could own property, they could not vote in any colony. Indentured servants and slaves could not vote either. In time, voting requirements changed. Church membership became less important in New England, and nonmembers were given the right to vote. Property

Governor William Tryon talks to a group of angry North Carolinians called Regulators. These people were from the frontier and believed the government of the colony did not care about their problems. What group in the 1600s had a similar complaint?

requirements also changed. In some colonies, a man could own property other than land. For example, a merchant who did not own his shop could claim ownership of his goods as property. In other colonies, in order to vote a man could pay a tax rather than own property.

The changing requirements also saw a change in the type of voter. The earliest colonial voters were mostly men of the upper class. Some members of the middle class could also vote. You may recall from the unit Colonial Beginnings that the wealthy planters' control of the House of Burgesses was one cause of Bacon's Rebellion. But in the 1700s, settlement spread onto the frontier. There, cheap and abundant land made it possible for more men to meet the property requirements for voting. By the mid-1700s, probably 85 percent of adult male colonists were qualified to vote.

LOOKING BACK

1. Why did Parliament want to have control over: **a.** colonial trade? **b.** colonial industry?
★ 2. Use the line graph to answer the following questions: **a.** Which year saw the least amount of taxes collected? **b.** Which year saw the largest amount? **c.** Did the tax revenue go up or down from 1765 to 1774?
3. List two advantages and disadvantages of the trade laws for the colonists.
4. **a.** How did the English government view the purpose of the colonies? **b.** Did the colonies agree or disagree with this? **c.** How do you think the colonists' view could lead to war?
5. Scanning pages 188-189 will help you answer these questions. What were the duties of each of the following parts of colonial government: **a.** governor? **b.** council? **c.** legislature?
6. List two changes in voting requirements in the colonies.

Chapter 2   The French in North America

LOOKING AHEAD

This chapter is about French settlements in North America. The French made their living by trading for furs with Native Americans. But the fur trade and European conflicts caused fighting between the French and British in North America. This rivalry was finally settled in the French and Indian War. After you study this chapter, you will be able to:

- compare and contrast French and British settlements in North America before the French and Indian War.
- ★ read pictures to make inferences about the French and Indian War.
- list the sequence of events in the French and Indian War.
- identify Pontiac's Rebellion as one effect of the French and Indian War.

Social Studies Vocabulary

proclamation

People

Robert Dinwiddie	William Pitt	Ottawa
George Washington	James Wolfe	George Grenville
Benjamin Franklin	Iroquois	

Places

Port Royal	Fort Duquesne
Ohio River valley	Louisbourg
St. Lawrence River valley	Quebec

Words and Terms

intendant	Albany Plan of Union	Proclamation
land speculation	Treaty of Paris	of 1763

Events

French and Indian War	Pontiac's Rebellion

Benjamin Franklin printed this snake in 1754 to show what would happen if the colonies did not unite. Why did they refuse to accept his plan of union?

As you may recall from the unit Europeans as Explorers, French explorers traveled along the St. Lawrence and Mississippi rivers in the 1600s. By the early 1700s, the French controlled these two important water routes into the interior of North America.

Unlike the British, few French followed the explorers to settle in North America. They preferred life in France to the hardships of

This painting shows the French influence on the Micmac people. Note the clothing and weapons. What other French influences do you see? What can you infer from the woman's cross?

frontier life. Also, land was not so available in New France as it was in the British colonies. Much of the best land belonged to friends of the French monarch. The little farming that was done was by tenant farmers. Like the Dutch, few French were interested in working another's land. As a result of the lack of colonists, New France depended on France for supplies, including food.

Like New Spain, New France was strictly controlled from Europe. French colonists had no self-government. A governor, appointed by the monarch, ruled. The monarch also appointed an intendant (in-TEN-duhnt), who reported directly to the monarch about what was going on in the colony. New France also had a council. It was made up of the governor, intendant, bishop of New France, and a few important colonists named by the monarch.

The French, like other Europeans, wanted to convert the Native Americans to Christianity. Roman Catholic missionaries came with the first explorers and later with the colonists. These missionaries lived among the Native Americans and tried to teach them Christianity and French ways of life.

FUR TRADE AND NATIVE AMERICANS

Although New France did not attract farmers, it did attract fur traders. They traded knives, guns, blankets, jewelry, and alcohol to the Native Americans for furs. The furs were then shipped to France and sold. Furs were the only profitable export New France had. To protect their fur trade, the French built a line of forts along the St. Lawrence and

Mississippi rivers. These forts offered protection to the traders and served as trading posts. Present U.S. cities such as Detroit, Michigan, and Green Bay, Wisconsin, grew out of these early forts.

Because the fur trade was so important, the French kept on friendly terms with many Native American peoples. The French traded with the Natchez and Quapaw (KWAW-paw) of the lower Mississippi, the Miami and Peoria of Illinois, and the Huron and Algonquin (al-GONG-kin) near the St. Lawrence, among other groups.

The French did not threaten the Native Americans the way the English did. There were few French colonists. Most were fur traders and missionaries who lived among the Native Americans. There were many more English and few were traders. Most were settlers who destroyed forests, drove away game, and cleared land for farming. Because the French were mainly interested in trade, they did not disturb the natural environment. Unlike the English coastal settlements, the interior remained unchanged and was still filled with game. By the mid-1700s, the Native Americans in the interior had not yet run out of furs for trade.

FRENCH-BRITISH RIVALRY

Like the French, English colonists in North America traded with the Native Americans. Throughout the 1600s and early 1700s, competition between traders of the two nations caused trouble. One problem in particular was trade with the Iroquois. You read in the unit Colonial Beginnings that the English took over the profitable Dutch fur trade in New York. In order to get more furs to trade with the English, the Iroquois kept pushing west. They soon ran into Native American peoples who traded with the French. This caused conflict between the Iroquois and Native Americans friendly to the French.

In addition, fur traders and settlers from the British colonies were moving west by the early 1700s. Some were crossing the Appalachians. The fur traders wanted more business while the settlers wanted land to farm. These colonists soon ran into the French.

Early Colonial Wars

French and British rivalry in North America was matched by their rivalry in Europe. From 1688 to 1763, England and France were either at war or preparing for war with each other. Often, these European wars spread to America and touched off fighting in areas claimed by both countries.

The first three wars in the colonies did not settle French and English claims. Much of the fighting took place on the frontier or at Port Royal. This was an important French fort in what is now Nova Scotia (NOH-vuh SKOH-shuh). The French and their Native American allies attacked the English in New England and New York. Much of the English war effort was spent trying to capture Port Royal or raiding Native

rivalry (RY-vuhl-ree): competition

193

American villages. The Native Americans received guns and supplies from the French. Because of this, the English knew they would have to defeat the French for a lasting peace.

FRENCH AND INDIAN WAR

Because of the explorations they financed, both France and Great Britain claimed four areas of North America. These areas were Nova Scotia, present-day northern New York, the Great Lakes area, and the Ohio River valley.

Few Europeans lived in the Ohio River valley. A few French forts housed some soldiers, traders, and missionaries. The British had several forts along their western frontier. Besides the profitable fur trade, however, the British were interested in the Ohio River valley for land speculation. Land speculation (spek-yuh-LAY-shuhn) is buying land in hope of selling it later at a profit. In the late 1740s, some British colonists began buying up land on the frontier at low prices. They hoped later to sell it to immigrants.

In 1753, to enforce their claim to the Ohio River valley, the French built forts at Presque Isle (presk YL), Le Boeuf (luh BUHF), and Venango (vih-NANG-goh) in what is now western Pennsylvania. Governor Robert Dinwiddie of Virginia, a land speculator, sent young George Washington to demand that the French leave. The land had been given to Virginia in its 1609 charter. The French refused.

The following year, Washington returned with some soliders to build Fort Necessity, near the French Fort Duquesne (doo-KAYN). A force of French and Native Americans captured Washington and his troops. They were later set free. Although war would not be declared until 1756, the French and Indian War had begun.

Fighting the War

At the beginning of the French and Indian War, British battle plans called for the capture of Fort Duquesne and of French forts along the St. Lawrence River. By 1757, the British had suffered defeat after defeat. In that year, William Pitt as secretary of state took over the war effort. He sent additional soldiers and supplies from Great Britain and replaced losing generals. Pitt also called for troops from the colonies.

In order to defeat the French, the British decided to capture their capital, Quebec. Before that could be done, however, several key French forts had to be taken. In 1758, the British captured Louisbourg (LOO-is-berg) and Fort Duquesne. In 1759, they took Forts Ticonderoga (ty-kahn-duhr-OH-guh), Crown Point, Frontenac (FRAHN-tuhn-ak), and Niagara. The way to Quebec was clear.

By July, the British under General James Wolfe reached Quebec. After several months of minor battles, the British captured the city in September. With the French capital taken, the war in America was over by 1760. However, fighting continued in Europe until 1763.

FRENCH AND INDIAN WAR: ADVANTAGES AND DISADVANTAGES OF EACH SIDE

	Advantages		Disadvantages	
	French Colonies	**British Colonies**	**French Colonies**	**British Colonies**
Military	Had the strongest army in the world Had more Native American allies than did the British colonies	Had most powerful navy so it could control the seas		Had only one Native American ally—the Iroquois
Political	Had one government to direct all activities			Had 13 separate governments
Economic		Were self-supporting and actually exported food and other goods	Were not self supporting; depended on supplies from France	
Population	Had one language so communication was easy	Were grouped along the coast Most people had families; were willing to fight for their homes	Had widely scattered settlements that were difficult to defend Had few colonists; most were fur traders who had no families	Had several immigrant groups, each speaking a different language

Albany Plan of Union

While Washington was fighting the French, delegates from seven British colonies met with Iroquois leaders at Albany, New York in 1754. The colonists asked the Iroquois to help them fight the French and their Native American allies. The Iroquois refused. They said the colonists were destroying their hunting grounds. By 1759, the Iroquois could see that the British were winning the war. As a result, they agreed to serve as guides and scouts for the British army.

The Albany meeting, however, was important for another reason. There, Benjamin Franklin, one of the delegates, suggested the Albany Plan of Union. It was based in part on the Iroquois League of Six Nations, which you may recall from the unit The First Americans. The Albany Plan called for a council of representatives chosen by the

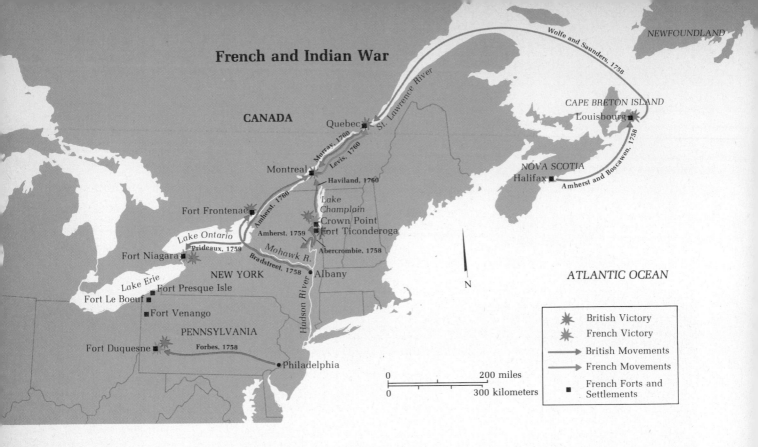

French and Indian War

NEWFOUNDLAND

CANADA

Wolfe and Saunders, 1758

CAPE BRETON ISLAND

Quebec

St. Lawrence River

Louisbourg

Murray, 1760

Montreal

Levis, 1760

Haviland, 1760

NOVA SCOTIA

Halifax

Amherst and Boscawen, 1758

Amherst, 1760

Fort Frontenac

Lake Champlain

Crown Point

Fort Ticonderoga

Lake Ontario

Amherst, 1759

Prideaux, 1759

Mohawk R.

Abercrombie, 1758

Fort Niagara

Bradstreet, 1758

Albany

ATLANTIC OCEAN

Lake Erie

NEW YORK

Fort Presque Isle

N

Fort Le Boeuf

Fort Venango

Hudson River

PENNSYLVANIA

Fort Duquesne

Forbes, 1758

Philadelphia

0   200 miles
0   300 kilometers

* British Victory
* French Victory
→ British Movements
→ French Movements
■ French Forts and Settlements

Left: This is one style of uniform worn by French soldiers. What problems might it have caused on the battlefield?

Right: This picture shows the retreat of General Edward Braddock and his troops from their attempt to capture Fort Duquesne in 1755. Which figures and what actions in the painting would help you see that it shows a retreat?

A British officer drew this view of the siege of Louisbourg. Based on this painting, what do you think it means to lay siege to a place?

BUILDING PICTURE SKILLS

In the last few units, you have been learning how to make inferences from written material. However, you can also make inferences from paintings, photographs, maps, charts, graphs, and cartoons. On these two pages are pictures of people and events of the French and Indian War. **Activity:** Look carefully at the pictures and then answer the questions in the captions.

Left: William Pitt's plan of attack on Canada changed the course of the war and led to a British victory. How can you tell he is an important person?

Below: The British victory at Quebec, shown in this 1760 engraving, ended French control in eastern North America. Where are the British and French troops located? Which side would you say had the greatest disadvantage? Why?

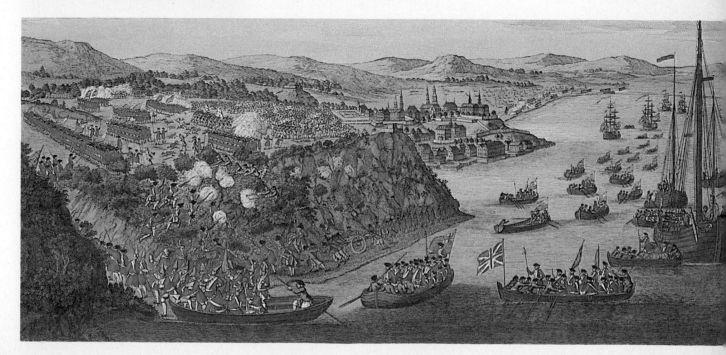

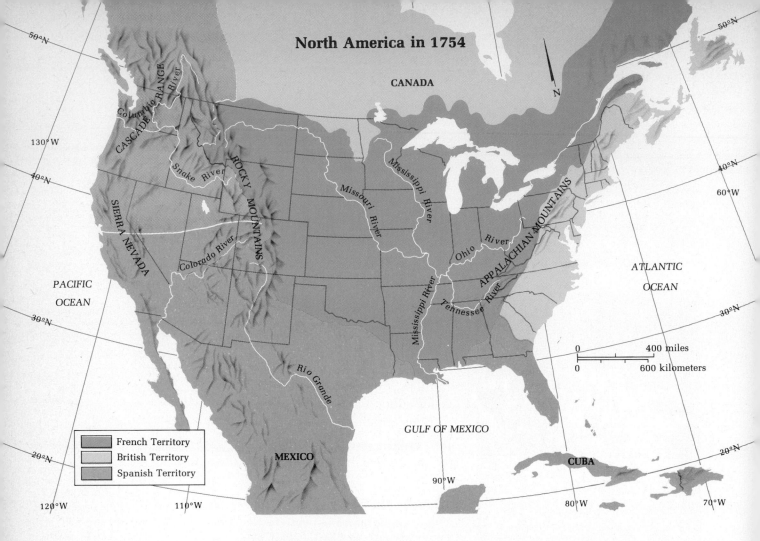

North America in 1754

CANADA

PACIFIC OCEAN

ATLANTIC OCEAN

CASCADE RANGE

Columbia River

Snake River

ROCKY MOUNTAINS

SIERRA NEVADA

Colorado River

Missouri River

Mississippi River

Ohio River

APPALACHIAN MOUNTAINS

Tennessee River

Mississippi River

Rio Grande

GULF OF MEXICO

MEXICO

CUBA

	French Territory
	British Territory
	Spanish Territory

0   400 miles
0   600 kilometers

legislature of each colony. A president-general would be named by the British monarch. The president-general and council would govern the affairs of the colonies when they needed to act together. For example, the president-general and council would make rules for trading with Native Americans.

The colonies rejected Franklin's plan. They did not want to give up any power even to a government of their own representatives. Like the New England Confederation, the Albany Plan of Union was a step toward uniting the colonies.

Results of the War

The Treaty of Paris in 1763 ended the fighting between the British and French. By the terms of the treaty, Great Britain gained Canada and all other French territory east of the Mississippi River. It also received French territories in India and the West Indies. Spain, France's ally, was forced to give Florida to the British. In return, France gave New Orleans and French lands west of the Mississippi to Spain.

For people in the British colonies, there were other results. The colonists had played a large role in fighting the war. By its end, thousands of colonists had fought alongside British soldiers. These colonial soldiers had seen British commanders make mistakes and lose

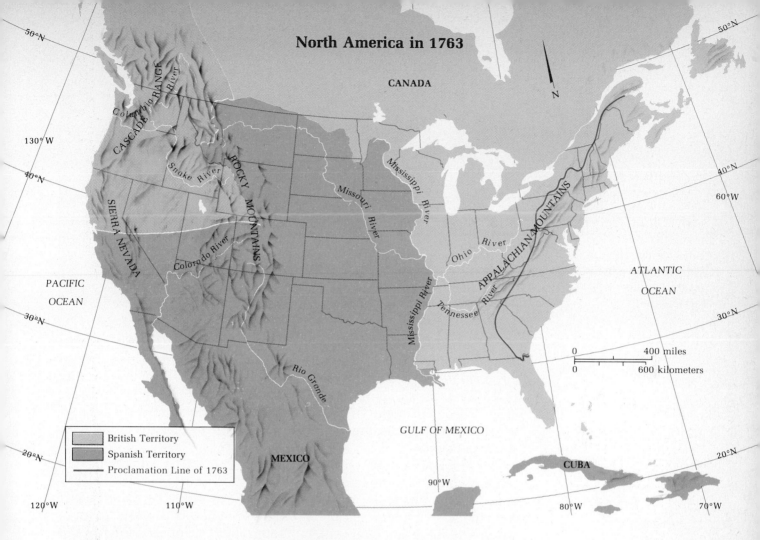

North America in 1763

British Territory
Spanish Territory
Proclamation Line of 1763

battles. The colonists knew the British could be defeated. In little more than 20 years, some of the colonists, such as Washington, would use the fighting skills that they had learned against the British.

The colonies were brought closer together by the French and Indian War. Even though the Albany Plan of Union had been rejected, colonial governments had worked together to defeat a common enemy. People from different colonies got to know one another as they fought side by side. Some of the fear that colonists felt about people from other colonies disappeared.

The war also ended the colonists' fear of the Native Americans on the frontier. The French were no longer there to supply the Native Americans in their attacks on the colonists. The colonists viewed the frontier as open for settlement.

PONTIAC'S REBELLION

Although colonists thought they were free to settle on the frontier, the Native Americans disagreed. In 1763, Pontiac (PAHN-tee-ak), a leader of the Ottawa (AHT-uh-wuh), organized the Ottawa, Lenni Lenape, and other Native Americans along the frontier of Pennsylvania, Maryland, and Virginia. They wanted to clear the land of Europeans.

In 1763, Pontiac, leader of the Ottawa, united a number of Native American peoples to fight colonial expansion on the frontier. Why did they fail?

Pontiac's followers captured eight of the ten forts on the western frontier. Many settlers were killed. The government of Great Britain sent British soldiers into the area and Pontiac's Rebellion was over by 1766. This threat, however, forced the British government under Prime Minister George Grenville to issue the Proclamation of 1763. A **proclamation** (prahk-luh-MAY-shuhn) is an official declaration or announcement.

The Proclamation of 1763 tried to keep the Native Americans and settlers apart. It forbade colonial settlement from west of the Allegheny Mountains to the Mississippi. Any Europeans living in the area were to leave. Traders, settlers, and land speculators protested. Often, farmers looking for land and fur traders and trappers violated the proclamation. However, they risked attacks by Native Americans and punishment by British soldiers. Pontiac's Rebellion had another result. It convinced the government of Great Britain that a British army was needed in the colonies to protect British interests.

LOOKING BACK

1. List the similarities and differences that existed between New France and the 13 British colonies before the French and Indian War. Consider population, government, relations with Native Americans, and economic activity.
2. Prepare a time line of the French and Indian War from the outbreak of fighting to the Treaty of Paris. The time line should include dates and names of major battles and the results of each. Here is an example: 1759, Battle of Quebec; British victory; Ends major fighting of the war.
★ 3. From reading the pictures on pages 196-97, state two things you learned about the way wars were fought in colonial times.
4. How did the end of the French and Indian War affect European-Native American relations on the frontier?

Chapter 3   Revolution in the Making

LOOKING AHEAD

This chapter describes the British government's attempts at tightening control over its North American colonies. You will read about the government's new tax laws and the colonists' protests. You will see how the colonists began to show their growing independence. After you study this chapter, you will be able to:

- describe the continuity and change in the colonial way of life.
- explain the reasons for Grenville's colonial policy.
- describe the idea of taxation without representation.
- describe the reasons for colonists' anger at the Townshend Acts.
- read a line graph to learn about tax revenue from the Sugar and Townshend Acts.
- explain the effects of the Boston Massacre.

Social Studies Vocabulary

boycott	repeal	revolution

People

George Grenville	Daughters of	John Dickinson
Patrick Henry	Liberty	Lord North
Samuel Adams	Sons of Liberty	Crispus Attucks

Words and Terms

writs of assistance	Sugar Act	tyranny
taxation without	Quartering Act	Declaratory Act
representation	Stamp Act	Townshend Acts

Events

Stamp Act Congress	Boston Massacre

The *Pennsylvania Journal* printed this stamp in 1765 to make fun of the Stamp Act. The paper went out of business rather than buy the stamps needed to sell each issue.

By the mid-1700s, the American colonies still shared many things with Great Britain. Most of the people had come from Great Britain or were descended from people who had. Their language was English. Their system of government was modeled after that of Great Britain. The first colonists had brought English law with them and set up the same court system.

In spite of these similarities, differences were developing in the 1700s, as you may recall from the unit Life in Colonial America. More non-English people were coming to the colonies. Their customs,

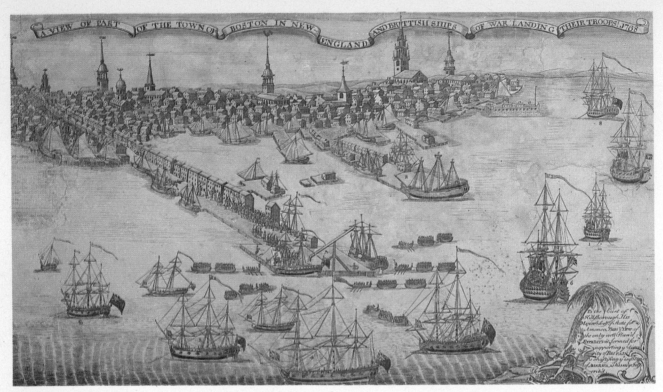

A VIEW OF PART OF THE TOWN OF BOSTON IN NEW ENGLAND AND BRITISH SHIPS OF WAR LANDING THEIR TROOPS! 1768

Paul Revere illustrated the arrival of British warships in Boston Harbor in this 1768 engraving. Why were the ships in the harbor? Is this a primary or a secondary source?

religions, and ways of life added to a growing American culture. The colonists had a better chance for social mobility than had people in Europe. Economically, the colonists were building their own industries and trade routes. The people were becoming able to solve their problems without help from the British government.

Out of these experiences, a new and different people—the Americans—were developing. This shows continuity and change at work. While all this was happening, however, the British government was attempting to tighten its control of the colonists.

GRENVILLE'S COLONIAL POLICIES

After the French and Indian War, the British Parliament took a new look at the laws governing its North American colonies. The war had helped the colonists by driving the French from North America. As a result, Parliament felt the colonists should be taxed to help pay the cost of the war. Many members of Parliament also felt the mercantile laws should be enforced.

Besides issuing the Proclamation of 1763 that you read about in the last chapter, Prime Minister Grenville had Parliament pass new laws to tax the colonies. He also called for strict enforcement of the Navigation Acts. In 1761, the British began using writs, or orders, of assistance to search for smuggled goods and collect unpaid customs duties. In addition, British warships were sent to patrol the coasts. Smugglers were to be captured and tried without a jury. This was against one of the basic rights of English subjects.

Taxation Without Representation

In 1764, Grenville had Parliament pass the Sugar Act. It was meant to strengthen the Molasses Act of 1733 that you read about in Chapter 1 of this unit. The new law reduced the tax on molasses brought into the colonies from British and non-British ports. Although this seemed to benefit colonial merchants, it did not. Before this, they had smuggled molasses from the French colonies as part of the Triangular Trade and never paid the tax. With stricter enforcement of the Navigation Acts, the colonists were no longer able to smuggle goods easily. They had to pay the tax or do without. Profits dropped sharply.

The colonists protested that the act was taxation without representation. Each colonial charter included the idea that people living in the colonies had the same rights as those living in England. One right of the English was the right to tax themselves through their representatives in Parliament. The monarch could not order a tax to be paid. Parliament had to vote on it. The colonists claimed they had no representation in Parliament. They claimed they could be taxed only by their own legislatures. Because colonial legislatures had not passed the Sugar Act, the colonists claimed it was taxation without representation. The British government rejected this argument. It claimed that Parliament made laws for British colonies as well as Great Britain.

The Quartering Act

After the Proclamation of 1763, Grenville sent a British army to the colonies. To save money, Grenville had Parliament pass the Quartering Act of 1765. Through it, the colonists had to provide housing and

quarter: to provide a place to live

Patrick Henry was a strong supporter of colonial self-rule. Here he speaks out in the Virginia assembly against taxation without representation. This engraving was done in 1856. Is it a primary or a secondary source?

supplies, such as bedding, candles, salt, beer, and rum, for the soldiers. Colonists feared that this law would lead to a permanent British army in the colonies. It would be an army the colonists would have to support.

The Stamp Act

Grenville went even further in his efforts to raise money from the colonists. He persuaded Parliament to pass a stamp act. Under this law, a special stamp had to be bought and placed on almost every kind of document colonists were likely to use. Wills, marriage licenses, newspapers, playing cards, advertisements, and even diplomas needed tax stamps. People in England had been paying this tax since 1694. The British government thought that through the Stamp Act the colonists would be paying their share of the cost of government.

The Sugar Act had been paid directly by only a few colonial merchants. The Stamp Act was felt by almost every colonist. It was also the first tax that the British government had placed on goods made and used in the colonies. The other taxes were on goods brought into or sent out of the colonies. Those taxes were supposed to regulate trade according to the policy of mercantilism.

The cry of taxation without representation rose again. In the House of Burgesses, Patrick Henry challenged the tyranny of Parliament. Tyranny (TIR-uh-nee) is rule by a person or persons without regard for justice. Henry declared that only the colonial legislatures had the right to tax the colonists. The other members of the House cheered. Samuel Adams voiced similar feelings in Massachusetts. Where would the British stop? "If our trade may be taxed, why not our lands?" he asked. The Massachusetts legislature asked for a meeting of all the colonies to discuss the Stamp Act. Nine sent delegates to a meeting in New York City.

Debate and Action

The meeting was known as the Stamp Act Congress. It was the first attempt by the colonies to discuss their common problems with the British. After days of debate, the Congress sent a petition to the government. They declared their loyalty to the monarch. They also agreed that the government had the right to regulate trade. But they restated their argument that the Sugar and Stamp acts were taxation without representation.

The statement from the Stamp Act Congress was not the only action the colonists took. Angry merchants in Boston, New York, Baltimore, and other cities decided to boycott British goods until the act was repealed. **Boycott** means to refuse to buy or sell a product, or deal with a group as a protest or punishment. **Repeal** (rih-PEEL) means to cancel a law. Colonial women organized into Daughters of Liberty to boycott British goods. Because of the boycott, British merchants began to lose customers and money. British unemployment rose as

This was one of the many stamps printed under the Stamp Act. Why were the stamps never used?

New Hampshire citizens are shown throwing stones at a figure representing a stamp collector. What effect did such actions have on stamp collectors?

unsold goods piled up. As their losses grew, British merchants began to ask Parliament to repeal the Stamp Act.

While this was happening some men took to the streets as Sons of Liberty. They overturned carriages, broke windows, and burned tax stamps. The mobs frightened both the merchants who would use the stamps and the tax collectors who would sell them. For example, a Boston mob attacked the home of Andrew Oliver, a tax collector, and the next day, he resigned.

Because of the opposition to the Stamp Act, most tax collectors had quit before the law ever went into effect. Most tax stamps remained locked in British forts and warships.

Repeal of the Stamp Act

Grenville lost his post as prime minister in 1765 and Parliament repealed the Stamp Act the next year. Parliament gave in because of the protests of British merchants and rising unemployment. However, the government insisted that it had the right to govern the colonies, including the right to tax them.

After the repeal, Parliament passed the Declaratory (dih-KLAR-uh-taw-ree) Act. This was a declaration, or statement, that "the American colonies have been, are, and of right ought to be controlled by and dependent on the King and Parliament of Great Britain. Parliament has full power to make laws for these colonies in all cases whatsoever." The repeal of the Stamp Act solved the immediate problem. However, the question of taxing the colonies was still unsettled.

TOWNSHEND ACTS

Colonists greeted the repeal of the Stamp Act with fireworks, dinners, and other celebrations. The boycott of British goods was lifted, and orders from the colonies flooded British manufacturers. Some colo-

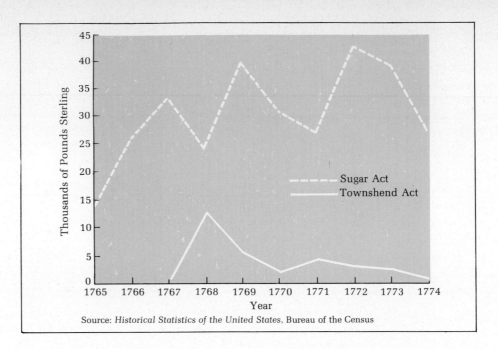

Tax Revenue from the Sugar and Townshend Acts

Source: *Historical Statistics of the United States*, Bureau of the Census

nial leaders even hoped for friendly relations with the British government. Little attention was paid to the Declaratory Act.

In May 1767, Parliament passed a new set of laws taxing the colonists. These laws came to be called the Townshend (TOWN-zuhnd) Acts. They were named for the head of the British treasury, Charles Townshend. Taxes were placed on many imported goods such as glass, lead, paper, and tea. Townshend mistakenly believed that the colonists would not oppose taxes on imported goods. He did not understand the taxation without representation problem.

The colonists were especially upset by the use of some of the money raised by the Townshend Acts. Some of it would pay the salaries of royal governors and judges in the colonies. As you may recall, colonial legislatures had the right to pay these officials. By withholding salaries, the legislatures could pass bills that the governors did not like. If the British government paid the governors directly, the colonial legislatures would lose this power. To the colonists, this meant loss of control over their most important officials.

Colonial Resistance

Once again, the colonists protested this attempt to take away their rights. Samuel Adams of Boston wrote articles attacking the British government. John Dickinson, a political leader in Pennsylvania and Delaware, spoke out against the Townshend Acts. In *Letters from a Farmer in Pennsylvania*, he described how many Americans felt about the Townshend Acts.

I am a farmer settled near the banks of the river Delaware in the province of Pennsylvania. My farm is small, and my servants are few and good. I spend a good deal of time in my library. I believe I have received a greater share of knowledge in history and the laws and constitution of my country than is generally gained by men of my class.

There is an act of Parliament which seems to me to destroy the liberty of these colonies. That law places duties on paper, glass, etc. It appears to me to be illegal. Parliament unquestionably holds the legal authority to regulate the trade of Great Britain and all its colonies. Such an authority is necessary for the common good of all. But Mr. Pitt's words are these [William Pitt, a member of Parliament],

'This kingdom, as the supreme governing and legislative power, has always bound the colonies by regulations and restrictions in trade, in navigation, in manufactures — in every thing except that of taking their money out of their pockets, without their consent.'

Hear then, let my countrymen rouse themselves, and behold the ruin hanging over their heads! If they once admit that Great Britain may lay duties upon exports to us for the sake of taxing us only, then American liberty is finished.

In addition to written protests, colonial merchants boycotted British goods as they had during the Stamp Act crisis. Colonial legislatures joined in the rising protest. The Massachusetts legislature sent a letter to the other colonies calling for resistance to the Townshend Acts. In New York, the legislature refused to supply British soldiers under the Quartering Act. The British government answered by dis-

crisis (KRY-sis): dangerous time

Paul Revere's engraving of the Boston Massacre shows British soldiers firing on unarmed citizens. The printing of this picture spread anti-British feeling throughout the colonies.

missing the legislatures of both colonies. British soldiers arrived in Boston from Canada to protect the royal governor from harm by the colonists.

By 1770, it seemed as though Great Britain and the colonies were headed toward armed conflict. To ease the tension, King George III appointed a new prime minister, Lord Frederick North. As a first step, Lord North proposed to repeal the Townshend Acts. However, on the day Parliament repealed the taxes, a fight broke out between colonists and British soldiers in Boston.

THE BOSTON MASSACRE

British soldiers had been sent to Boston to make sure colonial protests remained peaceful. The colonists were angered by armed soldiers on their streets. On March 5, 1770, a British soldier was being teased by a colonial mob. He called for help from nearby soldiers. The colonists began throwing snowballs, and the soldiers panicked. They fired into the crowd, killing five people and wounding six. Among those killed was a free black sailor and member of the Sons of Liberty, Crispus Attucks (AT-uhks).

The killing outraged Boston colonists, who called it the Boston Massacre (MAS-uh-kuhr). To calm colonial tempers, the British withdrew their troops to a fort in Boston Harbor. Tales of the Boston Massacre spread throughout the colonies, fanning the fires of revolution. **Revolution** (rev-uh-LOO-shuhn) means a basic change in or complete overthrow of a government, political system, or society.

LOOKING BACK

1. How was life in the British colonies in the mid-1700s both: **a.** the same as it had been? **b.** changing into something American?
2. Why did Grenville ask for: **a.** strict enforcement of the Navigation Acts? **b.** new taxes on the colonists?
3. **a.** What did the colonists mean by taxation without representation? **b.** What was the British government's answer to this idea?
4. **a.** What two things about the Townshend Acts angered the colonists? **b.** List two things the colonists did to protest them. **c.** List two things the British government did in answer to the protests.
5. Use the line graph in this chapter to answer the following questions: **a.** What years does the graph cover? **b.** Which year saw the greatest tax revenue? **c.** Which year saw the least? **d.** Compare the graph on page 185 that shows revenue for the Navigation Acts. Which set of acts, the Navigation or the Sugar and Townshend Acts, collected the most taxes?
6. What effect did the Boston Massacre have on: **a.** the colonists? **b.** the British?

A cartoon like a piece of writing has a topic. What is this cartoon about?

PRACTICING YOUR SKILLS

What If . . . One result of the French and Indian War was that France lost its North American empire. It lost present-day Canada and all its territory east of the Mississippi River. **What if** the French and their Native American allies had won the French and Indian War? How would the results of the war have been affected? Depending on where you live, how might your life be different?

Discussing Do you think the Boston Massacre was important? Or do you think it was a small incident used by those who favored independence to gain support? Be prepared to give reasons for your view.

Writing, Graphing, Researching, Making a Table

1. Write a paragraph comparing the purpose and the results of the Albany Plan of Union with those of the New England Confederation.
2. In Chapter 1 of this unit you read that Great Britain wanted a favorable balance of trade. You also learned about a line graph. Research in an almanac or the *U.S. Statistical Abstract* the U.S. balance of trade over the last ten years. Make a line graph to show it. Has the balance of trade been favorable or unfavorable?
3. In Chapter 2 of this unit you read that the French and the British fought three wars in the 1700s before the French and Indian War. Using reference materials, make a list showing the names of each of the colonial wars fought in America. Next to each war, write a brief statement of its results.

Exploring In Chapters 1 and 3 of this unit you read how the British government placed taxes on some items the colonists imported. Today, in the U.S., there are sales taxes, property taxes, and federal, state, and local income taxes. Sales tax is one of the most common forms of taxation. List five items that are subject to state sales tax in your state. What is the tax rate or percentage of sales tax in your state?

Building Study Skills

To **paraphrase** (PAR-uh-frayz) means to rewrite another's words into your own. Sometimes writing a paraphrase can be helpful in making the meaning of the original clearer. For example, paraphrasing some of the primary sources in this textbook might make them easier to understand. Paraphrasing is also an important skill in writing speeches, papers, and book reports. You may not use an author's exact words unless you clearly state by quotation marks that you are quoting the material, but you may paraphrase. Here are a few tips to help you with paraphrasing.

- Use your own words.
- Make sure you include the main idea and supporting details.
- Do not add your own ideas.
- Make your paraphrase shorter than the original material.

Activity: Paraphrase the passage from Dickinson's *Letters from a Farmer in Pennsylvania* on pages 206-207.

Reading

Dickinson, Alice. *Stamp Act: Taxation Without Representation is Tyranny.* New York: Watts, 1976.

Dobler, Lavinia and Edgar A. Toppen. *Pioneers and Patriots: The Lives of Six Negroes of the Revolutionary Era.* New York: Doubleday, 1965.

Knollenberg, Bernhard. *The Growth of the American Revolution, 1766-1775.* Riverside, New Jersey: Free Press, 1975. Primary sources.

Reeder, Colonel Red. *The French and Indian War.* New York: Elsevier/Nelson, 1972. As seen through the eyes of soldiers and settlers.

UNIT III **THE AMERICAN REVOLUTION**

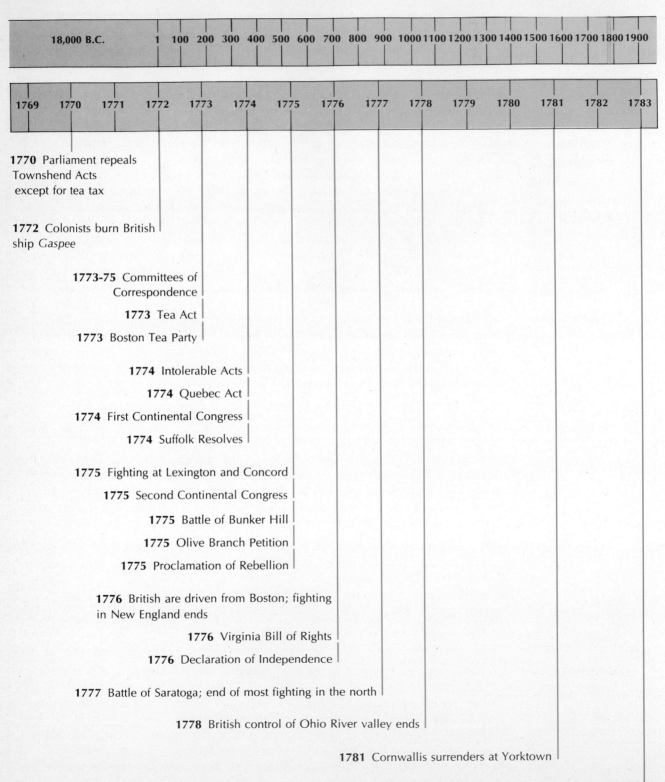

18,000 B.C.	1	100	200	300	400	500	600	700	800	900	1000	1100	1200	1300	1400	1500	1600	1700	1800	1900

1769	1770	1771	1772	1773	1774	1775	1776	1777	1778	1779	1780	1781	1782	1783

1770 Parliament repeals
Townshend Acts
except for tea tax

1772 Colonists burn British
ship *Gaspee*

1773-75 Committees of
Correspondence

1773 Tea Act

1773 Boston Tea Party

1774 Intolerable Acts

1774 Quebec Act

1774 First Continental Congress

1774 Suffolk Resolves

1775 Fighting at Lexington and Concord

1775 Second Continental Congress

1775 Battle of Bunker Hill

1775 Olive Branch Petition

1775 Proclamation of Rebellion

1776 British are driven from Boston; fighting
in New England ends

1776 Virginia Bill of Rights

1776 Declaration of Independence

1777 Battle of Saratoga; end of most fighting in the north

1778 British control of Ohio River valley ends

1781 Cornwallis surrenders at Yorktown

1783 Treaty of Paris

Chapter 1   From Protest to Warfare

LOOKING AHEAD

This chapter describes the events from 1770 to 1775 that led to the decision by the American colonies to break away from Great Britain. You will read about the laws that caused the Boston Tea Party, the First Continental Congress, and the fighting at Lexington and Concord in 1775. After you study this chapter, you will be able to:

- list the chronology that led to the Boston Tea Party.
- identify the restrictions placed on Massachusetts by the Intolerable Acts.
- identify actions taken by the First Continental Congress.
- describe the writer's point of view in the statement about the fighting at Lexington and Concord.

Social Studies Vocabulary

compromise

People

Thomas Hutchinson	Patrick Henry	King George III
Samuel Adams	Patriots	William Pitt
Thomas Gage	Tories	Edmund Burke

Places

Boston	Lexington	Concord

Events

Boston Tea Party   First Continental Congress

Words and Terms

Committees of Correspondence	Quebec Act province	Declaration of Rights and Grievances
Tea Act	Suffolk Resolves	
Intolerable Acts	militia	

Just as modern merchants do, merchants in the 1700s put identifying labels on the goods they sold. This label was used on the teas that came from the shop of Robert Fogg.

In spring 1770, Parliament repealed the Townshend Acts, except the tax on tea. That tax was kept to show the colonists Parliament had the right to tax them. With the repeal of the Townshend Acts, conditions in the colonies improved. Colonial trade increased and the profits of colonial merchants grew. However, it was a false peace. Problems between the British government and the colonists would continue as long as Parliament believed it could tax them.

In 1773, colonists dressed as Native Americans emptied 340 chests of tea into Boston Harbor. How did Parliament respond to the "tea party"?

FANNING THE FIRES OF REVOLUTION

Although relations between Great Britain and the colonies were generally peaceful, several events kept the colonists stirred up. The first involved the British ship, *Gaspee*. It was sent to the colonies to enforce British trade laws and prevent smuggling. In June 1772, the *Gaspee* ran aground off Providence, Rhode Island. That night, colonists burned the ship. The British government demanded that the guilty be tried in England for their crime. The colonists saw this as another attempt to take away their rights as British subjects. According to English law, all subjects had the right to a trial by a jury of their neighbors.

A second incident occurred at about the same time. Governor Thomas Hutchinson of Massachusetts claimed that he should be paid by the British government, not the legislature. This claim brought up the same issue that the Townshend Acts had. Who should control colonial governors—Parliament or the colonists?

Committees of Correspondence

Samuel Adams of Massachusetts was against the British government's paying colonial officials. More importantly, he believed in independence for the colonies. He was one of the first supporters of this idea. To encourage a break with Great Britain, Adams helped form Committees of Correspondence in New England in 1773.

Within two years, all the colonies had Committees of Correspondence. Their objective was to inform people about what was happening in other colonies. The letters from the committees reminded the colonists of their rights and of every wrong that Great Britain had

correspondence (kor-uh-SPAHN-duhns): communicating by letters

212

done or might do. The letters also supported the idea of independence. Throughout the colonies, the committees worked to unite public opinion against Great Britain. But action by Great Britain was needed before the colonists would turn to revolution.

Tea Act and a Tea Party

The fires of revolution burned brighter in spring 1773, when Parliament passed the Tea Act. This act gave the British East India Company a monopoly on exporting tea to the colonies. Under the Tea Act, the British East India Company also picked the colonial merchants who could sell East India Company tea. Other merchants in New York, Philadelphia, and Boston protested. They felt the Tea Act would put many of them out of business. In addition, they felt that if the tea could be controlled by hand-picked merchants, other products such as cloth, tools, and spices could be controlled, too.

The Tea Act let stand the tax on tea that was part of the Townshend Acts. The idea that the British government could tax the colonies on any item still angered many colonists. Colonial leaders who favored independence tried to stir the colonists to action. That action came on December 16, 1773. On that night, some 30 to 60 colonists, dressed as Native Americans, boarded three ships in Boston Harbor. In protest against the Tea Act, they dumped tons of tea overboard.

THE INTOLERABLE ACTS

In answer to the Boston Tea Party, Parliament passed several acts to punish Massachusetts. The colonists called these laws the Intolerable (in-TAHL-uhr-uh-buhl) Acts because the colonists thought they were so unfair. The first of these laws was the Boston Port Act. It closed the city's port until the colonists paid the East India Company for the tea.

Other Intolerable Acts were a new Quartering Act and the Administration of Justice Act. To see that the Intolerable Acts were obeyed, Great Britain was sending extra troops to Massachusetts. The Quartering Act required Massachusetts colonists to supply these troops. The Administration of Justice Act stated that a British soldier or official accused of a crime in Massachusetts could be tried outside the colony. The decision depended on whether Massachusetts' governor thought the person would receive a fair trial in the colony.

Another act gave much of the power of the governor of Massachusetts to the monarch. The monarch would now appoint members of the governor's council and other officials. The governor, however, was given the power to forbid town meetings. The British replaced Thomas Hutchinson, the American-born governor of Massachusetts, with General Thomas Gage. Gage was commander in chief of the British army stationed in the colonies.

By passing the Intolerable Acts, Parliament wanted to make an example of Massachusetts. Colonists that behaved like the people of

Boston would be harshly punished. Instead of creating respect for the British government, the Intolerable Acts angered people in all the colonies, not just in Massachusetts. Colonists again felt that their rights as British subjects were being taken away. If the Intolerable Acts could be used against Massachusetts, similar laws could be passed against any colony.

Most American colonists offered support to Massachusetts and the people of Boston. In spring 1774, the Boston Port Act went into effect. In sympathy, shops throughout the colonies closed their doors. Flags flew at half-mast and church bells rang. The Intolerable Acts united many colonists against British control of the colonies.

half-mast: halfway down a flag pole

THE QUEBEC ACT

About the same time the Intolerable Acts were passed, Parliament passed the Quebec Act. It expanded the Province of Quebec — the territory won from France in the French and Indian War — south to the Ohio River valley and west to the Mississippi River. A province (PRAHV-uhns) is a division of a country, similar to a state. The province was to have a government like that of New France. British officials would govern it directly. However, the people could keep their own laws and freedom of religion was allowed for the Roman Catholics in the region.

American colonists saw the law as an attack on their rights. According to the charters of several colonies, much of the area given to Quebec belonged to them. This act seemed to end their westward expansion. In addition, the lack of rights under the new government of Quebec frightened the colonists. French law did not guarantee the same rights as British law did. If the British could govern without such basic rights as trial by jury and the right to vote there, they might do the same to their own colonists. Also, some religious groups, such as the Puritans, resented giving any power to Roman Catholics.

FIRST CONTINENTAL CONGRESS

By mid-1774, the split between the colonies and Great Britain had become serious. Gage in Massachusetts was strictly enforcing the Intolerable Acts. Discontent was spreading to other colonies. Some people began to call for a central meeting or congress of the colonies to discuss the problems with Great Britain. Both the Massachusetts and Virginia legislatures suggested such a meeting.

The First Continental Congress, as it became known, met in Philadelphia in fall 1774. All the colonies except Georgia sent representatives. Georgia's royal governor prevented anyone from being sent. Among the 56 delegates were 30 lawyers, 9 farmers, 9 merchants, 3 millers, 3 public officials, 1 surveyor, and 1 carpenter. Only one delegate had not been born in the colonies. There were no women.

surveyor (suhr-VAY-uhr): one who measures land

214

The First Continental Congress met in 1774 in the Old State House in Philadelphia to discuss the colonies' problems with the British. Why is this building now called Independence Hall?

Each delegate represented his own colony. However, the delegates had to learn to think about what was best for the colonies as a whole. They had to think like Americans, rather than as members of a particular colony. This was one of the most important outcomes of the Congress. Patrick Henry said, "Virginians, Pennsylvanians, New Yorkers, and New Englanders are no more. I am not a Virginian but an American."

More people had been won over to the side of independence since Sam Adams had started the Committees of Correspondence. However, not all, or even most, colonists supported this idea. At the First Continental Congress though, there were a few more delegates who favored independence than were against it.

Suffolk Resolves

Although the delegates did not agree on independence, all opposed the harsh punishment of Massachusetts. To show its opposition, the Congress adopted the Suffolk (SUHF-uhk) Resolves. These four statements received their name from Suffolk County, Massachusetts, where Boston is located.

resolve (rih-ZAHLV): decision

The first of the resolves called for a boycott of British goods by the colonists. To enforce the boycott, an association was formed with committees in each colony. Another resolve refused to accept the British laws that had been passed as punishment for the Boston Tea Party. A third agreed to set up a government in Massachusetts, sepa-

This 1795 engraving shows Tories who have been tarred and feathered being paraded through the streets. Tories were colonists who remained loyal to Great Britain.

subject (SUHB-jikt): under control of

rate from the royal government of Gage. The last resolve asked all colonies to form their own militias. A militia (muh-LISH-uh) is an army made up of citizens rather than professional soldiers.

Declaration of Rights and Grievances

In October 1774, the First Continental Congress approved the Declaration of Rights and Grievances. This document listed the basic rights of British subjects in the colonies, as Congress saw them. Among these rights were the powers to make their own laws and to try criminals in colonial courts. Parliament's right to tax the colonies was rejected.

The delegates agreed that a second congress would meet in Philadelphia, if the British continued to pass laws like the Intolerable Acts. Much was to happen before the Second Continental Congress gathered in May 1775.

Reactions to the Congress

Many colonists, called Patriots, supported the work of the First Continental Congress. However, there were some who were indifferent to it. Others were not pleased with the actions taken by the delegates. They wanted improved relations with Great Britain, not independence. These people, called Tories, would later support Great Britain throughout the Revolutionary War. They would be persecuted by colonists who supported the war and, in the end, lose most of their wealth.

King George III wrote to his prime minister, Lord North, "The New England governments are in a state of rebellion, blows must decide whether they are to be subject to this country or independent." Although King George called for force against the colonies, some members of Parliament urged compromise. A compromise (KAHM-pruh-myz) is a settlement of a conflict by having all parties agree to give up some of their demands.

William Pitt, a British leader, called for the British troops to leave Boston. He also stated that Parliament should stop taxing the colonies. Another leader, Edmund Burke, thought a compromise should be reached because a war would hurt trade in the British empire. He also feared that people in other parts of the empire would want their independence.

LEXINGTON AND CONCORD

General Gage had arrived in Boston in May 1774 to take up his post as governor. He found the people opposing his army at every chance. The colonists were angry because the Boston Port Act had put 7,000 of them out of work. The colonists allowed no lumber for soldier's quarters to enter Boston. When soldiers did get lumber, colonists split the wooden planks so they could not be used. Straw for bedding was burned. Boston merchants refused to sell tools, blankets, or other goods to the army. British soldiers walked the city in groups, because they were not safe alone.

The colonists around Boston had collected guns and ammunition in case of trouble. Some of the supplies were stored at Concord, just outside Boston. Gage decided to remove the chance for violence by taking these supplies.

On the night of April 18, 1775, British troops marched out of Boston and toward Concord. Paul Revere and other Patriots rode into the countryside, announcing the British march. Church bells rang in every village the British passed through. There was no secret about their mission.

Early on the morning of April 19, the 700 British reached Lexington. There, they found about 70 armed colonists. Most were farmers. The British ordered the colonists to leave. They were about to when someone fired a musket. No one knows which side fired first. In 15 minutes, eight colonists were dead. The British moved on to Concord, a short distance away.

Between 300 and 400 colonial militia had gathered at Concord. They attacked the North Bridge, which the British were holding. The fight was over in five minutes and the British were retreating to Boston. All along the line of march, the militia fired on the British from behind trees, stone walls, and farmhouses. The sharpshooting continued all the way back to Boston.

Amos Doolittle made this engraving of the Battle of Lexington in 1775. What advantages did the British soldiers have over the colonists?

This cartoon from 1775 shows the British army looting and burning homes and barns as they retreat from Concord. Who do you think drew this cartoon — a Patriot or a Tory?

With the militia in the countryside, British soldiers did not dare move out of the city. Military support from other colonies helped the Massachusetts militia keep the British troops locked in Boston.

Not everyone supported Massachusetts. There were Tories who sided with the British government. A Tory view of Lexington and Concord was expressed by Peter Oliver, once the Chief Justice of Massachusetts' Superior Court.

After the Battle of Lexington, there was a general uproar which soon extended throughout the continent. Adams and his followers sounded the trumpet of rebellion. News of the battle flew rapidly. People told one another the sad story of the king's troops burning houses and putting the inhabitants of towns to death. No groups ever worked harder to spread the worst lies in order to make the colonists turn to violence. They added untrue details to the stories and suppressed the truth. At last, General Gage found ways to spread the truth to people who had kept their tempers cool. As for those who believed the lies, he could not change their minds.

suppress (suh-PRES): to hold back, to stop

LOOKING BACK

1. Scan pages 212-213 and list the events that led to the Boston Tea Party.
2. How did the Intolerable Acts punish the colonists of Massachusetts?
3. State two actions taken by the First Continental Congress that were steps toward independence.
4. a. In the reading about the fighting at Lexington and Concord, what was the writer's point of view? b. Was the writer a Tory or a Patriot? c. Paraphrase the passage to help you decide.

Chapter 2   Decision to Break Away

LOOKING AHEAD

This chapter is about the events from May 1775 to July 1776. During this time, the colonists and the British fought at Bunker Hill, Patriots wrote pamphlets for independence, and the Second Continental Congress moved toward a declaration of independence. After you study this chapter, you will be able to:

- identify actions taken by the Second Continental Congress.
- explain the continuity and change in the purpose of the First and Second Continental Congresses.
- identify the reasons why the Second Continental Congress moved toward independence so slowly.
- describe the chronology for writing the Declaration of Independence.

People

Ethan Allen	John Dickinson	Philip Freneau
Green Mountain Boys	King George III	Mercy Otis Warren
George Washington	Lord Dunmore	Abigail Adams
William Howe	Thomas Paine	Richard Henry Lee
William Prescott	James Otis	

Places

Boston	Fort Ticonderoga	Fort Crown Point

Words and Terms

Olive Branch Petition	*Common Sense*
Declaration of the Causes and Necessity of Taking Up Arms	pamphlets
	Virginia Bill of Rights
Proclamation of Rebellion	Declaration of Independence
mercenary	

Events

Second Continental Congress	Battle of Bunker Hill

As you read in the last chapter, thousands of militia gathered around Boston after Lexington and Concord. The British dared not move out of the city. A little less than a month later, the Second Continental Congress met in Philadelphia. Rebellion was in the air.

As members gathered on May 10 for the first meeting of Congress, they did not know that more fighting had occurred. That very morning before dawn, Ethan Allen, leading militia known as the Green Mountain Boys, had crossed Lake Champlain from what is now Vermont into New York. Surprising the British at Fort Ticonderoga, the militia ordered the fort to surrender "in the name of the Continental Congress." Later, they captured nearby Fort Crown Point. By taking these two forts, the Green Mountain Boys had freed from British control the most direct route to Canada. They had also taken cannon and supplies from the forts. These were dragged across the mountains to the militia around Boston.

SECOND CONTINENTAL CONGRESS

siege (SEEJ): long attack; surrounding a place in an effort to capture it

Even with the siege of Boston and the attack by the Green Mountain Boys, most colonists still wanted to make peace with Great Britain. But the British government had to recognize their rights as British subjects. The Second Continental Congress sent a statement of loyalty to the British government. However, Congress also took some actions that seemed to create a state of war with Great Britain.

One of Congress's first acts was to organize an army. It placed under its control the militia that had gathered around Boston and appointed George Washington commander in chief. This was a wise choice. Washington had military experience and was from a Southern colony. Placing him in command would attract soldiers from the Middle and Southern colonies. Up until that time, some colonists had felt that it was really New England's fight.

Throughout 1775, Congress took other steps that seemed like moves toward independence. It organized a navy and gave private ships permission to attack British shipping. Representatives of Congress were sent to France, Spain, and the Netherlands. They were looking for military and economic support in a possible war with Great Britain.

Battle of Bunker Hill

fortify (FOR-tuh-fy): to strengthen; to reinforce

Before Washington even left Philadelphia, the colonial army had gathered around Boston, shutting the British troops in the city. Gage knew that he had to keep the Americans from fortifying the hills around the city. If the Patriots placed cannon there, they could probably capture the city. Gage decided to take the hills himself.

After learning of the British plans, the Americans decided to fortify Bunker Hill. They changed plans and took Breed's Hill which was closer to the city. On the night of June 16, 1775, American soldiers began building fortifications. When Gage awoke on June 17 and saw cannon on Breed's Hill, he made plans to attack.

Under General William Howe, British soldiers moved slowly toward the hill. The Americans watched from above. The American commander, Colonel William Prescott, knew they had little ammunition. He ordered, "Don't fire until you see the whites of their eyes!"

When the British were almost upon them, the Americans opened fire. The British fell back. They regrouped and attacked again. Again, the Americans drove them from the hill. During the third attack, the Americans ran out of bullets and began firing nails and scraps of metal. Finally, the Americans had to retreat.

The Battle of Bunker Hill, as it came to be called, was a costly victory for the British. They lost about three times as many soldiers as the Americans did.

John Trumbull painted the *Battle of Bunker Hill* in 1786. He studied with Benjamin West and was an aide to George Washington during the Revolutionary War. The smoke in the painting is from the burning of Charles Town. Peter Salem, a former slave, is shown in the lower right.

Olive Branch Petition

Although the battle raised anger on both sides, Congress was not ready to declare independence. Through the summer of 1775, it tried to find a peaceful solution to the growing conflict. A committee headed by John Dickinson of Pennsylvania drew up the Olive Branch Petition. It stated that the colonists wished to remain loyal subjects of Great Britain and asked King George III to make peace with them.

Declaration of the Causes and Necessity of Taking Up Arms

In July 1775, Congress also approved the Declaration of the Causes and Necessity of Taking Up Arms. The declaration, like the Olive Branch Petition, stated that the colonists were not asking for independence. However, they were willing to fight to keep their rights as British subjects. They felt Parliament was taking away those rights.

Most Americans agreed with Congress. They were proud to be part of the British empire and proud of its history and traditions. Membership in the British empire also had trade advantages. The laws that

221

preference
(PREF-uhr-uhns):
first choice

limited trade also gave preference to colonial exports in Great Britain. Many non-British immigrants who had settled in the colonies also did not favor independence. They enjoyed British rights and they feared losing those rights under a new government.

The King's Answer

George III refused to receive the Olive Branch Petition. He did not believe the colonists were loyal British subjects. The king had heard that British soldiers were killed trying to enforce laws in the colonies. To him, the Patriot leaders were traitors who should be hung.

In August 1775, George III issued the Proclamation of Rebellion urging his "loyal subjects to oppose the rebellion." On December 22 at King George's request, Parliament passed an act forbidding all trade with the colonies. Parliament also increased the size of the British army. Mercenaries (MER-suh-ner-eez), soldiers from other countries, were hired to fight for Great Britain. The idea of the king's using foreign troops to take away their rights further angered the Americans.

rejection:
refusal to accept

The rejection of the Olive Branch Petition and George III's proclamation were great blows to American hopes for a peaceful settlement. Many colonists felt that Great Britain was responsible for the fighting. For them, the rejection of the Olive Branch Petition lifted the last block to independence.

STEPS TOWARD INDEPENDENCE

While these documents were making their way across the ocean, the colonists took more steps toward independence. In late summer 1775, an expedition left for Canada to try to win French-Canadian support. With Forts Ticonderoga and Crown Point in colonial hands, the colonial army moved easily into Canada. The Americans took Montreal but were unable to capture Quebec. The French-Canadians were not interested in joining the Americans. Under the Quebec Act, they were allowed to keep their laws, customs, and religion. Finding little success, the colonial army retreated.

In Virginia, the British governor, Lord Dunmore, acted to crush the rebellion in his colony. He offered freedom to any slave who would join his army. The Virginians defeated him. As he fled in January 1776, his army burned the town of Norfolk.

In Congress, almost all the delegates now agreed that soon they would have to make a declaration of independence. In New England, where troops were actually fighting British soldiers, the governments of New Hampshire, Massachusetts, Rhode Island, and Connecticut called for independence. Support for independence was also growing in the Southern and Middle colonies.

Still, not all American colonists favored independence. According to some historians, Patriots numbered about one third of the population. About one third of the colonists were Tories. The remainder did not support either side.

In late 1775, Colonel Benedict Arnold led 1,000 soldiers in an attack on Quebec. They were unsuccessful, and the weak and hungry soldiers retreated. Why did the colonists want to invade Canada?

Patriot Writers

In January 1776, a pamphlet appeared that further helped the move toward independence. In clear and stirring language, Thomas Paine's *Common Sense* explained why the colonies should be free from Great Britain. Paine asked why a small island should govern a large continent. He wrote that the colonies had received nothing but trouble as part of the British empire. "Everything that is right and reasonable pleads for separation. The blood of the slain cries out, 'Tis Time to Part." Finally, Paine predicted a bright and glorious future for an independent United States.

slain: those who have been killed

Paine was one of many writers who used pamphlets to speak out about the problems of the colonists. Perhaps as many as 2,000 pamphlets were written during the years Americans were gaining their independence. These little books were inexpensive to print and buy.

Among other pamphlet writers were Patriot leaders John Dickinson, author of *Letters from a Farmer in Pennsylvania*, and James Otis, who wrote *Rights of the British Colonies*. Philip Freneau (frih-NOH) used poetry as well as pamphlets to express his ideas.

Otis' sister, Mercy Otis Warren, turned to the theater as a way to criticize the British government for its treatment of the colonies. In the early 1770s, she wrote several plays that encouraged independence. She also corresponded with colonial leaders. She wrote to Washington, for example, about the organization that the new government should take.

criticize (KRIT-uh-syz): to disapprove; to find fault with

Abigail Adams was also interested in politics. In her letters to her husband John while he was attending the Continental Congress, she supported more rights for women.

By the way, in the new code of laws which I suppose it will be necessary for you to make, I desire you would remember the ladies and be more

223

generous and favorable to them than your ancestors! Do not put such unlimited power in the hands of husbands. Remember all men would be tyrants if they could.

tyrant (TY-ruhnt): cruel ruler

Her letters were also full of details of the things happening around her. Later historians have been able to learn much about the Battle of Bunker Hill and other events in Massachusetts because of her descriptions.

Closer to Independence

In March 1776, General Washington began fortifying a hill at Dorchester (DOR-ches-tuhr) Heights. This overlooked Boston from the south. By this time, General Howe had replaced General Gage. Howe felt it was useless to oppose the Americans. With 1,000 Tories, Howe and his soldiers sailed for Canada on March 17. The colonial army marched into Boston. As a result of Howe's actions, no major battles took place in Massachusetts during the Revolutionary War.

In April, North Carolina told its delegates to the Second Continental Congress to work for independence. Members of the Virginia House of Burgesses were angered in May at the news that King George was sending 12,000 mercenaries to help British troops. On May 15, the Virginia legislature told its delegates to Congress to vote for independence. A month later, the assembly adopted the Virginia Bill of Rights. This document became a guide for the later Bill of Rights to the U.S. Constitution.

DECLARATION OF INDEPENDENCE

By June 1776, the Second Continental Congress had been meeting for over a year. It met in the sometimes overcrowded rooms of the Pennsylvania State House, now called Independence Hall. As they worked, the delegates talked among themselves about independence. They were careful, however, not to use the word in any of their public statements. When they saw how popular Paine's *Common Sense* was becoming, they began to feel that the colonies were ready for independence.

resolution (rez-uh-LOO-shuhn): statement decided on; a formal expression of opinion

On June 7, Richard Henry Lee of Virginia introduced a resolution calling for independence. The delegates debated Lee's Resolution for about a month as its supporters tried to gain support. On July 2, the resolution passed.

Writing the Declaration

As you have read, many delegates had instructions from their governments to vote for independence. After Lee introduced his resolution, Congress chose a committee to write a Declaration of Independence.

224

Its members were John Adams of Massachusetts, Roger Sherman of Connecticut, Benjamin Franklin of Pennsylvania, Robert Livingston of New York, and Virginia's Thomas Jefferson. Jefferson was given the task of composing the Declaration. After Franklin and Adams made a few changes in Jefferson's work, the committee presented the Declaration to Congress on June 28.

Before approving the Declaration, Congress cut out the part that blamed George III for the slave trade. Delegates from colonies that earned money from the slave trade or used slave labor did not wish to threaten slave owners. After that, events moved quickly. Two days after accepting Lee's Resolution, Congress adopted the Declaration of Independence on July 4, 1776.

LOOKING BACK

1. State three actions by the Second Continental Congress that were steps toward independence.
2. **a.** List the actions of the First and Second Continental Congresses that show that the delegates to both meetings met for the same purpose.   **b.** What actions taken by the Second Continental Congress differed in purpose from actions of the First Continental Congress?
3. Why did the Second Continental Congress move so slowly toward independence?
4. List in order of their occurrence the events from May 1775 to July 1776 that led to the Declaration of Independence.

Chapter 3 — Declaration of Independence

LOOKING AHEAD

This chapter describes the reasons for the Declaration of Independence and examines the four parts of the document. After you study this chapter, you will be able to:

- identify the advantages the American colonies gained by declaring independence.
- explain the purpose of each of the four parts of the Declaration of Independence.
- describe the influence of European political thinkers on Jefferson's writing of the Declaration of Independence.

People

| Thomas Jefferson | Montesquieu | John Locke |

Words and Terms

| Preamble | unalienable rights | absolute despotism |

Pennsylvania paid £60 ($300) in 1752 for the bell that has become known as the Liberty Bell. When the British took Philadelphia, the bell was sent to Allentown to save it from being melted down for British weapons.

The Declaration of Independence declared that the 13 British colonies considered themselves free of British rule. By declaring independence, the colonies gained some important advantages. First, warfare had to be conducted by certain rules of war that most nations at the time agreed to. For example, colonial soldiers captured by the British had to be treated as prisoners of war. They could not be shot as rebels.

Second, the newly independent state governments and the Continental Congress found it easier to borrow money from foreign countries as well as from colonists. Finally, Congress hoped that the Declaration would unite people throughout the colonies in the cause of independence. However, those people who still opposed the break with Great Britain would now be considered traitors. Their property could be taken from them and sold to other colonists. The money would be used to finance the war.

The ideas in the Declaration of Independence were not new. However, Thomas Jefferson's writing was clear and moved the colonists to think carefully about freedom. His words still have meaning more than 200 years after they were written. There are four parts to the Declaration of Independence: the Preamble, or beginning; explanations of the political ideas in the document; a list of the charges against King George; and the statement in which the colonists declare their independence.

THE UNANIMOUS DECLARATION OF THE THIRTEEN UNITED STATES OF AMERICA

PREAMBLE

When, in the course of human events, it becomes necessary for one people to dissolve the political bands which have connected them with another, and to assume, among the powers of the earth, the separate and equal station to which the laws of nature and of nature's God entitle them, a decent respect to the opinions of mankind requires that they should declare the causes which impel them to the separation.

The Preamble (PREE-am-buhl), or first paragraph, of the Declaration explains why the colonists believed that independence was necessary. If a people were going to break away from the country that had ruled them, it was only right that they give reasons for their action.

POLITICAL IDEAS

We hold these truths to be self-evident: That all men are created equal; that they are endowed by their Creator with certain unalienable rights; that among these are life, liberty, and the pursuit of happiness. That to secure these rights, governments are instituted among men, deriving their just powers from the consent of the governed; that, whenever any form of government becomes destructive of these ends, it is the right of the people to alter or to abolish it, and to institute a new government, laying its foundation on such principles, and organizing its powers in such form, as to them shall seem most likely to effect their safety and happiness. Prudence, indeed, will dictate that governments long established should not be changed for light and transient causes; and accordingly all experience hath shown that mankind are more disposed to suffer while evils are sufferable, than to right themselves by abolishing the forms to which they are accustomed. But when a long train of abuses and usurpations, pursuing invariably the same object, evinces a design to reduce them under absolute despotism, it is their right, it is their duty, to throw off such government, and to provide new guards for their future security.

Jefferson borrowed many of the ideas in the Declaration from French and British political thinkers. Two such writers were Montesquieu (mahn-tuhs-KYOO) and John Locke. People live in societies, said Montesquieu and Locke, because life with rules is safer and more pleasant. To protect the rights of all members, groups select leaders and form governments. If leaders do not protect the rights of its members, a society should replace them with leaders who will. Since governments exist to serve the people, the people must take action when a government no longer serves them.

Jefferson pointed out that many people would rather suffer than oppose an evil government. Jefferson uses the term absolute despotism (AB-suh-loot DES-puht-iz-uhm) which means the complete control of a government. However, when evil acts continue, it is a people's duty to "throw off" that government and create a better one. This section helped win over some colonists who felt that fighting the monarch was wrong.

CHARGES AGAINST KING GEORGE

Such has been the patient sufferance of these colonies; and such is now the necessity which constrains them to alter their former systems of govern-

unanimous (yoo-NAN-uh-muhs): in complete agreement

transient (TRAN-shuhnt): passing quickly

usurpation (yoo-zuhr-PAY-shuhn): taking control by force

ment. The history of the present King of Great Britain is a history of repeated injuries and usurpations, all having in direct object the establishment of an absolute tyranny over these states. To prove this, let facts be submitted to a candid world.

He has refused his assent to laws the most wholesome and necessary for the public good.

He has forbidden his governors to pass laws of immediate and pressing importance, unless suspended in their operation till his assent should be obtained; and, when so suspended, he has utterly neglected to attend to them.

He has refused to pass other laws for the accommodation of large districts of people, unless those people would relinquish the right of representation in the legislature—a right inestimable to them, and formidable to tyrants only.

He has called together legislative bodies at places unusual, uncomfortable, and distant from the depository of their public records, for the sole purpose of fatiguing them into compliance with his measures.

He has dissolved representative houses repeatedly, for opposing, with manly firmness, his invasions on the rights of the people.

He has refused, for a long time after such dissolutions, to cause others to be elected, whereby the legislative powers, incapable of annihilation, have returned to the people at large for their exercise; the state remaining, in the mean time, exposed to all the dangers of invasions from without and convulsions within.

He has endeavored to prevent the population of these states; for that purpose obstructing the laws for the naturalization of foreigners, refusing to pass others to encourage their migration hither, and raising the conditions of new appropriations of lands.

He has obstructed the administration of justice, by refusing his assent to laws for establishing judiciary powers.

He has made judges dependent on his will alone for the tenure of their offices, and the amount and payment of their salaries.

He has erected a multitude of new offices, and sent hither swarms of officers to harass our people and eat out their substance.

He has kept among us, in times of peace, standing armies without the consent of our legislatures.

He has affected to render the military independent of, and superior to, the civil power.

He has combined with others to subject us to a jurisdiction foreign to our constitutions, and unacknowledged by our laws; giving his assent to their acts of pretended legislation:

For quartering large bodies of armed troops among us;

For protecting them, by a mock trial, from punishment for any murders which they should commit on the inhabitants of these states;

For cutting off our trade with all parts of the world;

For imposing taxes on us without our consent;

For depriving us, in many cases, of the benefits of trial by jury;

For transporting us beyond seas to be tried for pretended offenses;

For abolishing the free system of English laws in a neighboring province, establishing therein an arbitrary government, and enlarging its boundaries, so as to render it at once an example and fit instrument for introducing the same absolute rule into these colonies;

For taking away our charters, abolishing our most valuable laws, and altering fundamentally, the forms of our governments;

candid: fair; frank; sincere

depository (dih-PAHZ-uh-tor-ee): storehouse

annihilation (uh-ny-uh-LAY-shuhn): complete destruction

tenure (TEN-yuhr): length of time in office

jurisdiction (jur-is-DIK-shuhn): authority; power

mock: imitation

arbitrary (AR-buh-trer-ee): based on someone's desires rather than on laws or rules

228

For suspending our own legislatures, and declaring themselves invested with power to legislate for us in all cases whatsoever.

He has abdicated government here, by declaring us out of his protection and waging war against us.

He has plundered our seas, ravaged our coasts, burned our towns, and destroyed the lives of our people.

He is at this time transporting large armies of foreign mercenaries to complete the works of death, desolation, and tyranny already begun with circumstances of cruelty and perfidy scarcely paralleled in the most barbarous ages, and totally unworthy the head of a civilized nation.

perfidy (PER-fuh-dee): disloyalty; a breaking of trust

He has constrained our fellow citizens, taken captive on the high seas, to bear arms against their country, to become the executioners of their friends and brethren, or to fall themselves by their hands.

He has excited domestic insurrection among us, and has endeavored to bring on the inhabitants of our frontiers the merciless Indian savages, whose known rule of warfare is an undistinguished destruction of all ages, sexes, and conditions.

insurrection (in-suh-REK-shuhn): revolt

In every stage of these oppressions we have petitioned for redress in the most humble terms; our repeated petitions have been answered only by repeated injury.

redress (REE-dres): relief

A prince whose character is thus marked by every act which may define a tyrant is unfit to be the ruler of a free people.

Nor have we been wanting in attentions to our British brethren. We have warned them, from time to time, of attempts by their legislature to extend an unwarrantable jurisdiction over us. We have reminded them of the circumstances of our emigration and settlement here. We have appealed to their native justice and magnanimity; and we have conjured them by the ties of our common kindred to disavow these usurpations, which would inevitably interrupt our connections and correspondence. They, too, have been deaf to the voice of justice and consanguinity. We must, therefore, acquiesce in the necessity which denounces our separation, and hold them, as we hold the rest of mankind, enemies in war, in peace friends.

conjure (kuhn-JUR): to ask for

consanguinity (kahn-sang-GWIN-uh-tee): blood relationship

Much of the Declaration of Independence lists the ways in which King George III had taken away the rights of the colonists. Jefferson refers to the Navigation Acts, Townshend Acts, and the Quartering Act as examples.

Jefferson used harsh words to picture the king as responsible for the troubles that had occurred since 1764. Jefferson knew that British Parliament was as much at fault as George III. However, some members of Parliament had supported the colonists, and he did not want them to be blamed.

A NEW NATION AND ITS RIGHTS

We, therefore, the representatives of the United States of America, in General Congress assembled, appealing to the Supreme Judge of the world for the rectitude of our intentions, do, in the name and by the authority of the good people of these colonies, solemnly publish and declare, That these united colonies are, and of right ought to be, free and independent states; that they are absolved from all allegiance to the British crown, and that all political connection between them and the state of Great Britain is, and ought to be, totally dissolved; and that, as free and independent states, they have full power to levy war, conclude peace, contract alliances, establish commerce, and do all other acts and things which independent states may of right do. And, for the support of this declaration, with a firm reliance on the

rectitude (REK-tuh-tood): correctness

protection of Divine Providence, we mutually pledge to each other our lives, our fortunes, and our sacred honor.

In the last section of the Declaration, "these united colonies" are declared "to be free and independent states." Their rights include the power to declare war or peace, to make treaties, and to trade with other nations. This section left no doubt that the time for compromise had passed. Great Britain had to agree to colonial independence or defeat the colonists in battle. Benjamin Franklin summed up the feeling of the delegates who signed the Declaration when he said, "We must indeed all hang together, or most assuredly we shall hang separately."

assuredly
(uh-SHUR-id-lee):
certainly

John Hancock, President

Georgia
Button Gwinnett
Lyman Hall
George Walton

North Carolina
William Hooper
Joseph Hewes
John Penn

South Carolina
Edward Rutledge
Thomas Heyward, Jr.
Thomas Lynch, Jr.
Arthur Middleton

Maryland
Samuel Chase
William Paca
Thomas Stone
Charles Carroll
of Carrollton

Virginia
George Wythe
Richard Henry Lee
Thomas Jefferson
Benjamin Harrison
Thomas Nelson, Jr.
Francis Lightfoot Lee
Carter Braxton

Pennsylvania
Robert Morris
Benjamin Rush
Benjamin Franklin
John Morton
George Clymer
James Smith
George Taylor
James Wilson
George Ross

Delaware
Caesar Rodney
George Read
Thomas M'Kean

New York
William Floyd
Philip Livingston
Francis Lewis
Lewis Morris

New Jersey
Richard Stockton
John Witherspoon
Francis Hopkinson
John Hart
Abraham Clark

New Hampshire
Josiah Bartlett
William Whipple
Matthew Thornton

Massachusetts Bay
Samuel Adams
John Adams
Robert Treat Paine
Elbridge Gerry

Rhode Island
Stephan Hopkins
William Ellery

Connecticut
Roger Sherman
Samuel Huntington
William Williams
Oliver Wolcott

LOOKING BACK

1. List three advantages that the colonies gained by declaring their independence.
2. **a.** Name the four parts of the Declaration of Independence. **b.** What was the purpose of each?
3. Identify one main idea in the Declaration of Independence that Jefferson borrowed from European political thinkers.

Chapter 4   The Revolutionary War

LOOKING AHEAD

This chapter focuses on the years 1776 to 1783 when the colonists were fighting to establish a new nation. It describes the Revolutionary War mainly through maps and pictures. After you study this chapter, you will be able to:

- list the problems Congress faced in organizing to fight.
- ★ compare and contrast the British and colonial sides as they approached war.
- gather data about the Revolutionary War through interpreting text, maps, and pictures.
- read maps to locate colonial borders in the 1700s.

People

Salem Poor	Thaddeus Kosciusko
Deborah Sampson Gannett	Casimir Pulaski
Lydia Darragh	Robert Morris
Margaret Corbin	Haym Solomon
Mary Hays McCauley	John Burgoyne
Thayendanegea	George Rogers Clark
Silas Deane	Daniel Morgan
Arthur Lee	Francis Joseph de Grasse
Marquis de Lafayette	Lord Charles Cornwallis
Baron von Steuben	

Places

Trenton, New Jersey	Kaskaskia, Illinois
Philadelphia, Pennsylvania	Vincennes, Indiana
Saratoga, New York	Charles Town, South Carolina
Valley Forge, Pennsylvania	Cowpens, South Carolina
Monmouth, New Jersey	Yorktown, Virginia

Words and Terms

Continental Army   privateer   strategy

Events

Treaty of Paris

There are very few primary source pictures of Revolutionary War uniforms. This engraving appeared in Germany and is believed to show a colonial soldier in a uniform of blue cotton with a leather hat.

The Declaration of Independence did not guarantee independence for a United States. A war had to be won first. In order to do this, the Second Continental Congress had to overcome many problems. It had to organize an army and navy. Officials had to be sent to foreign countries to ask for aid. Most importantly, Congress had to find the money to finance the war.

BUILDING AN ARMY

recruit (rih-KROOT): to get to join

One problem Congress faced was recruiting enough Americans to fight the British. The first American soldiers were militia. Usually, members of the militia served for six months or fought only in battles near their homes. Most men did not want to leave their families for long periods of time.

In Chapter 2 of this unit, you read that Congress began organizing an army in spring 1775. Each state was asked to recruit men to form its own unit of the Continental Army. But Congress did not have the power to force the states to act. States could raise as few or as many volunteers as they wanted. Like the militia, the army had trouble getting soldiers to serve for long periods of time. Before the end of 1776, Congress set the term of enlistment at three years, but few men joined. Many Americans thought that the fighting with Great Britain would be over within a year. So, a year was the normal length of service volunteers served in the Continental Army.

Because it had trouble recruiting soldiers, the Continental Army was never very large. It reached its greatest size — 20,000 soldiers — early in 1778. At times, Washington had only 5,000 troops at his command. On the other hand, the British army numbered around 50,000. It was made up of British soldiers, Tories, and mercenaries. Besides recruiting soldiers, Congress faced problems in providing food, clothing, and supplies. Congress did not have the power to order states to supply the soldiers. It had to depend on voluntary state support.

Blacks in the War

Blacks were members of the militia that took part in the first battles of the Revolutionary War. Among them was Salem Poor, praised by his commanding officers for his courage at Bunker Hill. However, when Congress organized the Continental Army, it kept blacks out. Colonial leaders did not want the army to become a place for runaway slaves. But the main reason for not enlisting blacks was fear. Some colonists feared that armed slaves would turn on their owners.

Free blacks were angry at being kept out of the army. Late in 1775, they protested to General Washington. He placed the matter before Congress. It finally agreed to allow free blacks who had fought in the early battles to enlist. As the war dragged on, the Continental Army began recruiting blacks, both slave and free. There were blacks in units from most states, and blacks also served at sea. In all, 5,000 blacks served on the side of the Americans.

Some blacks also served in the British army. You may recall from Chapter 2 of this unit that Lord Dunmore offered freedom to black

slaves who joined the British. One reason Americans began recruiting black soldiers was in answer to this threat. Some black soldiers received their freedom for serving with the Americans.

Women Fighters

Women, too, took part in the Revolutionary War. Deborah Sampson Gannett (GAN-uht) joined the Continental Army, using a man's name. After she was dismissed once, she joined again under another male name. She left the Continental Army in 1783 with an honorable discharge. Other women such as Lydia Darragh (DAR-uh) of Philadelphia acted as messengers and spies. Margaret Corbin (KOR-bin) and Mary Hays McCauley, known as Molly Pitcher, took the places of their wounded husbands in battle.

Native Americans and the War

Many Native Americans did not take sides during the war. Some, such as the Oneida and about half of the Tuscarora, sided with the Americans. The rest of the Iroquois League remained loyal to Great Britain. As you may recall from the unit Becoming Americans, the League had fought with the British in the French and Indian War.

Led by Thayendanega (thuh-yen-duh-NAY-gee-uh), or Joseph Brant, the Iroquois carried out raids on frontier settlements in New York and Pennsylvania during the Revolutionary War. In 1779, the Americans decided to remove the threat of further Iroquois attacks. They sent an expedition against the Iroquois and destroyed many Iroquois villages in New York.

The frontier was the scene of many fights between Americans and Native Americans. Sometimes the fighting was caused or led by Tories. In South Carolina, the Cherokee, who earlier had fought against the British, now helped them. Like many Native Americans, the Cherokee feared the continued westward movement of Americans along the frontier. They sided with the British in an attempt to keep Americans from pushing onto their lands.

THE NAVY

Besides raising an army, Congress had to build a navy to defend American rivers and coasts. Because money was in short supply, Congress bought few ships during the war. However, the naval war was fought by American privateers (pry-vuh-TIRZ). These were ships owned by private citizens. Any British ships they captured they could keep. After 1780, the French navy entered the war. Without the help of the French fleet, the Americans would have been no match for the powerful British navy.

GAINING FOREIGN SUPPORT

The French fleet was only part of the support the Americans received from France. Congress sent Silas Deane, Arthur Lee, and Benjamin Franklin to France in 1776 to ask for aid. France answered with clothing, weapons, and money. Some of the money was a gift. Most of it was in the form of loans to be repaid after the war. Spain and the Netherlands also loaned Congress money.

Besides money and supplies, some Europeans came as volunteers to help the Americans. The Marquis de Lafayette (lah-fah-yet) from France became a general in the Continental Army before he was 20. Baron von Steuben (STOO-buhn) from Germany helped train American soldiers at Valley Forge. Thaddeus Kosciusko (kahs-ee-UHS-koh), a Polish army officer, commanded American troops. Casimir Pulaski (pyoo-LAS-kee), also from Poland, was a skilled engineer who built fortifications at West Point, New York.

FINANCING THE WAR

Paying for the war was another of Congress' problems. Between 1777 and 1779, Congress asked the states for a total of $95 million to carry on the war and to run the government. The states managed to raise only $54 million.

To pay the Continental Army and to carry out its work, Congress printed paper money, called Continental dollars. But it printed so much that the money lost its value. People soon began to say that something worthless was "not worth a Continental."

In 1781, the finances of Congress improved. In that year, Congress placed Robert Morris in charge of raising money for the war. Both Morris and Haym Solomon (SAHL-oh-muhn) gave large sums of their own money to Congress. Solomon also helped Morris raise money from European governments.

This seal is from a six dollar bill issued by the Second Continental Congress. Why were the bills considered worthless by the end of the war?

ADVANTAGES AND DISADVANTAGES OF EACH SIDE

As the British and colonial sides approached war, there were many military, political, and economic advantages and disadvantages on each side. Each nation also had its advantages and disadvantages in relation to its population.

Great Britain was a powerful country. Its population was three times as large and three times as wealthy as that of the colonies. It had a strong central government. However, the nation lacked unity in its fight against the Americans. Not everyone supported the war.

unity (YOO-nuh-tee): acting as one

The British had professional soldiers and officers as well as the money to hire mercenaries. The British also had the support of many Native American allies. The British army had better pay, food, uniforms, and supplies than did the Americans. Great Britain could produce all the supplies a large army and navy needed. Its navy was the strongest in the world. However, the British were never able to control more than the lands near the coast. Part of their problem was that they were fighting in unfamiliar places. Also, their supplies had to come from Great Britain, over 4,800 kilometers (3,000 miles) away.

The Americans had much greater problems. There were never enough soldiers in the army and militia. Of the troops there were, most were untrained and poorly supplied. Most soldiers served short terms and never gained much experience. But the Americans were fighting in familiar places and were close to their sources of supply. However, there were always shortages of food, clothing, blankets, weapons, and ammunition. The Americans had almost no navy and few Native American allies. The French and other foreign countries did not join the American side until late in the war.

Like the British, the Americans lacked unity of purpose. Not all Americans supported independence. Unlike the British, though, the Americans had a weak central government. Because Congress did not have the power to set taxes, the Americans lacked the money to fight the war. The fact that the Americans were fighting for a cause they believed in and were led by such leaders as Washington, Jefferson, Franklin, and Adams helped greatly.

You may recall from page 50 that in looking for comparisons and contrasts, you look for similarities and differences. Sometimes, they are stated clearly. Other times you have to infer some or all of the similarities and differences. In the section above, Advantages and Disadvantages of Each Side, the strengths and weaknesses of both the British and American sides are given. Reread the section. Decide which are strengths and which are weaknesses for each side in comparison to the other side. **1.** How do the two sides compare politically, economically, and militarily? **2.** Who seems to have more advantages? **3.** As a help, make a table similar to the one on page 195 in the unit Becoming Americans.

BUILDING READING SKILLS

Top left: British and American soldiers fought several battles in and around New York City in fall 1776. The British finally drove the Americans from the area. Where did the battles around New York City take place?

Center: After the French entered the war, the British retreated from Philadelphia. While marching to New York City, they were caught by Americans at Monmouth, New Jersey. In the confusion, American General Henry Lee ordered his soldiers to retreat. Washington urged the troops to fight on. What kinds of activity are shown in this battle scene?

John Trumbull painted this scene of General John Burgoyne surrendering to General Horatio Gates at Saratoga. News of the surrender prompted France to enter the war on the side of the Americans.

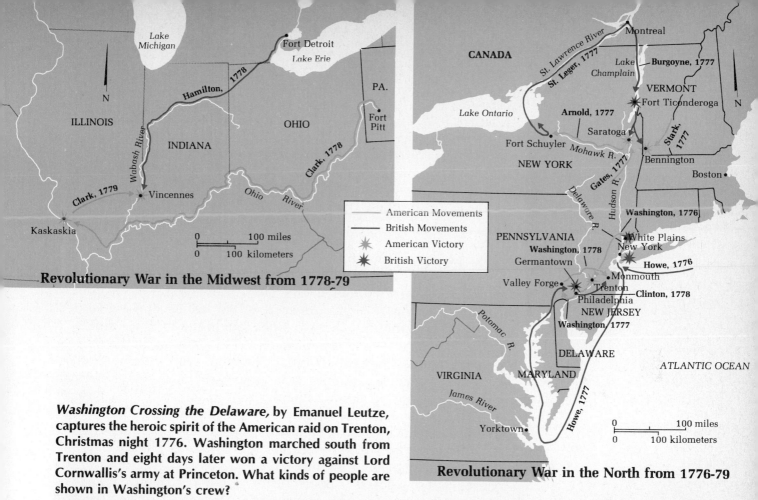

Revolutionary War in the Midwest from 1778-79

Lake Michigan
Fort Detroit
Lake Erie
N
ILLINOIS
OHIO
PA.
Hamilton, 1778
INDIANA
Fort Pitt
Wabash River
Clark, 1778
Clark, 1779
Vincennes
Ohio River
Kaskaskia
0   100 miles
0   100 kilometers

Revolutionary War in the North from 1776-79

CANADA
Montreal
St. Lawrence River
St. Leger, 1777
Lake Champlain
Burgoyne, 1777
VERMONT
Fort Ticonderoga
Lake Ontario
Arnold, 1777
N
Fort Schuyler
Mohawk R.
Saratoga
Stark, 1777
NEW YORK
Bennington
Boston
Gates, 1777
Hudson R.
Delaware R.
Washington, 1776
White Plains
New York
PENNSYLVANIA
Washington, 1778
Germantown
Howe, 1776
Valley Forge
Monmouth
Trenton
Clinton, 1778
Philadelphia
NEW JERSEY
Washington 1777
Potomac R.
DELAWARE
Washington 1777
MARYLAND
ATLANTIC OCEAN
VIRGINIA
James River
Howe, 1777
Yorktown
0   100 miles
0   100 kilometers

Legend:
— American Movements
— British Movements
✶ American Victory
✶ British Victory

Washington Crossing the Delaware, by Emanuel Leutze, captures the heroic spirit of the American raid on Trenton, Christmas night 1776. Washington marched south from Trenton and eight days later won a victory against Lord Cornwallis's army at Princeton. What kinds of people are shown in Washington's crew?

YEARS OF FIGHTING: 1776-79

In August 1776, British General William Howe made plans to move his troops into New York City. General Washington, however, learned of Howe's plans and moved into New York first. In several battles, the Americans were defeated. Washington was driven across New Jersey into Pennsylvania. The British had taken New York to try to cut New England off from the other colonies. They thought this would bring the war to a quick end. Their strategy (STRAT-uh-jee), or battle plan, did not work.

From their camp in Pennsylvania, American soldiers crossed the Delaware River on Christmas Day 1776. They won a victory over German mercenaries and British troops at Trenton, New Jersey. A few days later they won another at Princeton. These battles raised American hopes. During 1776, the Americans had lost several big battles. In the next nine months, the two sides fought no decisive battles.

decisive (dih-SY-siv): having a clear result

In September 1777, the Americans lost Philadelphia to the British. The next month, however, British General John Burgoyne (ber-GOYN) was forced to surrender at Saratoga, New York. The American victory ended most of the fighting in the Northern colonies. Besides the victory at Saratoga, the Americans were helped by France's entry into the war against Great Britain. Washington and his soldiers spent the winter of 1777-78 at Valley Forge, Pennsylvania. The soldiers suffered from the cold and from hunger. Shortages of food, clothing, and supplies caused soldiers to desert. In 1778, the British retreating from Philadelphia were beaten by Americans at Monmouth in New Jersey.

On the upper part of the western frontier, General George Rogers Clark defeated the British at Kaskaskia (kas-KAS-kee-uh), Illinois, and Vincennes (vin-SENZ), Indiana. Clark ended British control of the area, which included land claimed by several colonies.

CHESTER — William Billings

Treble Counter / Tenor (Tune) Bass

Let ty-rants shake their i- - ron rod, And Slav'-ry clank ____ her gall- -ing chains, We fear them not, ____ we trust ____ in God, New- eng-land's God ____ for ev- -er reigns.

Much fighting took place around Philadelphia. This painting shows the Battle of Germantown in 1777. Neither side won and Washington went into winter quarters at Valley Forge. In what other places around Philadelphia did fighting occur?

YEARS OF FIGHTING: 1779-81

By 1779, most of the fighting of the Revolutionary War had moved to the Southern colonies. British troops had already captured most of Georgia in 1778. In 1779, they planned to move into the Carolinas and Virginia. Charles Town, South Carolina, fell to them in May 1780.

Fighting continued throughout the Carolinas. Tories and their Cherokee allies raided American settlements on the frontier. Southern colonists answered with small, scattered attacks on the British. Most of this fighting took place in forests and swamps. In January 1781, General Daniel Morgan led the Americans to victory at Cowpens (KOW-penz), South Carolina.

In October 1781, the Americans under George Washington and the French navy under Admiral Francis Joseph de Grasse (duh GRAHS) trapped the British at Yorktown, Virginia. Lord Charles Cornwallis (korn-WAHL-is), commander of the British, surrendered his army to the Americans. American and British representatives met and wrote articles of surrender, some of which appear below.

The garrisons of York and Gloucester, including the officers and seamen of his Britannic Majesty's ships, will surrender to the forces of America and France. The land troops will be prisoners of the U.S., the navy to the naval army of the King of France.

The garrison of York will march out at two o'clock, with shouldered arms, and drums beating a British or German march. They are to lay their arms on the ground and return to camp. Two works on the Gloucester side will be delivered at one o'clock, to the American and French troops appointed to take them.

THE END OF THE WAR

After Cornwallis' defeat, the British government agreed to discuss an end to the fighting. American delegates, led by Benjamin Franklin,

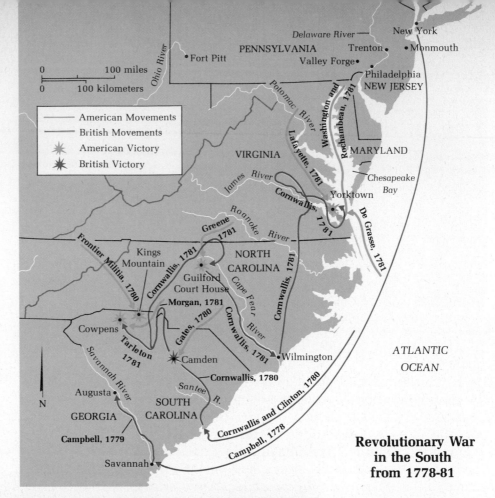

Revolutionary War in the South from 1778-81

In 1779 the American ship *Bonhomme Richard* met and defeated the larger and better armed *Serapis*. *Bonhomme Richard* was commanded by John Paul Jones. When asked to surrender, he answered, "I have not yet begun to fight." Which ship is the *Bonhomme Richard*? How can you tell?

Top: The Americans crushed the British at Cowpens, South Carolina. How does the artist show which troops are British and which are American? How did this battle fit into the strategy of the Americans?

Right: General Francis Marion led raids against the British in South Carolina. How did he earn the name, the Swamp Fox?

John Trumbull painted *The Surrender of Cornwallis* several years after the war. In fact, Cornwallis refused to surrender in person to Washington. Why might an artist change the facts?

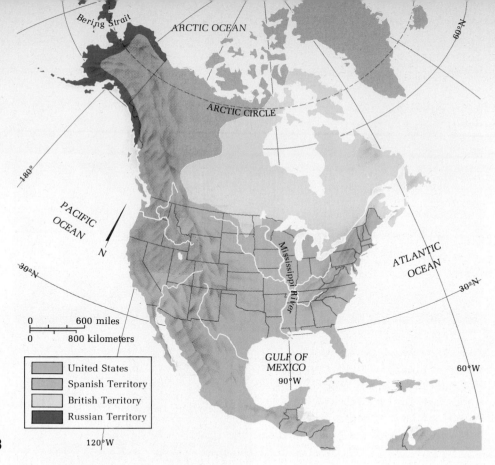

North America in 1783

Map legend:
- United States
- Spanish Territory
- British Territory
- Russian Territory

met the British in Paris. On April 13, 1783, Congress ratified the Treaty of Paris that officially ended the Revolutionary War.

Great Britain recognized the new nation. The U.S. received all former British lands east of the Mississippi River and from the Great Lakes to Florida. Florida, which Great Britain won in 1763, was given back to Spain. Spain had been an ally of France during the Revolutionary War. New Englanders could continue fishing off the coast of Newfoundland. Americans and the British agreed to pay each other any debts they owed from before the war. Congress agreed to persuade the states to return or pay for the property of Tories that had been taken. Great Britain agreed to remove all troops from the U.S.

LOOKING BACK

1. List three problems Congress faced in organizing to fight.

★ 2. Write a statement comparing and contrasting the British and colonial sides on each of the following: **a.** military training. **b.** help from outside forces. **c.** supplies. Remember you may have to infer some of the information.

3. **a.** List three key battles for the American side. **b.** Explain why they were important. **c.** From reading the maps on pages 237 and 240, what was the British battle strategy?

4. Use the maps on pages 198-99 and 240. **a.** What territory changed hands? **b.** How many times? **c.** Who took possession each time?

PRACTICING YOUR SKILLS

What If . . .   What if the colonists had lost the war? What kind of government would we have? Do you think the colonies would have expanded to the Pacific? Would Canada and the 13 colonies be one country?

Debating   Use the information above to arrange a debate on the following problem: The 13 colonies did not have to go to war to settle their disagreements with Great Britain.

Building Study Skills   Do you sometimes find that you cannot understand notes you have taken during a lecture? Below are some tips to make **taking and using lecture notes** more effective. The last five steps are similar to the SQ3R method you learned in How to Read Your Textbook.

- Draw a line down the left side of your notebook paper about 6.25 to 6.75 centimeters (2½ to 3 inches) from the edge.
- Listen carefully to the lecturer. Emphasis, pauses, and repetition of words are clues to main ideas. Take down only main ideas and supporting details. Do not take down everything the person says.
- Skip lines between ideas. Number supporting details.
- Write clearly. Use as few words as possible. Use abbreviations whenever possible.
- After the lecture, reduce the main ideas and supporting details to key words. Write them in the left-hand column.
- Cover the right-hand column, and using only the key words, recite what the lecture was about.
- Think back over the lecture to make sure you have the lecturer's views and not your own ideas and opinions.
- Spend time each week reviewing your notes.

Activity: Practice by taking notes while watching the nightly news.

Imagining, Making Tables, Researching, Writing

1. Would you have supported the Declaration of Independence if you had been living in 1776? Answer the question by imagining you are one of the following: **a.** a merchant in Boston;   **b.** a plantation owner in South Carolina;   **c.** a farmer on the frontier in Pennsylvania;   **d.** a slave in Virginia.
2. Make a table of the important land and sea battles of the Revolutionary War. List the date, place, and outcome of each battle.
3. Research Benedict Arnold's treason. Write a paragraph explaining why he chose the British side.

Exploring   If you live in a state where the Revolutionary War was fought, choose one battle. Research it. Then describe it in a paragraph, draw a picture of it, or make a map showing battle and supply lines.

Reading

Alderman, Clifford Lindsey. *The War We Could Have Lost.* New York: Scholastic Book Service, 1974. British errors in the Revolution.

Boardman, Fon W. *Against the Iroquois.* New York: Walck, 1978.

Davis, Burke. *Heroes of the American Revolution.* New York: Random House, 1971. Photos, prints, and maps.

Evans, Elizabeth. *Weathering the Storm: Women of the American Revolution.* New York: Scribner, 1975. Primary sources.

Quarles, Benjamin. *The Negro in the American Revolution.* New York: Norton, 1973. Paperback.

UNIT IV   A PLAN OF GOVERNMENT

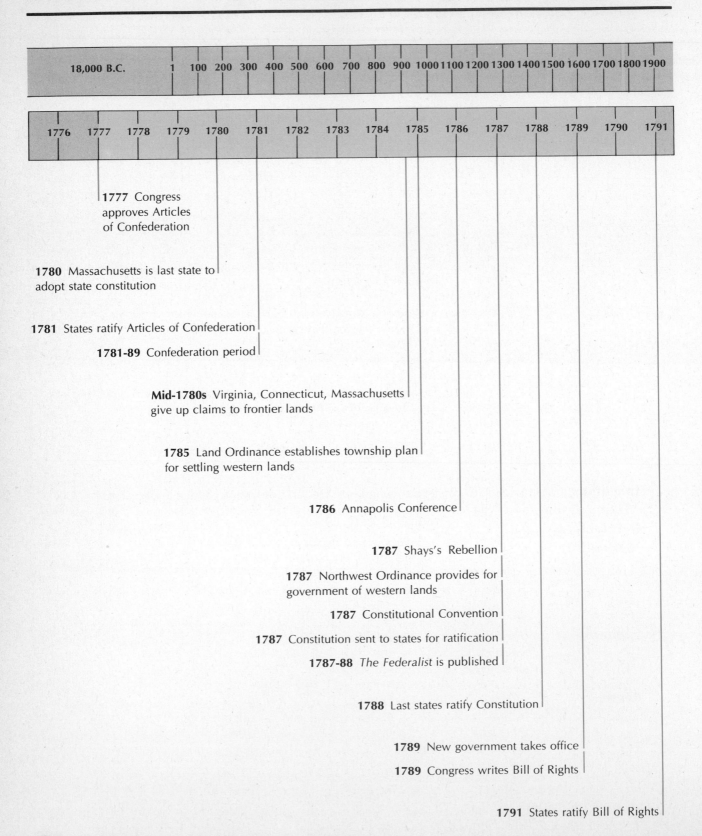

18,000 B.C.	1	100	200	300	400	500	600	700	800	900	1000	1100	1200	1300	1400	1500	1600	1700	1800	1900

1776	1777	1778	1779	1780	1781	1782	1783	1784	1785	1786	1787	1788	1789	1790	1791

1777 Congress
approves Articles
of Confederation

1780 Massachusetts is last state to
adopt state constitution

1781 States ratify Articles of Confederation

1781-89 Confederation period

Mid-1780s Virginia, Connecticut, Massachusetts
give up claims to frontier lands

1785 Land Ordinance establishes township plan
for settling western lands

1786 Annapolis Conference

1787 Shays's Rebellion

1787 Northwest Ordinance provides for
government of western lands

1787 Constitutional Convention

1787 Constitution sent to states for ratification

1787-88 *The Federalist* is published

1788 Last states ratify Constitution

1789 New government takes office

1789 Congress writes Bill of Rights

1791 States ratify Bill of Rights

Chapter 1   The Confederation Period

LOOKING AHEAD

When the American Revolution began, there was no central government for the 13 states. Yet some form of control was needed. In this chapter, you will read about the Articles of Confederation that the Second Continental Congress adopted. You will also learn about the economic and expansion problems of the country under the Articles. After you study this chapter, you will be able to:

- describe the influence of colonial experiences on the forming of state governments.
- list the weaknesses of the Articles of Confederation.
- describe the economic problems that faced the new nation after the Revolutionary War.
- describe how economic factors in the three geographical areas led to sectionalism.
- explain the land ordinances.

Social Studies Vocabulary

central government	judicial branch	credit
executive branch	interstate commerce	sectionalism
legislative branch	interest	

Places

Northwest Territory

Events

Confederation period	Shays's Rebellion
Congress of the Confederation	

Words and Terms

Articles of Confederation	arsenal
bankruptcy	Land Ordinance of 1785
creditor	Northwest Ordinance

The American Revolution ended British rule in the 13 colonies and began the United States of America. As we have seen, the Revolution was the end of a long series of events leading to independence. The changes that brought about the war had really begun in the late 1600s. But the Revolution was also just another event in the growth of American identity. It was followed by a time known as the Confederation period. As you may recall from the unit Colonial Beginnings, a confederation is a loose union of states.

STATE GOVERNMENTS

In May 1776, the Second Continental Congress had suggested that each colony set up its own government. New Hampshire and South Carolina had already done so. The other former colonies soon followed. Most wrote constitutions and then formed governments that followed their constitutions.

For the most part, the new constitutions were similar to the colonial charters. Power was divided among a governor, judges, and a legislature. Because of their experiences with royal governors, the colonists limited the power of the new governors. In each state, most power rested with the legislature. The new constitutions also included a bill of rights for the people. However, as had happened in colonial times, the wealthy controlled government.

A CENTRAL GOVERNMENT

Even though the states had their own governments, it was clear that these were not enough. A government was needed that could act for all the states. Some one group had to select commanders for the army, recruit soldiers, ask states for money and supplies, and hold discussions with European nations. The Second Continental Congress handled these matters during the war. But it realized that the new nation needed a more organized form of central government. A **central government** is one that acts for all the states in matters of common concern.

Late in 1776, Congress named a committee headed by John Dickinson of Pennsylvania to develop a plan for such a government. Congress approved the plan, known as the Articles of Confederation in 1777. Before they could become law, though, the Articles had to be approved by the states. Arguments over western land claims held this up until 1781.

article: a section of a written document

According to their colonial charters, Massachusetts, Connecticut, Virginia, North Carolina, South Carolina, and Georgia claimed lands west of the Appalachians. Maryland, whose charter did not give it any western lands, wanted these states to turn over their claims to the central government. Maryland refused to approve the Articles until this was done. The states finally agreed and Maryland voted *yes* in 1781. From 1781 until 1789, the central government of the new nation was based on the Articles of Confederation.

The Articles of Confederation

The Articles of Confederation gave the central government only limited power. The colonies were fighting the Revolution to free themselves from the laws and taxes of a strong central government. The colonies were determined to prevent any authority from interfering

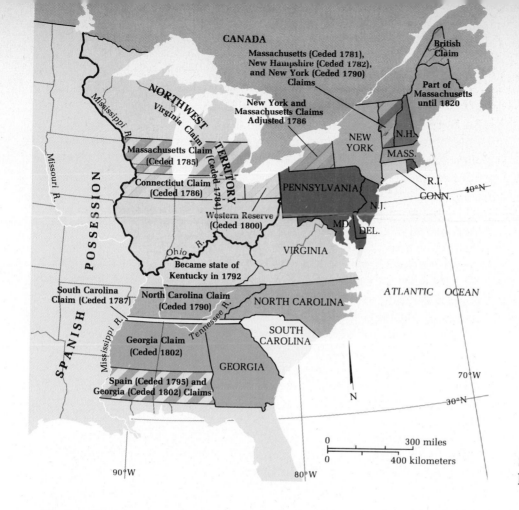

State Claims to New Lands

Map labels:
CANADA
Massachusetts (Ceded 1781), New Hampshire (Ceded 1782), and New York (Ceded 1790) Claims
British Claim
New York and Massachusetts Claims Adjusted 1786
Part of Massachusetts until 1820
NORTHWEST Virginia Claim
Massachusetts Claim (Ceded 1785)
TERRITORY (Ceded 1784)
Connecticut Claim (Ceded 1786)
Western Reserve (Ceded 1800)
NEW YORK
N.H.
MASS.
R.I.
CONN.
PENNSYLVANIA
N.J.
MD. DEL.
VIRGINIA
Mississippi R.
Missouri R.
Ohio R.
POSSESSION
Became state of Kentucky in 1792
South Carolina Claim (Ceded 1787)
North Carolina Claim (Ceded 1790)
NORTH CAROLINA
ATLANTIC OCEAN
SPANISH
Tennessee R.
Mississippi R.
Georgia Claim (Ceded 1802)
SOUTH CAROLINA
GEORGIA
Spain (Ceded 1795) and Georgia (Ceded 1802) Claims
40°N
70°W
30°N
N
0   300 miles
0   400 kilometers
90°W   80°W

with their local power. They considered themselves 13 separate states —each with its own constitution and government. Each wanted to remain free to govern itself.

Article II. Each state keeps its sovereignty, freedom, and independence, and every power, jurisdiction, and right, which is not by this confederation clearly given to the United States, in Congress assembled.

Article III. The states separately enter into a firm league of friendship with each other for their common defense, the security of their liberties, and their mutual and general good. They bind themselves to assist each other against all force offered to, or attacks made upon them, or any of them, on account of religion, sovereignty, trade, or any other reason.

sovereignty (SAHV-ruhn-tee): highest power; supreme authority

mutual: shared; taken together

Under the Articles, there was no President for the new nation. The Congress of the Confederation acted as both the executive and legislative branches. The **executive branch** of government runs the nation's affairs and carries out its policies. The **legislative** (LEJ-is-lay-tiv) **branch** makes laws. There was no **judicial** (joo-DISH-uhl) **branch** either—that part of government that tries court cases.

The Congress was made up of delegates from each state. The states had one vote apiece although they could send from two to seven delegates. Laws could be passed if nine of the thirteen states approved. The Articles themselves could be changed only with the approval of Congress and each state legislature.

According to the Articles, Congress had the power to make peace and war. Congress also could regulate affairs with Native Americans who lived in the newly won western lands. Among Congress' other powers were the rights to set up post offices and coin money. The Articles, however, did not give Congress the power to set taxes. The states kept this power. Congress also could not regulate **interstate commerce,** or trade between states. Because of this restriction, Congress could not regulate the collection of customs duties by the states. Because Congress had no control over this trade, each state acted separately. States without large ports had to buy and sell goods in neighboring states. Pennsylvania and New York, for example, demanded very high customs duties of New Jersey and Connecticut.

Under the Articles, the real power in the U.S. was still in the hands of the state governments. Congress could ask the states to do things but could not force them to act. As you may recall from the unit The American Revolution, Congress asked the states for money to run the war. The states raised only part of what Congress had asked for. There were some limits on state power, however. For example, states could not make agreements with foreign countries without the approval of Congress. No state could make laws that conflicted with treaties that Congress might make. However, states could object to a treaty and have it withdrawn. The states did not always obey the Articles. For example, after the war some states printed their own money, even though this power belonged to Congress.

THE NATIONAL ECONOMY

The nation's economy was very weak after the war. The government could not pay its bills because the states did not supply the money it asked for. Loans from foreign countries were difficult to get, and interest rates were high. **Interest** is a fee for borrowing money. Because Congress could not regulate trade, the money collected by the national government was not enough to meet expenses or settle its debts to other countries. The national government was near bankruptcy. It was dangerously close to being unable to pay its debts. The states, on the other hand, printed so much paper money that it was almost worthless. Prices rose.

During the war, many merchants and farmers had sold goods on credit. **Credit** is the promise of payment in the future. For example, farmers and merchants sold goods to the Continental army on Congress' promise to pay them after the war. When Congress could not pay, many people went bankrupt. The new nation faced serious economic problems. Many people grew angry at the government.

Shays's Rebellion

One example of the anger brought about by the economic conditions of the mid-1780s was Shays's Rebellion. Besides selling goods on credit, farmers also bought goods on credit. After the war, when the

This Howard Pyle illustration of Shays's Rebellion in 1787 is a secondary source. The work was not completed until the early 1900s. What kinds of sources might Pyle have used to paint his picture?

creditors, or people to whom the farmers owed money, demanded payment, the farmers could not pay. Many could not pay their land taxes either. Creditors took the farmers to court where judges often ordered the farmers' lands sold to pay their debts.

In 1786, farmers in Massachusetts demanded that the state pass a law to stop this. They wanted a law that would keep creditors from taking property in payment of debts. They also wanted an end to the heavy taxes on their land. The state refused and issued a proclamation making it illegal for people to assemble. The militia was called out to prevent gatherings. Daniel Shays, a bankrupt farmer, led 1,200 farmers in an attempt to seize the arsenal at Springfield, Massachusetts. An arsenal (AHR-suhn-uhl) is a place for storing weapons. The state sent its militia. On January 25, 1787, the state militia quickly defeated Shays's army.

The entire rebellion was over by the end of February. Few people were killed. But the rebellion showed many Americans that they needed a much stronger central government than the one the Articles gave them. The country needed a government that could improve economic conditions and help states in time of trouble.

Balance of Trade

After the war, Americans imported more goods than they exported and they bought much of these imported goods on credit. They wanted to make up for what they had done without during the war.

An unfavorable balance of trade developed for the new nation. The money being paid out for imports did not equal the money being brought in by American exports. Between 1784 and 1786, Americans bought goods worth £7.5 million from Great Britain. The symbol £ means pounds sterling, the basis for the British system of money. They sold goods to the British worth only £2.5 million. As a result, Americans owed British merchants £5 million. Nearly all the gold and silver in the U.S. was being paid to foreign merchants.

Before the war, Americans had a favored place in the economy of the British empire. Under the Navigation Acts, American goods were given preference over goods from outside the empire. After the war, American goods were no longer given this treatment. Nor could American ships carry British goods. For a time, Great Britain even closed its ports in the West Indies and Europe to American ships. This greatly hurt American trade. As you may recall from the unit Life in Colonial America, much of the colonists' trade had been with the West Indies.

New England was especially hard hit. Because its ships could no longer trade in British ports in the West Indies, its shipbuilding and trading centers declined. Before the war, Massachusetts had built 125 ships a year. After the war, it built fewer than 25 ships a year. The whaling and fishing industries also suffered. What had been the Middle colonies suffered from a loss of markets for their farm products.

The Southern states for a time lost their British markets for tobacco, rice, indigo, and naval stores. But because the British needed these goods, the South was the first area to recover.

An Improving Economy

By the mid-1780s, the U.S. economy was growing stronger. Without British regulations on trade and manufacturing, the Americans began to look around for new markets. The French had hoped to take over the American market from the British after the war. This did not happen because Americans continued to buy British goods. They wanted the things they were used to. However, trade with France did increase. New Englanders also found new markets and new trade goods in China.

With all this new business activity, Americans found they needed more government help than the Congress of the Confederation could give them. They needed a government that could regulate trade and the supply of money. They needed a government that could help them in their dealings with foreign countries.

Protection of Industry

Besides help with international trade, Americans wanted help with their industries. Manufacturers wanted economic protection from the cheaper goods imported from Europe. Without a tax on European goods, manufacturers believed that their industries would not grow.

This was similar to the position of British manufacturers in the mid-1700s. Then, the British asked for protection from the cheaper colonial goods imported into Great Britain.

The Congress of the Confederation had no power to act in this matter. The Articles kept for the states the power of setting customs duties. The states could not agree on one course of action. The different sections of the new nation had different interests.

These ships are tied up in Salem Harbor because after the war Great Britain would not let U.S. ships trade in British ports or carry British goods. What did this do to the new nation's economy?

SECTIONALISM

As you may recall from the unit Life in Colonial America, colonists in the different geographical regions were developing different economic and social systems in the 1700s. The Southern colonies were building a farming economy based on plantations. The Middle colonies had a mix of farming and manufacturing. New England was mainly a shipbuilding and trading center.

The continuation of these economic and social systems, however, led to a change in attitude called sectionalism. **Sectionalism** (SEK-shuhn-uhl-iz-uhm) is the division of a country or political group into sections whose objectives and interests differ from each other. It is loyalty to one's own section rather than to the whole group. In later units, you will see how sectionalism was one cause of the Civil War.

In the late 1700s, this growing sectionalism led to problems for the new nation. The states could not agree on certain things, and Congress did not have the power to force them to act together.

For example, Spain offered Congress a treaty giving the U.S. special trading rights. But there were two conditions. First, Spain would keep control of the port of New Orleans. Second, the U.S. would not use the Mississippi River for trade. As you may recall from the unit Colonial Beginnings, Spain had interests in Florida, Louisiana, and the Southwest. It did not want the new nation interfering.

The New England states were willing to give up control of the Mississippi because it was of no use to them. They wanted the trading

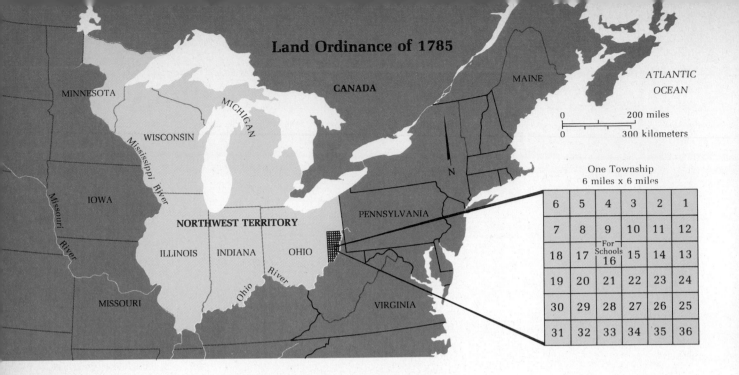

Land Ordinance of 1785

MINNESOTA

WISCONSIN

MICHIGAN

CANADA

MAINE

ATLANTIC OCEAN

IOWA

NORTHWEST TERRITORY

PENNSYLVANIA

ILLINOIS   INDIANA   OHIO

Mississippi River

Missouri River

Ohio River

MISSOURI

VIRGINIA

N

0   200 miles

0   300 kilometers

One Township
6 miles x 6 miles

6	5	4	3	2	1
7	8	9	10	11	12
18	17	For Schools 16	15	14	13
19	20	21	22	23	24
30	29	28	27	26	25
31	32	33	34	35	36

privileges with Spain. People on the frontier, on the other hand, saw control of the Mississippi as necessary to their trade and their expansion. They opposed the treaty. In response, Congress withdrew the treaty from further consideration.

EXPANSION

When the Revolution ended, the Treaty of Paris gave the U.S. all the land between the Appalachian Mountains and the Mississippi River. Based on their charters, several states claimed the area. By the mid-1780s, however, Virginia, Connecticut, and Massachusetts had given up their claims to the region north of the Ohio River. It then became public land. Congress had declared in 1780 that such public land would be settled and in time become states. These new states would have the same rights and freedoms as the older states.

Land-hungry settlers, army officers, and land companies raced to the area. They competed for ownership of this rich territory known as the Old Northwest and later the Northwest Territory. Native Americans already lived in the area and Congress wanted to avoid conflict with them. Congress wrote several treaties that guaranteed the rights of the Native Americans. As you will read in later chapters, the treaties meant little.

compete: to try hard to gain something

Land Ordinance of 1785

The new nation faced a shortage of money to run the government and to pay its debts. One way to get money was through the sale of these public lands. But first, it was necessary to decide how the land would be divided for sale.

The Land Ordinance of 1785 established a system for dividing and settling the lands of the Old Northwest. The ordinance (ORD-uhn-uhns), or law, stated that the government would survey the area. The land would then be divided into townships, each measuring 36 square miles. Each township was then to be subdivided into 36 sections measuring 1 square mile (640 acres). The sixteenth section of each town was to be set aside to support a public school. The townships were then to be sold at public auctions. The smallest amount that could be sold was a section. Land companies bought sections from the government at $1.00 an acre. They then divided the sections into smaller units and sold them to settlers.

Northwest Ordinance

Congress passed the Northwest Ordinance of 1787 to provide for the government of the Northwest Territory. This Territory was the land north of the Ohio River, west of Pennsylvania, and east of the Mississippi. From three to five districts could be created from it.

During the first period of settlement, each district was to have a governor, secretary, and three judges appointed by Congress. When the population reached 5,000 free adult males, the landholders could choose a legislature and a nonvoting delegate to Congress. When the population reached 60,000, the territory could adopt a constitution and ask for statehood. In time this area was divided into the states of Ohio, Indiana, Illinois, Michigan, Wisconsin, and part of Minnesota.

The ordinance outlawed slavery and guaranteed freedom of religion and trial by jury. Because of the land ordinances, the new territories of the Northwest received statehood on equal terms with the 13 original states. All states—old and new—had the same rights. While the ordinances were written for the Northwest Territory, the steps for statehood were later used for most of the new land the U.S. acquired.

LOOKING BACK

1. How did colonial experiences affect the way the states set up their governments?
2. List three weaknesses of the U.S. government under the Articles of Confederation.
3. What were three economic problems that the U.S. faced after the Revolutionary War?
4. **a.** List the economic systems that were developing in New England, the South, and the Middle colonies up to, through, and after the Revolutionary War. **b.** What is sectionalism? **c.** Why did sectionalism cause a problem for the government of the U.S.?
5. What was the purpose of the following laws: **a.** Land Ordinance of 1785? **b.** Northwest Ordinance?

Chapter 2   Decision for Change

LOOKING AHEAD

In the last chapter, you read that many Americans realized that the Articles of Confederation were not working. In this chapter, you will read how the Articles were put aside for a new constitution. You will also learn about the compromises that were made in order to write that constitution and about its ratification. After you study this chapter, you will be able to:

★ identify the differences in point of view between primary and secondary sources.
● compare and contrast a confederation form of government with a federal system.
● compare and contrast the features of the Virginia Plan and the New Jersey Plan.
● list four compromises made by the delegates.
● state two objections to the constitution.

Social Studies Vocabulary

convention	federal government	commerce
federalism	chief executive	ratification

People

George Washington	James Madison	Patrick Henry

Words and Terms

Virginia Plan	three-fifths clause
New Jersey Plan	overriding the President's veto
Connecticut Compromise	Federalist
Congress	Anti-Federalist
House of Representatives	*The Federalist*
Senate	

Events

Annapolis Conference	Constitutional Convention

The Articles of Confederation had serious weaknesses. It did not provide for an executive branch or for a central system of courts. It did not give the central government control of interstate commerce or the power to set taxes or enforce treaties. Under the Articles, Congress found the problems of the new nation almost impossible to solve. Congress had no way of forcing states to obey the laws it passed. Some people worried that the new nation would not last.

THE CONSTITUTIONAL CONVENTION

Meetings among the states in 1785 and 1786 to discuss trade problems convinced them that changes had to be made in the Articles. The Annapolis Conference of 1786 recommended a convention of all the states to make the needed changes. A **convention** (kuhn-VEN-shuhn) is a meeting held for a special purpose. The Congress of the Confederation agreed to the convention. The delegates were to be chosen by each state's legislature.

The 55 men who came to Philadelphia in May 1787 were among the ablest and most experienced leaders of the time. After years of experience with the Articles, they were very aware of the weaknesses. George Washington was selected to head the meeting. Among other members were Benjamin Franklin, James Madison, Alexander Hamilton, Roger Sherman, and Charles Pinckney. Patrick Henry refused to attend. He was against any plan to strengthen the central government. Rhode Island refused to send any delegates because it did not want a strong central government interfering in its affairs.

James Madison kept a full record of the debates. Because of his record, historians know much of what took place during the convention. In fact, historians know more than the people of 1787 did. Madison's notes were not published until 1840. The delegates voted to keep their discussions secret. They did not want news of their debates to reach the public until their decisions were final. In this way, the delegates were free of public arguments and influence. The following is from Madison's notes concerning the debate on the end of the slave trade to the U.S. His record is a primary source:

Wednesday, August 22
Mr. Sherman (Connecticut) disapproved of the slave trade. Yet as the states now had the right to import slaves, and as it was desirable to have

George Washington led the Constitutional Convention in its work. The chair that he sat in had a rising sun carved on it. Franklin compared the rising sun to the dawn of the new nation. How did the artist use this idea in his painting?

abolition
(ab-uh-LISH-uhn):
doing away with
something completely

prohibit (proh-HIB-it):
to forbid

as few objections to the government, he thought it best to leave the matter as we find it. He observed that the abolition of slavery seemed to be going on in the U.S. The good sense of the states would probably in time complete it.

Colonel Mason (Virginia). The present question concerns not the importing states alone, but the whole union. Maryland and Virginia he said had already prohibited the importation of slaves directly. North Carolina had done the same indirectly. All this would be useless, if South Carolina and Georgia be at liberty to import. The Western people are already calling out for slaves for their new lands. They will fill that country with slaves, if they can be got through South Carolina and Georgia. As to the states having the right to import, this was the case with many other rights, now to be given up.

contend (kuhn-TEND):
to argue

General Pinckney (South Carolina). South Carolina and Georgia cannot do without slaves. He contended that the importation of slaves would be for the interest of the whole union.

Mr. Sherman said it was better to let the Southern states import slaves, than to part with the states.

The following is a view of the Constitutional Convention by Max Farrand, an historian. Because he lived 150 years after the convention and had to use primary sources, his interpretation is a secondary source.

In 1787, slavery was not the important question. It might be said that it was not the moral question that it later became. The proceedings of the federal convention did not become known until the slavery question had grown into the supreme issue of the day. People naturally were eager to know what the framers of the Constitution had said and done upon this most interesting topic. This led to too much stress on the slavery question at the convention which has lasted to the present day. As a matter of fact, there was comparatively little said on the subject in the convention. Madison was one of the very few men who seemed to appreciate the real division of interests in this country. It is significant that in the debate on representation, he felt it necessary to warn the convention that it was not the size of the states, but that "the great danger to our general government is the great southern and northern interests of the continent being opposed to each other."

comparatively
(kuhm-PAR-uh-tiv-lee):
more or less

WORKING WITH SOURCES

James Madison's first-hand account of the debates on the slave trade shows several points of view among the delegates. **1.** What was Mr. Sherman's point of view? **2.** What was General Pinckney's view? **3.** Do these views show sectionalism? **4.** Is Max Farrand giving his opinion of slavery or describing what he thinks were people's reasons for the way they acted 150 years before?

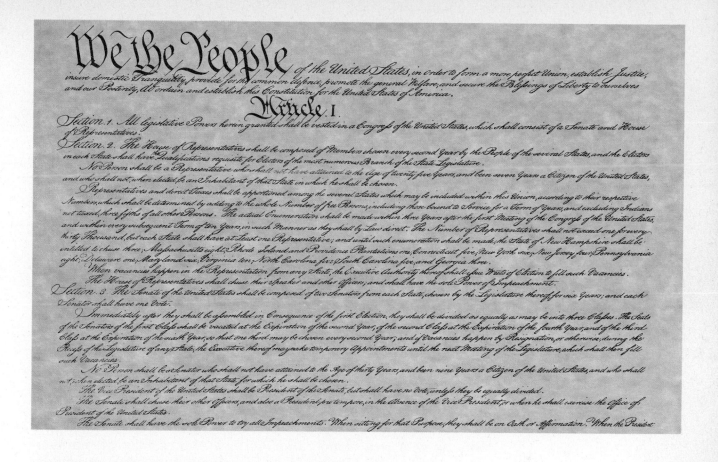

WRITING THE CONSTITUTION

The original objective of the convention was to revise, or change, the Articles of Confederation. It soon became clear that more than a few changes were needed. Governor Edmund Randolph of Virginia took the first step toward a new government with his Virginia Plan. It called for a central government completely different from the one in the Articles. From that point on, the delegates stopped trying to change the Articles and worked to create a new form of government. The result, after several months of discussing, arguing, and debating, became the U.S. Constitution.

Dividing the Power

Before the Constitution was completed, however, the delegates faced many problems and were forced to make many compromises. The first problem they faced was deciding on the kind of government that was needed. Should the central government be more powerful than the states? Or should the states have greater power? In other words, where would the highest authority rest: with the central government or with the states?

Delegates proposed two answers. One group of delegates wanted a strong union of states. They wanted Congress to make laws that all

propose: to suggest

states had to obey. Other delegates were afraid of a strong central government. This was the same fear that lay behind the writing of the Articles. These men proposed that the most important decisions be made in state legislatures.

With either solution, there would be problems. Without the power to act for everyone, the central government would face the problems of the Articles all over again. But if the states were not given enough power, they would not approve the new constitution. Nothing would be gained from the Constitutional Convention.

The problem was solved by creating a government based on federalism. **Federalism** (FED-uhr-uhl-iz-uhm) is a government system that divides power among national, state, and local authorities. In a **federal government,** the separate states unite under a central organization that controls matters of common interest and acts on behalf of the nation as a whole. Each state, however, controls affairs within its own borders. In other words, there is a strong central government, but the states have power, too.

Compromise on Representation

Another problem that faced the delegates was representation. How many representatives should each state have in the central government? Several plans were suggested. The Virginia Plan provided for a congress with two branches, or houses. The number of representatives a state would have in each house would be based on population. The more people in a state, the more representatives the state would have. Delegates from states with large populations favored this plan. It would give them more representatives and more power.

Delegates from states with small populations favored the New Jersey Plan. It called for a legislature of one house in which each state would have one vote. In this way, the states with small populations would have as much power as the more populated states.

The solution to the problem was the Connecticut Compromise, sometimes called the Great Compromise. According to it, the new Congress, the national lawmaking body, would have two houses. In the House of Representatives, or the lower house, the number of representatives would be based on population. This followed the Virginia Plan and pleased the more populated states. In the Senate, or upper house, each state would have the same number of representatives: two. This followed the New Jersey Plan and pleased delegates from the smaller states.

Another compromise had to be reached on how to count the population to decide the number of representatives. Delegates from southern states wanted slaves counted. Northern delegates opposed this because slaves could not vote. Some sectionalism may have entered into this argument. The slave population of the North had never been very large. After the Revolutionary War, slavery in the North was gradually dying out. The compromise that was reached allowed every

PLANS OF GOVERNMENT

	Virginia Plan	New Jersey Plan	U.S. Constitution
Representation	Based on population or wealth	Equal representation for each state	Lower house based on population; two representatives per state in upper house
Executive Branch	National executive chosen by Congress	Executive committee chosen by Congress	President chosen by electors; electors voted for by people
Judicial Branch	National judiciary chosen by Congress	National judiciary appointed by Executive committee	Supreme Court justices appointed by President confirmed by Senate; inferior courts established by Congress
Legislative Branch	Two houses: upper elected by the people; lower elected by the first house	One house: appointed by state legislatures	Two houses: upper based on equal representation; lower based on population

five slaves to be counted as three free men. This is called the three-fifths clause. As a result, the southern states gained additional members of the new House of Representatives.

Fear of a Chief Executive

A major weakness of the Articles was the lack of an executive branch led by a **chief executive**—head of state. This branch would be responsible for carrying out the work of the central government. But the delegates were afraid of a chief executive who had too much power. The Constitutional Convention limited the President's powers in several ways. For example, Congress had to approve by a two-thirds vote any treaty the chief executive made with a foreign country.

Another limit on the President's power was Congress' right to pass laws over the President's veto. The Constitution states that the President may veto a bill after Congress has passed it. However, Congress may vote again. If two-thirds of the members of both houses vote to pass the bill again, it becomes law. This is called overriding the President's veto.

Commerce

A final compromise dealt with **commerce,** the buying, selling, or trading of goods and services. Delegates from some states were afraid to give Congress the power to regulate trade. They feared that Congress would set taxes on imports and end the slave trade. Before the Con-

New York held a parade in 1788 to celebrate the state's ratification of the Constitution. The float honors Alexander Hamilton. Why?

vention would allow Congress power over commerce, it made two conditions. Congress could not tax exports nor end the slave trade until 1808.

RATIFICATION

The Constitutional Convention decided that the new Constitution would become law when nine of the thirteen states approved it. It was one thing for the delegates to approve the Constitution. They had debated it and reached compromises on key points. But **ratification** (rat-uh-fuh-KAY-shuhn), or approval, by the states was a very different matter.

There were several objections to the new Constitution. Many Americans felt it gave too much power to the central government. Others, including Jefferson, protested that the Constitution lacked a bill of rights. As you may recall from the unit Becoming Americans the English had had a bill of rights since 1689. Most of the new state constitutions also had such bills. The people wanted guarantees in the new Constitution of such rights as freedom from illegal searches and freedom of religion.

Federalists Versus Anti-Federalists

In spite of these objections, the ratification process began well. Each state called a convention of delegates to vote on whether to accept the Constitution. The delegates were chosen directly by the voters of each state. By June 1788, nine states had voted *yes*. The Constitution was law. However, it was clear that the new government would not work as long as four states did not join.

In Virginia, long and angry debates were held between Federalists and Anti-Federalists. Federalists (FED-uhr-uhl-ists) were those who supported the Constitution. Anti-Federalists were those who opposed it. Patrick Henry led the fight in Virginia against the Constitution. Virginia ratified it only after promises were made that Washington, a Virginian, would be the first President and that a bill of rights would be added quickly.

In New York, Hamilton, Madison, and John Jay defended the Constitution in a series of essays called *The Federalist*. Beginning in October 1787, these articles described the strengths of the Constitution and answered its critics. They pointed out, for example, that the people themselves would be voting for members of one house of Congress. These representatives of the people as well as the senators would have to approve every law that was passed.

The purpose of *The Federalist* was to bring about ratification in New York. The state did ratify the Constitution in June 1788. However, *The Federalist* found an audience beyond New York. Its arguments made sense to many people.

When the new government of the U.S. took office on March 4, 1789 only North Carolina and Rhode Island had not ratified the Constitution. They were surrounded by the new country but were not part of it. They saw no choice but to ratify. Approval came from North Carolina in November 1789 and from Rhode Island in May 1790. The Federalists' promise to add a bill of rights to the Constitution helped.

LOOKING BACK

★ 1. James Madison's first-hand account of the debates on the slave trade shows several points of view among the delegates. **a.** What was Mr. Sherman's point of view? **b.** What was General Pinckney's view? **c.** Is Max Farrand giving his opinion of slavery or describing what he thinks were people's reasons for the way they acted 150 years before? **d.** What is the difference between a primary and a secondary source?

2. In a paragraph, compare and contrast the government under the Articles of Confederation with the federal system of the Constitution. Use the following topics: chief executive, powers of the central government, powers of the states. You may have to infer some of the comparisons and contrasts.

3. Use the table to compare and contrast the Virginia and New Jersey plans as to: **a.** number of houses in the national legislature. **b.** type of executive. **c.** type of judiciary. **d.** method of choosing Congress.

4. Describe the four compromises that the delegates to the Constitutional Convention reached on each of the following: **a.** system of government. **b.** representation. **c.** chief executive. **d.** power to regulate commerce.

5. **a.** Explain two objections of Anti-Federalists to the Constitution. **b.** How did Federalists answer these questions?

Chapter 3   The Constitution

LOOKING AHEAD

In this chapter, you will learn about the basic principles and organization of the Constitution. You will read the Constitution along with notes that will help you understand its purposes. After you study this chapter, you will be able to:

- identify the four basic principles of the Constitution.
- list the enumerated powers of the federal government.
- ★ read a flow chart to learn how the system of checks and balances works.
- explain the reason for the Bill of Rights.
- explain how the Constitution is adaptable.
- ★ read a flow chart to learn how a bill becomes law.
- ★ read a flow chart to see how the federal court system works.
- ★ read a flow chart to learn how an amendment is proposed and ratified.

Social Studies Vocabulary

constitutional government	impeach	alliance
	flow chart	treason
amendment	excise tax	income tax

Places

District of Columbia

Words and Terms

enumerated powers	President pro tempore	petit jury
supremacy clause	chief justice	due process of law
system of checks and balances	quorum	cruel and unusual punishment
Supreme Court	pocket veto	naturalization
judicial review	writ of habeus corpus	equal protection of the laws
null and void	bill of attainder	
Bill of Rights	ex post facto law	Prohibition
elastic clause	electoral college	lame duck
implied powers	Cabinet	inauguration
Speaker of the House	trial by jury	
	probable cause	
	grand jury	

The Constitution that was finally written by the Constitutional Convention was the result of the work of delegates with many points of view. In order to be approved by these delegates and later by their states, the Constitution contained compromises. Only 42 of the 55 delegates were still at the convention when it ended on September 17, 1787. Of these, 39 signed the Constitution. Franklin expressed the feeling of most of them when, as he signed, he said: "Thus I consent, Sir, to this Constitution, because I expect no better, and because I am not sure that it is not the best."

The U.S. government today is one of the oldest constitutional governments in the world. A **constitutional government** is one in which law limits the power of the government. Many people in the 1780s did not believe a government built on such a constitution would last.

BASIC PRINCIPLES

Almost 200 years have passed since the writing of the Constitution. In these years, Americans have come to see that the Constitution is based on four principles. These are federalism, the separation of powers, the rights of individuals, and the adaptability of the Constitution to meet the needs of the times.

principle (PRIN-suh-puhl): basic rule

Federalism

As you read in the last chapter, the writers of the Constitution chose a federal system of government. They divided government powers among national, state, and local branches. The delegates then had to deal with the question of which of the three branches would be responsible for which activities. In Article I, Section 8, Clauses 1-17, the delegates listed the powers of the national government. These are called enumerated powers and include the rights to set taxes, coin money, regulate commerce, and maintain an army and navy.

maintain: to keep up; to continue

The Old State House in Boston, once the center of British rule in Massachusetts colony, represents one concern of the members of the Constitutional Convention — how to divide power among state and national governments.

The states kept the powers not directly given to the national government. The state governments in turn passed on some of their powers to local governments. For example, a state is responsible for education. But it usually turns much of its power over to local boards of education. They actually organize and operate the schools.

The Tenth Amendment to the Constitution, adopted in 1791, made clear the powers kept for the states: "Powers not delegated to the United States by the Constitution, nor prohibited by it to the states, are reserved to the states respectively, or to the people." An **amendment** is a change or addition.

The writers of the Constitution, however, also wanted to make it clear that the Constitution and federal law were considered higher than state law. They did this by including in Article VI, called the supremacy clause, a phrase declaring the Constitution "the supreme law of the land."

Separation of Powers

As you may recall from the last chapter, delegates to the Constitutional Convention wanted to make sure that no branch of government had too much power. As a result, they created three separate branches of government—executive, legislative, and judicial. Each has its own powers, and these powers limit one another. This separation of powers is called a system of checks and balances.

The President, for example, can make treaties with foreign nations. But the Senate must approve them. The President must report from time to time to Congress on the State of the Union—the progress of the nation. Although the President initiates budget bills, Congress must approve them. The House can **impeach,** or charge a President with wrongdoing. The Senate tries a President for such charges.

Congress as the legislative branch of the government has another check against the President's power. The President cannot make laws alone. As you may recall from the last chapter, the President has the right to veto a bill passed by Congress. Congress has the power to override the President's veto.

The judicial branch serves as a check on both the executive and legislative branches. The federal courts—with the Supreme Court as the highest court—can decide whether a law is constitutional, that is, whether it agrees with the Constitution. This is called judicial review. If the Supreme Court decides the law violates the Constitution, the law is declared null and void, without effect. It is no longer considered a law and cannot be enforced. However, only laws that have been challenged and are brought before the courts can be declared null and void.

Rights of Individuals

The delegates at the Constitutional Convention were aware that the Revolution was fought to protect certain rights of a free people. Some states had wanted a more detailed statement of the rights of the people than the new Constitution gave. During the first session of the new Congress, Madison proposed a bill of rights as the first ten amendments. Congress wrote the amendments during the summer of 1789. They were ratified by the necessary nine states before the end of 1791. The Bill of Rights guarantees the people of the U.S. certain rights as individuals. Among them are freedom of religion and of speech, freedom from illegal searches, and the right to a fair trial.

A **flow chart** shows, by pictures or a few words, the order of the steps in a process. A flow chart uses arrows to show direction. When reading a flow chart, always read the title to see what process is being shown. Then look for the start—the first arrow—to see which way the process flows. It may go from top to bottom, bottom to top, left to right, or in a circle. Look at the flow chart below. Some information is easier to read on one kind of flow chart than on another. **1.** Where does it begin? **2.** Which way does it read? **3.** Which branch of the federal government controls appropriations? **4.** Which branch can declare laws unconstitutional? **5.** Which branch can call special sessions of Congress? Look at the charts on pages 271, 281, and 284. **6.** Where does each begin? **7.** Which way does each read?

BUILDING SKILLS WITH CHARTS

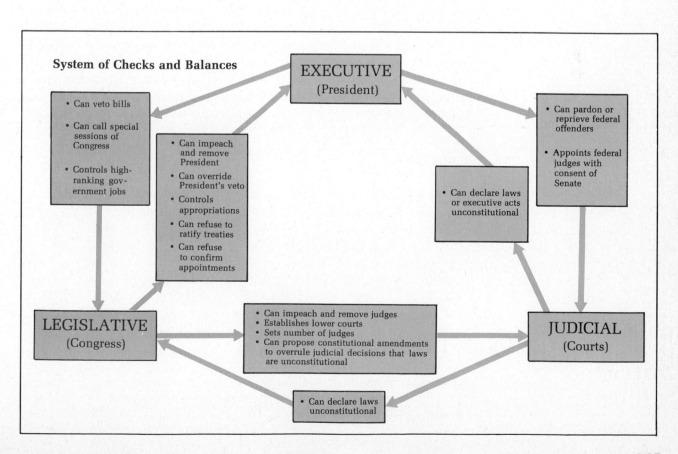

System of Checks and Balances

EXECUTIVE
(President)

- Can veto bills
- Can call special sessions of Congress
- Controls high-ranking government jobs

- Can impeach and remove President
- Can override President's veto
- Controls appropriations
- Can refuse to ratify treaties
- Can refuse to confirm appointments

- Can pardon or reprieve federal offenders
- Appoints federal judges with consent of Senate

- Can declare laws or executive acts unconstitutional

LEGISLATIVE
(Congress)

- Can impeach and remove judges
- Establishes lower courts
- Sets number of judges
- Can propose constitutional amendments to overrule judicial decisions that laws are unconstitutional

JUDICIAL
(Courts)

- Can declare laws unconstitutional

Adaptability of the Constitution

A document that has lasted as long as the Constitution has had to change to remain useful. This adaptability was built into the document by the delegates who wrote it. There are three ways the Constitution is flexible.

In Article I, Section 8, Clause 18, the delegates gave the federal government the right to stretch its powers when necessary. This is known as the elastic clause. According to it, Congress has the power "to make all laws which shall be necessary and proper" to carrying out its duties. This has allowed Congress to pass laws for many situations not specifically mentioned in the Constitution. For example, Congress created the Postal Service and a commission to regulate trade among the states.

The federal government also has implied powers. These are powers that can be inferred from the Constitution but are not actually listed in it. For example, the Preamble says that the Constitution is to "promote the general welfare." For this purpose, the federal government has created many programs to help people. It runs the Social Security System and can, for example, provide loans for college students and issue food stamps.

The amendment process is another way that makes the Constitution adaptable. The delegates to the convention recognized that amendments would be necessary in order to meet the needs of changing times and of future generations. Amendments can be proposed in one of two ways. One way is by a two-thirds vote of both houses of Congress. The second way is through a national convention called by Congress at the request of the "legislatures of two thirds of the states." Amendments must be ratified by the legislatures of three fourths of the states or by constitutional conventions called in three fourths of the states.

specifically
(spih-SIF-ik-lee):
particularly

STRUCTURE OF THE CONSTITUTION

Like the Declaration of Independence, the Constitution begins with a Preamble. This explains the purpose for writing the Constitution. Seven articles describing the main features of the government follow.

Articles I, II, and III describe the legislative, executive, and judicial branches of the government respectively. The next article explains the relationship of the states to one another and to the federal government. The fifth article explains the amendment process. Article VI deals with general ideas—the national debt, the authority of the Constitution, and officeholding. The last article tells how the Constitution is to be ratified.

Next come the amendments. As you have just read, the first ten amendments are known as the Bill of Rights. Since 1791, 16 amendments have been added. These show the concerns of the nation at various times in our history.

CONSTITUTION OF THE UNITED STATES

PREAMBLE
We the people of the United States, in order to form a more perfect union, establish justice, insure domestic tranquility, provide for the common defense, promote the general welfare, and secure the blessings of liberty to ourselves and our posterity, do ordain and establish this Constitution for the United States of America.

The Preamble states the reasons for writing the Constitution. These are to provide for: greater cooperation among states; equal justice for all; peace within the nation; an army and navy; a good life for all the people; and liberty now and in the future. The phrase *We the people* means that it is the people who are setting up the government.

Article I   LEGISLATIVE DEPARTMENT
Section 1   CONGRESS
Legislative powers. All legislative powers herein granted shall be vested in a Congress of the United States, which shall consist of a Senate and House of Representatives.

Article I describes Congress, the legislative branch of the federal government. Congress alone has the power to make laws for the nation, but the President and the courts are checks on this power.

Section 2   HOUSE OF REPRESENTATIVES
1. *Election.* The House of Representatives shall be composed of members chosen every second year by the people of the several states, and the electors in each state shall have the qualifications requisite for electors of the most numerous branch of the state legislature.

The members of the House are elected every two years by the voters of each state. Those who have the right to vote for state legislators also have the right to vote for federal representatives. According to this clause, each state has the power to decide who may vote. (See the 14th, 15th, 19th and 24th Amendments for limits on the power of states to make voting laws.)

2. *Qualifications.* No person shall be a representative who shall not have attained to the age of twenty-five years, and been seven years a citizen of the United States, and who shall not, when elected, be an inhabitant of that state in which he shall be chosen.

A representative must be at least 25 years old and have been a citizen of the U.S. for at least seven years. A representative must live in the state from which he or she is elected.

3. *Apportionment.* Representatives ~~and direct taxes~~ shall be apportioned among the several states which may be included within this Union, according to their respective numbers, ~~which shall be determined by adding to the whole number of free persons, including those bound to service for a term of years, and excluding Indians not taxed, three-fifths of all other persons.~~ The actual enumeration shall be made within three years after the first meeting of the Congress of the United States, and within every subsequent term of ten years, in such manner as they shall by law direct. The number of represen-

apportionment
(uh-POR-shuhn-muhnt):
division of representatives and taxes according to U.S. law

tatives shall not exceed one for every thirty thousand, but each state shall have at least one representative; ~~and until such enumeration shall be made, the state of New Hampshire shall be entitled to choose three, Massachusetts eight, Rhode Island and Providence Plantations one, Connecticut five, New York six, New Jersey four, Pennsylvania eight, Delaware one, Maryland six, Virginia ten, North Carolina five, South Carolina five, and Georgia three.~~

The number of representatives for each state depends on the state's population, which is counted every ten years in the census. Congress uses the census to decide the number of members each state should have in the House. Originally, each member was to represent no more than 30,000 people. However, our population has grown so much that in 1929 Congress fixed the size of the House at 435 members. Each member represents an average of 465,000 people. The least number of representatives a state can have is one. In deciding representation according to this clause, untaxed persons (Native Americans) were not counted, and a slave was counted as three fifths of a person. Native Americans are now taxed, and the three-fifths clause was replaced by the 13th Amendment and Section 2 of the 14th Amendment.

4. *Vacancies.* When vacancies happen in the representation from any state, the executive authority thereof shall issue writs of election to fill such vacancies.

When a representative dies or leaves office before her or his term is finished, the governor of the state orders a special election to choose a replacement. (See 17th Amendment for addition.)

5. *Officers; power.* The House of Representatives shall choose their speaker and other officers, and shall have the sole power of impeachment.

The House selects its own officers, including its chairperson, the speaker of the House. Only the House has the power to impeach high executive or judicial officers. If the House charges an official with wrongdoing, the trial is held in the Senate. The power of impeachment is a legislative check on the other two branches of government.

Section 3 SENATE
1. *Election.* The Senate of the United States shall be composed of two senators from each state, chosen ~~by the legislature thereof~~ for six years; and each senator shall have one vote.

Every state has two senators. Each serves for six years and has one vote. Originally, senators were not elected directly by the people but were chosen by each state's legislature. (See 17th Amendment for change.)

2. ~~*Term of service.* Immediately after they shall be assembled in consequence of the first election, they shall be divided as equally as may be into three classes. The seats of the senators of the first class shall be vacated at the expiration of the second year, of the second class at the expiration of the fourth year, and of the third class at the expiration of the sixth year, so that one-third may be chosen every second year; and if vacancies happen by resignation, or otherwise during the recess of the legislature of any state, the executive thereof may make temporary appointments until the next meeting of the legislature, which shall then fill such vacancies.~~

The senators elected in 1788 were divided into three groups so that elections could be held every two years. The 17th Amendment replaced the clause.

3. *Qualifications.* No person shall be a senator who shall not have attained to the age of thirty years, and been nine years a citizen of the United States, and who shall not, when elected, be an inhabitant of that state for which he shall be chosen.

A senator must be at least 30 years old and a U.S. citizen for nine years. A senator also must live in the state from which he or she is elected.

4. *President of Senate.* The Vice-President of the United States shall be president of the Senate, but shall have no vote, unless they be equally divided.

The president of the Senate is the Vice-President of the U.S. He or she may vote only to break a tie.

5. *Other officers.* The Senate shall choose their other officers, and also a president pro tempore, in the absence of the Vice-President, or when he shall exercise the office of President of the United States.

The Senate selects its own officers, including someone to preside if the Vice-President is absent or is serving as President of the U.S. That senator is called the president pro tempore (proh TEM-puh-ree).

6. *Impeachment trials.* The Senate shall have the sole power to try all impeachments. When sitting for that purpose, they shall be on oath or affirmation. When the President of the United States is tried, the chief justice shall preside: and no person shall be convicted without the concurrence of two thirds of the members present.

The Senate conducts the trials of officials impeached by the House. If the President is on trial, the Chief Justice of the Supreme Court presides. Otherwise, the Vice-President presides. To convict an official, two thirds of the senators present must vote guilty.

preside (prih-ZYD): to be in a place of authority; to direct

7. *Power in case of conviction.* Judgment in cases of impeachment shall not extend further than to removal from office, and disqualification to hold and enjoy any office of honor, trust, or profit under the United States: but the party convicted shall nevertheless be liable and subject to indictment, trial, judgment, and punishment, according to law.

If the Senate finds an impeached official guilty, it can only remove that person from office and forbid her or him from holding any other public office. The guilty person, however, may be tried in a regular court of law.

indictment (in-DYT-muhnt): legal statement accusing someone of a crime

Section 4 ELECTION AND MEETINGS
1. *Election.* The times, places, and manner of holding elections for senators and representatives, shall be prescribed in each state by the legislature thereof; but the Congress may at any time by law make or alter such regulations, ~~except as to the places of choosing senators~~.

According to this clause, states may decide when, where, and how to hold elections. Congress, however, may change the times and methods, except for the election of senators. (See 17th Amendment for change.) An example of

prescribe (prih-SKRYB): to order

Congress' use of this clause was the law that set the day for Congressional elections as the Tuesday after the first Monday in November in even numbered years.

2. *Sessions.* The Congress shall assemble at least once in every year, ~~and such meeting shall be on the first Monday in December,~~ unless they shall by law appoint a different day.

Congress must meet at least once a year. (See 20th Amendment for change.)

Section 5   ORGANIZATION OF CONGRESS

1. *Organization.* Each house shall be the judge of the elections, returns, and qualifications of its own members, and a majority of each shall constitute a quorum to do business; but a smaller number may adjourn from day to day, and may be authorized to compel the attendance of absent members, in such manner, and under such penalties as each house may provide.

Both the House and the Senate have the right to refuse to admit an elected member they think is unfit. But in 1969, the Supreme Court ruled that the House did not have the right to keep out a member who satisfies Article I, Section 2, Clause 2.

A quorum must be present for each house to do business. A quorum (KWAW-ruhm) is more than half the total number of members. Business often goes on with fewer members present, but both the Senate and House have rules to force members to attend.

proceedings
(pruh-SEED-ings).
meetings

2. *Rules.* Each house may determine the rules of its proceedings, punish its members for disorderly behavior, and, with the concurrence of two-thirds, expel a member.

The Senate and the House have the right to make their own rules for meetings and sessions and to punish members. By a two-thirds vote, members may even be expelled.

3. *Record.* Each house shall keep a journal of its proceedings, and from time to time publish the same, excepting such parts as may in their judgment require secrecy; and the yeas and nays of the members of either house on any question shall, at the desire of one fifth of those present, be entered on the journal.

Both houses must keep and publish a record of their activities. This journal is published daily and is called the *Congressional Record.* If Congress wants some activities kept secret, these are not published. Each member's vote on a particular question must be published if asked for by one fifth of the members present.

4. *Adjournment.* Neither House, during the session of Congress, shall, without the consent of the other, adjourn for more than three days, nor to any other place than that in which the two Houses shall be sitting.

Once in session, neither house can stop work for more than three days without the other house's approval. Both houses must meet in the same city.

Section 6   PRIVILEGES AND RESTRICTIONS

1. *Salary and rights.* The senators and representatives shall receive a compensation for their services, to be ascertained by law, and paid out of the

treasury of the United States. They shall in all cases, except treason, felony, and breach of the peace, be privileged from arrest during their attendance at the session of their respective houses, and in going to and returning from the same; and for any speech or debate in either house, they shall not be questioned in any other place.

Senate and House members set their own salaries and are paid by the U.S. government. When in session or traveling to or from a session, members cannot be arrested, except for treason, serious crimes, or breaking the peace. This is to prevent interference in their duties. Members also cannot be brought to trial for what they say in Congress or in a Congressional committee or publication. This is to allow a free debate of ideas.

2. *Limits on members.* No senator or representative shall, during the time for which he was elected, be appointed to any civil office under the authority of the United States, which shall have been created, or the emoluments thereof shall have been increased during such time; and no person holding any office under the United States shall be a member of either house during his continuance in office.

emolument
(ih-MAHL-yuh-muhnt): salary; fee

Senators and representatives cannot hold any job in the U.S. government that was created, or for which the salary was raised, during the member's term. A person already working for the government in another job may not serve as a member of either house.

Section 7 METHOD OF PASSING LAWS
1. *Tax bills.* All bills for raising revenue shall originate in the House of Representatives; but the Senate may propose or concur with amendments as on other bills.

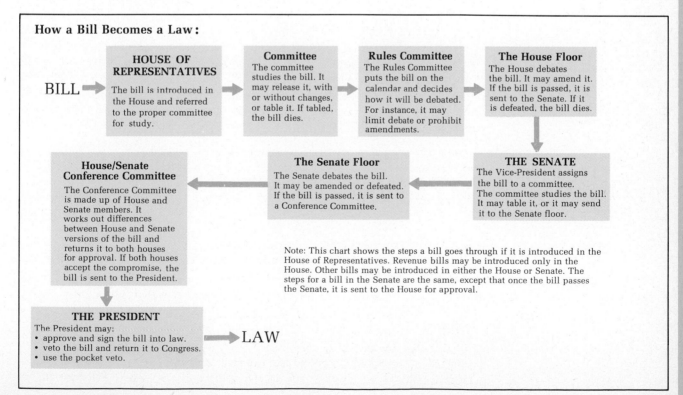

How a Bill Becomes a Law:

BILL →

HOUSE OF REPRESENTATIVES
The bill is introduced in the House and referred to the proper committee for study.

Committee
The committee studies the bill. It may release it, with or without changes, or table it. If tabled, the bill dies.

Rules Committee
The Rules Committee puts the bill on the calendar and decides how it will be debated. For instance, it may limit debate or prohibit amendments.

The House Floor
The House debates the bill. It may amend it. If the bill is passed, it is sent to the Senate. If it is defeated, the bill dies.

House/Senate Conference Committee
The Conference Committee is made up of House and Senate members. It works out differences between House and Senate versions of the bill and returns it to both houses for approval. If both houses accept the compromise, the bill is sent to the President.

The Senate Floor
The Senate debates the bill. It may be amended or defeated. If the bill is passed, it is sent to a Conference Committee.

THE SENATE
The Vice-President assigns the bill to a committee. The committee studies the bill. It may table it, or it may send it to the Senate floor.

Note: This chart shows the steps a bill goes through if it is introduced in the House of Representatives. Revenue bills may be introduced only in the House. Other bills may be introduced in either the House or Senate. The steps for a bill in the Senate are the same, except that once the bill passes the Senate, it is sent to the House for approval.

THE PRESIDENT
The President may:
• approve and sign the bill into law.
• veto the bill and return it to Congress.
• use the pocket veto.

→ LAW

Bills that involve raising money by taxes must start in the House of Representatives. The Senate, however, can, and often does, amend tax bills.

2. *How bills become laws.* Every bill which shall have passed the House of Representatives and the Senate, shall, before it becomes a law, be presented to the President of the United States; if he approve he shall sign it, but if not he shall return it, with his objections to that house in which it shall have originated, who shall enter the objections at large on their journal, and proceed to reconsider it. If after such reconsideration two thirds of that house shall agree to pass the bill, it shall be sent, together with the objections, to the other house, by which it shall likewise be reconsidered, and if approved by two thirds of that house, it shall become a law. But in all such cases the votes of both houses shall be determined by yeas and nays, and the names of the persons voting for and against the bill shall be entered on the journal of each house respectively. If any bill shall not be returned by the President within ten days (Sundays excepted) after it shall have been presented to him, the same shall be a law, in like manner as if he had signed it, unless the Congress by their adjournment prevent its return, in which case it shall not be a law.

Once a bill has been passed by the House and the Senate, it goes to the President for approval. The President may: a. sign the bill, making it a law; b. veto the bill; or c. hold the bill for ten days (not including Sundays). If Congress remains in session for that ten-day period, the bill becomes a law without the President's signature. If Congress adjourns, the bill does not become a law. This is called a pocket veto.

If the President vetoes a bill while Congress is in session, the bill is returned to Congress. If both the House and Senate again pass it by a two-thirds majority, the bill becomes a law. The *Congressional Record* must publish each member's vote in both houses. This clause is a legislative check on the executive branch.

3. *Presidential veto.* Every order, resolution, or vote to which the concurrence of the Senate and House of Representatives may be necessary (except on a question of adjournment) shall be presented to the President of the United States; and before the same shall take effect, shall be approved by him, or being disapproved by him, shall be repassed by two thirds of the Senate and House of Representatives, according to the rules and limitations prescribed in the case of a bill.

Except for adjournment, every action that needs the approval of both the House and the Senate must also be approved by the President. If any action is vetoed by the President, the item is sent back to Congress for a new vote. This is an executive check on the legislative branch.

Section 8   POWERS GRANTED TO CONGRESS
Enumerated powers. The Congress shall have power:
1. To lay and collect taxes, duties, imposts, and excises, to pay the debts and provide for the common defense and general welfare of the United States; but all duties, imposts, and excises shall be uniform throughout the United States;

Congress has the power to raise money by various kinds of taxes. Among them are excise taxes and imposts. *Excise* (ek-SYZ) *taxes* are taxes on goods made or sold within the country. An impost (IM-pohst) is a tax on imports. The revenue is used to pay government debts, keep an army and navy, and provide services. All federal taxes, duties, and excise taxes must be the same in each state.

This clause and the next 16 list the enumerated powers of Congress and, therefore, of the federal government.

2. To borrow money on the credit of the United States;

Congress has the power to borrow money for the nation's use. The Constitution sets no limit on the amount.

3. To regulate commerce with foreign nations, and among the several states, and with the Indian tribes;

Congress has the power to regulate trade with other countries, among states, and with Native American nations. Besides trade, Congress has used this clause to regulate interstate transportation, communications, and banking.

4. To establish a uniform rule of naturalization, and uniform laws on the subject of bankruptcies throughout the United States;

Congress decides how immigrants can become U.S. citizens and also makes laws to cover bankruptcy. Congress has the authority because bankruptcy cases deal with commerce.

5. To coin money, regulate the value thereof, and of foreign coin, and fix the standard of weights and measures;

Congress has the power to coin money and set its value. Congress also decides the value of foreign money in U.S. dollars. Congress sets the standards for weights and measures so they will be the same throughout the country. It is under this clause that the U.S. is changing to the metric system.

6. To provide for the punishment of counterfeiting the securities and current coin of the United States;

Congress has the power to make laws to punish those who make fake U.S. money, bonds, or stamps.

7. To establish post offices and post roads;

According to this clause, Congress was given the power to establish a postal system. At the time, this included the roads over which mail was delivered. In 1970, the post office became a government-owned corporation. Congress may veto changes in postal rates but cannot set these rates. Congress also has no power over workers' salaries.

8. To promote the progress of science and useful arts by securing for limited times to authors and inventors the exclusive right to their respective writings and discoveries;

To help the arts, sciences, and industry, Congress has the right to pass laws for copyrights and patents. Copyrights protect for a certain number of years the rights of artists, composers, and writers to their works. Patents give the same protection to inventors. During the time of a copyright or patent, no one may use a work without permission of the owner.

inferior
(in-FEER-ee-uhr):
lower in rank
or position

9. To constitute tribunals inferior to the Supreme Court;

Through Article III, the Constitution establishes the judicial system. This clause, however, gives Congress the power to establish courts that are lower in authority than the Supreme Court.

10. To define and punish piracies and felonies committed on the high seas, and offenses against the law of nations;

Congress may punish crimes committed on the high seas against the U.S. Congress may also punish U.S. citizens who violate international law.

11. To declare war, ~~grant letters of marque and reprisal~~, and make rules concerning captures on land and water;

Congress has the power to declare war. This clause also gave Congress the power to allow citizens to finance privateers. These ships could capture or destroy enemy ships without being guilty of piracy. Congress gave up this power in 1856 when it agreed to an international law against this practice. Congress, however, may still make laws about capturing enemy property.

appropriation
(uh-proh-pree-AY-shuhn):
money set aside for
a special purpose

12. To raise and support armies, but no appropriation of money to that use shall be for a longer term than two years;

Congress may recruit and finance an army. But all money bills for this purpose may be for a two-year period only. This is to make certain that the army remains under civilian control.

13. To provide and maintain a navy;

Congress has the power to recruit a navy and provide money for its needs. There is no time limit on money bills for the navy's use. The Constitutional Convention did not believe the navy was so great a threat to citizen's freedoms as an army.

14. To make rules for the government and regulation of the land and naval forces;

Congress has the power to make rules for the armed forces.

15. To provide for calling forth the militia to execute the laws of the Union, suppress insurrections, and repel invasions;

Each state has its own volunteer army. Until 1916, these troops were known as the militia. Now they are called the National Guard. Congress and the President have the power to call the National Guard into national service to enforce laws, put down rebellion, and stop invasions.

16. To provide for organizing, arming, and disciplining the militia, and for governing such part of them as may be employed in the service of the United States, reserving to the states respectively the appointment of the officers, and the authority of training the militia according to the discipline prescribed by Congress;

Congress has the power to organize, arm, and discipline the National Guard of each state. The states, however, appoint officers and train the Guard, according to rules made by Congress. When the National Guard is being used for national service, Congress and the President have power over it.

17. To exercise exclusive legislation in all cases whatsoever, over such district (not exceeding ten miles square) as may, by cession of particular states and the acceptance of Congress, become the seat of the government of the United States, and to exercise like authority over all places purchased by the consent of the legislature of the state in which the same shall be, for the erection of forts, magazines, arsenals, dockyards, and other needful buildings;

cession (SESH-uhn): giving up; handing over

According to this clause, Congress was given the power to govern an area bought from the states for the nation's capital. This became the District of Columbia which includes Washington. (See the 23rd Amendment.) This clause also gives Congress the right to govern all areas bought from the states for use as federal forts, arsenals, shipyards, and other necessary federal buildings.

Implied powers. 18. And to make all laws which shall be necessary and proper for carrying into execution the foregoing powers, and all other powers vested by this Constitution in the government of the United States, or in any department or officer thereof.

vested (VES-tid): given the control of

This is the elastic, or "necessary and proper," clause of the Constitution. It allows Congress to make any law needed to accomplish the above 17 clauses. Under this clause, Congress may also make laws to carry out other responsibilities the Constitution gives the federal government or its officials. Congress may not act as it wishes, however. It is limited by the Constitution.

Section 9   POWERS FORBIDDEN TO CONGRESS

1. The migration or importation of such persons as any of the states now existing shall think proper to admit, shall not be prohibited by the Congress prior to the year one thousand eight hundred and eight, but a tax or duty may be imposed on such importation, not exceeding ten dollars for each person.

Congress could not forbid the importing of slaves into the U.S. until 1808. Congress could, however, tax such imports as much as $10 a person. The word *slave* is not used. This clause was part of the compromise reached in writing the Constitution.

2. The privilege of the writ of habeus corpus shall not be suspended, unless when in cases of rebellion or invasion the public safety may require it.

Only in times of civil war or invasion, can Congress suspend the right to a writ of habeas corpus (HAY-bee-uhs KOR-puhs). This is a court order requiring that a person being held for a crime be brought before a judge. The judge must decide if there is enough evidence to keep the person in jail. If there is not, the judge orders the person released. The writ of habeas corpus is an important safeguard of personal freedom.

3. No bill of attainder or ex post facto law shall be passed.

Congress cannot pass laws that punish individual people and take away their right to a trial before a judge. Such a law is called a bill of attainder. This is another example of the separation of legislative and judicial powers. Ex post facto means something done after the fact. Congress may not pass a law declaring that an earlier action is illegal if, at the time it was performed, the action was not against the law.

4. No capitation, or other direct, tax shall be laid, unless in proportion to the census or enumeration herein before directed to be taken.

Direct taxes on individuals can be set by Congress only if they are the same for every person in every state. This clause prevented Congress from taxing slaves at a higher rate. (See the 16th Amendment for an addition.)

5. No tax or duty shall be laid on articles exported from any state.

Congress cannot tax goods sent out of state.

6. No preference shall be given by any regulation of commerce or revenue to the ports of one State over those of another: nor shall vessels bound to, or from, one State be obliged to enter, clear, or pay duties in another.

Congress is forbidden from passing laws that would give one state a trade advantage over another state. Also, Congress may not require a ship from one state to pay taxes to any other state it travels to. This clause was part of the compromises reached to have the Constitution ratified.

7. No money shall be drawn from the treasury, but in consequence of appropriations made by law; and a regular statement and account of the receipts and expenditures of all public money shall be published from time to time.

expenditure
(eks-PEN-duh-chur):
amount of money spent

The federal government may not spend money unless Congress has passed a law permitting it. The government must also make public the amount of money it receives and how it spends the money.

8. No title of nobility shall be granted by the United States: and no person holding any office of profit or trust under them, shall, without the consent of the Congress, accept of any present, emolument, office, or title of any kind whatever, from any king, prince, or foreign state.

No titles of nobility such as prince or countess can be given by the U.S. No U.S. official may accept a gift, money, job, or title from a foreign government without the permission of Congress. This clause was meant to prevent a class of nobles in the U.S. and discourage foreign governments from bribing — trying to buy off — U.S. officials.

Section 10 SECTION 10 POWERS FORBIDDEN TO STATES
1. No state shall enter into any treaty, alliance, or confederation; grant letters of marque and reprisal; coin money; emit bills of credit; make anything but gold and silver coin a tender in payment of debts; pass any bill of attainder, ex post facto law, or law impairing the obligation of contracts, or grant any title of nobility.

emit (ih-MIT):
to circulate

This clause lists eight things states cannot do. A state cannot make an alliance with a foreign government. An *alliance* (uh-LY-uhns) is a joining of groups by formal agreement to promote common interests. Through letters of marque (MAHRK) and reprisal (rih-PRYZ-uhl), a state cannot give its citizens permission to fight foreign countries. (See Article I, Section 8, Clause 11.) A state cannot make its own money. In addition, a state may not pass a law allowing bills of credit to be used in place of gold and silver. Bills of credit are notes promising to pay debts. Like Congress, a state may not pass bills of attainder or ex post facto laws. States may not interfere in contracts between individuals. Also, states may not grant titles of nobility.

2. No state shall, without the consent of the Congress, lay any imposts or duties on imports or exports, except what may be absolutely necessary for

executing its inspection laws: and the net produce of all duties and imposts laid by any state on imports or exports, shall be for the use of the treasury of the United States; and all such laws shall be subject to the revision and control of the Congress.

Unless Congress gives permission, states may not set taxes on goods entering or leaving their borders. States are, however, allowed to charge money to cover the cost of inspecting these goods. Congress has the right to change any of these state laws, and any money collected in this way goes to the federal government.

3. No state shall, without the consent of Congress, lay any duty of tonnage, keep troops, or ships of war in time of peace, enter into any agreement or compact with another state, or with a foreign power, or engage in war, unless actually invaded, or in such imminent danger as will not admit of delay.

Unless Congress approves, a state may not tax ships or keep warships or troops, except the National Guard, in peacetime. A state may not sign a treaty with another state or a foreign country unless Congress approves. A state may not wage war unless it has been invaded, or is about to be invaded, and cannot wait for the approval of Congress.

Article II EXECUTIVE DEPARTMENT
Section 1 PRESIDENT AND VICE-PRESIDENT

1. *Term.* The executive power shall be vested in a President of the United States of America. He shall hold his office during the term of four years, and, together with the Vice-President, chosen for the same term, be elected as follows:

The executive power is the power to see that the policies of the federal government are carried out. The President is the chief executive of the U.S. and is elected for four years. The Vice-President is also elected for four years.

2. *Electors.* Each state shall appoint, in such manner as the legislature thereof may direct, a number of electors, equal to the whole number of senators and representatives to which the state may be entitled in the Congress: but no senator or representative, or person holding an office of trust or profit under the United States, shall be appointed an elector.

3. *Original method of election.* The electors shall meet in their respective states, and vote by ballot for two persons, of whom one at least shall not be an inhabitant of the same state with themselves. And they shall make a list of all the persons voted for, and of the number of votes for each; which list they shall sign and certify, and transmit sealed to the seat of the government of the United States, directed to the president of the Senate. The president of the Senate shall, in the presence of the Senate and House of Representatives, open all the certificates, and the votes shall then be counted. The person having the greatest number of votes shall be the President, if such number be a majority of the whole number of electors appointed; and if there be more than one who have such majority, and have an equal number of votes, then the House of Representatives shall immediately choose by ballot one of them for President; and if no person have a majority, then from the five highest on the list the said house shall in like manner choose the President. But in choosing the President, the votes shall be taken by states, the representation from each state having one vote; a quorum for this purpose shall consist of a member or members from two thirds of the states, and a majority of all the

states shall be necessary to a choice. In every case, after the choice of the President, the person having the greatest number of votes of the electors shall be the Vice-President. But if there should remain two or more who have equal votes, the Senate shall choose from them by ballot the Vice-President.

4. *Date of choosing electors.* The Congress may determine the time of choosing the electors, and the day on which they shall give their votes; which day shall be the same throughout the United States.

Clauses 2, 3, and 4 explain the method of electing these officials. Clause 2 creates the electoral college. Americans do not vote directly for a President but for electors who in turn vote for President and Vice-President. The number of electors a state has is equal to the number of senators and representatives for that state in Congress. No senator, representative, or other government worker may be an elector.

Clause 3 was replaced by the 12th Amendment.

According to Clause 4, Congress has the power to choose the day on which the people vote for electors and the day the electors vote for the President and Vice-President. The first date is known as Election Day and is the Tuesday after the first Monday in November of every fourth year. The electors then meet on the Monday after the second Wednesday in December of that year.

eligible:
(EL-uh-juh-buhl):
qualified

5. *Qualifications for President.* No person except a natural-born citizen, or a citizen of the United States, at the time of adoption of this Constitution, shall be eligible to the office of President; neither shall any person be eligible to that office who shall not have attained to the age of thirty-five years, and been fourteen years a resident within the United States.

A person cannot be chosen President unless she or he was born a U.S. citizen or born of parents who were citizens at the time. An eligible person must be at least 35 years old and have lived in the U.S. for at least 14 years. Because the nation was new when the Constitution was ratified, foreign-born people who had become citizens were also eligible then.

said: mentioned before

6. *Vacancy.* In case of the removal of the President from office, or of his death, resignation, or inability to discharge the powers and duties of the said office, the same shall devolve on the Vice-President, and the Congress may by law provide for the case of removal, death, resignation, or inability, both of the President and Vice-President, declaring what officer shall then act as President, and such officer shall act accordingly, until the disability be removed, or a President shall be elected.

This clause was replaced by the 25th Amendment.

compensation
(kahm-puhn-SAY-shuhn):
pay; salary

7. *Salary.* The President shall, at stated times, receive for his services, a compensation, which shall neither be increased nor diminished during the period for which he shall have been elected, and he shall not receive within that period any other emolument from the United States, or any of them.

The salary of the President cannot be changed during a term in office. The President cannot receive any additional salary from the U.S. government or from any state. This is a check on the legislative branch which decides on the President's salary. Because of this clause, Congress cannot use the President's salary to influence Presidential policies.

8. *Oath of office.* Before he enter on the execution of his office, he shall take the following oath or affirmation:—"I do solemnly swear (or affirm) that I will faithfully execute the office of President of the United States, and will to the best of my ability, preserve, protect, and defend the Constitution of the United States."

execution: doing; putting into effect

With this oath, the President promises to do his or her best in seeing that the Constitution is followed.

Section 2 POWERS OF THE PRESIDENT

1. *Military powers; reprieves and pardons.* The President shall be commander in chief of the army and navy of the United States, and of the militia of the several states, when called into the actual service of the United States; he may require the opinion, in writing, of the principal officer in each of the executive departments, upon any subject relating to the duties of their respective offices, and he shall have power to grant reprieves and pardons for offenses against the United States, except in cases of impeachment.

The President is the head of the armed forces, including the National Guard when it is used in national service. The heads of the 13 executive departments, such as the Department of Education, must report to the President on their departments. This is the only mention in the Constitution of the heads of the executive departments, the Cabinet. The President may grant a reprieve (rih-PREEV), or delay, in carrying out the sentence of a person convicted in a federal court. The President also has the power to pardon, or set free, anyone convicted in a federal court. The President may not interfere in an impeachment.

2. *Treaties; appointments.* He shall have power, by and with the advice and consent of the Senate, to make treaties, provided two thirds of the senators present concur; and he shall nominate, and by and with the advice and consent of the Senate, shall appoint ambassadors, other public ministers and consuls, judges of the Supreme Court, and all other officers of the United States, whose appointments are not herein otherwise provided for, and which shall be established by law: but the Congress may by law vest the appointment of such inferior officers, as they think proper, in the President alone, in the courts of law, or in the heads of departments.

concur (kuhn-KER): to agree

The President may make treaties with foreign nations. But a two-thirds vote of the Senate is needed for a treaty to become effective. The President appoints Supreme Court justices, officials called ambassadors (am-BAS-uh-duhrz) to represent the U.S. in other nations, and other government officials, such as Cabinet members, whose jobs are not described in the Constitution. The Senate must confirm, or vote for, these appointments. Only the President, however, may fire Cabinet members. Congress may pass laws giving the President, the courts, or the heads of executive departments the right to make appointments to less important jobs without a Senate vote. This clause is a legislative check on the power of the executive branch.

3. *Appointments to vacancies.* The President shall have power to fill up all vacancies that may happen during the recess of the Senate, by granting commissions which shall expire at the end of their next session.

expire (ek-SPYR): to come to an end

The President may appoint officials to openings that occur when the Senate is not in session. They may serve until the end of the Senate's next session.

expedient
(eks-PEE-dee-uhnt):
desirable; suitable

Section 3   DUTIES OF THE PRESIDENT

He shall from time to time give to the Congress information of the state of the Union, and recommend to their consideration such measures as he shall judge necessary and expedient; he may, on extraordinary occasions, convene both houses, or either of them, and in case of disagreement between them with respect to the time of adjournment, he may adjourn them to such time as he shall think proper; he shall receive ambassadors and other public ministers; he shall take care that the laws be faithfully executed, and shall commission all the officers of the United States.

This section lists the President's legislative duties and balances some of Congress' lawmaking powers. The President has the duty to inform Congress of conditions in the nation. This is the President's State of the Union speech that is given each January when Congress begins its new session. The President must also make recommendations for laws and other changes in the government. The President may, in unusual circumstances, call special sessions of either or both houses of Congress. The President may also adjourn Congress if the two houses cannot agree on a time. The President also formally receives representatives of foreign nations. This right gives the President the power to recognize foreign governments. Congress does not share this power. This section gives the President the general duty of making sure all federal laws are carried out properly.

Section 4   IMPEACHMENT

The President, Vice-President, and all civil officers of the United States, shall be removed from office on impeachment for, and conviction of, treason, bribery, or other high crimes and misdemeanors.

misdemeanor
(mis-dih-MEEN-uhr):
breaking of a minor law

This section is a legislative check on the executive branch. Under it, Congress can impeach and remove from office the President, Vice-President, and government officials, except military officers or members of Congress. Members of Congress cannot be impeached, but they can be expelled. (See Article I, Section 5, Clause 2.)

Article III   JUDICIAL DEPARTMENT
Section 1   FEDERAL COURTS

The judicial power of the United States shall be vested in one Supreme Court, and in such inferior courts as the Congress may from time to time ordain and establish. The judges, both of the Supreme and inferior courts, shall hold their offices during good behavior, and shall, at stated times, receive for their services, a compensation which shall not be diminished during their continuance in office.

ordain: to decide;
to order

Only the Supreme Court is named in the Constitution. Congress, however, is given the power to establish lower federal courts such as courts according to geographical areas or for particular types of cases. The 91 district courts try cases in different areas of the nation and Puerto Rico. The 11 courts of appeals review cases sent to them from the district courts. Special federal courts, such as the Court of Military Appeals, hear cases of a particular kind. State and local courts are not covered in the Constitution.

Federal judges are paid by the U.S. government and serve for life unless they are convicted of a crime. The pay of a federal judge may not be lowered during her or his term of office. The last two items in Section 1 are checks on both the legislative and executive branches. The writers of the Constitution wanted federal judges to be free of pressure from the other branches.

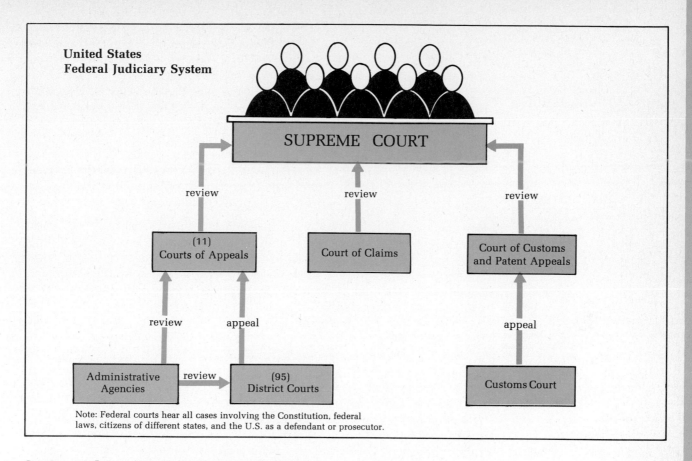

United States Federal Judiciary System

SUPREME COURT

review — review — review

(11) Courts of Appeals

Court of Claims

Court of Customs and Patent Appeals

review — appeal — appeal

Administrative Agencies — review → (95) District Courts

Customs Court

Note: Federal courts hear all cases involving the Constitution, federal laws, citizens of different states, and the U.S. as a defendant or prosecutor.

Section 2 JURISDICTION OF FEDERAL COURTS

1. *General power.* The judicial power shall extend to all cases, in law and equity, arising under this Constitution, the laws of the United States, and treaties made, or which shall be made, under their authority;—to all cases affecting ambassadors, other public ministers and consuls;—to all cases of admiralty and maritime jurisdiction;—to controversies to which the United States shall be a party;—to controversies between two or more States;—between a State and citizens of another State;—between citizens of different States,—between citizens of the same State claiming lands under grants of different States, and between a State, or the citizens thereof, and foreign States, citizens or subjects.

Federal courts deal with cases involving the Constitution, federal laws, treaties, and American ships at sea. The courts also deal with cases involving foreign representatives in this country. In addition, federal courts handle cases in which the U.S. government is involved and cases in which states or citizens of different states are involved. Other cases before a federal court can involve citizens of the same state who claim land in another state, or involve a state or its citizens and a foreign country or foreign citizen. (See the 11th Amendment for change.)

2. *Supreme Court.* In all cases affecting ambassadors, other public ministers and consuls, and those in which a state shall be party, the Supreme Court shall have original jurisdiction. In all the other cases before mentioned, the Supreme Court shall have appellate jurisdiction, both as to law and fact, with such exceptions, and under such regulations, as the Congress shall make.

equity (EK-wuh-tee): justice; fairness

Congress gave only to the Supreme Court the right to hear cases involving foreign representatives or states. This is what is meant by original jurisidiction. Under this clause, the Supreme Court also has appellate (uh-PEL-it) jurisdiction. It hears appeals on cases that were first tried in lower courts. Congress may make rules about the kinds of cases that can be appealed, however. Although it is not mentioned in the Constitution, the Supreme Court has the power to review laws and decide if they violate the Constitution.

3. *Trials.* The trial of all crimes, except in cases of impeachment, shall be by jury; and such trial shall be held in the state where the said crimes shall have been committed; but when not committed within any state, the trial shall be at such place or places as the Congress may by law have directed.

This clause guarantees a trial by jury to people accused of crimes against the federal government. The only exception is a trial of impeachment which is held in the Senate. Trials must be held in the state where the crime occurred. If the crime occurred outside any state, for example, in a federal territory, Congress decides where the trial will be held. This clause does not cover jury trials in state courts. That is covered in the 6th and 14th Amendments.

Section 3 TREASON

1. *Definition.* Treason against the United States, shall consist only in levying war against them, or in adhering to their enemies, giving them aid and comfort. No person shall be convicted of treason unless on the testimony of two witnesses to the same overt act, or on confession in open court.

2. *Punishment.* The Congress shall have power to declare the punishment of treason, but no attainder of treason shall work corruption of blood, or forfeiture except during the life of the person attainted.

According to this Clause 1, *treason* occurs when a U.S. citizen or permanent resident alien—foreigner—joins in war against the U.S. or helps the nation's enemies during wartime. Congress has also made it treason to spy; commit sabotage (SAB-uh-tahzh), that is, damage or destroy government property; try to overthrow the government; or join with others to do any of these acts in peacetime or wartime. Because of the seriousness of the crime, a person may be convicted of treason under one of only two conditions. Two witnesses must testify that the person committed such an act. Or the accused must confess in court.

Congress has the power to decide the punishment for treason. Punishment cannot include the person's family or the property he or she might leave to descendants. Punishing a traitor's family was common in Europe in the 1700s.

Article IV RELATIONS OF THE STATES
Section 1 PUBLIC RECORDS

Full faith and credit shall be given in each state to the public acts, records, and judicial proceedings of every other state. And the Congress may by general laws prescribe the manner in which such acts, records, and proceedings shall be proved, and the effect thereof.

States must honor the official records of other states. These records include birth certificates, wills, and court decisions. Congress may pass laws forcing states to recognize such records as legal.

Section 2 PRIVILEGES OF CITIZENS

1. *Privileges of citizens.* The citizens of each state shall be entitled to all privileges and immunities of citizens in the several states.

levy (LEV-ee): to set; to fix

forfeiture (FOR-fih-chuhr): loss or giving up of something as a punishment

A U.S. citizen visiting a state other than her or his own has the same rights as a citizen of that state. (See the 14th Amendment for additions.)

2. *Fugitives from justice.* A person charged in any state with treason, felony, or other crime, who shall flee from justice, and be found in another state, shall on demand of the executive authority of the state from which he fled, be delivered up to be removed to the state having jurisdiction of the crime.

If a person accused of a crime is found in another state, the governor of the state where the crime occurred has the right to demand the person be returned for trial. This is known as extradition (eks-truh-DISH-shuhn).

3. *Fugitive slaves.* No person held to service or labor in one state, under the laws thereof, escaping into another, shall, in consequence of any law or regulation therein, be discharged from such service or labor, but shall be delivered up on claim of the party to whom such service or labor may be due.

This clause became out-of-date with the passage of the 13th Amendment.

Section 3   NEW STATES AND TERRITORIES

1. *New states.* New states may be admitted by the Congress into this Union; but no new State shall be formed or erected within the jurisdiction of any other state; nor any state be formed by the junction of two or more states, or parts of states, without the consent of the legislatures of the states concerned as well as of the Congress.

Congress may admit new states into the U.S. New states, however, may not be formed from existing ones without the permission of those state legislatures and Congress. Only two states have been made from parts of existing states. Massachusetts gave up the area known as Maine in 1820. West Virginia was made from part of Virginia in 1863.

2. *Territory and property.* The Congress shall have power to dispose of and make all needful rules and regulations respecting the territory or other property belonging to the United States; and nothing in this Constitution shall be so construed as to prejudice any claims of the United States, or of any particular state.

construe (kuhn-STROO): to interpret; to explain

Congress has the power to govern all land and property belonging to the U.S. government. It makes rules for governing all territory that is not part of a state. Much of the frontier was governed as territories in the 1800s.

Section 4   PROTECTION OF THE STATES

The United States shall guarantee to every state in this Union a republican form of government, and shall protect each of them against invasion; and on application of the legislature, or of the executive (when the legislature cannot be convened), against domestic violence.

convene (kuhn-VEEN): to gather together; to meet

The U.S. guarantees to each state a government based on the right of its citizens to elect their own representatives. The U.S. will also protect states against invasion. If requested by a state's legislature or governor, the federal government will also send troops to stop violence within a state.

Article V   AMENDMENTS

The Congress, whenever two thirds of both Houses shall deem it necessary, shall propose amendments to this Constitution, or, on the application of the legislatures of two thirds of the several states, shall call a convention for proposing amendments, which, in either case, shall be valid to all intents and purposes, as part of this Constitution, when ratified by the legislatures of three fourths of the several states, or by conventions in three fourths thereof, as the one or the other mode of ratification may be proposed by the Congress; ~~Provided that no amendment which may be made prior to the year one thousand eight hundred and eight shall in any manner affect the first and fourth clauses in the ninth section of the first article~~; and that no state, without its consent, shall be deprived of its equal suffrage in the Senate.

Article V provides several ways for the Constitution to be amended and ratified. An amendment may be proposed by a two-thirds vote of each house of Congress. Or a national convention requested by two thirds of the states' legislatures may propose an amendment. Amendments can be ratified either by three fourths of the states' legislatures or by special conventions in three fourths of the states. Congress decides which method to use. The Constitution cannot be amended so a state loses its equal representation in the Senate unless the state agrees.

Article VI   THE SUPREME LAW OF THE LAND
1. *Public debt.* All debts contracted and engagements entered into, before the adoption of this Constitution, shall be as valid against the United States under this Constitution, as under the Confederation.

By this section, the U.S. government agrees to pay all debts and honor all agreements made by Congress before the Constitution was written.

2. *Supremacy clause.* This Constitution, and the laws of the United States which shall be made in pursuance thereof; and all treaties made, or which shall be made, under the authority of the United States, shall be the supreme law of the land; and the judges in every state shall be bound thereby, anything in the Constitution or laws of any state to the contrary notwithstanding.

This is perhaps the most important section in the Constitution. It is called the supremacy clause and places the Constitution, federal laws allowed under it, and treaties made by the U.S. above every other law in the nation. No state law, state constitution, or judicial ruling can be in opposition to them.

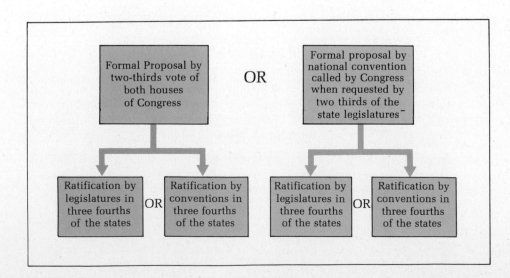

Amending the Constitution

3. *Oath of office*. The senators and representatives before mentioned, and the members of the several state legislatures, and all executive and judicial officers, both of the United States, and of the several states, shall be bound by oath or affirmation to support this Constitution; but no religious test shall ever be required as a qualification to any office or public trust under the United States.

All officials of the federal government and of the states must swear or affirm to support the Constitution. A person cannot be prevented from holding a government office or job because of his or her religious beliefs.

Article VII RATIFICATION OF THE CONSTITUTION
The ratification of the conventions of nine states shall be sufficient for the establishment of this Constitution between the states so ratifying the same.

The 13 states were to hold meetings to ratify the Constitution. When nine states ratified it, the Constitution would go into effect for those states.

Done in Convention by the unanimous consent of the states present the seventeenth day of September in the year of our Lord one thousand seven hundred and eighty-seven, and of the independence of the United States of America the twelfth. In witness whereof we have hereunto subscribed our names.

George Washington—
President and Deputy from Virginia.

Delaware
George Read
Gunning Bedford, Jr.
John Dickinson
Richard Bassett
Jacob Broom

Maryland
James McHenry
Daniel of St. Thomas Jenifer
Daniel Carroll

Virginia
John Blair
James Madison, Jr.

North Carolina
William Blount
Richard Dobbs Spaight
Hugh Williamson

South Carolina
John Rutledge
Charles Cotesworth Pinckney
Charles Pinckney
Pierce Butler

Georgia
William Few
Abraham Baldwin

New Hampshire
John Langdon
Nicholas Gilman

Massachusetts
Nathaniel Gorman
Rufus King

Connecticut
William Samuel Johnson
Roger Sherman

New York
Alexander Hamilton

New Jersey
William Livingston
David Brearley
William Paterson
Jonathan Dayton

Pennsylvania
Benjamin Franklin
Thomas Mifflin
Robert Morris
George Clymer
Thomas Fitzsimons
Jared Ingersoll
James Wilson
Gouverneur Morris

AMENDMENTS TO THE CONSTITUTION

abridge:
to decrease;
to lessen

Amendment 1 (1791) FREEDOMS OF RELIGION, SPEECH, PRESS, ASSEMBLY, AND PETITION

Congress shall make no law respecting an establishment of religion, or prohibiting the free exercise thereof; or abridging the freedom of speech, or of the press; or the right of the people peaceably to assemble, and to petition the government for a redress of grievances.

Congress may not set up an official religion for the U.S. or pass laws punishing anyone for practicing his or her religion. Congress may not prevent people from expressing their opinions freely, except in cases of libel (LY-buhl) and slander. These are false and knowingly vicious remarks. Libel refers to written remarks and slander to those spoken. People also have the right to hold peaceful meetings and to ask the government to correct any wrongs or injustices they see.

Amendment 2 (1791) RIGHT TO BEAR ARMS

infringe (in-FRINJ):
to violate; to trespass on

A well regulated militia, being necessary to the security of a free state, the right of the people to keep and bear arms, shall not be infringed.

Because people have the right to protect themselves by serving in state militias, civilians have the right to keep and carry weapons. Congress, however, has passed laws regulating the manufacture, sale, and use of weapons.

Amendment 3 (1791) QUARTERING OF SOLDIERS

No soldier shall, in time of peace, be quartered in any house, without the consent of the owner, nor in time of war, but in a manner to be prescribed by law.

In peacetime, Congress may not force civilians to give shelter in their homes and food to soldiers. In wartime, Congress may pass laws requiring private citizens to provide such housing.

Amendment 4 (1791) SEARCH AND SEIZURE

The right of the people to be secure in their persons, houses, papers, and effects, against unreasonable searches and seizures, shall not be violated, and no warrants shall issue, but upon probable cause, supported by oath or affirmation, and particularly describing the place to be searched, and the persons or things to be seized.

A person or a person's property cannot be searched without a warrant. This is a document issued by a judge who has been convinced there is good reason for a search. The federal law officer asking for a search warrant must show probable cause. He or she must give the reasons why a search is necessary, the person or evidence wanted, and the place to be searched. Evidence taken without a warrant may not be used in court.

Amendment 5 (1791) RIGHTS IN CRIMINAL CASES

infamous (IN-fuh-muhs):
very bad; wicked

No person shall be held to answer for a capital, or otherwise infamous, crime, unless on a presentment or indictment of a grand jury, except in cases arising in the land or naval forces, or in the militia, when in actual service in time of war or public danger; nor shall any person be subject for the same offense to be twice put in jeopardy of life or limb; nor shall be compelled in any criminal case to be a witness against himself, nor be deprived of life, liberty, or property, without due process of law; nor shall private property be taken for public use without just compensation.

A person cannot be tried in a federal court for a serious crime unless a grand jury first looks at the evidence and decides a trial is justified. A grand jury is made up of from 6 to 23 people to hear the evidence in secret. If the grand jury decides there is enough evidence, the person is tried before a petit (PET-ee) jury. This is a jury of 5, 6, 8, or 12 people who decide guilt or innocence. The only exception is cases involving the military in time of war or national emergency.

A person may not be tried a second time in a federal court for an offense he or she has already been found innocent of. Also, an accused person may not be forced to testify against himself or herself. In all cases, a person may not be punished by loss of life, liberty, or property without due process of law. Due process means that the law must be carefully followed. In addition, the federal government may not take private property for public use without paying the owner a fair price.

Amendment 6 (1791) RIGHT TO A FAIR AND SPEEDY TRIAL

In all criminal prosecutions, the accused shall enjoy the right to a speedy and public trial, by an impartial jury of the state and district wherein the crime shall have been committed, which district shall have been previously ascertained by law, and to be informed of the nature and cause of the accusation; to be confronted with the witnesses against him; to have compulsory process for obtaining witnesses in his favor, and to have the assistance of counsel for his defense.

compulsory (kuhm-PUHL-suh-ree): required

A person who is charged with a crime has the right to a speedy, public trial. The jury must be from the state and district where the crime was committed. The accused person must know why she or he is being charged and be present in court during the trial. The accused has the right to have witnesses appear in court, even if they do not wish to. Finally, a lawyer must be available for the accused. If the accused cannot afford a lawyer, the court will appoint one.

Amendment 7 (1791) RIGHT OF TRIAL BY JURY

In suits at common law, where the value in controversy shall exceed twenty dollars, the right of trial by jury shall be preserved, and no fact tried by a jury shall be otherwise reexamined in any court of the United States, than according to the rules of the common law.

When one person sues another over more than $20, there must be a jury trial if either person asks for one. Or both can agree not to have a jury trial. If a case is later appealed to a higher court, that court will reexamine the facts.

Amendment 8 (1791) BAIL, FINES, AND PUNISHMENT

Excessive bail shall not be required, nor excessive fines imposed, nor cruel and unusual punishments inflicted.

excessive (ek-SES-iv): too much; too large

The courts may not require a very large bail before setting free a person charged with a crime. Bail is an amount of money or property that an accused gives the court to guarantee that he or she will appear for trial. If the person does not appear, the court takes the money or property. If a person is found guilty, any fine — money the court requires a convicted person to pay as punishment — must not be too large. Punishments may not be cruel and unusual, such as cutting off the hand of a thief.

disparage (dis-PAR-ij): to make less important

Amendment 9 (1791)   RIGHTS RETAINED BY THE PEOPLE

The enumeration in the Constitution of certain rights shall not be construed to deny or disparage others retained by the people.

The rights listed in the Constitution are not the only rights that the people of the U.S. have. They have all the rights that are guaranteed under a free government. The rights that are not listed are in no way less important than those rights that are listed.

Amendment 10 (1791)   POWERS RESERVED TO THE STATES OR TO THE PEOPLE

The powers not delegated to the United States by the Constitution, nor prohibited by it to the states, are reserved to the states respectively, or to the people.

The Constitution gives certain powers to the U.S. government while denying certain other powers to the states. All other powers not mentioned in the Constitution rest with the individual states or the people. This amendment limits the possible power of the federal government. Through Article VI, Section 2, the possible power of the states is also limited. These two parts of the Constitution balance federal and state power.

Amendment 11 (1798)   SUING A STATE

The judicial power of the United States shall not be construed to extend to any suit in law or equity, commenced or prosecuted against one of the United States, by citizens of another state, or by citizens or subjects of any foreign state.

The federal courts may not act in cases in which a state is sued by citizens of another state or of a foreign country.

Amendment 12 (1804)   ELECTING A PRESIDENT AND VICE-PRESIDENT

distinct (dis-TINGKT): different; separate

The electors shall meet in their respective states, and vote by ballot for President and Vice-President, one of whom, at least, shall not be an inhabitant of the same state with themselves; they shall name in their ballots the person voted for as President, and in distinct ballots the person voted for as Vice-President, and they shall make distinct lists of all persons voted for as President and of all persons voted for as Vice-President, and of the number of votes for each, which lists they shall sign and certify, and transmit sealed to the seat of government of the United States, directed to the president of the Senate;—The president of the Senate shall, in the presence of the Senate and House of Representatives, open all the certificates and the votes shall then be counted;—The person having the greatest number of votes for President shall be the President, if such number be a majority of the whole number of electors appointed; and if no person have such majority, then from the persons having the highest numbers not exceeding three on the list of those voted for as President, the House of Representatives shall choose immediately, by ballot, the President. But in choosing the President, the votes shall be taken by states, the representation from each state having one vote; a quorum for this purpose shall consist of a member or members from two thirds of the states, and a majority of all the states shall be necessary to a choice. ~~And if the House of Representatives shall not choose a President whenever the right of choice shall devolve upon them, before the fourth day of March next following, then the Vice-President shall act as President, as in the case of the death or other constitutional disability of the President.~~ The person having

majority (muh-JOR-uh-tee): more than half

devolve (dih-VAHLV): to hand down to; to transfer

the greatest number of votes as Vice-President shall be the Vice-President, if such number be a majority of the whole number of electors appointed, and if no person have a majority then from the two highest numbers on the list, the Senate shall choose the Vice-President; a quorum for the purpose shall consist of two thirds of the whole number of senators, and a majority of the whole number shall be necessary to a choise. But no person constitutionally ineligible to the office of President shall be eligible to that of Vice-President of the United States.

The elections of 1796 and 1800 made it clear that the manner of selecting a President and especially a Vice-President needed to be changed from that described in Article II, Section 1, Clause 3. This amendment provides that the electors gather in each state and vote separately for President and for Vice-President. All the votes from the states are sent to the U.S. Senate. The individual receiving a majority of the electors' votes for President becomes President. The votes for Vice-President are also counted and the person receiving the majority of votes becomes Vice-President. (See 23rd Amendment.)

If no one receives more than one half of the electors' votes, the House of Representatives then chooses a President from among the top three candidates. Each state has one vote. At least one representative from two thirds of the states must be present for the vote. To be President, a candidate must receive the votes of a majority of all the states. If the House of Representatives cannot agree on a candidate before the date set for the new President to take office, the person who has been elected Vice-President serves as President. (See the 25th Amendment for the change.)

If a majority of the electors cannot agree on a Vice-President, the Senate selects a Vice-President in a similar manner — but selecting only from the top two candidates on the electors' lists.

The qualifications given by the Constitution for the office of President apply to the Vice-President as well.

Amendment 13 (1865)   ABOLITION

Section 1. Neither slavery nor involuntary servitude, except as a punishment for crime whereof the party shall have been duly convicted, shall exist within the United States, or any place subject to their jurisdiction.

Section 2. Congress shall have power to enforce this article by appropriate legislation.

appropriate
(uh-PROH-pree-it):
suitable; fitting

This and the following two amendments were the result of the Civil War. The 13th Amendment ended slavery in the U.S. and in any areas under its control. However, a person may be forced to work as punishment for a crime if a court has made that the punishment. This is not slavery. Congress has the power to make laws to enforce this amendment.

Amendment 14 (1868)   CIVIL RIGHTS AND THE STATES

Section 1. All persons born or naturalized in the United States, and subject to the jurisdiction thereof, are citizens of the United States and of the state wherein they reside. No state shall make or enforce any law which shall abridge the privileges or immunities of citizens of the United States; nor shall any state deprive any person of life, liberty, or property, without due process of law; nor deny to any person within its jurisdiction the equal protection of the laws.

This section defines citizenship as belonging to any person born or naturalized in the U.S. who is also subject to U.S. laws. Naturalization (nach-uh-ruh-luh-ZAY-shuhn) is the legal process for admitting a foreign-born person to citizenship. A U.S. citizen is also a citizen of the state in which she or he lives. This section of the Constitution prevents a state from setting up different requirements for citizenships for blacks and whites.

The key phrases in this section are privileges and immunities of citizens, due process of law, and the equal protection of the laws. The Supreme Court has interpreted these phrases as extending the Bill of Rights to the states. State government, like the federal government, may not take away basic rights. With this amendment, for example, no state can deny privileges and immunities—or civil rights such as freedom of speech or religion or assembly—to its citizens. The requirement for equal protection means that the law cannot treat citizens of the U.S. unequally.

immunity
(in-MYOO-nuh-tee):
protection; freedom

Section 2. Representatives shall be apportioned among the several states according to their respective numbers, counting the whole number of persons in each state, excluding Indians not taxed. But when the right to vote at any election for the choice of electors for President and Vice-President of the United States, representatives in Congress, the executive and judicial officers of a state, or the members of the legislature thereof, is denied to any of the ~~male~~ inhabitants of such state, being ~~twenty-one years of age, and~~ citizens of the United States, or in any way abridged, except for participation in rebellion, or other crime, the basis of representation therein shall be reduced in the proportion which the number of such ~~male~~ citizens shall bear to the whole number of ~~male~~ citizens ~~twenty-one years of age~~ in such State.

This section repeals Article I, Section 2, Clause 3 of the Constitution. That clause had counted a slave as three fifths of a person in deciding how many representatives a state would have in the House. With the 14th Amendment, everyone is counted equally. Under this amendment, a state's representation will be reduced if voting privileges are ever denied to anyone who is eligible and has not been convicted of a crime. This procedure has never been used.

Section 3. No person shall be a senator or representative in Congress, or elector of President and Vice-President, or hold any office, civil or military, under the United States, or under any state, who, having previously taken an oath, as a member of Congress, or as an officer of the United States, or as a member of any state legislature, or as an executive or judicial officer of any state, to support the Constitution of the United States, shall have engaged in insurrection or rebellion against the same, or given aid or comfort to the enemies thereof. But Congress may by a vote of two-thirds of each house, remove such disability.

Section 4. The validity of the public debt of the United States, authorized by law, including debts incurred for payment of pensions and bounties for services in suppressing insurrection or rebellion, shall not be questioned. But neither the United States nor any state shall assume or pay any debt or obligation incurred in aid of insurrection or rebellion against the United States, ~~or any claim for the loss or emancipation of any slave;~~ but all such debts, obligations, and claims shall be held illegal and void.

Section 5. The Congress shall have power to enforce, by appropriate legislation, the provisions of this article.

incur (in-KER):
to bring about

void: without
legal effect

This section prevented Confederate officers who had once held a federal office from being reelected to the federal government. Congress removed this barrier in 1898.

290

Under Section 4, Union debts from the Civil War were to be paid. Any debts owed to or by Confederate states were cancelled. No one was to receive payment for the loss of slaves. Congress has the power to make laws to enforce this amendment.

Amendment 15 (1870)   BLACK SUFFRAGE

Section 1. The right of citizens of the United States to vote shall not be denied or abridged by the United States or by any state on account of race, color, or previous condition of servitude.

Section 2. The Congress shall have power to enforce this article by appropriate legislation.

Congress proposed this amendment because of continued efforts to deny black Americans the right to vote. The federal government and the states are prevented from denying the vote to anyone because of race or because he or she may once have been a slave. Congress has the power to make laws to enforce this amendment.

Amendment 16 (1913)   INCOME TAX

The Congress shall have power to lay and collect taxes on incomes, from whatever source derived, without apportionment among the several states, and without regard to any census or enumeration.

derive (dih-RYV): to get

In 1895, the Supreme Court decided that an *income tax* was a direct tax and, according to Article I, Section 9, Clause 4, should be divided among the states according to population. This amendment allowed the federal government to tax Americans directly according to their rate of income rather than by population of each state. A tax on individual income was thought to be the fairest way of sharing the increasing cost of running the federal government.

Amendment 17 (1913)   DIRECT ELECTION OF SENATORS

Section 1. The Senate of the United States shall be composed of two senators from each state, elected by the people thereof, for six years; and each senator shall have one vote. The electors in each state shall have the qualifications requisite for electors of the most numerous branch of the State legislatures.

Section 2. When vacancies happen in the representation of any state in the Senate, the executive authority of such state shall issue writs of election to fill such vacancies: Provided, That the legislature of any State may empower the executive thereof to make temporary appointments until the people fill the vacancies by election as the legislature may direct.

Section 3. This amendment shall not be so construed as to affect the election or term of any Senator chosen before it becomes valid as part of the Constitution.

The 17th Amendment provides for the election of U.S. senators by direct vote of the people. The qualifications needed to vote for a senator are the same as those needed to vote for a member of the largest house of the state legislature. (See Article I, Section 3, Clause 1.)

If a senator dies or leaves office, the governor of the state is to call a special election. The state legislature may allow the governor to fill the position until an election can be held. (See Article I, Section 2, Clause 4; Article I, Section 3, Clause 2.)

Section 3 was added so that any senator elected under the old method would not be immediately affected by the new amendment. (See Article I, Section 3, Clause 1.)

concurrent
(kuhn-KER-uhnt):
having equal authority

Amendment 18 (1919)   PROHIBITION
~~Section 1. After one year from the ratification of this article the manufacture, sale, or transportation of intoxicating liquors within, the importation thereof into, or the exportation thereof from the United States and all territory subject to the jurisdiction thereof for beverage purposes is hereby prohibited. Section 2. The Congress and the several states shall have concurrent power to enforce this article by appropriate legislation.~~

One year after ratification, the 18th Amendment outlawed the manufacture, sale, and transportation of alcohol in the U.S. or between the U.S. and other nations. Under this amendment, both Congress and the states had to make laws to enforce prohibition. In 1919, Congress passed the Volstead (VAHL-sted) Act which allowed federal law officers to investigate and punish violations of the amendment.

inoperative
(in-AHP-ruh-tiv):
without effect;
not workable

~~Section 3. This article shall be inoperative unless it shall have been ratified as an amendment to the Constitution by the legislatures of the several states, as provided in the Constitution, within seven years from the date of the submission hereof to the states by the Congress.~~

This amendment was to go into effect only if ratified by the necessary three fourths of the states within seven years. The time limit on ratification was set to prevent many unratified or partially ratified amendments from remaining active. The time limit can be extended by Congressional vote.

Amendment 19 (1920)   WOMAN SUFFRAGE
Section 1. The right of citizens of the United States to vote shall not be denied or abridged by the United States or by any State on account of sex.
Section 2. Congress shall have power, by appropriate legislation, to enforce the provisions of this article.

The 19th Amendment gives women the right to vote in both national and state elections. Congress was given the power to enforce this amendment.

Amendment 20 (1933)   TERMS OF EXECUTIVE AND LEGISLATIVE OFFICERS
Section 1. The terms of the President and Vice-President shall end at noon on the 20th day of January, and the terms of senators and representatives at noon on the 3d day of January, of the years in which such terms would have ended if this article had not been ratified; and the terms of their successors shall then begin.

The term *lame duck* refers to people holding office who were not reelected. Their defeat in the November election resulted in "clipping their political wings." This means they had little influence during this time. This section shortens the period between the election and inauguration (in-aw-gyuh-RAY-shuhn) of officeholders. The President, Vice-President, and newly elected members of Congress take office in January, only two months after their election. Before this amendment, the President, Vice-President and members of Congress waited from November until March.

Section 2. The Congress shall assemble at least once in every year, and such meeting shall begin at noon on the 3d day of January, unless they shall by law appoint a different day.

This section sets January 3 as the date for Congress to assemble unless it passes a law naming a different day. (See Article I, Section 4, Clause 2.)

Section 3. If, at the time fixed for the beginning of the term of the President, the President-elect shall have died, the Vice-President-elect shall become President. If a President shall not have been chosen before the time fixed for the beginning of his term, or if the President-elect shall have failed to qualify, then the Vice-President-elect shall act as President until a President shall have qualified; and the Congress may by law provide for the case wherein neither a President-elect nor a Vice-President-elect shall have qualified, declaring who shall then act as President, or the manner in which one who is to act shall be selected, and such persons shall act accordingly until a President or Vice-President shall have qualified.

Section 4. The Congress may by law provide for the case of the death of any of the persons from whom the House of Representatives may choose a President whenever the right of choice shall have devolved upon them, and for the case of the death of any of the persons from whom the Senate may choose a Vice-President whenever the right of choice shall have devolved upon them.

If a President-elect dies before assuming office, the Vice-President-elect becomes President. If a President-elect has not been selected or is not qualified, the Vice-President-elect serves as President until a qualified candidate is chosen. Congress decides who will serve or how such selection will be made. Congress has the same power if both fail to qualify. Congress has the power to make a law for cases in which a President selected by the House or a Vice-President selected by the Senate dies before taking office.

Section 5. Sections 1 and 2 shall take effect on the 15th day of October following the ratification of this article.

Section 6. This article shall be inoperative unless it shall have been ratified as an amendment to the Constitution by the legislatures of three fourths of the several states within seven years from the date of its submission.

Sections 1 and 2 of this amendment went into effect on October 15 after ratification. The same seven-year limit on ratification was placed on this amendment as was first used in the 18th Amendment.

Amendment 21 (1933)   REPEAL OF PROHIBITION

Section 1. The eighteenth article of amendment to the Constitution of the United States is hereby repealed.

Section 2. The transporation or importation into any state, territory, or possession of the United States for delivery or use therein of intoxicating liquors, in violation of the laws thereof, is hereby prohibited.

The 18th Amendment is repealed and national prohibition ended.

States have the right to forbid the delivery and use of alcohol within their borders. Under this amendment, violation of a state law against alcohol is a crime against the U.S. also.

Section 3. This article shall be inoperative unless it shall have been ratified as an amendment to the Constitution by conventions in the several states, as provided in the Constitution, within seven years from the date of submission hereof to the states by the Congress.

293

This amendment became effective when it was ratified within seven years by state conventions of three fourths of the states. This is the only amendment that has been presented to state conventions rather than to state legislatures to ratify.

Amendment 22 (1951)   LIMITING PRESIDENTIAL TERMS
Section 1. No person shall be elected to the office of the President more than twice, and no person who has held the office of President, or acted as President, for more than two years of a term to which some other person was elected President shall be elected to the office of the President more than once. ~~But this article shall not apply to any person holding the office of President when this article was proposed by the Congress, and shall not prevent any person who may be holding the office of President, or acting as President, during the term within which this article becomes operative from holding the office of President or acting as President during the remainder of such term.~~
~~*Section 2.* This article shall be inoperative unless it shall have been ratified as an amendment to the Constitution by the legislatures of three fourths of the several states within seven years from the date of its submission to the states by the Congress.~~

No one may serve more than two terms as President. Anyone who serves for more than two years in place of an elected President can be elected for only one term. The amendment did not apply to Harry S Truman who was President when the amendment was proposed and ratified. This amendment was proposed because of the four terms in office by Franklin D. Roosevelt. Congress felt that so many years in office for one person was not necessarily good for the country. This amendment became effective when three fourths of the state legislatures ratified it within seven years.

Amedment 23 (1961)   ELECTION IN THE DISTRICT OF COLUMBIA
Section 1. The District constituting the seat of government of the United States shall appoint in such manner as the Congress may direct:
   A number of electors of President and Vice-President equal to the whole number of senators and representatives in Congress to which the District would be entitled if it were a state, but in no event more than the least populous state; they shall be in addition to those appointed by the states, but they shall be considered, for the purposes of the election of President and Vice-President, to be electors appointed by a state; and they shall meet in the District and perform such duties as provided by the twelfth article of amendment.
Section 2. The Congress shall have power to enforce this article by appropriate legislation.

Before this amendment, people living in the District of Columbia could not vote for President and Vice-President. Now, the District has three electors, the least number the District would have if it were a state.

Amendment 24 (1964)   POLL TAX BANNED
Section 1. The right of citizens of the United States to vote in any primary or other election for President or Vice-President, for electors for President or Vice-President, or for senator or representative in Congress, shall not be denied or abridged by the United States or any state by reason of failure to pay any poll tax or other tax.

populous
(PAHP-yuh-luhs):
full of people

Section 2. The Congress shall have the power to enforce this article by appropriate legislation.

Neither the U.S. nor any state may deny anyone the right to vote because of non-payment of any tax, including poll taxes. Some states used to charge such taxes to prevent blacks and poor people from voting. This section applies to primary and other elections for President or Vice-President, their electors, or members of Congress. Congress has the power to make laws to enforce this amendment.

Amendment 25 (1967)   PRESIDENTIAL DISABILITY AND SUCCESSION
Section 1. In case of the removal of the President from office or his death or resignation, the Vice-President shall become President.
Section 2. Whenever there is a vacancy in the office of the Vice-President, the President shall nominate a Vice-President who shall take the office upon confirmation by a majority vote of both houses of Congress.

If the President is removed from office, dies, or resigns, the Vice-President then becomes President. Any vacancy in the office of Vice-President is filled by the President nominating someone. A majority of both houses of Congress must confirm the nomination.

Section 3. Whenever the President transmits to the president pro tempore of the Senate and the speaker of the House of Representatives his written declaration that he is unable to discharge the powers and duties of his office, and until he transmits to them a written declaration to the contrary, such powers and duties shall be discharged by the Vice-President as Acting President.

This section provides for a case of temporary Presidential disability. If the President notifies the Senate and the House that she or he cannot do the job, the Vice-President becomes Acting President. The Vice-President continues in that position until the President indicates an ability to do the work again.

Section 4. Whenever the Vice-President and a majority of either the principal officers of the executive departments or of such other body as Congress may by law provide, transmit to the president pro tempore of the Senate and the Speaker of the House of Representatives their written declaration that the President is unable to discharge the powers and duties of his office, the Vice-President shall immediately assume the powers and duties of the office as Acting President.

Thereafter, when the President transmits to the president pro tempore of the Senate and the speaker of the House of Representatives his written declaration that no inability exists, he shall resume the powers and duties of his office unless the Vice-President and a majority of either the principal officers of the executive department or of such other body as Congress may by law provide, transmit within four days to the president pro tempore of the Senate and the speaker of the House of Representatives their written declaration that the President is unable to discharge the powers and duties of his office. Thereupon Congress shall decide the issue, assembling within 48 hours for that purpose if not in session. If the Congress, within 21 days after receipt of the latter written declaration, or, if Congress is not in session, within 21 days after Congress is required to assemble, determines by two thirds vote of both houses that the President is unable to discharge the powers and duties

receipt (rih-SEET): something that is received; the action of receiving

295

of his office, the Vice-President shall continue to discharge the same as Acting President; otherwise, the President shall resume the powers and duties of his office.

This section deals with cases in which the President thinks he or she is able to work, but others disagree. If the Vice-President and a majority of heads of executive departments or other government officers named by Congress decide the President is unfit, they must notify the leaders of both houses of Congress in writing. The Vice-President steps in at once as Acting President. When the President decides he or she is able to carry out the duties of the office, he or she declares this in writing to the leaders of both houses and returns to office. If the Vice-President and other leaders still feel the President is not able to do the job, they have four days to write to Congress. Congress must then decide the question of fitness by a two-thirds vote of each house. This amendment was passed after President Dwight Eisenhower suffered several serious ilnesses while in office.

Amendment 26 (1971) VOTING BY EIGHTEEN-YEAR-OLDS
Section 1. The right of citizens of the United States, who are eighteen years of age or older, to vote shall not be denied or abridged by the United States or any state on account of age.
Section 2. The Congress shall have the power to enforce this article by appropriate legislation.

Anyone 18 years of age or older cannot be denied the right to vote because of age. Congress has the power to make laws to enforce this amendment.

LOOKING BACK

1. Explain each of the following principles of the Constitution: **a.** federalism; **b.** separation of powers; **c.** rights of individuals; **d.** adaptability.
2. List the enumerated powers of the federal government as given in the Constitution.
★ 3. Explain in a paragraph how the system of checks and balances works. Use the flow chart on page 265 as your guide.
4. Why did Americans in the 1780s want a Bill of Rights?
5. **a.** Define the elastic clause. **b.** Define implied powers. **c.** Why did the delegates create an amendment process for the U.S. Constitution?
★ 6. Explain in a paragraph how a bill becomes law. Use the flow chart on page 271 as your guide.
★ 7. Explain in a paragraph how the appeals system of the federal courts work. Use the flow chart on page 281 as your guide.
★ 8. **a.** How are Constitutional amendments proposed? **b.** How are Constitutional amendments ratified? Use the flow chart on page 284 as your guide to answer these questions.

PRACTICING YOUR SKILLS

What If . . .

The Constitution provides for a federal government in which power is shared among national, state, and local governments. Yet, people opposed the Constitution. They thought it gave too much power to the national government. **What if** the Constitution had given the states the rights to raise armies, make foreign treaties, and coin money? How might this have affected the future of the U.S.?

Discussing

The delegates to the Constitutional Convention met in secrecy. They feared arguments if the public knew what was happening during the meetings. Yet, the Preamble begins with the phrase "We the people of the United States." Do you agree or disagree with the delegates' wish for secrecy? Discuss whether you agree or disagree with the view that some government meetings must be held in secret.

Imagining, Charting, Researching

1. Imagine you are a member of a state legislature in 1787-89 and must vote on the new Constitution. Make a list of the features that would make you vote for the Constitution. Then list things that would make you vote against it. Think about the advantages and disadvantages of the Constitution. Write a statement giving your vote and the reasons for it.
2. Using information in this unit, make a flow chart showing the sequence of events for writing and ratifying the Constitution.
3. Use an almanac to find the number of representatives your state has in the House of Representatives. Check statistics from the last three censuses to see if your state has lost, gained, or kept the same number of representatives.

Exploring

Laws are rules of conduct set up by people and enforced by authority. All areas of your life are affected by laws. There are laws about your health, safety, environment, and your rights as a student. To discover how laws affect your life, go through an ordinary day and list the ways laws regulate your life.

Reading

Bates, Elizabeth. *The Making of the Constitution*. New York: Viking, 1973. Primary source materials.

Cooke, Donald E. *America's Great Document, the Constitution*. Maplewood, New Jersey: Hammond, 1970. The people involved in creating the Constitution.

Falkner, Leonard. *For Jefferson and Liberty: The United States in War and Peace, 1800-1815*. New York: Knopf, 1972. Primary sources.

Katz, William L. and Bernard Gaughran. *The Constitutional Amendments*. New York: Watts, 1975. Paperback. Describes amendment procedures.

Kelly, Alfred H. and Winfred A. Harbison. *The American Constitution*. 5th ed. New York: Norton, 1976. English and colonial origins.

Kohn, Bernice. *The Spirit and the Letter: The Struggle for Rights in America*. New York: Viking, 1974.

Lawson, Don. *The Changing Face of the Constitution*. New York: Watts, 1979.

Morison, Samuel E., ed. *Sources and Documents Illustrating the American Revolution, 1764-1788, and the Formation of the Federal Constitution*. 2nd ed. New York: Oxford University Press, 1969.

Peterson, Helen Stone. *Making of the U.S. Constitution*. Champaign, Illinois: Garrard, 1974. Constitutional convention to Washington's election.

Sanderlin, George. *A Hoop to the Barrel: The Making of the American Constitution*. New York: Coward, 1974.

Smith, Page. *The Constitution: A Documentary and Narrative History*. New York: Morrow, 1978.

Section III THE NATION COMES OF AGE

Unit I
The New Nation

Unit II
New Role for the Nation

Unit III
New Technology

ERA

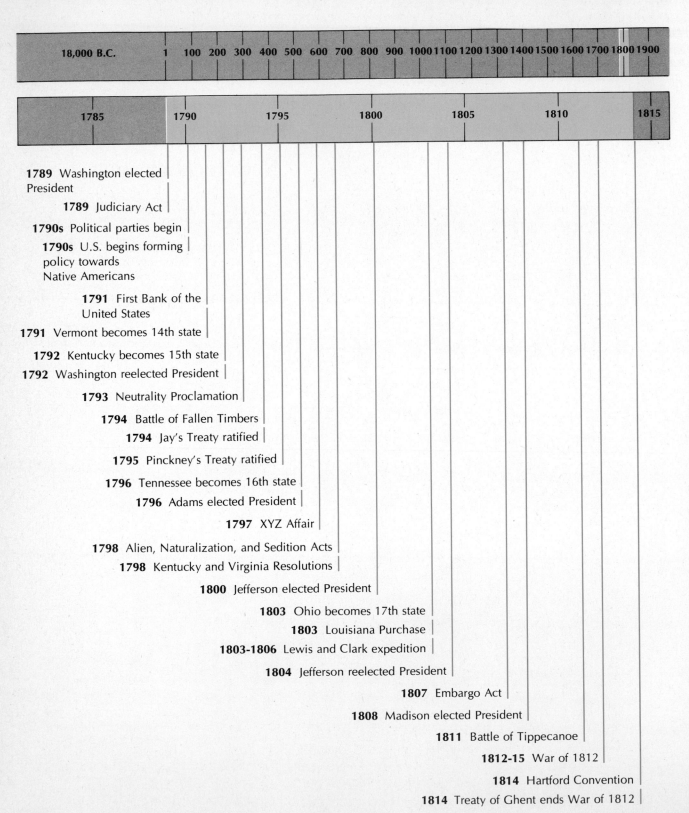

18,000 B.C. 1 100 200 300 400 500 600 700 800 900 1000 1100 1200 1300 1400 1500 1600 1700 1800 1900

1785 1790 1795 1800 1805 1810 1815

1789 Washington elected President

1789 Judiciary Act

1790s Political parties begin

1790s U.S. begins forming policy towards Native Americans

1791 First Bank of the United States

1791 Vermont becomes 14th state

1792 Kentucky becomes 15th state

1792 Washington reelected President

1793 Neutrality Proclamation

1794 Battle of Fallen Timbers

1794 Jay's Treaty ratified

1795 Pinckney's Treaty ratified

1796 Tennessee becomes 16th state

1796 Adams elected President

1797 XYZ Affair

1798 Alien, Naturalization, and Sedition Acts

1798 Kentucky and Virginia Resolutions

1800 Jefferson elected President

1803 Ohio becomes 17th state

1803 Louisiana Purchase

1803-1806 Lewis and Clark expedition

1804 Jefferson reelected President

1807 Embargo Act

1808 Madison elected President

1811 Battle of Tippecanoe

1812-15 War of 1812

1814 Hartford Convention

1814 Treaty of Ghent ends War of 1812

Chapter 1   Starting the New Government

LOOKING AHEAD

This chapter describes the beginning of the new nation under its first President, George Washington. You will read how the President's Cabinet and the court system were created. You will learn how different views on building the nation's credit led to the development of political parties. This chapter also describes the nation's expansion on the western frontier. After you study this chapter, you will be able to:

- list the problems facing Washington as the first President.
- explain Hamilton's economic program.
- compare and contrast the beliefs of the Federalists and Democratic-Republicans.
- ★ read a population density map to learn where the greatest and least areas of settlement were in 1790.
- describe the new nation's policy toward Native Americans.

Social Studies Vocabulary

minister	competition	strict constructionist
bond	political party	population density
tariff	loose constructionist	states' rights

People

George Washington	Thomas Jefferson	Democratic-
John Adams	Henry Knox	Republicans
John Jay	Alexander Hamilton	Anthony Wayne
Edmund Randolph	Federalists	

Places

Old Southwest

Words and Terms

Judiciary Act of 1789   First Bank of the United States
credit risk

Events

Whiskey Rebellion   Battle of Fallen Timbers

These one-cent pieces were used in New Jersey and Massachusetts in the late 1780s. Why did the states stop coining their own money in 1791?

Once the Constitution was ratified by nine states, the electoral college gathered to choose a President and a Vice-President. According to the Constitution, electors gather in their respective states on the same day and vote. The first electors met in February 1789. When their votes were counted, all had voted for George Washington who was named

On the way to his inauguration as the first President of the U.S., George Washington arrives in New York Harbor amid cannon salutes and the cheers of fellow citizens.

President. John Adams received the next highest number of votes and was named Vice-President. They took the oaths of office on April 30, 1789, in New York City, the temporary capital.

WASHINGTON, THE FIRST PRESIDENT

As the hero of the Revolutionary War, Washington had the respect of the people. He set out, as President, to win their respect for the new government. Washington knew that difficult times were ahead. The federal government had been given the job of protecting the Constitution. Keeping a careful balance between the powers of the federal government and the rights of the people and of the states would not be easy. The new government also had to deal with foreign governments and with Native Americans. Just as important, the first government would be setting customs and traditions for later Presidents and federal officeholders to follow.

Judiciary Act of 1789

The first job Washington and Congress faced was filling in the details of government under the Constitution. For example, the Constitution called for a Supreme Court but gave no details. The Constitution also gave Congress the power to set up lower courts but did not say what kind or how many.

In 1789, Congress passed the Judiciary (joo-DISH-ee-er-ee) Act. It called for a Chief Justice and five Associate Justices. The first Chief Justice was John Jay who had written some of *The Federalist*. The act also set up 13 district courts and 3 circuit courts. Since 1789, the number of Supreme Court justices and lower courts has increased as the country has grown.

The Cabinet

The Constitution states that the heads of departments in the executive branch should report to the President. But it does not say what the departments should be or how many. In 1789, Congress created three departments in the executive branch: Treasury, State, and War. The fourth, that of Attorney General, was created by the Judiciary Act. It is the job of the Attorney General to advise the federal government on legal matters. The first Attorney General was Edmund Randolph. He had proposed the Virginia Plan at the Constitutional Convention.

As the first Secretary of State, Washington chose Thomas Jefferson. Jefferson was experienced in dealing with foreign nations. He had been minister to France under the Articles of Confederation. A **minister** (MIN-is-tuhr) is a person who represents his or her government in a foreign nation. Washington asked General Henry Knox, Secretary of War during the Confederation Period, to continue in that job. Alexander Hamilton, who had written some of *The Federalist*, was named Secretary of the Treasury.

Washington often consulted these department heads. By 1793, they were meeting almost weekly and had become known as the President's Cabinet, or advisors. Since then, the number of departments has grown to 13, and each department head belongs to the Cabinet.

consult (kuhn-SULT): to ask advice or information from

BUILDING THE NATION'S CREDIT

Many of the new nation's problems dealt with money. The U.S. owed more than $50 million in war debts to foreign countries and to American citizens. The states owed about $25 million. The Constitution gave the federal government the power to set taxes and to create a money system but did not say how. As Secretary of the Treasury, Hamilton had to solve these problems.

Payment of Debts

Hamilton knew that only a nation that pays its debts can establish credit. He wanted the federal government to pay its debts and any that state governments owed because of the war.

Hamilton suggested that this be done by the sale of federal bonds. **Bonds** are notes that promise payment of the selling price with interest within a certain period of time. Hamilton proposed a 20-year limit. By paying its debts, the U.S. would establish itself as a good credit risk. That is, the government would be able to borrow money in the future because creditors knew they would be repaid. The plan had another purpose. Owning government bonds would encourage support for the new nation. If the bonds were to be repaid, the government had to succeed.

Some of the states were against Hamilton's plan. Virginia and most of the southern states had already paid all or most of their debts. They did not want to pay the debts of the rest of the nation. Hamilton

This watercolor by William Birch shows the Capitol building as it looked when first used by Congress in 1800. The Capitol was rebuilt after the British burned it in 1814.

proposed a compromise to Jefferson, Madison, and members of Congress from Virginia. If they would agree to the federal government's taking over state debts, he would work to have the new nation's capital built in the South. The Virginians agreed. In 1790, Congress voted to locate the capital along the Potomac River. Until the new city was built, Philadelphia became the temporary capital.

The Tariff

As part of Hamilton's economic program, he also proposed increasing the **tariff** (TAR-if), or tax on imports. In 1789, Congress had passed a small tariff. However, Hamilton thought that the tariff was not high enough. Besides raising money, he wanted the tariff to encourage and protect the nation's infant industries.

Hamilton hoped to see the U.S. become an industrial country like Great Britain. Before this could happen, though, U.S. industries needed protection from foreign competition. **Competition** (kahm-puh-TISH-uhn) is the effort of producers or sellers of similar goods to win more business by offering the lowest prices or the best conditions. A high tariff would increase the price of foreign goods. As a result, people would buy the cheaper American-made goods. Congress, however, failed to pass Hamilton's tariff. The members saw no need for it.

The First Bank

The third part of Hamilton's program involved setting up a national bank. It would be larger than the state banks and would have branch banks. Money for the national bank would come from two sources: the sale of shares in the bank and the tax money the government collected.

The bank would serve as a place for Americans to deposit their money. It would lend money to the government and to industry. Besides receiving deposits and making loans, the bank would also be the government's banker. It would issue money for the federal government and provide a single money system for the nation rather than each state issuing its own money.

Some members of Congress opposed Hamilton's bank plan. They felt that nothing in the Constitution gave the government the power to establish a bank. Hamilton argued that it was implied in the powers given Congress under the elastic clause. He persuaded Washington to support the plan. As a result, Congress passed a law giving a charter to the First Bank of the United States in 1791.

RISE OF THE TWO-PARTY SYSTEM

The U.S. Constitution made no provisions for political parties. A **political** (puh-LIT-uh-kuhl) **party** is a group of people with similar views who unite to promote their goals. The first U.S. political parties began in the 1790s. They grew out of differences between those who agreed with Hamilton's program for the new nation and those who opposed it.

Hamilton's program was based on a loose constructionist's view of the Constitution. **Loose constructionists** believe in an interpretation of the U.S. Constitution that supports an expansion of the powers of the federal government. Hamilton and his followers argued that the Constitution could not possibly spell out all the powers of the government. They claimed that the Constitution's "necessary and proper" clause gave the federal government certain implied powers. They claimed also that the federal government could use these implied powers to carry out the powers actually stated in the Constitution. Hamilton's proposal for a national bank is an example of the idea of implied powers.

The following is from a letter Alexander Hamilton wrote to George Washington. In this passage, the Secretary of the Treasury outlines reasons for the national bank.

February 23, 1791

It is a question of what is constitutional, and of what is not. This question is the purpose of the bill. If the purpose is within any of the specified powers of the Constitution, and if the bill is related to that purpose, and is not forbidden by any section of the Constitution, it may safely be thought to come within the power of the national authority. There is also this further question: Does the proposed bill abridge the right of any state or of any individual? If it does not, there is a strong argument in favor of its constitutionality.

specified (SPES-uh-fyd): described in detail

Federalists

The loose constructionists, Hamilton and his supporters, formed the first political party—the Federalists. The name was first used for people who favored a strong federal government and ratification of the Constitution. After the Constitution was ratified, the Federalists continued to work for a strong central government. They were strongest in New England and New York where manufacturing and trade were important. Federalists wanted the government to help build the nation's industry. They supported Hamilton's program, including the national bank and the tariff. Most members of the first Congress were Federalists.

Democratic-Republicans

Opposed to Hamilton were **strict constructionists.** These people do not support expansion of the federal government's power beyond what is actually stated in the Constitution. Thomas Jefferson became the leader of the early strict constructionists. In 1791, he wrote:

> I consider the foundation of the Constitution as laid on this ground: That "all powers not delegated to the United States, by the Constitution, nor prohibited by it to the States, are reserved to the States or to the people." To take a single step beyond the boundaries thus specially drawn around the powers of Congress, is to take possession of a boundless field of power.

Jefferson had supported ratification of the Constitution because he believed it was the best way to guard freedom. But he did not want the power of the federal government to grow at the expense of states' rights. **States' rights** are the rights and powers belonging to the states rather than to the federal government. These include all the powers the U.S. Constitution does not actually give the federal government or deny the states. Jefferson and his supporters argued that strong state governments would best protect the freedom of the people.

Jefferson's followers were called Democratic-Republicans or simply Republicans. That name lasted until the mid-1820s when party members began calling themselves Democrats. While the Federalists favored an industrial society, the Democratic-Republicans believed that the best society was one that was based on farming. "When people get piled upon one another in large cities," Jefferson wrote, "they shall become corrupt." Instead of building their own factories, Americans should remain farmers and buy their manufactured goods from Europe. The Democratic-Republicans were strongest in the farming regions of the South and on the frontier.

Washington did not belong to either party. He appointed followers of both Hamilton and Jefferson to his first Cabinet. In 1792, Washington and Adams were reelected. During Washington's second term, more Federalists held office, and Washington found himself siding more and more with them.

corrupt (kuh-RUHPT): evil; bad

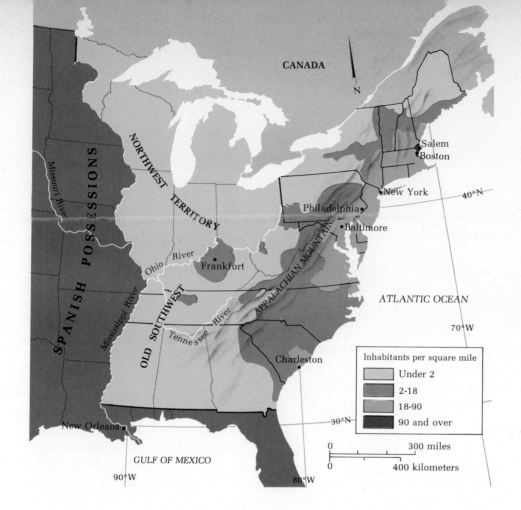

CANADA

Salem
Boston

New York

Philadelphia

Baltimore

SPANISH POSSESSIONS

NORTHWEST TERRITORY

Missouri River

Ohio River

Frankfort

Mississippi River

OLD SOUTHWEST

APPALACHIAN MOUNTAINS

Tennessee River

ATLANTIC OCEAN

40°N

70°W

Charleston

New Orleans

30°N

90°W   80°W

GULF OF MEXICO

Inhabitants per square mile

Under 2
2-18
18-90
90 and over

0   300 miles
0   400 kilometers

The Frontier in 1790

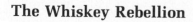

The map Frontier in 1790 shows **population density.** This is the average number of people living in a given area. The map above shows the average number of people per square mile in the newly formed United States and its territories. The areas of highest population density are usually cities and large towns. **1.** In 1790, which areas—coastal plains, Appalachians, Piedmont, and so on—of the U.S. had the largest populations? **2.** What factors do you think caused this? **3.** Which areas were the least settled? **4.** What factors do you think caused this? **5.** Where was the frontier located in 1790?

BUILDING MAP SKILLS

The Whiskey Rebellion

In time, the division between the Federalists and the Democratic-Republicans became sharper. In addition to the tariff, Hamilton asked for an excise tax on whiskey. The tax, passed in 1791, was especially hard on farmers on the frontier. They made more money turning their corn crop into whiskey than selling it as grain. In 1794, farmers in western Pennsylvania rebelled against the tax.

Washington called out the militia of four states to put down the rebellion. Hamilton led the soldiers in a show of force. He wanted the

The frontier was settled in cycles. Pioneers came to clear small patches of land, build log cabins, and plant a few crops. Fences were made of logs. There were no barns and few other farm buildings.

rural (RUHR-uhl): of or from the country

farmers to see that the federal government was powerful and its laws had to be obeyed. The rebellion ended with the arrest of 200 rebels. As a result of the government's action, many farmers and small business owners turned against the Federalists and supported the Democratic-Republicans.

THE FRONTIER

When the first census was taken in 1790, the U.S. population was about four million. Most people lived in rural settlements and small towns along the Atlantic coast. Only 3 percent of the population lived in the six largest cities: Philadelphia, New York, Boston, Charleston, Baltimore, and Salem, Massachusetts. Only about 1 person in 25 lived beyond the Appalachians.

Ten years later, the population was over seven million. By 1830, it had grown to almost ten million. As the population increased, land in the settled areas became scarce. The Appalachians had been the western boundary of the frontier during the early and mid-1700s. During the Revolutionary War, fighting between Americans and Native Americans on the other side of the Appalachians had kept many settlers from moving into the area.

After the war, people pushed beyond them into the Northwest Territory and the Old Southwest. The Old Southwest was the land south of the Ohio River, between the Appalachians and the Mississippi. It included what would become the states of Kentucky, Tennessee, Alabama, and Mississippi. As more people went south and west, new states were added: Kentucky (1792), Tennessee (1796), and Ohio (1803). The Mississippi became the new boundary of the frontier. In 1791, Vermont was also admitted to statehood when New York and New Hampshire gave up claims to the region.

Native Americans and the New Nation

As settlers moved onto the frontier, they often asked the federal government for protection from Native Americans. Sometimes, the government and Native Americans signed a treaty, then soldiers were sent to enforce it. Or, soldiers defeated Native Americans in battle, then made them sign a treaty. Most often, the treaties forced Native Americans to give up their lands and move.

The U.S. dealt with the leaders of Native American groups as it would with leaders of foreign nations. However, the government of most Native American peoples was not organized the way other governments were. Native Americans did not give their leaders the power to act without the group's agreement. If most Native Americans within a nation did not agree to a treaty, they would not obey it. There was also a conflict between the way Native Americans and the U.S. government viewed land. Native Americans felt that no one owned the land. It was free for everyone's use, so no one had the right to give it away or sell it.

In the Old Southwest, the U.S. made treaties with the Creek, Cherokee, and Seminole. Despite the treaties, trouble continued into the early 1800s. The Spanish hoped to stop U.S. expansion southward. They gave the Native Americans weapons and supplies and encouraged attacks on American frontier settlements.

In the Northwest Territory, the British armed the Native Americans. They hoped the Native Americans would form a barrier to further expansion by the new nation. In 1790 and 1791, the U.S. Army marched into Native American lands north of the Ohio River. Both times, they were badly defeated. In 1794, Washington sent General Anthony Wayne into the Northwest Territory. Wayne and his soldiers met Shawnee (shaw-NEE), Miami (my-AM-ee), Ottawa, Potawatomi (pahd-uh-WAHT-uh-mee), Ojibwa, Fox, Sauk (SAWK), and others at

After the pioneers, came settlers who cleared more land, built bigger houses, put up farm buildings such as barns, and planted large fields. Some settlers even planted orchards.

despite (dih-SPYT): regardless of

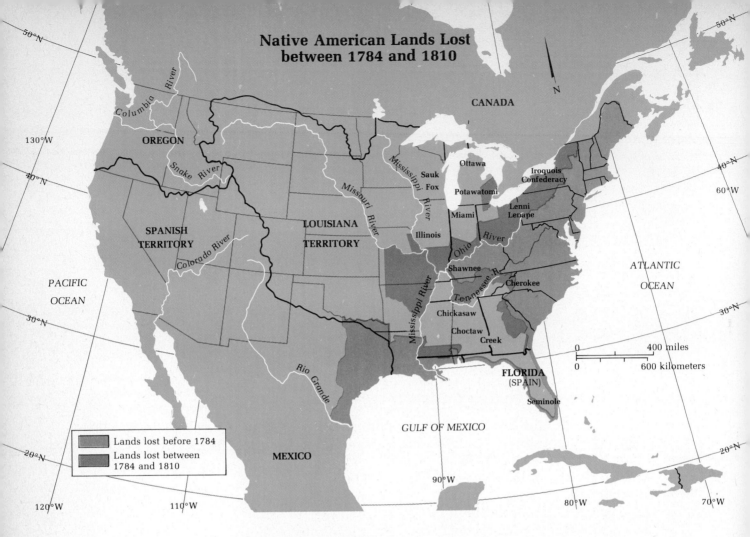

Native American Lands Lost between 1784 and 1810

CANADA

OREGON

SPANISH TERRITORY

LOUISIANA TERRITORY

Columbia River

Snake River

Colorado River

Missouri River

Mississippi River

Ottawa

Sauk Fox

Potawatomi

Miami

Illinois

Iroquois Confederacy

Lenni Lenape

Ohio River

Shawnee

Tennessee R.

Cherokee

Chickasaw

Choctaw

Creek

Mississippi River

Rio Grande

MEXICO

FLORIDA (SPAIN)

Seminole

GULF OF MEXICO

ATLANTIC OCEAN

PACIFIC OCEAN

- Lands lost before 1784
- Lands lost between 1784 and 1810

0   400 miles
0   600 kilometers

Fallen Timbers near present-day Toledo, Ohio. The Native Americans were greatly outnumbered and were unable to hold off the better-armed U.S. Army. The Battle of Fallen Timbers lasted less than two hours, but its effects have lasted to the present. In 1795, the Native Americans of the area were forced to sign the Treaty of Greenville, which gave up most of their lands in the Northwest Territory. This treaty cleared the way for settlers to go west of the Appalachians.

LOOKING BACK

1. **a.** List three problems Washington faced when he became President. **b.** Choose one and explain how it was solved.
2. **a.** List two objectives of Alexander Hamilton's economic program. **b.** Describe his plans for meeting each.
3. Compare and contrast the beliefs of the Federalists and Democratic-Republicans on: **a.** interpreting the Constitution. **b.** the best type of economy for the U.S. **c.** states' rights.
4. Use the map on page 307 to answer: **a.** What area had the greatest population? **b.** Why did the territories have small populations?
5. **a.** Describe how the U.S. government made treaties with Native Americans. **b.** State two effects of the Treaty of Greenville.

Chapter 2   Washington's Foreign Policy

LOOKING AHEAD

To survive, the new nation had to avoid foreign wars. Yet problems with other countries developed that troubled many Americans. Meeting the needs of some sections of the U.S. depended on solving these problems. This chapter tells how the new nation handled differences with France, Great Britain, and Spain. After you study this chapter, you will be able to:

- compare and contrast the views of the Federalists and Democratic-Republicans on the French Revolution.
- ★ read a cartoon to learn about historical issues and events.
- explain how the U.S. solved its problems with Great Britain and Spain.
- identify the main point Washington made about foreign policy in his Farewell Address.

Social Studies Vocabulary

foreign policy	neutrality
republic	parallel

People

Edmond Genet

Words and Terms

the Union	impressment	right of deposit
Neutrality	Jay's Treaty	
Proclamation	Pinckney's Treaty	

The main goal of Washington's foreign policy was peace. **Foreign (FOR-uhn) policy** is a government's plan for dealing with other countries. At the same time, Washington had to preserve the Union—the United States—by meeting the needs of Americans in each section of the country. Almost at once, Washington faced his first challenge.

THE FRENCH REVOLUTION AND THE U.S.

In 1789, a revolution broke out in France. The monarchy was overthrown, and a republic was formed. A **republic** is a government in which officials and representatives are elected by the people, and certain rights are guaranteed to the people. By 1793, the French were calling for uprisings against all monarchs. European kings and queens became alarmed that the French Revolution might spread to their countries. As a result, Prussia—parts of the modern nations of East and West Germany, of Poland, of the Soviet Union—and Austria declared war against France. Then France declared war on Great Britain, Spain, and the Netherlands who were allies of Prussia and Austria at the time.

According to the alliance that France and the U.S. had signed in 1778, the U.S. should have come to France's aid. Although the French had helped win the Revolutionary War, Americans were divided over whether they should now help the French. Hamilton and the Federalists said no. They felt the U.S. had no duty to help the French spread revolution. They said that the treaty of 1778 had been made with the king—Louis XVI. Now that the French had overthrown the monarchy, the treaty was no longer in effect.

Jefferson and the Democratic-Republicans, on the other hand, argued that the treaty should be honored. They felt that the French Revolution was just and they wanted it to succeed. The Democratic-Republicans called on the government to help the French.

Washington wanted the French to succeed, too, but he also wanted to keep the U.S. out of war. He realized that the new nation was still weak. Its economy, for example, was just beginning to grow and depended greatly on trade with Great Britain. War with Great Britain would cut off this trade and with it the money it earned Americans and the manufactured goods it brought them.

In 1793, Washington issued a proclamation of neutrality. **Neutrality** (noo-TRAL-uh-tee) is the refusal to take sides or become involved. The Neutrality Proclamation stated that the U.S. and its citizens would not become involved in the war. Congress quickly made the proclamation law by passing the Neutrality Act.

On July 14, 1789, French citizens stormed the Bastille, a hated symbol of the monarch. The revolutionaries captured the prison and later destroyed it. Which Americans supported the French Revolution and which did not? Why?

The Cannibals are landing

This cartoon illustrates differences between Democratic-Republicans and Federalists over the French Revolution. Why are the French labeled as cannibals? Did the cartoonist support Jefferson?

Cartoons can express opinions about events and issues. They often use symbols to represent their meaning. A symbol is a sign or an object that stands for something else. Historical cartoons can be difficult to understand because you may not recognize the symbols used in a certain period. When you look at a cartoon, first identify the subject. Second, identify the symbols. Finally, try to recognize the artist's point of view. **Activity:** Study the cartoon above and then answer the questions in the caption.

BUILDING PICTURE SKILLS

Genet

At about this time, Edmond Genet (zhuh-NE), the new minister to the U.S. from France, arrived in America. He began recruiting soldiers for the French army and organizing raids on the ships of France's enemies. These actions violated the Neutrality Act. The Cabinet asked the French government to replace Genet. At first, Jefferson had thought Genet would win new support for the Democratic-Republicans and the French. But in time, even Jefferson wanted him sent home. He felt Genet was damaging the Democratic-Republicans. In 1794, the French government changed, and Genet's enemies came to power. The French ordered him home, but he chose to remain in the U.S. as a private citizen.

RELATIONS WITH GREAT BRITAIN

Even while trade with Great Britain was growing, problems were developing between the U.S. and that nation. As you may recall, the

Treaty of Paris ended the Revolutionary War. According to the treaty, Great Britain was to give up its forts and trading posts in the lands between the Ohio and Mississippi rivers. By 1793, however, the British still had not left all their forts and were continuing to trade for furs. Americans living on the frontier believed the British were also encouraging Native American raids on their settlements.

The British, for their part, said they would not leave until the U.S. paid its war debts. They also wanted the U.S. to repay Tories for property taken from them during the Revolutionary War. Although the U.S. had agreed in the Treaty of Paris to make these payments, it was now resisting.

Another problem with Great Britain concerned its attacks on U.S. ships in the Caribbean. After France declared war on Great Britain, the British navy began capturing ships thought to be trading with French colonies. The U.S. government protested. Since the U.S. was neutral, the government said that American ships should be allowed to trade with all nations. As part of its policy of neutrality, the U.S. would not sell guns, ammunition, or other war goods to either side.

The capturing of U.S. ships led to another problem—impressment. Impressment is the seizing of sailors and forcing them to work. When the British boarded U.S. ships, they took sailors that they suspected of having deserted the British navy. Some were deserters, but others were American citizens. When news of this reached Americans, many were ready to go to war.

Jay's Treaty

In 1794, Washington sent Chief Justice John Jay to Great Britain to find a peaceful solution to the problems. The treaty he signed covered

When at war with France, Great Britain seized U.S. ships thought to be trading with the French and often forced U.S. sailors into service in the British Navy. What excuse did the British use?

the most important points. The British agreed to leave the western frontier by June 1796. They also agreed to grant the U.S. trading rights in the British islands of the Caribbean. Other problems, such as U.S. payment of war debts and interference with U.S. shipping, were left to a joint committee to decide.

The Democratic-Republicans strongly objected to the treaty. They felt that the Federalists supported the treaty because they were only interested in increasing trade with Great Britain. Over the protests of Democratic-Republicans, Jay's Treaty was ratified in June 1795. Later, a committee worked out the question of war debts. But a committee was not able to end the taking of U.S. ships or impressment. You will read more about these problems in Chapter 4 of this unit.

TREATY WITH SPAIN

As you may recall from the unit The American Revolution, the British returned Florida to Spanish rule after the Revolutionary War. Spain also ruled the area called Louisiana. Like the British, the Spanish decided they needed protection from the expanding U.S. They gave guns and ammunition to Native Americans for raids on American settlements in the Old Southwest. The Spanish also began building forts on the eastern side of the Mississippi. Washington sent Thomas Pinckney to Spain to persuade the Spanish to stop building on U.S. land.

While Pinckney was there, news came of Jay's Treaty. Spain feared that as allies the U.S. and Great Britain would try to seize Spanish colonies in the Americas. To win U.S. friendship, Spain agreed to American demands. In Pinckney's Treaty, the two countries agreed that the southern boundary between Georgia and Spanish Florida would be set at the 31st parallel. A **parallel** (PAR-uh-lel) is an imaginary line that represents a degree of latitude. Spain also agreed to prevent Native American raids from Florida into Georgia. Most importantly, Americans were guaranteed the use of the Mississippi. They were also guaranteed the right of deposit at New Orleans. This meant Americans could leave trade goods awaiting shipment on the docks of New Orleans.

WASHINGTON'S FAREWELL ADDRESS

In 1797, Washington's second term as President came to an end. Jay's Treaty had stirred a loud protest among Democratic-Republicans who wanted to go to war against the British. Washington and the Federalists had been strongly criticized for supporting the treaty. Washington decided to retire.

As he prepared to leave office, Washington wrote a message to the people describing his feelings about the dangers of political parties,

Congress ratified Jay's Treaty in 1795 to avoid war with Great Britain. To show their dislike of the treaty, opponents burned figures of Jay. Who opposed the treaty?

THE PRESENT State of our COUNTRY.

William Charles drew this cartoon to illustrate the spirit of Washington's Farewell Address. What symbols does the artist use? What is the point of view of the artist?

sectionalism, and alliances with foreign countries. In his Farewell Address, he wrote the following about foreign policy:

> The great rule of conduct for us, in regard to foreign nations, is to have with them as little political connection as possible. As far as we have already formed engagements, let them be carried out with perfect good faith. Here let us stop.
>
> Our distant situation invites and allows us to follow a different course. If we remain one people, under an efficient government, the period is not far off when we may choose peace or war, as our interest, guided by justice, shall counsel.
>
> Why give up the advantages of so peculiar a situation? Why, by interweaving our future with that of any part of Europe, entangle our peace and prosperity in the toils of European ambition, rivalry, interest, humor, or caprice?

efficient (uh-FISH-uhnt): getting the best results without wasting energy, time, and so on

caprice (kuh-PREES): a sudden change without reason

LOOKING BACK

1. What were the views of each of the following about the French Revolution: **a.** the Federalists? **b.** Democratic-Republicans?
★ 2. Use the cartoon on page 313 to answer: **a.** What subject does the cartoon illustrate? **b.** What is the artist's point of view? **c.** What are the three steps in reading a cartoon?
3. **a.** What problems nearly led to war with Great Britain? **b.** How were they solved? **c.** What problems between Spain and the U.S. were solved by Pinckney's Treaty?
4. **a.** State the main point Washington made in his Farewell Address about the kind of foreign policy the new nation should have. **b.** What details from his speech support your answer?

Chapter 3   Change and Expansion

LOOKING AHEAD

The years from 1796 to 1806 were a time of growth for the new nation. In this chapter, you will read about the presidencies of John Adams and Thomas Jefferson. The U.S. doubled in size and avoided another war. After you study this chapter, you will be able to:

- list the chronology of the undeclared war between the U.S. and France.
- explain why the Federalists wanted the Alien, Sedition, and Naturalization Acts passed.
- read a cartoon to identify how some people felt about the Alien, Sedition, and Naturalization Acts.
★ identify the assumption made in the Kentucky and Virginia Resolutions.
- describe how the elections of 1796 and 1800 resulted in the 12th Amendment.
- identify the importance of *Marbury* v. *Madison*.
- list the states that were made from the Louisiana Purchase.

Social Studies Vocabulary

assumption

People

John Adams	John Marshall	William Clark
Thomas Jefferson	Pierre Toussaint	York
Napoleon Bonaparte	L'Ouverture	Sacajawea
Aaron Burr	Meriwether Lewis	Zebulon Pike

Places

Columbia River

Words and Terms

XYZ Affair	Kentucky Resolution	midnight judges
Alien Act	Virginia Resolution	*Marbury* v. *Madison*
Naturalization Act	12th Amendment	Louisiana Purchase
Sedition Act	revolution of 1800	

Lewis and Clark kept journals during their exploration of the Louisiana Purchase. This page from Clark's journal illustrates and describes in detail a trout they caught.

For eight years, Washington held the presidency and supported most Federalist programs. During that time, Jefferson's Democratic-Republicans were growing in strength. When Washington refused a third term, they challenged Federalist control of the government.

THE ELECTION OF 1796

The election of 1796 was the first U.S. presidential election in which candidates from different parties competed. The major issue was Jay's Treaty. The Federalists supported it, while the Democratic-Republicans were against it. For President, the Federalists chose John Adams and for Vice-President, Thomas Pinckney. The Democratic-Republicans chose Jefferson and Aaron Burr.

According to the electoral system, the person with the highest number of votes would become President. The person with the second highest number would become Vice-President. Adams had 71 electoral votes and Jefferson had 68. Adams became President, and Jefferson, with the second highest number, was named Vice-President. Because of the electoral system, a Federalist President took office with a Democratic-Republican Vice-President.

CONFLICT WITH FRANCE

Soon after taking office in 1797, Adams faced his first foreign policy problem. Jay's Treaty had angered the French who thought that the U.S. and Great Britain had become allies against France. The French began capturing American ships in the Caribbean. By mid-1797, they had captured over 300 — more than the British had seized. The Democratic-Republicans, opposed to both the British and the treaty, encouraged the French attacks. They hoped the U.S. would side with France to end the attacks.

Adams wanted to avoid war. Looking for a peaceful solution, he sent Charles C. Pinckney, Elbridge Gerry (GER-ee), and John Marshall to France. Before any discussion could begin, Charles Talleyrand (TAL-ee-rand), the French foreign minister, sent three agents to the Americans to demand money. The Americans refused. When they reported to Adams, they referred to the agents only as X, Y, and Z.

Reports of the XYZ Affair were printed in American newspapers, and people were angered. Americans said they would spend "millions for defense but not one cent for tribute." Federalists in Congress called for war. A Navy Department was formed. Washington was asked to take command of the army. Because the Democratic-Republicans had sided with the French, they lost many supporters.

Americans expected France to declare war. However, Talleyrand called the XYZ Affair a misunderstanding, and Adams reopened peace talks. For the next two years, France and the U.S. fought an undeclared war at sea while talks continued. The fighting ended in 1800 when the French agreed that the treaty of 1778 was no longer in effect.

ALIEN, NATURALIZATION, AND SEDITION ACTS

During this time, the Federalists in Congress tried further to weaken the Democratic-Republican party. They passed the Alien, Natural-

tribute (TRIB-yoot): money paid to a nation to ensure peace or protection

318

Debate over the Alien, Sedition, and Naturalization Acts became heated at times as this cartoon from 1798 shows. Congressmen Griswold and Lyons actually came to blows over the issues.

ization, and Sedition Acts. The Alien Act gave the government the power to arrest and deport any alien believed to be dangerous. The Naturalization Act raised from 5 to 14 years the length of time an alien had to live in the U.S. before becoming a citizen. These laws were aimed at the many French immigrants in the U.S. Most supported the pro-French Democratic-Republicans.

deport (dih-PORT): to send out of the country

The Sedition (suh-DISH-uhn) Act called for punishment of anyone who opposed laws or made false or critical statements about the President or Congress. Because of this law, a number of Democratic-Republican writers and printers were jailed by Federalist judges. This angered many Americans who believed the Sedition Act violated the First Amendment rights of freedom of speech and of the press.

The acts were so unpopular they increased Democratic-Republican support. Two state legislatures—Kentucky and Virginia—passed resolutions declaring the Alien and Sedition Acts unconstitutional. Jefferson wrote Kentucky's resolution and Madison wrote Virginia's. The resolutions said that if a state believed a federal law to be unconstitutional, the state could declare the law null and void. Whether states had this right was a question that would arise again.

The Kentucky and Virginia Resolutions are based on an assumption. An **assumption** (uh-SUMP-shuhn) is what a person thinks or takes for granted to be true. It may or may not be true. For example, as you may recall from the unit The New Nation, Jefferson made an assumption in the quote, "When people get piled upon one another in large cities, they shall become corrupt." He assumed that cities made people corrupt. You must read carefully to see if an author is making an assumption or drawing a conclusion based only on facts. **1.** What is an assumption? **2.** In the Kentucky and Virginia Resolutions, what assumption did Jefferson and Madison make about the rights of states?

BUILDING READING SKILLS

319

REVOLUTION OF 1800

As the election of 1800 neared, Jay's Treaty was still an issue. To make matters worse, Adams in 1799 had made peace with France's new leader, Napoleon Bonaparte (nuh-POH-lih-uhn BOH-nuh-pahrt). Adams thought that war with France would damage the growing U.S. economy. Americans who favored war with France were unhappy with the President's decision. Yet it was the unpopular Alien and Sedition Acts that cost the Federalists more support than any other issue.

Jefferson, in the meantime, was working to build support. He argued that not all Democratic-Republicans had to be farmers. Southern farmers could work with New England merchants for changes that would benefit both groups. Jefferson's running mate was again Aaron Burr of New York. John Adams and Charles C. Pinckney were the Federalist candidates for President and Vice-President.

In the electoral college, Jefferson and Burr both received 73 votes. Although Burr had run for the vice-presidency, he wanted the presidency. Under the Constitution, the election went to the House of Representatives. After seven days and 36 ballots, Jefferson was chosen President and Burr, Vice-President. Because of this situation the 12th Amendment was added to the Constitution. As you may recall from the unit A Plan of Government, this amendment calls for separate elections in the electoral college for President and Vice-President.

Jefferson called his election the "revolution of 1800." He meant that the people had changed a government that they felt no longer served their needs and they had done so peacefully.

Jefferson began his term by putting into practice his Democratic-Republican policies. He had Congress repeal the Naturalization Act. The Alien Act had expired in 1800, and the Sedition Act expired in 1801. Jefferson pardoned those who had been jailed under the Sedition Act. The excise tax that caused the Whiskey Rebellion was also repealed. Jefferson wanted to give greater power to the people and the states, but he knew there were limits to what he could change. Although he disagreed with the idea of the First Bank, it would have been dangerous to the economy to try to close it.

Marbury v. *Madison*

One of Jefferson's first problems in office concerned the midnight judges. These were last-minute judicial appointments made by Adams. All the judges were Federalists, and Adams's act angered Jefferson. When he took office, a few of the appointed judges had not actually received their commissions. Following Jefferson's directions, Secretary of State James Madison refused to deliver their papers. One of the men, William Marbury, asked the Supreme Court for an order forcing Madison to give him his commission. Marbury based his request on a section of the Judiciary Act of 1789.

The Chief Justice of the Supreme Court was John Marshall, also an Adams appointee. In the case of *Marbury* v. *Madison*, Marshall ruled

commission
(kuh-MISH-uhn):
document giving a
person duties, powers, and
privileges

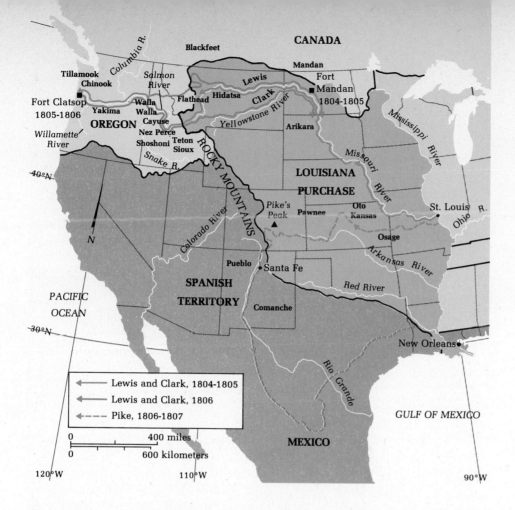

Within the map:

CANADA

Blackfeet

Mandan

Columbia R.

Tillamook
Chinook

Salmon
River

Lewis

Fort
Mandan
1804-1805

Fort Clatsop
1805-1806

Flathead   Hidatsa   Clark

Yakima   Walla Walla
Cayuse
Nez Perce
Shoshoni   Teton
Sioux

OREGON

Willamette
River

Yellowstone River

Arikara

Mississippi River

Missouri River

Snake R.

ROCKY MOUNTAINS

LOUISIANA
PURCHASE

40°N

N

Colorado River

Pike's
Peak

Pawnee

Oto
Kansas

St. Louis

Ohio R.

Osage

Arkansas River

Pueblo   Santa Fe

SPANISH
TERRITORY

PACIFIC
OCEAN

Red River

Comanche

30°N

New Orleans

Rio Grande

GULF OF MEXICO

⟵ Lewis and Clark, 1804-1805
⟵ Lewis and Clark, 1806
⟵ --- Pike, 1806-1807

0   400 miles
0   600 kilometers

120°W   110°W   90°W

MEXICO

**Exploration of the
Louisiana Purchase
from 1803 to 1807**

that the part of the Judiciary Act that Marbury referred to was unconstitutional. Because the Constitution had not given this power to the Supreme Court, Congress could not give this power to the Court either. Marshall's decision established the power of judicial review. This is the power of the Supreme Court to review a legislative act and, if necessary, declare it unconstitutional. This right provided a check on both the President and Congress.

LOUISIANA PURCHASE

In the last chapter, you read that Spain controlled New Orleans and the area known as Louisiana. In 1800, Spain gave Louisiana to France. Napoleon, the French emperor, planned to create a French empire in North America. Late in 1802, officials in Louisiana refused to allow Americans to use New Orleans. This angered frontier settlers for whom the port was the main route for their trade goods. Federalists called for war but Jefferson wanted to avoid conflict.

In 1803, he sent James Monroe and Robert Livingston to Napoleon with an offer to buy New Orleans. If the French refused, they were to ask that the right of deposit be restored. If this were denied, the two men were to ask for British support in any fight with the French for control of the Mississippi.

This is New Orleans as it looked in 1803 when the U.S. purchased Louisiana from France. Why was New Orleans important to settlers on the frontier?

Meanwhile, Napoleon's plans for a North American empire were going badly. He had not been able to get Florida from Spain. In the Caribbean, blacks had rebelled against the French in St. Domingue (san daw-MANG), now the nation of Haiti (HAY-tee). Led for a time by Pierre Toussaint L'Ouverture (TOO-san loo-ver-TYOOR), the revolt eventually won the colony's independence in 1804. An important part of Napoleon's planned empire was lost.

Napoleon also found himself in need of money. When Monroe and Livingston made their offer, Napoleon said he would sell all of Louisiana for $15 million. Jefferson accepted. In 1803, the two countries signed the treaty of cession. Using the Northwest Ordinance of 1787 as a guide, Jefferson made Louisiana a territory. People living in the area were given the rights of U.S. citizens and could in time ask for statehood.

Lewis and Clark Expedition

The Louisiana Purchase almost doubled the size of the U.S. The most important gains at the time were control of the Mississippi and of New Orleans. But Jefferson wanted to know what more he had bought for the nation. In 1803, he sent two army officers, Meriwether Lewis and William Clark, to explore the new territory. Jefferson hoped they would find an all-water route to the Pacific.

Lewis and Clark traveled to Pittsburgh and then down the Ohio and Mississippi rivers to St. Louis, near the mouth of the Missouri River. The expedition left St. Louis in May 1804 with a small group of soldiers, civilians, and Clark's slave, York. York proved very helpful in establishing good relations with Native Americans along the way. He won his freedom during the trip.

The group traveled up the Missouri River to what is now North Dakota and spent the winter with the Mandan. In spring 1805, they headed west. With the help of Sacajawea (sak-uh-juh-WEE-uh), a young Shoshoni who was married to one of the group's interpreters, they moved into what are now the states of Montana and Idaho. There, Sacajawea was reunited with her brother, a Shoshoni leader, and the expedition received much-needed supplies.

The group then crossed the Rocky Mountains and entered the land of the Nez Perce. They followed several westward-flowing rivers into the Columbia that brought them to the Pacific in November 1805. They camped along the coast for the winter and returned to St. Louis the following year.

Although Lewis and Clark did not find an all-water route to the Pacific, they did bring back useful information. They mapped the lands they crossed and brought back descriptions of the animals and plants they saw. The expedition also provided helpful information about the Native Americans they met. Lewis and Clark's exploration of the Columbia River became part of the basis for the later American claim to Oregon. The following is from the *Journal of Meriwether Lewis*. It describes the horses the expedition saw near the Columbia River.

> The horses appear to be of an excellent race, beautifully formed, active and strong. Some of them are spotted with large scattered patches of white mixed with dark brown. They are allowed to run loose in the plains. Whether the horse was originally a native of this country or not, the soil and climate appear to be perfectly well adapted to this animal. The abundance and cheapness of horses will be extremely advantageous to those who may attempt the fur trade to the East Indies by way of the Columbia River and the Pacific Ocean.

After Lewis and Clark, other explorers went west. Jefferson sent another army officer, Zebulon Pike, to search for the sources of the Mississippi, Red, and Arkansas rivers. Pike reached what is now Colorado and attempted but failed to climb the mountain now named for him: Pike's Peak. Pike and his followers were captured by Spanish troops in New Mexico and returned to the American border. The information Pike gathered about Spanish territory added to American interest in expanding into these lands.

Members of the Lewis and Clark expedition kept records. This woodcut of a meeting with Native Americans is from the published journal of Patrick Gass.

The Barbary States of North Africa had been demanding tribute from U.S. and European ships in the Mediterranean for years. In the early 1800s, the U.S. fought back. This shows the U.S.S. *Constitution* bombarding Tripoli, one of the Barbary States. The next year, Tripoli agreed to end piracy.

ELECTION OF 1804

As the election of 1804 neared, Jefferson and the Democratic-Republicans were sure of winning. However, Jefferson did not want Burr as his running mate. He had not forgiven Burr for trying to claim the presidency in 1800. George Clinton was chosen instead, and Jefferson and Clinton won easily.

Burr became a Federalist, but he could not win the trust of Alexander Hamilton. Angered by a remark Hamilton made about him, Burr challenged him to a duel in 1804. Hamilton was killed, and Burr's political career was destroyed.

LOOKING BACK

1. List in chronological order the events that led to the undeclared war between the U.S. and France.
2. Why did the Federalists think that each of the following would help their party: **a.** Alien Act? **b.** Naturalization Act? **c.** Sedition Act?
3. Study the cartoon on page 319. **a.** How are others in Congress reacting? **b.** How does the artist view Congress?
★ 4. What assumption about states rights was made in the Kentucky and Virginia Resolutions?
5. **a.** In the election of 1796, what problem occurred because of the way the electoral college was set up? **b.** What problem occurred in the election of 1800? **c.** How did the 12th Amendment solve the problem?
6. What principle of law was established in *Marbury* v. *Madison?*
7. Using the map on page 321: **a.** List the states and parts of states that were made from the Louisiana Purchase. **b.** While exploring the Louisiana Purchase, what Native American lands did Lewis and Clark pass through?

Chapter 4   The New Nation Under Fire

LOOKING AHEAD

This chapter describes the difficulties the U.S. had in trying to stay neutral during the events leading up to the War of 1812. You will read about that war and learn why it was unpopular with some Americans. After you study this chapter, you will be able to:

- list the sequence of events that led to the War of 1812.
- state Tecumseh's reasons for wanting to unite Native Americans on the western frontier.
- compare the advantages and disadvantages of the U.S. and Great Britain in the War of 1812.
- list the results of the War of 1812.
- identify the assumption made in the resolution of the Hartford Convention.

Social Studies Vocabulary

embargo   market   depression   secede

People

James Madison	Tecumseh	Oliver H. Perry
War Hawks	William Henry Harrison	Francis Scott Key
Henry Clay	Tenskwatawa,	Andrew Jackson
John C. Calhoun	the Prophet	

Places

Detroit	Lake Erie	Washington, D.C.
Fort Dearborn	Lake Champlain	Fort McHenry

Words and Terms

Embargo Act   "The Star-Spangled Banner"

Events

Chesapeake incident	War of 1812	Hartford Convention
Battle of Tippecanoe	Battle of the Thames	
	Battle of New Orleans	
	Treaty of Ghent	

In the early 1800s, under the leadership of Napoleon, the French were trying to conquer Europe. France's most powerful enemy was Great Britain. In waging war, both countries violated U.S. rights at sea. Jefferson, however, was determined to remain neutral. Americans had developed a highly profitable trade with both Great Britain and

France, and Jefferson wanted it to continue. However, as the wars dragged on, Great Britain and France were making trade difficult for the U.S. Each country was seizing American ships headed for enemy ports. The British were still impressing American sailors. In June 1807, the British Ship *Leopard* fired on the U.S. naval ship *Chesapeake* off the Virginia coast. Three men were killed and 18 injured. The British boarded the *Chesapeake* and took four of its crew.

EMBARGO ACT

The *Chesapeake* incident angered Americans. Jefferson called for an embargo. An **embargo** (em-BAHR-goh) is a government's refusal to allow trade with other countries. The act closed U.S. ports to all foreign ships, and U.S. ships could trade only along the U.S. coast. Jefferson hoped that the need for American goods and markets would force Great Britain and France to respect U.S. rights. A **market** is not only a place to buy or sell but also a demand for a particular item.

The embargo, however, had little effect on Great Britain and France, but it badly damaged the U.S. economy. Merchants, shipowners, and sailors were especially hard hit. Industries, such as lumbering, that were related to shipping were also hurt. Farmers suffered because they lost their foreign customers. The nation entered a **depression,** a time of little business activity. Prices are low, profits are few, unemployment is high, and there is little demand for goods. Many businesses and banks fail.

The unpopular Embargo Act was a major issue in the election of 1808. Federalists blamed the Democratic-Republicans for the loss of

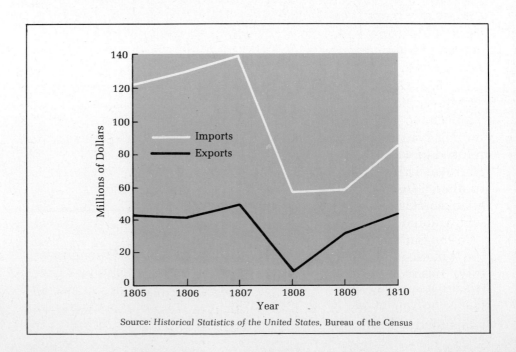

United States Foreign Trade from 1805 to 1810

Source: *Historical Statistics of the United States,* Bureau of the Census

trade. Even though the problem was nationwide, Federalists had strong support only in New England. Most Americans in rural areas still supported the party of Jefferson. In 1808, they elected Jefferson's choice, James Madison, as President.

WAR HAWKS

In 1809, Congress replaced the Embargo Act with a milder law. It reopened trade with all countries except France and Great Britain. Trade with these two nations would begin again when they agreed to respect U.S. rights. In 1810, Madison renewed trade with France. He was misled by Napoleon into believing that France would honor U.S. neutrality. The French continued to violate U.S. sea rights.

During this time, anti-British feeling was growing in the country. Impressment and attacks on U.S. shipping were two reasons. The third reason involved the frontier. Frontier settlers believed Native Americans were attacking them from bases in Canada. A group in Congress called War Hawks strongly favored war. They were looking for an excuse to drive the British from Canada and open that land to American settlement. Their leaders were Henry Clay of Kentucky and John C. Calhoun of South Carolina. The War Hawks became even louder in their demands for war in 1811 after a conflict with followers of Tecumseh (tih-KUHM-suh).

TECUMSEH

A few years earlier, Tecumseh, a Shawnee, had begun working to unite Native Americans along the frontier from the Great Lakes to the Gulf of Mexico. He wanted them to form an alliance and refuse to sell settlers any more land. Tecumseh believed that if the Native Americans could form a powerful enough alliance, they could stop the spread of frontier settlements. He found support among Ojibwa, Winnebago (win-uh-BAY-goh), Potawatomi, and other peoples.

In 1811, General William Henry Harrison, governor of the Indiana Territory, led a group of Americans to Tecumseh's village near the Tippecanoe (tip-uh-KUH-noo) River. As governor, Harrison had been forcing Native Americans to sell their lands, and Tecumseh had refused to accept these sales. Tecumseh was not in the village when Harrison arrived. He had gone to ask the Creek for their support. His brother, Tenskwatawa (ten-SKWAH-tah-wah), known as the Prophet, attacked Harrison's army. This was against the orders of Tecumseh, who wanted to avoid conflict.

prophet (PRAHF-it): one who predicts the future

In the Battle of Tippecanoe, both sides had heavy losses. However, the Americans burned the village and declared the battle their victory. Harrison's men claimed to have found British weapons in the village. When Tecumseh learned of the battle, he joined the British in Canada. When word of the battle reached the War Hawks, they demanded war. Giving in, Congress declared war in 1812.

In the Battle of Tippecanoe, U.S. troops and Shawnee fought over the forced selling of Native American lands. Who claimed victory? How did this battle lead to the War of 1812?

THE WAR OF 1812

The vote that declared war showed the growing sectionalism in the U.S. Most members of Congress from the South and from frontier states voted for war while those from New England voted against it. The New Englanders feared the loss of trade that a war would bring. The war actually began because of poor communications. By the time war was declared, the British had changed their policies toward the U.S. but word had not yet come.

Fighting the War

American strategy called for an invasion of Canada. However, the American surrender of Detroit and British victories at Fort Dearborn, now Chicago, and in northern New York delayed this plan. In April 1813, the Americans captured and burned York, now Toronto, in Canada. A few months later, Oliver Hazard Perry's ships defeated the British on Lake Erie. With Lake Erie under control, the Americans invaded Canada. In October 1813, Harrison defeated the British and their Native American allies at the Battle of the Thames (TEMZ). Tecumseh was killed, and his death ended Native American hopes of resisting American settlers.

Early in 1814, the British and their European allies defeated Napoleon. Great Britain then turned its full attention to the U.S. The British had a threefold plan of attack: a drive south from Canada into northern New York; an attack on Washington, D.C.; and an attack on New Orleans. The Americans stopped the British on Lake Champlain. The second British force captured and burned Washington, D.C. However, it was stopped by the Americans at Fort McHenry, near Baltimore. During the battle, Francis Scott Key wrote "The Star-Spangled Banner." At the Battle of New Orleans, the British were defeated by General Andrew Jackson. This battle was fought two weeks after the war had officially ended. However, the American victory was important because had the British captured New Orleans, they might not have been willing to give it up.

threefold: having three parts

328

THE WAR OF 1812: ADVANTAGES AND DISADVANTAGES OF EACH SIDE

	Advantages		Disadvantages	
	American	British	American	British
Military	At war only in North America; did not have to send troops overseas	Had large navy able to block U.S. ports	Had few ships or trained sailors	At war with France; unable to send extra troops for war against U.S.
		Had soldiers and people in Canada able to defend the land	Had small, poorly trained army spread over a huge land area	
		Had Native American allies on frontier	Had to fight Native American allies of both Great Britain and Spain	
Political		Continued to trade with New England	New England unwilling to help war with either money or troops	
Economic			Lost tax revenue because of loss of foreign trade	Had high unemployment and high prices caused by loss of foreign trade
Population	Had large population			Had small British population in North America

Results of the War

On December 24, 1814, the U.S. and Great Britain signed the Treaty of Ghent (GENT). The War of 1812 ended Native American efforts to stop westward expansion. But the war did not settle the problems between the U.S. and Great Britain. Both countries kept the boundaries they had before the war. However, the war marked a change in relations between the countries. The U.S. had fought a war with the most powerful nation in the world, Great Britain. Although the U.S. had not won the war, neither had Great Britain. Americans gained a new confidence and pride in their country.

THE HARTFORD CONVENTION

In December 1814, a group of New Englanders had met in a secret convention at Hartford, Connecticut. Some of the delegates wanted

War of 1812

American Movements
British Movements
American Victory
British Victory

0   200 miles
0   300 kilometers

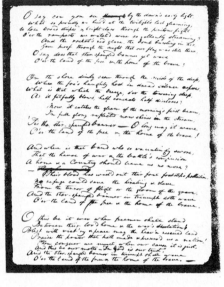

Francis Scott Key wrote this poem while watching the British bombard Fort McHenry. In 1931, Congress approved it as the national anthem— "The Star-Spangled Banner." Would you consider this a primary source?

General Andrew Jackson led U.S. troops into the Battle of New Orleans. Although fought after the war had ended, the battle was important. Why?

The British captured and burned Washington, D.C., in August 1814. The rebuilding of the Capitol and White House was completed in 1819.

U.S. troops were defeated at Queenston when reinforcements refused to cross the Niagara River. The artist mistakenly put U.S. troops in red and the British in blue. How can you tell this from the painting?

During the fight for Lake Erie, Oliver H. Perry's own ship was badly damaged. He rowed to another American ship that had been kept out of the battle and continued to command the fighting from there. What clues to this story can you find in the painting?

American and British delegates met at Ghent, Belgium, in 1814 to draw up the treaty that ended the War of 1812. What issues were not settled by the treaty?

the member states to secede from the U.S. and make a separate peace with Great Britain. **Secede** (sih-SEED) means to withdraw from membership.

The war had never been popular in New England, especially among Federalists. The governors of the New England states had refused to let their militias join the invasion of Canada. They feared that capturing Canada would mean more political power for the states made from the British territory. Merchants in New England were also angered at the loss of foreign trade.

The delegates to the convention adopted a resolution much like the Virginia and Kentucky Resolutions. The resolution declared that if a state found a law of Congress to be unconstitutional, it could declare the law null and void. By the time the Hartford Convention made its resolution public, the Treaty of Ghent had been signed. Some Americans considered the talk of secession to be treason. The convention caused the Federalists to lose more support. Never again would the party have a strong influence in national affairs.

LOOKING BACK

1. Beginning with 1807, list the events that led to the War of 1812.
2. Why did Tecumseh want to unite the Native Americans on the western frontier?
3. **a.** What were the advantages of the U.S. in the War of 1812? **b.** What were its disadvantages? **c.** What were the advantages of Great Britain in the War of 1812? **d.** What were its disadvantages? **e.** Based on this comparison, do you think the two sides were about equal? **f.** Which advantages do you think outweighed the disadvantages for the U.S.?
4. What were three results of the War of 1812?
5. What assumption was made in the resolution of the Hartford Convention?

PRACTICING YOUR SKILLS

What If . . .

Chapter 1 described how political parties developed during Washington's administration. Americans divided politically over Hamilton's program for building American credit. **What if** Hamilton's program had been accepted? What effect might this have had on the development of American political parties? Would southern farmers and planters have always agreed with New England merchants and manufacturers?

Discussing

Chapter 4 describes how poor communications influenced the War of 1812. Today, communication systems are much faster. Do satellites, television, radio, newspapers, books, and so on help to unite or divide people? Do they prevent or cause conflict?

Researching, Making a Table, Making a Time Line, Writing

1. In an encyclopedia or almanac, research the number of departments now in the Cabinet. Make a table showing the name of each department, the date of its beginning, its current head, and its major responsibilities.
2. Research the relationship between the U.S. and Native Americans from 1778 to 1812. Make a time line listing major events.
3. In 1815, Stephen Decatur defeated the Barbary Pirates. Research and write a paragraph about the events that led to this defeat.
4. Research one battle of the War of 1812, and write a paragraph describing it. Identify the leaders of each side and whether it was an American or British victory. Explain what effect, if any, the battle had on the course of the war.

Exploring

If you live in one of the original 13 states or in an area that became a state between 1787 and 1812, research in history texts how electors for your state voted in presidential elections during those years. Make a table showing this data.

Building Study Skills

On page 24 you learned some tips for taking notes during a lecture. But you will also need notes for writing papers, for giving a speech, or for use in a debate. This skill section will help you learn to **take notes from your reading.**

- Use index cards, if possible, to record information. Use one index card per topic.
- Write the title, author, and page numbers of your source on the top of each index card.
- Read the source for main ideas and supporting details.
- Write down the main ideas for each paragraph or section.
- Write down any details that clarify the main ideas. You may record direct quotations from sources or paraphrase them. Be accurate.

Activity: Practice this skill by taking notes on one of the books listed below, or on a book from the library about some event in American history from 1789 to 1814.

Reading

Barry, James P. *The Louisiana Purchase, April 1803: Thomas Jefferson Doubles the Area of the U.S.* New York: Watts, 1973.

Burt Olive Wooley. *Sacajawea.* New York: Watts, 1978.

Coit, Margaret L. *The Growing Years: 1789-1820.* Morristown, New Jersey: Silver Burdett, 1974. Social, political, and military history.

Hawke, David Freeman. *Those Tremendous Mountains: The Story of the Lewis and Clark Expedition.* New York: Norton, 1980.

Starkey, Marion. *Lace Cuffs and Leather Aprons: Popular Struggles in the Federalist Era, 1783-1800.* New York: Knopf, 1972. Illustrations, maps, and songs.

Tucker, Glenn. *Tecumseh: Vision of Glory.* New York: Atheneum, 1973.

UNIT II NEW ROLE FOR THE NATION

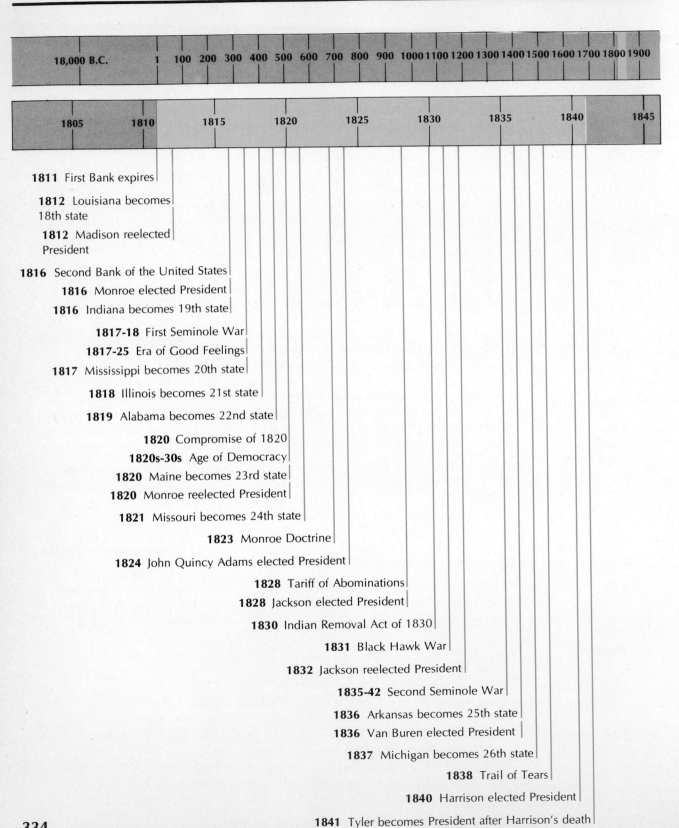

| 18,000 B.C. | 1 | 100 | 200 | 300 | 400 | 500 | 600 | 700 | 800 | 900 | 1000 | 1100 | 1200 | 1300 | 1400 | 1500 | 1600 | 1700 | 1800 | 1900 |

| 1805 | 1810 | 1815 | 1820 | 1825 | 1830 | 1835 | 1840 | 1845 |

1811 First Bank expires

1812 Louisiana becomes 18th state

1812 Madison reelected President

1816 Second Bank of the United States

1816 Monroe elected President

1816 Indiana becomes 19th state

1817-18 First Seminole War

1817-25 Era of Good Feelings

1817 Mississippi becomes 20th state

1818 Illinois becomes 21st state

1819 Alabama becomes 22nd state

1820 Compromise of 1820

1820s-30s Age of Democracy

1820 Maine becomes 23rd state

1820 Monroe reelected President

1821 Missouri becomes 24th state

1823 Monroe Doctrine

1824 John Quincy Adams elected President

1828 Tariff of Abominations

1828 Jackson elected President

1830 Indian Removal Act of 1830

1831 Black Hawk War

1832 Jackson reelected President

1835-42 Second Seminole War

1836 Arkansas becomes 25th state

1836 Van Buren elected President

1837 Michigan becomes 26th state

1838 Trail of Tears

1840 Harrison elected President

1841 Tyler becomes President after Harrison's death

Chapter 1　　　New Directions for the U.S.

LOOKING AHEAD

This chapter is about the years following the War of 1812 when the young nation moved in new directions, at home and abroad. The years 1817 to 1825 saw the U.S. occupied with the American System, the Panic of 1819, the Missouri Compromise, and a new role in world affairs. After you study this chapter, you will be able to:

★ explain what a historical time period is using the *Era of Good Feelings* as an example.
- describe how the American System appealed to each section of the nation.
- list the sequence of events that led to the Panic of 1819.
- identify the problem that led to the Missouri Compromise.
- explain U.S. foreign policy during the Era of Good Feelings.

Social Studies Vocabulary

nationalism	protective tariff	doctrine
historical time period	panic	

People

James Monroe	Henry Clay	John C. Calhoun

Places

Middle Atlantic States	Maine
Missouri	Florida

Events

Panic of 1819	First Seminole War

Words and Terms

American System	Rush-Bagot Agreement
Second Bank	Adams-Onis Treaty
internal improvements	Monroe Doctrine
Missouri Compromise	

The years following the War of 1812 were ones of peace and growing **nationalism** (NASH-uhn-uhl-iz-uhm)—loyal or patriotic feeling for one's nation. Americans began to feel that they could fight anyone and anything—Europeans, Native Americans, the frontier—and win. Industry was on the rise, and people were on the move. In politics, it was a time of little party rivalry, although sectionalism was growing.

ERA OF GOOD FEELINGS

succeed:
to come after

James Madison, who had been reelected in 1812, was succeeded as President in 1816 by James Monroe. Monroe, a Democratic-Republican from Virginia, had been Madison's Secretary of State. Soon after taking office, Monroe made a tour of New England. He told the people there that he would protect their interests as well as those of the other sections of the country. He was so convincing that a Boston newspaper gave his presidency the name: Era of Good Feelings.

In 1820, Monroe was reelected without opposition. The Federalists had lost much of their support because of the Hartford Convention. Democratic-Republicans controlled the federal government and most state governments. But even though the Federalists were gone, some of their policies were taken over by the Democratic-Republicans.

BUILDING CHRONOLOGICAL SKILLS

You have just read that Monroe's presidency was called the Era of Good Feelings. An era is a **historical time period** that is marked by the work of an important person, such as President Monroe, or by a particular event or period, such as a time of peace after a war. This definition is true of any historical period whether it is called an era, an age, a time, or a period. There is no set time limit for an historical period. It may last 5 years or 25 or longer. Look at the time line on page 334 and find the Era of Good Feelings. **1.** What were its dates? **2.** How many years was this? One historical time period may overlap another. In the next chapter, you will read about a period that began during the Era of Good Feelings and ended after it.

THE AMERICAN SYSTEM

After the War of 1812, Henry Clay and John C. Calhoun proposed a plan that was similar in some ways to the ideas of Alexander Hamilton. The goals of Clay and Calhoun's plan—called the American System—were to encourage U.S. economic growth and to unite the country. The plan offered something for each section of the country.

Protective Tariff

For the shippers and manufacturers of the Northeast, the American System proposed a protective tariff. A **protective tariff** is a tax on foreign goods which raises their prices and protects the taxing country's producers of the same goods. Before the War of 1812, Americans had bought most of their manufactured goods from Europe. Most came from Great Britain. After Jefferson ordered the embargo in 1807, Americans would not import these goods. They could either buy American-made goods, or do without. Merchants and ship-owners began to use their money to build factories and shops. You will read more about American industry in the unit New Technology.

After the war ended in 1815, British goods were again shipped to the U.S. American manufacturers, finding they had competition, asked the government to place a tax on imported goods that were also made in the U.S. In 1816, Congress passed a small protective tariff, but it was unpopular. Some Americans were angered at having to pay more for goods to protect American manufacturers.

Second Bank

Another part of the American System called for a Second Bank. The charter for the First Bank had not been renewed in 1811 because of resistance by Democratic-Republicans in Congress. They felt that the bank gave too much power to wealthy shippers and manufacturers. When the First Bank closed, its activities were taken over by state banks. Americans did not have much confidence in these banks. They had seen too many fail, and depositors lose their savings.

In 1816, Congress established the Second Bank in an effort to restore confidence in the country's banking system. The Second Bank became the government's banker again. It received all moneys paid to the government and paid all its debts.

Internal Improvements

For farmers of the South and frontier states, the American System proposed a national system of roads and canals paid for by the federal government. These internal improvements would help farmers carry their goods to market and obtain supplies from coastal merchants and manufacturers more quickly. You will read more about internal improvements in the unit New Technology.

Effect of a Protective Tariff

internal (in-TER-nuhl): inside

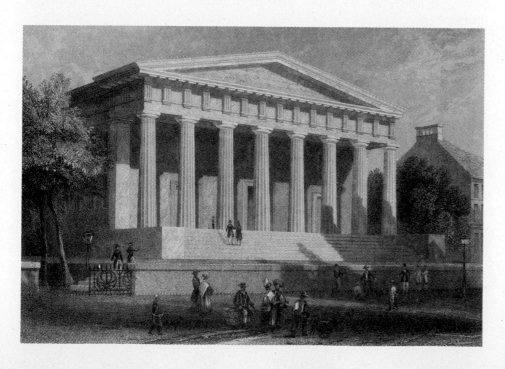

The Second Bank of the United States was chartered in 1816. What was the bank's purpose?

Opposition to the American System

Clay and Calhoun felt that the American System had something to offer each section of the nation. They expected it to be supported by *all* sections. However, this did not happen. People from frontier states were against the Second Bank. They thought that the bank would be controlled by wealthy easterners who would not lend them money. New Englanders were against using federal money for internal improvements. They felt that mostly the South and frontier states would be helped by them.

At first, Southerners supported a protective tariff. Later, they opposed it. Southerners felt the protective tariff would raise the prices that they paid for manufactured goods without giving them any economic advantages. The Middle Atlantic states—New York, New Jersey, and Pennsylvania—supported all three parts of the American System because the section believed it would benefit from each part of the plan.

PANIC OF 1819

The years right after the War of 1812 were prosperous for Americans. Many people bought land or built factories on credit. They hoped to repay their loans with the large profits they would make from their investments. The Second Bank and state banks were eager to lend money. They hoped to make large profits from the interest they charged on their loans.

The directors of the Second Bank became concerned about the amount of buying on credit that Americans were doing. Late in 1818, they decided not to make any new loans. The directors also demanded that loans be repaid in gold or silver instead of paper money. Many state banks had been issuing their own paper money. Much of it was not backed by gold or silver and was worthless. This means that the banks did not hold a certain amount of the value of each dollar they printed in gold or silver.

People had trouble repaying their loans. A panic gripped the country. A **panic** is an economic crisis in which people lose confidence in the banking system. Depositors began to demand their money. Since many banks had lent all their funds, they could not pay their depositors. These banks closed. Unable to repay their loans, many businesses and farmers went bankrupt. The U.S. sank into an economic depression that lasted for three years.

MISSOURI COMPROMISE

Toward the end of Monroe's first term in office a serious problem developed over the admission of new states. The problem arose not because of party rivalry but sectional rivalry. When the Constitution

The Missouri Compromise

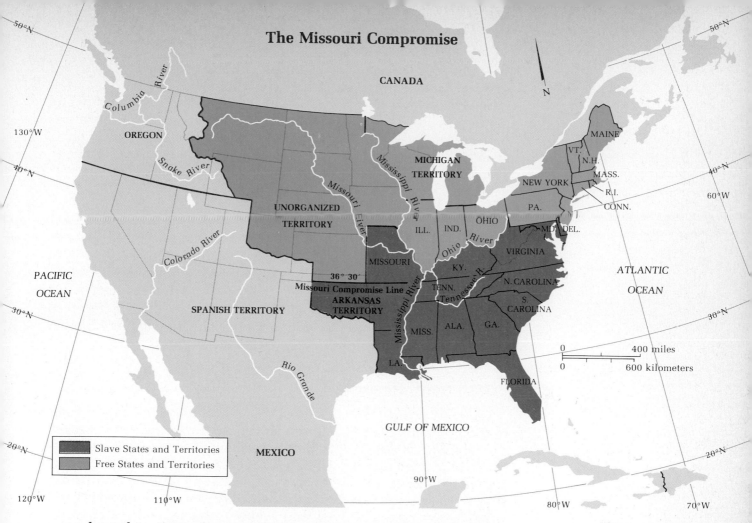

was adopted in 1789, there were seven free, or nonslave, states and six slave states. As new states entered the Union, a balance developed between slave and free states. By 1819, there were 11 free states and 11 slave states.

This balance was important because it kept equal the number of votes northern free states and southern slave states had in the Senate. The northern states, with their large populations, had many more votes in the House of Representatives. However, as long as the southern states could hold their equality in the Senate, they could keep antislave laws from being passed.

In 1818, Southerners faced a serious challenge. Missouri, part of the Louisiana Purchase, applied for statehood. It asked that slavery be allowed to continue within its borders. Northerners demanded that Missouri enter as a free state. At about the same time, Maine requested admission as a free state. Southerners said Maine could enter as a free state only if Missouri were allowed to enter as a slave state. This would keep the balance.

The question became a constitutional one. Northerners claimed that since Congress controlled the territories, it had the constitutional right to decide whether they should enter the Union as free or slave states. Southerners felt that each territory had a constitutional right to decide that question for itself.

A stormy debate followed. Mostly through the efforts of Henry Clay, an agreement was reached. Called the Missouri Compromise, it provided that Missouri would enter the Union as a slave state and Maine as a free state. For the time being, the slave-free balance was protected. But the problem would arise again. The Missouri Compromise said that any future state created from the Louisiana Purchase, north of the 36°30′ line, would be free. By the 1850s, many people would disagree with this solution.

A NEW ROLE

As the U.S. grew in size and power, its relationships with its neighbors changed. Arguments between the U.S. and Canada—then called British North America—were settled. To the south, the U.S. received Florida from Spain. The U.S. also turned its attention to Spain's other former American colonies.

British North America

After the War of 1812 ended, the U.S. and Great Britain solved some of the problems the war had not solved. In 1817, the two countries signed the Rush-Bagot (BAG-uht) Agreement. It stated that neither nation would keep warships on the Great Lakes. In 1818, the two countries set the boundary between the Louisiana Purchase and British North America at the 49th parallel. However, disagreement over Oregon remained unsolved and would become a problem in the 1840s.

U.S. troops fought the Seminole in 1818 during the First Seminole War. The war led to the U.S. purchase of Florida from Spain. What finally happened to the Seminole? See the map on page 354.

Florida

During Monroe's first term, the U.S. reached an agreement with Spain over Florida. As you may recall from the unit Growth of American Identity, Spain had given Florida to Great Britain after the French and Indian War. The British then divided the colony into East Florida and West Florida. In 1779, Spain, as an ally of the British colonies in the Revolutionary War, occupied West Florida. After the war, Great Britain turned over control of both East and West Florida to Spain.

The area remained under Spanish rule until 1819. During that time, Florida attracted many Americans. Some were settlers who wanted to work their own land. Others were criminals, runaway slaves, and Native Americans forced off their lands in the new nation. Most of these people ignored Spanish control. Spain had been weakened by years of war in Europe and could do little to enforce its control over Florida. In time, American settlers in Florida demanded that the U.S. take over the colony. In 1810, settlers in West Florida declared their independence, and President Madison accepted West Florida as part of the U.S. He then offered to buy East Florida but the Spanish monarch refused.

Trouble along the U.S.-Florida boundary was constant. Seminole (SEM-uh-nohl) from Florida often attacked U.S. settlements. In 1817, U.S. soldiers were sent to drive the Seminole back across the border. In 1818, President Monroe ordered Andrew Jackson to put an end to the raids. These conflicts are known as the First Seminole War. Jackson led his soldiers into East Florida where they attacked the Seminole and captured two Spanish forts. Jackson believed Spain was supplying and encouraging the Native American raids.

Still weak from European wars, Spain agreed to give up Florida. In 1819, Spain and the U.S. signed the Adams-Onis Treaty that created a boundary line between all Spanish and U.S. claims west of the Mississippi. The U.S. recognized Spanish control of Texas, and Spain recognized the U.S. claim to the Oregon country.

Monroe Doctrine

Florida was not the only American territory that Spain lost. While Spain was fighting in Europe in the early 1800s, several Spanish colonies in the Americas declared their independence. After the fighting in Europe was over, Spain was too weak to take these colonies by force. Austria, Prussia, Russia, and France offered to help Spain.

The British opposed this alliance because they did not want to see Spain powerful again. They asked the U.S. to join in making a statement against European interference in the Americas. However, President Monroe decided that the U.S. should issue its own statement. A joint one would increase British influence in the Americas, which would be against the interests of the U.S.

In 1823, the President issued the Monroe Doctrine. A **doctrine** (DAHK-truhn) is a statement of policy. Monroe told European nations

Miguel Hidalgo, a priest, began the revolt that led to Mexican independence from Spain in 1821. The U.S. would use the Monroe Doctrine in 1867 to free Mexico from a French takeover.

acknowledge
(ak-NAHL-ij):
to accept

not to interfere with the nations of the Americas. In return, the U.S. would not interfere in Europe. The Monroe Doctrine reads in part:

> We owe it to fairness and to the friendly relations existing between the U.S. and the European powers to declare that we should consider any attempt on their part to extend their system to any part of this hemisphere as dangerous to our peace and safety. With the existing colonies of any European power we have not interfered and shall not. But with the governments who have declared their independence and kept it, and whose independence we have acknowledged, we view any interference by a European power as an unfriendly act toward the U.S.

The Monroe Doctrine was a bold statement by the young nation. Monroe knew that the U.S. did not have the military power to keep other nations out of the Americas. But Monroe's statement was a sign that the U.S. was determined to have a voice in world affairs. In years to come, the Monroe Doctrine would be quoted by several U.S. Presidents seeking to keep foreign influence out of the Americas.

LOOKING BACK

★ 1. **a.** Why was Monroe's presidency called the Era of Good Feelings? **b.** List three events that occurred during this era that made this a time of good feelings for most people.

2. **a.** What were the three parts of the American System? How were they designed to appeal to: **b.** the South? **c.** the frontier states? **d.** New England?

3. What events led to the Panic of 1819?

4. **a.** What problem led to the Missouri Compromise? **b.** How did it solve the problem? **c.** For which present-day states does the 36°30' line serve as a boundary?

5. How did the U.S. settle its disagreements with: **a.** British North America? **b.** Florida? **c.** European nations? In answering **c.** paraphrase the quote from the Monroe Doctrine above.

Chapter 2

Age of Democracy

LOOKING AHEAD

This chapter is about the changes that took place in American politics during the early 1800s. The changes included increased power for the average American voter, more American voters, and a new two-party system. After you study this chapter, you will be able to:

- describe how American politics changed in the early 1800s.
- ★ distinguish fact from opinion in Tocqueville's view of American democracy.
- define and state the length of the Age of Democracy.
- explain Andrew Jackson's appeal to average Americans.
- explain how and why the method of choosing presidential candidates changed.

Social Studies Vocabulary

opinion   caucus   platform

People

Andrew Jackson   Henry Clay   Democrats
John Quincy Adams   John C. Calhoun   National Republicans

Words and Terms

Age of Democracy   corrupt bargain
Jacksonian Democracy   party conventions

In 1826, Americans celebrated the 50th anniversary of their independence, and they had much to celebrate. The nation was more than twice the size it had been in 1789. Other nations recognized it as a world power. Since the 1770s, the nation had not had a violent change of government. Each change of President had been brought about by voting. In addition, by the 1820s more Americans were able to vote.

POLITICAL PARTICIPATION

As you may recall from the unit Colonial Beginnings, the colonies had voting restrictions. Even after independence, some states continued to limit the kind of men who could vote. Some states refused to allow a man to vote if he was Catholic, Jewish, or a Quaker. Other states required men to own land or have a certain amount of money.

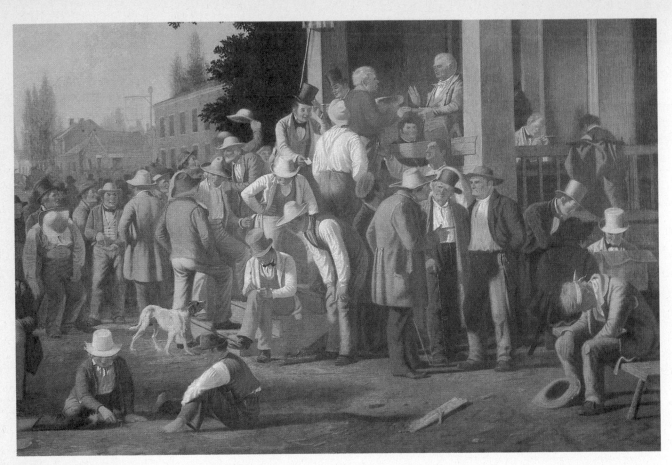

In the early 1800s, more male citizens were able to vote. In his *County Election,* George Caleb Bingham showed candidates making last minute attempts to win these new voters.

More Voters

The frontier movement began to change these requirements. On the frontier, people were judged by what they could do, not by the amount of wealth they had. As these areas became states, property and religious requirements for voting were dropped. Between 1812 and 1837, nine states were added to the Union. Mississippi (1817) and Alabama (1819) had been part of the Old Southwest. Maine (1820) had been part of the frontier within the U.S. at the end of the Revolutionary War. Louisiana (1812), Missouri (1821), and Arkansas (1836) were carved out of the Louisiana Purchase. Indiana (1816), Illinois (1818), and Michigan (1837) were made from the Northwest Territory.

The older states were soon dropping qualifications for voting, too. By the 1820s, most states gave the right to vote to most free white men. Free black males could vote in some northern states. However, women and slaves could not vote in any state. Only New Jersey from 1790 to 1807 permitted women to vote.

As more voters came from the middle and lower classes, political power became more widespread. A new age in American politics was beginning—the age of the common man, meaning the average citizen. In 1831, Alexis de Tocqueville (duh tawk-VEEL), a Frenchman, visited the U.S. After traveling and studying the country for almost a year, he wrote a book about his experiences. The following is taken from that book *Democracy in America* written in 1835.

The political activity which exists everywhere in the United States must be seen in order to be understood. No sooner do you set foot upon American soil, than you are stunned by the sound of voices demanding the satisfaction of their social wants. Everything is moving around you. Here, the people of one part of a town are meeting to decide upon the building of a church. There, the election of a representative is going on. A little further on, the delegates of a district are writing a petition to the town asking for some local improvements. In another place, the laborers of a village quit their plows to discuss a matter.

Interest in politics ranks high among the activities of a citizen in the United States. Almost the only pleasure an American knows is to take part in the government, and to discuss it. Even the women frequently attend public meetings, and listen to political speeches and debates as a recreation from their household labors.

This passage by Alexis de Tocqueville gives his view of democracy in America. His view is based on the fact that people did have a voice in government. But much of what he says is opinion. An **opinion** is a belief that is based on what a person thinks rather than a proven fact. Did all the laborers actually quit their plowing to discuss a matter? Was the discussion of government the only pleasure an American knew? You must read carefully to distinguish fact from opinion. If a statement can be proved, then it is a fact. If a statement expresses how a person feels and cannot be proved, it is an opinion. **1.** What are some of Tocqueville's opinions? **2.** Why are they opinions and not facts?

BUILDING READING SKILLS

More Power

There were other changes in the election process during the early 1800s. As you may recall from the unit The New Nation, the ratification of the 12th Amendment was one. It changed the method that electors used in choosing the President and the Vice-President. During this time, the method for choosing the electors themselves changed.

In the early 1800s, most states did not have elections to choose electors. State legislators or party organizations chose them. They picked either members of their own legislatures or other public officials. Around the 1820s, because of the increase in voter interest, states began to give the right to choose electors to the people. The type of electors that were picked did not change. But average citizens felt they had a voice in deciding who would be their President.

During this time, more state and local offices became elective. Before this, an elected official, such as a mayor, would name people to lesser posts, such as treasurer or sheriff. By the 1820s, more people were able to vote for more of the people who governed them.

An important factor that increased voter power as well as participation was education. Public education became more available in cities and towns in the early 1800s. More and more people were able to read and write. Newspapers and books reached larger audiences. Interest in politics increased along with education. You will read more about public education in the unit Life at Mid-Century.

AGE OF DEMOCRACY

These changes in the election process happened slowly. Each state passed different laws at different times. By the mid-1820s, however, these changes were well underway. Some historians call the 1820s and 1830s the Age of Democracy because of increased voter interest and participation. Others call the new interest and participation Jacksonian Democracy, because of Jackson's appeal to ordinary Americans.

They saw Jackson as one of the people. He was the son of a poor pioneer family and a hero of the War of 1812. He had gone to Tennessee when it was still frontier to make his living. However, Jackson had become a wealthy landowner with many slaves. As a member of the House of Representatives and later of the Senate, he had not been known as a reformer or a supporter of the average citizen. However, Jackson's rough frontier ways and toughness appealed to ordinary citizens in all sections of the country.

Election of 1824

Beginning in 1800, Democratic-Republicans controlled the presidency. As you read in Chapter 1 of this unit, Federalist power began to weaken after the party opposed the War of 1812. By 1824, there were few Federalists left. However, the U.S. was far from being a nation with only one political party. Democratic-Republicans were dividing into groups, often along sectional lines. The groups disagreed over the direction the U.S. should take: strong federal government or strong state governments.

All the candidates in the presidential election of 1824 were Democratic-Republicans. A Democratic-Republican caucus picked William H. Crawford of Georgia to run for President. A **caucus** (KAW-kuhs) is a meeting of party leaders to decide on candidates, policies, and party strategy. Crawford became ill but remained in the race. Three other Democratic-Republicans also ran. Tennessee's Andrew Jackson was popular in all sections of the nation. John Quincy Adams of Massachusetts, the son of John Adams, had strong support from the manufacturing and shipping interests of New England and New York. The supporters of Henry Clay of Kentucky were mainly in the Ohio River valley. John C. Calhoun of South Carolina also wanted to be President but withdrew to become a vice-presidential candidate.

When the election was over, Calhoun was the only clear winner and was named Vice-President. Jackson had won the most popular and electoral votes for President. However, he did not have a majority

The election of 1824 was decided by the House of Representatives in agreement with the 12th Amendment. Why was Jackson not chosen as President?

of electoral votes. So, according to the 12th Amendment, the election was decided in the House of Representatives. Clay gave his support to Adams, and Adams was elected President. When Adams made Clay his Secretary of State, Jackson's supporters claimed that a "corrupt bargain" had been made between Adams and Clay. However, the two shared similar views on governing the nation. Both believed in the American System and a strong federal government.

Jackson's Election

Early in Adams's administration Jackson's supporters began laying plans for the next election. Because of the bitterness over the election of 1824, the election of 1828 became a contest of personalities, not of issues. Across the country, Jackson's supporters painted Adams as a member of the upper class. They claimed that he did not care about the needs and worries of ordinary Americans. Jackson easily defeated Adams. Calhoun, who had supported Jackson, was reelected Vice-President.

During the election, people who supported Jackson began calling themselves Democrats. The Democratic party still exists. Supporters of Adams and Clay became known as National Republicans. The Democratic-Republicans disappeared as a party.

Party Conventions

Besides the rise of a new two-party system, the method of selecting presidential candidates also changed during the time of Jackson. Before 1830, presidential hopefuls did not run for their party's nomination the way they do today. The candidate was chosen by a caucus of his party's members in Congress. By the 1820s, people were becoming dissatisfied with the caucus, or King Caucus as they called it. Some claimed the system kept qualified people from becoming

In 1831, national political parties began using conventions to select their candidates. How were candidates chosen before this?

candidates. Others throught that the caucus system was undemocratic, because it did not give many Americans a voice in selecting their leaders.

Beginning in 1831, both the Democrats and National Republicans began using conventions to choose presidential and vice-presidential candidates. Under the new convention system, party members in local communities met and selected delegates to their party's national convention. The convention selected the presidential and vice-presidential candidates and decided on the party's platform. A **platform** is a political party's statement of goals and policies. The convention system was more democratic than the caucus. It represented a party's membership rather than just its leaders. However, local political leaders had much to say about the choice of delegates.

LOOKING BACK

1. **a.** How did more Americans gain the right to vote in the early 1800s? **b.** State two changes in voting rights that gave Americans more political power.
★ 2. **a.** How is an opinion different from a fact? **b.** List three statements of Tocqueville that are opinions. **c.** On what facts did he base his opinions?
3. **a.** When was the Age of Democracy? **b.** Why was this period called the Age of Democracy?
4. Why did Andrew Jackson appeal to average Americans?
5. **a.** How were presidential candidates selected before the 1830s? **b.** How did that method change in the early 1830s? **c.** Why did the change come about?

Chapter 3   Jackson as President

LOOKING AHEAD

This chapter is about the major events of Andrew Jackson's presidency — the spoils system, nullification, Native American removal, the bank war, the rise of the Whig party, and the Panic of 1837. After you study this chapter, you will be able to:

- identify Jackson's reasons for using the spoils system.
- recognize the points of view of South Carolina and Jackson on the issue of nullification.
- describe the sequence of events for the removal of Native Americans.
- list Jackson's reasons for opposing the Second Bank.
- state the main reason for forming the Whig party.
- compare and contrast the causes of the Panic of 1837 with those of the Panic of 1819.

Social Studies Vocabulary

political patronage   reservation

People

Andrew Jackson	Cherokee	Martin Van Buren
John C. Calhoun	Creek	Osceola
Henry Clay	Choctaw	Whigs
Sauk	Chickasaw	
Fox	Seminole	

Words and Terms

spoils system	Indian Removal	Trail of Tears
Tariff of Abominations	Act of 1830	pet banks
ordinance of nullification	Indian Territory	

Events

Black Hawk War	Second Seminole War	Panic of 1837

Many people in the 1830s referred to Jackson as "King Andrew." Why?

In March 1829, Andrew Jackson became President. As the hero of the average citizen, he was against government run by a small group of wealthy Americans. He believed that ordinary people should fill most public offices. After his election, Jackson began using political patronage to fill federal government jobs. **Political patronage** (PAY-truhn-ij) is the giving of government jobs to supporters of the party in power. A person may or may not be qualified for the job. Jackson's use of political patronage has been called the spoils system. He believed

Senators Daniel Webster and Robert Hayne debated the nullification issue in 1830. Here, Webster speaks to the Senate against nullification, calling for "Liberty and Union, now and forever, one and inseparable!"

that "to the victor belongs the spoils." Because he had won the presidency, he could give spoils, or rewards in the form of jobs, to his Democratic party supporters.

Jackson was not the first to use political patronage. Local and state politicians had been doing it for years. However, he was the first President to make wide use of it in the federal government.

THE NULLIFICATION CRISIS

One of the strongest challenges to the Union occurred during Jackson's time in office. You may recall from Chapter 1 of this unit that Congress passed a protective tariff in 1816. It angered Southerners and did not give northeastern manufacturers as much protection as they had wanted. The manufacturers began a fight for a higher tariff.

When the Tariff of 1824 was passed, the South reacted more angrily than it had in 1816. Southerners felt that if Europeans could not find American markets for their goods, they would stop buying such raw materials as cotton, tobacco, and indigo. The South's economy was built on these crops. In 1828, the tariff was raised again over southern protests. It was so high that Southerners called it the Tariff of Abominations.

South Carolina's Stand

The cotton planters of South Carolina were especially hurt by high protective tariffs. By the late 1820s, the planters were facing serious economic troubles. The price of cotton was down. South Carolina's soil was losing its fertility and producing less cotton. The state's population was declining. More and more of its people were moving to the new states of Alabama, Louisiana, and Mississippi in search of fertile land.

In 1832, Congress passed another tariff bill. Because it lowered the tax on some items, it received some southern support. South Carolinians, however, believed the tariff had not been reduced enough. In addition, many feared that the tariff was a first step toward outlawing slavery. They saw the tariff as a sign that the federal government was becoming too strong. "Yield on the tariff issue," warned the newspaper *Charleston Mercury* "and abolition (of slavery) will become the order of the day."

The South Carolina legislature called a convention to take action against the tariff. The members first considered seceding but adopted an ordinance of nullification instead. In the ordinance, South Carolina declared the tariff to be "null, void, and no law; nor binding upon this state, its officers, or its citizens." South Carolina argued that states could refuse to obey federal laws that states decided were unjust and unconstitutional. This was the same issue that had been raised in the Hartford Convention and in the Kentucky and Virginia Resolutions.

nullification (nuhl-uh-fuh-KAY-shuhn): the act of cancelling

Jackson's Position

As a Southerner, Jackson agreed with the South about many things. However, he refused to accept the idea that a state could disobey the federal government. If a state was allowed to nullify a federal law, Jackson reasoned, the Union would be destroyed. Vice-President Calhoun disagreed and supported the idea of nullification. He resigned from the vice-presidency in December 1832 to run for the Senate from South Carolina. As a Senator, he became a leading spokesman for southern interests.

Jackson acted quickly to meet South Carolina's challenge to the Constitution. In December 1832, he issued a statement to the people of South Carolina informing them that secession, the act of seceding, was treason. He declared that the federal union of states could not be broken. Acting to back his words with force, Jackson in March 1833 asked Congress for the authority to use the army and navy, if necessary, to collect the tariff in South Carolina. Meanwhile, Henry Clay, the Great Compromiser, persuaded Congress to pass a lower, compromise tariff. When South Carolina accepted the compromise, the nullification crisis was over—for a time.

NATIVE AMERICAN REMOVAL

Another major event of Jackson's presidency was the removal of many Native Americans to reservations west of the Mississippi River. **Reservations** (reh-zer-VAY-shuhnz) are lands set aside by the government for Native American use. Members of the Iroquois League had been on reservations since 1788. Despite the early attempts of the U.S. government to protect Native American rights, land-hungry settlers wanted more and better land. The Native American hunting economy, which needed the forests, often got in the way of development.

In 1832, Sauk and Fox fought to keep their land in Illinois and Wisconsin. They were badly defeated by the Illinois militia. What finally happened to the Sauk and Fox? See the map on page 354.

Conflict erupted between the two groups. Through treaties, sales, and force, Native Americans were gradually pushed off their lands in the area east of the Mississippi. Some Native Americans were uprooted more than once. Each time they were moved, they were told it would be the last time. Sometimes after moving into an area, a group had to fight other Native Americans who had been there first.

Sauk and Fox

In 1804, the U.S. government had forced Sauk and Fox leaders to sign a treaty giving up their lands in Illinois and Wisconsin. But Black Hawk, a Sauk leader, challenged the treaty. In 1831, the government under Jackson forcibly removed most of the Sauk and Fox across the Mississippi to Iowa. Black Hawk refused to go. In what has become known as the Black Hawk War, the U.S. Army and the Illinois militia fought Black Hawk and his followers for several months. At the Battle of Bad Axe, Wisconsin, the soldiers massacred many of Black Hawk's people, including women and children. Black Hawk surrendered, and the remaining Sauk were sent to Iowa.

Five Civilized Tribes

In the early 1800s, the Cherokee, Creek, Choctaw, Chickasaw, and Seminole occupied lands in Florida, the Carolinas, Georgia, Alabama, and Mississippi. Most had become farmers and had accepted Christianity in the 1700s. Despite these changes, the Five Civilized Tribes, as they have been called, were removed from their lands.

As American settlers poured into the Old Southwest, they pressured the U.S. government to move the five groups out. The settlers found a friend in Andrew Jackson. During his presidency, Jackson signed over 90 treaties that transferred Native American lands to new owners. He urged Congress to pass the Indian Removal Act of 1830. This act gave him the power to remove Native Americans by force to land west of the Mississippi in what is now the state of Oklahoma. This area was named the Indian Territory.

In 1831, the Choctaw became the first of the five peoples to be taken to the Indian Territory. They were followed by the Creek in 1836 and the Chickasaw in 1837. Some resisted and were either killed or removed in chains by the army. Some Creek escaped notice and stayed in central Florida.

The Cherokee held out longer against removal. Since 1790, they had been recognized by the U.S. as a separate nation. In 1827, they adopted a constitution that set up a government with an elected leader, a senate, and a house of representatives. The Cherokee hoped that by adapting to American ways, they would be able to keep their lands. They were successful until 1828 when the government of Georgia declared Cherokee lands to be part of the state. The Cherokee lost their status as a nation, and they also lost their right to make laws. They had to obey Georgia laws, which could be used to take away their lands. After gold was discovered on Cherokee land in 1829, the state government was more eager than ever to have the Cherokee removed. In his yearly message to Congress in December 1829, Jackson declared his support for the State of Georgia's position.

The Cherokee appealed to the Supreme Court. In a decision written by Chief Justice John Marshall in March 1832, the Court ruled the Cherokee should keep their lands. Following is a part of that ruling.

From the beginning of our government, Congress has passed acts to regulate trade and activities with the Indians. These acts treat them as nations, respect their rights, and have as a firm purpose to give them the protection promised them in the treaties. All these acts consider the several Indian nations as distinct political communities, having territorial boundaries, within which they have authority. They also have the right to all the lands within those boundaries. This is accepted and guaranteed by the United States.

The Cherokee nation is a distinct community with its own territory and boundaries. Within it, the laws of Georgia can have no force, and the citizens of Georgia have no right to enter, but with the agreement of the Cherokee themselves, or in keeping with treaties, and with the acts of Congress.

Georgia disagreed with the court's opinion and began giving Cherokee lands away. The Cherokee appealed to Jackson for help. The President advised the Cherokee to move. Feelings among the Cherokee were divided. Some were willing to move, while others insisted on staying. In 1835, those in favor of moving signed a treaty with Jackson's representative. They agreed to give up their lands and move to the Indian Territory.

About 2,000 of the 16,000 Cherokee were gone by 1838. That year, President Martin Van Buren sent the army to move the rest. Some walked, and others rode on horseback or in wagons. With U.S.

In 1821, Sequoyah, a Cherokee, completed an alphabet for his people. Before Europeans came, Native Americans did not use written languages. They passed their history by word of mouth from generation to generation.

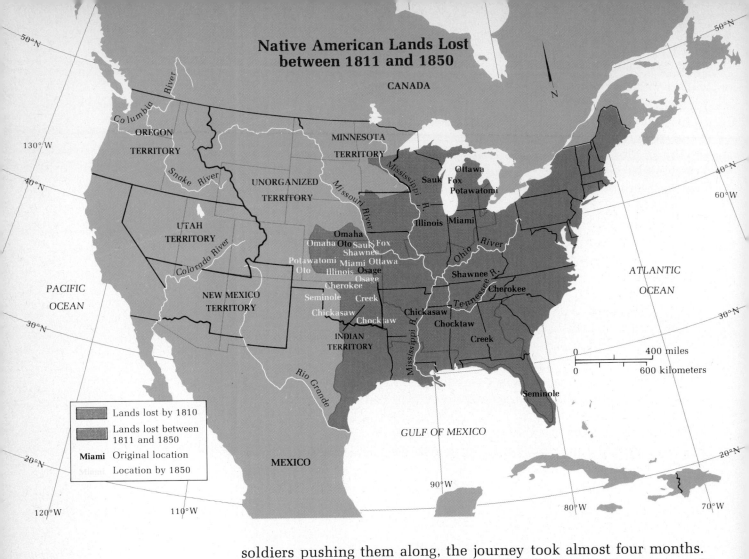

Native American Lands Lost between 1811 and 1850

CANADA

OREGON TERRITORY

MINNESOTA TERRITORY

UNORGANIZED TERRITORY

UTAH TERRITORY

NEW MEXICO TERRITORY

PACIFIC OCEAN

ATLANTIC OCEAN

Columbia River

Snake River

Colorado River

Missouri River

Mississippi

Ottawa
Sauk Fox
Potawatomi

Omaha
Omaha Oto
Potawatomi
Oto
Sauk Fox
Shawnee
Miami Ottawa
Illinois Osage
Osage
Cherokee
Seminole
Chickasaw
Choctaw

Illinois Miami

Ohio River

Shawnee R.

Cherokee

Tennessee R.

Chickasaw

Chocktaw

Creek

Creek

Seminole

INDIAN TERRITORY

Rio Grande

MEXICO

GULF OF MEXICO

	Lands lost by 1810
	Lands lost between 1811 and 1850
Miami	Original location
Miami	Location by 1850

0 — 400 miles
0 — 600 kilometers

soldiers pushing them along, the journey took almost four months. Some of it was made in snow and freezing weather. About 4,000 of those who started the trip died of sickness or hunger before ever reaching the Indian Territory. Because the Cherokee buried so many along the way, the march has been called the Trail of Tears. Some Cherokee went into the mountains of North Carolina rather than be moved. Their descendants still live in the area.

The last people to be moved west were the Seminole. Following the First Seminole War, the Seminole were forced to live in a swampy area of southern Florida called the Everglades. But even there settlers pressured the Seminole to leave. Led by Osceola (ahs-ih-OH-luh), the Seminole fought back. The conflict, known as the Second Seminole War, lasted from 1835 to 1842. Osceola was captured, and most of the Seminole were removed to the Indian Territory. A few remained in the Everglades where their descendants live today.

pressure (PRESH-uhr): to try to influence or force

THE BANK WAR

Jackson distrusted banks in general, but he had a special dislike for the Second Bank. He felt that the bank placed too much power in the

354

hands of the federal government. He also claimed that the bank was run by wealthy people who used it for loans to themselves and their friends. The average person had difficulty obtaining a loan. For these reasons, Jackson considered the bank a threat to the rights of the states and of poorer Americans.

When the bank's charter came up for renewal in 1836, Jackson decided he would oppose it. However, Henry Clay, who was running for President in 1832, wanted to make the bank a major issue in that year's election. Clay persuaded the bank's president, Nicholas Biddle, to apply for early renewal of the bank's charter. Clay thought that he would gain voters if he became the chief supporter of the bank.

In summer 1832, Congress agreed to recharter the bank. Jackson vetoed the bill. When Congress failed to override the President's veto, the bank's charter was not renewed. During the campaign of 1832, Clay called for renewal of the charter. He and the bank's supporters claimed that the nation's economy depended on the bank. But most voters agreed with Jackson, and the President easily won reelection. Jackson's Secretary of State, Martin Van Buren, was elected Vice-President.

Jackson, however, would not allow the bank to die a natural death in 1836. He destroyed it in 1833 by removing all federal money and placing it in state banks, called "pet banks" by his enemies. They claimed that the President selected these banks because they were run by people loyal to him.

ANOTHER POLITICAL PARTY

During the presidential election of 1832, the National Republicans, some Democrats, and others who opposed Jackson formed a new political party. They called themselves Whigs, and Henry Clay became their presidential candidate. Before the Revolutionary War, people who opposed George III called themselves Whigs. In the 1830s, the new party took this name because it opposed "King Andrew," as Jackson was sometimes called. His enemies gave him this nickname because they claimed he disregarded the law. Not all Whigs supported the bank or the rest of Clay's American System. But they had one thing in common—dislike for Jackson.

PANIC OF 1837

Jackson's actions against the Second Bank brought on the kind of economic problems he was trying to avoid. Using federal money, the "pet banks" began making loans to land buyers, most of whom bought the land for speculation. There was no longer a national bank to regulate the nation's money supply. So some state banks began issuing paper money that was not backed by gold or silver.

During the Panic of 1837 and the resulting depression, many people were faced with the same problem as the man in this painting, *The Long Bill* by James Henry Beard. What caused the Panic of 1837?

In 1836, Jackson acted to slow land speculation. He ordered all payments for land be made in gold or silver. Land buyers then demanded that state banks exchange their paper money for gold or silver. Many banks could not and failed. Money became scarce and prices for everything dropped. Many people lost their savings, farms, businesses, and jobs.

When the new President, Martin Van Buren, took office in 1837, the U.S. was in the midst of a panic. Following the panic, the nation sank into an economic depression as it had after the Panic of 1819.

TIPPECANOE AND TYLER, TOO!

In the election of 1840, the Whigs blamed Van Buren for the panic and depression. They picked General William Henry Harrison, the hero of Tippecanoe, to oppose him. John Tyler was chosen to run for Vice-President. Harrison was shown as a man of the people, in much the same way that the Democrats had presented Jackson. "Tippecanoe and Tyler, Too!" was the campaign slogan of the Whigs. Harrison easily defeated Van Buren but the general died a month after taking office. Tyler became President and faced a difficult time.

Tyler was the first Vice-President to reach the highest office upon a President's death. Some Americans thought he should be only an acting President, with little power. Tyler thought differently. Although a Whig, Tyler opposed some Whig ideas supported by Henry Clay, the party leader. Clay proposed a new bank and a higher protective tariff. Congress passed both bills but could not override Tyler's veto. The Whigs were unhappy with Tyler and tried to impeach him in 1843. They failed but refused to nominate him for a second term.

LOOKING BACK

1. Why did President Jackson use the spoils system?
2. On the issue of nullification, what was: **a.** South Carolina's point of view? **b.** President Jackson's point of view? **c.** Clay's compromise?
3. **a.** Why did American settlers want the Native Americans removed from their lands? **b.** Why was Black Hawk's War fought? **c.** What did each of the Five Civilized Tribes do?
4. Reread the section The Bank War and: **a.** list Jackson's reasons for opposing the Second Bank. **b.** describe how Jackson destroyed the Second Bank.
5. **a.** Why was the Whig party formed? **b.** What details support your answer?
6. Reread pages 338 and 355 to help you answer these questions. **a.** What causes of the Panic of 1837 were similar to those of the Panic of 1819? **b.** Which causes were different? **c.** What generalization can you make about what may cause a panic?

PRACTICING YOUR SKILLS

What If . . .

In Chapter 3 of this unit, you read that the nullification crisis passed after Henry Clay, the Great Compromiser, persuaded Congress to pass a lower, compromise tariff. **What if** Henry Clay had not worked out a compromise? How might nullification have been settled?

Discussing

Using the spoils system, Jackson placed some of his supporters in government positions. Today, political patronage still exists. Do you think public officials have a right to fill government positions with their political supporters? Why or why not?

Researching, Writing

1. The U.S. banking system is very different today from what it was in the 1800s. Today, a large part of it is controlled by the Federal Reserve System. Research and write a paragraph either about requirements for Federal Reserve Banks, or advantages and disadvantages of Federal Reserve membership.
2. John Marshall served as Chief Justice of the Supreme Court from 1801 to 1835. During that time he worked to build a powerful Supreme Court and a strong federal government. Research and write a paragraph about John Marshall's effect on the growth of power of the Supreme Court.

Exploring

In Chapter 2 of this unit you read how American voters gained more political power in the 1820s and 1830s. For example, more public offices became elective. Make a list of local government offices in your community. Note whether they are elective or appointive. If they are appointive, who names people to them? What are the terms of office for each post?

Building Study Skills

On page 209 you learned how to paraphrase. Summarizing is a similar but slightly different skill. **Summarizing** material means to state what you have read in more general terms and with fewer details than the original material. Deciding which details are the most important to include is one part of summarizing. The skill can help you in writing reports or studying for tests. Here are a few tips to help you write summaries.

- Read the passage, article, or book carefully.
- Take notes in your own words. Do not copy sentences directly from the material.
- Include the main ideas and the most important supporting details.
- Do not add your own ideas.
- After putting your notes in paragraph form, make sure your summary is short, complete, and accurate.

Activity: Summarize that part of Chapter 2 of this unit that shows the relationship between increased voter participation and the election of Andrew Jackson.

Reading

Chidsey, Donald B. *Andrew Jackson, Hero.* New York: Elsevier-Nelson, 1977. Emphasizes politics of the day.

Coit, Margaret L. *The Sweep Westward, 1829-1849.* Morristown, New Jersey: Silver Burdett, 1974. Political, social, and military history.

Fleischmann, Glen H. *The Cherokee Removal, 1838: An Entire Indian Nation Is Forced Out of Its Homeland.* New York: Watts, 1971.

Hoople, Cheryl G., ed. *As I Saw It: Women Who Lived the American Adventure.* New York: Dial, 1978. Writings of 40 women of the 1800s.

Jackson, Florence. *Black Man in America* Series. 6 vols. New York: Watts, 1971-75. Abolitionists and black churches during Jackson's time in vol. 2.

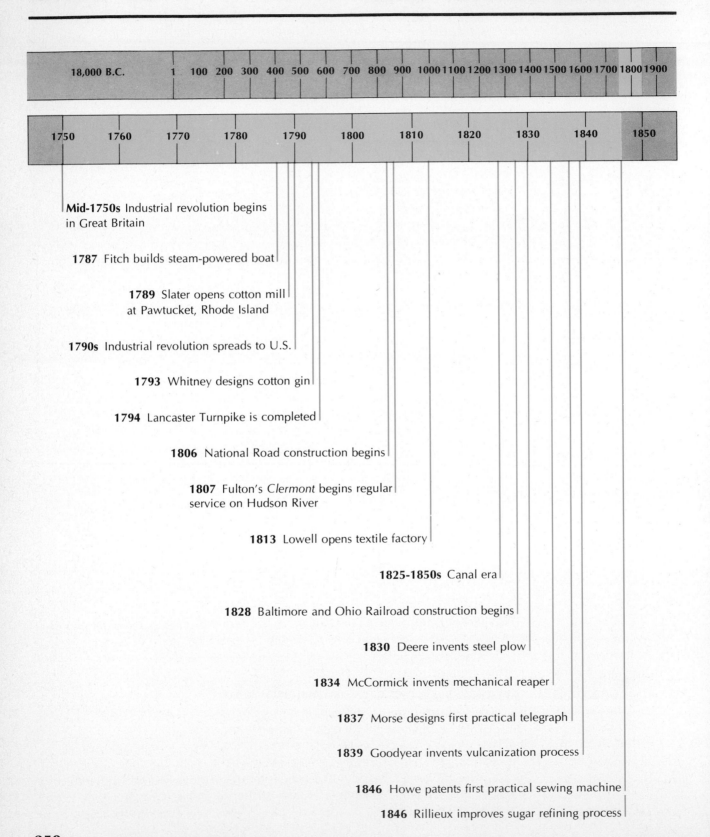

18,000 B.C.   1   100   200   300   400   500   600   700   800   900   1000 1100 1200 1300 1400 1500 1600 1700 1800 1900

1750   1760   1770   1780   1790   1800   1810   1820   1830   1840   1850

Mid-1750s Industrial revolution begins in Great Britain

1787 Fitch builds steam-powered boat

1789 Slater opens cotton mill at Pawtucket, Rhode Island

1790s Industrial revolution spreads to U.S.

1793 Whitney designs cotton gin

1794 Lancaster Turnpike is completed

1806 National Road construction begins

1807 Fulton's *Clermont* begins regular service on Hudson River

1813 Lowell opens textile factory

1825-1850s Canal era

1828 Baltimore and Ohio Railroad construction begins

1830 Deere invents steel plow

1834 McCormick invents mechanical reaper

1837 Morse designs first practical telegraph

1839 Goodyear invents vulcanization process

1846 Howe patents first practical sewing machine

1846 Rillieux improves sugar refining process

Chapter 1   New Machines, New Industry

LOOKING AHEAD

In the early 1800s, the U.S. began to change from a farming country to an industrialized nation. In this chapter, you will learn how this change came about. You will also learn how different sections of the country were affected by it. After you study this chapter, you will be able to:

- contrast the domestic system and the factory system.
- explain how the industrial revolution began and then spread to the U.S.
- identify the continuity and change in U.S. industry as a result of the industrial revolution.
- describe how different parts of the U.S. were affected by industrialization.

Social Studies Vocabulary

industrialization	factory system
industrial revolution	corporation
domestic system	law of supply and demand

People

John Kay	Eli Whitney	Norbert Rillieux
Richard Arkwright	Catherine Greene	Charles Goodyear
Edmund Cartwright	John Deere	Samuel F. B. Morse
Samuel Slater	Cyrus McCormick	
Francis Cabot Lowell	Elias Howe	

Places

Lowell, Massachusetts	Midwest

Words and Terms

Boston Associates	interchangeable	steel plow
cotton gin	parts	mechanical reaper

In the 1790s, Hamilton had a vision of the nation as a center of manufacturing and trade. He believed that Americans had a special talent for "mechanical improvements". They soon proved him right. But to understand how U.S. industry grew, it is necessary to look at the sequence of events in Great Britain in the 1700s. In those years, Great Britain turned from an economy based on farming to one based on industry. This process is called **industrialization** (in-duhs-tree-uhl-uh-ZAY-shuhn). The change occurred so quickly that it is called the **industrial revolution**.

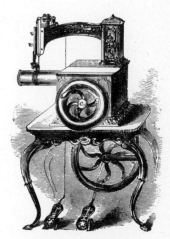

Elias Howe is credited with making the first practical sewing machine in 1846. This is one of his later improved models.

INDUSTRIAL REVOLUTION IN GREAT BRITAIN

With the growth of shipping and overseas colonies, Great Britain's markets grew, especially for British-made cloth. But the way cloth was made could not meet the growing demand. Under what was called the **domestic system,** all work was done at home. Merchants bought raw cotton or wool from farmers and then took it to spinners who turned it into thread. After paying them, the merchants took the thread to weavers. They used hand-operated looms to weave the thread into cloth. When the cloth was finished, merchants sold it for the highest price.

The domestic system worked well for centuries. But in 1733, John Kay invented a machine that helped weavers weave cloth much faster. The result was a demand for more thread. In 1769, Richard Arkwright (AHRK-ryt) designed a spinning machine that greatly speeded up thread-making. Now, weavers could not keep up with spinners. In 1786, Edmund Cartwright (KAHRT-ryt) designed a power loom that could turn out many times more cloth in a day than a hand-operated loom.

As machine power began to replace hand power, work was no longer done in the homes of spinners and weavers. Machines were too costly and complicated for individual craftworkers to buy and repair. Merchants became manufacturers and began to build factories. Workers who had no skills were trained to run the machines. Soon the factory system had replaced the domestic system. The **factory system** is a method in which workers and machines produce goods in a building set aside for such work.

SPREAD OF THE INDUSTRIAL REVOLUTION

The British wanted to keep the plans for their spinning and weaving machines secret. As long as Great Britain was the only nation with these machines, it would lead the world in cloth production. However, Samuel Slater (SLAY-tuhr), a British worker, spent several years learning to operate and repair Arkwright's spinning machine. At the same time, Slater was memorizing every detail of it. In 1789, he came to the U.S. and built the first successful cotton mill at Pawtucket (paw-TUHK-et), Rhode Island.

America's Textile Industry

The power loom did not reach the U.S. until the 1800s. Francis Cabot Lowell (LOH-uhl) of Massachusetts had seen Cartwright's loom while in England. In 1813, under Lowell's direction, the first American power loom was built at Waltham (WAHL-thum), Massachusetts.

Lowell's factory marked the beginning of America's textile industry. In 1822, Lowell and others formed a corporation known as the Boston Associates. A **corporation** (kor-puh-RAY-shuhn) is a group

This woodcut illustrates the domestic system. These women are carding and spinning fiber into thread at home. The carding, or combing, step cleans and untangles the fiber so it can be spun.

textile (TEKS-tuhl): woven cloth

Lawrence, Massachusetts, was one of the many industrial centers that grew up in New England in the early 1820s. What factors led to the rise of industry in the North but not in the South?

acting legally as an individual for business purposes. Each member of the corporation invests money in exchange for shares of stock. The stock gives the person the right to a share of any profits the corporation makes. This is similar to the joint-stock companies that financed the first English colonies in North America.

In time, the Boston Associates wanted to expand and needed greater energy resources than Waltham offered. The group moved to a place near Boston at the falls of the Merrimack (MER-uh-mak) River. Water flowing over the falls created the power needed to run the machines. This was the beginning of the city of Lowell, one of America's earliest industrial centers.

Industry and Cities

Besides Lowell, such cities as Lawrence and Fall River sprang up in Massachusetts because of the textile industry. Other industries gave rise to cities, too. Brockton, Lynn, and Haverhill (HAY-vruhl), in Massachusetts, were built around the growing shoe and boot industry. New England was not the only area to feel the effects of industrialization. Cities in Pennsylvania, New York, New Jersey, and Maryland grew because of factories.

Industry developed in the North because the area had the natural resources and the labor supply that the factory system needed. Because early factories depended on coal or water for energy, most factories were near coal mines or near rivers along the fall line. The falling water produced power to turn water wheels, and later generators, to operate the machinery. As you will read later in the unit Life at Mid-Century, the increase in European immigrants from the 1830s on provided northeastern manufacturers with a large labor supply. In the South, some industry developed. But there was no large supply of unemployed workers and little money to invest. Most of the work force, money, and land were tied up in farming.

The cotton gin in this illustration is run by steam power. How did the invention of the cotton gin change the economy of the South? What else did the cotton gin affect?

The Cotton Gin

The growing textile industry in the North and in Europe created a great demand for raw cotton from the South. But this made a problem in itself. When cotton is picked, the boll (BOHL), or ball, is filled with seeds as well as raw cotton. The seeds have to be removed, but removing them by hand is a very slow process.

In 1793, Eli Whitney designed a machine that removed the seeds from cotton. Whitney had learned of the problem while working as a tutor for the Greene family of Georgia. Catherine Greene, the owner of the plantation, suggested a faster way to clean cotton. Whitney's machine was based on her suggestion. The cotton gin, as it was called, could be run either by hand, water power, or horses. With Whitney's cotton gin, a worker could clean more than 45 kilograms (about 100 pounds) of cotton in a day. As cotton farming became more profitable, it spread across the South and with it slave labor.

Interchangeable Parts

Whitney later turned to the manufacture of muskets, or guns. In 1798, he received an order to make several thousand for the federal government. Until that time, guns were made by hand, and no two were exactly the same. A barrel from one might not fit the handle of another. Whitney decided to make his guns by machine. In this way, they could have interchangeable parts. A part from one gun could be used in place of the same part in another of his guns. Because Whitney's machines could turn out identical parts, a worker could put together a gun in very little time.

Whitney's system of interchangeable parts was an important step in the industrialization of America. If guns could be made from interchangeable parts, so could other items. American industry continued to make the same kinds of goods. But a change in methods and machines affected the time and number of workers needed.

BETTER FARM MACHINERY

The steel plow and the mechanical reaper—a machine for cutting grain—did for the farmers of the Midwest what the cotton gin had done for the South. Before 1860, the term Midwest meant the states made from the Northwest Territory—Illinois, Indiana, Ohio, Michigan, and Wisconsin—and states that had been formed from part of the Louisiana Purchase—Kansas, Minnesota, Iowa, and Missouri. Today the Midwest also includes Nebraska and North and South Dakota. In the mid-1800s, however, they were not yet states.

Before the 1830s, farmers used wooden or iron plows to turn over the hard-packed soil of the plains. The work was difficult and not very profitable. Since farmers ate or used most of what they raised, they had little to sell. They realized that in order to raise cash crops, they needed better farm equipment. But the system of interchangeable parts was necessary before this equipment could be made.

When John Deere invented the steel plow in 1830, farmers quickly accepted it. The steel blade of the plow made it possible to cut deep into the hard soil. More land was opened to farming. By 1858, Deere's factory was making 13,000 plows a year.

In addition to the steel plow, wheat farmers needed an effective tool for cutting grain. They were using sickles or scythes (SYTHZ), long-handled tools with curved blades, to harvest their crops. Because the season was short and the sickles were not very effective, farmers could cut only a small amount of grain. Cyrus McCormick solved their problem in 1834 with his mechanical reaper. Using a McCormick reaper, one person and a team of horses could cut as much grain as five people with sickles. The reaper allowed farmers to grow larger amounts of wheat for sale. By 1869, nearly 80,000 reapers had been sold.

OTHER IMPORTANT INVENTIONS

The amount of goods that could be made by machine was much greater than the amount that could be made by hand. As a result, manufactured goods were cheaper for Americans to buy than handmade goods had been. As goods became cheaper, Americans wanted more of them. This is an example of the economic **law of supply and demand.** The law states that prices for goods rise when there is increased demand. Prices fall when the supply of goods increases.

To help them produce more goods, manufacturers began looking for ways to speed up production. The sewing machine was one such invention. Elias Howe is credited with inventing the first practical sewing machine in 1846. Beginning in the 1850s, sewing machines were put in factories and revolutionized the clothing industry.

practical
(PRAK-tuh-kuhl):
useful

An invention by Norbert Rillieux (rihl-YOO) revolutionized the sugar industry. Rillieux, a black engineer, developed an improved machine that removed water from sugar cane. His machine greatly reduced the cost of producing sugar.

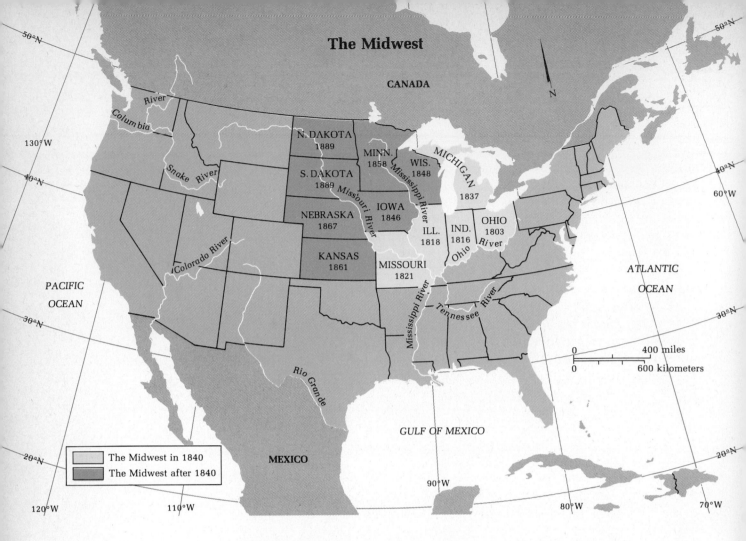

The Midwest

CANADA

N. DAKOTA
1889

MINN.
1858

S. DAKOTA
1889

WIS.
1848

MICHIGAN
1837

IOWA
1846

NEBRASKA
1867

ILL.
1818

IND.
1816

OHIO
1803

KANSAS
1861

MISSOURI
1821

Columbia River

Snake River

Missouri River

Mississippi River

Colorado River

Ohio River

Tennessee River

Mississippi River

Rio Grande

PACIFIC
OCEAN

ATLANTIC
OCEAN

MEXICO

GULF OF MEXICO

The Midwest in 1840
The Midwest after 1840

0   400 miles
0   600 kilometers

50°N 40°N 30°N 20°N

130°W 120°W 110°W 90°W 80°W 70°W 60°W

In 1839, Charles Goodyear found a way to make rubber more useful. Before he invented his vulcanization (vuhl-kuh-nuh-ZAY-shuhn) process, rubber was sticky in hot weather and easily broken in cold weather. His process made rubber usable in all climates and at all times of the year.

In 1837, Samuel F. B. Morse made the first practical telegraph. However, it took him seven years to convince Congress to give him the money to build a telegraph line. But in 1844, he linked Baltimore and Washington by telegraph. By 1866, telegraph lines reached to California.

LOOKING BACK

1. How did the domestic system differ from the factory system?
2. **a.** How did the industrial revolution begin? **b.** How did it spread to the U.S.? **c.** Why is it called a revolution?
3. **a.** What remained the same about U.S. industry during the industrial revolution? **b.** What changes occurred as a result of it?
4. How did the industrial revolution affect: **a.** the North? **b.** the South? **c.** the Midwest?

Chapter 2   A Transportation Revolution

LOOKING AHEAD

In this chapter, you will read about the transportation problems Americans once faced, and how they solved them. You will also learn how the revolution in transportation affected the different sections. After you study this chapter, you will be able to:

- describe how the steamboat and the clipper ship affected trade and travel.
- summarize the issue of internal improvements.
- read a map to find routes to different parts of the U.S.
- describe what is meant by the term *canal era.*
- distinguish fact from opinion in Strong's description of the steam locomotive.
- describe how the railroad helped the economic growth of the Northeast and Midwest.
- ★ find for the mid-1800s the average number of railroad tracks built in the U.S.

Social Studies Vocabulary

mean

People

James Watt	John Fitch	Robert Fulton

Places

Appalachian Mountains	Cumberland Gap	National Road
	Natchez Trace	Braddock's Road
Wilderness Road	Lancaster Turnpike	Erie Canal

Words and Terms

Clermont	Baltimore and Ohio Railroad
turnpike	South Carolina Canal and Railroad Company
canal fever	

During the first few decades of the new nation, travel from one part of the country to another was slow and difficult. People used pack animals and wagons on dirt roads and mountain trails. In wet weather, the roads turned to mud. At other times, they were dusty and full of potholes. On the nation's rivers, rafts and boats carried people and goods downstream. Upstream travel—travel against the river current—was difficult.

In the early 1800s, Americans were moving west in large numbers, and industry was growing. People began to see that they needed bet-

decade (DEK-ayd): a ten-year period

For centuries Japan had been closed to people of other nations. Before the U.S. could open a profitable Asian trade, Commodore Matthew Perry landed in Japan in the early 1850s to convince the Japanese to trade with other nations. From this picture, what means do you suppose he used?

ter kinds of transportation. Like the industrial revolution, one invention in the field of transportation led to another until a revolution was happening. This revolution helped the economy grow as farmers and manufacturers found it easier to get their goods to market.

STEAMBOATS AND CLIPPER SHIPS

The first step in the transportation revolution was the development of a practical steam engine in the 1760s by James Watt of Scotland. In 1787, John Fitch, an American, built a boat that was powered by a steam engine. In 1790, his steamboat began regular service on the Delaware River between Philadelphia and Burlington, New Jersey. But there were not enough users, and service was discontinued.

Successful steamboat service began in 1807, when Robert Fulton's *Clermont* made its first trip up the Hudson River. With considerable noise and smoke, it steamed from New York City to Albany in 32 hours. It made the return trip downstream in 30 hours. Four years later, the steamboat *New Orleans* was shipping passengers and goods up and down the Mississippi. It was the first of many.

Because of its location near the mouth of the Mississippi, New Orleans became the port of entry for goods shipped to the South and Midwest from the Northeast, Europe, Latin America, and Asia. Producers in the South and Midwest shipped their sugar, cotton, grain, and livestock to New Orleans where they were put on ocean-going ships. After the 1840s, canals and railroads brought most midwestern products to the cities of the Northeast. However, New Orleans continued as a major port for the southern cotton, sugar, and slave trade.

Steamboats revolutionized transportation because they could travel both upstream and downstream easily. They also greatly lowered transportation costs, which helped farmers and manufacturers. Before regular steamboat service between Cincinnati and New Orleans, it cost $5 to ship 100 pounds of goods. By 1842, the rate was 25¢.

Changes in ocean-going transportation also helped the economy. As you may recall from the unit A Plan of Government, Americans began trading in Asia during the Confederation period. The long ocean voyage was dangerous yet highly profitable. American ship-owners began to look for a ship design that was faster. The clipper ship was the result. It had a narrow hull, or body, with tall masts and as many as 35 sails. It was called a clipper ship because it clipped off the distance four or five times faster than older, wider ships. The first clipper *Rainbow* was launched in 1845. Clipper ships were in wide use in the late 1840s and 1850s.

Using clipper ships, New England merchants took the lead in world trade. Much of the money that they made was used to build American factories and railroads. Besides trading with Asia, clipper ships carried goods and passengers between the U.S. and Europe. California and Oregon were brought closer to the Atlantic coast by clipper ships.

FEW ROADS WEST

As you may recall from the unit Life in Colonial America, the Appalachian Mountains had few passes and acted as a natural barrier to early westbound travel. As a result, there were few land routes west. Most people traveled inland by water. The Great Wagon Road was one of the first roads through this area. Another early route, the Wilderness Road, was opened in 1775. It cut through the Appalachians at the Cumberland Gap and opened up the area beyond North Carolina and Virginia. The road led to the settlement of the region that became the states of Kentucky and Tennessee.

The Natchez (NACH-ez) Trace, another early road, was once a Native American trail. It cut through the lands of the Chickasaw and

The development of the steamboat and the construction of canals in the 1840s led to the steady growth of such cities as Pittsburgh.

Canals and Roads in 1850

Choctaw and connected Natchez, Mississippi with Nashville, Tennessee. In 1801, Jefferson had the army clear and widen the trail. The new road allowed faster travel for people and goods moving into the Old Southwest.

Turnpikes

The first improvement in road travel occurred with the building of turnpikes. A turnpike is a road with tollgates where tolls, or fees, are collected from those using the road. The Lancaster Turnpike, one of America's first turnpikes, was completed in 1794. It connected Philadelphia with the farm area around Lancaster, Pennsylvania, about 96 kilometers (60 miles) to the west.

The National Road

As more people moved into the Ohio and Mississippi valleys, the need for better routes to these areas became a national concern. One solution was a national road—one that would be built with federal money. After careful study, it was decided that the road should run from the Potomac River in Cumberland, Maryland to the Ohio River at Wheeling, now part of West Virginia. Part of the road would follow Braddock's old military route. Braddock's Road was built during the

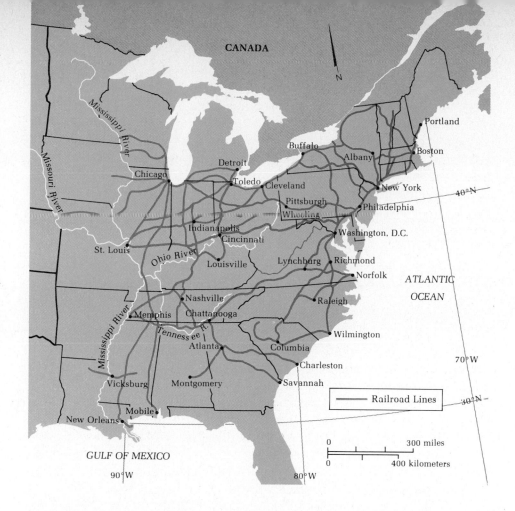

CANADA

Mississippi River

Missouri River

Portland
Buffalo
Boston
Albany
Detroit
Chicago
Toledo
Cleveland
New York
40°N
Pittsburgh
Philadelphia
Wheeling
Indianapolis
Washington, D.C.
St. Louis
Cincinnati
Ohio River
Louisville
Lynchburg
Richmond
Norfolk
ATLANTIC
OCEAN
Nashville
Raleigh
Memphis
Chattanooga
Tennessee R.
Wilmington
Atlanta
Columbia
70°W
Charleston
Vicksburg
Montgomery
Savannah
Railroad Lines
30°N
Mobile
New Orleans
GULF OF MEXICO
0   300 miles
90°W
80°W
0   400 kilometers

Railroads in 1860

French and Indian War to connect Maryland with Fort Duquesne in Pennsylvania.

In 1806, Congress appropriated money for the National Road and construction began. Within 13 years, the road reached to Wheeling. Later, it was extended to Vandalia (van-DAYL-yuh), Illinois. The National Road did much to encourage movement westward. The road also added to the economic growth of the western frontier. It tied the Ohio Valley with Maryland, New York, New Jersey, and Pennsylvania and gave both the western frontier and the eastern states markets for each other's goods.

Internal Improvements

In time, providing money for such internal improvements as roads and canals became a major political issue. As you may recall from the unit The New Nation, Henry Clay and John C. Calhoun proposed the American System. One part of it called for the federal government to pay for internal improvements. In 1816, their plan won support in the southern, western, and Middle Atlantic states. However, New Englanders opposed it. They thought they would lose people to the West once it was opened for settlement. You may also recall that they were against using federal money for internal improvements. One of the people who shared this view was President Madison. His last act in office was the veto of an internal improvements bill. Such a bill, he claimed, violated states' rights.

The South, with Calhoun as its spokesman, at first supported internal improvements. By 1824, however, many Southerners had changed their views. The protective tariff passed in 1816 hurt their economy. Taxes for internal improvements would only add to their troubles. Also, federal money for internal improvements was seen as increasing the power of the federal government. This, in turn, would threaten states' rights. The South felt that protecting states' rights meant protecting its economic system.

THE CANAL ERA

The National Road linked the Ohio Valley with the Northeast. But a link was also needed between the Northeast and the Great Lakes. People and goods needed an easier way to reach the regions being settled around the lakes. Since federal money was not available, it was up to the states to pay for internal improvements.

In 1817, the New York State legislature granted Governor DeWitt Clinton's request to build a canal through the state. Work began in 1817 and was finished in 1825. Named the Erie Canal, it was successful beyond all hopes. In the canal's first nine years, toll charges paid off the construction costs. In addition, the canal greatly reduced transportation costs. The fee for shipping a ton of freight between New York City and Buffalo dropped from $100 to under $10. In central New York State, cities and towns sprang up along the canal. New York City grew as a center of commerce and shipping.

"Canal fever" spread to other states. By 1840, a network of canals grew up linking some of the older, northeastern states with the newer ones farther west. Canals in the states of Ohio, Indiana, Kentucky, and Illinois allowed river traffic on the Ohio and Mississippi rivers to flow to the Great Lakes. Traders in the western parts of New York and Pennsylvania were linked through canals with eastern ports as well as with the Great Lakes. The period of great canal activity lasted until the 1850s when railroads began to overshadow canals.

RAILROADS

Canals and roads added greatly to the industrial growth of America. But both connected only parts of the country. A transportation system was needed that would connect all parts of the nation in a giant network. This means of transportation had to be usable in all kinds of weather. It had to be cheap enough so that goods could be shipped great distances at low rates. It had to be convenient, dependable, and comfortable. The railroad answered all these needs.

The earliest railroads were built in British coal mines to carry coal to the surface. The cars were horse-drawn and traveled on wooden

Miles of Railroad Track Built 1835–1850

Year	Miles of Track
1835	138
1836	280
1837	348
1838	453
1839	386
1840	491
1841	606
1842	505
1843	288
1844	180
1845	277
1846	333
1847	263
1848	1056
1849	1048
1850	1261

Source: *Historical Statistics of the U.S.,* Bureau of the Census

The *Best Friend of Charleston* was the first steam-powered locomotive built in the U.S. for regular service on a railroad. In 1831, it began carrying passengers and goods between Charleston and Hamburg, South Carolina.

tracks. Later, iron was used for the tracks. In the early 1800s, a few small horse-drawn railroads were built in New England. In 1828, work was begun on the Baltimore and Ohio Railroad, the first large railroad. It had horse-drawn cars and carried its first passengers in 1830. The route was 20.9 kilometers (13 miles) long. But between 1835 and 1850, an average of 495 miles of track was being built each year.

Around 1830, the steam engine was adapted to train use. The first regularly scheduled steam-powered railroad was the South Carolina Canal and Railroad Company. The following is from the diary of George Templeton Strong, dated July 1, 1839. Strong is describing a new invention, the steam locomotive.

It's a great sight to see a large train get under way. I know of nothing that would more strongly impress our great-great-grandfathers with an idea of their descendants' progress in science. Just imagine it rushing by a stranger to the invention on a dark night, whizzing and rattling and panting, with its fiery furnace gleaming in front, its chimney vomiting fiery smoke above, and its long train of cars rushing along behind like the body and tail of a gigantic dragon — and all darting forward at the rate of twenty miles an hour. Whew!

Because of problems with early steam locomotives, railroads did not overtake canals as a major means of transportation until the 1850s. To encourage construction, the federal government gave land to railroad companies. By 1860, four million hectares (about ten million acres) of land had been given to 45 railroads. When the Civil War began in 1861, more than 48,000 kilometers (30,000 miles) of track had been built. Much of it was in the Midwest.

Railroads greatly affected the movement of settlers. Because the railroads gave quick, cheap transportation between sections, land in the Midwest became more valuable. Cheaper transportation meant lower prices and new markets for midwestern food products and northeastern manufactured goods. Both sections prospered because each had a market for its goods. Cities that were not near major waterways began to grow once a railroad was built nearby. In the South, Atlanta, Georgia; Richmond, Virginia; and Chattanooga, Tennessee, became rail centers. Detroit, Michigan; Chicago; and Cleveland, Ohio, grew because of their closeness to railroads. Railroads also helped the growth of mining because they used large amounts of coal and iron.

BUILDING STATISTICAL SKILLS

You have just read about the average miles of railroad track built between 1835 and 1850 in the U.S. The average in a series of numbers is called the **mean.** To find the mean, add all the numbers in the series and divide by the number in the series. For example, $7 + 9 + 2 + 4 + 3 = 25$; $25 \div 5 = 5$. The answer 5 is the mean.

The mean is a useful tool for social scientists. They use it to get a general idea of the size of a group without having to look at each item. For example, they can use the mean to find the size of an average family's income in New York City in any year. The mean can also be used to compare the average size of one group with the average size of another. For example, average family income in New York City can be compared with average family income in Dallas.

1. Use the table on page 370 to find the mean for railroad tracks built between 1835 and 1839. **2.** What was the average miles of track built between 1840 and 1844? **3.** What does this tell you about the economy of the U.S. in these two periods? **Hint:** How would the Panic of 1837 have affected railroad building?

LOOKING BACK

1. How did each of the following affect travel and trade: **a.** the steamboat? **b.** clipper ships?
2. **a.** Why was the National Road built? **b.** How was it paid for? **c.** What were two views on internal improvements?
3. Use the maps on pages 368-69 to see how a western farmer might ship goods from Cincinnati to: **a.** Boston. **b.** Charleston.
4. **a.** When was the canal era in the U.S.? **b.** Why was this time period called the canal era? **c.** Can you recall from the unit New Role of the Nation an era that overlaps it?
5. Reread the selection from George Strong's diary and: **a.** list the factual information. **b.** list the statements that are based on his opinions. Do not be confused by his writing style.
6. Describe how both the Northeast and Midwest prospered because of the railroads.
7. **a.** Use the table Miles of Railroad Track to find the mean for miles of track built from 1845 to 1850. **b.** What can you infer about the economy of the U.S. during those years?

Compare and contrast how the growth of railroads affected each section of the nation.

PRACTICING YOUR SKILLS

What If . . .

In Chapter 1, you read that many of the earliest factories were located in the Northeast. An important reason for the industrialization of this area was the availability of water and coal for energy. **What if** the first factories had been located in the southern states wherever water or coal was plentiful? How might the economy of the southern states have been affected? Would the South's views on banking, protective tariffs, and slavery have been different?

Discussing

In Chapter 1, you read how corporations were formed to build some of the early factories. In Chapter 2 you read about the states' rights view of internal improvements. Discuss how people in favor of states' rights might have viewed the idea of allowing corporations to build and operate roads. How would they have paid for the roads?

Imagining, Researching, Charting

1. You read in Chapter 2 how an American viewed one of the first steam locomotives. Imagine you have just watched Robert Fulton's *Clermont* make its first voyage up the Hudson River. In a letter, describe what you might have seen.
2. In the unit A Plan of Government, you read flow charts to find out how a bill becomes a law and how the judiciary works. Using information from Chapter 1 of this unit and from reference materials, make a flow chart showing the steps involved in the domestic system for making cloth. With each step of the domestic system, place the invention or inventions that eventually improved that step.
3. Besides those mentioned in this unit, other important inventions were developed in the late 1700s and early 1800s. Use an encyclopedia or other reference book to research and summarize in one paragraph the invention of one of the following: spinning jenny, macadam, smelting process.

Exploring

Inventions improve ways of doing things in businesses, on farms, or in homes. To find out how inventions have changed daily life, make a list of the things you use that were not known 100 years ago. Check off those that did not exist 20 years ago.

Building Study Skills

Outlining is a useful skill that will help you organize your ideas for studying, writing a paper, or giving an oral report. An outline consists of main topics and subtopics arranged in order from the most general to the most specific. Here is the form for an outline and a few tips to help with outlining.

- Keep your wording simple but clear.
- Have at least two topics in your outline and two subtopics under each topic.
- Begin the first word of each topic and first subtopic with a capital letter.
- Begin the first word of a second subtopic with a small letter.

> I.   Topic
>   A. First subtopic
>   1. second subtopic
>   2. second subtopic
>   B. First subtopic
> II. Topic

Activity: Practice by outlining this unit to help you study.

Reading

Ebeling, Walter. *The Fruited Plain: The Story of American Agriculture.* Berkeley, California: U. of California Press, 1980.

Fisher, Leonard Everett. *The Factories.* New York: Holiday House, 1979.

Franchere, Ruth. *Westward by Canal.* Riverside, New Jersey: Macmillan, 1972.

Langdon, William C. *Everyday Things in American Life, 1776-1876.* New York: Scribner, 1941. Roads, turnpikes, covered bridges, canals and so on.

Snow, Richard. *The Iron Road: A Portrait of American Railroading.* New York: Scholastic Book Service, 1978.

Ward, Ralph T. *Steamboats: A History of the Early Adventure.* Indianapolis, Indiana: Bobbs Merrill, 1973.

Section IV NATION IN CONFLICT

Unit I
Life at Mid-Century

Unit II
Manifest Destiny

Unit III
Coming of the Civil War

Unit IV
Civil War & Reconstruction

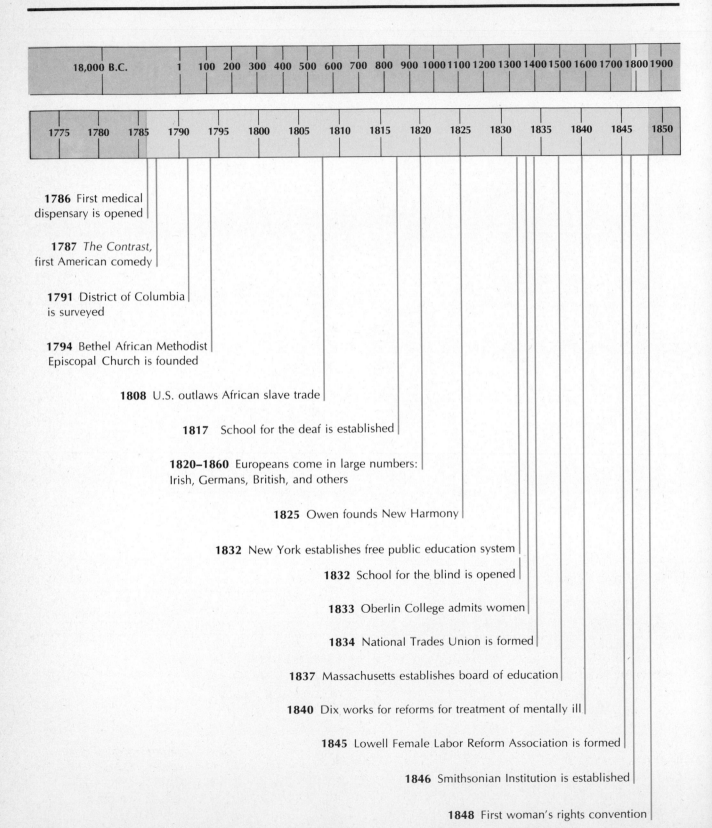

18,000 B.C.	1	100	200	300	400	500	600	700	800	900	1000	1100	1200	1300	1400	1500	1600	1700	1800 1900

1775	1780	1785	1790	1795	1800	1805	1810	1815	1820	1825	1830	1835	1840	1845	1850

1786 First medical dispensary is opened

1787 *The Contrast,* first American comedy

1791 District of Columbia is surveyed

1794 Bethel African Methodist Episcopal Church is founded

1808 U.S. outlaws African slave trade

1817 School for the deaf is established

1820–1860 Europeans come in large numbers: Irish, Germans, British, and others

1825 Owen founds New Harmony

1832 New York establishes free public education system

1832 School for the blind is opened

1833 Oberlin College admits women

1834 National Trades Union is formed

1837 Massachusetts establishes board of education

1840 Dix works for reforms for treatment of mentally ill

1845 Lowell Female Labor Reform Association is formed

1846 Smithsonian Institution is established

1848 First woman's rights convention

Chapter 1   The Peopling of America

LOOKING AHEAD

This chapter is about the movement of peoples from northern and western Europe to the U.S. from 1820 to 1860. You will learn why they left their homes and why they chose to settle in the U.S. You will also read about where the immigrants settled and about the prejudice they met. After you study this chapter, you will be able to:

- distinguish between the pull and push forces that influenced groups of European immigrants to come to America.
- identify similarities and differences among immigrant groups.
- explain why British immigrants met less prejudice than other groups.
- ★ read a pie graph to learn the percent of immigrants from different countries in northern and western Europe.
- list the reasons for the prejudice of some native-born Americans against immigrants in the mid-1800s.

Social Studies Vocabulary

heritage	pie graph	nativist
emigrate	prejudice	

People

Irish	Scandinavians	Know-Nothings
Germans	Swiss	
British	Dutch	

Events

Great Potato Famine	Revolutions of 1830 and 1848

Words and Terms

push forces	pull forces

From 1790 to 1815, about 250,000 Europeans immigrated to the U.S. Between 1820 and 1860, over 4.6 million more came, most of them after 1840. These new immigrants came for many of the same reasons that brought the first colonists to the Americas. Historians classify these reasons into two groups, push forces and pull forces.

Push forces were those conditions in Europe that made people want to leave. Push forces, such as famine and religious persecution, differed from group to group. Pull forces, on the other hand, were conditions in the U.S. itself that attracted Europeans. These, too, differed from group to group.

famine (FAM·uhn): great shortage of food that affects a large number of people

Immigrants setting out for America wave to friends and relatives on shore. What pull forces attracted immigrants to the U.S.?

The chief pull force was the growing U.S. economy of the early 1800s. Industrialization, the growth of cities, the transportation revolution, and westward expansion created many opportunities. People were needed to work in factories, build roads, dig canals, lay railroad tracks, and build ships. The idea of owning land also brought Europeans to the U.S.

COMING TO AMERICA

In the 1800s, books and pamphlets on life in America flooded Europe. Shipping companies and railroads paid for advertisements and published guidebooks to attract immigrants. The guidebooks listed wages, prices, geography, climate, and crops for different parts of the U.S. However, nothing influenced Europeans more than letters from friends and relatives who had already gone to America. These letters often described the U.S. as a land of golden opportunity. Anyone who worked hard, was honest, and saved his or her money could be successful. A Welsh immigrant addressed the following letter, dated 1846, to his minister in Wales:

I found the country better than I expected. I have bought a farm with house, buildings, and 18 acres of wheat already sown. There is only one farm between my brothers-in-law. I am about three miles from Mr. Rice and two miles from Mr. Hughes. The land appears rich and fruitful and I am happy to say that I feel quite at home. I would not, for a considerable sum, return to Wales. This is a country for a man with a family, where supplies are cheap and of the best kind. We can eat beefsteaks or ham every morning with our breakfast.

In 1830, the trip from Ireland to the U.S. cost about $12. Immigrants could save that in less than a year and then send it home so that another family member could come. Unlike colonial times, family members often came alone to work, save, and send for relatives.

The trip across the Atlantic usually took six weeks but the time varied, depending on the weather. The immigrants were packed into the lower decks of the ships. Food, water, and fresh air were limited. Sometimes, diseases swept through the ships, killing many of the immigrants. Some immigrants died just from the hardships of the trip. Others were so weakened that they died soon after arriving in the U.S.

IRISH

Almost two million Irish entered the U.S. between 1820 and 1860. This was the largest group of European immigrants to come to the U.S. during the 40 years before the Civil War. It was about 20 percent of Ireland's population. Most left Ireland because of economic and farming problems.

Most of the Irish were tenant farmers who rented land from a few wealthy landowners. After 1815, the landowners began combining the small farms into large ones. The larger farms were more profitable to run. The Irish who were forced off the farms had no place to go. The English in the 1600s and the Scotch-Irish in the early 1700s had faced the same problem. As many of these earlier people had done, many Irish came to America. But the great migration of Irish did not begin until the 1840s. From 1845 to 1849, the potato crops—the chief

This woodcut from about 1851 shows a priest blessing Irish emigrants. What push forces caused people to leave Ireland?

food of the Irish—were destroyed by disease. Over 750,000 people starved to death during the Great Potato Famine, as it was called. More than a million left Ireland, many for the U.S.

Although most Irish immigrants were farmers, they were too poor to buy land. Most settled in the port cities of New York, Philadelphia, Baltimore, and Boston. Many who arrived in Boston moved inland to New England factory towns. In the cities, the Irish had to learn new ways of making a living. The few skilled workers, such as bricklayers, found construction jobs in the growing cities. But most Irish men were unskilled. They had to take whatever jobs they could find. Some worked loading and unloading ships or in factories. Many took jobs laying tracks for the new railroads. Because families could not live on the wages an unskilled worker made, women and children worked, too. Many found factory jobs. Irish women also worked as maids in hotels or in homes—jobs that native-born white women would not take.

In Ireland, the Irish had lived in small farm villages. Relatives, friends, neighbors, and their church were nearby. Like the immigrants you read about in the unit Life in Colonial America, the Irish settled among their people who were already in the U.S. Many Irish neighborhoods grew up around people who had come from the same village.

For hundreds of years, the Roman Catholic church had been an important part of Irish life. To keep their heritage, the Irish built churches and schools. **Heritage** (HER-uh-tij) means something that is passed from one generation to the next, such as religion or traditions.

The Irish also formed new organizations to help immigrants adapt to their new life. Immigrant societies and benevolent associations gave food and shelter to new immigrants and help to the sick and to victims of accidents. The Irish also began their own newspapers.

The Irish quickly learned the power of politics. Most Irish became members of the Democratic party because it helped them find housing and jobs. In return, the Irish gave the party their votes. By the mid-1800s, the Irish were a powerful political force in many northeastern cities. Irish politicians held many local offices and handed out political patronage jobs to supporters.

benevolent
(buh-NEV-uhl-uhnt):
kindly, helpful

GERMANS

Farming and economic problems were the chief reasons for German immigration. Between 1820 and 1860, over 1.5 million Germans came to the U.S. They were Catholics, Protestants, and Jews.

Beginning in the early 1800s, German tenant farmers found it difficult to borrow money to buy new equipment. Much of the money in Germany was being used to expand industry and transportation. Besides a lack of credit, crop failures in the 1840s drove out many tenant farmers. In addition, as the industrial revolution spread

through Germany, many craftworkers, such as spinners and spinning-wheel makers, were losing their jobs to machines.

Another force that caused Germans to emigrate was political. **Emigrate** (EM-uh-grayt) means to leave one's homeland to live somewhere else. During the 1800s, there was no East Germany and West Germany as we know them today. The area was made up of a number of German states. Following Napoleon's defeat in 1815, the rulers of these states, as well as other European monarchs, wanted to wipe out any influences of the French Revolution. As you may recall from the unit The New Nation, the French had called for revolutions against all monarchs. The rulers of the German states began to limit such rights as freedom of the press and freedom of assembly. Some Germans wanted greater freedoms and a unified nation similar to the U.S. In 1830 and again in 1848, revolutions broke out in Germany. Both times the revolutions were crushed, but many revolutionaries escaped to the U.S.

Once in the U.S., the Germans, like the Irish, faced the problem of earning a living. However, German immigrants, unlike the Irish, were not all poor. Some were wealthy farmers, craftworkers, or professionals. Most Germans settled in Ohio, Illinois, Wisconsin, and Missouri, where good farmland was available. Wealthier Germans bought thousands of hectares of land. By working for others and saving, poorer families also were able to buy farms. Many German craftworkers and professionals also settled in the Midwest. They were able to find work in the growing cities of the region. By 1850, for example, one third of the population of St. Louis was German-born. Like the Irish, the Germans built separate neighborhoods and communities. They also formed immigrant societies and benevolent associations and began their own German-language newspapers.

In the mid-1800s, farmers came to the U.S. in search of good farmland. Many settled in the Midwest. Which states or territories did they go to? See the map on page 364.

unified (YOO-nuh-fyd): united; made one

381

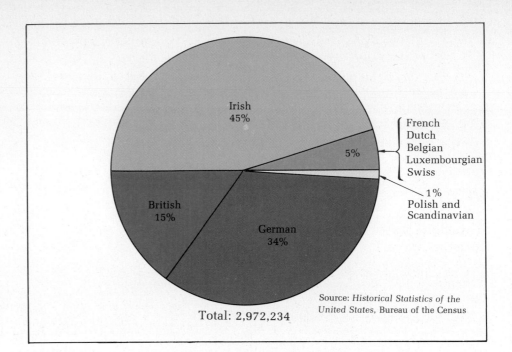

Irish
45%

5%
French
Dutch
Belgian
Luxembourgian
Swiss

1%
Polish and
Scandinavian

British
15%

German
34%

Total: 2,972,234

Source: *Historical Statistics of the United States*, Bureau of the Census

Immigrants from Northwestern and Central Europe between 1845 and 1855

 BUILDING GRAPH SKILLS

The graph on this page is called a **pie graph.** A pie graph is round and shows parts of a whole. Each part, or section, of the pie represents a part, or percent, of the total number. Each section of a pie graph is always labeled so you will know who or what, as well as how much of the whole, a particular part represents. For example, this pie graph shows the whole, or total number, of immigrants to the U.S. from each of 12 nations of northern and western Europe from 1845 to 1855. The British section represents 15 percent of the total number of immigrants shown in the graph. **1.** What percent does the Irish part represent? **2.** What percent of the total number of immigrants was German?

BRITISH

After Ireland and Germany, the next largest group of immigrants came from Great Britain. Between 1820 and 1860, almost 800,000 people emigrated from England, Scotland, and Wales to the U.S. Some were farmers, but most were skilled workers. Their skills played an important part in spreading the industrial revolution in the U.S.

Most of the English, Scots, and Welsh were pulled to the U.S. rather than pushed out of Great Britain. Unlike the Irish and Germans, they were not escaping poverty or political unrest. Most were making a good living, but reports of golden opportunities in the U.S. convinced many they could do better.

Like many Germans, many British immigrants arrived with money. As a result, they were able to move beyond the port cities. The Welsh

poverty (PAHV-uhr-tee): being poor

settled mostly in Pennsylvania where Welsh had settled in the late 1600s and in Ohio, New York, Massachusetts, and Wisconsin. The English and Scots settled wherever there were jobs.

Unlike other immigrants, the British did not need to build separate communities or neighborhoods to feel at home. They shared the same culture as most native-born Americans. They spoke the same language and most were Protestants. The British blended easily into American society.

OTHER GROUPS

Although most immigrants from Scandinavia—Norway, Sweden, and Denmark—came after the Civil War, some did immigrate to the U.S. before 1860. Norwegians began arriving in the late 1830s and the Swedes about 1852. The number of Danish immigrants was never very large. Most Scandinavian immigrants were farmers. They were pulled to America by the promise of better land, rather than pushed by economic or political forces. Most settled in the Midwest and bought farms.

Small numbers of Swiss and Dutch also came to the U.S. Both Switzerland and the Netherlands are small countries with little farmland. Most Swiss and Dutch immigrants came in hopes of owning land and settled in the farm areas of the Midwest.

IMMIGRANTS AND PREJUDICE

By the mid-1800s, some native-born Americans were becoming alarmed by the growing number of immigrants. Some concerns of Americans were real. But some were based on prejudice. **Prejudice** (PREJ-uh-dis) is dislike for or intolerance of others without knowledge to support or disprove one's opinion.

Some native-born Americans saw the immigrants as threats to their jobs. Immigrants were desperate for work and employers knew this. Owners of some businesses eagerly replaced native-born workers with immigrants and then paid them less. Some Americans thought that because the Irish and Germans built separate communities and kept their customs and traditions, they did not want to become part of American society. They saw the immigrants as threats to American life. Also, because of the revolutions of 1830 and 1848, some Americans looked upon all German immigrants as revolutionaries.

Most prejudice before the Civil War was directed against Roman Catholics, many of whom were Irish. Germans, Scandinavians, Swiss, and Dutch suffered less because most were Protestants like the majority of Americans. As in colonial days, some Americans feared the power that Roman Catholics might gain. In 1834, an anti-Catholic mob burned a convent in Charlestown, Massachusetts. Local brick-

disprove:
to prove false

Nativists battle militia called to restore law and order in Philadelphia after two Roman Catholic churches were burned.

layers took part in the burning in anger against Irish competition for jobs. In 1844, several Catholic churches were burned in Philadelphia. A number of people were killed and as many as 100 hurt.

People who called themselves nativists formed organizations to fight immigration. A **nativist** (NAYT-iv-uhst) is one who believes that native-born people should be favored over immigrants. These groups opposed the appointment of immigrants and Roman Catholics to public office. One group, the Order of the Star-Spangled Banner, held its meetings in secret. Because members answered "I don't know" when questioned about their activities, they were called Know-Nothings. By 1852, they had grown into a political party called the American party. It quickly became known as the Know-Nothing party. The Know-Nothings won a few elections in northern states during the 1850s and had some southern members. But the party divided over the slavery issue and had disappeared by 1860.

LOOKING BACK

1. What push and pull forces influenced each of the following groups to come to America: **a.** Irish? **b.** Germans? **c.** British? **d.** Scandinavians? **e.** Swiss and Dutch?

2. **a.** What were some similarities among the groups of European immigrants once they got to the U.S.? **b.** What were some differences?

3. Why did the British find it easier to adjust to life in America than did the Irish and Germans?

★ 4. Use the pie graph on page 382 to find the percent of immigrants to the U.S. from: **a.** Germany. **b.** Poland, Norway, Sweden, and Denmark. **c.** Great Britain and Ireland combined.

5. State two reasons why some native-born Americans were prejudiced against immigrants. Be careful to distinguish between facts and people's opinions.

Chapter 2   Sectional Differences

LOOKING AHEAD

This chapter describes the different economies that had developed in the three sections of the U.S. by the mid-1800s. The Northeast was building factories while the South was becoming a center for cotton farming. The Midwest was mainly a food-producing area. You will read how technology was chiefly responsible for the differences. After you study this chapter, you will be able to:

- describe the economic system of the Northeast.
- find the mean number of workers in manufacturing.
- explain the cause-and-effect relationship of the cotton gin on the southern economy.
- read a pie graph to find the percent of U.S. cotton exported in 1820 and 1860.
- describe the effects of technology and transportation on the growth of the Midwest.

Social Studies Vocabulary

goods and services   labor union   strike

People

Sarah G. Bagley

Places

New Bedford, Massachusetts   Cincinnati   Detroit
Nantucket Island, Massachusetts   Toledo, Ohio   Milwaukee
Providence, Rhode Island   Cleveland   Chicago

Words and Terms

Lowell Female Labor Reform Association   Cotton Kingdom

By the mid-1800s, two thirds of America's population was working on farms. Most of the nation's exports were farm products. In many areas, especially in the Midwest, more farmers were raising such cash crops as corn and wheat. Even though most Americans worked on farms, the economy was changing. Farmers and other Americans were buying goods and services they had once produced themselves. **Goods and services** are things made and activities done for others for a price.

As Americans began to demand cheaper machine-made goods, more and more factories were built, especially in the Northeast. Better farm machinery and transportation were creating a demand for land

How did cotton become so important to the southern economy?

in the Midwest. The cotton gin had already turned much of the South into the Cotton Kingdom. Roads, railroads, canals, and rivers linked the sections of the U.S. into a huge trade network.

THE NORTHEAST

As you read in the unit New Technology, the first factories were built in the Northeast. But trade and whaling were also important to the economy of the Northeast in the mid-1800s. They were perhaps more important than they had been in the 1700s.

Trade and Whaling

By the mid-1800s, merchants from the Northeast were trading with Europe, Asia, and the West Indies, as well as with other sections of the U.S. Passengers as well as goods were carried to Europe on regularly scheduled voyages. New York became the busiest of the northeastern ports, but Philadelphia, Boston, and other New England ports also grew.

The activity of the port cities created many jobs. Sailors, dockworkers, warehouse workers, clerks, craftworkers, and shopkeepers were needed. Construction jobs increased as these people had to have places to live and do business. Restaurants, hotels, and taverns multiplied. Churches and schools were also built.

One of the major trade items that went through these ports was whale oil. It was still an important fuel in the mid-1800s. New England whaling ships sailed the North Atlantic, the Pacific and Indian oceans, and as far as the Arctic Circle and Antarctica. Voyages often lasted three to four years. New Bedford and Nantucket Island in Massachusetts and Providence, Rhode Island, became centers of the whaling industry.

The art of carving on whalebone or whale ivory is called scrimshaw. Sailors on long whale hunts made many fine pieces of scrimshaw. From this picture what do you think a whale hunt was like?

Manufacturing

Much of the money made by the wealthy in trade and whaling was invested in factories. In the early 1800s, there were only a few factory owners such as the Boston Associates, which you read about in the unit New Technology. But by the mid-1800s, factories were an important part of the Northeast's economy. Factory owners, along with bankers, shipowners, and owners of transportation systems, were among the wealthiest people in the Northeast. They belonged to the upper class and supported public officials who would protect their business interests. Among these interests were a high tariff and no labor unions. A **labor union** is an organization of workers, formed to deal with employers.

From the textile mills of Lowell, people quickly adapted the factory system to the making of glass, woolen goods, firearms, and furniture. More and more Americans found jobs in manufacturing. Factory workers had only to be taught to run the machines. The machines did the jobs that skilled craftworkers had once done.

The factories of the mid-1800s were usually large wooden buildings of several floors. They were very hot in summer and cold in winter. Employees worked 12 to 14 hours a day, six days a week. Lamps were the only light, but they were also fire hazards. The air, especially in textile mills, was filled with dust. Many of the machines were unsafe, and accidents were frequent. The following is from a letter by a young woman describing factory work in Lowell:

hazard (HAZ-uhrd): danger

It makes my feet ache and swell to stand so much, but I suppose I shall get accustomed to that too. The girls generally wear old shoes to work;

387

but they almost all say that when they have worked here a year or two they need shoes a size or two larger than before they came. The right hand, which is the one used in stopping and starting the loom, becomes larger than the left.

We go in at five o'clock; at seven we come out for breakfast; at half-past seven we return to our work, and stay until half-past twelve. At one, or quarter-past one, we return to our work, and stay until seven at night. Then the evening is all our own.

Most early factory workers were women. They came from the farms of New England and were unmarried. Their wages gave their families extra money to pay mortgages or send brothers to school. Some women took factory jobs to save for their weddings, to escape life on the farm, or to live in the city.

To encourage families to send their daughters to Lowell, the mill owners opened dormitories for the women. These were run by matrons (MAY-truhnz), or house mothers. Strict rules of behavior were enforced. Two or three women shared a room, and meals were healthful and filling. The Lowell system was followed by other mill owners throughout New England.

By the mid-1800s, however, factory life was changing. European immigrants were streaming into the U.S. Factory owners saw them as a huge supply of unskilled and cheap labor—cheaper labor than native-born women. Because the immigrants had little choice, they accepted the low pay that factory owners offered. As a result, many native-born women workers were replaced by immigrants, especially

mortgage (MOR-gij): a claim on property in exchange for a loan

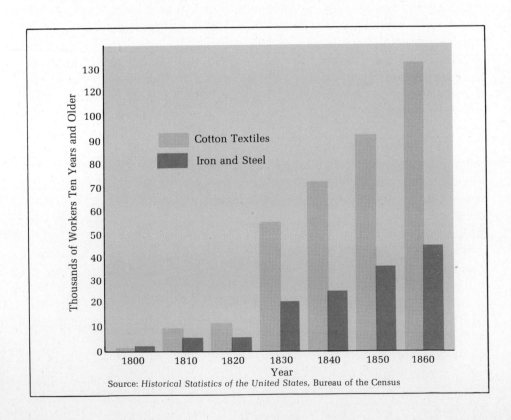

Workers in Selected Manufacturing Industries from 1800 to 1860

Thousands of Workers Ten Years and Older

Cotton Textiles
Iron and Steel

Year

Source: *Historical Statistics of the United States*, Bureau of the Census

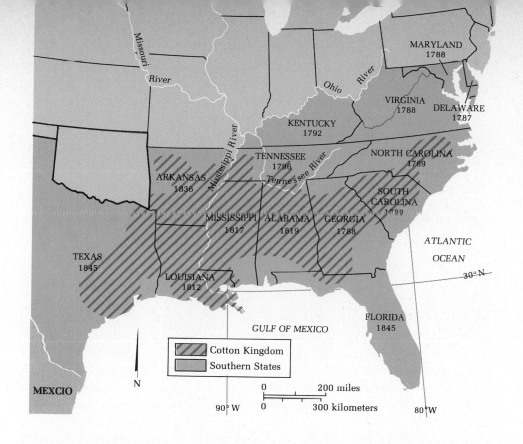

The Cotton Kingdom

Irish immigrants. Even Lowell changed. In the 1830s, the mill owners began to demand more and more work from each woman. Instead of running one loom, they had to run two or three. Instead of raising wages, the owners cut them whenever the demand for goods declined. This happened, for example, after the Panic of 1837. Because the owners were so interested in profits, life in the company-owned dormitories suffered, too. Women were crowded six or eight to a room. After a long day at the mill, supper was often bread and gravy.

In the 1830s and 1840s, the Lowell mill workers went out on strike several times. A **strike** is the refusal to work until an employer agrees to certain worker demands. However, the workers in Lowell were forced back to the mills each time without gaining their demands. The mill owners always threatened to replace the strikers with people eager for work. In 1845, under Sarah G. Bagley, a group of Lowell workers formed the Lowell Female Labor Reform Association. The LFLRA could not organize enough workers, however, and had disappeared by 1847. You will read more about labor unions in the next chapter.

THE COTTON KINGDOM

The southern states were also affected by changes in technology. As you may recall from the unit New Technology, the cotton gin allowed southern planters to grow more cotton. Cotton farming spread from

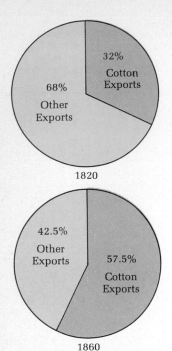

Total United States Exports v. Cotton Exports in 1820 and 1860

Source: *Historical Statistics of the United States*, Bureau of the Census

idle: not working

the states along the Atlantic to the new states along the Mississippi. By the 1840s, the South was known as the Cotton Kingdom.

As the Cotton Kingdom spread, so did slavery. Cotton farming needed great numbers of workers, so slavery became more profitable. From 1808 to 1860, the number of slaves in the U.S. rose from just under one million to almost four million. Although the importing of slaves ended in 1808, a large market in buying and selling slaves within the U.S. developed. Planters, especially in the older southern states, often broke up black families to sell members to planters in the newer states. This caused great suffering and hardship among black families.

Plantations

As they had since colonial days, plantation owners and their families belonged to the highest social class in the South. They also controlled the southern economy and political life. Planters elected men to office, especially to Congress, who supported their interests.

On large plantations, cotton planting was divided into five steps. Each step was done by a different work gang. A gang was made up of 20 to 30 slaves of both sexes and all ages. They were managed by an overseer paid by the planter. At planting time, in January, the different gangs moved through the fields doing their jobs. First, the soil was plowed. Then clumps of dirt were broken up. The ground was made level. Holes were dug, and the seeds were dropped in and covered with dirt. Planting was usually finished by late March.

When it rained or when the planting was done, male field hands cut and hauled wood, fixed fences, and repaired buildings and tools. Female field hands made thread, wove cloth, and sewed clothes for their families. In April, the cotton plants began to appear. The slaves looked after the fields, hoeing and weeding, until the cotton was ready to pick. In August, the work of harvesting began and did not end until around Christmas.

In his book *Twelve Years a Slave*, Solomon Northrup relates his experience as a field hand on a cotton plantation. Northrup, a free black, was kidnapped in 1841 and sold as a slave to a Louisiana planter. He was rescued in 1853.

> The hands are in the cotton fields as soon as it is light in the morning. With the exception of ten or fifteen minutes at noon, they are not permitted to be idle until it is too dark to see. They do not dare to stop, even at dinner time, until the order to halt is given.
>
> The day's work over, the baskets are carried to the gin-house, where the cotton is weighed. No matter how tired, a slave never approaches the gin-house with his basket of cotton but in fear. If it falls short in weight, he knows he will suffer. If it is over by ten or twenty pounds, then the owner will demand the same amount the next day. After weighing, follow the whippings. Then, the baskets are carried to the cotton-house, and the contents stored away.

This done, the labor of the day is not yet ended. The slaves attend to their chores. One feeds the mules, another the pigs and another cuts the wood. At a late hour, the slaves reach their quarters. Then a fire must be built, the corn ground, and supper and also dinner for the next day prepared.

Small Farms and Industry

Only about 50,000 Southerners were planters. However, hundreds of thousands of Southerners owned small farms. They raised food crops, such as corn and wheat, and some livestock. Although some of these farmers owned slaves, many did not. In North Carolina, for example, three fourths of the families owned no slaves at the time of the Civil War.

By the mid-1800s, the South had only about 10 percent of the nation's industry. These factories were not part of the trade network between the different sections of the country, however. They were built to supply local needs only. For example, a flour mill would be built in a town to fill the need for flour of the town and nearby farms. Much of the iron, rope, and lumber used in the South was produced in similar small factories.

Manufacturing in the South lagged behind the Northeast for several reasons. Planters felt that farming was more profitable than manufacturing. As a result, they put most of their money into land and slaves. Because of the lack of industry and lack of a large trade network, southern cities did not grow as quickly as cities in the Northeast, or even in the Midwest, did. By 1860, the South was still a farming area with an economy based mainly on cotton. The South needed only a

The southern economy was based on cotton farming and slave labor. Reread the passage by Solomon Northrup. Does this picture support the reading?

Cincinnati, on the Ohio River, was a prosperous city in 1835 when this watercolor was done. River trade was important to its growth. What other factors led to the growth of midwestern cities?

few large cities, such as New Orleans, Savannah, and Charleston, to handle its cotton trade with the Northeast and Great Britain.

Economics of Slavery

Although slavery was spreading in the mid-1800s, the system created a number of economic problems for the South. First, planters had to provide food, clothing, and shelter for their slaves. Slaves could not be fired during hard times the way free workers could. Because planters invested much of their money in land and slaves, they could not afford to invest in new labor-saving machines, such as mechanical cotton pickers. As a result, planters could not decrease their use of slaves. Slavery became a cycle that seemed to have no end. Yet, while it was costly, slave-run plantations often produced large profits for their owners.

cycle:
a series of events
that repeats

GROWTH OF THE MIDWEST

During the mid-1800s, the Northeast developed close ties with the new states of the Midwest. As you may recall from the unit New Technology, these two regions were joined by a network of canals, roads, and railroads. They were linked economically, too. The Midwest supplied the Northeast with such raw materials as farm products and lumber. Until the Midwest began building its own factories in the 1830s, it bought its manufactured goods from the Northeast.

After the Revolutionary War, the Midwest was a wilderness and considered part of the frontier. Pioneers made trails and cleared small patches of land for farms. Settlers came next. Instead of log cabins, they built permanent homes and farmed larger pieces of land. They also built roads, bridges, and villages.

By the mid-1800s, much of the land in the Midwest had been settled. As you may recall from the unit New Technology, beginning in the early 1800s, the area between the Ohio and Mississippi rivers quickly filled with settlers. These fertile lands attracted people from the worn-out farms of the Northeast, as well as immigrants. By the end of the 1850s, for example, the five states made from the Northwest Territory had a population of almost seven million.

Unlike the South where slave labor was so important, farm families themselves provided the labor on midwestern farms. Large families were common. For one thing, more children meant more workers. In the beginning, midwestern farms were self-sufficient. Farmers raised their own food and made most of their own clothes and tools. Two inventions, the steel plow and the mechanical reaper, changed this. Farmers began to grow cash crops and use the income to buy manufactured goods.

Gradually, villages grew into towns where farmers could sell their crops and buy goods and services. Shopkeepers, merchants, doctors, and so on, moved to the Midwest to open shops and provide services to the growing population. Often the towns grew into cities, especially if they were along railroad lines or major waterways, such as the Great Lakes. Cincinnati; Toledo, Ohio; Cleveland; Detroit; and Milwaukee, among other cities, became important during this time. From these cities, farmers shipped their grain and other food products to states along the Gulf of Mexico and the Northeast. In time, factories appeared. In Chicago, for example, factories were built to make Deere plows and McCormick reapers. Cincinnati, by the 1850s, had become a major center for steamboat building.

LOOKING BACK

1. **a.** What were the major ways people earned their livings in the Northeast? **b.** How did the factory system create jobs for unskilled workers?
2. Use the bar graph Workers in Selected Manufacturing Industries to find the mean number of workers for the years: **a.** 1800. **b.** 1810. **c.** 1820. **d.** 1830. **e.** 1840.
3. **a.** How did the cotton gin affect slavery in the South? **b.** Why did the South remain mainly a farming region?
4. Use the pie graph on page 390 to answer the following. What percent of total U.S. exports was cotton in: **a.** 1820? **b.** 1860? **c.** From this graph, what could you say about cotton's importance to the U.S. economy before the Civil War?
5. How was the growth of the Midwest affected by: **a.** the invention of better farm machinery? **b.** the location of cities along railroads or major waterways?

Chapter 3   A Changing Society

LOOKING AHEAD

This chapter is about the changes that were taking place in American society during the early and mid-1800s. Groups formed to improve working conditions, work for woman's rights, fight abuse of alcohol, provide free public education, and help the disabled. Free blacks, who were prevented from fully taking part in American society, set up their own organizations. After you study this chapter, you will be able to:

- compare and contrast the problems faced by free blacks in the North and in the South.
- explain the rise of labor unions in the early 1800s.
- list rights that were denied women in the early 1800s.
- ★ identify bias toward women's activities in the mid-1800s.
- list and explain other reform movements of the mid-1800s.
- state changes that occurred in free public education in the mid-1800s.

Social Studies Vocabulary

craft union   bias

People

Richard Allen	Pauline Wright	Catherine Beecher
Absalom Jones	Davis	Thomas Gallaudet
Lucretia Mott	Susan B. Anthony	Samuel Gridley
Elizabeth Cady	Robert Owen	Howe
Stanton	Horace Mann	Dorothea Dix
Lucy Stone	Emma Hart Willard	

Places

Oberlin College   Mount Holyoke   University of Iowa

Words and Terms

African Methodist Episcopal Church   Seneca Falls Convention
National Trades Union   temperance movement
    utopian community

OWL   O

This illustration is from a children's picture book of ABCs, printed around 1850.

In the early and mid-1800s, Americans in greater numbers were interested in reforming what they saw as the evils of American life. Many joined reform movements. Some people felt society could not be changed so they chose to live away from it. Free blacks, however, seemed to have little choice. They had to make their living in American society, but the interest in freedom and equality did not reach to them. Because they were prevented from fully participating in society, free blacks began building their own organizations. There was also a movement for abolition of slavery during these years. You will read about it in the unit Coming of the Civil War.

FREE BLACKS

One change in American society during the early to mid-1800s was an increase in the number of free blacks. Their numbers rose from about 59,500 to 488,000 during the first 70 years of the nation. There were several reasons for this. During and after the Revolutionary War, most northern states passed laws that gradually freed slaves. In addition, some slaveowners set their slaves free as a reward for service. A few owners allowed slaves to buy their freedom. As you may recall from the unit Life in Colonial America, owners often rented their slaves to others. Some owners let their slaves keep part of the money they made and save it to buy their freedom. Also, some blacks gained their freedom by running away.

Free blacks faced many of the same problems as slaves. In the South, laws prevented free blacks from moving within a state or from one state to another. Except for a short time in North Carolina and Tennessee, free blacks could not vote. They could not serve on juries or testify in court. At any time, free blacks could be stopped and asked for proof of their freedom. If found without it, a free black could be claimed as a slave.

The treatment of free blacks in the North was not much better. In most northern states, they could not vote, serve on juries, or hold

Mrs. Juliann Jane Tillman preached in the African Methodist Episcopal Church in Philadelphia in the 1840s. What purposes did black churches serve?

conduct (KAHN-dukt):
behavior

public office. Before free blacks could settle in some northern states, they had to give $500 as a guarantee of good conduct. In towns and cities, free blacks were forced to live in areas apart from whites. Churches, schools, hospitals, restaurants, theaters, concert halls, steamboats, and trains either had separate sections for blacks or did not allow them at all. Because so many restrictions were placed on free blacks, they established their own organizations. The most important was the black church. Black churches grew rapidly in the North before the Civil War.

The idea began one Sunday morning in 1787 in Philadelphia. White church officials pulled Richard Allen and two other blacks from pews at the front of the church. They were told to go to the section for blacks. Instead, the three walked out. As a result of their treatment, Allen and Absalom (AB-suh-luhm) Jones organized the Free African Society that became the Mother Bethel African Methodist Episcopal Church (AME) in 1794. The AME Church spread from Philadelphia to other parts of Pennsylvania and into New Jersey, Delaware, and Maryland. By 1816, the separate churches were joined together with Allen as bishop. Other black churches, such as the African Methodist Episcopal Zion (ZY-uhn) Church, were soon founded. In the South, laws against the gathering of free blacks prevented the growth of black churches until after the Civil War.

Besides serving the spiritual needs of its members, black churches had other purposes. They were the training ground for black leaders. In towns that kept black children from public schools, the churches set up their own schools. Churches helped members find jobs. Picnics and church dinners gave free blacks opportunities to socialize. Some black churches sponsored newspapers. Finally, the church was the place where blacks met to talk about their roles in the antislavery movement and in politics.

socialize
(SOH-shuhl-yz):
to take part
in group activities

LABOR UNIONS

While restrictions kept free blacks from becoming full members of society, some Americans were trying to change society by improving working conditions. Before the industrial revolution, craftworkers needed only a few tools to start their own businesses. They worked in their homes or in small shops. After the industrial revolution, successful craftworkers such as tailors or shoemakers enlarged their shops to employ many others of their craft. As you may recall from the unit New Technology, the wealthy also invested in factories. Factories employed both skilled and unskilled workers. Craftworkers were needed to repair machines or for those jobs that machines could not do.

Since many workers no longer owned their own tools or place of work, they began joining together to protect their rights. As you read in Chapter 2 of this unit, factory workers, such as those in Lowell, joined together temporarily to ask for better working conditions, shorter hours, and better pay. However, the first lasting labor unions

On the left is Lucretia Mott; on the right, Elizabeth Cady Stanton. Why did they call the first woman's rights convention?

were organized among craftworkers in larger shops. To cut costs, employers began dividing skilled workers into teams. In a tailor shop, for example, one team sewed on sleeves and another team attached buttons. Employers also began hiring women and children who worked for one fourth or one half the wages of men.

The first craft unions appeared as early as the 1790s. A **craft union** is an organization of skilled workers who work at the same job. These early unions fought against the division of labor and the hiring of cheap labor. Membership was limited to white men. The craftworkers would not train women or blacks.

In the 1820s and 1830s, some local craft unions, such as the Journeymen Tailors of New York City, were able to organize many of the craftworkers in their industries. In 1834, the National Trades Union was formed to try to organize all craftworkers across the country, regardless of craft. But the National Trades Union and most local craft unions were destroyed by the Panic of 1837. Local unions reappeared in the 1840s. But not until the 1850s did national craft unions appear once again. Most lasted only a few years.

Employers usually opposed labor unions. Using their money as a tool, they elected legislators who supported their views. For example, in 1847, the New Hampshire legislature passed a law providing for a ten-hour workday. However, the law allowed owners to hire workers for longer workdays if the workers were willing. Most were—if it meant the difference between having a job or not having one.

WOMAN'S RIGHTS

In the early 1800s, women had few rights. Most girls did not attend school beyond the elementary grades. Nor did women enter professions, such as medicine or law. While single women could own property, married women could not. At marriage, they gave to their husbands their right to own property. Mothers had no legal rights to their children. Women could not vote and were unable to hold office. It was considered unladylike for a woman to speak in public or offer prayers in church. Many men held the same beliefs as Orestes (uh-RES-teez) Brownson, the author of the following:

> Extend now to women suffrage and eligibility; give them the political right to vote and be voted for; make it possible for them to enter the arena of political life, to become canvassers in elections and candidates for office, and what remains of family union will soon be dissolved. Woman was created to be a wife and mother; that is her destiny. Her proper place is home, and her proper function is the care of the household, to manage a family, to take care of children, and attend to their early training.

canvasser
(KAN-vuhs-er):
one who asks
for votes

Like men, women took an interest in reform movements of the time. But men set limits to their participation. For example, women could set up chairs for meetings but were not allowed to speak. In 1840, the men who controlled the World Anti-Slavery Convention in London refused to seat Lucretia Mott and other women delegates. At the meeting, Mott met Elizabeth Cady Stanton. Angered by the men's action, the two women pledged to work for woman's rights.

In July 1848 at Seneca Falls, New York, Mott and Stanton led the first woman's rights convention. Delegates to this convention adopted a resolution modeled after the Declaration of Independence. In this resolution, the women asked for all their rights as U.S. citizens, including the right to vote. The resolution ended with the statement: "We insist that they [women] have immediate admission to the rights and privileges which belong to them as citizens of the United States."

Another important woman's rights meeting was held at Worcester, Massachusetts, in 1850. Led by Lucy Stone and Pauline Wright Davis, this was the first national meeting on equal rights for women. It was open to both men and women.

Other important leaders in the woman's rights movement were Sojourner Truth and Susan B. Anthony. Truth was also active in the antislavery movement. Anthony believed that women should be able to support themselves. She fought for more women teachers—one of the few jobs open to educated women—and equal pay for them with men teachers.

 BUILDING READING SKILLS

The Brownson reading above is an example of bias. **Bias** is a strong feeling for or against a person or thing without any facts to support the feeling. Bias is based on opinion. A biased person usually refuses to accept any facts that conflict with his or her opinion. The author of this reading believes that all women have only one role in life. **1.** Does the author give facts to support this belief? **2.** What is the author's view of woman's suffrage? **3.** Is this an example of bias? **4.** Why or why not? **5.** If it is not bias, what facts does the author give to support his view? **6.** If it is bias, what kind of facts would the author have to give to support his view?

398

TEMPERANCE

In the early 1800s, drinking and drunkenness were becoming serious problems. Many people blamed the increase in poverty, crime, accidents, and mental illness on heavy drinking. A temperance movement began. Temperance (TEM-puhr-uhns) means moderation in one's habits, actions, and so on. Reformers organized temperance societies to fight heavy drinking. At their meetings, temperance reformers gave emotional speeches and sang anti-drinking songs. The reformers also flooded the country with literature describing the harmful effects of alcohol. The movement continued to grow after the Civil War. You will read more about it in the unit Industrialism and the West.

UTOPIAN COMMUNITIES

Some Americans of the early 1800s were not satisfied with reforming only a part of society. They thought it should be completely reformed. To show that this could be done, these people built their own communities apart from society. These utopian communities, as they were called, reached their peak in the 1840s. Utopian (yoo-TOH-pee-uhn) means a perfect social or political system.

Most utopian communities were small, and members supported themselves by running their own businesses. The Amana (uh-MAN-uh) Society in Iowa, for example, built seven communities that farmed and made woolen goods, especially blankets. One of the most famous communities was New Harmony in Indiana. It was founded in 1825 by Robert Owen who had been a factory owner in Scotland. He believed that people could build a perfect society based on farming and manufacturing. New Harmony failed because some members refused to work and others disliked Owen's ideas about religion.

A mid-1800s class recites for the teacher. What were Horace Mann's contributions to public education?

All the utopian communities of the 1800s failed for various reasons. But they are important because they show that Americans were interested in improving society and were prepared to take the responsibility to make those improvements.

CHANGES IN EDUCATION

As you may recall from the unit Life in Colonial America, some colonies started public schools for their children. But in other colonies, such as New Netherland, schools were set up and run by religious groups. However, education was not widespread in the 1700s. Before the 1830s, elementary schools were found mainly in New England. In 1832, New York City established free public elementary schools. Two years later, Pennsylvania passed a law that divided the state into 1,000 school districts. Each was to set up a school system. In 1837, Massachusetts established a board of education to supervise its schools. The first secretary for education in Massachusetts was Horace Mann.

Mann, who was a lawyer and a politician, believed that in a democracy everyone should receive an education. He felt that schools should prepare people to take part in community life and in politics. To improve education, Mann organized local school districts into a statewide system. He also set up schools for teacher training, lengthened the school year, and raised teachers' salaries. By 1850, through

Mann's efforts and those of other educational reformers, public education had become part of life in the Northeast.

In the South, free public education did not begin until the 1850s. For the most part, southerners still lived in widely scattered settlements as they had in colonial days. Sending children to school was difficult. In the Midwest, because of the Northwest Ordinance, each township set aside land for a school. As a result, free public education grew quickly.

Education for women above elementary school, however, grew slowly. In the 1820s, Emma Hart Willard and Catherine Beecher began schools for women called female seminaries. These were like high schools. In 1833, Oberlin College in Ohio became the first college to admit women. In 1837, Mary Lyons opened Mount Holyoke in Massachusetts. It was the first college founded only for women. In 1856, the University of Iowa became the first state university to admit women.

OTHER REFORMERS

Reformers also took up the cause of disabled people. In 1817 at Hartford, Connecticut, Thomas Gallaudet (gal-uh-DET) established the first school for the deaf. Samuel Gridley Howe in 1832 opened a school for the blind in Boston.

Dorothea Dix worked to improve the treatment of the mentally ill. At that time, mentally ill people were not treated for their illnesses. They were shut off from society in prisons, jails, and poorhouses. After Dix visited these places in Massachusetts, she reported her findings to the state legislature. Dix asked the legislators for laws to protect and help the mentally ill. During the 1840s, she carried her reform work across the country. Through her efforts, hospitals for the mentally ill were set up in 15 states.

LOOKING BACK

1. What problems did free blacks face in the: **a.** North? **b.** South? **c.** Were the problems the same or different?
2. **a.** Why did craftworkers form unions? **b.** How did the Panic of 1837 affect craft unions? **c.** How did factory owners oppose labor unions?
3. What rights were denied women in the early 1800s?
4. List two examples of bias in the reading on page 398.
5. What changes occurred in free public education in the early 1800s?
6. Describe the purpose of each of the following: **a.** temperance movement. **b.** utopian communities. **c.** the work of Gallaudet. **d.** the work of Howe. **e.** the work of Dix.

Chapter 4

An Emerging Culture

LOOKING AHEAD

This chapter is about the cultural life of the new nation. It describes the development of American themes and styles in literature, painting, theater, and music of the early to mid-1800s. It also discusses science, higher education, and leisure activities in the U.S. during this time. After you study this chapter, you will be able to:

- explain how romanticism influenced American literature.
- describe the rise of American newspapers.
- explain the effect of romanticism on American painting.
- identify advances that took place in science.
- state a change that took place in higher education.
- identify two influences on theater and music of the period.
- identify two leisure activities of these decades.

Social Studies Vocabulary

folk song

People

Henry David Thoreau	John Trumbull
Ralph Waldo Emerson	Gilbert Stuart
Nathaniel Hawthorne	Charles Wilson Peale
Edgar Allan Poe	Sarah Peale
Washington Irving	Joshua Johnston
James Fenimore Cooper	Thomas Cole
James Russell Lowell	Asher B. Durand
Henry Wadsworth Longfellow	Robert S. Duncanson
Walt Whitman	John James Audubon
Angelina Grimke	George Caleb Bingham
Sarah Grimke	George Catlin
Elizabeth Cady Stanton	Benjamin Rush
Lydia Child	Benjamin Banneker
Frances Harper	Maria Mitchell
Frederick Douglass	Royall Tyler
Solomon Northrup	Stephen Foster
Sojourner Truth	

Places

Smithsonian Institution

Words and Terms

romanticism	penny dailies	spiritual
Knickerbocker school	Hudson River school	

This portrait of a father and son was painted in 1810 by Joshua Johnston. Have the clothes changed very much since the 1700s when the Beardsleys were painted? See page 176.

In this painting, Thomas Cole portrays a scene from *The Last of the Mohicans*. In the novel, James Fenimore Cooper wrote sympathetically of Native Americans and the American wilderness.

As you may recall from the unit Life in Colonial America, colonists in the 1600s and early 1700s copied much from European culture. By the early 1800s, however, Americans were creating their own culture. They were becoming wealthier and, as a result, had more free time for the arts, education, and entertainment. More Americans were able to afford the works of professional writers and artists. Folk art continued, however, especially in frontier regions where craftworkers could still make a living. With increasing numbers of people receiving an education, interest in science grew.

LITERATURE

As you may recall from the unit Life in Colonial America, much of colonial literature was in the form of diaries, journals, and histories. These continued to be the major forms of writing in the early years of the new nation. But in the 1800s, novels, short stories, essays, and poems became popular.

essay (ES-ay): a short composition

Two well known authors were Henry David Thoreau (THOR-oh) and Ralph Waldo Emerson. Both believed in living a simple life, close to nature, in order to appreciate life fully. *Walden*, Thoreau's best known book, was published in 1850. It tells of his experiences and thoughts while living in a cabin on Walden Pond near Boston. In his essays and poems, Emerson wrote about self-sufficiency and about people fighting for their beliefs.

One idea that greatly influenced the literature as well as the painting of the early to mid-1800s was romanticism (roh-MAN-tuh-siz-uhm). Romantic artists disliked the world of factories and cities. To escape, the romantics turned for themes to faraway places, the past, legends, nature, and the ordinary citizen. Romantics were also drawn to supernatural subjects. Some romantics wrote stories filled with violence and supernatural happenings. Novels of this type include *The Scarlet Letter* and *The House of the Seven Gables* by Nathaniel

supernatural: beyond or above natural things

403

What might this reader of the early 1800s expect to find in his newspaper? How had newspapers changed by the mid-1800s?

Hawthorne. Edgar Allan Poe used similar themes in such short stories as "The Fall of the House of Usher."

A group of writers living in and near New York City in the first half of the 1800s became known as the Knickerbocker (NIK-er-bahk-er) school. They wrote about America and Americans. Among the group were Washington Irving and James Fenimore Cooper. Irving wrote a number of short stories, including "The Legend of Sleepy Hollow" and "Rip Van Winkle." Cooper wrote about Native Americans and early settlers in such works as *The Leatherstocking Tales*.

American poets of the early and mid-1800s include James Russell Lowell, Henry Wadsworth Longfellow, and Walt Whitman. Lowell's poems were political or antislavery in theme. Longfellow used historical events and legends as topics for his poems. Whitman shared many of Emerson's beliefs in self-sufficiency and the rights of the individual. *Leaves of Grass*, published in 1855, is about American pioneers and the bright future that Whitman saw for the nation.

Literature by women and blacks found an audience among some Americans. Women found readers in the newspapers and pamphlets of antislavery, temperance, and woman's rights groups. Angelina and Sarah Grimke penned attacks on slavery while Elizabeth Cady Stanton wrote in favor of temperance and woman's rights. Lydia Child wrote one of the first antislavery books *An Appeal in Favor of that Class of Americans Called Africans*.

In the early 1800s, blacks also found readers. Frances Harper is considered the most famous black poet after Phillis Wheatley. Many of her poems were directed against slavery. An important body of black works grew from the stories of former slaves. Among these were the experiences of Frederick Douglass, Solomon Northrup, and Sojourner Truth. Historians find these important sources of information about slavery.

NEWSPAPERS

emphasis (EM-fuh-sis): special force; importance

In the first years of the new nation, people began newspapers to support one political party or another. For example, the New York *Evening Post* was begun to support Hamilton and the Richmond, Virginia, *Enquirer*, to back Jefferson. The Age of Democracy saw the rise of even more political newspapers. The abolitionist and temperance movements had their own papers, too. The emphasis in these papers was on news of interest to the movement.

With new technology, newspapers became easier and cheaper to print. They began selling for a penny a copy and were called penny dailies because they were printed each day. The first successful penny daily was the New York *Sun*, which appeared in 1833. It covered horse races and prize fights but little other news. By the mid-1800s, newspapers had many of the same features they have today, except for photographs. Drawings were used instead. Photographs in newspapers would have to wait for another series of inventions.

A class in astronomy meets at Vassar College, in the late 1880s. The professor, Maria Mitchell is standing next to the telescope. How did she further scientific knowledge?

PAINTING

Professional painting during the late 1700s and early 1800s was similar in themes and style to painting during the later colonial period. In time, new themes were added — scenes from the Bible, myths, and ancient history. John Trumbull, Gilbert Stuart, and Charles Wilson Peale were famous American painters of the period. Trumbull painted Revolutionary War battles. Stuart and Peale were chiefly portrait painters who painted such heroes as Washington and John Paul Jones. Sarah Peale, sister of Charles, was the first successful American woman artist. Like Charles, she was a portrait painter. Joshua Johnston, or Johnson, was another popular portrait painter. It is not known where Johnston, a former slave, received his training. Some art historians think he was trained by Charles Wilson Peale. Johnston painted portraits of wealthy merchants.

In the mid-1800s, American artists, like American writers, were influenced by romanticism. Artists turned to nature. Thomas Cole was the most famous artist of the Hudson River school of landscape painters. The group was so named because of the many artists who painted in the romantic style in New York and northern New England. Other members of the Hudson River school were Asher B. Durand and Robert S. Duncanson.

Other artists of the mid-1800s, while not considered romantics, painted scenes from nature. John James Audubon (AW-duh-bahn) was one of the first to study and paint American birds. George Caleb Bingham and George Catlin painted scenes of the frontier. Catlin is especially known for his paintings of Native Americans.

SCIENCE

By the late 1700s, more people were making scientific research and experimentation their careers. This was one result of the new emphasis on practical knowledge in colleges and universities. Dr. Benjamin

Top: *Fur Traders Descending the Missouri* was painted by George Caleb Bingham in 1845. What can you learn about frontier life at mid-century from this picture?

Left: George Catlin painted the Mandan leader Mah-to-pa, *Four Bears,* in 1865. Could this be considered a primary source?

Right: *Blazing Tree* was painted by Hannah Cohoon, an untrained artist, after she saw it in a dream. Why is this folk art?

Top left: Sarah Peale painted *Still Life with Watermelon* in 1820. A still life pictures objects, usually household items, not people.

Top right: Shakers—a religious group—produced plain, sturdy furniture such as this. What generalizations can you make about the Shakers' life-style from the objects shown in this photograph?

Bottom: How do you know Robert Duncanson's midwestern landscape, *Blue Hole, Little Miami River,* is a romantic work?

dispensary
(dis-PEN-suh-ree):
place that gives
free or low-cost
health care

Rush, who taught medicine at the University of Pennsylvania, set up the first medical dispensary in the U.S. in 1786.

Accomplishments were made in other areas of science, too. In 1791, Benjamin Banneker was one of those who surveyed the boundaries of the District of Columbia. Banneker, a black astronomer and mathematician, published an almanac from 1791 to 1796. In it, he charted the movement of stars and planets, listed the tides, and made weather predictions. This information was useful to farmers and sailors. In the early 1800s, Joseph Henry experimented with electricity. He invented the electromagnet that later made it possible to use electricity for power and light in industry. Other people were working in such fields as astronomy. In 1847, Maria Mitchell discovered the comet that bears her name. She taught at the Vassar Female College.

One event that greatly helped scientific research in the U.S. was the opening of the Smithsonian Institution. In 1829, James Smithson donated money to the new nation to be used to spread scientific knowledge. Congress accepted the money but debated for ten years how it should be spent. Finally, in 1846, Congress established the Smithsonian Institution, the first institution for scientific research in the Americas.

HIGHER EDUCATION

Between the late 1700s and the mid-1800s, many colleges added schools of law, medicine, and science. Religious groups continued to found colleges as they had in colonial days. The first Roman Catholic college in the U.S., Georgetown, was founded in 1789 in what is now Washington, D.C. Nonreligious colleges and universities were also established. The University of North Carolina, founded in 1789, was the first university set up by a state. Rensselaer Polytechnic (ren-suh-LEER pahl-ee-TEK-nik) Institute opened in Troy, New York, in 1824 and provided a course of study in engineering and technology.

THEATER AND MUSIC

As you may recall from the unit The New Nation, the population of the U.S. grew rapidly after the Revolutionary War. More people were living in towns and cities and, as a result, cities were able to support more entertainment. Many theaters and music halls were built. In 1787, the first American comedy, *The Contrast*, written by Royall Tyler, was produced in New York. It poked fun at royalty by contrasting the royal way of life with the life of the ordinary American.

In music, the late 1700s and early 1800s showed growing American nationalism. "Hail Columbia," composed in 1798, was inspired by the undeclared naval war with France. As you may recall from the unit The New Nation, the "Star-Spangled Banner" was written during

the War of 1812. It did not become the national anthem until 1931. In 1831, the song "America" was written to the music of the British "God Save the King."

Among many Americans, folk songs became popular. A **folk song** is a song passed down from generation to generation. Stephen Foster, born in Pennsylvania, wrote nearly 200 songs, many of which were based on black folk songs. Many of his compositions tell of unhappiness and poverty. Two of his more popular are "Oh! Susanna," sung by forty-niners working on their gold claims, and "Old Folks at Home." You will read more about the forty-niners in the next unit.

Blacks created two types of folk songs—spirituals and work songs. Spirituals had religious themes and were sung to make life more bearable. The regular beat of work songs helped the members of the work gangs work together. There was a song for almost every job, for example, songs for picking cotton and others for chopping wood. Slaves expressed much of their resentment against slavery in their work songs and spirituals.

LEISURE ACTIVITIES

Increased wealth and more free time encouraged the growth of leisure activities in the mid-1800s. Baseball, much as we know it today, developed around the 1830s or 1840s. Many people wrongly credit Abner Doubleday with the invention of the game. However, baseball developed from an English game called rounders. Rounders involved hitting a ball and then running around bases. New England colonists played rounders in the early 1700s. Football, in one form or another, was popular among male college students by the mid-1800s. The ball was usually a bag filled with sawdust. Golf was popular in the northeastern part of the U.S.

Among the many leisure activities that Americans participated in during the 1800s was baseball. From what game did it develop? What other sports did Americans play?

In rural areas, building a house or barn was the occasion for a social gathering, as it had been in colonial times. Camp meetings also became times for socializing. People came to hear rousing sermons, sing, pray, and meet their neighbors. In the cities, attending lectures, swimming in public baths, and exercising in gyms were becoming popular pastimes.

Of all leisure activities, dancing was the most popular everywhere. New dance steps were introduced in the cities and spread into the country. Newer city hotels had dance floors and orchestras for their customers' entertainment. The polka (POHL-kuh) and the waltz were popular in the mid-1800s.

LOOKING BACK

1. **a.** How did the romantic authors try to escape from the world of factories and cities? **b.** What themes did the Knickerbocker school use?

2. What sequence of events in American society gave rise to American newspapers?

3. **a.** What changes took place in American painting from colonial days to the mid-1800s? **b.** What themes did the Hudson River school use? **c.** What are the themes of the paintings on pages 406–407?

4. **a.** Identify three scientific accomplishments made in the U.S. during the late 1700s and early 1800s. **b.** Why was the founding of the Smithsonian Institution important?

5. What change took place in higher education between the late 1700s and the mid-1800s?

6. **a.** Why were more theaters and music halls built in the late 1700s to mid-1800s? **b.** What influenced music during these same years?

7. **a.** What were two popular leisure activities of the period? **b.** Why were Americans able to develop many leisure activities in these years?

PRACTICING YOUR SKILLS

What If . . . In Chapter 1, you read how economic and political conditions in Europe during the early 1800s forced many to leave their homelands. **What if** conditions in Europe had been better and people had stayed? How might the labor supply in the U.S. have been affected? How might this have affected industrial development and territorial expansion? How might wages and working conditions in the U.S. have been changed?

Building Communication Skills

Before giving an oral report or speech, review paraphrasing, summarizing, and outlining. The following tips will help you give an informative and interesting talk.
- Read about and take notes on the topic you will present.
- Organize your notes into an outline.
- Write your outline on note cards. Do not read from the note cards or memorize them. Glance at them from time to time as you speak.
- Make your introduction interesting so you will get your audience's attention.
- Practice your speech in front of your family or friends.
- Look at your audience and speak in a normal, relaxed tone. Smile.
- Speak clearly and loudly. Avoid *you know, um, er, like,* and so on.
- If you are using visual aids, such as posters, be sure they can be read from the back of the room. When you practice your talk, practice using the visual aids, too.
- End your report or speech by pausing and then saying *thank you.*

Activity: In Chapter 4, you read about some forms of entertainment popular in the U.S. in the 1800s. Imagine that you are an historian living 100 years from now. Prepare a brief oral report on modern American entertainment.

Researching, Writing, Graphing

1. Europeans were attracted to the U.S. in the early 1800s because jobs were plentiful and the U.S. enjoyed a higher standard of living. Using reference materials, compare the standard of living in the U.S. for the last five years. Has it increased or declined? For each of the last five years, how does the U.S. compare with other countries in the top five? What changes were there? When?
2. In Chapter 2 of this unit, you read how the economies of the different parts of the country developed differently. Because of these differences, members of Congress from these sections voted differently on issues. In a short paragraph, describe what you think representatives from the Northeast, South, and Midwest might have thought about giving bank loans to new industry.

Exploring

In Chapter 1, you read that some of our ancestors came from Europe. Along with their belongings, our ancestors brought many customs with them. Whether your ancestors came from Europe or elsewhere, write a paragraph about a custom that has been passed down in your family. Or choose a custom you find interesting from another culture and write a paragraph about it.

Reading

Barton, H. Arnold, ed. *Letters from the Promised Land: Swedes in America, 1840–1914.* Minneapolis: University of Minnesota Press, 1975.

Erickson, Charlotte. *Invisible Immigrants: The Adaption of English and Scotch Immigrants in Nineteenth-Century America.* Miami: University of Miami Press, 1972.

Fisher, Leonard Everett. *The Factories.* New York: Holiday, 1979. New England.

Hymowitz, Carol, and Michaele Weissman. *A History of Women in America.* New York: Bantam, 1978. Paperback.

Murphy, Eugene, and Timothy Driscoll. *An Album of the Irish Americans.* New York: Watts, 1974. From the Revolution to the present.

Myron, Robert, and Abner Sundell. *Art in America: From Colonial Days Through the Nineteenth Century.* New York: Macmillan, 1973.

Rippley, LaVerne J. *The German-Americans.* Boston: Twayne, 1976.

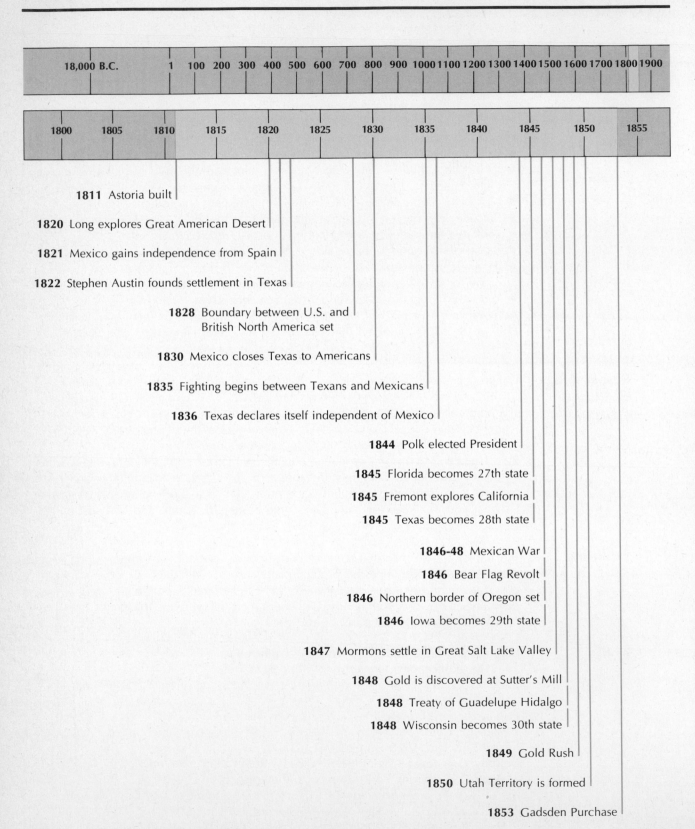

| 18,000 B.C. | 1 | 100 | 200 | 300 | 400 | 500 | 600 | 700 | 800 | 900 | 1000 | 1100 | 1200 | 1300 | 1400 | 1500 | 1600 | 1700 | 1800 | 1900 |

| 1800 | 1805 | 1810 | 1815 | 1820 | 1825 | 1830 | 1835 | 1840 | 1845 | 1850 | 1855 |

1811 Astoria built

1820 Long explores Great American Desert

1821 Mexico gains independence from Spain

1822 Stephen Austin founds settlement in Texas

1828 Boundary between U.S. and British North America set

1830 Mexico closes Texas to Americans

1835 Fighting begins between Texans and Mexicans

1836 Texas declares itself independent of Mexico

1844 Polk elected President

1845 Florida becomes 27th state

1845 Fremont explores California

1845 Texas becomes 28th state

1846-48 Mexican War

1846 Bear Flag Revolt

1846 Northern border of Oregon set

1846 Iowa becomes 29th state

1847 Mormons settle in Great Salt Lake Valley

1848 Gold is discovered at Sutter's Mill

1848 Treaty of Guadelupe Hidalgo

1848 Wisconsin becomes 30th state

1849 Gold Rush

1850 Utah Territory is formed

1853 Gadsden Purchase

Chapter 1   The Southwest

LOOKING AHEAD

This chapter describes the changing frontier and American interest in Mexican land. You will read how that interest led to war with Mexico and the addition of large parts of Mexican territory to the U.S. After you study this chapter, you will be able to:

- pick out the assumption in the idea of manifest destiny.
- read a map to explain how settlers traveled west.
- identify the reasons for U.S. interest in Mexican borderlands.
- explain the sequence of events that made Texas a state.
- state the causes of the Mexican War.
- describe the importance of the Mexican Cession and the Gadsden Purchase to U.S. expansion.
- read a map to explain how U.S. territory expanded.

Social Studies Vocabulary

manifest destiny	dictatorship	negotiate
expansionism	annexation	

People

Moses Austin	Comanche	Stephen Kearney
Stephen Austin	Kiowa	John C. Fremont
Santa Anna	Apache	Winfield Scott
Sam Houston	James K. Polk	
Karankawa	Zachary Taylor	

Places

Santa Fe Trail	The Alamo	Monterrey, Mexico
Old Spanish Trail	Rio Grande	Veracruz
Texas	Nueces River	Mexico City

Words and Terms

Southwest	Treaty of Guadalupe	Gadsden Purchase
Battle of San Jacinto	Hidalgo	
Republic of Texas	Mexican Cession	

Economically, the 1840s were a good time for the U.S. As you read in the unit New Technology, factories, inventions, railroads, and canals were changing the U.S. and its economy. New methods in industry were turning out more goods and services. New means of transportation were uniting farmers and manufacturers with new markets. Immigrants were streaming into the U.S. from Europe. Much of the land east of the Mississippi had been settled. Along with immigrants and

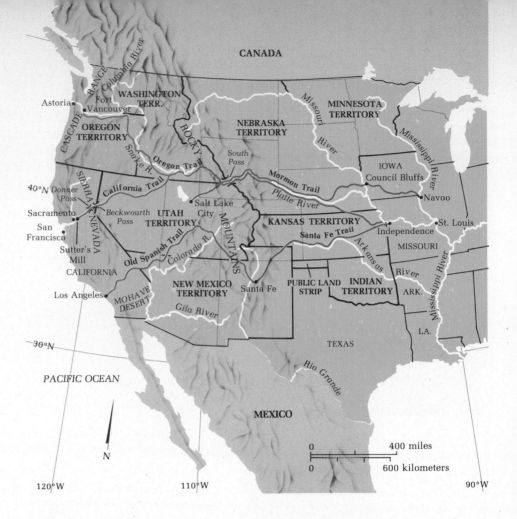

Trails West

Easterners who wanted to move, some of the settlers near the Mississippi wanted to go farther west.

In 1845, the editor of the *New York Morning News* said the U.S. had a "manifest destiny to overspread the continent allotted by Providence...." **Manifest destiny** (MAN-uh-fest DES-tuh-nee) was the belief of Americans of the mid-1800s that they had the right to expand across the continent. This belief in the idea of increasing a country's territory is also called **expansionism** (eks-PAN-shuhn-iz-uhm). Before the end of the 1840s, Americans would be using the term *manifest destiny* as an excuse for their expansion into the Southwest — the present states of Arizona, New Mexico, Texas, and Oklahoma — as well as into the Far West — the present states of California, Oregon, and Washington.

allotted
(uh-LAHT-uhd):
given as a share

MEXICAN BORDERLANDS

As you may recall from the unit Colonial Beginnings, New Spain north and west of the Rio Grande was thinly settled. There were some missions, presidios, and a few colonists. Spain kept the region as a barrier to U.S. expansion.

While the Southwest was under Spanish control, Americans had little contact with the area. You may recall from the unit The New Nation that when Zebulon Pike crossed the border into New Mexico, he was captured and sent back to the U.S.

In 1821, these lands became part of Mexico after that country won its independence from Spain. That same year, the first American trader, William Becknell (BEK-nuhl) was allowed to enter Santa Fe. By 1824, a regular trade route, the Santa Fe Trail, had been established between Missouri and Santa Fe. Merchants traveled the 1,260 kilometers (780 miles) from Independence, Missouri, to Santa Fe with pack animals or in Conestoga (kahn-is-TOH-guh) wagons loaded with trade goods. Business was sometimes interrupted by fighting between traders and Native Americans.

Because of the Santa Fe Trail, trade with Americans became very important to the economy of New Mexico. The trail remained a profitable link between the Southwest and U.S. traders until the railroad reached Santa Fe in 1880. An extension of the Santa Fe Trail, the Old Spanish Trail, ran from Santa Fe to Los Angeles in California.

profitable:
giving good results, especially financial gain

AMERICANS IN TEXAS

As early as the 1820s, the Mexican province of what is now Texas began attracting settlers from the U.S. These settlers, mostly from the southern states, found parts of Texas well suited for raising cotton and sugar. In 1820, Moses Austin asked permission of the Spanish in Mexico to build a settlement in East Texas. Austin died shortly after, but in 1821 the newly formed Mexican government gave his son, Stephen, permission. The following year, he led 300 families into the area between the Brazos (BRAZ-uhs) and Colorado rivers.

By 1830, there were about 25,000 Americans and 4,000 Spanish-speaking Mexicans in Texas. Many of the Americans were blacks who

province (PRAHV-uhns): a political division of a country

A trade caravan arrives in Santa Fe in 1844. Where else was trade a factor in the development of a thinly settled area?

415

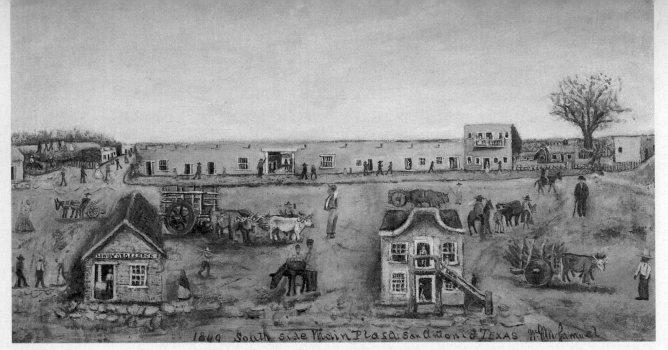

This is a view of the Main Plaza of San Antonio, painted in 1849. What can you learn from this painting about the economy of the area?

had been brought there as slaves to work the cotton and sugar plantations. The Mexican government became concerned that it might lose Texas with so many Americans living there.

In 1830, Mexico refused to allow any more Americans to enter Texas, and it outlawed the importing of slaves. Texans—both Americans and Mexicans living in Texas—protested. Without slaves, they could not work their plantations. The Mexican government sent soldiers to enforce the law and collect customs duties along the Texas-U.S. border. Stephen Austin went to Mexico City in 1833 to ask that the laws against slavery, American immigration, and customs duties be repealed. The government refused. Austin was jailed after he wrote a letter to the people of Texas telling them to form their own government. He was freed in 1835 and returned to Texas to command its army against Mexico.

Revolution and Independence

In 1834, General Antonio Lopez de Santa Anna (SAHN-tah AH-nah) had become President of Mexico. He abolished the Mexican constitution and set up a dictatorship. A **dictatorship** (DIK-tay-ter-ship) is a government system in which one person exercises complete authority. The Texans again asked the Mexican government to consider their requests. But the talks failed. By late 1835, Texans and Mexican soldiers were fighting. The most famous battle was the siege of the Alamo in San Antonio. A force of 182 Texans, under the command of Colonel William B. Travis, died at the Alamo. More than 1,000 Mexican soldiers were killed.

In March 1836, about 60 American and Mexican Texans met and declared the Republic of Texas. They formed a government similar to that of the U.S., with a president, congress, and a supreme court.

Although slaves had fought for Texas's independence, the new government did not give them their freedom. In April, an army led by Sam Houston defeated a Mexican army at the San Jacinto (san juh-SIN-toh) River and captured Santa Anna. Santa Anna signed a treaty recognizing Texas's independence.

After the Battle of San Jacinto, the Texans elected Sam Houston President. They also approved a constitution and sent a representative to the U.S. to ask for annexation. **Annexation** (an-ek-SAY-shuhn) is the addition of territory to a nation. A new government in Mexico replaced Santa Anna and refused to recognize the treaty. However, Mexico was not strong enough to force Texas to return to Mexican rule.

recognize
(REK-uhg-nyz):
to admit

Native Americans and Texans

Many of the Southerners who came to Texas had helped drive Native Americans from the southern U.S. After they arrived in Texas, the Southerners fought Native Americans living there. By the late 1840s, Texans had destroyed most of the Karankawa (kuh-RANG-kuh-waw) and several other nations.

North and west of the Texas settlements, the situation was different. The Comanche, Kiowa (KY-oh-wah), and Apache fiercely resisted. Texans and U.S. soldiers repeatedly fought the Comanche and Kiowa until 1867 when both peoples were moved to the Indian Territory. Fighting with the Apache lasted until the 1870s.

Annexation: A Political Issue

The U.S. government refused the offer to annex Texas. It knew that annexation could mean war with Mexico. American citizens, however, were divided in opinion. Because Texas allowed slavery, those who believed in slavery supported annexation. Those opposed to slavery were against admitting Texas to the Union. Because the U.S. government had refused, Texas withdrew its request in 1838 and prepared to remain an independent nation.

President Tyler, seeking reelection, made the annexation of Texas a major issue in the election of 1844. Tyler knew many voters wanted annexation and he hoped to gain their support. The Whig party, which was antislavery, opposed annexation. It was against adding any territory that might increase the number of slave states. The Whigs turned away from Tyler and nominated Henry Clay. The Democrats nominated James K. Polk who ran on a platform of annexation.

Polk defeated Clay and, in 1845, the U.S. annexed Texas and also received the Public Land Strip, which later became part of Oklahoma. Texas entered the Union as a slave state. Florida was also admitted as a slave state that year. But the free-slave ratio did not remain uneven for long. Iowa was admitted as a free state in 1846 and Wisconsin as a free state in 1848. There were now 15 free and 15 slave states.

MEXICAN WAR: ADVANTAGES AND DISADVANTAGES OF EACH SIDE

	Advantages		Disadvantages	
	Mexico	U.S.	Mexico	U.S.
Military	Had a much larger army			Were outnumbered in every major battle
			Had poorly equipped soldiers and officers	Had trouble getting soldiers and supplies to the right place at the right time
		Had well-trained officers and soldiers	Had poorly trained officers and soldiers	
	Were fighting to defend their homes			Were fighting to gain territory
Political		Had a strong and stable* government	Had a weak and unsteady government	
Economic		Had many factories for supplying troops	Had few factories for supplying troops	
Population	War popular throughout nation			War popular mainly in Mississippi Valley

*stable (STAY-buhl): lasting; steady; unchanging

MEXICAN WAR

In 1845, the Mexican government still claimed Texas. It warned that it would look on annexation as a declaration of war. Some Americans welcomed war as a way to add more land to the U.S. A disagreement over the boundary between Texas and the U.S. gave expansionists their excuse for war.

The U.S. accepted Texas's claim that the Rio Grande formed its southwestern boundary. Mexico claimed the Nueces (nyoo-AY-suhs) River farther north as the true boundary. At that time, General Zachary Taylor and a small U.S. force were camped along the Nueces. In January 1846, Polk ordered them to move to the east bank of the Rio Grande. When Taylor sent out a scouting party, it was attacked by Mexican soldiers who had crossed the river.

Giving in to the rising war fever, Polk sent a war message to Congress. He claimed that Mexico had crossed the U.S. border and shed American blood on American soil. On May 12, 1846, Congress declared war on Mexico.

Fighting the War

There were three major campaigns of the war: Northern Mexico; New Mexico and California; and Mexico City. In northern Mexico, General Taylor pushed the Mexicans south and west of the Rio Grande. He took the Mexican town of Monterrey (mahn-tuh-RAY) and turned to Veracruz (ver-uh-KROOZ). On the way, Taylor's army met Santa Anna at Buena Vista (BWAY-nah VEES-tah). In a fierce battle that lasted two days, the U.S. won its biggest victory of the war.

In the second campaign, Colonel Stephen Kearny (KARH-nee) marched to Santa Fe and claimed New Mexico without losing a soldier. Kearny then turned westward but learned that California was already in American hands. Captain John C. Fremont had raised the American flag from Sonoma (soh-NOH-muh) to San Diego without opposition.

The Americans directed their final campaign against Mexico City. In March 1847, General Winfield Scott landed a large army at Veracruz and fought his way to Mexico City. In September, the Americans captured the city. Santa Anna, again the Mexican leader, fled. It was months before a Mexican government was formed to negotiate peace with the Americans. **Negotiate** (nih-GOH-shee-ayt) means to discuss a problem in order to work out a solution.

Results of the War

The Treaty of Guadalupe Hidalgo (gwahd-uh-LOO-pay ee-DAHL-go), which officially ended the war, was signed in February 1848. Under the treaty, Mexico gave up its claims to the land between the Nueces River and the Rio Grande. Mexico also gave up a huge area known as the Mexican Cession. It included parts of the present states of Colorado, Wyoming, New Mexico, and Arizona and all the states of California, Nevada, and Utah. In exchange, the U.S. paid Mexico $15 million. The U.S. also agreed to settle American claims against Mexico that came to $3.5 million.

GADSDEN PURCHASE

More land was added to the U.S. in 1853. In that year, James Gadsden (GADS-duhn), the U.S. minister to Mexico, arranged the purchase of a strip of land south of the Gila (HEE-luh) River for $10 million. This is known as the Gadsden Purchase. The U.S. wanted this land for a transcontinental railroad. Without it, the railroad would have to be built across the Rocky Mountains. With the addition of the Mexican

transcontinental: across the continent; from coast to coast

The Mexican War

After defeating the Mexicans on his march from Veracruz, General Winfield Scott and his army rode into Mexico City. It was the last campaign of the war. Note the American flag flying over the city. Artist Carl Nebel illustrated the capture for a history of the war written by George Kendall, a war correspondent. Is Nebel's painting a primary or secondary source? Which is Kendall's book?

Top: Stephen Kearny's troops are shown passing through the New Mexico Territory. Where were they headed?

Right: American soldiers cross the Rio Grande. Judging from these pictures, what kinds of problems might the surrounding country have created for the army?

Left: Nebel also illustrated the Battle of Buena Vista. Soldiers at this time marched out in columns, faced each other within range, and fired. As the first row fell, the next took its place. Where are the Americans' fresh troops and supplies located?

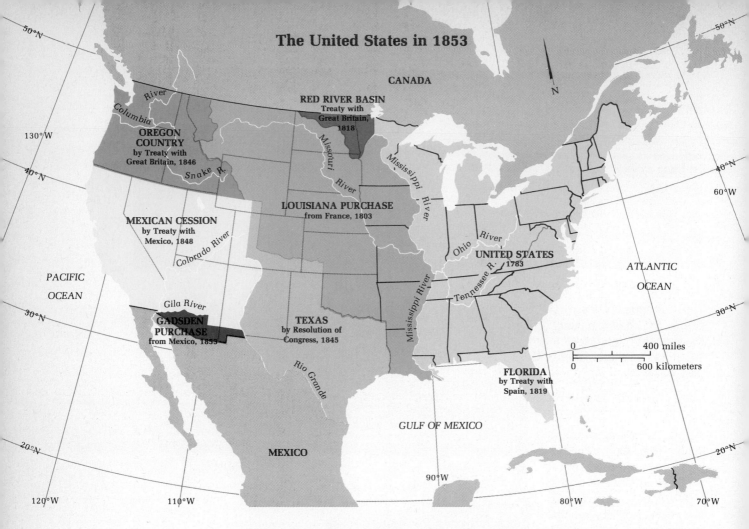

The United States in 1853

CANADA

RED RIVER BASIN
Treaty with
Great Britain,
1818

River

Columbia

OREGON
COUNTRY
by Treaty with
Great Britain, 1846

Snake R.

Missouri River

Mississippi River

MEXICAN CESSION
by Treaty with
Mexico, 1848

Colorado River

LOUISIANA PURCHASE
from France, 1803

Ohio River

UNITED STATES
1783

Tennessee R.

Mississippi River

ATLANTIC
OCEAN

130°W
50°N

40°N

30°N

PACIFIC
OCEAN

Gila River

GADSDEN
PURCHASE
from Mexico, 1853

TEXAS
by Resolution of
Congress, 1845

Rio Grande

FLORIDA
by Treaty with
Spain, 1819

0   400 miles
0   600 kilometers

MEXICO

GULF OF MEXICO

90°W

120°W   110°W   80°W   70°W

20°N

60°W

N

Cession and the Gadsden Purchase, about 1,440,000 square kilometers (about 556,000 square miles) were added to the U.S. This additional land set off a new westward movement and reopened the slavery issue. It also brought problems to the Mexicans living in the area.

LOOKING BACK

1. On what assumption is the idea of manifest destiny based?
2. Use the map on p. 414 to answer: **a.** What physical feature did many trails follow?   **b.** Where did travelers cross the mountains?   **c.** In what present-day states did each Trail end in?
3. Why were Americans interested in Mexican borderlands?
4. **a.** Why were Americans attracted to Texas?   **b.** What problems did Americans in Texas face?   **c.** What were the results of the Texans' war for independence?   **d.** How did annexation of Texas become a political issue in the U.S.?
5. State two causes of the Mexican War.
6. What area did the U.S. receive as a result of the Mexican Cession?   **b.** Why was the Gadsden Purchase important?
7. Use the map on p. 422 to explain how the U.S. acquired the lands west of the Mississippi.

Chapter 2   Beyond the Rockies

LOOKING AHEAD

This chapter is about U.S. expansion beyond the Rocky Mountains in the mid-1800s. You will read about the addition of Oregon and California to the U.S., as well as Mormon settlement in what is now the state of Utah. After you study this chapter, you will be able to:

- identify the bases of British and U.S. claims to Oregon.
- ★ explain the methods used to attract people to Oregon.
- describe what happened to the Native Americans as a result of U.S. expansion into Oregon.
- explain Polk's plan for adding Oregon to the U.S.
- describe U.S. annexation of California.
- explain the effect of the gold rush on California.
- identify the sequence of events and people important to the settlement of the Utah Territory.
- read a map to explain how the western frontier changed.

Social Studies Vocabulary

propaganda

People

Stephen Long	John C. Fremont	Mormons
Robert Gray	James Marshall	Joseph Smith
John Jacob Astor	James Beckwourth	Brigham Young

Places

Oregon	California	Great Salt Lake
Columbia River	Sutter's Mill	Valley
Oregon Trail	Beckwourth Pass	Utah Territory

Words and Terms

Great American Desert	Bear Flag Revolt	forty-niners
"Fifty-four forty or fight"	gold rush	

In 1820, President Monroe sent Captain Stephen Long to explore the Rocky Mountain area. On his way to the Rockies, Long passed through flat, mostly treeless plains. Because of so few trees and the dryness of the climate, Long felt the area was unsuited to farming. He called it the Great American Desert. The name was used by others and began to appear on maps of the natural region that we now call the Great Plains. Because of Long's report, Americans moving west went either to the Southwest or to Oregon and California. The Great American Desert was not settled until the late 1800s.

What do you think was the point of view of the cartoonist who drew this picture of a gold hunter?

Both Roman Catholic and Protestant groups established missions for the Native Americans in Oregon. How were they similar to the earlier Spanish missions?

OREGON

The Oregon country lay west of the Rockies. It stretched from the northern border of California to the southern border of Alaska. The area was claimed by Spain, Russia, the U.S., and Great Britain. Spain gave up its claim as part of the Adams-Onis Treaty in 1819. Russia withdrew its claim in 1824 in answer to the Monroe Doctrine. Then only the U.S. and Great Britain were left to decide the ownership of the Oregon country.

The U.S. wanted Oregon as far north as the 49th parallel. Great Britain insisted on the 46th parallel as the northern boundary between the U.S. and British North America. The British claim rested on a number of British explorations of the area between the 1500s and 1700s. The U.S. claim dated to 1792 when Robert Gray, a Boston fur trader, had explored the Columbia River. The Lewis and Clark expedition of the early 1800s further supported the U.S. claim.

You may recall from the unit New Role for the Nation that in 1818 the two nations met to discuss the boundary problem. They set the 49th parallel as the boundary between the U.S. and British North America east of the Rockies. But the Oregon boundary question was not settled. Each nation wanted the Columbia River because of its importance to the fur trade. As a compromise, they agreed to hold Oregon jointly for ten years. In 1827, the agreement was renewed for an indefinite time.

indefinite
(in-DEF-uh-nit):
not limited

Traders, Missionaries, Settlers, and Native Americans

British fur traders had been in Oregon since the 1790s and had established a profitable fur trade. In 1811, John Jacob Astor, an American, built Astoria (as-TOHR-ee-uh), a trading post at the mouth of the Columbia River. Other American trappers and traders soon followed. Some lived and traded with the Native Americans year-round. Others wintered in Oregon and returned to St. Louis in the spring with their furs. Missionaries, too, lived among the Native Americans trying to convert them to Christianity.

As Native Americans became more dependent on trade goods, they moved closer to the trading posts. They gave up some of their own ways of life to trap animals for the fur trade. This was similar to what had happened to the Woodlands Native Americans in the 1600s. Unlike that situation, Native Americans and traders in Oregon remained friendly through the 1830s. However, the movement of groups closer to trading posts often caused fighting with Native American groups already living in an area.

Missionaries and traders sent back to the U.S. reports describing the beauty and resources of Oregon. These reports attracted many Americans to Oregon. Reverend Gustavus Hines wrote the following about Oregon:

> From a personal experience of more than five years, the writer is prepared to express the opinion that the climate of Oregon is decidedly favorable to health. It is good for growing wheat, barley, oats, peas, apples, potatoes, turnips, and all other vegetables which are cultivated in the Middle States. In addition with the vast amount of salmon which may be barreled annually and dairy products which the country is well suited to, the exports of Oregon, in proportion to the number of inhabitants, *may* equal those of any portions of the United States. Individuals have, in some instances, arrived in this country in the month of September, have settled immediately on some of the fine prairies, and, with little but good health, have harvested, the following year, from fifty to one hundred and fifty acres of wheat.

Most of the new settlers traveled over the Oregon Trail. It began in Independence, Missouri, and reached about 3,200 kilometers (2,000 miles) to Astoria. By the 1840s, the Oregon Trail was heavily traveled.

Native Americans became alarmed at the number of settlers coming to Oregon. They feared the loss of their lands. Because of greed and rivalry between trading companies, fur traders began to cheat the Native Americans. Some groups fought back after their people began to die from diseases brought by the Americans. The Cayuse (KY-yoos), for example, attacked American settlements after many of their people died from measles.

Reverend Hines's report about Oregon is an example of propaganda. **Propaganda** is the deliberate spreading of information, beliefs, and ideas to influence people for or against another cause or person. Propaganda does not always tell the whole truth and often shows bias. Reverend Hines reports only the good things about living in Oregon. He does not warn settlers about the difficult journey to Oregon or possible trouble with Native Americans. By publishing his report, Reverend Hines hoped that people would move to Oregon. **1.** Reread his report and state the information he uses to urge people to move to Oregon. **2.** What propaganda might Reverend Hines have used to keep people from moving to Oregon? **3.** Which of his statements do you feel show his bias towards Oregon?

BUILDING READING SKILLS

Fifty-four Forty or Fight!

As more settlers moved into the Oregon country, Americans began to think about annexation. Elected on a platform of annexation, President Polk was eager to add Oregon to the U.S. In 1845, he repeated the U.S. offer to set the Oregon border at the 49th parallel. Again, Great Britain refused, but Polk had a plan.

Some Americans had been demanding that the U.S. take Oregon up to 54° 40′ north latitude. This gave rise to the slogan "Fifty-four forty or fight!" Polk led the British to believe that he agreed. He announced that the U.S. would not renew the agreement to hold the land jointly. Faced with Polk's strong stand, the British gave in. The fur trade on the Columbia River was not important enough to risk war.

In 1846, Great Britain agreed to set the northern border of Oregon at the 49th parallel. Oregon became a territory in 1848. In 1853, the lands of the Oregon Territory north of the Columbia River organized separately as the Washington Territory.

Photography had become popular by the mid-1800s. Photographs such as the ones on these pages are excellent primary sources for studying events since then.

CALIFORNIA

Before 1845, Americans knew little about California. The few Americans who had settled there were trappers, traders, and fishers. In that year, John C. Fremont, called the Pathfinder, explored California. He wrote a book that became an important source of information about the region. Because of Fremont's description, Americans began to think of California as part of their manifest destiny.

Americans in California

When California was first settled, the Spanish monarch had given large land grants to friends and important people. After 1821, the Mexican government, too, began giving away land to encourage settlement. For example, soldiers who served in California received land. Americans who came to California seeking a new life were also given land.

In the 1820s and 1830s, Americans who came to California adapted to the culture of the Spanish already living there. Americans received land grants, became Mexican citizens, intermarried, and held public offices. But the Americans who came in the 1840s were different. Many came with their families and did not want to become Mexican citizens. They settled in areas far from government control and considered themselves Americans, not Mexicans. They looked forward to annexation by the U.S.

President Polk also wanted California to become part of the U.S. In 1845, he offered to buy California from Mexico, but Mexico refused. After losing Texas, it did not want to lose California, too. Later that year, Polk encouraged the Americans in California to revolt. If the rebels asked for annexation, he would grant it. In June 1846, a month

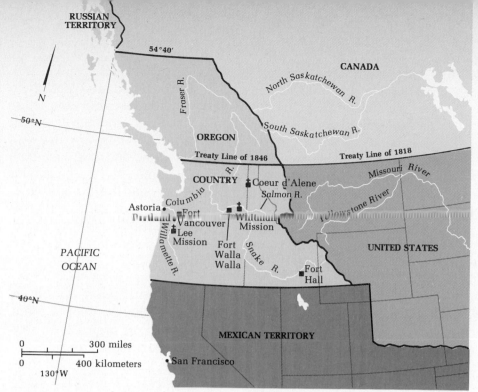

RUSSIAN
TERRITORY

54°40'

CANADA

North Saskatchewan R.

Fraser R.

South Saskatchewan R.

50°N

OREGON

Treaty Line of 1846   Treaty Line of 1818

Missouri River

COUNTRY   Coeur d'Alene
Salmon R.

Astoria   Columbia
                Fort
Portland   Vancouver   Whitman
                Lee   Mission
                Mission

PACIFIC
OCEAN   Fort
                        Walla
                        Walla   Snake R.

40°N   Fort
                                       Hall

Yellowstone River

UNITED STATES

N

0   300 miles
0   400 kilometers
    130°W

San Francisco

MEXICAN TERRITORY

Oregon Boundary Settlement

after the Mexican War broke out, a group of American settlers captured the Mexican outpost at Sonoma. The rebels proclaimed California a republic and raised a homemade flag. It had a single star and the figure of a grizzly bear. Because of this symbol, the rebellion became known as the Bear Flag Revolt.

The next month, the U.S. Navy occupied Monterey and declared California part of the U.S. The Americans showed little respect for the Spanish of California and placed harsh restrictions on them. The people of southern California rebelled and retook Monterey. Negotiations ended the revolt in January 1847. Through the Treaty of Guadalupe Hidalgo the following year, California became part of the U.S.

Gold!

In January 1848, John Sutter, a Swiss immigrant to the Sacramento Valley, decided he needed a sawmill. He hired James Marshall to build one on the American River, which ran through his land. As Marshall was working, he spotted small, shiny flakes of gold in the stream. Marshall looked more closely and found the riverbed sparkling with gold. At first, Sutter and Marshall tried to keep the discovery at Sutter's Mill a secret. But word soon spread. Within four months, many Californians, armed with picks, shovels, and shallow pans, were searching the hills and streams of California. Because much of the gold was easily found in rivers and streams, many prospectors panned for gold. They would make holes in the bottom of a pan and then dip it into the stream bed. They let water flow through the pan leaving sand, stones, and, they hoped, gold in the pan.

Walter Colton, the mayor of Monterey, California, described the beginning of the gold rush. In his diary, Colton wrote of the townspeople's reactions to the news of gold.

Prospectors sometimes ran water from streams through flumes, or troughs, to wash the gold from rocks and soil. Their tools show clearly in these photographs.

427

intense (in-TENS):
very strong

mason (MAY-suhn):
one who builds
with stones or bricks

Tuesday June 20. My messenger has returned with samples of the gold. As he brought the yellow lumps from his pockets and passed them around the eager crowd, the doubts about the discovery of gold left.

The excitement produced was intense. Many were soon busy in their hasty preparations for a departure to the mines. The family who had kept house for me caught the moving infection. Husband and wife were both packing up; the blacksmith dropped his hammer, the carpenter his plane, the mason his trowel, the farmer his sickle, and the baker his loaf.

All were off for the mines, some on horses, some on carts, and some on crutches. An American woman, who had recently opened a boarding-house here, pulled up stakes, and was off before her lodgers had even time to pay their bills.

By summer 1849, people from all over the world were coming to California. By the end of the year, there were 100,000 people there. Because so many people came in 1849, the miners are called forty-niners, but there were many goldhunters in the 1850s, too.

Goldhunters from the eastern U.S. traveled to California by three routes. The first was overland, across the Great Plains and Rocky Mountains. The other two routes to California were by sea. Clipper ships left the East Coast and headed south to Cape Horn at the tip of South America. After rounding the cape, the ships continued north to California. Another route was by ship from the East Coast to Central America and then overland to the Pacific. There, the forty-niners continued north by ship.

Once in California, most of the goldhunters lived in temporary mining camps where life was rough and laws were few. Many of the forty-niners were single men who did not plan to settle in California. They expected to find gold and return home. But some goldhunters brought their families, and some single women traveled to California looking for a better life. They went to work as cooks and launderers in the mining camps.

Blacks, both slave and free, went to California. Some slaves won their freedom by finding gold for their owners. By 1852, California had the wealthiest black community in the U.S. A free black, James Beckwourth, was the first American to explore a pass across the Sierra Nevada to the Sacramento Valley, in 1850. Goldhunters used the Beckwourth Pass, as it was called, on their way to California.

Most forty-niners did not find gold. Instead, they found a mild climate and rich, fertile land well suited to farming. Many prospectors decided to stay. Cities, such as San Francisco and Sacramento, grew first because of the gold rush but then continued to attract settlers. Smaller towns developed in the fertile valleys and along the coast. Farming, ranching, and trade became major economic activities of the new territory.

Native Americans and Californians

The Americans who poured into California in the gold rush had little interest in the Native Americans who lived there. They overran their

San Francisco rapidly became a city during the gold rush. In this lithograph, made in 1851, the bay is crowded with ships. How did they get there from the East?

villages and hunting and gathering grounds. As in Oregon, the diseases of the settlers killed many Native Americans. With their economy almost destroyed, many Native Americans struggled to survive. In desperation, some turned to robbery. For protection, miners formed armed bands and attacked Native Americans.

In time, the settlers distrusted all Native Americans and used any excuse to attack them. Women and children were murdered. Many men were made slaves. In the 1850s, the government of California forced Native Americans to give up their lands and live on reservations. In most cases, the reservations were small areas of infertile land that the settlers did not want.

UTAH AND THE MORMONS

Many of the forty-niners who traveled the overland route to California stopped at the Mormon settlement in the Great Salt Lake Valley. The Mormons are a religious group also called the Church of Jesus Christ of Latter-Day Saints. They were founded by Joseph Smith in 1830.

Before settling in the Great Basin, the Mormons had lived in Ohio, Missouri, and Illinois. In each state, the Mormons had tried to build a community in which they could freely practice their beliefs. But each time they failed. Their non-Mormon neighbors were angered by Mormon claims of revelations from God. They also opposed the Mormon practice of polygamy (puh-LIG-uh-mee), having more than one spouse at a time. In each place they settled, the Mormons were attacked and some killed.

In July 1847, the Mormons moved to the Great Salt Lake Valley. At the time, the land was still under Mexican control. In 1848, the Mexican War ended, and the land became part of the U.S. The Mormons irrigated the desert and turned it into fertile farmland. In 1849, they formed the state of Deseret (dez-er-ET). They set up a government with Brigham Young, the Mormon leader, as governor and adopted a

revelation
(rev-uh-LAY-shuhn):
something made known,
especially a religious
truth

429

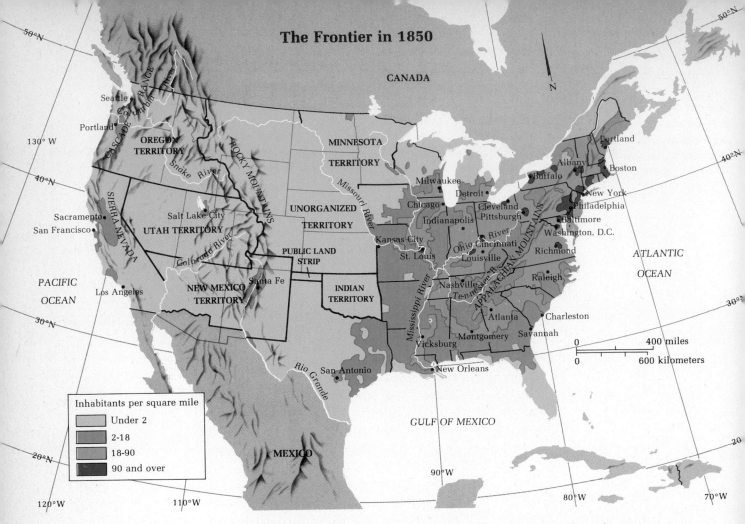

The Frontier in 1850

CANADA

Seattle

Portland

OREGON TERRITORY

MINNESOTA TERRITORY

Milwaukee

Chicago   Detroit

UNORGANIZED

TERRITORY

Indianapolis   Cleveland   Pittsburgh

Kansas City

St. Louis   Ohio   Cincinnati

Louisville

Sacramento

San Francisco

Salt Lake City

UTAH TERRITORY

Los Angeles

PACIFIC OCEAN

PUBLIC LAND STRIP

NEW MEXICO TERRITORY

Santa Fe

INDIAN TERRITORY

Nashville   Tennessee R.

Atlanta   Charleston

Montgomery   Savannah

Vicksburg

San Antonio

Rio Grande

New Orleans

GULF OF MEXICO

Portland   Albany   Boston   Buffalo   New York   Philadelphia   Baltimore   Washington, D.C.   Richmond   Raleigh

ATLANTIC OCEAN

MEXICO

Inhabitants per square mile
- Under 2
- 2-18
- 18-90
- 90 and over

0   400 miles
0   600 kilometers

constitution. They asked Congress for statehood, but the request was turned down. Congress was arguing over whether to allow slavery in the territories. As part of the Compromise of 1850 that you will read about in the next unit, the U.S. formed the Utah Territory. Brigham Young was named governor.

LOOKING BACK

1. **a.** On what basis did Great Britain rest its claim to the Oregon country? **b.** On what was the U.S. claim based?
2. **a.** How was propaganda used by Reverend Hines in the reading on p. 425? **b.** Which statements show bias toward Oregon?
3. How did the coming of each of the following affect Native Americans in Oregon: **a.** traders? **b.** settlers?
4. How did President Polk solve the problem of Oregon?
5. **a.** Why was the U.S. interested in California? **b.** What steps did the U.S. take to add California to the Union?
6. How did the gold rush affect California's: **a.** population? **b.** economic growth? **c.** Native Americans?
7. Why did the Mormons migrate to Utah?
8. Use the map on p. 427 to explain how westward movement changed: **a.** the frontier. **b.** population density.

430

PRACTICING YOUR SKILLS

What If . . .

In Chapter 1, you read how the people of the Republic of Texas favored annexation by the U.S. But Great Britain was also interested in Texas. **What if** the people of Texas had decided not to become a part of the U.S.? Would they have remained independent? Might they have become a colony of Great Britain?

Building Communication Skills

A **debate** is a formal argument of two sides of a problem. The signers of the Declaration debated the document but not quite in this formal way. In a formal debate, one side is pro, or for the issue, and one side is con, or against it. The statement of the problem or issue is given first. Then the two sides try to persuade the audience or judges either to accept or reject it. After the first round of speeches, there is a rebuttal period. A rebuttal (rih-BUT-uhl) is an argument that tries to prove the other side incorrect. The last speaker on each team ends her or his speech with a summary of the main issue and proofs. To prepare for a debate, each team member should:
- Read as many sources as possible to build a case of facts for his or her side.
- Take notes.
- Work together to decide on the arguments.
- Prepare a speech on his or her share of the debate.
- Rehearse her or his speech.

Activity: Debate: The U.S. had a manifest destiny to expand from ocean to ocean.

Researching, Writing, Making a Table, Imagining

1. When Stephen Long labeled the Great Plains as the Great American Desert, he assumed the land was worthless. Later settlement proved him wrong. Today, the Great Plains are an important part of the U.S. economy. Using what you learned from the introduction Life in America and from reference books, write a paragraph describing the geography and climate of the Great Plains.
2. Using reference materials, make a table showing the two most important economic activities of each of the Great Plains states.
3. Using reference materials, write a paragraph on gold. Tell where and how it is mined in the U.S. today, its uses, and current value.
4. Imagine that you are going to Oregon in the late 1850s. Write a letter to your family describing your journey. Tell how you traveled, what you saw, and what you found in Oregon.

Exploring

The gold rush of 1849 was an important reason for people to move to California. Many towns and cities in the U.S. grew because of one or two major developments. Perhaps a major industry located there or a large amount of some natural resource was found. Research the history of your town or city. Write a brief report describing when it was founded, by whom, and for what purpose.

Reading

Bauer, K. Jack. *The Mexican War, 1846–1848.* New York: Macmillan, 1974.
Billington, Ray Allen, and Henry E. Huntington Library & Art Gallery. *Westward Expansion: A History of the American Frontier.* 4th ed. New York: Macmillan, 1974.
Deloria, Vine, Jr. *Indians of the Pacific Northwest.* New York: Doubleday, 1977.
———. *The Way West.* New York: Bantam, 1972. Fiction. Paperback.
James, Marquis. *The Raven: A Biography.* Indianapolis: Bobbs-Merrill, 1976. A biography of Sam Houston.
Katz, William Loren. *Black People Who Made the Old West.* New York: Crowell, 1971. Thirty-five black men and women who helped settle the frontier.
Parkman, Francis. *Oregon Trail.* New York: Airmont, 1964. Paperback.
Seidman, Laurence. *The Fools of '49: The California Gold Rush, 1848–1856.* New York: Random House, 1976.

UNIT III   COMING OF THE CIVIL WAR

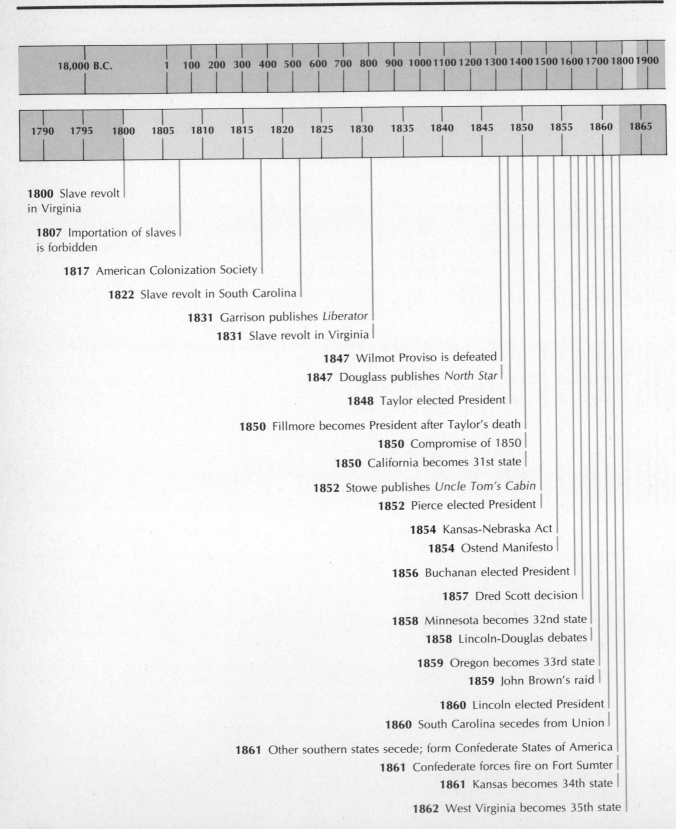

| 18,000 B.C. | 1 | 100 | 200 | 300 | 400 | 500 | 600 | 700 | 800 | 900 | 1000 | 1100 | 1200 | 1300 | 1400 | 1500 | 1600 | 1700 | 1800 | 1900 |

| 1790 | 1795 | 1800 | 1805 | 1810 | 1815 | 1820 | 1825 | 1830 | 1835 | 1840 | 1845 | 1850 | 1855 | 1860 | 1865 |

1800 Slave revolt in Virginia

1807 Importation of slaves is forbidden

1817 American Colonization Society

1822 Slave revolt in South Carolina

1831 Garrison publishes *Liberator*

1831 Slave revolt in Virginia

1847 Wilmot Proviso is defeated

1847 Douglass publishes *North Star*

1848 Taylor elected President

1850 Fillmore becomes President after Taylor's death

1850 Compromise of 1850

1850 California becomes 31st state

1852 Stowe publishes *Uncle Tom's Cabin*

1852 Pierce elected President

1854 Kansas-Nebraska Act

1854 Ostend Manifesto

1856 Buchanan elected President

1857 Dred Scott decision

1858 Minnesota becomes 32nd state

1858 Lincoln-Douglas debates

1859 Oregon becomes 33rd state

1859 John Brown's raid

1860 Lincoln elected President

1860 South Carolina secedes from Union

1861 Other southern states secede; form Confederate States of America

1861 Confederate forces fire on Fort Sumter

1861 Kansas becomes 34th state

1862 West Virginia becomes 35th state

Chapter 1   Compromise Again

LOOKING AHEAD

This chapter describes the continuing sectional differences over slavery that many Americans thought had been solved by the Missouri Compromise. You will read about the problem caused by the addition of Mexican land to the U.S., the presidential election of 1848, and the Compromise of 1850. After you study this chapter, you will be able to:

- identify the problem the Wilmot Proviso was supposed to solve.
- state each presidential candidate's view on the spread of slavery into the new territories.
- summarize the Compromise of 1850 and its results.
- ★ gather data by comparing maps.

Social Studies Vocabulary

popular sovereignty	commissioner	abolitionist movement

People

John C. Calhoun	Zachary Taylor	Daniel Webster
Lewis Cass	Henry Clay	Stephen A. Douglas
Free-Soil party	Millard Fillmore	

Places

New Mexico Territory	Utah Territory	Washington, D.C.

Words and Terms

Wilmot Proviso	Fugitive Slave Law
Compromise of 1850	personal liberty laws

General Zachary Taylor ran not on the issues in the election of 1848 but on his military record.

Sectional interests had threatened the Union since the early days of the new nation. You may recall from the unit The New Nation such threats as the Virginia and Kentucky Resolutions and the Hartford Convention. Another serious threat to the future of the Union occurred when Missouri applied for statehood in 1818. A long and bitter debate finally ended in the Missouri Compromise that kept the balance between free and slave states at 12 each. In 1832, South Carolina threatened to ignore a protective tariff and secede from the Union. The crisis passed when Congress approved Clay's compromise tariff the following year. But as the U.S. entered the 1850s, slavery was becoming the greatest danger to the security of the Union.

Henry Clay, speaking in the Senate, proposes a compromise to settle debate over whether new territories should be admitted to the Union as free or slave states.

WILMOT PROVISO

In 1846, when war broke out between the U.S. and Mexico, sectional interests reappeared. Many Northerners opposed the war because they saw it as a southern plot to spread slavery to any new territory the U.S. might gain. To prevent this, David Wilmot (WIL-muht), a Representative from Pennsylvania, introduced the Wilmot proviso. It stated that slavery should be forbidden in any former Mexican territory. Speaking for the South, John C. Calhoun argued that the proviso was unconstitutional.

proviso (pruh-VY-zoh): requirement in a document or contract

According to Calhoun, Congress had a duty to protect the rights of slaveowners to take their property into new territory. The Wilmot Proviso passed the House of Representatives but was rejected by the Senate. In 1848, the Mexican War ended, and the issue raised by the Wilmot Proviso became real. But it would not be faced by President Polk and an expansionist Congress. This was an election year, and a new President and a new Congress would have to solve the problem of the spread of slavery.

ELECTION OF 1848

President Polk had wanted to solve the slavery issue by extending the Missouri Compromise line of 38°30′ to the Pacific Ocean. But Polk, tired from the Mexican War, refused to run for reelection. The Democrats were then divided over Calhoun and Van Buren. As a compromise candidate, they selected Lewis Cass, former governor of the Michigan Territory and a Senator from Michigan. He favored **popular sovereignty** (SAHV-ruhn-tee)—allowing people to vote on questions themselves—in this case, whether slavery should be allowed in the territories.

Those Democrats who opposed Cass joined the new Free-Soil party. The Free-Soilers opposed the spread of slavery into the territories acquired from Mexico. They nominated Martin Van Buren for President. His slogan was "Free Soil, Free Speech, Free Labor, Free Men."

The Whigs chose General Zachary Taylor, the hero of the Mexican War. Taylor had no experience in politics so Americans did not know his views on such issues as the spread of slavery. However, the Whigs hoped Americans would elect Taylor as they had other military heroes: Washington, Jackson, and Harrison. The Whigs were right, and Taylor won by 36 electoral votes.

COMPROMISE OF 1850

The new President was soon forced to deal with the issue of slavery's spread into the new territories. Because of the gold rush, California's population had grown quickly and the territory asked for statehood. At that time—1850—there were 15 slave and 15 free states. If admitted as a free state, California would tip the balance against the slave states. But this was only the beginning. Each time one of the terri-

Debate in the Senate over the issue of the spread of slavery into the new territories was not always so peaceful. In this lithograph from the period, Vice-President Millard Fillmore calls for order as one Senator threatens another.

435

tories that was made from former Mexican lands asked for statehood, the nation would face the same question. Should the new state be free or slave?

After much debate in Congress. Henry Clay proposed a compromise designed to please all sections of the nation. It dealt with the Texas boundary problem as well as the issue of slavery. According to the compromise, California would be admitted as a free state. The people of New Mexico and Utah, however, would decide by popular sovereignty if the areas would be organized as free or slave territories. Texas, which had been claiming a large area of land also claimed by New Mexico, would give up this claim. In return, Congress would pay Texas $10 million. The slave trade, but not slavery, would be abolished in the District of Columbia. Finally, Congress would pass a Fugitive Slave Law.

fugitive
(FYOO-juh-tiv):
runaway

According to the Fugitive Slave Law, commissioners would be appointed with special powers to hunt runaways. A **commissioner** (kuh-MISH-uhn-er) is a government representative. The commissioners would be able to hold hearings, issue arrest warrants for suspected runaways, and return suspected runaways to their owners. During the hearings, suspected runaways would not be permitted to testify on their own behalf. Commissioners would receive $10 for each suspected fugitive they returned South but only $5 when they set a black free.

John C. Calhoun opposed the compromise. His view was that the balance in Congress between free and slave states was being destroyed. As a result, the South was losing its political power. The following is from a speech Calhoun made to the Senate on March 4, 1850:

preserve (prih-ZERV):
to keep safe;
to keep unchanged

How can the Union be preserved? There is but one way. That is by a full and final settlement on the principle of justice. The South asks for justice, simple justice, and less she should not take. She has no compromise to offer but the Constitution, and no concession or surrender to make.

But can this be done? Yes, easily. The North has only to do justice by giving the South an equal right in the acquired territory. And, to do her duty by having the laws relating to fugitive slaves be fulfilled. The North should also end agitation on the slavery question.

agitation
(aj-uh-TAY-shuhn):
a stirring up;
a protest

Calhoun died in March 1850. President Taylor, who opposed the compromise because he disliked the concessions to the South, died in July. He was succeeded by Vice-President Millard Fillmore. Fillmore supported Clay's plan. Daniel Webster of Massachusetts, one of the most powerful speakers in the Senate, also supported Clay's compromise. Webster pleaded with Northerners to end their disagreement with the South and preserve the Union. With the added support of Senator Stephen A. Douglas of Illinois, Congress accepted Clay's compromise.

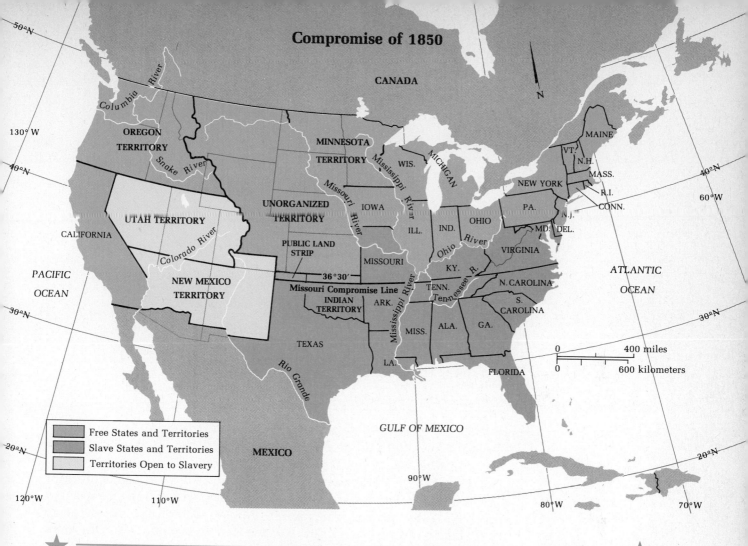

Compromise of 1850

Free States and Territories
Slave States and Territories
Territories Open to Slavery

By comparing maps of the same area drawn to show different time periods you can actually see the effects of wars, treaties, and legislative acts. Look at the map Compromise of 1850. It shows the effects of the compromise Congress reached over the spread of slavery into the territories. The map is similar to the Missouri Compromise map on page 339. Comparing these two maps can help you see the changes that occurred as a result of Congress's action. **1.** Which states and territories were formed from lands acquired from Mexico and Great Britain? **2.** How many free states were created after the Missouri Compromise? **3.** How many slave states were created after the Missouri Compromise? **4.** List the states admitted to the Union after 1820. **5.** Which areas would be allowed to decide the slavery question?

BUILDING MAP SKILLS

Results of the Compromise

The Compromise of 1850 had been designed to give something to every section of the nation, and it did delay a civil war for ten years. However, the compromise settled nothing. Allowing the people in the Utah and New Mexico territories to decide on the slavery question

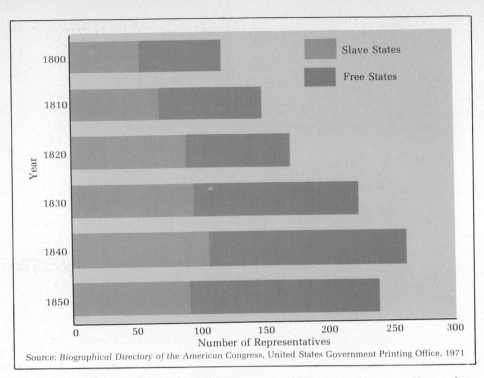

House of Representatives: Free States v. Slave States from 1800 to 1850

Year

1800
1810
1820
1830
1840
1850

Slave States
Free States

Number of Representatives

0   50   100   150   200   250   300

Source: *Biographical Directory of the American Congress*, United States Government Printing Office, 1971

did not solve the problem of whether slavery should be allowed to spread. The Fugitive Slave Law was difficult to enforce because so many Northerners refused to obey it.

Some northern states passed personal liberty laws to protect former slaves. These laws provided for jury trials to decide on the freedom of fugitive slaves. Several times angry mobs took fugitive slaves away from slave chasers. The Fugitive Slave Law drove many Northerners to join the **abolitionist** (ab-uh-LISH-uhn-ist) **movement**—a movement to end slavery.

Southerners were angered by the northern refusal to obey the law. They accused Northerners of ignoring the compromise and the right of Southerners to reclaim their property. The increase in abolitionist activities hardened southern opposition to abolition.

LOOKING BACK

1. **a.** What problem did the addition of Mexican land to the U.S. create? **b.** How was the Wilmot Proviso supposed to solve it?
2. How did the following presidential candidates feel about slavery's spread into the new territories: **a.** Cass? **b.** Van Buren? **c.** Taylor?
3. **a.** Summarize the six parts of the Compromise of 1850 in your own words. **b.** What was the northern reaction to the Fugitive Slave Law? **c.** How did Southerners react to these actions of Northerners?
★ 4. Look at the maps Compromise of 1850 and Missouri Compromise. How did the Compromise of 1850 change the decision about slavery reached in the Missouri Compromise?

Chapter 2   The Antislavery Movement

LOOKING AHEAD

By 1850, the argument over slavery was becoming the biggest problem between the North and South. This chapter describes the activities of those who opposed slavery. It describes colonization, abolition, slave revolts, and the growing tensions in the nation caused by the movement against slavery. After you study this chapter, you will be able to:

- identify the ways in which Americans tried to end slavery.
- describe the work of the underground railroad.
- describe an important result of slave revolts.
- recognize the use of propaganda in slavery arguments.

People

William Lloyd Garrison	Sarah Grimke	Gabriel Prosser
Frederick Douglass	Angelina Grimke	Denmark Vesey
David Ruggles	John Quincy Adams	Nat Turner
William Still	Quakers	Elijah Lovejoy
Sojourner Truth	Harriet Tubman	

Places

Liberia

Words and Terms

American Colonization Society	underground railroad
gag rules	conductor
"moral suasion"	

As the 1700s came to a close, many Americans predicted that slavery would soon die out. By 1804, most northern states had abolished it. As you may recall, slavery was not important to the economies of New England or of most Middle Atlantic states. In the South, planters were finding it difficult to pay their debts. In Virginia and North Carolina, for example, the soil of many plantations was wearing out from years of raising tobacco. In Georgia and South Carolina, planters were making little profit from rice and indigo. Remember that this was before the invention of the cotton gin turned the South into the Cotton Kingdom.

Although Congress had forbidden the importing of slaves after 1808, many Americans were not satisfied with this. They saw slavery as morally wrong and were determined to do away with it completely. Their efforts took several forms.

COLONIZATION

One form was colonization. Some Americans thought that the U.S. had a duty to blacks to pay for their return to Africa and to help them set up communities there. Other Americans saw this as a way to rid the country of free blacks. Southern slaveowners, especially, wanted their slaves protected from the influence of free blacks.

In 1817, the American Colonization Society was founded to send blacks to Africa. In the next few decades, the society paid for several thousand blacks, most of them free, to go to Africa. These people founded the nation of Liberia (ly-BEER-ee-uh). Most blacks, however, angrily opposed colonization. They had been born in the U.S. and felt that they had a right to remain. By the 1830s, white abolitionists also began attacking the idea.

ABOLITION

immoral (ih-MOR-uhl): wicked; wrong

One of the first white abolitionists to see that colonization was not the answer was William Lloyd Garrison. In 1831, he began publishing the abolitionist newspaper *Liberator*. In 1832, he helped organize the New England Anti-Slavery Society. Garrison and his followers used a nonviolent method called "moral suasion." They used words to try to convince people that slavery was immoral and unjust. Garrison believed that once enough people believed this there would be a nationwide demand for an immediate end to slavery. His call brought many people to the movement for abolition. In 1833, he helped organize the American Anti-Slavery Society. By 1840, the society had about 1,400 local groups in the North and Midwest and about 250,000 members. Garrison also supported equality for women workers in the abolitionist movement.

Blacks, both free-born blacks and former slaves, played important roles in abolition. Perhaps the best-known black was Frederick Douglass. Born a slave in 1817, he escaped to the North when he was 21. He became a speaker for the Massachusetts Anti-Slavery Society. In 1845, he published his autobiography *Narrative of the Life of Frederick Douglass*, which gave a full account of his sufferings under slavery. In 1847, he began the abolitionist newspaper *North Star*. One of Douglass's goals was to get more free blacks involved in the movement. Among free black abolitionists were David Ruggles and William Still. Ruggles led the New York movement, and Still was active in Philadelphia. Both were conductors on the underground railroad. Sojourner Truth, a former slave, traveled the country speaking in favor of rights for blacks and women. She told movingly of her experiences in *Narrative of Sojourner Truth*.

In the early 1800s, the abolitionist movement had some support in all sections of the nation. By about 1830, however, this was changing. Southern opposition to slavery was lessening as cotton farming was becoming more profitable. Among southern abolitionists were Sarah

Frederick Douglass, a gifted speaker and writer against slavery, was self-educated. Name three other abolitionists.

440

and Angelina Grimke (GRIM-kee), daughters of a Charleston slave-owner. Because of her experiences as a teacher in a black Sunday school, Sarah opposed the law that forbade teaching slaves to read. In time, the sisters moved North to work for abolition. When they met opposition to their speaking in public because they were women, the Grimkes joined the woman's rights movement.

Other abolitionists wrote pamphlets and sent petitions to state legislatures and to Congress asking for an end to slavery. By 1836, abolitionists' petitions were flooding Congress. Debating them all would have taken much of Congress's time. In addition, Southerners in Congress did not want any debate on slavery. With support coming mostly from southern members, both houses of Congress passed gag rules. According to these rules, petitions were rejected without discussion. Later, Northerners in Congress fought to repeal the gag rules and in 1844 were successful. Massachusetts Representative John Quincy Adams, the former President, led the fight for repeal.

The underground railroad was neither underground nor a railroad but a well-organized system to help slaves to freedom. Escaping North, however, was filled with danger and the trip took great courage as this painting by Thomas Moran shows.

The Underground Railroad

Some abolitionists attacked slavery with more than words. They helped runaway slaves escape on what became known as the underground railroad. This was a secret network of people called conductors who helped slaves flee to northern states or to Canada. Quakers were especially active in the underground railroad. During the journey, slaves were hidden in cellars, attics, old mills, church towers, and other places provided by the conductors. Sometimes the runaways were transported from one stop to another in false-bottom wagons covered with hay. If caught, runaway slaves were brutally punished. Conductors were fined and/or jailed if found helping run-aways. The Mother Bethel A.M.E. Church that you read about in the unit Life at Mid-Century was just one of the hundreds of stops on the underground railroad.

The most famous conductor was Harriet Tubman. She was born a slave on a Maryland plantation around 1820. When she was in her twenties she ran away. By day, she hid in caves and cemeteries. At night, she traveled north. Tubman settled in Philadelphia where she became part of the underground railroad. Risking her life and free-dom, she returned to the South 19 times to lead more than 300 men, women, and children to freedom.

In their spirituals, black slaves often expressed their desire for freedom. One such spiritual, "Go Down, Moses," is often linked to Har-riet Tubman and her trips into the South. The words of the song tell the Bible story of Moses leading the Israelites (IZ-ree-uhl-yts) out of Egypt to the Promised Land. In this spiritual, Moses is a symbol for Harriet Tubman. The slaves used religious symbols so that slave-owners would not know they were singing about freedom.

Slave holders once offered $40,000 for the capture of Harriet Tubman. Why is she often compared to the Moses in the Bible?

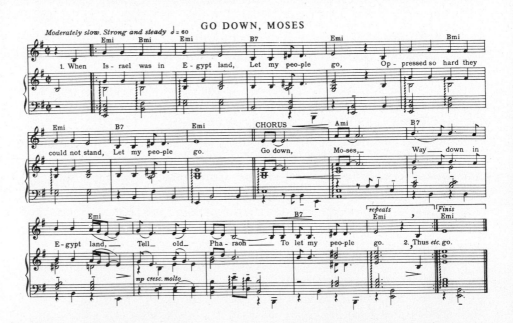

GO DOWN, MOSES

1 When Israel was in Egypt land,
   Let my people go,
   Oppressed so hard they could not stand,
   Let my people go.
        Go down, Moses,
        Way down in Egypt land,
        Tell old Pharaoh
        To let my people go.

2 'Thus spoke the Lord' bold Moses said,
   'Let my people go,
   If not, I'll smite your first-born dead,
   Let my people go.' *(Chorus)*

3 'Your foes shall not before you stand,
   Let my people go,
   And you'll possess fair Canaan's land,
   Let my people go.' *(Chorus)*

4 'You'll not get lost in the wilderness,
   Let my people go,
   With a lighted candle in your breast,
   Let my people go.' *(Chorus)*

chorus (KOR-uhs): part of a song that is repeated

442

SLAVE REVOLTS

As you may recall from the unit Life in Colonial America, blacks protested their slavery in several ways. During the 1800s, the most dramatic method was rebellion. Slave revolts, however, were difficult to carry out because of the secrecy needed. Slaveowners expected trouble and tried to keep slaves from gathering. Nevertheless, slaves attempted a number of revolts.

In 1800, Gabriel Prosser (PRAH-ser), a 24-year-old blacksmith, led a plot to set up a black nation in Virginia. On August 30, Prosser and over 1,000 slaves met to begin their rebellion with an attack on Richmond. A storm arose, and Prosser postponed the attack. Two slaves told their owners who, in turn, notified the state government. The governor ordered 600 soldiers to crush the rebellion before it began. Many slaves were arrested, and 35 were hanged, including Prosser.

plot (PLAHT):
secret plan

Other revolts followed. Denmark Vesey (VEE-zee) spent several years planning a rebellion among slaves around Charleston. A former slave himself, he had bought his freedom by working as a carpenter. In 1822, whites learned of Vesey's plan from some of the slaves involved, and 139 blacks, free and slave, were arrested. Thirty-seven were executed. Four whites who had helped the blacks were fined and jailed.

Another revolt was led by Nat Turner in Virginia in 1831. He and his followers began the revolt by killing Turner's owner and his family. Within a day, Turner's group had killed 60 whites. In putting down the revolt, state and federal soldiers killed 100 blacks. Fourteen more, including Turner, were hanged.

Following these revolts, some southern states passed harsh laws to try to frighten slaves into obedience. For robbing a house or store, for example, a slave could be whipped and his or her ears cut off. For small offenses, such as refusing to work, slaves were whipped, branded, or disabled in some way. A toe or a finger might be cut off.

FANNING THE FLAMES OF WAR

For a number of reasons, Americans in both the North and South opposed the antislavery movement. Merchants and planters feared the fight against slavery would hurt trade between North and South. Others feared the abolitionists would force the South to secede and so destroy the Union. Northern workers feared they would lose their jobs to freed blacks.

These fears often led to violence in both sections of the country. In 1835, a mob dragged Garrison through the streets of Boston with a rope around his neck. In 1837, Elijah Lovejoy, editor of an antislavery newspaper, was killed by a mob in Alton, Illinois.

The antislavery movement caused even bitterer feelings in the South. A white man was whipped in Virginia for saying that blacks

443

deserved their freedom. A Georgian who subscribed to the *Liberator* was dragged from his house, tarred and feathered, set afire, dunked in a river, and whipped.

Some Southerners responded to abolitionist charges that slavery was immoral and unjust with several arguments. One argument tried to justify slavery on the grounds that blacks were thought to be naturally inferior to whites. Southerners argued that blacks could not handle the responsibilities of freedom. Some Southerners claimed that most slaves were content and happy. In 1846, Matthew Estes (ES-teez) of Columbus, Mississippi, published a defense of black slavery. In it, he describes his view of slavery's benefit to the U.S.

> There are benefits to the country from slavery. It must be admitted as a fact, that without slave labor, the larger and more fertile portion of the South would be left uncultivated. Destroy slavery and you destroy Southern agriculture and the blessings that flow from it. The cotton, tobacco, rice, and sugar of the South, all the products of slave labor, are the bases of much of the wealth of this country, North and South, and also of Europe.

A different southern view of slavery was presented in Hinton R. Helper's *The Impending Crisis of the South: How to Meet It*, published in 1857. Helper, a North Carolinian, wrote the book for southern lower- and middle-class whites who did not own slaves. It describes the terrible effects slavery had on all parts of southern life. The following gives Helper's view of slavery's effects on the southern economy:

uncultivated
(uhn-KUHL-tuh-vayt-id): not developed; wild

Slaves were considered personal property by slave holders. They were bought and sold at auctions like this one. What effect could this have on slave families?

It is a well-known fact that Southerners must go to the North for almost every good and service, from matches and paintings to cotton-mills and steamships. From want of profitable employment at home large numbers of us must move to the West. The free states keep their large populations. Everything made in the North is sold while there is no demand for Southern products. We depend on Northern capitalists for money to build our railroads, canals, and other improvements.

And now, to the point. In our opinion, the reason why the progress of the South has been held back; our trade has decreased; large portions of our people live in poverty; some have been driven away from their homes; and we are dependent on the free states can be traced to the source—slavery.

Because of the ideas in the book, Helper was unable to have it published in the South. Southern speakers and writers attacked it. Some people were even arrested for buying a copy. In the North, this southern case against slavery was widely read.

It was often dangerous to be an abolitionist, even in the North. The editor of this newspaper office in Illinois was killed and his building burned by a proslavery mob.

LOOKING BACK

1. **a.** What was one early solution to ending slavery that was opposed by most blacks? **b.** How did Garrison hope to end slavery? **c.** Choose two other abolitionists and explain how each worked to end slavery.
2. **a.** What was the purpose of the underground railroad? **b.** How did it operate?
3. **a.** What did some southern states do as a result of slave revolts? **b.** What was the purpose of the laws?
4. **a.** State the propaganda Estes uses to support his idea that slavery was good for the U.S. **b.** How does Helper's view of the effect of slavery differ from Estes's view?

Chapter 3   Growing Tensions

LOOKING AHEAD

In this chapter, you will learn why the Compromise of 1850 did not settle the issue of the spread of slavery. Abolitionist activities, such as the publication of *Uncle Tom's Cabin,* and the desire of expansionists for more land added to the growing problems between North and South. You will also read about how the Kansas-Nebraska Act led to more conflict and a new political party. After you study this chapter, you will be able to:

★ identify some stereotypes in *Uncle Tom's Cabin.*
● explain how expansionism added to the tensions between North and South.
● explain how the Kansas-Nebraska Act led to a Bleeding Kansas
● state the main reason for the rise of the Republican party.

Social Studies Vocabulary

stereotype

People

Harriet Beecher Stowe	John Brown	John C. Fremont
Franklin Pierce	Republican party	
Stephen A. Douglas	James Buchanan	

Places

Cuba	Kansas Territory	Pottawatomie Creek
Nebraska Territory	Lawrence, Kansas	

Words and Terms

Uncle Tom's Cabin   Ostend Manifesto   Kansas-Nebraska Act

135,000 SETS, 270,000 VOLUMES SOLD.

UNCLE TOM'S CABIN

FOR SALE HERE.

The Greatest Book of the Age.

How did *Uncle Tom's Cabin* increase the tensions between North and South?

Although a great many Americans saw the Compromise of 1850 as a solution to the slavery issue, many did not. As you have just read, many Northerners so disliked the Fugitive Slave Law that they became abolitionists. The publication of Harriet Beecher Stowe's novel *Uncle Tom's Cabin* in 1852 brought more followers to the cause of abolition. Expansionists' wish for more territory and the possibility of a transcontinental railroad added to the problems between North and South.

UNCLE TOM'S CABIN

In *Uncle Tom's Cabin* Harriet Beecher Stowe described slaves being whipped, bought and sold, and separated from their families. The author had little personal knowledge of slavery. Her book was based on information given her by runaway slaves.

Uncle Tom's Cabin stirred bitter feelings in both North and South. A year after its publication, *Uncle Tom's Cabin* had sold more than 300,000 copies. The book, together with plays based on it, turned many Northerners against slavery. Southerners considered the book insulting and said that it presented an unfair view of slavery. The book describes the experiences of Tom, a black slave, and his three owners. The first two treat him kindly. The third, Simon Legree (lih-GREE), mistreats Tom and eventually kills him. Legree, the chief villain of the novel, is a Northerner who went South to make his fortune. Both blacks and whites have criticized the book as being biased and filled with propaganda. The following is an example of Stowe's point of view.

In order to appreciate the sufferings of the Negroes sold South, it must be remembered that their affections are very strong. They are not naturally daring and enterprising but home-loving and affectionate. Add to this all the terrors of the unknown, and the fact that being sold South is set before the Negro from childhood as the worst punishment. The threat of being sent down river terrifies more than whipping or torture of any kind. We have heard this feeling expressed by them and seen the horror with which they tell of frightful stories of down river.

A missionary among the fugitives in Canada told us many of the fugitives confessed themselves to have braved the danger of escape because of the desperate horror with which they regarded being sold South—a doom which was hanging either over themselves or their husbands, wives or children. This nerves the African, naturally patient, timid, and unenterprising, with heroic courage, and leads him to suffer hunger, cold, pain, the danger of the wilderness, and the more dread penalties of recapture.

enterprising (EN-ter-pryz-ing): ready to try new things; adventurous

nerve (NERV): to give courage to

BUILDING READING SKILLS

The passage you have just read from *Uncle Tom's Cabin,* is an example of stereotyping. A **stereotype** is an idea about a person or thing that is based on an oversimplified view. A stereotype makes all people within a group the same. It does not take into consideration individual differences. Nor is a stereotype based on facts. It is most often based on secondhand information rather than direct experience. Someone who holds a stereotyped view of others usually will not change his or her view when presented with accurate information. In the passage above, Stowe stereotypes all black slaves as being naturally patient, timid, and unheroic. She does not consider those blacks who deliberately damaged their work or who rebelled openly against their owners. **1.** What is a stereotype? **2.** Find and state two stereotypes in this passage. **3.** According to the above description of her novel, did Stowe have firsthand experience of what she wrote about?

CUBA

Following the war with Mexico, some Americans believed the U.S. should expand into North and South America. Cuba was especially attractive to American expansionists. If the U.S. took Cuba, it would give the nation control of the Caribbean and the Gulf of Mexico. The South wanted Cuba because it would add another slave-holding territory to the Union.

President Polk had offered to buy Cuba in 1848, but Spain had refused. In 1852, Franklin Pierce, a Democrat, defeated the Whig candidate General Winfield Scott. Pierce had run on a platform of expansion. After his election, he made the addition of Cuba a national objective. This was not popular in the North. Northerners did not want any more slave-holding territory added to the U.S.

In 1854, those Americans who wanted Cuba received what seemed to be an excuse for taking the island. In February, the Spanish seized an American ship that had stopped at the port of Havana. The Spanish thought the ship was delivering weapons to Cubans who wanted to rebel against Spanish rule. Some Americans called for war. The affair could have ended when the Spanish released the ship, but Pierce wanted Cuba.

manifesto
(man-uh-FES-toh):
declaration
of objectives

The President sent representatives to negotiate with Spain for Cuba's purchase. The U.S. representatives met at Ostend (ahs-TEND), Belgium, in October 1854. Their report, called the Ostend Manifesto, recommended that the U.S. offer Spain $120 million for Cuba. If Spain refused, the U.S. should take Cuba by force. Great Britain and France, allies of Spain at the time, were angered. The U.S. Congress and the American public were also angered. Embarrassed, the government refused to accept the Ostend Manifesto even though the ministers had done what Pierce wanted. It would be almost 50 years before Cuba would become U.S. territory. You will read more about this in the unit Reform and Expansion.

KANSAS-NEBRASKA ACT

Besides adding foreign territory, many Americans wanted a transcontinental railroad. But this issue, too, added to the tensions between North and South. Northerners wanted the railroad to follow a central route across the Great Plains. Southerners wanted the railroad built across the land the U.S. had received in the Gadsden Purchase. The greatest barrier to the central route was the vast Native American lands between the Missouri River and the Rockies. By the 1850s, Midwesterners were asking the government to allow white settlement there. The fertile lands of the Native Americans attracted them because the best land east of the Mississippi River had been settled. Railroad officials and land speculators also asked the government to open Native American lands to settlement.

In 1854, Senator Stephen A. Douglas of Illinois proposed such a plan. It would not only open most of these lands to white settlement

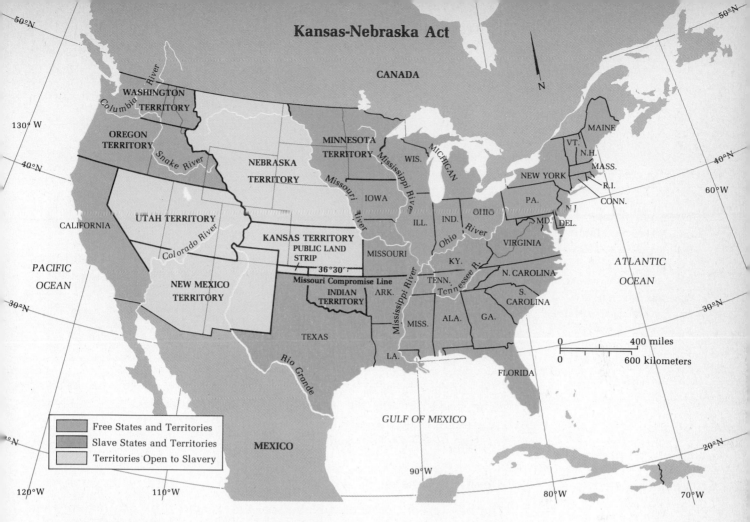

Kansas-Nebraska Act

Free States and Territories
Slave States and Territories
Territories Open to Slavery

but would also help the cause of a central route for the railroad. Douglas was a leading supporter of this route. Like a number of politicians of the day, he owned land in the area and had invested money in railroad stock.

The area that Douglas suggested settling was north of the 36° 30′ line of the Missouri Compromise. The Compromise of 1850 had not affected this area, and slavery was still outlawed there. Southerners in Congress insisted that instead of one large territory, as Douglas proposed, the region be divided into two—Kansas and Nebraska. Southerners also insisted that slavery be allowed.

Douglas accepted these changes—perhaps because he hoped to win southern support for his nomination for President. Douglas tried to convince Northerners that slavery would not spread into these territories. They were not suited to plantation farming. Douglas also said that allowing the territories to decide for themselves the issue of slavery was only democratic.

The Kansas-Nebraska Act, as Douglas's plan was called, created much debate in Congress. Most Southerners approved of the bill because it repealed the Missouri Compromise by allowing popular sovereignty. Northerners opposed the bill for the same reason. In spite of northern opposition, Congress passed the bill in May 1854. What is now the state of Kansas became the Kansas Territory. The Nebraska Territory included what is now the state of Nebraska and

The group in this picture rescued Johnny Doy, a convicted slave liberator, from jail in St. Joseph, Missouri. Feelings ran so high among those for and those against the spread of slavery that both sides often broke the law.

parts of the states of Montana, North Dakota, South Dakota, Wyoming, and Colorado. By 1863, Congress had created several more territories from Nebraska. The Nebraska Territory was then reduced to the size of the present state.

Bleeding Kansas

The passage of the Kansas-Nebraska Act created little excitement in the South. However, its passage caused bitterness in the North and violence in the Midwest. When the time came to vote, people in the Nebraska Territory voted against slavery, as Douglas had thought they would. But in Kansas both antislavery and proslavery forces were determined to control the government. Antislavery groups in the North sent money and guns to antislavery settlers, or Free-Soilers. Proslavery settlers also received money and guns from their supporters. The territory became known as Bleeding Kansas.

In March 1855, an election was held to elect a government for the Kansas Territory. During the election, 5,000 armed Missourians rode across the border and took over the Kansas polls. They kept Free-Soilers from voting. After helping to elect a proslavery government, they rode back to Missouri. Angry Free-Soilers then held their own election and chose a government. Kansas now had two governments.

On May 21, 1856, a proslavery group attacked the Free-Soil capital, Lawrence. They looted and burned the town. One person was killed. In answer to the attack, John Brown, an abolitionist, led an attack on the proslavery settlement of Pottawatomie Creek. Brown and his men dragged five proslavery settlers from their cabins and murdered them. In the warfare that followed, nearly 200 people died.

Federal soldiers restored order late in 1856, but the future of Kansas —slave or free—remained unsettled. The new President, James Buchanan (byoo-KAN-uhn), supported the proslavery government, but

the Congress did not. In 1858, the people of Kansas elected an antislavery government in fair elections. In 1861, Kansas entered the Union as a free state.

ANOTHER CHANGE IN POLITICAL PARTIES

Since the 1830s, the two major U.S. political parties had been the Whigs and the Democrats. Both had support in all sections of the nation. But the Kansas-Nebraska Act split the parties apart. Northern Whigs and Democrats opposed the act while Southerners of both parties supported it. Many Southerners left the Whig party and became Democrats. Many northern Democrats left their party and, in 1854, with northern Whigs and some small antislavery parties, formed the Republican party. By 1860, the Whig party had disappeared.

The Republicans did not want to abolish slavery. But they did want to keep it from spreading into the new territories. The Republican party quickly gained members but only in the North. In the 1854 congressional elections, the Republicans elected more than 40 legislators. By 1856, the Republicans were strong enough to nominate a candidate for President.

Election of 1856

The Democrats decided not to renominate President Pierce. They feared that he could not win in the northern states because of his position on Kansas. Instead, the Democrats nominated James Buchanan of Pennsylvania. He had served as Polk's Secretary of State and later as minister to Great Britain. He had taken no public position on the Kansas issue but favored the southern position on slavery. Democrats supported the Compromise of 1850 and the Kansas-Nebraska Act.

In 1856, the Republicans nominated John C. Fremont for President. They were against the spread of slavery and for the admission of Kansas as a free state. They lost the election but expected to win in 1860. Why?

The Republicans nominated John C. Fremont of California. They campaigned against the spread of slavery and for the admission of Kansas as a free state. Millard Fillmore ran with the support of the remaining Whigs and the Know-Nothings.

Buchanan won the election with the support of the southern states. He received the electoral votes of only five northern states. Fremont showed strength in the North. However, some Northerners had not voted for him because they feared a Republican victory would split the nation. Fillmore received some northern support but received the electoral votes of only one state. Although the Republicans lost the election, the strong support they received encouraged them to look to victory in the election of 1860.

LOOKING BACK

★ 1. **a.** Identify three stereotypes in the passage from *Uncle Tom's Cabin.* **b.** Based on the description of the novel in this textbook and the passages quoted, why do you think *Uncle Tom's Cabin* would be considered propaganda for abolition? **Hint:** Question **b** asks you to infer your answer based on what you have just read.

2. **a.** Why did Southerners want to add Cuba to U.S. territory? **b.** Why did Northerners oppose this expansionism?

3. **a.** Why did a proposed transcontinental railroad politically divide the North and South? **b.** How was the Kansas-Nebraska Act supposed to help solve the split? **c.** Why did the act further increase tensions between North and South? **d.** Why was Kansas called Bleeding Kansas?

4. **a.** How did the slavery issue affect the Whig party in the mid-1850s? **b.** What caused the founding of the Republican party? **c.** State one reason to support your answer.

Chapter 4   War Comes

LOOKING AHEAD

This chapter is about the final conflicts between North and South in the late 1850s that led to the Civil War. You will read about the Dred Scott decision, the Lincoln-Douglas debates, John Brown's raid, the election of 1860, and the first shots of the Civil War. After you study this chapter, you will be able to:

- explain the effect of the Dred Scott decision on slaves, slaveowners, and the Missouri Compromise.
- explain the effects of John Brown's raid on the North and South.
- describe the views of the presidential candidates in the election of 1860.
- compare and contrast the positions and actions of Buchanan and Lincoln on southern secession.
- ★ test a hypothesis about the causes of the Civil War.

Social Studies Vocabulary

hypothesis

People

Dred Scott   John C. Breckinridge
Abraham Lincoln   Constitutional Union party
Stephen A. Douglas   John Bell
John Brown   Jefferson Davis

Places

Harper's Ferry, Virginia   Montgomery, Alabama
Charleston   Fort Sumter
Baltimore

Events

Panic of 1857   John Brown's raid
Lincoln-Douglas debates

Words and Terms

Dred Scott decision   Confederate States of America

James Buchanan took office on March 4, 1857. Shortly after, a panic gripped the nation. Buying on credit and land speculation had brought on the Panic of 1857 as they had earlier panics. As in past economic crises, the panic was followed by a depression. This one lasted for three years.

The North was harder hit than the South. Many Northerners had invested their money in industry and transportation, while wealthy Southerners had most of their money tied up in land and slaves. Northerners blamed southern control of Congress for their economic problems. They said Southerners had prevented the passage of such government-sponsored programs as free western lands and government aid to railroads.

Besides facing economic problems, the nation still faced the issue of the spread of slavery into the new territories. No solution that Congress had proposed had settled the issue. So, in 1857 the Supreme Court tried to settle the argument.

DRED SCOTT DECISION

Dred Scott was a black slave who was living in Missouri at the time of his owner's death. His owner, an army doctor, had moved several times while he owned Scott. They had lived in Illinois and the Wisconsin Territory. Slavery was illegal in Illinois according to the Northwest Ordinance and in the Wisconsin Territory because of the Missouri Compromise. After the doctor died, Scott sued his new owner for his freedom. He based his lawsuit on the grounds that he had lived on free soil and was, therefore, free.

A local Missouri court decided in favor of Scott, but the Missouri State Supreme Court ruled against him. With his legal costs paid by antislavery groups, Scott took his case to the U.S. Supreme Court. On March 6, 1857, Chief Justice Roger B. Taney (TAW-nee) read the Court's decision. Taney said that no slave nor descendant of a slave could be a U.S. citizen. For that reason, a slave could not sue anyone nor attempt to gain freedom through the courts. Moreover, the Court found that the restrictions on slavery in the Northwest Ordinance and the Missouri Compromise were unconstitutional. According to the decision, the Constitution protected the right of slaveowners to take their slaves anywhere in the U.S.

The South was jubilant over the Dred Scott decision. Northerners were outraged. Many condemned the decision as a plot to spread slavery throughout the nation. Rather than settling the issue, the Dred Scott decision added to the widening split between North and South.

jubilant
(JOO-buhl-uhnt):
rejoicing

LINCOLN-DOUGLAS DEBATES

The new Republican party, made up mostly of antislavery Northerners, opposed the Dred Scott decision. Its stand attracted new members, among them Abraham Lincoln. Born in 1809, Lincoln was the son of a poor, uneducated frontier farmer. Lincoln had little schooling but educated himself by reading. Among his early jobs were store clerk, mail carrier, and surveyor. His political career began in 1832 when he won a seat in the Illinois legislature as a Whig. At the age of 27, Lincoln became a lawyer. In 1846, he was elected to the U.S.

In a series of debates with his opponent, Stephen Douglas, during the 1858 campaign for the Senate, Abraham Lincoln attracted much attention. What issues and feelings are expressed by the banners in the crowd?

House of Representatives as a Whig. But after the Kansas-Nebraska Act, be became a Republican.

In June 1858, Illinois Republicans selected Lincoln to run for the U.S. Senate against Stephen A. Douglas. After accepting the nomination, Lincoln challenged Douglas to a series of debates. Douglas accepted, and seven debates were held. The main issue was the spread of slavery into the new territories.

Douglas accused Lincoln and the Republicans of being abolitionists. Douglas argued in favor of popular sovereignty. Lincoln, for his part, denied being an abolitionist. He said Republicans would not interfere with slavery in areas where it already existed. But, Lincoln added, Republicans would not allow slavery to spread into new territories. Lincoln declared that the territories were mainly for poor whites. There, they had a chance to own farms or businesses and make better lives for themselves. They would not be able to do this if they had to compete with slave labor.

In the debate at Freeport, Illinois, on August 27, Lincoln forced Douglas to admit that the Dred Scott decision did not guarantee the spread of slavery into the territories. Douglas said that if the people in an area did not want slavery, they could keep it out. This answer caused some southern Democrats to turn against Douglas. Douglas needed their support to further his chances for the presidency in 1860. Lincoln lost the election for senator to Douglas. But because of the debates, Lincoln won a national reputation as a leader of the Republican party.

JOHN BROWN'S RAID

While others debated, John Brown, the abolitionist, decided to take his war against slavery into the South. In 1859, after Kansas voters

Under guard, John Brown rides to his hanging. What had he tried to do? The painting is by Horace Pippin, a black artist whose mother is said to have witnessed the hanging. How did Pippin show this in his painting?

chose to become a free state, Brown moved near Harper's Ferry, Virginia (now West Virginia). He received several thousand dollars from northern abolitionists to continue his antislavery activities. Brown used the money to buy weapons for his small group of followers. He had 18 men, including three of his sons and five blacks.

On October 16, 1859, Brown and his followers seized the federal arsenal at Harper's Ferry. Brown planned to arm the slaves that would join him once they heard of his raid. He would then set up a string of bases in the mountains of Virginia and Maryland. From these bases, his followers would wage war on slaveowners. However, federal troops commanded by Colonel Robert E. Lee captured Brown and his group the following day. Brown was tried for treason against the state of Virginia, found guilty, and hanged in December 1859.

John Brown's raid aroused the fear among Southerners that there might be a general slave rebellion. Their fear turned to anger when they learned that Brown had the support of some northern abolitionists. The raid convinced many in the South that Northerners were not willing just to stop the spread of slavery. They meant to end slavery where it already existed. For the most part, Northerners condemned Brown's violence. But he became a hero to many who shared his desire to abolish slavery.

ELECTION OF 1860

The Democratic Convention met at Charleston in April 1860. Among northern Democrats, Stephen A. Douglas was the leading candidate for the presidential nomination. Southern delegates were determined to block his nomination, however. They now opposed the idea of popular sovereignty, which Douglas supported. Southern delegates also demanded a platform supporting the Dred Scott decision and federal protection of slavery in the territories. Northern delegates wanted the convention to support popular sovereignty. When the two sides refused to compromise, the convention broke up.

In June, the Democrats met again in Baltimore but in two conventions. Northern Democrats nominated Douglas to run for President on a platform of popular sovereignty. Southerners chose Buchanan's Vice-President John C. Breckinridge of Kentucky. His platform supported federal protection of slavery in the territories.

In May, the Republicans had met in Chicago. In their platform, they pledged to allow slavery where it already existed but to stop its spread into the new territories. The Republicans nominated Abraham Lincoln for President.

Former Whigs and Know-Nothings formed the Constitutional Union party. Sidestepping the slavery question, the party stood for the Constitution, the Union, and the enforcement of U.S. laws. The party nominated former Secretary of War and U.S. Senator John Bell of Tennessee as its presidential candidate.

sidestep (SYD-step): to avoid

The outcome of the presidential election of 1860 was decided by sectional interests. As you may recall from Chapter 1 of this unit, there were 18 free states and 15 slave states. California had been admitted as a free state in 1850. Minnesota had been admitted in 1858 and Oregon in 1859 also as free states. Lincoln carried every free state and won the majority of electoral votes. Douglas was second in popular votes but won only Missouri. Breckinridge won Delaware and all the southern states except Tennessee, Kentucky, and Virginia. Bell won the states in which opinions on slavery were sharply divided.

carry (KAR-ee): to win

Secession and War

During the 1860 election campaign, South Carolina had threatened to leave the Union if Lincoln were elected. As soon as the election's results were known, South Carolina prepared to secede. On December 20, 1860, a state convention passed an ordinance of secession. The convention also issued a statement explaining why the state was leaving the Union. Among the reasons given were: abolitionist propaganda, the underground railroad, northern personal liberty laws, and the formation of a political party — the Republican party — opposed to the southern way of life.

Frederick Douglass, the abolitionist and newspaper editor, had a different opinion. He believed slavery was the chief cause of the Civil War. The following is from an editorial he wrote in the February 1861 issue of *Douglass' Monthly*.

Now, what disturbs, divides and threatens to bring on civil war, and to break up and ruin this country, but slavery. Who but one morally blind

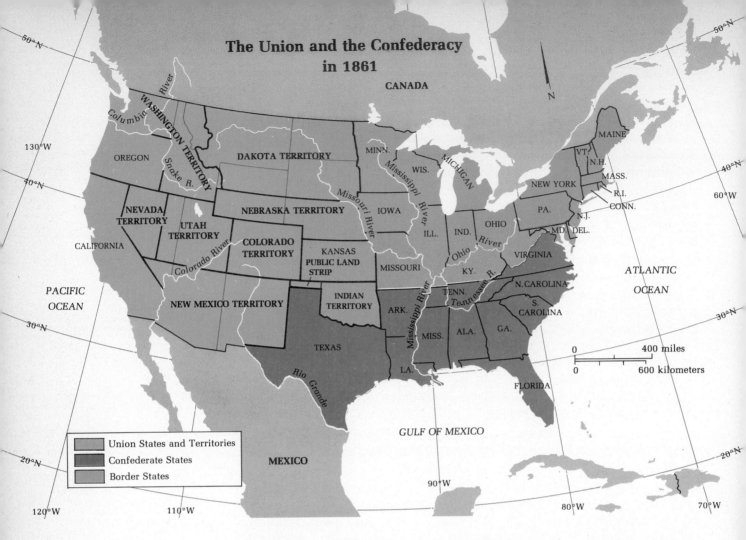

The Union and the Confederacy in 1861

CANADA

WASHINGTON TERRITORY

Columbia River

OREGON

Snake R.

NEVADA TERRITORY

UTAH TERRITORY

CALIFORNIA

COLORADO TERRITORY

Colorado River

NEW MEXICO TERRITORY

DAKOTA TERRITORY

NEBRASKA TERRITORY

KANSAS PUBLIC LAND STRIP

Missouri River

MINN.

WIS.

IOWA

ILL.

MICHIGAN

MISSOURI

INDIAN TERRITORY

ARK.

TEXAS

Rio Grande

Mississippi River

LA.

MISS.

ALA.

IND.

OHIO

Ohio River

KY.

TENN.

Tennessee R.

GA.

N. CAROLINA

S. CAROLINA

NEW YORK

PA.

N.J.

MD.

DEL.

VIRGINIA

MAINE

VT.

N.H.

MASS.

R.I.

CONN.

FLORIDA

GULF OF MEXICO

MEXICO

PACIFIC OCEAN

ATLANTIC OCEAN

N

	400 miles
0	
0	600 kilometers

Union States and Territories
Confederate States
Border States

50°N • 130°W • 40°N • 30°N • 20°N • 120°W • 110°W • 90°W • 80°W • 70°W • 60°W • 50°W • 30°N • 20°N

can fail to see it. Fifteen states are determined to continue this system of wickedness. They want to either make it the law of the whole country, or destroy the government. Here is the cause of the trouble. Slavery is the disease, and its abolition in every part of the land is necessary to the future quiet and security of the country.

By early February 1861, Mississippi, Florida, Alabama, Georgia, Louisiana, and Texas had joined South Carolina in seceding from the Union. In spring 1861, Arkansas, North Carolina, Tennessee, and Virginia also seceded. However, Virginians in the western part of the state stayed loyal to the Union. In 1863, western Virginia was admitted to the Union as West Virginia. On February 4, delegates from the southern states met in Montgomery, Alabama, and organized the Confederate States of America, also called the Confederacy. They elected Jefferson Davis of Mississippi as President and Alexander H. Stephens of Georgia as Vice-President.

President Buchanan insisted that secession was unconstitutional. However, he was unwilling to force the South back into the Union. The President hoped for a compromise and waited for the states to return.

On March 4, 1861, Abraham Lincoln became President. Like Buchanan, he declared secession to be unconstitutional. But unlike Buchanan, Lincoln made it clear that he would use force, if necessary, to bring the South back into the Union. He would enforce U.S. laws and protect U.S. property, such as military bases, in the South.

One of the military bases was Fort Sumter in the harbor at Charleston. South Carolinians surrounded the fort and demanded its surrender. Lincoln refused and announced that he was sending a ship to resupply the fort with food. On April 12, 1861, a Confederate force fired on the supply ship and the fort. With the firing on Fort Sumter the Civil War had begun.

During and after the war, Americans would argue over the reasons for the conflict. One person who thought that opposing ideas on government—states rights versus a strong central government—caused the Civil War was Alexander H. Stephens of Georgia, former Vice-President of the Confederacy. In his book *A Constitutional View of the Late War Between the States*, published in 1868, Stephens gave his view of the beginning of the Civil War.

That the Civil War was caused by opposing principles is an unquestionable fact. The conflict arose from opposing ideas as to the nature of the General Government. The contest was between those who thought it was strictly federal and those who thought it was wholly national. It was a conflict between the principles of Federation, on the one side, and Centralism on the other. Slavery was only the question which brought the opposing principles of government into actual collision with each other on the field of battle.

BUILDING THINKING SKILLS

In the unit The Nation Comes of Age, you learned about assumptions. As historians study primary and secondary sources, they often make assumptions based on the data they have gathered and analyzed. They call these assumptions hypotheses. A **hypothesis** (hy-PAHTH-uh-sis) is an educated guess or prediction. It is a reasonable possible answer. What may seem reasonable now, may not prove to be if new evidence is found. Historians usually agree on historic facts such as dates and participants in events because the evidence supporting them is unquestionable. However, historians often disagree on the meaning and significance of the facts. Historians construct and test hypotheses to prove or disprove the validity of their assumptions. A hypothesis may be considered valid when there is more evidence to support it than to contradict it.

As you read history, you can come to your own conclusions or assumptions about events, too. For example, in this unit you have read three different opinions about what caused the Civil War. Choose one of the following hypotheses and test its validity:

- The struggle over political power between North and South caused the Civil War.
- The struggle to end slavery caused the Civil War.
- The struggle over states' rights versus a strong central government caused the Civil War.

Reread the unit for evidence that both supports and contradicts the hypothesis. Classify your data in a table with columns labeled, "Evi-

contradict
(kahn-truh-DIKT): to disagree with

Union soldiers inside Fort Sumter return southern fire. Who owned Fort Sumter? What had President Lincoln said he would do if U.S. property was in danger?

dence Supporting the Hypothesis" and "Evidence Contradicting the Hypothesis." **1.** Is all your data relevant to the hypothesis? Do not include any data that is not directy related to the hypothesis. **2.** Is your information accurate? Make sure you stated the information correctly. **3.** Is your data adequate? List at least three examples for each side of your table. **4.** Review the data you have gathered and weigh the evidence supporting and contradicting the hypothesis. Decide whether the hypothesis you chose is valid, and write a statement either supporting it or contradicting it.

LOOKING BACK

1. How did the Dred Scott decision affect: **a.** rights of slaves? **b.** rights of slaveowners? **c.** the Missouri Compromise?
2. What was the reaction to John Brown's raid: **a.** in the South? **b.** in the North?
3. What was the political platform of each of the following presidential candidates: **a.** Lincoln? **b.** Douglas? **c.** Breckinridge? **d.** Bell?
4. Write a paragraph comparing and contrasting the positions and actions of Presidents Buchanan and Lincoln on the issue of southern secession. Be sure to state clearly the reasons for any actions each president took.
5. How do historians use hypotheses? **b.** Restate the hypothesis you chose from page 459. **c.** State the evidence you gathered to support or contradict it. **d.** Do you think the hypothesis is valid or not?

PRACTICING YOUR SKILLS

What If . . . The invention of the cotton gin changed the southern economy dramatically. **What if** the cotton gin had not been invented? Do you think slavery would have died out by itself? Would there still have been a need for abolitionists to make people see that slavery was immoral? How might the southern economy have developed?

Debating Debate the issue: Popular sovereignty was a fair and democratic way of solving the issue of slavery in the territories.

Researching, Making a Table Writing

1. Using reference materials, research the executive, legislative, and judicial branches of the Confederate government. Make a table listing the similarities and differences between the governments of the U.S. and of the Confederacy.
2. In the election of 1860, Lincoln won the largest number of popular and electoral votes. Douglas received the second largest popular vote but the least number of electoral votes. Using reference materials if needed, explain how the U.S. electoral system made this outcome possible.
3. Using reference materials, write a report on the underground railroad. Include major routes, methods of hiding runaways, means of transportation, noted conductors, and years of major underground railroad activity.

Exploring

1. If you live in a former Confederate state, prepare a brief written report on your state's joining the Confederacy. Include who decided on secession, who opposed leaving the Union, and where and when the decision was made.
2. If you live in a state that stayed in the Union during the Civil War, prepare a brief written report on abolitionist activity in your state before the Civil War.

Building Writing Skills

An essay is a short composition on one topic. Short reports are essays and many tests are made up of essay questions. The topic of an essay should not be too big. For example, Native Americans is too broad, but Some Customs and Traditions of the Shoshoni would be small enough to focus on. Here are some tips to help you.

- Identify your purpose. Are you attempting to inform, amuse, anger, or persuade.
- Before you write, make an outline listing main ideas and supporting details.
- Make your introduction interesting so you will catch your readers' interest. Beginning with a question is one way.
- Be sure to keep your purpose in mind as you write.
- Tie all the main points of your essay together in a conclusion.

Activity: Using the information from Unit III about the hypothesis you tested, write an essay of three to five paragraphs. State the hypothesis as your topic. Use as supporting details the evidence you gathered to prove or disprove it. **Hint:** When answering an essay question, restate the question and use facts as supporting details.

Reading

Barry, James P. *Bloody Kansas, 1854-65: Guerrilla Warfare Delays Peaceful American Settlement.* New York: Watts, 1972.

Davis, Ossie. *Escape to Freedom: A Play About Young Frederick Douglass.* New York: Viking Press, 1978.

Dillon, Merton. *The Abolitionists: Growth of a Dissenting Minority.* New York: Norton, 1979. Role played by free blacks.

Mitgang, Herbert. *The Fiery Trial: A Life of Lincoln.* New York: Viking Press, 1974.

Potter, David M. *The Impending Crisis: 1848-1861.* New York: Harper & Row, 1976.

Webb, Robert N. *Raid on Harper's Ferry, October 17, 1859: A Brutal Skirmish Widens the Rift Between North and South.* New York: Watts, 1971.

UNIT IV CIVIL WAR & RECONSTRUCTION

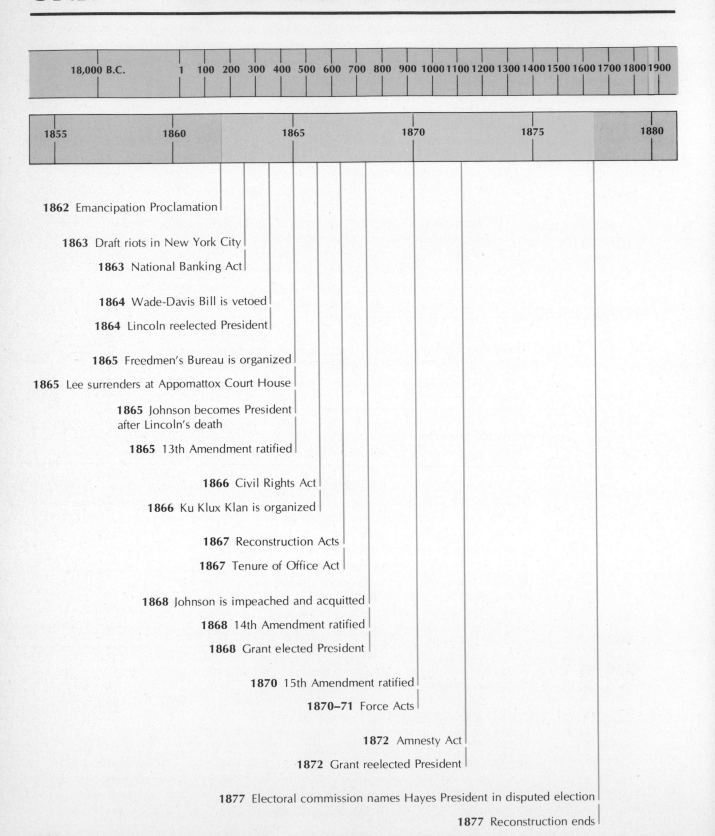

18,000 B.C. 1 100 200 300 400 500 600 700 800 900 1000 1100 1200 1300 1400 1500 1600 1700 1800 1900

1855   1860   1865   1870   1875   1880

1862 Emancipation Proclamation

1863 Draft riots in New York City

1863 National Banking Act

1864 Wade-Davis Bill is vetoed

1864 Lincoln reelected President

1865 Freedmen's Bureau is organized

1865 Lee surrenders at Appomattox Court House

1865 Johnson becomes President after Lincoln's death

1865 13th Amendment ratified

1866 Civil Rights Act

1866 Ku Klux Klan is organized

1867 Reconstruction Acts

1867 Tenure of Office Act

1868 Johnson is impeached and acquitted

1868 14th Amendment ratified

1868 Grant elected President

1870 15th Amendment ratified

1870–71 Force Acts

1872 Amnesty Act

1872 Grant reelected President

1877 Electoral commission names Hayes President in disputed election

1877 Reconstruction ends

Chapter 1   Battlefront

LOOKING AHEAD

This chapter describes the fighting of the Civil War. You will learn about the advantages and disadvantages of each side as war approached and about the war plans of each. The chapter also discusses the problems each side faced in drafting soldiers and the contributions to the war by women, blacks, and Native Americans. After you study this chapter, you will be able to:

- compare and contrast the advantages and disadvantages of the Union and Confederacy.
- describe the war plans of each side.
- identify the problems each side faced in building an army.
- identify the sequence of events in fighting the Civil War.
- ★ gather data about strategy through maps.

Social Studies Vocabulary

blockade   draft   discrimination

People

Irvin McDowell	Dorothea Dix
Pierre G. T. Beauregard	Ely S. Parker
Thomas "Stonewall" Jackson	Stand Watie
George McClellan	Albert Johnston
Ulysses S. Grant	Henry W. Halleck
William H. Carney	David Farragut
Robert Smalls	Joseph E. Johnston
Pauline Cushman	Robert E. Lee
Belle Boyd	John Pope
Sally Louisa Tompkins	Ambrose Burnside
Clara Barton	Joseph Hooker
Elizabeth Blackwell	William T. Sherman

Places

Bull Run (Manassas)	Gettysburg	Richmond
Shiloh (Pittsburgh Landing)	Vicksburg	Appomattox Court
Antietam (Sharpsburg)	Chattanooga	House
Chancellorsville	Petersburg	

Words and Terms

bounty   draft riot

Confederate soldiers wore light brown, or butternut, uniforms like this one. Officers' uniforms were gray.

At the beginning of the Civil War, neither side expected or was prepared for a long fight. Each side expected to win the war with a few easy victories on the battlefield. Throughout spring 1861, Union and Confederate soldiers trained and paraded to shouts of "On to Richmond" or "On to Washington."

The first battle, fought in July 1861 at Bull Run (Manassas: muh-NAS-uhs), Virginia, was a shock to both sides. Union forces led by General Irvin McDowell (muhk-DOW-uhl) attacked a Confederate force under General Pierre G. T. Beauregard (BOH-ruh-gahrd). Members of Washington society made the 32-kilometer (20-mile) trip to sit in the shade and watch the fighting. They expected to see the firing of a few shots and a quick northern victory.

But Confederate reinforcements under General Thomas "Stonewall" Jackson were rushed to the battlefield. With steady gunfire, the Confederates pushed the Union forces back. The retreat quickly became a rout. Throwing away their rifles, the inexperienced Union troops began running back to Washington, tripping over the shocked civilians. The Confederates, surprised by the collapse of the enemy, did not follow. They celebrated instead.

This first battle of the war greatly boosted southern morale. It also made Northerners realize that defeating the Confederacy would not be quick and easy. The table listing the advantages and disadvantages of each side as the Civil War began should help you understand why the war lasted so long. The table should also help you to see why the Union was the eventual winner.

WAR PLANS

After Bull Run, the Union mapped out a strategy with three objectives. The first was to capture the Confederate capital at Richmond. By taking the enemy capital, the Union hoped to weaken southern morale badly. The second Union objective was to gain control of the Mississippi. This would divide the South and cut off one of its most important transportation routes. Finally, the Union would blockade Confederate ports. **Blockade** (blahk-AYD) means to prevent passage in or out. Closing southern ports would keep the South from shipping cotton to Europe in exchange for supplies.

To meet its goals, the Union created two main army groups. East of the Appalachians, the army was under the command of General George B. McClellan (muh-KLEL-uhn). West of the Appalachians, the Union fielded an army led by General Ulysses S. Grant. After McClellan failed to put pressure on the Confederates, Lincoln replaced him.

As commander in chief of U.S. armed forces, Lincoln controlled the conduct of the war. He appointed top army officers and suggested strategy. After removing McClellan, Lincoln had trouble finding a general that would bring him the battle victories he wanted. Lincoln replaced the commander of the army in the east several times before giving the command to Grant. Grant had won the President's confidence through a series of victories on the western battlefront.

The South planned to fight a defensive war on its own territory. It hoped that such a war would wear down the Union will to fight. Southern leaders expected to receive economic help from Great Britain, the chief importer of its cotton.

BUILDING AN ARMY

At the beginning of the war, both the Union and the Confederacy tried to fight the war with volunteers. In the North, state and federal governments each paid a bounty, or sum of money, to attract volunteers. But by 1862, even bounties could not recruit enough soldiers. The Confederacy also found it difficult to fill its army with volunteers.

After a year of fighting, the South passed its first draft law. A **draft** is a government's call on its citizens to serve in the military. The law stated that every white man between the ages of 18 and 35 could be called for military service. But a drafted man could hire a substitute, and certain men were exempted—those who owned 20 or more slaves or those who worked in weapons or ammunition factories. Many Southerners objected to the unfairness of the law.

exempt (eg-ZEMPT): to free from a duty

The Confederacy passed additional laws in 1863 and 1864 that changed some of the unfair practices. The new laws stopped the hiring of substitutes, cut the number of exemptions, and included white men between the ages of 17 and 50. By war's end, more than one million men had volunteered or been drafted into the Confederate Army.

On March 3, 1863, the Union passed its first draft law. This law made white men between the ages of 20 and 45 eligible for military

465

CIVIL WAR: ADVANTAGES AND DISADVANTAGES OF EACH SIDE

	Advantages		Disadvantages	
	Union	Confederacy	Union	Confederacy
Military	Had twice as many soldiers Had a small navy	Had more and better officers Had only to fight a defensive war to win	Had to conquer the South to win	Had no navy so used private vessels
Political	Had a strong, established government			Had to build a new government
Economic	Had almost all U.S. industry Had almost all U.S. supplies of coal, iron, copper, gold Had most U.S. rail routes for transporting and supplying troops Had almost all U.S. banking and financial centers Traded with foreign nations for needed supplies			Had little industry Had few natural resources Had few rail routes for transporting and supplying troops Had few banking and financial centers Had limited foreign trade because of northern blockade
Population	About 22 million			About 9 million including 3½ million slaves

service. As in the South, the law allowed a man to hire a substitute. The Union law also allowed a drafted man to pay the government $300 rather than serve. Many Northerners were angered because the law seemed to favor the wealthy.

Draft riots broke out in several cities. The most serious were in New York City in July 1863. For four days, mobs roamed the streets stealing, burning homes, and killing people. What began as an antidraft riot turned into racial violence. Blacks were beaten to death, and some were even burned alive. Most of the rioters were immigrants who feared losing their jobs to freed slaves. Before federal troops restored order, 76 people were dead. Despite such opposition to the draft, about 300,000 white male draftees out of a total of two million soldiers served in the Union Army.

Women and the War

On the home front, women on both sides worked in recruiting centers and raised money for the poor and injured. On the battlefront, women served as scouts, smugglers, and spies. Pauline Cushman was a Union spy. Belle Boyd acted as one of General "Stonewall" Jackson's messengers. Historians also think she may have been involved in blockade running. Estimates put at 400 the number of women who fought in the war disguised as men.

Not far from the battle lines, women freed men for battle by laundering clothes, cooking, and nursing the wounded. Sally Louisa Tompkins was made an honorary captain in the Confederate Army for her work as a nurse. Clara Barton nursed wounded Union soldiers at Bull Run, Antietam (an-TEE-tuhm), and Fredericksburg. In 1881, Barton helped organize the American Red Cross. Dr. Elizabeth Blackwell, the first woman graduate of an American medical college, recruited nurses for the Union Army. Dorothea Dix, whom you may recall from the unit Life at Mid-Century, supervised all Union Army nurses.

Blacks and the War

During the early months of the war, neither side allowed blacks—free or slave—to serve. Slaves who ran away to the Union lines were usually returned to their owners. A few northern generals kept runaways and used them as cooks, drivers, nurses, scouts, or spies. By 1862, however, Union casualties were mounting and it was becoming difficult to recruit white soldiers. That summer the Union began accepting black volunteers into its army and navy. Blacks enlisted with enthusiasm. However, once in uniform they met with much discrimination and resistance from white soldiers and officers alike. **Discrimination** (dis-krim-uh-NAY-shuhn) means unequal treatment. Most blacks were given jobs as cooks or drivers. They did not receive as much military training or medical care as white soldiers.

Until 1864, black soldiers were paid less than whites. A white soldier received $13 a month, while a black soldier was paid $7. White soldiers refused to serve in the same regiments as blacks. Some states, such as Massachusetts, formed all-black regiments. Most of these, however, were led by white officers, because only a small number of blacks were allowed to become officers. However, two regiments under General Benjamin Butler were led by blacks as were several other regiments. Officers's commissions were given to a number of black doctors and chaplains.

In all, over 186,000 blacks served the Union. About 30,000 saw action in the navy. After the opening months of the war, few battles were fought in which blacks did not take part. Many blacks were awarded medals for their bravery under fire. For example, a Massachusetts soldier, William H. Carney, was awarded the Congressional Medal of Honor for his part in the Union attack on Fort Wagner in South Carolina. Carney was one of twenty blacks during the war who received this honor. There were many such acts of bravery,

Mathew Brady took this picture of a Union soldier wearing a Zouave uniform. The cap is red with a blue band, the shirt red, the jacket and pants gray. A more common Union soldier's uniform was dark blue shirt and jacket with gray pants.

Union Movements
Confederate Movements
Union Victory
Confederate Victory
Union Area
Confederate Area
Area gained by Union

Ohio River

Fort Donelson

Fort Henry
Nashville

Memphis
Chattanooga

Shiloh
(Pittsburg Landing)
Grant, 1862
Tennessee R.
Atlanta

Birmingham
Montgomery

Fort Sumter
Charleston

Natchez
Savannah

Baton Rouge
New Orleans
Jacksonville

Farragut, 1862

GULF OF MEXICO

Union
Blockade

Mississippi River

N

**Civil War from
1861 to 1862**

0   200
0   300 kilometers

Antietam
Sharpsburg
Lee, 1862
Baltimore
Harper's Ferry
Burnside, 1862
McClellan, 1862
Bull Run
Washington, D.C.
Bull Run
(Manassas)
Pope 1862
Fredericksburg
Lee 1862
Chesapeake Bay
McClellan, 1862
Jackson 1862
Richmond
Seven Days Battles
Merrimac v. Monitor

0   30 miles
0   50 kilometers

Above, left: "Tenting Tonight on the Old Campground" was composed by a New Hampshire ballad singer. It describes a soldier's longing for peace and loved ones at home. Why do you think this song became popular among both Union and Confederate soldiers?

Above: Blacks enlisted in the Union Army in large numbers. Many came from the South. Those shown here belong to the Second Light Artillery Regiment.

Top: The U.S. S. *Merrimac* fought the C.S.S. *Monitor* to a draw off Norfolk.

Bottom, left: This sketch shows Union and Confederate soldiers in battle at Antietam. What was the outcome of that one-day battle?

Bottom, right: Alfred R. Waud did the sketch at left for *Harper's Weekly*. The technology for using photographs in publications was not available.

During the Civil War, both sides used blacks in the war effort. How did their use differ between North and South?

especially among runaway slaves who fought for the Union. Robert Smalls was a slave who piloted boats in Charleston Harbor before the war. In 1861, he sailed one of these boats out of the harbor and turned it and himself over to the Union. The Union Navy used Smalls and the boat in the northern war effort.

The South did not enlist blacks as soldiers until March 1865, and few actually fought. However, had it not been for the slaves who took the place of white males, the South could not have fielded so large a white army. Slaves were either hired from their owners or forced into service. They built trenches and earthworks for defense and worked as butchers, drivers, and nurses. Some slaves were sent from their plantations to work in factories and mines. Iron works in Virginia and Alabama used slave labor throughout the war.

Native Americans and the War

Some Native Americans fought for the Union or the Confederacy though most saw the fighting as a white war. Each side promised to protect Native American land and property if Native Americans would fight. They could not be drafted since they were not citizens. Some Native American nations were divided in their loyalties. Creeks, Chickasaws, Cherokees, Choctaws, and Seminoles had supporters of both sides.

Two Native Americans who took part in the war were Ely S. Parker and Stand Watie (WAH-tee). Parker, a Seneca, was Grant's military secretary during the war. Later, when Grant was elected President, Parker was named U.S. Commissioner of Indian Affairs. Watie, a Cherokee, was the only Native American brigadier general in the Confederate Army. He led a unit of Cherokee volunteers called the Cherokee Mounted Rifles. At the end of the war, Watie was one of the last Confederate officers to surrender.

YEARS OF FIGHTING: 1862

After Bull Run, no major battles took place until early 1862. During this break, General McClellan began building his army. While he slowly trained his troops, General Grant led Union soldiers in an invasion of western Tennessee. They captured Forts Henry and Donelson on the Tennessee and Columbia rivers and took 14,000 prisoners. Grant then marched into Mississippi.

Early in the morning of April 6, a Confederate force of 40,000 led by General Albert Johnston surprised Grant's army at Shiloh (SHY-loh; Pittsburgh Landing) in northeastern Mississippi. Many Union soldiers were caught dressing or making their morning coffee. The Confederates were close to victory when fresh Union troops arrived and turned the near massacre into a Union victory. The casualties — 13,000 Union and 10,700 Confederates — hurt morale on both sides. After Grant failed to follow the retreating Confederates, Lincoln replaced him with General Henry Halleck.

During this time, Admiral David Farragut (FAR-uh-guht) of the Union Navy had captured New Orleans, Baton Rouge (BAT-uhn ROOZH), and Natchez on the Mississippi. The lower part of the Mississippi was now under Union control.

In March, the first battle between armored warships had taken place. The U.S.S. *Monitor* had defeated the C.S.S. *Merrimac* off the coast of Virginia. With a water route to southern Virginia open, McClellan moved his troops along the coast and up the James River. While moving toward Richmond, part of his force was attacked near the Chickahominy (chik-uh-HAHM-uh-nee) River by Confederates under General Joseph E. Johnston. Neither side gained a victory, but Johnston was seriously wounded. He was replaced by General Robert E. Lee. Several days later, Lee struck at McClellan's forces. For seven days, the armies were locked in battle around Richmond. The fighting ended with no clear-cut victory but with 15,800 Union and 20,000 Confederate casualties. McClellan retreated to the James River. President Lincoln, displeased with McClellan, placed him under the command of General Halleck.

Then, in the second Battle of Bull Run in August 1862, Lee's army struck at Union soldiers under General John Pope. The Union forces were again defeated. Lee continued north crossing the Potomac into Maryland. At Antietam (Sharpsburg), McClellan attacked; 70,000 Union troops faced 40,000 Confederates. By the end of the day, 22,000 soldiers lay dead, and the Confederate line held. Instead of advancing, McClellan allowed Lee to retreat across the Potomac to Rich-

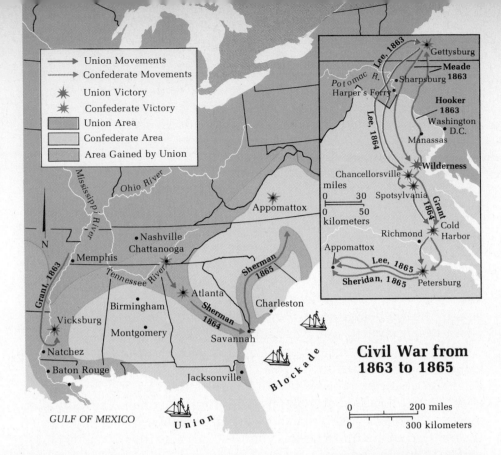

Civil War from 1863 to 1865

Union Movements
Confederate Movements
Union Victory
Confederate Victory
Union Area
Confederate Area
Area Gained by Union

Above: The Battle of Gettysburg began when Confederate soldiers looking for shoes ran into Union cavalry. On the third day, Lee ordered General George Pickett to storm the Union lines. Confederate troops, marching in formation, were beaten back. Who was the Union general in this battle? Why is it considered a turning point in the war?

Opposite, top: A Confederate concert singer wrote this patriotic song.

Opposite, bottom: Grant's soldiers cut a canal opposite Vicksburg. How is the kind of terrain shown in the picture shown on the map?

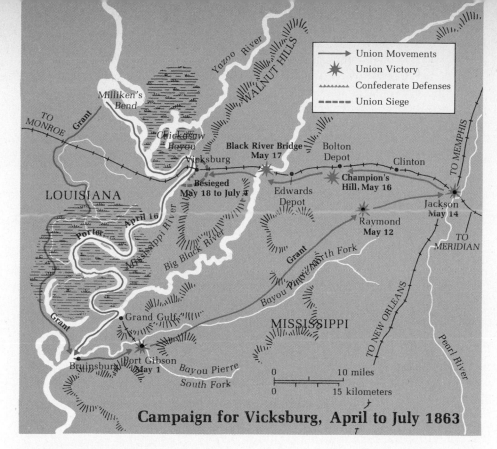

Campaign for Vicksburg, April to July 1863

Map legend:
- → Union Movements
- ✹ Union Victory
- Confederate Defenses
- Union Siege

⭐ **BUILDING MAP SKILLS**

The map above illustrates strategy, or a plan of attack. It shows terrain (physical features), troop movements, and defenses. Study the map of Vicksburg. **1.** What physical features made Vicksburg easy to defend? **2.** Describe Grant's route. **3.** What was his goal in taking the railroad?

mond. In November, Lincoln removed McClellan and replaced him with General Ambrose Burnside. When he failed to take Richmond in December, Lincoln replaced him with General Joseph Hooker.

YEARS OF FIGHTING: 1863–65

In April 1863, Hooker's army moved into Chancellorsville, Virginia, on its way toward Richmond. Lee, camped a short distance away, sent "Stonewall" Jackson against Hooker. Jackson's forces, attacking at six o'clock the evening of May 2, surprised the Union troops. Nightfall brought a break in the fighting, but the battle continued the next day. It lasted for three days, until Hooker retreated.

With northern morale at a new low after Chancellorsville, Lee took his army into the North. With an invasion and victory, he hoped to convince the Union to end the war. On July 1, 1863, near Gettysburg (GET-iz-berg), Pennsylvania, a Confederate expedition looking for shoes met a Union cavalry unit. Both sides called for reinforcements. After three days of fighting, Lee retreated. The Battle of Gettysburg was a turning point in the war. It showed that Lee's plan to end the war with an invasion would not work. The battle however, did end southern hopes for British help. After this costly defeat, the British were convinced that the Confederacy could not win.

At the same time as the Battle of Gettysburg, Union forces under Grant won an important victory at Vicksburg, Mississippi. In mid-May 1863, Grant had laid siege to the city. Cut off from food, supplies, and reinforcements, the city surrendered on July 4. With Vicksburg

Many of the wounded were cared for in field hospitals near the battlefront. The more seriously wounded were taken to hospitals behind the lines. This is a Union field hospital after a battle near Savage Station, Virginia.

under Union control, the North now controlled the Mississippi. Supplies and reinforcements from Texas and Arkansas could not reach the other states of the Confederacy. Lincoln, pleased with Grant, gave him command of all the western army groups. In November, Grant captured Chattanooga (chat-uh-NOO-guh), Tennessee, an important rail center. In March 1864, Lincoln promoted Grant to commander of all Union armies.

That spring, Grant moved against Richmond. Along the way, Grant fought Lee's army at the battles of the Wilderness, Spotsylvania Court House, and Cold Harbor. Both sides suffered heavy losses. With 60,000 Union soldiers killed during these battles, some Northerners demanded Grant's removal. Lee finally dug in around Petersburg, 37 kilometers (23 miles) from Richmond, and Grant placed the city under siege.

While Grant was applying pressure to Lee's army, General William T. Sherman fought his way against General Joseph Johnston's forces from Tennessee to Atlanta, Georgia. On September 2, Sherman took Atlanta. In November, he marched from Atlanta to Savannah, destroying along the way everything that Southerners could use to continue fighting—railroads, bridges, crops, and even houses. In December, Sherman reached Savannah and turned north to meet Grant.

By April 1865, Lee's forces could no longer hold out against the siege of Petersburg. They retreated toward Richmond with Grant following. Richmond fell to Grant on April 3, 1865. With only 30,000 soldiers to face Grant's 115,000, Lee saw the hopelessness of fighting. On April 9, he surrendered to Grant at Appomattox (ap-uh-MAT-uhks) Court House, Virginia. The fighting was over.

LOOKING BACK

1. Write a paragraph comparing and contrasting the following for both the Union and the Confederacy: **a.** army and navy. **b.** economies. **c.** population. **d.** politics.

2. Write one statement describing the strategies of each: **a.** the Union. **b.** the Confederacy. Be sure to include Lincoln's role in Union war plans.

3. What problems did each of the following face in drafting soldiers: **a.** the Union? **b.** the Confederacy? **c.** What were the reasons behind the New York City draft riots? **d.** What kinds of discrimination did blacks face in the Union Army? **e.** How did the Confederate Army use blacks? **f.** How did women serve the war effort on both sides? **g.** How did most Native Americans see the war?

4. Using the material in this chapter, make a time line showing the major events of the Civil War.

★ 5. Study the map on p. 473 to answer: **a.** What physical features made Vicksburg difficult to attack? **b.** What route did Grant take to reach it? **c.** How did he cut off supplies to the city?

Chapter 2

Home Front

LOOKING AHEAD

This chapter describes the effects of the Civil War on the home fronts of both the Union and the Confederacy and each side's efforts to raise money to fight the war. You will also learn about the Emancipation Proclamation and the presidential election of 1864. After you study this chapter, you will be able to:

- state the reasons behind opposition to the war in both the Union and the Confederacy.
- list two effects of the war on the home fronts of both the North and the South.
- describe how each side financed the war.
- explain the events that led to issuing the Emancipation Proclamation.
- identify the main issue in the 1864 presidential election.

Social Studies Vocabulary

| war bond | inflation | emancipation |

People

Copperheads	Charles Sumner	George B. McClellan
Radical Republicans	Thaddeus Stevens	
	Andrew Johnson	

Words and Terms

| border states | greenbacks | Emancipation |
| profiteers | National Banking Act | Proclamation |

As you may recall from the unit Coming of the Civil War, Lincoln's goal in fighting the Civil War was to reunite the nation. During the first two years of the war, Lincoln made little progress toward his goal. But, beginning in 1863, the tide of battle began to turn in favor of the Union. Helped by military victories, President Lincoln won reelection in 1864. Besides winning a military advantage, the Union was also strengthening its economic advantage over the Confederacy.

THE UNION

Not everyone in the Union—or in the Confederacy—supported the Civil War. Most Northerners wanted the Union preserved, but some Northerners believed that fighting a war over secession was wrong. In

Congress, a few Democratic members, called Copperheads after the snake, opposed the war policy of Lincoln and the rest of Congress. They wanted peace and hoped it could be brought about through negotiations. As a result, they voted against all bills to help the Union war effort. Most Copperheads were from Ohio, Illinois, and Indiana or from the Union border states—Delaware, Kentucky, Maryland, and Missouri. The border states were slave states that remained in the Union.

While some Northerners opposed the war itself, others opposed the way it was being fought. They wanted the Union to defeat the Confederacy completely. This view was represented in Congress by members of Lincoln's own party. A group of Republicans called Radicals wanted to go further than Lincoln and add abolition as a goal for fighting the war. In 1861, the Radicals called for the immediate freeing and arming of slaves. While the Radicals were united in their goal, they were divided in their motives. One group, led by Senator Charles Sumner of Massachusetts and Representative Thaddeus Stevens of Pennsylvania, favored abolition because they thought slavery was wrong. These Radicals wanted to make freed slaves U.S. citizens with all the rights of citizens. Other Radicals blamed Southerners for starting the war and wanted to punish the South by freeing the slaves.

motive (MOH-tiv): reason for acting

Behind the Lines

In 1861, the Civil War caused a depression in the North. At first, the loss of southern trade badly hurt northern manufacturers and bankers. Without southern cotton, many New England textile mills closed. In time, the mills reopened to make woolen goods such as army blankets and uniforms. Other manufacturers also began to produce goods to meet the demands of the army. By late 1862, northern factories were turning out thousands of uniforms, boots, blankets, tents,

Women working in northern factories aided the Union war effort. What was one bad result of the large numbers of women in the labor force?

saddles, rifles, cannon, and bullets. Farmers benefited from the increasing need of the army for food, wool, and leather. With increased demand came increased prices—and profits—for farmers. Shipbuilding, mining, railroading, and meat-packing industries expanded to meet the growing demands of a wartime economy.

People called profiteers took advantage of the war to become rich. They sold the Union rotten meat, uniforms and blankets of poor quality, rifles that jammed or misfired, and poorly built ships. Some profiteers smuggled goods to the Confederacy in return for cotton.

Not all Northerners shared in the prosperity, however. The families of many Union soldiers suffered great hardships. As prices for goods rose, some poorer families were unable to buy food and clothing. Many women were forced to find factory jobs at any wage. As had happened before, with so many women working, factory owners lowered the pay of all employees.

Financing the War

The Union raised money in several ways. Beginning in 1861 and continuing throughout the war, Congress raised the tariff. The added tax on foreign goods brought in some money but not enough. In 1861 and again in 1862, Congress passed income tax laws. Most of the money the Union raised at this time, however, came through the sale of war bonds. A **war bond** is a bond issued by a government to raise money for fighting a war.

The federal government also issued a small amount of paper money, not backed by gold or silver. The paper dollars were known as greenbacks because the back of the paper was green. Since greenbacks could not be exchanged for gold or silver, some merchants would not take them in payment. Or, they demanded more greenbacks than if the purchaser was using gold or silver. Inflation resulted. **Inflation** is a rapid increase in the price of goods and services. During times of inflation, the same amount of money buys less than it would have bought earlier. Inflation in the North, however, never became as severe as it did in the South.

To raise additional money for the war and to improve the U.S. banking system, Congress passed the National Banking Act in 1863. Under this act, private citizens could invest money to open a national bank. At least one third of their investment had to be used to buy government bonds. In return for the bonds, the bank could issue bank notes, or paper money, backed by the government.

THE CONFEDERACY

In the South, as in the North, not everyone supported the war. Many Southerners thought that southern rights could be protected only by leaving the Union. But there were other Southerners who did not think this was important enough to fight for. As the war dragged

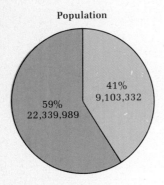

Population

59%
22,339,989

41%
9,103,332

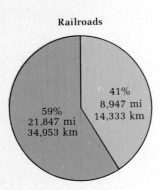

Railroads

59%
21,847 mi
34,953 km

41%
8,947 mi
14,333 km

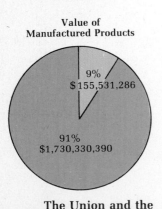

Value of
Manufactured Products

9%
$ 155,531,286

91%
$1,730,330,390

**The Union and the
Confederacy in 1860**

■ Union

▨ Confederacy

Source: *Eighth Census of the United
States,* Bureau of the Census

The Union blockade and the destruction of many rail lines caused shortages of food and other necessities. The desperation of the people for food is shown in this illustration. Like cartoons, other artwork also has a point of view. What do you think the artist thought of these people?

on, southern opponents of the war gained support. Especially after 1862, defeats on the battlefield and economic troubles on the home front caused many to wonder whether they should keep fighting.

Behind the Lines

One of the biggest problems the Confederacy faced was supplying the army. As you may recall from the unit Life at Mid-Century, the South had little industry. Southerners depended on the North and on Europe for their manufactured goods. They paid for these goods with the money from selling their cotton. The war ended most of this trade.

In 1861, the Union blockaded Confederate ports. In the first three years of the war, the blockade was not very effective. Southerners used blockade runners to break through it. These ships brought weapons and manufactured goods such as machinery from Europe. But the Confederate Army always suffered from shortages of shoes and uniforms. During the last two years of the war, the Union added more ships to the blockade line. The amount of smuggled weapons and other goods fell as more and more blockade runners were captured. As a result, Southerners were forced to set up their own weapons factories. The few factories that were built made only small amounts of cannon, rifles, and ammunition.

Because almost all the war was fought in the Confederacy, Southerners found it difficult to move what goods and supplies they had. Union forces destroyed much of the southern railway system. In addition, many southern waterways, especially after 1863, were under Union control.

By the middle of the war, shortages of goods for use on the home front were also a problem. Southerners no longer enjoyed such luxu-

Bales of cotton pile up on a southern dock as a result of the Union blockade. Is a photograph always better for learning about an event than a sketch or a painting?

ries as coffee or tea. Also, many necessities—clothing, soap, pots and pans, and medicine—were not available. When machines broke down or wore out, there were no spare parts to repair or replace them. A number of cities, among them Vicksburg and Richmond, were under siege by Union troops and went for long periods without food, medicine, and other supplies.

With husbands and sons away in the war, southern women managed plantations, farms, and businesses. Because of shortages and inflation, southern women had to make clothing and household goods last. When an item wore out, Southerners on the home front went without or used a substitute. For example, when clothing wore out, southern women made their own cloth and colored it with dyes made from plants. For coffee, they drank a liquid made from sweet potatoes and grain.

Financing the War

The South found it difficult to raise money to fight the war. Because of the blockade, the South could not raise money through tariffs. Income taxes produced little revenue because most southern wealth was tied up in land and slaves. For the same reason, the sale of Confederate war bonds brought little money. Some money came through loans to the South from foreign governments.

Income from these sources was not nearly enough to pay for the war, however. To pay its bills, the Confederacy was forced to issue paper money with no gold or silver to back it. As in the North, Southerners lost faith in the paper money that their government printed. But inflation in the South was much more severe than in the North. As the war dragged on and hopes of a Confederate victory faded, Confederate money declined drastically in value. By 1865, a Confederate

drastically
(DRAS-tik-lee):
severely

480

dollar was worth only about one cent in gold. As the Confederate dollar declined in value, prices soared. Most Southerners, but especially those who worked for wages, were hurt by inflation. Their wages did not increase to match the rising prices for whatever food and clothing were available.

EMANCIPATION PROCLAMATION

From the start of the war, abolitionists had urged Lincoln to make immediate freedom for slaves a Union war goal. But Lincoln, although he hated slavery, had been unwilling. He feared that **emancipation** (ih-man-suh-PAY-shuhn), or freeing the slaves, would drive the border states into the Confederacy. He also realized that many northern workers opposed emancipation. They feared freed blacks would move North and take their jobs by agreeing to work for lower wages. As you read in the last chapter, this was one reason for the draft riots. Finally, Lincoln himself differed with abolitionists on one point. He believed that slaveowners as property owners should be paid for the slaves they freed.

As the war dragged on, pressure grew for Lincoln to free the slaves. More and more Northerners joined with Radicals in calling for emancipation. Some wanted to punish the South for the war by freeing the slaves. Others hoped that emancipation would encourage the slaves to revolt and possibly end the war more quickly.

By summer 1862, Lincoln was convinced that he had to make some statement about freeing the slaves. He wanted to satisfy the growing number of Americans who favored emancipation. But he also wanted to win support from Great Britain. Because the British government opposed slavery, Lincoln hoped emancipation would discourage British merchants from trading with the Confederacy.

At first, Lincoln offered to have the federal government pay slaveowners in the border states to free their slaves. But the slaveowners refused the money and refused to free their slaves. On September 22, 1862, five days after the Union victory at Antietam, Lincoln issued the Emancipation Proclamation. The President had waited for a Union victory so that he would appear to be issuing the proclamation from a position of strength. The proclamation promised to free all slaves in those states or parts of states still in rebellion on January 1, 1863.

The Emancipation Proclamation did not affect slaves in border states or in southern areas occupied by Union troops. In reality, the proclamation had no effect on slaves in areas controlled by the Confederacy either. Lincoln's purpose in issuing the proclamation was to pressure those parts of the Confederacy that were still fighting. He hoped the proclamation would force them into ending the war.

Southerners saw the proclamation as an attempt to create slave revolts. Northern abolitionists cheered but thought that the proclama-

After the Emancipation Proclamation, many blacks left the plantations and crossed to the freedom and safety of Union lines. What was Lincoln's purpose in issuing the Proclamation?

tion did not go far enough. They argued that it should have included slaves in border states. Democrats accused the President of changing the goal of the war from restoring the Union to freeing slaves.

ELECTION OF 1864

In the presidential election of 1864, the Republicans nominated Lincoln over the protests of the Radicals in the party. To broaden the party's support, the Republicans chose Andrew Johnson of Tennessee, a Democrat, for vice-presidential candidate. The Democrats based their campaign on the North's growing desire for peace. In their platform, they called for an end to the fighting and for peace talks. The Democrats chose General George B. McClellan, the war hero, as their candidate. Lincoln won easily. The Republicans had opened western lands for settlement, reorganized the banking system, and raised the tariff. These acts won support from all parts of the Union.

LOOKING BACK

1. Why were some people opposed to the war in: **a.** the Union? **b.** the Confederacy?
2. **a.** How did the northern economy change during the war? **b.** Give two examples. **c.** What were two problems the South faced? **d.** How did Southerners attempt to solve each?
3. How was the war effort financed in: **a.** the Union? **b.** the Confederacy?
4. **a.** What events led Lincoln to issue the Emancipation Proclamation? **b.** What effects did the proclamation have on slaves?
5. What was the main issue in the presidential election of 1864? **Hint:** You will have to infer the answer from the motives or actions of members of the two parties.

Chapter 3   Debate Over Reconstruction

LOOKING AHEAD

This chapter describes some of the problems facing the U.S. after the Civil War. Presidents Lincoln and Johnson disagreed with Congress on the way the reconstruction of the Union should be carried out. After you study this chapter, you will be able to:

- identify the problems facing the U.S. after the Civil War.
- compare Lincoln's view of how Reconstruction should be handled with Congress's view.
- identify the conflict between Johnson and Congress.
- list the laws that were passed to protect the rights of former slaves.
- describe the sequence of events that led to Johnson's impeachment and acquittal.
- explain the reason for Grant's victory in the presidential election of 1868.

Social Studies Vocabulary

amnesty   civil rights

People

Abraham Lincoln	Andrew Johnson	Edwin M. Stanton
John Wilkes Booth	Ulysses S. Grant	Horatio Seymour

Words and Terms

Reconstruction	freedmen	Reconstruction Acts
Wade-Davis Bill	Freedmen's Bureau	Tenure of Office Act
13th Amendment	Civil Rights Act	
black codes	14th Amendment	

As the Civil War ended, the nation faced three problems:

- readmitting the seceded states to the Union;
- deciding how to treat ex-Confederate leaders;
- determining the rights of former slaves.

President Lincoln, his successor Andrew Johnson, and Congress all had different views on how to solve these problems. Southerners and freed slaves also had their views. In the end, it was Congress that guided Reconstruction. Reconstruction is the term used to describe the rebuilding of the nation after the Civil War. It describes that period in U.S. history when the states of the former Confederacy were controlled by the federal government.

successor
(suhk-SES-uhr):
one who comes after

This view of Atlanta by Mathew Brady shows some of the destruction that city suffered during the war. This is the railroad yard. Why did the Union destroy southern rail lines?

LINCOLN'S PLAN

In December 1863, while the war was still being fought, President Lincoln announced his plan for Reconstruction. Ex-Confederate states could be readmitted when the number of people in a state who had taken a loyalty oath to the Union equaled one tenth the number of voters in the 1860 election. The state could then form a government, hold a constitutional convention, and adopt a new constitution.

Lincoln's plan promised amnesty for most ex-Confederates if they were willing to take the loyalty oath. **Amnesty** (AM-nis-tee) is a general pardon, especially for offenses against the federal government. Amnesty would be granted to high-ranking ex-Confederate officials only if they asked the President individually for pardons.

According to Lincoln's plan, new state constitutions had to forbid slavery. States had to provide free public education for blacks. However, his plan did not include giving blacks the right to vote.

Under the first part of Lincoln's plan, new governments were set up in Tennessee, Arkansas, Virginia, and Louisiana before the war ended. But Congress refused to seat the newly elected Senators and Representatives from these states.

Opposition

The Republican-controlled Congress opposed Lincoln's plan for several reasons. Many thought the terms for readmitting the seceded states should be harsher. Others thought that Reconstruction came under the powers given to Congress, not to the President. They believed the President had gained too much power during the war and wanted to reestablish the balance of power between Congress and the presidency. Some Republicans were moved by political reasons.

They feared the majority of southern white voters would become Democrats. These same members of Congress feared that if former Confederates were allowed to return to Congress, they might vote against such Republican programs as high tariffs, the national banks, and money for railroad construction. Some members of Congress opposed Lincoln's plan because it did not establish the rights of newly freed blacks.

In 1864, Radical Republicans introduced the Wade-Davis Bill as their plan for Reconstruction. Before a state could be readmitted, a majority of a state's citizens who had voted in the 1860 election would have to swear loyalty to the Union. Only those whites who had not voluntarily fought against the Union would be allowed to vote and to attend the constitutional conventions. The new constitutions would have to outlaw slavery and deny the right to vote to all ex-Confederate officials.

After the bill passed Congress, President Lincoln vetoed it. He said that under the Constitution he alone had the responsibility for Reconstruction. According to Lincoln, Reconstruction was part of the Union war effort and came under his duties as commander in chief. He did not need Congress's approval.

Congress also took up the matter of the rights of the former slaves. In January 1865, it proposed the 13th Amendment to the Constitution. This amendment abolished slavery in the U.S. It was ratified in December by the necessary 27 states.

Lincoln's Death

On April 9, 1865, the fighting ended, but the Union's victory was soon clouded by tragedy. On April 14, President Lincoln was attending a play at Ford's Theatre in Washington. During the performance, John Wilkes Booth, a supporter of the Confederacy, entered the presidential box unnoticed. He shot the President, leaped to the stage shouting "Thus ever to tyrants!" and escaped by a back door. He was later shot trying to escape from a hiding place in Virginia.

The mortally wounded President was carried to a boardinghouse across from the theater where he died the next morning. Only a month before, in his second inaugural address, Lincoln had asked Americans to "bind up the nation's wounds; to do all which may achieve and cherish a just and a lasting peace."

mortally:
leading to death

JOHNSON AS PRESIDENT

Vice-President Andrew Johnson, a former Senator from Tennessee, succeeded Lincoln. Johnson had been the only Senator from a Confederate state to remain in the U.S. Senate after his state had seceded. When Union soldiers captured Tennessee in 1862, Lincoln made him military governor of the state. Two years later, Lincoln chose him as his vice-presidential running mate to attract Democratic voters.

Johnson was a Jacksonian Democrat who believed strongly in states' rights. He argued that neither Congress nor the President should interfere in the internal affairs of states. Johnson also favored protecting the interests of small southern farmers. In his view, they were the people who would make the South democratic and loyal to the Union. He hoped to take the leadership of the South from the wealthy planters and place it in the hands of small farmers.

In spring 1865, while Congress was in recess, Johnson decided to go ahead with Reconstruction. Like Lincoln, he believed that the approval of Congress was not needed. Johnson followed Lincoln's plan with a few small changes. Amnesty was offered to all ex-Confederates except the highest officials and people who owned property worth more than $20,000. These Southerners were not permitted to vote or to hold state or federal offices. However, they could ask the President for individual pardons. The states also had to ratify the 13th Amendment before readmission.

For the seven months that Congress was in recess, Johnson carried out his plans for Reconstruction. During this time, all the southern states except Texas set up governments and elected representatives to Congress. When Congress met in December 1865, Johnson announced that new state governments had been established in the South. The Union had been restored.

More Opposition

Congress did not agree. Radical Republicans argued that Johnson had gone beyond his powers as President. Under the Constitution, only Congress had the power to make laws. Other members of Congress were angry that many of the newly elected southern representatives were the same men who had led the Confederacy. For example, Alexander H. Stephens, Vice-President of the Confederacy, was the new Senator from Georgia. Among the new members from the South were Confederate generals, colonels, Cabinet members, and 58 members of the Confederate Congress. The Republican-controlled Congress refused to allow the southern members to take their seats.

Instead, Congress appointed a committee to investigate whether any of the former Confederate states should be represented in Congress. The committee looked into the mistreatment of freed slaves across the South. In its report, the committee found that no state was entitled to representation and that presidential Reconstruction was a mistake. Congress should determine Reconstruction policy in order to make sure that the new governments would be loyal and democratic.

entitle (en-TY-tuhl): to give a right to

Black Codes

Most Northerners right after the Civil War had been willing to allow the President to guide Reconstruction. However, a series of laws passed by the new southern governments in 1865 and 1866 changed the minds of many Northerners. Called the black codes, they varied from state to state. Most states, however, allowed former slaves to choose their employers, use the courts, and marry legally. But other parts of the black codes greatly limited the rights of newly freed blacks.

For example, most states passed laws that provided for the arrest and fining of unemployed blacks. Those who could not afford the fine could be hired out to an employer who would pay it. Other laws kept former slaves from serving on juries, voting, carrying weapons, holding public office, and owning land. A former slave had to buy a license to work in a craft.

Southerners claimed that the black codes were needed to keep law and order. Many southern whites feared that former slaves would turn to violence in revenge for past mistreatment. Northerners, however, viewed the black codes as an attempt to keep blacks in slavery. Since colonial days, Southerners had depended on slave labor to run their plantations. When slavery ended, plantation owners still needed large amounts of labor. The black codes enabled them to keep their supply of cheap, unskilled workers.

Freedmen's Bureau

When the war ended, thousands of former slaves, called freedmen at the time, began leaving southern farms and plantations. Many traveled across the South searching for family members separated by the slave trade. Others went to Union Army camps, towns, and cities. For many former slaves, migration was their way of proving their newly gained freedom. At first, many former slaves refused to work for their

Public education for southern blacks began after the war. The Freedmen's Bureau, which helped blacks with the change to freedom, established some schools, as did various private groups. Not all the students were children. Many adults wanted to learn to read and write.

former owners. They hoped to become independent farmers themselves. They believed the federal government would take the land away from former slaveowners and give it to them.

In March 1865, while the war was still going on, Congress created the Freedmen's Bureau to help both blacks and whites left homeless and jobless by the war. The Freedmen's Bureau was under the control of the War Department. However, it was staffed by both military and civilian workers. The bureau helped people find homes and jobs, settled disagreements between blacks and their employers, provided medical care, set up schools, and gave legal help. Among the schools aided by the bureau were Fisk University in Tennessee and Hampton Institute in Virginia.

confiscate
(KAHN-fis-kayt):
to take and keep

The act setting up the Freedmen's Bureau raised hopes among blacks that they would receive "40 acres and a mule." A section of the act gave the bureau the power to give away abandoned or confiscated land to former slaves. According to the act, former slaves would be allowed to rent the land for three years and then buy it at its 1860 value. But even the Freedmen's Bureau became a battleground between the President and Congress. Johnson ended the black dream of "40 acres and a mule" by ordering all land returned to its original owners.

In December 1865, Congress passed a second Freedmen's Bureau Act. The bureau was given additional powers to protect former slaves from the black codes. President Johnson vetoed the bill in February 1866. He said it was unconstitutional because it continued wartime laws into peace time. The Radicals were angered but did not have enough votes to pass the act over Johnson's veto. By July, the Radicals had pulled together enough votes, and the Freedmen's Bureau Act was passed.

The activities of the bureau ended in 1869. By then, most of the southern states had been readmitted to the Union under Congress's plan for Reconstruction. Although a small number of the bureau's officials were dishonest or inefficient, the bureau was an important part of Reconstruction. It helped thousands of poor Southerners, black and white, to find homes and jobs. It did not help many blacks to own land, but it did protect thousands of blacks in their dealings with employers.

hostile (HAHS-tuhl):
very unfriendly

Across the South, many white Southerners were hostile to the bureau. Some felt that, as part of the federal government, the bureau was interfering in matters better left to the states. Other Southerners accused the bureau of stirring up hatred between blacks and whites. Southern Democrats were especially angered by politicans' use of the bureau to register black voters as Republicans.

Civil Rights Act

In March 1866, Congress passed the Civil Rights Bill to nullify the black codes. **Civil rights** are rights guaranteed to citizens by law. The bill stated that all persons born in the U.S. were citizens of the U.S. In

This illustration from *Harper's* magazine shows a black campaigning for office. What three groups were active in southern government during Reconstruction?

addition to granting citizenship rights to former slaves, the bill gave them the right to testify in court, buy land, make contracts, and exercise the same civil rights as whites. The President said the bill interfered with the rights of states and vetoed it. However, the Radicals were joined by other Republicans, and the Civil Rights Act was passed over Johnson's veto.

Fourteenth Amendment

Many besides the President thought the Civil Rights Act was unconstitutional. In order to settle the issue, Congress approved the 14th Amendment to the Constitution in June and sent it to the states for ratification. According to the amendment, persons born or naturalized in the U.S. were citizens both of the U.S. and of the state in which they lived. If a state denied any adult male the right to vote, that state was to be denied representation in Congress in proportion to the number of citizens who had been denied the vote. Ex-Confederate leaders could not hold federal or state office unless pardoned by a two-thirds vote of Congress. No Confederate debts could be collected. Former slaveowners could not sue for payment for the loss of their slaves.

proportion (pruh-POR-shuhn): direct relation in size or number of parts

The 14th Amendment was really a plan for Reconstruction. But Johnson insisted that the southern states had already been reconstructed under his plan. He advised the South to reject the amendment. He wanted to make ratification and Reconstruction the chief issues of the 1866 congressional elections. Except for Tennessee, the ten southern states followed Johnson's advice. However, the 14th Amendment became part of the Constitution when it was ratified by the northern states in 1868.

CONGRESSIONAL RECONSTRUCTION

In the congressional elections of 1866, Johnson was handed a major defeat. Many Northerners were angered by violence toward freed blacks in the South and convinced that presidential Reconstruction had not worked. Republicans captured more than two thirds of both houses of Congress. With the Radicals in control, Republicans now had the necessary majority to override a presidential veto. Led by Thaddeus Stevens and Charles Sumner, Congress set out to finish the Reconstruction plan it had begun with the Freedmen's Bureau, the Civil Rights Bill, and the 14th Amendment.

Reconstruction Government

Over President Johnson's veto, Congress passed the first of a series of Reconstruction Acts in March 1867. The acts declared illegal the governments of the ten southern states that opposed the 14th Amendment. Tennessee, because it had ratified the amendment, was allowed to keep its government and constitution. The other ex-Confederate states were divided into five military districts. Each district was controlled by a major general who reported to General Ulysses S. Grant, as head of the Union Army. The major general could take any steps necessary, including force, to protect civil rights and keep order.

According to the Reconstruction Acts, the state governments set up under Johnson's Reconstruction plan were disbanded. The former Confederate states were to call new conventions to write new constitutions. The members of the constitutional conventions were to be elected by all adult males—black and white—in each state. Under the

In the summer of 1866, President Johnson went to the voters in search of support for his Reconstruction plans. How is this similar to modern politics? Was Johnson successful?

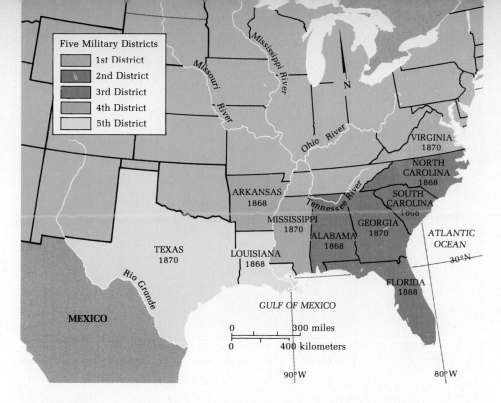

Five Military Districts
- 1st District
- 2nd District
- 3rd District
- 4th District
- 5th District

VIRGINIA 1870
NORTH CAROLINA 1868
SOUTH CAROLINA 1868
ARKANSAS 1868
MISSISSIPPI 1870
GEORGIA 1870
ALABAMA 1868
TEXAS 1870
LOUISIANA 1868
FLORIDA 1868
ATLANTIC OCEAN
30°N
Rio Grande
MEXICO
GULF OF MEXICO
Mississippi River
Missouri River
Ohio River
Tennessee River

0   300 miles
0   400 kilometers

90°W   80°W

14th Amendment, former Confederate officials were not allowed to hold federal or state office. As a result, they were to have no part in writing the new constitutions. These constitutions were to give the right to vote to all male citizens—black and white. The southern states were also required to ratify the 14th Amendment.

IMPEACHMENT OF JOHNSON

As part of the battle between Congress and the President, the Radicals decided to place a limit on the President's constitutional powers. On March 2, 1867, over the President's veto, Congress approved the Tenure of Office Act. The President had to obtain Senate consent before removing Cabinet members or other federal officials who had been approved by the Senate.

In February 1868, Johnson fired Secretary of War Edwin M. Stanton. Stanton had opposed Johnson's Reconstruction policies. He had also become an ally of the Radical Republicans. As a result of Stanton's dismissal, the House of Representatives voted to impeach Johnson. As you may recall from the unit A Plan of Government, to impeach means only to accuse a person formally of a crime, not to convict. President Johnson was accused of violating the Tenure of Office Act. However, the Radicals really wanted to remove Johnson because he had opposed their Reconstruction policies.

For the first time in U.S. history, the Senate held an impeachment trial of a President. The trial began in March and lasted six weeks. The Senate voted three times, but each time the vote was 35 to 19 in favor of conviction. This was one vote short of the two-thirds majority needed to convict Johnson. Although he was acquitted, the trial left

acquit (uh-KWIT): to declare not guilty

491

The impeachment trial of President Johnson took place in the Senate, with the Chief Justice of the Supreme Court presiding as judge. Although Johnson was acquitted, how did the trial affect Reconstruction?

Johnson disgraced and powerless. Neither the Republicans nor the Democrats nominated him for reelection in 1868.

ELECTION OF 1868

In 1868, the Republicans chose General Grant, the hero of the Civil War, to run for President. The Democrats nominated Horatio Seymour (SEE-mor), who had served as governor of New York during the war.

In the campaign, the Republicans used a strategy known as "waving the bloody shirt." They presented themselves as the party that had saved the Union and the Democrats as the party of secession. Grant won the election by a large majority in the electoral college. In the popular vote, however, his lead was small. The electoral votes that gave Grant his victory came from the South. There, former slaves, grateful to the Republicans, voted Republican in large numbers.

LOOKING BACK

1. Identify the problems the U.S. faced after the Civil War.
2. **a.** How did Lincoln think Reconstruction should be handled? **b.** What was Congress's view of Reconstruction?
3. **a.** On what important issue did Johnson and the Congress disagree? **b.** What was the view of each side on this issue?
4. **a.** Why did southern states pass black codes? **b.** What were some of the restrictions placed on former slaves by the codes? What was the purpose of the following: **c.** Freedmen's Bureau? **d.** 13th Amendment **e.** 14th Amendment?
5. List the sequence that led to Johnson's impeachment and acquittal. Begin with his readmission of the southern states.
6. **a.** Who gave Grant his electoral victory in 1868? **b.** Why?

Chapter 4   The Nation Reconstructed

LOOKING AHEAD

This chapter is about the Reconstruction of the former Confederate states under the plan of the Radical Republicans. The chapter describes the economy and government of the South, resistance to Reconstruction, and the results of Reconstruction. After you study this chapter, you will be able to:

- describe the problems of southern landowners and former slaves after the Civil War.
- identify the groups involved in Reconstruction politics in the South.
- explain how the outcome of the election of 1876 was settled.
- list the results of Reconstruction.
- test a hypothesis about the successfulness of Congressional Reconstruction.

Social Studies Vocabulary

segregation

People

Francis L. Cardoza	J. H. Rainey	Victoria Woodhull
P. B. S. Pinchback	Robert Smalls	Rutherford B. Hayes
Jonathan Gibbs	Ku Klux Klan	Samuel J. Tilden
Hiram R. Revels	Horace Greeley	Peter Cooper
Blanche K. Bruce	Liberal Republicans	

Words and Terms

15th Amendment	carpetbagger	poll tax
sharecropper	scalawag	literacy test

Radical Republicans had won the battle with President Johnson over Reconstruction, and Johnson left office in 1869. When the Republicans realized how important the black vote had been in electing Grant to the presidency, the Republican-controlled Congress approved the 15th amendment. It stated that no one could be denied the right to vote because of race. The amendment was ratified in 1870.

By then, all the former Confederate states had been brought back into the Union. Alabama, Florida, Louisiana, North Carolina, and South Carolina had been readmitted by 1868. Georgia, Mississippi, Virginia, and Texas took longer to ratify the 14th Amendment. They also had to ratify the 15th Amendment before they were readmitted.

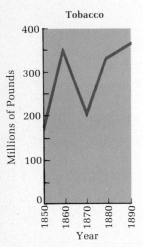

Cotton

(graph: y-axis "Millions of Bales" from 0 to 8; x-axis "Year" from 1850 to 1890)

Tobacco

(graph: y-axis "Millions of Pounds" from 0 to 400; x-axis "Year" from 1850 to 1890)

Cotton and Tobacco Production in the South from 1850 to 1890

Source: *Abstract of the Eleventh Census,* 1890, Bureau of the Census

holdings: property

RECONSTRUCTION IN THE SOUTH

Because almost all the fighting of the Civil War had taken place in the South, large areas of the South lay in ruins in April 1865. The homes of planters, poor farmers, and former slaves alike had been deliberately burned by Union soldiers or had been caught in the middle of fighting. Fields were trampled, and crops burned or left to rot. Some of the land had gone unplowed for several years. Hard work would be needed to clear it and make it productive again. Many cities, such as Richmond, Vicksburg, and Atlanta, were burned-out ruins. Most of the South's railroads had been destroyed, either to keep them from falling to the Union or to cut off supplies to the Confederates.

Besides the destruction, there was great human suffering. Many Southerners, black and white, were without food, clothing, and shelter. Many people had lost family members in the fighting.

The Southern Economy

After the Civil War, the North's economy was booming. The economy of the South, which had always lagged behind the North's, was almost destroyed. The end of the Confederacy had made Confederate money and bonds worthless. Southerners who had lent money to the government lost it all. In addition, the end of slavery cost slaveowners their means of making money—slave labor to work their fields.

Landowners had little or no money to pay freed slaves who now worked for wages or even to buy farm tools and supplies. The landowners had to borrow money from northern banks, but money was scarce. Most bankers preferred to lend money to businesses in the North and West, areas that were expanding. For their part, former slaves worked for wages but were paid less than white workers. Their one hope of economic independence was owning land. But as you have read, the Radical Republicans' plan of "40 acres and a mule" was killed. Even if former slaves had been given land, they would not have been able to farm it without money for tools, farm animals, seed, and other supplies.

As a result of these problems, a new system of farming developed in the South. Many southern landowners broke their holdings into small units. On each unit, the landowner settled a family of sharecroppers. A sharecropper is a person who farms someone else's land in return for part of the crops. Sharecropping is similar to tenant farming. The landowner supplied the house, tools, and seed. The sharecropper provided the labor. Generally, the landowner received half the crops that the sharecropper raised. If the sharecropper provided the supplies, then less of the crops were paid to the landowner.

The system did not work well. The money that sharecroppers made from their share of the crop was usually not enough to provide their families with food, clothing, and household goods. As a result, the sharecroppers were constantly in debt either to their landowner or to local merchants. Landowners often cheated their sharecroppers. The following is historian Leon Litwack's description of sharecropping:

While politicians fought over governing the South, the South's economy slowly recovered. These are iron furnaces in operation near Rock Woods, Tennessee. How did business interests help to bring an end to Reconstruction?

To many freedmen, the new arrangement—tenant farming—seemed promising at first glance because of the feelings of independence it gave. As if to stress such feelings, the new tenant might move his cabin from the old slave village out onto the plot of land he had rented or else build a new cabin to symbolize his new independence. In opting for this arrangement, moreover, he fully expected to make this plot of land his own through hard work and saving. But in most instances, such hopes remained unfulfilled and the tenant found himself little better off than he had been. The great mass of laboring freedmen, whether they rented lands or worked for wages or shares, remained laborers—landless agricultural workers.

The sharecropping system was not limited to former slaves. Poor white farmers also found themselves sharecropping in the post-Civil War South.

Even former slaves who were skilled in such crafts as carpentry and blacksmithing had a difficult time. The black codes required that they buy licenses, which could be difficult if they had little money. Even blacks who had never been slaves were required to have a license. Like former plantation workers, freed black craftworkers lacked the money to buy tools and open shops. If they managed to open a small business, they often had trouble attracting customers. Many blacks did not have the money to pay to have work done, and many whites would not patronize a black-owned business. They viewed these craftworkers as threats to the jobs of whites.

In some areas, the southern economy made some gains during Reconstruction and into the 1880s. Cotton production increased slowly until by 1879 the South was producing more cotton than it had before the war. After the war, loose tobacco for rolling cigarettes became popular. To meet the demand, more landowners in Virginia and North Carolina turned their land into tobacco farms. In Alabama, coal and iron industries developed, and by the late 1870s Birmingham was growing rapidly. Additional railroad track was laid in the South, and textile mills were opened.

patronize
(PAY-truhn-iz):
to trade with

The first two sessions of Congress after the Civil War had one black Senator, Hiram H. Revels on the left, and six black Representatives: Turner, De Large, Walls, Long, Rainey, and Elliott. How many blacks served in Congress between 1869 and 1901?

supposedly
(suh-POHZ-id-lee): said to be true

Politics

The political system of the South was in a state of confusion after the Civil War. As you may recall from the last chapter, the Republican-controlled Congress kept ex-Confederate leaders from holding office. Also, many southern leaders had been killed in the war. Finally, some white Southerners refused to participate in the new governments. These men were angered by the control that the federal government held over their lives and by its protection of the rights of blacks. Some Southerners, however, were willing for various reasons to take part in Reconstruction government.

Three groups were important in the new southern governments. The first group were Northerners who settled in the South after the war. Ex-Confederates called them carpetbaggers because they supposedly carried all their belongings in a suitcase made of carpet. These Northerners were often accused of taking advantage of the South for their own benefit. While some of these people were dishonest, many were hardworking teachers, missionaries, and government officials. Some worked for the Freedmen's Bureau.

A second group were southern whites who supported the Radicals' plan for Reconstruction. Many ex-Confederates referred to these people as scalawags (SKAL-uh-wagz) and accused them of being traitors. This group included many Southerners who had disapproved of slavery, opposed secession, and remained loyal to the Union during the Civil War. The group also included Southerners who wanted to make a profit from Reconstruction.

Blacks—free born and former slaves—were the third group to play a role in Reconstruction politics. Some like Francis L. Cardoza (kahr-DOH-zuh), who served as Treasurer and Secretary of State of South Carolina, and P. B. S. Pinchback, who was lieutenant governor of

Louisiana, were well educated. Many, though, were former slaves and as such were poor, uneducated, and lacking in political experience. However, blacks never controlled southern politics during Reconstruction. Northerners and southern whites held most of the important political offices. For example, while blacks were a majority in the lower house of the South Carolina legislature until 1874, the upper house and the governorship were always controlled by whites. Blacks never controlled either house of any other state legislature. Every state, however, had blacks who held positions such as state legislators or heads of departments. Jonathan Gibbs, for example, was Secretary of State of Florida.

A few blacks held office at the federal level. Between 1869 and 1901, two blacks became U.S. Senators and 20 were elected to the House of Representatives. Hiram R. Revels and Blanche K. Bruce represented Mississippi in the U.S. Senate. South Carolina elected eight blacks to the House; North Carolina, four; Alabama, three; Georgia, Mississippi, Florida, Louisiana, and Virginia, one each. Of these, J. H. Rainey and Robert Smalls, the pilot who turned over a ship to the Union Navy in 1861, served for 10 years each. Eight other black members of the House were elected for two and three terms.

Resistance

Many white Southerners resented Reconstruction and organized secret societies as early as 1866 to fight it. Among these groups were the Knights of the White Camelia (kuh-MEEL-yuh), the White League, and the Ku Klux Klan (KKK). The KKK was the largest. It used terror to keep blacks and their white supporters from voting or holding public office.

Southern state governments outlawed the organizations but were unable to stop their activities. In 1870 and 1871, Congress passed a series of Force Acts. These acts gave the President the power to suspend the writ of habeas corpus, use federal troops to keep order, and use federal officials to supervise elections. As a result of the Force Acts, hundreds of whites were arrested and brought to trial.

END OF RECONSTRUCTION

As you may recall from the last chapter, Ulysses S. Grant was elected President in 1868. In 1872, he was reelected over Horace Greeley (GREE-lee). Greeley, the editor of the *New York Tribune*, ran as the candidate of the Democrats and Liberal Republicans. Liberal Republicans had left the Republican party because of government corruption under Grant. You will read more about this in the next unit Industrialism and the West. Victoria Woodhull also ran for President as the candidate of the Equal Rights party. She campaigned for giving women the right to vote.

During Grant's second term in office, Reconstruction was coming to an end. Congress had gained a number of moderate Republicans who

Klan members wore robes and masks. They rode out at night, burning crosses and whipping and lynching blacks and their white supporters. What steps did the government take against the KKK?

did not agree with the Radicals' harsh attitude toward the South. The Radicals lost power for several reasons. The deaths of Charles Sumner and Thaddeus Stevens weakened Radical influence in Congress. Also, many Northerners had supported the Radicals only because they disliked President Johnson's policies. When he left office in 1869, the Radicals lost much of this support.

Some Northerners were becoming disgusted with Reconstruction because of the stories they heard about corruption in southern state governments. Also, as the years went by, northern interest in protecting the rights of blacks faded. Other, more personal problems such as the Panic of 1873 took its place. Finally, a growing number of northern business leaders realized that continuing Reconstruction would only delay normal business between North and South. As more and more Northerners grew tired of Reconstruction, it seemed best to return control of the South to its own leaders.

In May 1872, with the support of moderate Republicans, Congress passed the Amnesty Act. This restored voting and office-holding rights to most former Confederates. After Congress approved the act, southern whites gradually regained control of their governments. By 1876, only Louisiana, Florida, and South Carolina had Reconstruction governments.

The Disputed Election

As the presidential election of 1876 approached, the corruption in the Grant administration seemed to make a Democratic victory certain. The Republicans nominated Rutherford B. Hayes. Hayes was the popular, three-term Governor of Ohio. The Democrats turned to Samuel J. Tilden (TIL-duhn) of New York. Tilden, a lawyer, had won fame by exposing corruption in New York City government. Peter Cooper was the candidate of the Greenback party. Its platform called for the government to issue more paper money.

The Democrats ran on a platform of ending government corruption. The Republicans again waved the bloody shirt. A favorite Republican slogan was, "Every man that shot Union soldiers was a Democrat." As the votes were counted, it first appeared that Tilden had been elected. However, the votes in South Carolina, Florida, and Louisiana were in doubt. They were originally counted for Tilden. But the Republican leaders of those states threw out large numbers of Democratic votes and declared Hayes the winner.

Congress appointed a commission of eight Republicans and seven Democrats to investigate. The commission was made up of five Senators, five Representatives, and five Supreme Court Justices. A compromise was worked out. In return for supporting Hayes, the Democrats wanted an end to Reconstruction. In addition, the Republicans would see that money was given to help build the Texas and Pacific railroad. A Southerner would be appointed to Hayes's Cabinet.

On March 2, 1877, the electoral commission voted eight to seven in favor of Hayes. Reconstruction ended that year when President Hayes withdrew the last federal troops from the South.

In 1877, an electoral commission was named to decide the winner of the 1876 presidential race. What caused the disputed election? How did the commission resolve it?

THE RESULTS OF RECONSTRUCTION

Reconstruction had both good and bad effects. The state governments set up under the congressional plan of Reconstruction adopted a number of reforms. Black and poor white males were able to vote and hold office for the first time. The new governments built hospitals, orphanages, and places to care for the disabled. Roads, bridges, and railroads were repaired. More rail lines were opened, and existing railroads were extended.

Perhaps the most important result was the establishment of the first public school systems in most southern states. Before the Civil War, only North Carolina had free public education. By the early 1870s, Reconstruction governments had taken control of the schools opened by the Freedmen's Bureau and set up more. At first, southern whites stayed away from the public schools because blacks attended. By 1885, however, most southern school districts had segregated whites and blacks in their own schools. **Segregation** (seg-ruh-GAY-shun) is keeping groups separated from each other by law or custom.

Although Reconstruction governments introduced a number of reforms, some states had corrupt governments. Legislatures approved large sums for state house furniture, government printing jobs, and travel, but much of this money really went to the legislators themselves. Some officials took bribes in return for doing favors for businesses. Often the money that was supposed to be used to help freed blacks was taken by dishonest officials and their friends.

Reconstruction did not help blacks to own land or to better themselves financially. It also did not help blacks protect their rights. During Reconstruction, the Republican-controlled Congress granted certain rights by law to former slaves. In practice, however, the secret white societies used fear to keep many blacks from exercising these

The jury to try Jefferson Davis for treason was selected from this group of citizens reporting for jury duty. It was the first mixed jury ever called in the U.S. Why was it the first?

rights. After Reconstruction ended, southern states used various legal means to deny former slaves their voting rights. Poll taxes and literacy tests were two. A poll tax is a tax that has to be paid in order to vote. A literacy test determines whether a person can read and write.

LOOKING BACK

1. **a.** Why did southern landowners need to borrow money? **b.** What problems did former slaves face in trying to buy land after the war? **c.** Why did the system of sharecropping develop? **d.** Was sharecropping fair to both former slaves and landowners? **e.** Why or why not?
2. Who were three groups that were involved in Reconstruction politics?
3. How was the election of 1876 settled?
4. **a.** List three results of Reconstruction. **b.** Classify them as good or bad.
5. Use what you have learned in Chapters 3 and 4 to test the hypothesis: Congressional Reconstruction was successful in solving the problems the nation faced after the Civil War. **a.** As a help, go through the two chapters and look for evidence to answer the questions: Did Congressional Reconstruction have a solution for each problem? If so, was it a lasting solution? Find evidence that supports or contradicts your answers. Be sure that your evidence is relevant, accurate, and adequate. **b.** Weigh the evidence and decide if the hypothesis is valid. Write a statement, based on your evidence, that either supports or contradicts the hypothesis.

PRACTICING YOUR SKILLS

What If . . .   In Chapter 3 of this unit you read about the conflict between President Johnson and Congress over Reconstruction. In December 1865, Johnson informed Congress that Reconstruction in the South had been completed according to his plan. **What if** Congress had agreed to Johnson's plan? How might this have affected: **a.** ex-Confederate officials? **b.** former slaves? **c.** southern politics? **d.** national political parties? **e.** the presidential election of 1868?

Discussing   In Chapter 2 of this unit, you read how the war improved the economy of the North. Why did this happen?

Researching, Making a Table, Writing, Graphing

1. Using the information in Chapter 1 of this unit and additional research, make a table of the major battles of the Civil War. Table headings should include where the battles were fought, when, army commanders, and results.
2. Using reference materials, make two pie graphs illustrating the presidential election of 1868 or of 1876. One graph should show the percentages of the popular vote each candidate received. The other graph should show the percentages of candidates' electoral votes.
3. Using reference materials, prepare a brief report on the purpose of the Freedmen's Bureau and its accomplishments.

Exploring

1. If you live in a former Confederate state, research and write a report on when and how your state was readmitted to the Union. Include constitutional conventions, approval of the constitution, and ratification of constitutional amendments.
2. If you live in a state that remained in the Union during the Civil War, research and write a report on when your state ratified the 13th, 14th, and 15th Amendments. Include the number of votes for and against each amendment.

Building Writing Skills

A book report involves the skills of paraphrasing and summarizing. Your report should give an overall picture of what the book is about and explain why you did or did not like the book. Here are some tips to help you write a book report.

- Include book title, author, publisher, date of publication, and type of book—fiction, nonfiction, biography—in the first paragraph of your report.
- Do not retell the entire story. Summarize the main events and main characters. Discuss the author's purpose and the ideas he/she wanted to communicate.
- State your opinion about the book in the last paragraph. Tell why you did or did not enjoy the book.

Activity: Choose a book about the Civil War or Reconstruction and write a two-page book report about it following the above guidelines.

Reading

Catton, Bruce, and American Heritage Eds. *American Heritage Pictorial History of the Civil War*. New York: Doubleday, 1960.

Davis, Burke. *Sherman's March*. New York: Random House, 1980.

Eaton, Clement. *Jefferson Davis*. New York: Free Press, 1979. Paperback.

Franklin, John H. *From Slavery to Freedom: A History of Negro Americans*. New York: Knopf, 1980. Paperback.

Ribbons, Ian. *The Battle of Gettysburg: 1 3 July 1863*. New York: Oxford University Press, 1978. A day-by-day description.

Sterling, Dorothy. *The Trouble They Seen: Black People Tell the Story of Reconstruction*. New York: Doubleday, 1976. Primary sources.

Section V   BIG BUSINESS AND WORLD POWER

Unit I
Industrialism and the West

Unit II
Reform and Expansion

UNIT I INDUSTRIALISM AND THE WEST

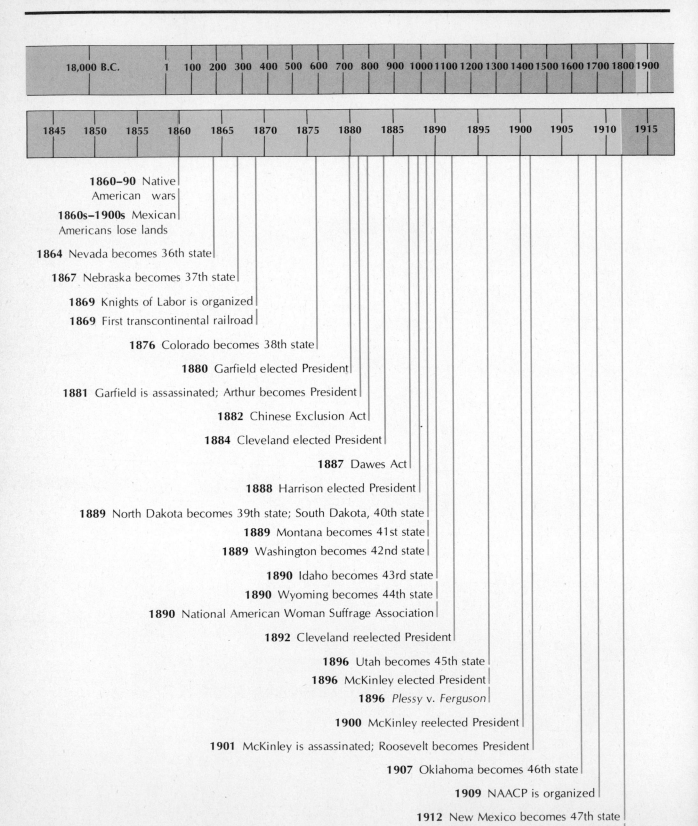

| 18,000 B.C. | 1 | 100 | 200 | 300 | 400 | 500 | 600 | 700 | 800 | 900 | 1000 | 1100 | 1200 | 1300 | 1400 | 1500 | 1600 | 1700 | 1800 | 1900 |

| 1845 | 1850 | 1855 | 1860 | 1865 | 1870 | 1875 | 1880 | 1885 | 1890 | 1895 | 1900 | 1905 | 1910 | 1915 |

1860–90 Native American wars

1860s–1900s Mexican Americans lose lands

1864 Nevada becomes 36th state

1867 Nebraska becomes 37th state

1869 Knights of Labor is organized

1869 First transcontinental railroad

1876 Colorado becomes 38th state

1880 Garfield elected President

1881 Garfield is assassinated; Arthur becomes President

1882 Chinese Exclusion Act

1884 Cleveland elected President

1887 Dawes Act

1888 Harrison elected President

1889 North Dakota becomes 39th state; South Dakota, 40th state

1889 Montana becomes 41st state

1889 Washington becomes 42nd state

1890 Idaho becomes 43rd state

1890 Wyoming becomes 44th state

1890 National American Woman Suffrage Association

1892 Cleveland reelected President

1896 Utah becomes 45th state

1896 McKinley elected President

1896 *Plessy* v. *Ferguson*

1900 McKinley reelected President

1901 McKinley is assassinated; Roosevelt becomes President

1907 Oklahoma becomes 46th state

1909 NAACP is organized

1912 New Mexico becomes 47th state

1912 Arizona becomes 48th state

Chapter 1   Native Americans: Last Stand

LOOKING AHEAD

This chapter describes the final struggle between western Native Americans and the federal government for their lands. You will read about the laws that broke up their landholdings and the armed conflicts between Native Americans and soldiers and settlers. The chapter also describes several champions of Native American rights. After you study this chapter, you will be able to:

- explain why Native Americans were forced onto reservations.
- read a table to interpret the causes of the conflicts between Native Americans and settlers and soldiers.
- describe reservation life.
- identify a stereotype of Native Americans.
- explain the effects of the Dawes Act on Native Americans.
- explain the sequence of events that led to the end of the Indian Territory.
- compare and contrast maps of lands lost by Native Americans.

People

George A. Custer	Black Kettle	Quanah Parker
Winnemucca	White Antelope	Chief Joseph
Mangas Coloradas	Red Cloud	Morning Star
Cochise	Kintpuash	Little Wolf
Geronimo	Crazy Horse	Ouray
Victorio	Sitting Bull	Big Foot
Little Crow	Gall	Sarah Winnemucca
Manuelito	Spotted Tail	Helen Hunt Jackson

Places

Great Sioux Reservation	Guthrie, Oklahoma
Indian Territory	Oklahoma City

Words and Terms

Indian Appropriation Act	Medicine Lodge Treaty
Laramie Treaty	Ghost Dance
Plains Wars	Massacre at Wounded Knee
Sand Creek Massacre	Bureau of Indian Affairs
Battle of the	Dawes Act
Little Bighorn	Dawes Commission

By the mid-1800s, American settlement still reached only slightly beyond the Mississippi River. Some Americans had moved to California

While attacking a Sioux and Cheyenne camp on the Little Bighorn River, in Montana, Custer and many of the Seventh Cavalry were killed. Kicking Bear who fought there drew this picture of this attack. Is the drawing accurate or does it show bias? What are your reasons?

and to Oregon in the 1840s, and there were Mormon settlements in Utah. But the Rocky Mountains and the northern and southern Plains were still occupied mostly by Native Americans. As long as people east of the Mississippi and beyond the Rockies thought of much of this area as the Great American Desert, Native Americans there were safe.

SETTLERS ON NATIVE AMERICAN LANDS

In the late 1850s, miners began to move into what are now the states of Colorado, Nevada, Idaho, Montana, and South Dakota. In the 1870s and 1880s, gold and silver miners also settled in the regions that are now the states of Arizona, Wyoming, Utah, and New Mexico. After the Civil War, increasing numbers of ranchers and farmers began settling in Texas and what are now the states of Nebraska, Colorado, Wyoming, Washington, Arizona, Idaho, New Mexico, North Dakota, and South Dakota.

The lands that these people claimed were often the hunting grounds of Native Americans. Settlers in the late 1800s showed as little respect for the rights of Native Americans as had earlier settlers. The nations were forced to fight for their lands against settlers and the U.S. Army. Eventually, however, the Native Americans were defeated. They were mistreated by the law and outnumbered on the battlefield.

Government Action

On March 3, 1871, Congress passed the Indian Appropriation Act. According to the act, the U.S. government would no longer recognize any Native American group as an independent nation. The government would not make any more treaties with Native Americans. However, treaties made before that date would be honored. Unfortunately, as farmers and miners moved onto Native American lands, this did not always happen.

For example, the Laramie (LAR-uh-mee) Treaty of 1868 had established the Great Sioux Reservation, which covered most of what is now South Dakota. In 1874, Colonel George A. Custer and the Seventh Cavalry violated this treaty when they were sent to find out if the reports of gold in the Black Hills were true. Within two years, miners were pouring into the area. When the Sioux fought back to protect themselves, they were defeated and forced to sign a new treaty giving up the Black Hills.

In 1866, the government had redivided the Indian Territory to establish reservations for more Native American nations. Eventually, the Osage (oh-SAYJ), Arapaho (uh-RAP-uh-hoh), Cheyenne, Wichita, Kiowa, Pawnee, and Comanche were settled in this area. More and more Native American groups were forced onto reservations as settlers moved onto their lands. By 1880, reservations had also been established in Oregon, Colorado, and Nevada and in what are now the states of Washington, South Dakota, New Mexico, Idaho, Arizona, Oklahoma, and Utah.

Native American Conflicts

A number of conflicts took place between Native Americans and soldiers and settlers during this period. The Native Americans usually fought in small groups and had no overall battle plan. Young men left reservations to attack whatever settlers and soldiers were nearby. Many of the young men were killed in these battles, and the rest were forced back to their reservations. Often soldiers and settlers attacked peaceful villages. Occasionally, bands of Native Americans would join together to fight but their successes were limited.

By 1890, with the massacre at Wounded Knee, most of the fighting was over. In the end, the Native Americans had lost to the better organization of the government troops and to their larger numbers and newer weapons. The table on pages 508 and 509 lists major conflicts.

RESERVATION LIFE

In some areas, such as the Midwest and Northwest, the lands used as reservations were suited to farming. However, not all Native Ameri-

NATIVE AMERICAN WARS FROM 1860 TO 1890

Nation	Leaders	Causes	Results
PAIUTE Original location: Nevada and Utah	Winnemucca	Game is scarce; Paiute steal cattle from settlers and soldiers; corrupt agents steal supplies and Paiute starve	1860: Soldiers attack and kill women and children while Paiute men on hunt; Paiute sent to reservations in Oregon and Washington
CHIRICAHUA APACHE Original location: Arizona and New Mexico (part of Western Apache)	Mangas Coloradas Cochise Geronimo Victorio	Apache raid cattle and horses of settlers; Apache sold into slavery by Spanish and Mexicans; 1861: Cochise attacked by troops under flag of truce	1861-70: Apache fight U.S. troops; forced by other Native Americans to make peace; Geronimo imprisoned in 1886; Apache forced onto reservations in Florida, Arizona, and New Mexico; Mangas Coloradas tortured and killed
SANTEE SIOUX Original location: Minnesota	Little Crow	Corrupt agents steal food; settlers killed in fight over ownership of one chicken	1862: Army defeats and scatters Sioux; many Sioux killed or imprisoned; others escape to Canada or Dakota plains; Plains War begins; ends 1891
NAVAJO Original location: Southern Plains	Manuelito	Navajo raid settlers' horses and cattle to discourage gold mining; soldiers seize flocks, destroy gardens, orchards, try to starve Navajo out	1864: Kit Carson and troops defeat Navajo; force them to walk 480 kilometers (300 miles) to reservation near Fort Sumner, New Mexico; 1868: moved to Arizona
CHEYENNE Original location: Oklahoma	Black Kettle White Antelope	Game is scarce; hunting grounds ruined by settlers; Cheyenne ambush settlers, raid cattle and supplies; troops attack while Cheyenne seek peace	1864: About 450 Cheyenne men, women, and children killed by soldiers at Sand Creek, Colorado; remaining Cheyenne scatter
OGLALA SIOUX Original location: Northern Plains (part of Teton Sioux)	Red Cloud	Army builds Bozeman Trail and forts on Sioux hunting grounds to protect settlers; Sioux attack wagon trains and refuse to let settlers use trail	1867-68: Forts abandoned after Sioux siege; government signs treaty to close trail and destroy forts
MODOC Original location: Oregon and California border	Kintpuash (Captain Jack)	Modoc denied reservation in homeland; forced on reservation in Oregon; escape to California	1872: Army tries to arrest Kintpuash; eight soldiers die; 1873: Kintpuash kills general; Kintpuash and three men are hanged; Modoc forced onto Indian Territory reservation

NATIVE AMERICAN WARS FROM 1860 TO 1890

Nation	Leaders	Causes	Results
OGLALA SIOUX HUNKPAPA SIOUX Original location: Dakota (part of Teton Sioux) BRULE SIOUX Original location: Nebraska (part of Teton Sioux) CHEYENNE Original location: Northern Plains	Crazy Horse Sitting Bull Gall Spotted Tail	1875: Government orders all Native Americans onto reservations by spring; not enough time to move; Cheyenne attacked on way to reservation by soldiers; Sioux refuse to sell land to miners or to go to reservation	1875: Sioux and Cheyenne join forces; 1876: attacked by Custer and Seventh Cavalry at Battle of Little Bighorn; Sioux and Cheyenne scatter; 1877: Oglala Sioux forced by hunger to surrender; Hunkpapa Sioux settle in Canada; 1878: Oglala Sioux moved to Pine Ridge Reservation; 1881: Hunkpapa return to U.S. when promised amnesty; forced onto Standing Rock Reservation in Dakota Territory; Brule Sioux settle on Rosebud Reservation in Dakota Territory
COMANCHE Original location: Texas	Quanah Parker	1867: Comanche refuse to sign Medicine Lodge Treaty and move to reservation; settlers slaughter buffalo; Comanche attack settlers	1875: U.S. troops attack Comanche; move them to reservation in Indian Territory
NEZ PERCE Original location: Oregon, Washington, Idaho	Chief Joseph	Troops attack Nez Perce and order them to reservation in Idaho; Nez Perce refuse to leave lands granted to them in 1863 treaty	1877: Chief Joseph leads 800 Nez Perce on retreat from army; captured near Canada; sent to Indian Territory reservation; moved to reservations in Washington and Idaho in 1885
CHEYENNE Original location: Montana, Minnesota	Morning Star (Dull Knife) Little Wolf	Cheyenne exiled to Indian Territory; try to return to Montana hunting grounds	1878: Cheyenne overtaken by troops; many killed; rest are returned to reservation
UTE Original location: Colorado	Ouray	Uprising on reservation in Colorado because of corrupt and cruel agent	1879: Ute kill agents of White River Agency; peace treaty signed
HUNKPAPA SIOUX	Sitting Bull Big Foot	Sioux perform Ghost Dances thought by army to stir up trouble	1890: Sitting Bull killed while resisting arrest; over 200 men, women, and children killed at Wounded Knee, South Dakota; last major battle between Native Americans and U.S. government

can groups were farmers. Some were hunters or fishers, as you may recall from the unit The First Americans. The government's attempts at forcing these people to farm did not always work.

On the Plains, even if the peoples had wanted to live and hunt as they once had, they could not. Most of the buffalo were gone. Estimates put as high as 15 million the number of buffalo on the Plains in the mid-1800s. After the Civil War, hunters killed buffalo to feed the construction crews of the railroads. Others shot buffalo for sport. Hunters also supplied buffalo hides to tanneries to make leather goods. The hunters left the meat to rot. By 1880, the buffalo on the southern Plains were gone. By 1904, only 34 were left on the northern Plains.

Bureau of Indian Affairs

Especially on the Plains reservations, Native Americans had to depend on the Bureau of Indian Affairs for survival. Corrupt bureau agents often sold to settlers the supplies meant for the Native Americans. Sometimes the food the Native Americans did receive was rotten and moldy.

The Bureau of Indian Affairs had been created in 1824, as part of the War Department. In 1849, it was transferred to the Department of the Interior. The bureau forbade Native American religious ceremonies on the reservations and encouraged Native Americans to speak English, rather than their own languages. Children were sent away to boarding schools where they had to dress and speak like white people and follow their customs. For many Native Americans, life lost much of its meaning as they saw their traditions and customs being pushed aside.

Native Americans Speak Out

Native Americans protested their treatment. One group, the Nez Perce, carried their protest to the President. In 1877, they had been ordered to move to a reservation. A series of fights with the soldiers accompanying them forced them to flee to Canada. At the border, they were caught by the army. After five days of fighting, the Nez Perce surrendered. Instead of being sent to a reservation in the Northwest as they had been promised, they were sent to the Indian Territory.

In 1879, Chief Joseph of the Nez Perce went to Washington, D.C., to ask President Hayes to send his people to the promised reservation. In his speech, Chief Joseph spoke for many Native Americans:

All men were made by the same Great Chief Spirit. They are all brothers. The earth is the mother of all people, and all people should have equal rights upon it. Let me live to be a free man—free to travel, free to stop, free to work, free to trade where I choose, free to choose my own teachers, free to follow the religion of my fathers, free to think and talk and act for myself—and I will obey every law, or submit to the penalty.

This photograph of a Piegan camp was taken by Edward Curtis. Since this is a photograph, what can you infer about the date of the scene?

Chief Joseph and his people were eventually allowed to return to the Northwest.

Another Native American who spoke against government mistreatment was Sarah Winnemucca (win-uh-MUHK-uh), a Paiute. She lectured in eastern cities and in 1883 wrote *Life Among the Paiute: Their Claims and Wrongs*, a book pointing out the hardships of the Paiute. In 1880, she had met with President Hayes and received permission for her people to move to a reservation in Oregon. They were living on a reservation in Washington state where they were being mistreated by the government agent.

White Reaction

In 1881, Helen Hunt Jackson wrote *A Century of Dishonor* to expose the mistreatment of Native Americans. She also wanted to show the falseness of the stereotypes that many whites held about Native Americans.

> Why should the Indian be expected to plant corn, fence lands, build houses, or do anything but get food from day to day, when experience has taught him that the product of his labor will be seized by the white man tomorrow? The most industrious white man would become a drone under similar circumstances. Nevertheless, many of the Indians are already at work, and furnish ample proof of the falseness of the idea that 'the Indian will not work.' So long as they are not citizens of the United States, their rights of property are insecure. While they continue individually to gather the crumbs that fall from the table of the United States, idleness, and debt will be the rule, and hard work, saving, and freedom from debt the exception.

drone: one unwilling to work

ample (AM-puhl): enough

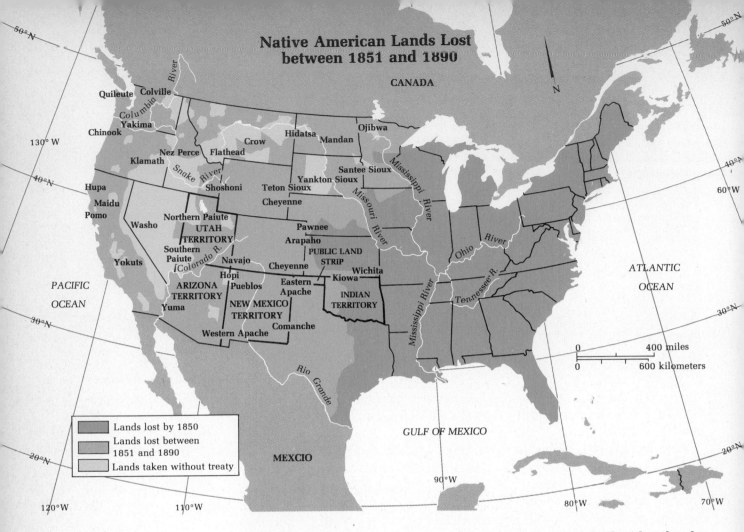

Native American Lands Lost between 1851 and 1890

CANADA

N

Quileute Colville

Columbia River

Yakima

Chinook

Nez Perce Flathead

Klamath

Snake River

Hupa

Shoshoni

Maidu

Pomo

Washo

Northern Paiute

UTAH TERRITORY

Southern Paiute

Colorado R.

Navajo

Yokuts

Hopi

ARIZONA TERRITORY

Pueblos

Yuma

NEW MEXICO TERRITORY

Western Apache

Crow

Hidatsa Mandan

Ojibwa

Santee Sioux

Yankton Sioux

Teton Sioux

Cheyenne

Pawnee

Arapaho

Cheyenne

Eastern Apache

PUBLIC LAND STRIP

Kiowa

Wichita

INDIAN TERRITORY

Comanche

Rio Grande

Mississippi River

Missouri River

Ohio River

Mississippi River

Tennessee R.

ATLANTIC OCEAN

PACIFIC OCEAN

GULF OF MEXICO

MEXCIO

50°N
130° W
40°N
30°N
20°N
120° W
110°W
90°W
80°W
70°W
50°N
40°N
60°W
30°N
20°N

0   400 miles
0   600 kilometers

■ Lands lost by 1850
■ Lands lost between 1851 and 1890
□ Lands taken without treaty

Some Easterners were upset by what Jackson described in her book. In 1887, as a result of pressure by these people, Congress passed the Dawes (DAWZ) Act.

Dawes Act

The Dawes Act was supposed to solve the problems of Native Americans. Under this act, the reservations were broken up, and each head of a household received 64 hectares (160 acres) of land. Individual families could not sell their land for 25 years. All Native Americans who received land would become citizens of the U.S. after 25 years. Any land that was not held by individual families would be sold to white settlers and the money used to educate Native American children. Not all Native American groups obeyed the law. Some, especially in the Southwest, ignored it.

In passing the Dawes Act, the government hoped to make Native Americans independent farmers and to assimilate them into white American culture. The act was not successful. As you have already read, many Native Americans were not farmers and were not familiar with farming methods. The breakup of the reservations left Native Americans without their traditions and culture and eventually much of their land.

In time, many families sold their land and lived on the money they received. When the money ran out, they had no means of support. Others were cheated out of their land. By 1932, non-Native Americans claimed two thirds of the 55 million hectares (138 million acres) of land held by Native Americans in 1887. As a result of the Dawes Act, Native Americans became more and more dependent on the U.S. government.

INDIAN TERRITORY

Not even Indian territory remained safe. By the late 1880s, settlers were asking the federal government to open more western land for settlement. Much of what the government decided to open was in the Indian Territory.

In 1889, the government bought land from the Creek and Seminole. In April of that year, 50,000 settlers prepared to race for land claims as the government opened 769,000 hectares (1.9 million acres). The pistol announcing the beginning of the land rush went off at noon. By nightfall, 10,000 people had settled in each of the new cities of Guthrie (GUHTH-ree) and Oklahoma City. The next year the U.S. government set up the Oklahoma Territory with Guthrie as its capital.

In 1893, 2.6 million hectares (6.5 million acres) more were opened on the Tonkawa (TAHNG-kuh-wah) and Pawnee reservations. Over 50,000 people claimed land on the first day of settlement. Wanting still more land, settlers began to ask that the rest of the Indian Territory be opened. Congress created the Dawes Commission to bargain for the land and disband the Native American nations. The earlier Dawes Act did not apply to the Indian Territory. In 1907, Oklahoma became a state, and the Indian Territory ceased to exist.

LOOKING BACK

1. Why were Native Americans forced onto reservations?
2. What generalization can you make from the table about the causes of the conflicts between Native Americans and settlers and soldiers?
3. What effect did reservation life have on Native American: **a.** religion? **b.** language? **c.** children?
4. **a.** What stereotype of Native Americans does the reading from Helen Hunt Jackson's book attempt to change? **b.** What arguments does she offer to show its falseness?
5. Why did the Dawes Act make it difficult for Native Americans to support themselves?
6. List the events that led to the end of the Indian Territory.
7. Study the maps on pages 354 and 512. **a.** How did the way land was taken between 1851 and 1890 differ from before 1850? **b.** What had happened to the Indian Territory by 1890?

Chapter 2   Settling the Last Frontier

LOOKING AHEAD

This chapter describes the settling of the last frontier—the area bounded by the Missouri River and the eastern borders of Oregon and California. As the Native Americans were being forced onto reservations, miners, ranchers, and farmers were streaming into the area. You will also read about the hardships Mexican Americans suffered because of this flood of newcomers. After you study this chapter, you will be able to:

- interpret data by comparing population density maps.
- list the developments that opened the West to settlement.
- describe how Mexican Americans lost their lands.
- explain how a mining camp became a permanent settlement.
- identify the cause that led to the decline of open-range cattle ranching.
- describe the effects of Plains' geography and climate on farming equipment and methods.

Events

Panic of 1873

Words and Terms

last frontier	open range
Homestead Act	sodbuster
Court of Private	Department of Agriculture
Land Claims	Morrill Land-Grant Act

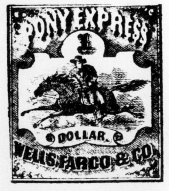

The Pony Express carried mail between Missouri and California in 10 days. The service lasted a little over a year. With the completion in 1861 of coast-to-coast telegraph lines, there was no need for the Pony Express.

In the unit Manifest Destiny, the population density map shows that less than two people per square mile lived in the area between the Plains and the Rocky Mountains in 1850. This was the last frontier. In 1890, the Census Bureau declared the frontier closed. The U.S. had fulfilled its manifest destiny and spread from sea to sea.

NEW STATES

Several major developments took place after the Civil War that opened this area to settlement. As you read in Chapter 1, many Native Americans in the area were forced onto reservations in the 1870s and 1880s. Settlers going west felt safer. The discovery of gold and silver in the Rockies brought miners and merchants. Many stayed to build permanent towns and cities.

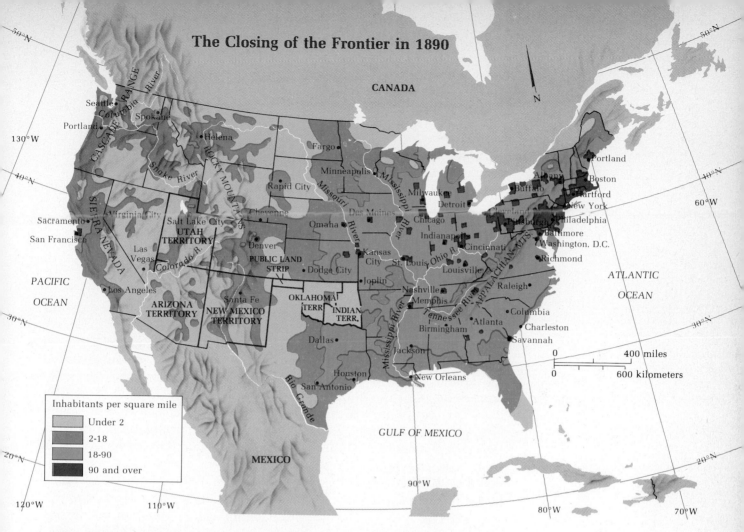

The Closing of the Frontier in 1890

Inhabitants per square mile
- Under 2
- 2–18
- 18–90
- 90 and over

The Homestead Act of 1862 encouraged settlement of the Great Plains. Under this act, the U.S. government gave 64 hectares (100 acres) of land to any citizen or immigrant who promised to live on and work the land for five years. Because most of the fertile farmland east of the Mississippi had been settled, many native-born Americans and immigrants took advantage of this offer.

The opening of the Indian Territory added more land for settlement. The chief factor that made all this westward movement possible was the completion of the first transcontinental railroad in 1869. You will read more about it in Chapter 4 of this unit. As the western territories added population, they were divided into states. Between 1864 and 1912, 13 new states were admitted to the Union.

STATES ADMITTED TO THE UNION FROM 1864 to 1912

State	Date	State	Date	State	Date
Nevada	1864	Montana	1889	Oklahoma	1907
Nebraska	1867	Washington	1889	New Mexico	1912
Colorado	1876	Idaho	1890	Arizona	1912
N. Dakota	1889	Wyoming	1890		
S. Dakota	1889	Utah	1896		

MEXICAN LAND GRANTS

Native Americans were not the only ones to lose their land to settlers. By the Treaty of Guadalupe Hidalgo after the Mexican War, former Mexicans had been guaranteed citizenship and the right to keep their property. Some of these property claims dated back to the land grants given by the Spanish monarchs when the area was part of the Viceroyalty of New Spain. Other grants of land had been given to soldiers who fought against Spain in the Mexican Revolution. At the time of the Treaty of Guadalupe Hidalgo, 75,000 Mexicans lived in the Southwest—60,000 in what is the present state of New Mexico.

As settlers moved into New Mexico in the 1850s and 1860s, the former Mexicans began to lose their land. Settlers acquired Mexican American land through purchase, violence, and the occasional help of corrupt politicians. The cattle boom in the 1870s created a demand for large areas of land for cattle grazing.

In the 1880s, politicians, lawyers, and bankers formed the Santa Fe Ring. The Ring used its power to influence judicial and legislative decisions over Mexican American lands. Many former Mexicans were confused by the U.S. form of government and U.S. tax laws. The Ring used this confusion to their benefit. Dishonest surveys were made that took parts of land grants away from Mexican Americans. This land was then sold to settlers. Spain and Mexico had taxed what was grown on the land, not the land itself. In 1895, the government decided to collect back taxes from 1848 to 1895. Many landowners could not pay these huge sums, and their land was sold at auction.

deed: document that proves ownership

In 1891, a Court of Private Land Claims was established to confirm ownership of the land claimed by Mexican Americans. Proving ownership was difficult because so many of the deeds had been lost or destroyed over the years. By the time the court disbanded in 1904, many Mexican Americans who could not show proof of ownership lost their lands to the federal government. The government set aside 3.6 million hectares (9 million acres) of the land to establish national forests. Much of the remaining land was sold or rented to settlers.

MINERS

In the late 1850s, miners were heading to the Rockies where gold and silver had been discovered. Mining camps sprang up from what is now Montana to Arizona and New Mexico. Miners set up tents, and shopkeepers and saloonkeepers went into business as soon as they could unpack their goods. If gold or silver was not found, a tent city could disappear as quickly as it had appeared. Sometimes when a strike was big, mining camps became permanent. Towns and cities of wooden homes, stores, and churches were built to provide for the needs of the miners.

strike: a discovery

A number of mining camps, among them Virginia City; Denver; Cheyenne, Wyoming; and Helena, Montana, are prosperous western cities today. In the 1880s, however, many mining towns were abandoned when the mines were worked out. The last big gold and silver strike was at Cripple Creek, Colorado, in 1891-94.

Many people came to mining camps with hopes of "striking it rich." Only a few did, and most spent their money as quickly as they mined or panned it. Once a city grew up in place of tents, those who could not make a living from mining often stayed and became merchants. As in California, most of the miners were men. A few women came to earn money doing laundry and cooking. Occasionally, a family took up mining, but this was rare. Martha Jane Canary, also known as Calamity Jane, grew up in mining camps and became an expert horsewoman and sharpshooter.

calamity
(kuh-LAM-uh-tee):
disaster

CATTLE RANCHERS

The Great Plains were well suited to cattle raising on the open range, that is, unfenced grassland. Much of this land was government land that the ranchers did not own or even rent. The first cattle had been brought in from Mexico. Mexicans taught cowhands about cattle raising, branding, and round ups. By the end of the Civil War, cattle ranching was booming on the Texas plains. By the 1870s, it had spread to the northern plains.

In the 1840s and 1850s, cattle ranchers drove their herds from Texas overland to New Orleans or to the gold fields. After the Civil War, they drove their herds north over several trails to rail lines in Kansas and Nebraska. There, the cattle were sold and shipped by rail to meat-packing factories in Chicago. In the 1870s, the railroads extended their lines to Texas.

In this painting by Charles Russell you can see some of the skills a good cowhand needed. A steer has become tangled in the rope and pulled the cowhand's horse to the ground. See how the roper has shifted his weight to help his horse.

Cattle Trails

Many of the cowhands who worked on these ranches were black. Perhaps as many as 5,000 blacks became cowhands after the Civil War. Some were freed slaves who went west. Others were freed slaves from Texas who stayed to work for wages. Good cowhands were scarce so most blacks were welcomed. But few became foremen or trail bosses. Nat "Deadwood Dick" Love and Bose Ikard were two of the most famous black cowhands.

By 1890, the days of open-range cattle ranching were over. In the late 1860s and 1870s, farmers moving west began buying and fencing in land and damming up rivers and streams. By the early 1880s, sheep herders were also taking over land and water sources. Range wars broke out over land and water rights. To add to these problems, beef prices fell in the mid-1880s because the supply was greater than the demand. Two severe winters and a drought between 1885 and 1887 killed thousands of cattle. Many ranchers went broke.

However, cattle ranching did not end. Ranchers formed associations to cooperate with one another. To end range wars, they bought or rented government land. So that supply would not be greater than demand, they kept their herds small. Ranchers also began to grow hay to feed their herds in future droughts or blizzards.

FARMERS

Attracted by cheap land, farmers from the East, Midwest, and South headed west after the Civil War. In 1879, a crop failure in the South sent many blacks west. Other blacks went to escape the black codes and similar laws. Blacks homesteaded in Missouri, Iowa, Nebraska, and in what later became Oklahoma.

Plains farmers were called sodbusters because of the hard-packed soil they had to break up before they could plant. New equipment and farming methods were needed before it was even possible to grow crops on this land. Steel plows were invented that dug deeper and faster into the soil. Threshing machines that could separate wheat grains from stalks were combined with harvesters. In 1878, the twine binder was added to the reaper. This new machine cut wheat, picked it up, and tied it into bundles.

The Plains receive about only 25 centimeters (10 inches) of rain a year. To grow crops, farmers began to practice dry farming. In this method, a field is planted every other year. In the year the field lies unplanted, the soil soaks up precipitation and stores it for the next year's crop. Plains farmers also tried irrigation. But drilling for water and then pumping it to the fields was too expensive for most farmers.

Besides the hard-packed soil and little rainfall, Plains farmers faced other problems. Because of the herds of cattle and sheep that roamed across the Plains, farmers needed fences. But there were few trees to use for fence wood. The invention of barbed wire in 1873 provided a substitute. Barbed wire fences also led to range wars. Cattle that tried to break through the fences were caught on the barbs. They either died there or tore their hides trying to free themselves.

The early families were isolated on their farms and rarely saw other people. Often farming was not very profitable. The prices that farmers received for their crops depended on the general business activity of the country. When business was bad, as it was after the Panic of 1873, farmers made little money.

The federal government made several attempts to help farmers. It established the Department of Agriculture in 1862. Its many bureaus carry on research and collect information of importance to farmers. Its pamphlets about new farming techniques, soil conservation, and plant diseases are available to farmers at low cost.

In 1862, Congress also passed the Morrill Land-Grant Act. Each state and territory was given a large tract of land to sell. The money from the sale of the land was to be used to set up agricultural and mechanical arts, that is, mining and engineering, colleges. Eventually, 69 colleges were established under the Morrill Act.

The Shores family, homesteaders in Nebraska, were photographed in front of their sod house and barn. Why did many Plains settlers use sod bricks for their buildings?

tract (TRAKT): area of land or water

LOOKING BACK

1. Look at the map The Frontier in 1850 on page 430 and then at the one in this chapter. **a.** What states and territories west of the Mississippi had few settlers in 1850? **b.** Estimate how much of the West had been settled between 1850 and 1890. **c.** Look at the map The Frontier in 1790 on page 307. What changes in population density have taken place along the East coast in 100 years? **d.** Look at the map Natural Regions of the United States on page 13. Why do you think some areas of the U.S. had fewer than two people per square mile?
2. What developments took place in the mid-1800s that opened the West to settlement?
3. How were Mexican American lands taken away?
4. How did mining camps become permanent cities or towns?
5. What three events led to the end of open-range cattle raising?
6. **a.** State three problems that Plains farmers faced in the late 1800s. **b.** Describe how farmers overcame each one.

Chapter 3   Immigrants and the City

LOOKING AHEAD

This chapter describes the growth of cities in the late 1800s. You will learn about life in the city for the poor, the middle class, and the wealthy and about the corruption in city government. You will also read about immigration during this period. After you study this chapter, you will be able to:

★ explain the difference between percent of population and actual number.
● list the reasons for the growth of cities.
● compare city life for the poor, middle class, and wealthy.
● describe the corruption in city governments.
● list the push and pull forces for immigrant groups.
● describe how immigrants in the late 1800s adapted to their new lives.
● explain how native-born Americans and earlier immigrants reacted to the immigrants of the late 1800s.

Social Studies Vocabulary

urbanization	kickback	ethnic group

People

Jacob Riis	Jane Addams	Samuel J. Tilden
Stanton Coit	Ellen Starr	Dennis Kearney
Lillian Wald	William Tweed	Workingmen's party

Places

Neighborhood Guild	Henry Street Settlement House	Hull House

Events

Panic of 1873	Panic of 1893

Words and Terms

percent	party boss	Gentlemen's Agreement
slum	Immigration	
tenement	Restriction League	
ward leader	Chinese Exclusion Act	

Jane Addams was a co-founder of Hull House in Chicago. One of a number of settlement houses in the U.S., it helped immigrants adapt to their new life. How?

Between 1860 and 1900, the U.S. became a nation of city dwellers. **Urbanization** (er-buhn-uh-ZAY-shuhn), the changing of an area from a rural to a city society, was taking place. Before the Civil War, only 20 percent of the population lived in cities. By 1900, the percentage had doubled. The number of city dwellers had risen from 6 million to 30 million.

BUILDING STATISTICAL SKILLS

The word *percent* means the number of parts per hundred. For example, if 30 percent of 500 people are farmers, then 30 out of every 100 people—or 150 out of 500—are farmers. To find the actual number of farmers, multiply the percent, using the decimal form, by the total population: $.30 \times 500 = 150$. You have just read that the percent of the population living in cities doubled between 1860 and 1900. But the actual city population more than tripled—from 6 million to 30 million.

Year	Total Population	Percent in Cities	Population in Cities
1860	31,443,321	20%	6,288,664
1900	75,994,575	40%	30,397,830

Do not assume that because a percent is doubled, the actual number also doubles. Remember, the total population also increased between 1860 and 1900. **Activity:** In 1920, the total population of the U.S. was 105,710,620. If 70 percent of the population lived in cities, what was the actual number of people living in the cities that year?

THE GROWTH OF CITIES

Cities grew for a number of reasons. Improved farm machinery put many owners of small farms and many farm hands out of work. The Panic of 1873 and the depression that followed also caused many farmers to lose their lands. The panic had been brought about by the overexpansion of railroads and industry after the Civil War. These farm people had nowhere to go but to cities to look for homes and jobs. Southern blacks also swelled the population of cities, especially in the Northeast. But the largest number of new urban dwellers were immigrants. Most of those who came to the U.S. at the end of the 1800s stayed in the cities. By then the last frontier had closed, and there were few job opportunities outside the cities.

    The Northeast had the largest number of cities because it was the oldest area of the country and had the most industry. But some of the fastest-growing cities were in the Midwest: Omaha, Nebraska; Minneapolis, Minnesota; Cleveland; and Detroit. Chicago became a rail center as well as an industrial and financial center. Railroads played a large role in the growth of such western cities as San Francisco, Los Angeles, and Portland, Oregon. Although southern cities developed more slowly, the population of older cities, such as Charleston, Rich-

urban (ER-buhn): having to do with cities

521

mond, and New Orleans, grew rapidly in the late 1800s. Newer cities, such as Birmingham with its steel industry, grew as the demand for their products grew. You will read more about industry and railroads in the next chapter.

CITY LIFE

The quality of life in the city depended on whether a person was an immigrant, a black, or a native-born American. It also depended on whether the person was rich, middle class, or poor. The following is a general description of what life was like for these three groups in the cities of the late 1800s.

The Poor

The poor—immigrants, blacks, and whites from farm areas—had few job skills and were often out of work. Because they had so little money, these people were forced to live in areas of cities known as slums. Their homes were tenements. These were buildings of three, four, or more stories that received little sun or fresh air and were often without running water or heat. Each floor was divided into many small rooms. Sometimes a family of five or six lived in one room. Often, if a family was lucky enough to have two rooms, they rented the second room to add to their income.

The owners of tenements did not live in them and rarely, if ever, made repairs. The tenements became run-down quickly and were un-

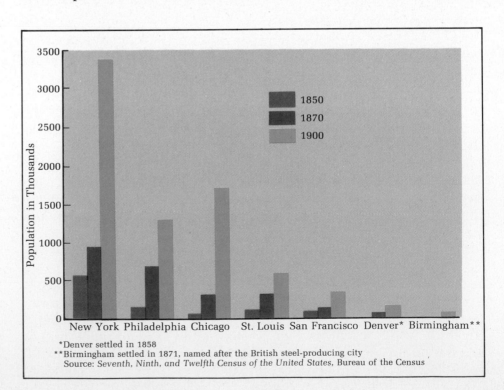

Population Growth in Selected Cities from 1850 to 1900

*Denver settled in 1858
**Birmingham settled in 1871, named after the British steel-producing city
Source: *Seventh, Ninth, and Twelfth Census of the United States*, Bureau of the Census

This photograph of Hester Street on New York's Lower East Side shows a typical street scene from around the late 1800s. What does the photograph tell you about the part of the city shown and the lives of the people there?

safe and unhealthy. They lacked such safety features as fire escapes. Garbage was thrown out the windows into alleys, and rats ran through the buildings. Sewage spilled into streets. Disease and malnutrition were common among tenement dwellers who had little or no money for doctors.

Most tenement dwellers shopped from pushcarts that lined the streets. From these carts, they could buy second-hand clothing, day-old bread, and bruised fruits and vegetables. Most of the people could not afford meat. Because of the overcrowding and poverty, some people turned to crime to help support their families. Some stole only food, but others turned to robbery and even murder to get money. In the 1880s, the number of people in prisons had increased by 50 percent and the murder rate had tripled.

malnutrition
(mal-noo-TRISH-uhn):
illness from eating
too little food

The Middle Class and the Wealthy

The middle class—clerks, managers of businesses, and shop owners—lived away from the downtown part of the city. In these areas, neat painted houses were set back from the street and had small yards. Some streets were lined with shops. There was usually a meat market, barber shop, bank, fruit stand, and a candy store.

Lawyers, doctors, and owners of large businesses lived in the farthest parts of the city. Their large homes were surrounded by trees and wide lawns. By the 1870s and 1880s, cable cars and electric street cars had made it possible for these people to go to work each day downtown and return home at night. Cities continued to expand outward from downtown as transportation systems improved.

Reforms

The growth of slums in the cities caused many Americans to react. Jacob Riis (REES), a journalist and social reformer, wrote and lectured on slum conditions. In the 1880s and 1890s, settlement houses were opened in major cities to help immigrants. Stanton Coit (KOYT) opened Neighborhood Guild on the lower east side of New York City in 1886. In 1892, Lillian Wald opened Henry Street Settlement House, also in New York. The following year Jane Addams and Ellen Starr started Hull House in Chicago.

Volunteers at settlement houses taught immigrants to speak, read, and write English. They took care of small children so their parents could work, and they provided health care for adults and children. Settlement house workers also tried to brighten the lives of the poor with recreational, sports, and cultural activities such as concerts.

CORRUPT CITY GOVERNMENTS

A number of cities in the late 1800s were run by dishonest politicians — both Democratic and Republican. The late 1860s and 1870s were a time of political corruption across the country, as you will read in the next chapter.

Many people blamed the corruption on business. Politicians did favors, such as giving contracts to businesses, in exchange for bribes and kickbacks. A **kickback** is a sum of money given by a business to a politician in return for a contract for government work. The company overcharges the city, state, or federal government and then "kicks back" the extra to the politician who made the contract.

Other people blamed the corruption in city government on immigrants. Some neighborhood politicians, called ward leaders, did favors for them in exchange for votes. A ward was a political unit of a city. It was usually a number of blocks square and often made up of people from the same ethnic group. An **ethnic group** is a group of people who share social and political ties, a common culture, and/or come from the same geographic region.

Each political party chose a leader for its party from each ward. The ward leader looked out for the interests of the party in his ward. For example, ward leaders helped immigrants adapt to life in the U.S. Their new country could be very confusing to immigrants. They came to depend on their ward leader to help them find jobs and housing and deal with the legal system. Ward leaders also helped immigrants file for citizenship. Once immigrants became citizens, they repaid the helpfulness of the ward leader by voting as he wished.

Party Bosses

The most powerful politician in a city or state was the party boss. Party bosses controlled the decisions and actions of their political

The cartoon of the Tweed Ring by Thomas Nast is captioned "Who stole the people's money? 'Twas he." According to the cartoon, who besides politicians were involved in the ring?

parties and of the governments that their parties ran. The party boss could influence the choice of candidates for office, the acts of elected officials, the giving of political patronage, and even the decisions of judges.

Democratic Party Boss William Tweed of New York City was one of the worst of the corrupt city politicians and party bosses. Between 1865 and 1871, he robbed the city of millions of dollars. Boss Tweed, as he was called, was Superintendent of Public Works. As such he handled all the city's contracts for new construction and he awarded the contracts to companies that gave him the largest bribes. Tweed also overstated the amount of money needed to run the city and then pocketed the extra. He drove the city to the edge of bankruptcy. Samuel J. Tilden, a New York lawyer, was largely responsible for breaking up the Tweed Ring. As you may recall from the unit Civil War and Reconstruction, Tilden became the Democratic candidate for President in 1876 as a result of his reform efforts.

IMMIGRANTS

Between 1860 and 1920, more than 27 million immigrants entered the U.S. As you may recall from the unit Life at Mid-Century, most immigrants who came before 1860 were from northern and western Europe. This was also true between 1860 and 1890. But by 1900 over 70 percent of all immigrants were eastern and southern Europeans — Italians, Russians, Austrians, Hungarians, Poles, Bulgarians, Serbians (from what is now part of Yugoslavia), Rumanians, Greeks, and Turks.

The first law limiting immigration to the U.S. was passed in 1882. It was designed to keep out criminals, the insane, and those who might not be able to take care of themselves. Here two immigration workers at Ellis Island give intelligence tests to immigrants.

Northern and Western Europeans

Many push forces were at work encouraging immigrants from northern and western Europe to leave their homelands. Most of the forces were economic. Because of large wheat harvests elsewhere in the world, the demand for European wheat declined in the 1870s and 1880s. This caused a depression in farming, especially in Great Britain, Scandinavia, and Germany. These countries also had a series of industrial problems that led to a decline in manufacturing. As a result, many unemployed craftworkers, miners, and iron and textile workers came in search of jobs. They usually had little or no money.

Those who were drawn to the U.S. by pull forces, however, had some money. After the Civil War, Wisconsin, Minnesota, and Iowa were among the states that advertised for Europeans to buy land. During this period, the federal government was giving large grants of land to the western railroads to sell. The profits were used to extend the tracks. The railroads encouraged immigrants, especially Germans and Scandinavians, to buy land. The railroads offered to pay part of their passage. Some even provided housing for the immigrants until they bought land.

Immigrants from northern and western Europe began to decrease in the 1890s. The last frontier had been settled. Most of the good farmland was claimed. Also, farm profits were declining. The Panic of 1893 was especially hard on farmers. Conditions in northern and western Europe were also changing. The birth rate was declining. Fewer people were competing for available jobs. Because employers had a smaller labor force to choose from, wages and working conditions improved. In the late 1890s, Germany and Sweden experienced rapid industrial growth, which created many new jobs. Governments also stepped in to slow emigration by developing social and economic reforms to keep their people at home. Great Britain encouraged those who wanted to emigrate to settle within the British Empire—Canada, Australia, New Zealand, or South Africa.

U.S. IMMIGRANTS FROM 1860 TO 1920

Nationality	Number	Where They Lived	How They Lived
Germans	4,645,279	Midwest, Northeast	Farmers; factory and steel workers
Italians	4,183,106	Northeast	Miners; farmers; farm and construction workers
Austrians and Hungarians	4,074,117	Midwest, Northeast	Miners; farmers
Russians	3,623,811	Midwest, Northeast	Farmers; railroad and factory workers
British	3,130,929	Midwest, Northeast, South	Farmers; factory and steel workers
Irish	2,450,430	Northeast	Miners; factory, construction, and railroad workers
Scandinavians	2,107,030	Midwest	Farmers; machinists; skilled workers
Canadians	1,860,058	West	Miners; farmers
Chinese	311,362	West	Miners; farmers; farm, construction, and railroad workers
Mexicans	288,613	Southwest	Farm workers
Bulgarians, Serbians, Rumanians, Turks	273,920	Midwest, Northeast	Unskilled workers
Japanese	242,181	West	Farmers; farm and railroad workers
Poles	168,418	Northeast, Midwest	Miners; farmers; steel workers
Greeks	188,500	Northeast, Midwest, West	Unskilled and railroad workers

areas, through no fault of their own, these immigrants were forced to live in dirty, crowded tenements. The earlier immigrants also feared that the many newcomers would take away their jobs. As had happened before, employers began hiring new arrivals at lower wages.

Organizations were formed to limit the number of immigrants coming into the U.S. In 1893, the Immigration Restriction League convinced Congress to pass a bill admitting only people who could read and write. President Cleveland vetoed it.

Efforts to exclude particular immigrant groups met with more success. When the Chinese in California began farming, Californians began to protest. They were afraid of the competition. They could not grow as much as cheaply as the Chinese did with their farming methods. In the late 1800s, Dennis Kearney (KAHR-nee) formed the Workingmen's party to rid the U.S. of Chinese. Pressure by this group led to the passage of the Chinese Exclusion Act of 1882. This act prevented any Chinese from entering the U.S. or becoming U.S. citi-

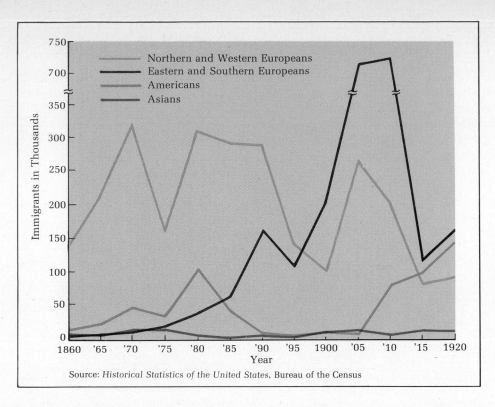

Immigration
from 1860 to 1920

Source: *Historical Statistics of the United States*, Bureau of the Census

exclusion
(eks-KLOO-zhuhn):
keeping out;
shutting out

zens for ten years. Additional acts were passed in 1888 and 1892. In 1902, Congress made the exclusion of all Chinese immigrants permanent. The Gentlemen's Agreement of 1907 excluded all Japanese immigrants from the U.S.

LOOKING BACK

⭐ 1. **a.** If you are given percentage of population, how do you find the actual number of people? **b.** If the population doubles does the percentage necessarily double? **c.** Why or why not?

2. List and explain three factors that helped cities to grow.

3. Describe the areas of the cities in which: **a.** the poor lived. **b.** the middle class lived. **c.** the wealthy lived.

4. How did each of the following contribute to corruption: **a.** politicians and business? **b.** politicians and immigrants?

5. **a.** List the push forces that encouraged northern and western Europeans to emigrate. **b.** List the pull force. **c.** Why did emigration from these two areas decline in the 1890s? **d.** List the push forces that encouraged eastern and southern Europeans to emigrate. **e.** What was the major pull force?

6. **a.** How did immigrants in the late 1800s adapt to their new lives? **b.** Were these similar to ways immigrants in the early 1800s had adapted? Reread pages 379-84 to help you answer.

7. **a.** Why did native-born Americans and earlier immigrants resent the immigrants of the late 1800s? **b.** What laws were passed restricting immigration?

Chapter 4   Growth of Industry

LOOKING AHEAD

This chapter describes changes in American industry after the Civil War. You will learn the reasons for U.S. industrial growth and for the spread of corruption that came with the rise of big business. You will also learn about the reasons for the rise of labor unions and the use of strikes. After you study this chapter, you will be able to:

- recognize continuity and change in U.S. industry.
- ★ read a map to explain U.S. time zones.
- describe how corporations came to control big business.
- state two laws passed to regulate big business.
- explain the reason for the rise of nationwide labor unions in the late 1800s.
- read a table to make a generalization about the causes of strikes in the late 1800s.

Social Studies Vocabulary

time zone	trust	industrial union
rebate	subsidy	collective bargaining

People

Henry Bessemer	J. Pierpont Morgan	Terence V. Powderly
William Kelly	William Sylvis	Mary O'Sullivan
John D. Rockefeller	Isaac Meyers	Mary Kehew
Andrew Carnegie	Frederick Douglass	

Events

Haymarket Riots	Homestead Strike	Pullman Strike

Words and Terms

Pacific Railway Act	National Labor	Women's Trade
Sherman Antitrust	Union	Union League
Act	National Colored	yellow-dog contract
Whiskey Ring	Labor Union	blacklist
Credit Mobilier	Knights of Labor	
Interstate	AFL	
Commerce Act	ILGWU	

This drawing illustrated an article describing the interest shown in the telephone at the Centennial Exposition in Philadelphia. How might developments in communications have helped industry's growth?

In the 1870s, Reconstruction was coming to an end and so was the rural farm life of most Americans. With each new invention, the industrialization that had begun in the early 1800s became more widespread. Large corporations were replacing small businesses. Workers began to organize into labor unions to demand better wages and working conditions. Many of the members of these new unions were immigrants. Business leaders fought against unions and against the laws that would protect the public from the dishonest practices of some big businesses.

FROM FARMING TO INDUSTRY

In the unit New Technology, you read about the beginning of industrialization in the U.S. Within 20 years after the Civil War, the nation had changed from a farming economy to one based on industry.

Railroads

Several factors allowed industry to grow rapidly. One of the most important was the expansion of railroads. As you may recall from the unit New Technology, trains were traveling over more than 48,000 kilometers (30,000 miles) of track by 1861. But much of this track was in the Midwest. To grow, industry needed an efficient system of transportation. Raw materials had to be carried from the West and South to factories in the Midwest and Northeast. The manufactured goods then had to be carried to markets across the country.

In 1862, Congress passed the Pacific Railway Act. It gave the Central Pacific and the Union Pacific the right to build a transcontinental railroad. The act also gave the two companies large amounts of land to sell to raise money for laying track. The Central Pacific built east from Sacramento, California, and the Union Pacific built west from Council Bluffs, Iowa. The work was done mostly by Irish immigrants on the Central Pacific and Chinese immigrants on the Union Pacific.

The two companies linked up on May 10, 1869 at Promontory (PRAH-muhn-toh-ree) Point, Utah. A golden spike was used to join the last rails. By 1900, there were 419,230 kilometers (258,784 miles) of track across the U.S.

Oil, Coal, and Steel

Another development that helped industry was the discovery of the process for refining oil, or petroleum, into kerosene, gasoline, and lubricants. In time, industry used these products to light and heat factories and to keep machines in working order. In 1859, the first oil well in the U.S. was drilled in Pennsylvania. By 1880, Pennsylvania, Kentucky, Ohio, Illinois, and Indiana were the biggest oil-producing states. It was not until the early 1900s that oil was discovered in the South and West, in Texas, Louisiana, Oklahoma, and California.

From the early 1800s to the early 1900s, coal was the chief source of energy for manufacturing and transportation. It powered steam engines in factories and locomotives. By the late 1800s, the U.S. had replaced Great Britain as the leading producer and user of coal.

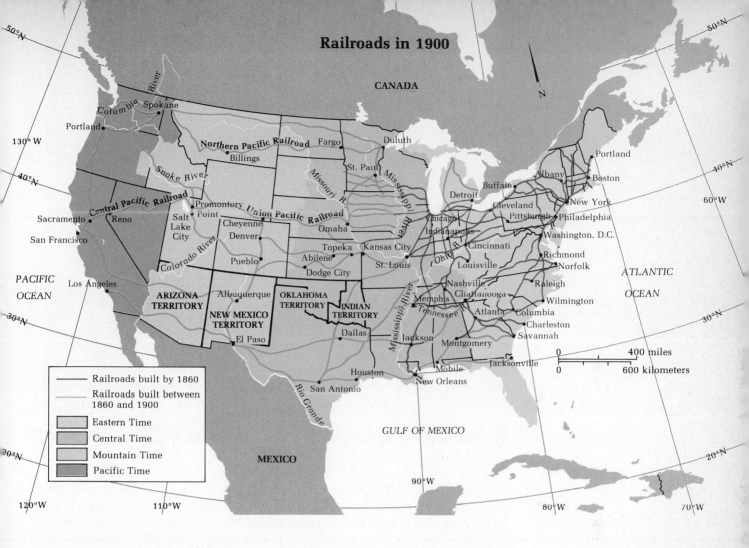

Railroads in 1900

CANADA

Columbia River
Spokane
Portland
Northern Pacific Railroad
Fargo
Duluth
Billings
St. Paul
Snake River
Missouri R.
Mississippi
Portland
Albany
Boston
Buffalo
Detroit
Cleveland
New York
Central Pacific Railroad
Promontory Point
Union Pacific Railroad
Pittsburgh
Philadelphia
Sacramento
Reno
Salt Lake City
Cheyenne
Washington, D.C.
San Francisco
Denver
Omaha
Chicago
Indianapolis
Cincinnati
Richmond
Colorado River
Topeka
Kansas City
Ohio R.
Louisville
Norfolk
Los Angeles
Pueblo
Abilene
St. Louis
Nashville
Raleigh
Dodge City
Memphis
Chattanooga
Columbia
Wilmington
ARIZONA TERRITORY
Albuquerque
OKLAHOMA TERRITORY
INDIAN TERRITORY
Tennessee R.
Atlanta
Charleston
NEW MEXICO TERRITORY
Dallas
Savannah
PACIFIC OCEAN
ATLANTIC OCEAN
El Paso
Jackson
Montgomery
Jacksonville
Houston
Mobile
New Orleans
San Antonio
Rio Grande
GULF OF MEXICO
MEXICO

Legend:
- Railroads built by 1860
- Railroads built between 1860 and 1900
- Eastern Time
- Central Time
- Mountain Time
- Pacific Time

Scale: 0–400 miles / 0–600 kilometers

Clocks in various sections of the U.S. do not all show the same time. For example, when it is 8:00 a.m. in New York city, the sun has not risen in San Francisco. This time difference caused scheduling problems for the railroads. So that everyone would know when the trains arrived and departed, the railroads established railroad time along their routes. By 1883, the U.S. was divided into 100 time zones. A **time zone** is an area in which the same time is used. The borders are crooked so that counties and nearby communities can share the same time.

In 1884, the railroads divided the country into four time zones: Eastern, Central, Mountain and Pacific. Today, there are three more: Yukon and Bering for Alaska and Alaska-Hawaii. Use the map above to answer these questions about time zones for the 48 contiguous states. **1.** In which time zone do you live? **2.** What is the time difference between neighboring zones? **3.** When it is 9:30 p.m. in Philadelphia, what time is it in Denver? **4.** When it is 4:15 a.m. in Houston, what time is it in Miami?

contiguous
(kuhn-TIG-yoo-uhs):
touching; in contact

The Bessemer process made steel by forcing blasts of hot air over melted iron to burn away the impurities. The oval shapes are the converters in which the process took place. Why was steel important to industry?

The production of large quantities of steel at low cost also made rapid industrialization possible. Steel is harder and stronger than iron. It replaced iron in machinery and in building bridges, railroads, and skyscrapers. In the 1850s, Henry Bessemer (BES-uh-mer), of England and William Kelly, an American, discovered a process that removed the impurities from iron to make steel. American industry quickly made use of the Bessemer process and later improvements in steelmaking. By 1885, the U.S. was the world's major steel producer.

Workers

By 1900, two thirds of the workers in industry were immigrants. As employers in the 1830s and 1840s had looked on immigrants as a cheap source of labor, so did employers in the late 1800s. By 1890, the average native-born male worker made $12.50 a week. Women made half that for the same amount of work. Immigrants and blacks made less. Children made almost nothing. In the garment, or clothing industry, for example, they earned about 50 cents a week for sewing on buttons or pulling loose threads from finished garments. By 1900, almost two million children under the age of 16 were working in the garment industry alone.

After the Civil War, some blacks moved North looking for a better life than sharecropping and the black codes offered. They were often disappointed. Many employers would not hire them because they were black. They were often forced to take jobs no one else would do, such as cleaning meat-packing plants.

RISE OF BIG BUSINESS

As you may recall from the unit New Technology, a corporation is a group acting legally as an individual for business purposes. Although stockholders own the company, they have little control over the board of directors who run it. In the late 1800s, some directors managed corporations for their own gain and cheated stockholders out of their dividends. Directors of railroads were notorious for this.

In the late 1800s, the struggle for survival caused many companies to close their doors. Because large corporations were able to produce more items more cheaply, they were able to force prices so low that smaller businesses could not compete. Corporations that produced the same product often joined together in a monopoly. The monopoly could charge any price it wished for a product because it was either the only producer of the product or the largest. For example, in the late 1800s, Standard Oil monopolized the oil industry.

notorious (noh-TOH-ree-uhs): well-known; having a bad reputation

Captains of Industry or Robber Barons

Some of the largest American businesses of the late 1800s and early 1900s were controlled by men who have been called captains of industry by some. Others call them robber barons. These men had national power and were ruthless if not dishonest.

ruthless (ROOTH-luhs): without mercy; cruel

John D. Rockefeller was one of the wealthiest of these men. In 1863, he opened a small oil refinery near Cleveland, Ohio, the center of oil refining in the 1860s. In 1870, he organized the Standard Oil Company and sold stock in it. Competitors were forced to join with Standard Oil in a monopoly, sell out, or be forced out of business. Rockefeller forced the railroads to use the rebate system. A **rebate** is a refund of part of a payment. Railroads paid back to Standard Oil part of the cost that Standard Oil paid for having its oil shipped.

In time, Rockefeller controlled all the refineries in Ohio, Pennsylvania, Maryland, and New York. By 1882, he controlled 95 percent of the nation's oil refineries, as well as oil fields and pipelines. In that year, he organized Standard Oil's holdings into the Standard Oil Trust. In a **trust,** all the stock of the corporations involved is turned over to a single board of managers, or trustees, who run the trust. Other corporations followed Standard Oil's lead and formed trusts until the Sherman Antitrust Act was passed by Congress in 1890.

Andrew Carnegie (kahr-NAY-gee), another captain of industry, had emigrated from Scotland as a boy. In 1864, he started an iron-making business in Pittsburgh and added a steel company to his holdings in the early 1870s. Later, he added ownership of iron ore deposits. In 1899, he formed the Carnegie Steel Corporation. It was the largest industrial organization in the world, employing over 20,000 people. His tactics, like those of Rockefeller, included rebates and ruthlessness. Carnegie dominated the steel industry. When he retired in 1901, he sold his company to United States Steel Corporation. He and the stockholders in Carnegie Steel shared in almost a half billion dollars from the sale.

The United States Steel Corporation was organized in 1901 with the help of J. Pierpont Morgan. Morgan was a wealthy banker and a member of the board of directors of a number of banks, railroads, and other corporations. During the early 1900s, Morgan's banking house lent money to start such corporations as General Electric and International Harvester. During the Panic of 1907, Morgan used his power to increase his holdings. You will read more about Morgan's business practices in the unit Reform and Expansion.

The captains of industry were important members of the Democratic and Republican parties and were often influential in choosing presidential and congressional candidates. They controlled much of the wealth of the nation. Some gave money away to charitable organizations. Carnegie and Rockefeller gave large sums to establish schools, libraries, and various charities. Other wealthy men, however, did not feel they had a responsibility to share their wealth with the less fortunate.

Corruption

As U.S. industries grew, many of the people who controlled them became corrupt. Corruption was widespread and reached its peak in the 1870s during Grant's administrations. The corruption involved business and local, state, and federal governments. In the last chapter, you read about problems in city government. On the federal level, there was the Whiskey Ring and Credit Mobilier (moh-BEEL-yer).

Whiskey manufacturers and government officials, including the head of Internal Revenue and the President's secretary, formed the Whiskey Ring. Its purpose was to cheat the government out of taxes placed on liquor. More than 200 government officials and whiskey distillers were eventually convicted, but the leaders escaped with only light sentences.

Credit Mobilier was a construction company that laid track for the Union Pacific Railroad. It was owned by the same men who owned the railroad. They made sure that the construction company overcharged the railroad which, in turn, got its money from federal land grants and federal subsidies. A **subsidy** (SUHB-sid-dee) is money granted by the government to aid non-government organizations. To keep the federal government from investigating the company's practices, some government officials and members of Congress were allowed to buy stock at low prices. These were really bribes. When Credit Mobilier was paid for its work, the extra money went directly to these stockholders. When the company was eventually investigated, no government official or company director ever was convicted.

Federal Regulations

In the late 1880s, the U.S. government began to regulate industry. The Interstate Commerce Act of 1887 outlawed some practices of the railroads. The act stated that interstate railroads could not charge a

interstate: between states; from state to state

536

higher rate for a short trip than for a long trip. All rates had to be fair, and rebates became illegal.

In 1890, Congress passed the Sherman Antitrust Act. This law stated that any monopoly, trust, or conspiracy organized to restrict free trade and competition was illegal. Also, any person who attempted to form a monopoly was guilty of a crime. The Sherman Antitrust Act was not well enforced because it was unclear. No one was sure what the terms *monopoly, trust,* and *conspiracy* meant or to whom they applied. Those found guilty of violating the act were given only light punishment.

Also, the Presidents during this period—Harrison, Cleveland, and McKinley—supported big business. The Supreme Court of Ohio did use the Sherman Antitrust Act to break up the Standard Oil Trust in 1892. By 1899, however, the company had been reorganized as Standard Oil of New Jersey. It was not until the early 1900s that the federal government began to enforce the law. You will read more about this in the unit Reform and Expansion.

LABOR UNIONS

As you may recall from the unit Life at Mid-Century, some labor unions were organized in the 1830s and 1840s, but they did not last. These early unions usually met personally with the owners of factories and businesses to ask for higher wages or better conditions. With the rise of big corporations after the Civil War, workers had no contact with their employers. Fighting in small groups for their rights, workers lacked the power to gain their demands. They began to see the need for large, powerful unions that could act on their behalf against big business.

These photographs by Lewis Hine are typical industrial scenes. The boy is carrying a load of coats that are to be finished at home. The girl stands between two thread machines she is responsible for operating. How old do you think these children are? Why did such children have to work?

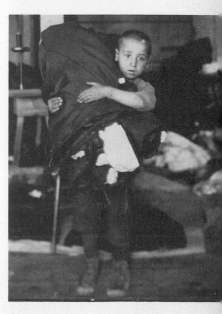

One of the first such unions was the National Labor Union formed in 1866. Under the direction of William Sylvis, the union fought for an eight-hour day for workers. Although the union said it welcomed blacks, it recommended that they form separate local organizations. To avoid the hostility of many whites in the National Labor Union, Isaac Meyers and Frederick Douglass organized the National Colored Labor Union in 1869.

Knights of Labor

The first union that had any great success in working for its members was the Knights of Labor. It was organized in 1869 by a group of Philadelphia garment workers. The union reached the height of its power between 1879 and 1887 under the leadership of Terence V. Powderly. The Knights of Labor was an industrial union open to all factory workers — male and female, black and white. An **industrial union** is made up of skilled and unskilled workers in the same industry, such as the steel industry. At one time, 10 percent of the union's members were black.

The Knights of Labor supported an eight-hour day and health and safety regulations. Its slogan was "An Honest Day's Pay for an Honest Day's Work." The union was able to force several state legislatures to pass child labor laws. Children were limited to an eight-hour workday and could not do any job considered dangerous. It was not until 1938, however, that child labor laws were passed on a national basis. The Knights of Labor began to lose members after the nationwide strike that led to the Haymarket Riots in 1886. A series of unsuccessful strikes led to the end of the Knights of Labor's power by 1900.

American Federation of Labor

A union that still exists is the American Federation of Labor (AFL), organized in 1886. Led by Samuel Gompers (GAHM-perz) until 1924, the AFL began as a craft union for native-born white, male workers. As you may recall from the unit Life at Mid-Century, a craft union is an organization of skilled workers who work at the same job in different industries. Although unskilled workers, women, immigrants, and blacks made up the largest part of the labor force, they were not represented by the AFL until 1890.

The AFL was the first union to attach labels to all products made by its members and to encourage shoppers to buy union-made goods. The AFL used collective bargaining to gain higher wages and shorter working hours. In **collective bargaining,** representatives of the union and the employer meet to set up conditions of employment — wages, hours, and so on — acceptable to both sides.

Other Unions

A number of unions, both craft and industrial, were created in the 1880s and 1890s. The International Ladies' Garment Workers Union

IMPORTANT LABOR STRIKES OF THE LATE 1800s

Who	Where	When	Causes	Results
Baltimore & Ohio Railroad Workers	Martinsburg, W. Va.	1877	Wage cut by management during economic depression	Rails torn up; stations burned; freight cars smashed; strike broken by federal troops; workers go back to work
Factory workers throughout city (Haymarket Riots)	Haymarket Square, Chicago	1886	Protest police action against strikers at a local factory	Bomb thrown into crowd; seven police killed; eight labor leaders sentenced to death and four hanged for bombing
Carnegie Steel Company workers (Amalgamated Association of Iron, Steel and Tin Workers) (Homestead Strike)	Homestead, Pa.	1892	Wage cut and 70-hour work week demanded by management	Employees' union calls strike; Pinkerton guards called in; several workers and detectives killed; strike broken by state militia; union disbanded; workers return to jobs
Pullman factory workers and American Railway Union (Pullman Strike)	Pullman, Ill.	1894	Wage cut and union leader fired by management	Railroad traffic in and out of Chicago stopped for two months; train service interrupted in 27 states; federal troops sent in; 22 workers killed; strike broken

(ILGWU) was organized in 1900 to represent garment workers, most of whom were women. However, men in the industry were also eligible to join. The Women's Trade Union League was organized by Mary O'Sullivan and Mary Kehew in 1903. Its purpose was to unite women workers to fight for better wages and working conditions. The league organized laundry, garment, and telephone workers.

While unions were trying to recruit new members, the economy and big business were scaring workers away. Many people had been hurt by the Panic of 1873 and the depression that followed. They feared they would lose their jobs if they belonged to a union. Many employers saw unions as threats to their businesses and tried to destroy them. To get a job, workers were often forced to sign a yellow-dog contract. This was a statement promising not to join a union. Employers also circulated blacklists. These were lists of workers suspected of belonging to a union. If a worker's name appeared on a

Members of the Women's Trade Union League demonstrate. Notice the sign on the left. When was a federal child labor law passed?

blacklist, he or she would be unable to find a job. Blacklists are illegal today. Other people did not join unions because they were frightened by the violence of labor strikes.

The Strike

The most effective weapon that labor had was the strike. During the late 1800s, however, there were few successful strikes. Usually workers were forced back to their jobs without winning their demands. Employers often used black or immigrant workers as strikebreakers. Strikes often ended in violence when police or federal troops were brought in. The table lists major strikes of the late 1800s and their results. Workers found strikes more effective in the 1930s when they began using the sitdown strike.

LOOKING BACK

1. **a.** What changes occurred in industry after the Civil War? **b.** How were these changes a part of the continuing process of industrialization?
2. **a.** Why did railroads establish time zones in the 1880s? **b.** What are the seven time zones in the U.S.? Use the time zone map to find the time in: **c.** New York when it is noon in Denver. **d.** Chicago when it is 2:45 p.m. in Houston.
3. **a.** List two practices of corporations that allowed them to control business in the late 1800s. **b.** How did John D. Rockefeller use his power over railroads and competitors?
4. What was the purpose of each of the following: **a.** Interstate Commerce Act? **b.** Sherman Antitrust Act?
5. **a.** Why were nationwide labor organizations formed in the late 1800s? **b.** Why were people afraid to join labor unions?
6. Read the table of major strikes and make a generalization about the causes of strikes in the late 1800s.

Chapter 5

Political Issues

LOOKING AHEAD

This chapter is about the national political issues of the late 1800s. You will read about civil service reform, the money supply, the tariff, populism, woman suffrage, and black civil rights. After you study this chapter, you will be able to:

- describe the sequence that led to civil service reform.
- explain why some people wanted lower tariffs.
- explain why farmers wanted more money in circulation.
- list five populist reforms.
- identify the bias in Bryan's "Cross of Gold" speech.
- describe gains women made in their fight for suffrage in the late 1800s.
- describe the effects of *Plessy* v. *Ferguson* on blacks.

Social Studies Vocabulary

third party	suffrage	referendum
civil service system	initiative	recall

People

Chester A. Arthur	Populist party	Elizabeth Cady
Half-Breeds	Mary Elizabeth	Stanton
James G. Blaine	Lease	Lucy Stone
Stalwarts	Ignatius Donnelly	Julia Ward Howe
James A. Garfield	William McKinley	Carrie Chapman Catt
Greenback-Labor	William Jennings	Albion Tourgee
party	Bryan	Booker T.
Grover Cleveland	Theodore Roosevelt	Washington
Benjamin Harrison	Susan B. Anthony	W.E.B. Du Bois

Words and Terms

Civil Service	cooperative	"separate but
Commission	Panic of 1893	equal"
Bland-Allison Act	Gold Standard Act	Niagara Movement
Sherman Silver	National American	NAACP
Purchase Act	Woman Suffrage	National Urban
gold standard	Association	League
McKinley Tariff Act	Jim Crow laws	National Association
National Grange	*Plessy* v. *Ferguson*	of Colored Women

The elephant is the symbol of the Republican party. After the election of 1876, Thomas Nast drew this cartoon of the victorious but bruised elephant. After you read this chapter, decide if the elephant was still victorious by 1900.

National politics in the late 1800s was affected by western settlement, the rise of big business, corruption in public office, and the denial of rights to certain members of American society. Several major political

In this silver mill in Virginia City, Nevada, silver ore was shovelled into tubs to be washed before being made into silver bars for shipment. What role did silver play in the politics of the period?

issues grew out of these developments. Throughout the period, people dissatisfied with both major parties formed third parties. A **third party** takes its membership from disappointed members of the major political parties and usually lasts for only a short time. The third parties of the late 1800s elected some candidates to office. However, their greatest contribution was the influence their demands had on the two major parties. Many of the reforms the third parties worked for were eventually adopted by either the Democrats or the Republicans.

CIVIL SERVICE REFORM

As you may recall from the unit Civil War and Reconstruction, Republican Rutherford B. Hayes was named President in the disputed election of 1876. His first act as President was to order the withdrawal of all federal troops from the South.

After his election, Hayes announced that he would serve as President for only one term. Since he did not have to give out government jobs to win support for the next election, Hayes was able to work for reform of the **civil service system.** This system handles the regulations governing the hiring and firing of government employees. Wherever he could, Hayes tried to fill posts with capable men and remove those who were not. For example, he fired three Republicans from posts in the New York Customs House for hiring friends under the spoils system. One of the officials that he removed was Chester A. Arthur, a future President of the U.S. Although Hayes had much public support for civil service reform, he did not have the support he needed in Congress.

Assassination and Reform

Even if Hayes had wanted a second term, the Republicans would not have renominated him. The leaders of his party were strong supporters of the spoils system. For the presidential nomination in 1880, the Republicans were divided into two groups. The Half-Breeds supported Senator James G. Blaine of Maine. The Stalwarts (STAWL-wuhrts) supported former President Grant. At the Republican National Convention, neither man received enough votes to win the nomination. As a compromise, the convention chose James A. Garfield, U.S. Representative from Ohio.

The Democrats nominated Winfield Scott Hancock, a Civil War hero, to oppose Garfield. The Greenback-Labor party nominated Iowa Representative James B. Weaver. This party had been formed by members of the Greenback and National Labor Reform parties after the 1876 election. The party's platform called for an eight-hour workday, woman suffrage, and an income tax. **Suffrage** is the right to vote.

Garfield narrowly won the election. As President, he favored the Half-Breeds in giving out government jobs. The Stalwarts received only minor posts. On September 10, 1881, Garfield was shot and killed by a disappointed office seeker.

Chester A. Arthur became the fourth Vice-President to succeed to the presidency. As a result of Garfield's assassination, Arthur, who had once been fired for handing out patronage, began to work for civil service reform. Through his efforts, the Pendleton Act of 1883 established the Civil Service Commission to test applicants. Employees would no longer be hired or fired based on party loyalty. In 1883, only 10 percent of federal jobs were under the control of the Civil Service Commission. Many Presidents after Arthur added to the number of jobs governed by Civil Service. Today, 90 percent of all federal jobs are included.

THE TARIFF AND MONEY

After the Civil War, many Americans began urging the government for tariff reform and the printing of more paper money. As you may recall from Chapter 2 of this unit, farmers were facing difficult times in the 1870s. They were among the loudest in their calls for lower tariffs and more paper dollars.

Those who wanted tariff reform argued that when the nation and its industries were new, there had been a reason for high protective tariffs. By the 1880s, however, U.S. industries were among the largest in the world. The lack of foreign competition allowed manufacturers to charge high prices. Tariff reformers asked that tariffs be lowered. This would allow some foreign competition and help drive down prices of American-made goods. However, American manufacturers would still be able to make a profit. In 1883, President Arthur appointed a

reduction
(ri-DUHK-shuhn):
making less

commission to study the question. The commission recommended a general reduction of tariffs. Republicans did not agree and the new bill that was passed much like the old one. Because tariff reformers were not satisfied, the debate continued throughout the 1880s.

Besides lowering tariffs, many people wanted the government to put more paper money into circulation. These people, especially farmers, hoped that having more money, in this case greenbacks, in circulation would bring about prosperity. Although prices would rise, paying debts would be easier. What such people as the Greenback-Labor party were asking for was government-sponsored inflation.

Bland-Allison Act

As you read in the unit New Role for the Nation, U.S. currency was backed by gold and silver. In 1873, the U.S. government stopped buying and coining silver. Silver had become too scarce to use in coins. But silver strikes in Colorado and Nevada made silver plentiful. Because the government was no longer buying silver, the value of the metal dropped. The owners of silver mines were furious. They insisted that the government begin buying silver again, and use it to back U.S. currency.

currency
(KER-uhn-see):
money in use

At this time, farmers, who had been calling for more greenbacks, joined forces with the mine owners. Farmers reasoned that by uniting with the wealthy silver interests, their combined forces could pressure the government for the coinage of silver. With silver coins and silver-backed paper dollars, there would be more money in circulation. In response to farmers' and mineowners' demands, Congress passed the Bland-Allison Act in 1878. Under this law, the government agreed to buy and coin small amounts of silver. However, the hoped for prosperity did not occur. Farm prices remained low.

Presidential Reactions

Grover Cleveland, a Democrat, was elected to the presidency in 1884. In his first year in office, he asked Congress to repeal the Bland-Allison Act. Congress refused. Congress also refused Cleveland's request two years later to lower the tariffs.

Cleveland's position on the issues pleased no one. Eastern bankers and industrialists wanted a high tariff to guarantee high prices and a money system backed by gold. Farmers in the South and West wanted a low tariff and money backed by silver. Although the Democrats renominated Cleveland, he lost the 1888 presidential election to Benjamin Harrison. Harrison was the grandson of former President William Henry Harrison. He opposed tariff reductions and supported issuing money backed by silver.

In 1890, Harrison signed the Sherman Silver Purchase Act, which increased the amount of silver that the government bought and used.

This meeting of grangers near Winchester, Illinois, in 1873, is typical of National Grange meetings. From the signs, what do you think the purpose of the National Grange was?

The act gave little help to farmers and greatly harmed the U.S. economy. Because the government did not buy all the silver that was mined, the price for the metal fell. Americans who had silver-backed money felt they would be safer if they had gold. They turned in their silver for gold. The government's supply of gold to back its currency fell drastically.

During Harrison's term, the McKinley Tariff Act was passed. It set the highest tariffs yet on foreign manufactured goods. The tariff allowed the prices of American-made goods to rise, and the American public, especially farmers, suffered greatly.

THE POPULIST ERA

In 1867, the National Grange was established by Oliver H. Kelley. The purpose of the organization was to give farmers an opportunity to discuss their problems and to learn about advanced farming methods. Because of the depression following the Panic of 1873, the organization had grown to 850,000 members by 1875.

The National Grange introduced farmers to the idea of cooperatives. A cooperative is a business owned by the people who use its services. In this case, farmers bought directly from suppliers as a group. This lowered farmers' costs and, as a result, the prices they charged. Farmers could still make a profit. The granges also fought against the high rates charged by railroads and grain storage operators.

In the 1870s and 1880s, farmers also formed alliances, which were similar to the granges. Alliances fought against high freight rates and

During the election of 1896, Republican candidate William McKinley campaigned from his front porch. What were the issues in this campaign? Who supported McKinley?

high interest rates for farm loans. The alliances called for the government to increase the money supply. As you have just read, farmers believed that more money would increase crop prices and get them out of debt.

In 1892, some farmers' alliances and granges joined with the Knights of Labor, miners, industrial workers, and small business owners to form the Populist (PAHP-yuh-list), or People's party. Their platform called for unlimited coinage of silver money, government ownership of railroads, a federal income tax, limits on immigration, an eight-hour workday, and popular election of U.S. Senators. As you may recall from the unit A Plan of Government, Senators were elected by state legislatures.

Populists wanted other voting reforms. The party called for initiative, referendum, and recall. **Initiative** (ihn-NISH-ee-uh-tive) gives citizens the right to propose laws to a legislature. **Referendum** (ref-uhr-EN-duhm) allows a legislature to have citizens vote on issues. **Recall** (REE-kawl) permits voters to remove elected officials from office. Populists also called for the use of the secret ballot. In this system, each person receives a printed ballot and marks it in private. Up to this time, people voted in public.

Mary Elizabeth Lease and Ignatius Donnelly helped to establish the Populist party and write its first campaign platform. Lease was an author, public speaker, and reformer. She later left the Populist party to work for woman suffrage. Donnelly was a politician, reformer, and writer.

Election of 1892

In the presidential election of 1892, the Populists nominated James B. Weaver. The Republicans renominated Harrison and made support of a high protective tariff their major campaign promise. The Democrats nominated Grover Cleveland, who promised to lower the tariff if elected.

Farmers, who were still deep in debt, turned to the new Populist party. The Populists carried four states and elected governors in Kansas, North Dakota, and Colorado. They also elected five Senators and ten Representatives. Factory workers, however, stayed with the Democrats, and Cleveland won the election. He became the first and only President to serve two nonconsecutive terms.

Two months after Cleveland took office, a severe financial panic swept the nation. The Panic of 1893 was caused by the continuing farm depression, a European business slump that cut U.S. exports, and the continuing drain on the Treasury's gold supply. Investors withdrew their money from businesses. Prices and wages fell as four million people lost their jobs.

nonconsecutive
(nahn-kuhn-SEK-yuh-tiv): not in order

"Cross of Gold"

Faced with the growing dissatisfaction of voters, Democrat Cleveland did not seek reelection in 1896. The Republicans nominated William McKinley, Governor of Ohio. He hoped to make the support of high protective tariffs the key issue of the campaign.

However, the new Democratic candidate changed the campaign's focus. William Jennings Bryan, a noted public speaker and politician, delivered his now-famous "Cross of Gold" speech at the Democratic convention in 1896. The speech resulted in his nomination for President. He said in part:

> You come to us and tell us that the great cities are in favor of the gold standard. We reply that the great cities rest upon our broad and fertile prairies. Burn down your cities and leave our farms, and your cities will spring up again as if by magic. But destroy our farms and the grass will grow in the streets of every city in the country. Having behind us the producing masses of this nation and the world, supported by the business interests, the laboring interests, and the workers everywhere, we will answer their demand for a gold standard. We will say: You shall not press down upon the brow of labor this crown of thorns, you shall not crucify mankind upon a cross of gold.

The Populists had to decide whether to support the Democrats, who had adopted a platform almost identical to theirs, or to nominate their own candidate. If they supported Bryan, they felt the Democrats would win. However, the Populist party might begin to disappear without its own candidate. The Populists gave their support to Bryan. To show that they were still an independent party, they nominated Thomas Watson of Georgia for Vice-President.

Because he favored a high protective tariff and the gold standard, McKinley was supported by the bankers and industrialists of the Northeast. The Democrats, with Populist support, did well in the South, Midwest, and West. But it was not enough. McKinley won the election by more than 600,000 votes. After this election, the Populist party lost support. By 1900, it was no longer a political power.

McKinley as President

McKinley kept his two major campaign promises. In 1897, he had Congress pass a protective tariff that sent tariff rates higher than ever. In 1900, he approved the Gold Standard Act that officially placed the U.S. on the gold standard. All paper money would be backed only by gold.

The Republicans nominated McKinley to run for a second term in 1900. The Democrats again nominated Bryan and they continued to campaign for unlimited silver coinage. This issue was no longer important, however. Gold had been discovered in Alaska in 1896, and the nation's money supply increased greatly.

Under McKinley, the nation had recovered from the Panic of 1893 and was experiencing a period of prosperity. Even farmers were seeing a rise in the prices of farm products. Most Americans believed McKinley would bring four more years of prosperity, and he won the election by almost a million votes.

mentally (MEN-tuhl-ee): involving the mind

McKinley did not complete his second term. He was shot and killed by a mentally disturbed person in September 1901. Vice-President Theodore Roosevelt, at age 42, became the youngest President in U.S. history. Roosevelt had been governor of New York.

WOMAN SUFFRAGE

In May 1869, Susan B. Anthony and Elizabeth Cady Stanton founded the National Suffrage Association to oppose the 15th Amendment. This amendment granted suffrage to all men but not to women. The single goal of the National Suffrage Association was to get women the right to vote.

In 1870, Lucy Stone and Julia Ward Howe formed the American Woman Suffrage Association. This group saw the vote as a means to an end—gaining full rights for women. They also attacked the problem differently. Rather than trying to persuade Congress to give women the right to vote, they worked to persuade state legislatures. In 1890, the two groups solved their differences and formed the National American Woman Suffrage Association. The organization was led by Elizabeth Cady Stanton, Susan B. Anthony, and Carrie Chapman Catt.

In 1869, Wyoming had given women the right to vote, hold office, and serve on a jury. In 1870, Wyoming voters elected the first woman justice of the peace. By 1890, women could vote in local elections in

Women won the right to vote in Wyoming elections in 1869. This polling place is in Cheyenne. Why did it take until 1920 for women to win national suffrage?

Wyoming, Colorado, Utah, and Idaho. Progress on the national level, however, was slow. You will read more about woman suffrage in the unit Between the Wars.

BLACK CIVIL RIGHTS

As you may recall from the unit Civil War and Reconstruction, despite the 15th amendment, black men were not always guaranteed the right to vote. Poll taxes, literacy tests, and fear of such groups as the Ku Klux Klan kept blacks from voting. In the 1890s, southern states passed Jim Crow laws that restricted the civil rights of blacks. The laws were named after a black character in a song. These laws called for separate facilities for blacks and whites. For example, blacks could not stay in the same hotels nor eat in the same restaurants as whites.

"Separate but Equal"

In 1890, Louisiana passed a law providing for separate railroad cars for blacks and whites. Some blacks in the state decided to test the legality of the law. They hired a lawyer, Albion Tourgee (toor-ZHAY), to plead their case. Then Homer Plessy (PLES-ee), a black man, bought a railroad ticket and deliberately sat in a car for whites. The conductor asked him to move to a car for blacks. When Plessy refused, he was arrested.

The Louisiana courts upheld the law, and Tourgee took the case through the appeals system to the U.S. Supreme Court. In *Plessy* v. *Ferguson*, Tourgee argued that the law violated the 13th and 14th Amendments. The Supreme Court ruled that separate cars for blacks and whites were within the law as long as the cars were of equal quality. This case opened the way for more Jim Crow laws calling for "separate but equal" facilities. The Supreme Court ruling was not overturned until 1954.

Black Leaders

One of the most influential black leaders of the late 1800s was Booker T. Washington. He encouraged blacks to concentrate on getting along with whites rather than on demanding equal rights. He was willing to put up with inequality and segregation in exchange for economic advancement. Blacks, he believed, could benefit more from practical, vocational education than from a college education.

W.E.B. Du Bois (doo-BOYS), a historian and sociologist, disagreed with Washington's educational and political philosophy. He supported college training for blacks and feared that vocational schools would limit the development of higher education for blacks. Du Bois believed blacks should fight openly for their rights, especially for the right to vote. Washington's influence began to decline in the early 1900s as Du Bois and other leaders formed organizations to help blacks.

At left is W.E.B. Du Bois in the *Crisis* office. At right is a picture of the farm at Tuskegee. Booker T. Washington, who founded Tuskegee, believed that blacks should improve their status through vocational education. What was Du Bois's view?

Black Organizations

In 1905, Du Bois founded the Niagara (ny-AG-uh-ruh) Movement. The group fought discrimination by demanding voting rights and desegregated schools. The members worked to elect candidates who promised to fight prejudice. At one time, the movement had 30 branches in U.S. cities. The movement failed to win the support of most blacks, however, and disbanded in 1910.

The year before, the National Association for the Advancement of Colored People (NAACP) had been founded by some members of the Niagara Movement and whites to fight violence against blacks. Among its goals were the enforcement of antilynching laws and the end of job discrimination. Du Bois joined in 1910. He became editor of the magazine *Crisis*, which published articles about the racial situation and about successful blacks in the arts, business, science, and other fields.

The National Urban League was established for both blacks and whites in 1911. Members conducted community projects that provided health care, housing, job training and placement, and voter education. They often appeared before legislative bodies to influence public opinion and make their causes more widely known. Both the NAACP and the Urban League are still active.

When the General Federation of Women's Clubs was founded in 1890, black women were excluded. As a result, Mary Church Terrell, Josephine Ruffin, and Margaret Murray Washington organized the National Association of Colored Women in 1896. The group set up clubs across the country. They helped organize schools and hospitals. The black clubs were eventually admitted to the General Federation.

LOOKING BACK

1. **a.** What events led to the reform of the civil service system? **b.** How did the Civil Service Commission reform the spoils system?
2. Why did some Americans of the late 1800s call for lower protective tariffs?
3. Why did some Americans, especially farmers, want to have more money in circulation?
4. **a.** List five Populist goals of the late 1800s. **b.** What were the issues in the presidential election of 1896?
5. Reread Bryan's "Cross of Gold" speech. **a.** Which group is he biased toward? **b.** Which group is he biased against?
6. **a.** What women's organizations were formed in the late 1800s to work for woman suffrage? **b.** In what area of the country did women first win the right to vote? **c.** Why do you think this happened in that area?
7. **a.** How did the outcome of *Plessy* v. *Ferguson* harm blacks? **b.** Compare and contrast the educational and political philosophies of Washington and Du Bois.

Chapter 6

A Changing Culture

LOOKING AHEAD

This chapter is about the culture that developed as the nation changed in the late 1800s. You will read about the writers and artists of this period and about the music, theater, and other kinds of entertainment available to people. You will also learn about some of the inventions that brought changes in daily living, work, and leisure activities. After you study this chapter, you will be able to:

- list three themes that writers of the 1800s used.
- explain the reason for the increase in the number of newspapers.
- compare and contrast realism and impressionism in art.
- explain four changes in education in the late 1800s.
- list three leisure activities that people enjoyed.

People

Samuel Clemens	Mary Wilkins	Winslow Homer
Stephen Crane	Freeman	Thomas Eakins
Hamlin Garland	Louisa May Alcott	Henry Ossawa Tanner
Theodore Dreiser	Edward Eggleston	Edmonia Lewis
Frank Norris	Charlotte Gilman	Daniel Chester
William Dean	Paul Laurence	French
Howells	Dunbar	August Saint-Gaudens
Thomas Nelson Page	Emily Dickinson	Frederic Remington
George Washington	Joseph Pulitzer	Louis Tiffany
Cable	William Randolph	Booker T. Washington
Joaquin Miller	Hearst	Mary McLeod Bethune
Helen Hunt Jackson	John Singer Sargent	George Washington
Bret Harte	James McNeil	Carver
Sarah Orne Jewett	Whistler	John Philip Sousa
	Mary Cassatt	Scott Joplin

Events

Philadelphia Centennial	World's Columbian
Exposition	Exposition

Words and Terms

the Gilded Age	linotype	nickelodeon
realist	vaudeville	dime novel
impressionist	ragtime	medicine show

This is a cover from *Harper's Weekly* magazine of the late 1800s. What kinds of magazines were popular in this period?

The years after the Civil War brought great social and economic changes to the U.S. These changes were reflected in the cultural and leisure activities of the late 1800s. New inventions affected not only the way people earned their livings but also how they spent their free time. Many writers and artists used themes from life around them — the frontier, the city, factory life, and politics.

LITERATURE

In 1873, Samuel Clemens (KLEM-uhnz), under the pen name of Mark Twain, wrote *The Gilded Age.* This novel ridiculed greedy industrialists and corrupt politicians. People began to use the term *Gilded Age* to describe the period during and just after the Grant administrations. Twain used many different subjects to illustrate his theme of the corrupting effect of society on people. In his most famous novel, *The Adventures of Huckleberry Finn,* Twain comments on society from the viewpoint of a young, as yet uncorrupted, boy.

Twain belonged to no particular school of literature. However, he was influenced by the times he lived in as were other writers. In the last half of the 1800s, romanticism gave way to realism. Realism portrays life as it is, not as people would like it to be. Ordinary people and their problems were the subject matter of these writers. Some authors wrote novels and short stores about inner reality — fear, love, loneliness. Others wrote about the outer world as they saw it. Big business and the frontier were often themes. Some realists wrote about the customs, manners, speech, and dress of people in a particular region of the country. The table on page 554 lists representative novelists and short story writers and their works.

Two well-known poets from the late 1800s are Paul Laurence Dunbar and Emily Dickinson. Dunbar was a black poet who wrote about life in the South. Most of Dickinson's works were not published until after her death. She often wrote of everyday things, such as a sunset or reading a book, but she painted word pictures with a special talent.

As you can see from the table, a number of women were writing and being published by the end of the 1800s. Woman's rights was still an important issue. The leading writer on the subject was Charlotte Gilman. In *Women and Economics,* she urged women to work outside the home to gain economic independence.

NEWSPAPERS AND MAGAZINES

In 1870, there were only 600 daily newspapers in the U.S. By 1900, the number had increased to 2,000. This was made possible by the invention of the linotype (LY-nuh-typ) machine in 1884. This machine set type mechanically rather than by hand, which is a slow process. Besides these general interest newspapers, foreign-language newspapers and newspapers for black readers were available in many large cities in the late 1800s.

Two of the most influential newspapers were Joseph Pulitzer's New York *World* and William Randolph Hearst's New York *Journal.* While

ridicule
(RID-uh-kyool):
to make fun of

representative
(rep-ri-ZEN-tuh-tiv):
like others
of one's kind;
similar

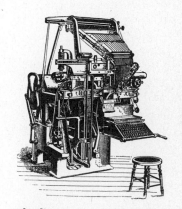

The linotype machine set type mechanically much faster than could be done by hand. How would this affect the cost of newspapers and magazines?

REPRESENTATIVE AUTHORS AND THEIR WORKS OF THE LATE 1800s

Author	Work	Theme
Stephen Crane	*Red Badge of Courage*	Death and fear in war; set during Civil War
Hamlin Garland	*Main-Travelled Roads*	Isolation and hardship on the Plains
Theodore Dreiser	*The Financier*	An industrialist who claws his way to power
Frank Norris	*The Octopus*	Railroads' control over farmers
William Dean Howells	*The Rise of Silas Lapham*	Big business and the families behind it
Thomas Nelson Page	*Red Sock*	South during the Civil War and Reconstruction
George Washington Cable	*Old Creole Days*	Short stories about Louisiana
Joaquin Miller	*Life Amongst the Modocs*	Native Americans
Helen Hunt Jackson	*Ramona*	California Native Americans
Bret Harte	*The Luck of Roaring Camp*	Short stories about the California gold rush
Sarah Orne Jewett	*The Country of Pointed Firs*	Life and customs of rural New England
Mary Wilkins Freeman	*A New England Nun and Other Stories*	Women of rural New England
Louisa May Alcott	*Little Women; Little Men*	New England life
Edward Eggleston	*The Hoosier (HOO-zhuhr) Schoolmaster*	Midwestern life

Pulitzer (POOL-it-ser) reported mostly human-interest stories that is, stories about ordinary people. Hearst used his paper to support social reform. Both papers helped create public opinion, especially in the late 1890s as you will read in the unit Reform and Expansion.

Magazines were very popular by the late 1800s. The first magazine in the U.S. had been published in 1741 but lasted only a few months. One of the first successful ones was *Godey's* (GOH-deez) *Lady's Book*, which began publishing in 1830. Several magazines devoted to reporting news and publishing social comment began around the mid-1800s. Among these were *Leslie's Weekly, Atlantic Monthly,* and *Harper's Weekly.* In the late 1800s, social reformers began writing for magazines. Among the most popular magazines was the *Ladies' Home Journal,* which began in 1883. Besides articles on home decorating, cooking, and child rearing, the magazines used its pages to call attention to serious problems of the times. It campaigned against the use of harmful drugs such as morphine in some medicines.

ART

The art of the late 1800s was as varied as the literature. Some artists were realists. They painted portraits and scenes of ordinary people. They paid close attention to accuracy in lighting, color, and detail. Other artists were impressionists. They were not interested in reality but in their feelings about it. They tried to capture with paints an impression of the scene before them. They used soft colors and hazy outlines of objects to show how they felt about the scene.

Among the realists of the period were John Singer Sargent, Winslow Homer, Thomas Eakins (AY-kinz), and Henry Ossawa Tanner. Sargent, a portrait painter, paid close attention to accuracy and detail but tried to show each person in the most flattering way. Homer began his career with sketches and paintings of the Civil War. He later painted pictures of the sea and the New England coast. Eakins painted portraits and scenes of outdoor life and sporting events. Tanner studied under Eakins. Although his paintings of southern blacks were popular, Tanner moved to Europe to escape discrimination.

Mary Cassatt (kuh-SAT) and James McNeill Whistler were impressionists. Cassatt is best known for her portraits of mothers and children. Whistler painted portraits and landscapes.

Edmonia Lewis was the first black sculptor to receive recognition in the U.S. Her sculpture of poet Henry Wadsworth Longfellow is in the Harvard College Library. Both Daniel Chester French and Augustus Saint-Gaudens (saynt-GOH-duhnz) did lifelike sculptures of famous Americans. Frederic Remington is known for his action paintings, illustrations, and sculptures of cowhands and Native Americans.

EDUCATION

In Chapter 2, you read about the Morrill Land-Grant Act which encouraged the building of agricultural and mechanical arts colleges. Many of these new colleges admitted women. By the late 1800s, women were finding it easier to enter liberal arts or teaching colleges. But they continued to face strong opposition in business, law, and medical schools. Although some women graduated from law schools in the late 1800s, women were not allowed to practice law in most states until 1920. The exception was Iowa. The first woman lawyer was licensed to practice there in 1869. Ten years later the first woman was admitted to practice before the U.S. Supreme Court.

Although blacks attended land-grant colleges, only a few private black colleges existed. Howard University in Washington, D.C., had been founded in 1867 for freed blacks. Hampton Institute in Virginia had been opened in 1868 with the help of the American Missionary Society. Booker T. Washington started Tuskegee (tuhs-KEE-gee) Institute in Alabama in 1881. Along with academic subjects, blacks learned practical skills needed to earn a living. In 1904, Mary McLeod Bethune (bay-THYOON) opened a school for young women in

The creator of this piece, Edmonia Lewis, a woman and a black, was a noted sculptor of the period. One of her works won an award at the Centennial Exposition.

555

Left: These vases are examples of Favrile (fuhv-REEL) glassware created by Louis Comfort Tiffany in the late 1800s. They show the flowing and twisting lines typical of the artistic movement called *art nouveau* (noo-VOH). Why do you think these are considered professional art?

Below: Thomas Eakins thought art should be scientifically accurate. *Max Schmidt in a Single Scull* was painted in 1871. What features make this a painting of the realist school?

Top: Cassatt's *Mother and Child* shows the light and airy colors typical of impressionist works.

Left: John Singer Sargent painted *The Daughters of Edward Darley Boit* in 1882. Compare and contrast this portrait with the ones on page 176.

Bottom: Like many professional artists of the time, Henry O. Tanner studied in France. He is best known for his scenes of black life and biblical themes such as *Abraham's Oak*.

REPRESENTATIVE INVENTIONS OF THE LATE 1800s

Inventor	Invention	Date
Elisha Graves Otis	Elevator	1852
George Westinghouse	Railroad air brake	1863
Christopher Sholes	Typewriter	1867
Joseph Glidden	Barbed wire	1873
George F. Green	Dental drill	1875
Alexander Graham Bell	Telephone	1876
Thomas Edison	Phonograph	1877
	Light bulb	1879
Thomas L. Rankin	Indoor ice-skating rink	1879
George Eastman	Photographic film	1880
W. Johnson	Egg beater	1884
Ottmar Mergenthaler	Linotype	1884
George Eastman	Kodak camera	1888
John Loud	Ball point pen	1888
William Burroughs	Adding machine	1888
Sarah Boone	Ironing board	1892
Jesse W. Reno	Escalator	1892
Whitcomb L. Judson	Zipper	1893
J. A. Burr	Lawn mower	1899

Florida. In 1923, it merged with a school for young men to form Bethune Cookman College.

New types of schools began to appear in the late 1800s. The first public kindergarten was opened in St. Louis in 1873. By 1900, more than 200,000 children attended public kindergartens each year. High schools increased in number in the late 1800s as more people needed skills for office work.

SCIENCE AND TECHNOLOGY

The late 1800s was a time of practical research and inventions. The work of George Washington Carver in the late 1800s and early 1900s changed southern farming dramatically. He developed several hundred products, such as candy and shoe polish, from peanuts, sweet potatoes, and pecans. Carver convinced southern farmers to grow these crops instead of cotton. This saved the fertility of the soil and provided better income for farmers.

The table above lists some representative inventions of the late 1800s. Some made life easier, others helped industry grow, and some were just for fun.

fertility
(fer-TIL-uh-tee):
ability to
produce growth

THEATER AND MUSIC

The first vaudeville theater opened in Boston in 1883. Vaudeville (VAW-duh-vil) was a series of separate musical, singing, dancing, and animal acts. There was usually a skit, or short play, too. As vaudeville became popular, theaters opened across the country. The first motion picture theater, called a nickelodeon (nik-uh-LOH-dee-uhn), opened in the late 1800s. Admission was a nickel, and piano music accompanied the silent movies.

Cowboy songs, marches, and ragtime were popular music of the day. Such John Philip Sousa (SOO-suh) marches as "The Stars and Stripes Forever" were often played at public ceremonies and parades. Scott Joplin (JAHP-luhn) was a popular composer of ragtime, an early form of jazz. Among the pieces he wrote was "The Entertainer."

LEISURE ACTIVITIES

During the late 1800s, about one eighth of the families in the U.S. controlled seven eighths of the nation's income. The wealthy amused themselves by attending charity balls and giving parties. They held horse races and yacht races. The men played golf, billiards, and polo. The women enjoyed archery, croquet (krow-KAY), and tennis.

People with less money attended vaudeville shows and nickelodeons. They had bicycle races and played volleyball. Barnum's circus and "Buffalo Bill" Cody's Wild West Show starring Annie Oakley were popular. People also read dime novels such as Horatio Alger's (AL-jer) tales of moral young men who worked hard and became successful. These novels reinforced the U.S. as the land of golden opportunity.

With the invention of motion pictures, people found a new form of entertainment. This audience is watching the Keystone Cops. Because the first movies were silent, live piano music accompanied the action on the screen.

559

This scene is Fifth Avenue, New York, but it could have been any street in America in the late 1800s or early 1900s. Why would the scene be different after about 1910?

Expositions and state fairs were popular. To celebrate the country's 100th birthday, Philadelphia hosted the Centennial Exposition. All kinds of new inventions were shown including Alexander Graham Bell's telephone. The World's Columbian Exposition in Chicago in 1893 showed a ferris wheel among its many steam engines and other inventions celebrating the nation's progress.

Besides state fairs, people in the West had rodeos, quilting bees, and square dances. Travelling vaudeville shows came to larger towns, and medicine shows travelled all over. A medicine show had a few actors who performed all the parts in a play.

LOOKING BACK

1. **a.** List the three themes that were most often used in novels and short stories in the late 1800s. **b.** Identify one writer for each theme.
2. Why was there an increase in the number of newspapers published in the late 1800s?
3. **a.** How do realism and impressionism in art differ? **b.** How are they the same?
4. **a.** What problems did women face in education in the late 1800s? **b.** How did higher education for blacks improve? **c.** What new kinds of schools developed or increased in numbers?
5. Read the table on inventions and choose three inventions. Explain how each might have helped industry, made life easier, or added to the types of entertainment available.
6. **a.** How did the wealthy entertain themselves? **b.** List three kinds of activities other people enjoyed. **c.** What kinds of things did fairs and expositions show?

PRACTICING YOUR SKILLS

What If . . . In Chapter 3, you read about the immigrants that came to the U.S. in the late 1800s. **What if** these immigrants had not come? What effect would this have had on the development of industry? How might it have affected the growth of cities in the 1800s?

Discussing In Chapter 6, you read about some inventions that changed the lives of many Americans from the 1860s to the late 1800s. Discuss how your life today would be different if the items mentioned in this chapter had not been invented.

Researching, Imagining, Making a Table, Making a Map, Writing

1. In Chapter 4, you read about the first labor unions. Using an encyclopedia or other reference books, research one of the AFL unions that interests you. Make a list of accomplishments of this union.

2. Imagine that you are a miner, farmer, or cattle rancher living on the Plains in the late 1800s. Make a table with two columns and label them "Problems" and "Solutions." Under the "Problems" column, list five difficulties you would have encountered. In the other column, show how you would have solved each problem.

3. Draw a map of the U.S. and fill in the states. Use the time lines from your textbook to label the date each state was admitted to the U.S.

4. Read a book by one of the authors in Chapter 6 and write a book report.

Building Writing Skills

Writing a research paper puts into practice many of the study and writing skills you have learned in this text. Once you have gathered your data, use the following tips to help you write your paper:

● Sort your index cards into two groups: important facts, ideas, statistics, details, and quotations in the first group, and less useful information in the second.

● Outline the information in the first group. Make sure the topics and subtopics cover your subject and are arranged in order.

● Write the first version, or draft, of your paper. Write only on every other line. You will use the extra space for additions, changes, and improvements.

● Read your first draft carefully. Does it make sense? Is it clear and interesting? See if you can use any data from your second group.

● Edit and rewrite until you are satisfied with the first draft.

● When you copy out the final draft, make sure you use footnotes for quotations.

Activity: Select one person from the tables in this unit and write a research report describing where that person grew up, how he or she became famous, and what works he or she completed.

Reading
Brown, Dee. *Wounded Knee: An Indian History of the American West.* Edited by Amy Ehrlich. New York: Dell, 1975.

Brownstone, David M., et al. *Island of Hope, Island of Tears.* New York: Rawson, Wade, 1979. Interviews with immigrants.

Meltzer, Milton. *Bread and Roses: The Struggle of American Labor, 1865-1911.* New York: New American Library, 1977. Paperback.

Rifkind, Carole. *Main Street: The Face of Urban America.* New York: Harper & Row, 1979. Paperback. Development of the city.

Seidman, Laurence. *Once in the Saddle: The Cowboy's Frontier.* New York: Knopf, 1973. The cattle business from 1866 to 1896.

Wertheimer, Barbara. *We Were There: The Story of Working Women in America.* New York: Pantheon, 1977. Paperback.

Young, Alida E. *Land of the Iron Dragon.* New York: Doubleday, 1978. Fiction. Chinese Americans and the Central Pacific Railroad.

UNIT II   REFORM AND EXPANSION

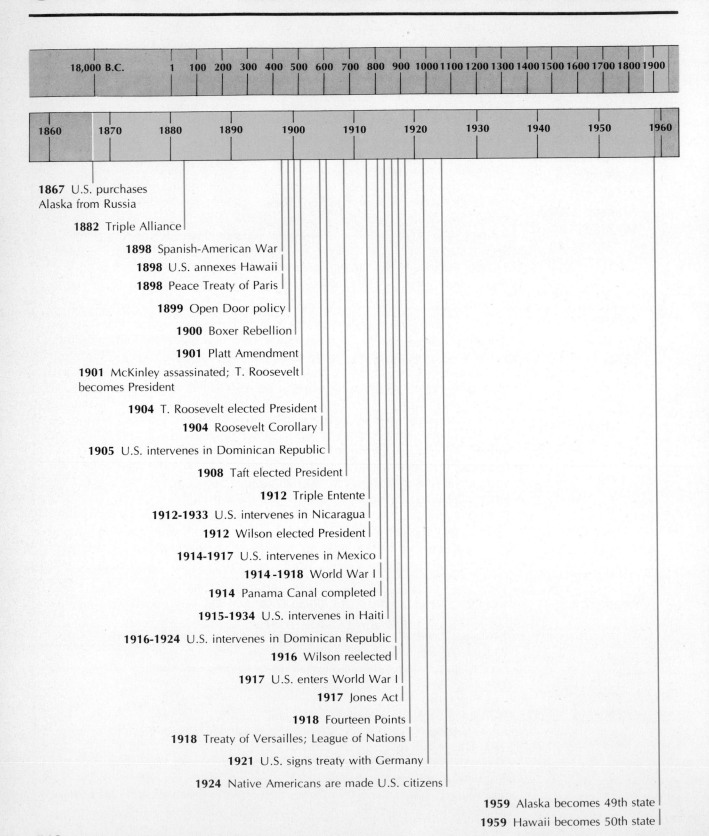

| 18,000 B.C. | 1 | 100 | 200 | 300 | 400 | 500 | 600 | 700 | 800 | 900 | 1000 | 1100 | 1200 | 1300 | 1400 | 1500 | 1600 | 1700 | 1800 | 1900 |

| 1860 | 1870 | 1880 | 1890 | 1900 | 1910 | 1920 | 1930 | 1940 | 1950 | 1960 |

1867 U.S. purchases Alaska from Russia

1882 Triple Alliance

1898 Spanish-American War

1898 U.S. annexes Hawaii

1898 Peace Treaty of Paris

1899 Open Door policy

1900 Boxer Rebellion

1901 Platt Amendment

1901 McKinley assassinated; T. Roosevelt becomes President

1904 T. Roosevelt elected President

1904 Roosevelt Corollary

1905 U.S. intervenes in Dominican Republic

1908 Taft elected President

1912 Triple Entente

1912-1933 U.S. intervenes in Nicaragua

1912 Wilson elected President

1914-1917 U.S. intervenes in Mexico

1914-1918 World War I

1914 Panama Canal completed

1915-1934 U.S. intervenes in Haiti

1916-1924 U.S. intervenes in Dominican Republic

1916 Wilson reelected

1917 U.S. enters World War I

1917 Jones Act

1918 Fourteen Points

1918 Treaty of Versailles; League of Nations

1921 U.S. signs treaty with Germany

1924 Native Americans are made U.S. citizens

1959 Alaska becomes 49th state

1959 Hawaii becomes 50th state

Chapter 1   The Progressives

LOOKING AHEAD ⎯⎯⎯⎯⎯⎯⎯⎯⎯⎯

This chapter describes the progressives and the reforms they helped to make law in the early 1900s. You will read about the reform administrations of Presidents Roosevelt, Taft, and Wilson. After you study this chapter, you will be able to:

- compare and contrast the Populists and progressives.
- read a table to make a generalization about the objectives of muckrackers.
- identify three progressive reforms enacted under Roosevelt.
- explain why Roosevelt ran as a candidate of the Progressive party in 1912.
- identify two reforms enacted under Wilson.

Social Studies Vocabulary

progressive	conservative	injunction

People

Lincoln Steffens	Jacob Riis	Theodore Roosevelt
Ida M. Tarbell	Ray Stannard Baker	William H. Taft
Upton Sinclair	John Spargo	Progressive party
David Graham	Gustavus Myers	Woodrow Wilson
Phillips	Josiah Flynt Willard	Eugene V. Debs

Events

Panic of 1907

Words and Terms

muckraker	Hepburn Act	Underwood Tariff
square deal	Pure Food and	Federal Reserve Act
Northern Securities	Drug Act	Federal Trade
Company	Payne-Aldrich Act	Commission
Department of	16th Amendment	Clayton Antitrust Act
Commerce and Labor	17th Amendment	price discrimination

Demands for economic, political, and social reform became louder during the depression that struck the country between 1893 and 1897. Many city governments and some state governments responded to the challenge and made changes. Reform on the national level was more difficult. By the early 1900s, reformers were calling themselves progressives. A **progressive** (pruh-GRES-iv) is a person who favors reform, improvement, and progress through government action.

THE REFORM MOVEMENT

The progressives took many of their goals from the Populist platforms of the 1890s. However, the Populists and the progressives were different. For the most part, the Populists were farmers, factory workers, and owners of small businesses. The progressives included these groups but also included many college-educated, middle- and upper-class city dwellers.

The Populists organized into a political party, and except for a time in 1912, the progressives did not. They were Republicans, Democrats, or members of some third party. The Populists were united around two issues — tariff and cheap money. The progressive movement, on the other hand, was made up of separate groups, each working for its own particular cause. Some worked to reform government corruption and inefficiency. Others were more interested in regulating big business. Some wanted to help the poor. Among the progressives were a group of journalists and writers called muckrakers (MUHK-rayk-erz). They wrote books and articles for magazines and newspapers to expose the corruption and evils of government, big business, and the cities.

The progressives had their greatest successes on the local and state level. For example, Wisconsin became the first state to provide for the direct election of U.S. Senators. In 1898, South Dakota adopted initiative, referendum, and recall. Although opposition to reform was stronger on a national level, Congress did not adopt some reforms.

A PROGRESSIVE IN THE WHITE HOUSE

As you may recall from the unit Industrialism and the West, Theodore Roosevelt became President after McKinley's assassination. Roosevelt was the first President to carry out the reforms of the Populists and progressives. He wanted what he called a "square deal" for everyone. One of Roosevelt's first acts was aimed at big business. He set out to limit the size and number of trusts. His reputation as a "trust buster" rested largely on the breakup of the Northern Securities Company. This trust was formed by J. P. Morgan in 1902. He had merged all railroad systems from Lake Michigan to the Pacific into one company, eliminating all competition. Roosevelt's Attorney General brought suit against the company and it was found in violation of the Sherman Antitrust Act. The Supreme Court ordered the company broken up into three small ones. In 1903, Roosevelt set up the Department of Commerce and Labor to oversee business and labor activity.

Roosevelt also believed that more care should be given to conserving our natural resources. He supported the establishment of national parks and wildlife preserves. The National Reclamation Bill of 1902 provided for saving water resources and set aside money from the sale of public land to finance dams in Wyoming and Arizona. Roosevelt

inefficiency (in-uh-FISH-uhn-see): lack of ability to get the best results without wasting time, energy, and so on

eliminate (ih-LIM-uh-nayt): to do away with; to get rid of

preserve: safe place set aside for wildlife

564

SOME REPRESENTATIVE MUCKRAKERS AND THEIR WORKS

Writer	Work	Purpose
Lincoln Steffens	"Shame of the Cities"	To describe corruption of politicians, police, and business in cities
Ida M. Tarbell	History of the Standard Oil Company	To expose Rockefeller's methods in driving his competition out of business
Upton Sinclair	The Jungle	To call attention to the unhealthy conditions in the meat-packing industry
David Graham Phillips	The Treason of the State	To charge Senators with passing ineffective laws regulating railroads in order to continue receiving bribes
Jacob Riis	How the Other Half Lives	To expose corruption, vice, and crime in slum areas of New York City
Ray Stannard Baker	The Spiritual Unrest Following the Color Line	To describe problems of blacks in slums To expose problems of blacks
John Spargo	The Bitter Cry of the Children	To expose child labor in factories
Gustavus Myers	History of the Great American Families	To condemn families whose fortunes were built on corruption and exploitation
Josiah Flynt Willard	"The World of Graft"	To expose Western Union's involvement in illegal betting

also set aside 3.6 million hectares (9 million acres) of land in the Southwest for a national forest. As you may recall from the unit Industrialism and the West, much of this land had been taken from Mexican Americans.

When Roosevelt won the 1904 election, he announced he would not run again. He felt this would free him to push for more reforms without having people think he was seeking personal power.

In 1906, Roosevelt signed the Hepburn Act to strengthen the Interstate Commerce Commission that you read about in the unit Industrialism and the West. The ICC had the authority to prevent railroads from giving rebates, but progressives felt that the ICC needed additional power. The Hepburn Act allowed the ICC to set maximum rail rates and all railroads had to lower their rates within 30 days.

Upton Sinclair's The Jungle prompted Roosevelt to appoint a commission to investigate the meat-packing industry. The commission found that stories of contaminated meat were true. In 1906, Congress passed the Pure Food and Drug Act. This forbade the sale, manufacture, or transporting of spoiled or mislabeled food or drugs. Also, labels on packages could not contain false or misleading information.

contaminated
(kuhn-TAM-uh-nayt-uhd): spoiled, dirty

In 1907, another financial panic hit the U.S. The causes were similar to the causes of earlier panics. Businesses overextended their credit, and banks loaned too much money.

This cartoon is titled "The Bosses of the Senate." What is the cartoonist's point of view? Notice the *People's Entrance.*

THE TAFT ADMINISTRATION

Roosevelt, as the leader of the Republican party, chose the Republican nominee for President in the 1908 election: his Secretary of War, William Howard Taft. The Democrats again nominated William Jennings Bryan. Both parties had platforms that condemned monopolies and pledged tariff reductions. Roosevelt's record as a progressive helped Taft, and he won. Shortly after the inauguration, Roosevelt set off on a hunting trip to Africa. He was confident that the progressive reforms he had begun would be continued by Taft.

Steadily rising prices had made the tariff the chief issue that Taft faced as President. Many people thought high prices were caused by high tariffs. In 1909, the Payne Bill, which reduced the tariffs on a number of items, passed the House. But when the bill reached the Senate, Nelson Aldrich (AWL-drich) attached several amendments that restored most of the tariffs to their original levels. Taft signed the Payne-Aldrich Bill into law to please some conservative Republicans. A **conservative** (kuhn-SER-vuh-tiv) is a person who wants to keep things the way they are and who is against making changes too quickly. The progressives were outraged.

Although progressives felt that Taft had deserted them, a number of reforms were undertaken during his administration. Twice as many antitrust suits were filed during Taft's one term in office than had been filed in Roosevelt's two terms. Taft did not go after small corporations as Roosevelt had but attacked large corporations such as General Electric, International Harvester, U.S. Steel, and Standard Oil. In 1910, Taft supported a bill to place telephone, telegraph, wireless, and cable companies under the jurisdiction of the ICC.

Two other reforms were brought about through amendments to the Constitution. The 16th Amendment allowed for a federal income tax, and the 17th Amendment called for direct election of Senators. Both had been supported by the Populists and progressives.

566

Election of 1912

When Roosevelt returned from Africa, he found that Taft had not continued his "square deal" programs. Roosevelt blamed Taft for the split in the Republican party. Roosevelt began touring the country making speeches urging a minimum wage for women, child labor laws, worker's compensation, and a federal health program. He sounded very much like a candidate for office. However, the Republicans picked Taft as their presidential nominee in 1912.

Angered that they could not take the nomination away from Taft, the progressives in the Republican party formed their own political party—the Progressive party. They nominated Roosevelt for President. When a reporter asked Roosevelt how he felt, the former President answered "as strong as a bull moose." After that, the Progressive party became known as the Bull Moose party.

The Democrats chose Woodrow Wilson their presidential candidate. He had received national attention in 1910 for reforms he had begun as governor of New Jersey. Eugene V. Debs, who ran in 1900, 1904, and 1908, again ran on the Socialist ticket. Because of the Republican split, Wilson had little trouble winning.

WILSON AS PRESIDENT

Shortly after he was inaugurated, Wilson called a special session of Congress to lower tariffs. The 1913 Underwood Tariff reduced the rates on many imports. It completely removed the tariffs on such items as wool, sugar, iron ore, and steel rails. However, the tariff actually did little to help the economy. In the same year, Congress passed the Federal Reserve Act. This act divided the country into 12

Theodore Roosevelt speaks to a group of bankers. Why did Roosevelt run as the candidate of the Progressive party in 1912? On what issues did he campaign?

Accompanied by supporters and a newsman or two, Woodrow Wilson goes to the polls to vote in the election of 1912. Why did he win the election so easily?

regions and set up a national bank in each region. The 12 national banks would be supervised by a Federal Reserve Board appointed by the President. These banks would make loans to private banks and the board would set the interest rates at which private banks could borrow money. The board would also control the amount of money in circulation. Congress hoped this would prevent future panics and depressions.

During his campaign, Wilson had promised to strengthen antitrust laws. He kept this promise in 1914 when Congress established the Federal Trade Commission (FTC). Its purpose was to investigate unfair business practices.

Additional antitrust measures became law under the Clayton Antitrust Act. This act outlawed price discrimination, or the charging of one price to one customer and a different price to another. The new laws also stated that antitrust laws could no longer be applied to labor unions. Injunctions could not be used against strikes, except to prevent property damage. An **injunction** is a court order commanding a person or group to do, or stop doing, something.

LOOKING BACK

1. Compare and contrast the Populists and the progressives in each of the following areas: **a.** their backgrounds. **b.** programs. **c.** organizations.
2. Read the table and make a generalization about the objectives of the muckrakers.
3. What progressive reforms were enacted under Roosevelt in: **a.** big business? **b.** food and drugs? **c.** conservation?
4. List and explain the sequence of events that led to Roosevelt's running as a Progressive party candidate for President in 1912.
5. What progressive reforms were enacted under Wilson in the areas of: **a.** tariff? **b.** big business? **c.** banking?

Chapter 2   U.S. as a World Power

LOOKING AHEAD

This chapter describes how the U.S. acquired Alaska and territory beyond North America in the late 1800s and early 1900s. You will also read about U.S. relations with Asia and U.S. involvement in Central America and the Caribbean. After you study this chapter, you will be able to:

- explain why Alaska was a valuable addition to the U.S.
- identify reasons for U.S. imperialism in the late 1800s.
- explain the role of propaganda in the Spanish-American War.
- explain the Open Door policy.
- state the importance of the Panama Canal.
- describe ways in which the Roosevelt Corollary was used.
- list the sequence of events that led to U.S. involvement in Mexico in the early 1900s.

Social Studies Vocabulary

imperialism   autonomy

People

William Seward	Theodore Roosevelt	Pancho Villa
Queen Liliuokalani	Emilio Aguinaldo	John J. Pershing
George Dewey	John Hay	
Pascual Cervera y Topeta	Victoriano Huerta	
	Venustiano Carranza	

Places

Alaska	Santiago, Cuba	Panama Canal Zone
Hawaii	El Caney, Cuba	Dominican Republic
Cuba	San Juan Hill	Nicaragua
Puerto Rico	Guam	Haiti
the Philippines	China	Mexico
Manila Bay	Panama	

Events

Boxer Rebellion

Words and Terms

yellow journalism	Foraker Act	Open Door policy
U.S.S. *Maine*	Jones Act	Roosevelt Corollary
Rough Riders	Commonwealth of	"big stick" policy
Platt Amendment	Puerto Rico	

This is the uniform of an officer in the U.S. Army in 1890. Why is a soldier in uniform a good symbol of this period in U.S. history?

During the 1800s, the U.S. had spread from a strip along the Atlantic across to the Pacific and from the Gulf of Mexico to the Canadian border. The purchase of Alaska completed the nation's growth on the continent. The U.S. then started to reach beyond these borders.

ALASKA

In 1867, the U.S. purchased Alaska from Russia. The Secretary of State at the time, William Seward (SOO-erd), was aware of the area's rich natural resources and had arranged for the purchase. But most Americans referred to the area as "Seward's Folly." In 1880, gold was discovered and prospectors poured in. Within four years, Congress had made Alaska a federal district. Federal officials were sent in to govern the district and regulate gold claims. In the 1890s, most of Alaska's gold had been mined. However, many miners stayed because of the abundance of timber, fish, coal, and iron they found. Alaska was made a territory in 1912 and a state in 1959.

IMPERIALISM

In the 1890s, U.S. expansion overseas was part of a worldwide movement called imperialism. **Imperialism** (im-PIR-ee-uhl-iz-uhm) means to extend economic or political control over other nations, sometimes by force. In the late 1800s, Great Britain, France, and Germany were taking over areas in Asia, the Middle East, and Africa. Many Americans believed the U.S. should do the same. They believed European nations would not recognize the U.S. as a world power until it controlled colonies overseas. Manufacturers also needed new markets and new sources of raw materials. The U.S. frontier had closed and

In addition to news stories that stirred American support for a war with Spain, there were also cartoons that encouraged it. What are the symbols in this cartoon? What do they represent? What is the cartoonist's viewpoint?

570

wealthy bankers and industrialists were looking for new opportunities in which to invest their money.

Hawaii

Americans had settled in the Hawaiian Islands as early as the 1820s. By the late 1800s, American citizens owned a number of large sugar plantations and were among the most powerful people in the Islands. In 1887, they were able to gain control of the Hawaiian legislature.

But in 1891, Queen Liliuokalani (li-lee-oo-aw-kah-LAH-ni) came to the throne. She was a strong opponent of foreign rule. She rallied her people to try to regain control of their nation. Fearing they might lose their profitable sugar plantations, the planters in 1893 demanded that the queen give up her throne. Aided by marines from a U.S. warship, the Americans set up their own government. They asked the U.S. to annex Hawaii.

President Cleveland did not believe in imperialism and asked that the queen be restored to power. The planters refused and continued to run the government and push for annexation. Changing politics in the Pacific and the Spanish-American War increased mainland support for annexation. In 1898, President McKinley annexed the Hawaiian Islands. Hawaii became a territory in 1900 and a state in 1959.

Queen Liliuokalani, shown here in Western dress, came to the U.S. twice after losing her throne. Her song, "Aloha Oe," later became the Hawaiian song of farewell. Why might the song have special meaning for Hawaiians and the Queen?

SPANISH-AMERICAN WAR

By the 1890s, Spain still controlled Cuba, Puerto Rico, and the Philippines. But there were frequent revolts against Spanish rule. The Spanish denied these people their political rights, taxed them heavily, and limited their foreign trade. In 1895, a major rebellion began in Cuba. The Spanish-controlled government put the rebels in prison.

This happened at the same time that a battle was raging between the New York *Journal* and the New York *World* over which could sell more newspapers. To try to win the battle, the owners of each paper printed sensational stories. They sent reporters to Cuba to seek out such stories among the jailed rebels. This kind of sensational reporting that may distort facts is called yellow journalism. Many Americans demanded the U.S. stop Spanish mistreatment of Cubans.

In February 1898, the U.S.S. *Maine* was sent to Cuba to protect American lives and property in case of violence. The ship was anchored in Havana (hah-VAH-na) Harbor. On the night of February 15, the *Maine* exploded and 260 American sailors were killed. No one knew then nor has later research shown if the explosion was an accident or whether the Spanish were responsible.

With emotions whipped up by yellow journalists, members of Congress and ordinary citizens urged President McKinley to declare war. "Remember the Maine" was their slogan. Congress demanded Spain's withdrawal from Cuba. Spain broke diplomatic relations. The U.S. answered with a blockade of Cuba. Spain then declared war.

distort (dis-TORT): to change from the truth

SPANISH-AMERICAN WAR: ADVANTAGES AND DISADVANTAGES OF EACH SIDE

	Advantages		Disadvantages	
	U.S.	**Spanish**	**U.S.**	**Spanish**
Military	Had modern navy	Had large army already established in Cuba	Had small army of mostly volunteers who were untrained and disorganized	Had small navy
			Wool uniforms, inadequate drinking water and medical supplies, rotten food, high rate of disease	Poor transportation could not get soldiers to strategic spots
Political	Had strong government with popular support for policy of imperialism			Power struggle between political parties and ruling monarch
Economic	In a period of prosperity			Depressed economies in Cuba and Spain
Population	War popular with Americans who felt they were saving suffering people			Spanish Empire collapsing; people not interested in war

Fighting the War

The first military move was in the Philippines (FIL-uh-peenz)—far from Cuba. On May 1, 1898, a U.S. fleet commanded by Commodore George Dewey steamed into Manila Bay. Within a few hours, it had destroyed ten Spanish warships. By August, Spanish troops in the city of Manila had surrendered. The Philippines were under American control.

The war in the Caribbean centered on Cuba. In May, seven Spanish warships commanded by Admiral Pascual Cervera y Topeta (ser-VER-uh ee toh-PAY-tuh) arrived. They were quickly trapped in Santiago (sahn-TYAH-goh) Harbor by a U.S. fleet. On July 1, U.S. troops defeated the Spanish at El Caney (el ka-NE-uh) and San Juan Hill. The Ninth and Tenth Cavalry, made up entirely of black soldiers, led the attack on San Juan Hill. They were joined by the Rough Riders, a group of untrained white volunteers organized by Lieutenant Colonel Theodore Roosevelt. The Spanish fleet, fearing capture, steamed out of Santiago Harbor on July 3 and was destroyed by U.S. ships. On July 17, the city of Santiago surrendered.

Spanish-American War

American Movements →
Spanish Movements →
American Victory ✳

CHINA
Hong Kong
Dewey
Merritt
PACIFIC OCEAN
Luzon
Manila
SOUTH CHINA SEA
PHILIPPINES
Mindanao
N

ATLANTIC OCEAN
FLORIDA
GULF OF MEXICO
Havana
CUBA
Sampson
Shafter
Schley
San Juan Hill
Santiago de Cuba
CARIBBEAN SEA
Cervera
DOMINICAN REPUBLIC
HAITI
N

0   200 miles
0   300 kilometers

Right: U.S. soldiers easily defeated the Spanish at Santiago, the major battle in the Caribbean. The army, however, was not prepared to fight in the Caribbean. It lost more men to disease than to battle.

Bottom: In the Philippines, Admiral George Dewey destroyed the Spanish fleet without losing a sailor. In Cuba, the Navy blockaded the Spanish in Santiago harbor, then sank their ships as they ran the blockade.

BATTLE OF SANTIAGO JULY 1ST AND 2ND 189

A few days later, American troops took the Spanish island of Puerto Rico against little resistance. Puerto Rico had received autonomy from Spain in November 1897, only to be forced to give it up eight months later. **Autonomy** (aw-TAHN-uh-mee) is the right of self-government.

In October 1898, U.S. and Spanish representatives met in Paris. Although Cuba received independence from Spain, it was placed under U.S. control. The U.S. also took possession of Puerto Rico and the island of Guam (GWAHM) in the Pacific. The U.S. paid Spain $20 million for the Philippines.

Occupation and Revolt

The peace treaty did not end the fighting. In the Philippines, Emilio Aguinaldo (ah-gee-NAWL-doh) had led an unsuccessful revolt against Spanish rule in 1896. When he learned that the treaty gave the Philippines to the U.S., he led a revolt against the Americans. War followed, but the Filipino (fil-uh-PEE-noh) rebels were poorly armed and had to surrender in 1901. The U.S. gradually gave Filipinos more self-rule until they received independence in 1946.

In Cuba, the U.S. set up a government and established schools and hospitals. In 1901, Congress added the Platt Amendment to the Cuban constitution. The amendment forbade interference by any foreign power in Cuba. The amendment also stated that the U.S. had a right to keep order in Cuba. The Cubans accepted these conditions reluctantly. Cuba received independence in 1934 when the Platt Amendment was withdrawn.

reluctantly
(ri-LUHK-tuhnt-lee):
unwillingly

Puerto Rico became a territory of the U.S. in 1900 under the Foraker (FAHR-uh-ker) Act. The act stated that trade between Puerto Rico and the U.S. was to be free of tariffs and that Puerto Ricans were to pay no federal taxes. Both provisions are still in effect. In 1917, under the Jones Act, Puerto Ricans became U.S. citizens and were given the right to elect their own legislators. In 1947, the Jones Act was amended to allow Puerto Ricans to elect their own governor. Puerto Rico adopted its own constitution and became a commonwealth in 1952. The Commonwealth of Puerto Rico is self-governing and its association with the U.S. is voluntary.

provision
(pruh-VIZH-uhn):
part of a document

CHINA AND FOREIGN POWERS

Once the U.S. had the Philippines, some Americans felt the U.S. should take a more active role in Asia. China had long been a profitable trading partner for the U.S. However, Great Britain, Germany, Russia, France, Italy, and Japan were carving China up into areas of special interest. Within an area, a nation such as Germany forced the government to give it special trading privileges. American business people feared that these countries could prevent the U.S. from trading in China.

In this scene painted by a Japanese artist, U.S. troops march through Peking after the Boxer Rebellion. Why were the soldiers in China? Why were Japanese there? Do you think this painting is a primary or a secondary source?

To avoid this, John Hay, Secretary of State for both McKinley and Roosevelt, proposed in 1899 what came to be known as the Open Door policy. This guaranteed that every nation trading in China would have equal rights to the use of seaports and railroads. No foreign power could try to limit any privileges given to another country by the Chinese government. In March, Hay announced that the foreign powers had agreed. This was not true. However, to deny it would have made a nation appear a threat to China's independence.

In spring 1900, a group of Chinese patriots, called Boxers, revolted against foreign influence in China. Many people were killed, and much foreign property was destroyed. An international armed force of soldiers crushed the Boxer Rebellion. Hay now feared that the foreign powers would try to divide China in payment for the damages the Boxers had done. He advised these nations that the U.S. wanted to preserve China's independence. These countries finally agreed to accept money in payment for the damages.

PANAMA CANAL

During the 1800s, both Americans and Europeans dreamed of a canal that would cut across Central America and connect the Atlantic and Pacific. Without such a canal, ships had to sail around South America. A canal would cut shipping time and costs. A French company had begun work on a canal in Panama in the 1880s but had gone bankrupt. In 1902, the U.S. agreed to pay $40 million for the work that had already been done. Because Panama was a territory of Colombia, President Roosevelt offered to pay Colombia to allow the U.S. to complete the canal. Colombia refused.

Panama Canal

intervene
(in-tuhr-VEEN):
to come in to help
settle a dispute

In November 1903, the Panamanians (pan-uh-MAY-nee-uhnz) broke away from Colombia. Roosevelt sent an American warship to support the rebels and quickly recognized the new Republic of Panama. In February 1904, the Senate approved a treaty with Panama that gave the U.S. control of a strip of land called the Panama Canal Zone. Panama received $10 million and a yearly payment of $250,000 for use of the land. The U.S. also agreed to guarantee the independence of the new nation. Work began and the Panama Canal was completed in 1914.

ROOSEVELT COROLLARY

In 1902, conflict in Venezuela brought warships from Great Britain, Germany, and Italy to South America. Because of growing U.S. interest in Central and South America and the U.S. investment in the Panama Canal, Roosevelt felt he needed to declare the nation's intention of keeping peace in that region. In 1904, he issued a corollary to the Monroe Doctrine. A corollary (KOR-uh-ler-ee) is an addition to an existing document. In the Roosevelt Corollary, the President said the U.S. would act as a police officer and settle any trouble in the Americas. Outside help would not be needed. The U.S. role would be backed by armed force. He believed, as he said, that the U.S. should "speak softly and carry a big stick."

In the early 1900s, Roosevelt and other U.S. Presidents used this "big stick" policy to intervene in several Caribbean and Central American nations. In 1905, the U.S. took over customs houses in the Dominican Republic to force that nation to pay its European debts. To keep peace between rival political groups, U.S. marines later occupied the Dominican Republic from 1916 to 1924. Marines also occupied Nicaragua from 1912 to 1933 to collect debts owed U.S. banks and to keep order. In 1915, President Wilson sent troops to restore order in Haiti. The soldiers remained until 1934.

MEXICAN REVOLUTION

Superior U.S. force did not always work. In 1913, the President of Mexico, Francisco Madero (mah-THAY-roh), was assassinated by General Victoriano Huerta (oo-ER-tuh). Americans with businesses in Mexico urged Wilson to recognize Huerta's government. Wilson refused because he believed Huerta did not represent the Mexican people. He promised U.S. support to Venustiano Carranza (kah-RAHN-sah) who led the resistance to Huerta.

In April 1914, Huerta's soldiers arrested some American sailors who had wandered into a restricted area. The sailors were later released, but Wilson was angered. He wanted an apology, and Huerta refused. Wilson then ordered U.S. marines and sailors to land in Veracruz to prevent a delivery of weapons to Huerta. At the same

The cartoonist has drawn Theodore Roosevelt as a policeman from whom all nations ask help. What does the nightstick labeled "The New Diplomacy" mean? What statement by Roosevelt is the cartoonist picturing?

time, Huerta was losing his political support. In July, he was forced to resign, and Carranza took control of the Mexican government.

After an unsuccessful attempt to overthrow Carranza, Pancho Villa (VEE-yah) who also wanted to rule Mexico set out to discredit Carranza with the U.S. government. In January 1916, he killed 16 Americans who were in Mexico at Carranza's request. In March, Villa crossed the border into New Mexico and murdered 17 more Americans. President Wilson responded by sending General John J. Pershing and several thousand soldiers into Mexico. They chased Villa across northern Mexico, but he was never caught. The troops were recalled in 1917 at Carranza's request.

discredit
(dis-KRED-it):
to cast doubt on;
to harm reputation of

LOOKING BACK

1. Why did Alaska prove to be a valuable addition to the U.S.?
2. **a.** State two reasons why Americans wanted the U.S. to expand its possessions in the late 1800s.   **b.** Explain how Hawaii was added to the U.S.
3. **a.** How did propaganda lead to U.S. involvement in the Spanish-American War?   **b.** List the results of the war.
4. **a.** What was the Open Door policy?   **b.** Why did John Hay think it was necessary?
5. **a.** Why was a canal across Central America important in the early 1900s?   **b.** How did Panama gain independence? **c.** What were the terms of the treaty with Panama that gave the U.S. control of the canal?
6. How did U.S. Presidents use Roosevelt's "big stick" policy in the early 1900s?
7. List the sequence of events that led to U.S. involvement in Mexico in the early 1900s.

Chapter 3   The U.S. in World War I

LOOKING AHEAD

This chapter describes the role of the U.S. in World War I. You will read why war broke out in Europe in 1914, how the U.S. became involved, how the war was fought, and how peace was made in 1919. After you study this chapter, you will be able to:

- explain the causes of World War I.
- describe how the U.S. became involved in the war.
- explain the assumption behind the way some Americans reacted to German Americans during World War I.
- list the sequence of battles that led to Germany's defeat.
- explain the conditions of the Treaty of Versailles.
- explain U.S. opposition to the League of Nations.

Social Studies Vocabulary

armistice

People

Archduke Franz Ferdinand	Woodrow Wilson	Herbert Hoover
	Charles Evan Hughes	John J. Pershing

Places

Sarajevo	Belleau Wood	Meuse-Argonne
Bosnia	Chateau-Thierry	
Serbia	Saint-Mihiel	

Words and Terms

Triple Alliance	Food Administration	Fourteen Points
Triple Entente	Committee on Public Information	Treaty of Versailles
Allied Powers		League of Nations
Central Powers	Espionage Act	
U-boat	Sedition Act	
Zimmermann Note	Selective Service Act	
War Industries Board	trench warfare	
	Big Four	

This poster advertises Liberty Loans, which were war bonds. The government raised $40 million in five loan drives to finance World War I.

In 1914, many people believed that a long war involving many nations was impossible. The wars of the past 50 years had been brief. A few major battles had decided the outcomes. In August 1914, however, a long war did begin. Before it ended four years later, all the world's most powerful nations had fought and millions had died.

WORLD WAR I BEGINS

The roots of the war lay in the competition among European nations for power in Europe and for colonies overseas. In 1882, Germany, to protect itself against its old enemies France and Russia, joined with Austria-Hungary and Italy to form the Triple Alliance. Over the next 25 years, Great Britain, France, and Russia formed the Triple Entente to balance the Triple Alliance. Entente (ahn-TAHNT) is another word for alliance. Smaller European nations chose sides and joined the alliances, too. By 1914, all that was needed to set off the explosive situation was a spark.

The spark was the assassination of Archduke Franz Ferdinand and his wife Sophie in June 1914. They were visiting Sarajevo (SAH-rah-ye-voh), the capital of Bosnia, which is now part of Yugoslavia. At the time, it was part of Austria-Hungary, and the Archduke was next in line to rule Austria-Hungary. While riding through the city, the royal couple were shot and killed. The murder suspect was a young Serbian. Many Serbians felt Bosnia should belong to Serbia.

Austria-Hungary blamed Serbia for the murders and declared war on July 28. Russia came to Serbia's aid. Because Germany supported Austria-Hungary, it declared war on Russia on August 1. Italy broke relations with the Triple Alliance and joined the Allies. Germany, Austria-Hungary, Bulgaria, and the Ottoman Empire—the present countries of Turkey, Syria, Lebanon, Israel, and parts of the Armenian Soviet Socialist Republic, Jordan, and Iraq—became known as the Central Powers.

Most Americans in 1914 considered this a European conflict and wanted to stay out of it. As Jefferson had done over 100 years before, the President declared the U.S. a neutral nation.

At first, the U.S. supplied food, clothing, weapons, and manufac-

Germany used a new weapon in World War I—the U-boat or submarine. This painting shows the sinking of a U.S. freighter by a German U-boat. How did German use of U-boats lead to the involvement of the U.S. in the war?

tured goods to both sides. Very soon, however, the U.S. was trading almost completely with the Allies. Generally, Americans favored the Allies, especially Great Britain. The U.S. and Great Britain shared much of the same heritage and for years the two countries had had close economic ties. Another reason for supplying the Allies was that Great Britain controlled the Atlantic. The British navy had quickly driven German warships from the seas and blockaded German ports.

Germany struck back with a blockade of its own. Germany, however, used a new weapon—the submarine or U-boat. In February 1915, Germany declared a war zone around Great Britain and announced that its U-boats would attack without warning all Allied ships—passenger and merchant—in the war zone. The Germans would not guarantee the safety of ships of neutral nations. The German's ignored Wilson's protest and warned Americans that it would be dangerous to travel on Allied ships. On May 7, 1915, a German submarine sank the British passenger ship *Lusitania*. Over 1,000 men, women, and children, including 128 Americans, lost their lives.

Americans called for war. Wilson implied war was a possibility if more Americans died. Germany, fearing the U.S. would join the Allies, said it would not sink passenger ships without warning.

THE U.S. ENTERS THE WAR

In 1916, the Democrats nominated Wilson for another term. Their slogan was, "He kept us out of war," a boast of Wilson's policy of neutrality. The Republicans chose Supreme Court Justice Charles Evans Hughes. While not coming out for or against American involvement in the war, the Republicans criticized Wilson's foreign policy. Wilson defeated Hughes in the closest presidential election since 1876.

In February 1917, Germany again began attacking ships without warning. In March, German U-boats sank three American merchant ships. That same month, Americans learned of the Zimmermann Note. This was a secret message sent to the President of Mexico by the German government. According to the note, Germany would allow Mexico to take New Mexico, Arizona, and Texas in return for declaring war on the U.S. On April 2, 1917, President Wilson asked Congress for a declaration of war against Germany.

Home Front

The government immediately set up the War Industries Board to organize American industry. It made sure that there were enough workers and materials to keep factories working at full speed. The government also set up among other agencies a Food Administration headed by a future President, Herbert Hoover. The agency encouraged farmers to grow more, and people to eat less. There were "Wheatless Mondays" and "Meatless Tuesdays" to save food to send to the troops.

As men went off to war, many jobs opened up. Between 1915 and 1918, more than one million women entered the labor force. Thou-

In army camps across the country, enlisted and drafted former civilians trained for combat. These troops are having target practice.

sands of blacks migrated north in search of jobs and better lives. Most found work that paid more than they had earned in the South. However, they found that they had not escaped discrimination by moving north.

Although many Americans supported the war, others were unenthusiastic and some opposed it. To gain support, President Wilson established the Committee on Public Information. The committee used well-known people—artists, actors, musicians, writers—to spread propaganda in support of U.S. war efforts. Congress also passed the Espionage (ES-pee-uh-nahzh) and Sedition Acts. These were meant to discourage Americans from spying or speaking out against the war effort or recruitment. All these activities built up anti-German feeling. Some schools stopped teaching German. Occasionally, people with German names lost their jobs. Libraries banned books about Germany, and sauerkraut was renamed "liberty cabbage."

Building the Armed Forces

The first job Wilson and Congress faced was bringing the armed forces to fighting strength. In May, Congress passed the Selective Service Act. It required all men between the ages of 21 and 30 to register for the draft. Almost three million men were eventually drafted. Along with enlistments, almost five million men and women served in the army, navy, and marines.

The marines and the navy refused to enlist blacks, but the army recruited more than 370,000 black soldiers. Of these, 1,400 served as officers. However, they served in segregated units. Native Americans also served in World War I. In 1924, the U.S. gave citizenship to all Native Americans in recognition of their service in the war. Over 20,000 Puerto Ricans also fought.

These shoulder patches identify different armies and divisions within the U.S. Army. The top patch is from the Third Army and the other from the Eighth Division.

FIRST IN
THE FIGHT~
ALWAYS
FAITHFUL~
BE A U.S. MARINE!

The Western Front in 1918

- – – – Front in March
- ••••• Front in July
- ——— Armistice Line
- ——▶ German Movements
- ▲▲▲▲ German Defenses
- ——▶ Allied Movements

NORTH SEA

NETHERLANDS

Cologne •
GERMANY

Calais
Belgians
• Brussels
BELGIUM

ENGLISH CHANNEL

British

LUXEMBOURG

British and Americans

French
• Paris
FRANCE

French and Americans

Americans

0   50 miles
0   60 kilometers

Left: Five million men and women served in the armed forces during World War I. How did posters such as this influence people to enlist?

Bottom, left: Blacks who were sent to Europe were usually in construction or other labor battalions. Those in combat served in segregated units. How did their treatment in World War I compare to earlier wars?

Bottom, right: Musicians, actors, and artists were all part of the effort to organize support for the war at home. Composer George M. Cohan's song "Over There" was written in French and English and became the most popular patriotic song of World War I.

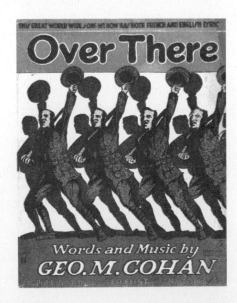

Over There

Words and Music by
GEO. M. COHAN

Top: The American Red Cross provided medical care and a link with home for soldiers in Europe. At home, Red Cross volunteers encouraged Americans to support the war effort. During the war, women also worked as mechanics, in steel mills, and in weapons factories, among other jobs.

Bottom: *Aeroplane Flight Over the Verdun Front* by Farré depicts a common scene during the war. Many dog fights, or air battles, took place over the Western Front. At the beginning of the war, planes had been used only for spying, but they were soon armed. The Germans also used zeppelins (ZEP-uh-luhns), or large blimps.

WORLD WAR I: ADVANTAGES AND DISADVANTAGES OF EACH SIDE

	Advantages		Disadvantages	
	Allied Powers	**Central Powers**	**Allied Powers**	**Central Powers**
Military	Had twice as many in the armed forces Had powerful navy for blockading enemy ports	Had better military organization Had U-boats to attack supply ships Had better lines of communication in Europe	Had to transport much of their troops and supplies by sea	
Economic	Industry in Great Britain and the U.S. able to supply armed forces	German industry able to supply its armed forces		
Political			Russia out of the war after Russian Revolution in 1917	Weak government in Austria-Hungary
Population	Overwhelming support of war effort			Many peoples in Austria-Hungary and Ottoman Empire working to establish their own nations at expense of war effort

Fighting the War

By 1917, the ground war was almost at a standstill. The fighting centered in northern France along what was called the Western Front. The French had stopped the German invasion in fall 1914. But neither the French nor the British were able to drive the Germans back. Each side finally dug in, and trench warfare began. The two sides faced each other across an empty "no man's land" protected by barbed wire and machine guns. Fighting on the Eastern Front, the German and Austro-Hungarian border with Russia, ended in December 1917. In early 1917, a revolution occurred in Russia, and the new government pulled Russia out of the war.

As soon as war was declared, President Wilson named General John J. Pershing to command all U.S. troops on the western front. He had been in charge of the attempt to capture Pancho Villa in Mexico. Pershing arrived in France in early June 1917 with only 190 officers and troops. It would take many months to train the million soldiers that Pershing wanted in France. Pershing also wanted U.S. troops to fight together as a separate army along their own section of the front.

Fearing the arrival of hundreds of thousands of fresh troops, the Germans began a major attack in March 1918. They broke through the British and French lines in several places and threatened the city of Paris. Americans held the front near Belleau (BEL-oh) Wood. In July, 275,000 American soldiers stopped a huge German attack at Chateau-Thierry (shah-TOH tye-REE). By the end of July, the Allies had completely stopped the Germans. To help their ground forces, the U.S. used airplanes for observation and to drop bombs. With World War I, the airplane had entered the arsenal of modern warfare.

In September, the Allies began their own attack. American troops won bitterly fought battles at Saint-Mihiel (SAHN mee-YEL) and Meuse-Argonne (MUZ ar-GAWN). The German armies retreated, falling back across France toward the German border. The German government asked for an **armistice**—an agreement to stop the war. On November 11, 1918, the fighting stopped. Over 100,000 Americans died in the fighting, but that was a small number compared to the ten to thirteen million Europeans killed.

TREATY OF VERSAILLES

In January 1919, delegates from the allied nations gathered in Versailles (ver-SY), France, to write a peace treaty. But the major decisions were made by the Big Four—France, Great Britain, Italy, and the U.S. President Wilson wanted a peace treaty that would not punish the losers. A year earlier he had announced to Congress what he thought would make a fair and just peace. His plan became known as the Fourteen Points. In the last point of this document, Wilson proposed that all the nations organize into a league so that future conflict could be settled peacefully rather than by war. The other Allied leaders, however, wanted to punish Germany. The final treaty was hard on Germany, but it did contain some of Wilson's principles.

In the Treaty of Versailles, Germany accepted responsibility for the war and agreed to pay $33 billion in damages to the Allies. Germany also lost its colonies in Asia and Africa. The Allies insisted that Germany be allowed only a small army and navy. Germany lost Alsace (AHL-sahs) and Lorraine and the Saar (SAHR) Valley, an important coal region. The treaty also created a number of new European nations from territory that once belonged to the defeated nations. Finally, the treaty created Wilson's League of Nations.

U.S. Opposition

Wilson and the Democrats in Congress supported the Treaty of Versailles and the League of Nations. Important Republicans in Congress opposed the treaty. They viewed it as a Democratic document because they had not been asked for advice. They also opposed joining the League. They did not want to commit the U.S. to aid other nations

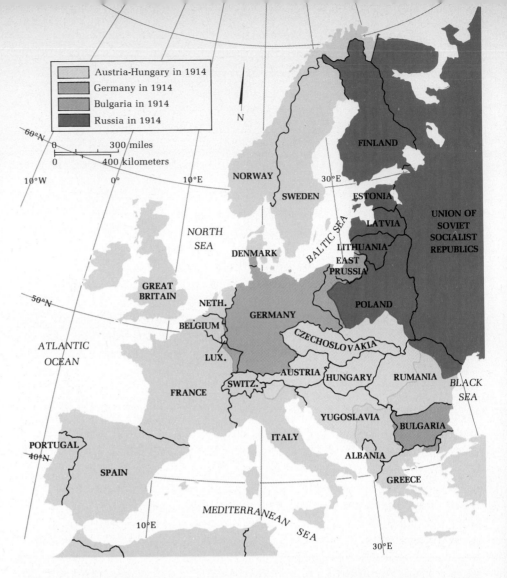

**Europe after
World War I**

automatically in time of war. The U.S. Senate voted on ratification of the Treaty of Versailles several times between November 1919 and March 1920. But Wilson's supporters could not gather enough votes. The U.S. eventually signed a separate peace treaty with Germany in 1921. However, the U.S. never joined the League of Nations.

LOOKING BACK

1. **a.** Why did powerful European nations make alliances in the years before World War I? **b.** What event sparked World War I?
2. **a.** Why did the U.S. trade with the Allies? **b.** How did the German use of U-boats violate U.S. neutrality? **c.** What two events caused the U.S. to enter the war?
3. What assumption did some Americans make about German Americans during World War I?
4. Beginning with U.S. entry into the war, describe the sequence of battles that led to Germany's defeat.
5. **a.** List five parts of the Treaty of Versailles. **b.** Why did Republicans in Congress oppose the Treaty and the League of Nations?

PRACTICING YOUR SKILLS

What If . . .

In Chapter 2 you read about the completion of the Panama Canal. **What if** the canal had not been built? How would this have affected the cost of goods sent from Europe to the west coast of the U.S.? How would the U.S. have been affected in a sea war with an Asian nation? Is the canal as important now that there are airplanes?

Researching, Writing, Making a Time Line

1. In Chapter 2, you read that Puerto Rico had autonomy for a brief period. Write a short research paper describing the changes in government of the island from 1898 to the present.
2. Read a book by one of the muckrakers listed in Chapter 1 and write a book report.
3. Airplanes were among the new weapons used for the first time during World War I. Use encyclopedias and other reference books to draw pictures for a bulletin board display of U.S. and German airplanes used in World War I.
4. Use additional sources to make a time line listing the reform legislation passed by Congress between 1880 and 1916.
5. The Lafayette Escadrille (es-kuh-DRIL) was a famous flying group in World War I. Research and write a brief report on it.

Exploring

You read about the Food and Drug Act in Chapter 1. State and local governments also supervise the quality, cleanliness, and purity of foods. Contact your local or state health department and find out what standards have been set for your area.

Building Communication Skills

Negotiating is the settlement of a disagreement by discussing and compromising. The Treaty of Versailles was negotiated in this way. Sometimes one person will act as the negotiator to design a settlement that is acceptable to all parties. Here are some tips to help you negotiate a successful settlement.

- Have each side present their demands and the reasons they feel their demands should be met.
- Review the demands to make sure they are reasonable.
- Plan a settlement that is fair. Each side should get and give up some of its demands.
- Present your compromise. If one side is not satisfied with the settlement, then you must redesign your settlement.

Activity: Pick a topic on which the members of your class disagree. Have each side present their demands and the reasons they should be met. As the negotiator, you must negotiate a settlement that is satisfactory to both sides.

Reading

Henri, Florette, and Richard Stillman. *Bitter Victory.* New York: Doubleday, 1970. Paperback. Black soldiers in World War I.

Hoobler, Dorothy and Thomas. *An Album of World War I.* New York: Watts, 1976.
———. *Fighting on the Western Front in World War I.* New York: Putnam, 1978.

Lawson, Don. *The United States in the Spanish-American War.* New York: Abelard-Schumann, 1976.

May, Ernest R. *The Progressive Era: 1901-1917.* Morristown, New Jersey: Silver Burdett, 1974. Political, social, and military history.

Morris, Edmund. *The Rise of Theodore Roosevelt.* New York: Ballantine, 1980.

Tentler, Leslie Woodcock. *Wage-Earning Women: Industrial Work and Family Life in the United States, 1900-1930.* New York: Oxford University Press, 1979.

Walworth, Arthur Clarence. *America's Moment: 1918.* New York: Norton, 1977.

Section VI MODERN AMERICA

ERA

PEACE

GIVE US B
OUR LA

NO
MORE

LOWER
PRICES

AIM

BOYCOTT
GRAPES

GRAY
POWER

BLACK
POWER

EQUAL RIGHTS, EQUAL PAY

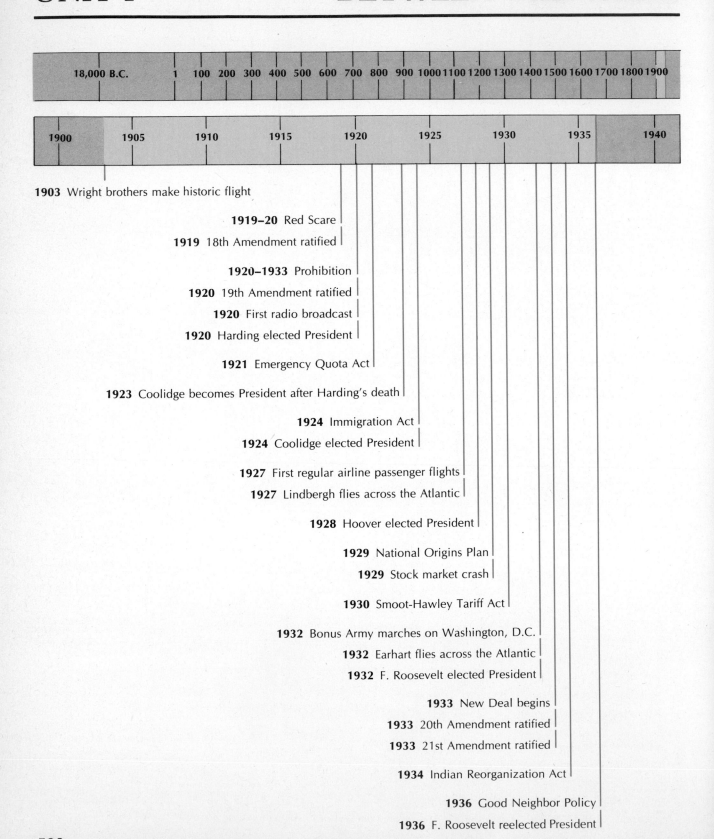

18,000 B.C. 1 100 200 300 400 500 600 700 800 900 1000 1100 1200 1300 1400 1500 1600 1700 1800 1900

1900 1905 1910 1915 1920 1925 1930 1935 1940

1903 Wright brothers make historic flight

1919–20 Red Scare
1919 18th Amendment ratified

1920–1933 Prohibition
1920 19th Amendment ratified
1920 First radio broadcast
1920 Harding elected President

1921 Emergency Quota Act

1923 Coolidge becomes President after Harding's death

1924 Immigration Act
1924 Coolidge elected President

1927 First regular airline passenger flights
1927 Lindbergh flies across the Atlantic

1928 Hoover elected President

1929 National Origins Plan
1929 Stock market crash

1930 Smoot-Hawley Tariff Act

1932 Bonus Army marches on Washington, D.C.
1932 Earhart flies across the Atlantic
1932 F. Roosevelt elected President

1933 New Deal begins
1933 20th Amendment ratified
1933 21st Amendment ratified

1934 Indian Reorganization Act

1936 Good Neighbor Policy
1936 F. Roosevelt reelected President

Chapter 1   The Twenties

LOOKING AHEAD

This chapter describes the changes in the U.S. after World War I. You will read about woman suffrage, new forms of transportation, and new kinds of entertainment in the 1920s. You will also read about the nationwide unrest and discrimination that lay under the glitter of the age. After you study this chapter, you will be able to:

- describe the conditions that led to national prohibition and the factors that caused it to fail.
- list two ways women worked for suffrage in the early 1900s.
- explain the problems in Harding's presidency.
- identify causes of unrest during the 1920s.
- identify the bias in the immigration laws of the 1920s.
- list two technological advances that changed American life.
- classify the themes of writers in the 1920s.

Social Studies Vocabulary

suffragist	communism	suburbs
prohibition	quota system	materialism
cost of living	assembly line	

People

Warren G. Harding	Henry Ford	Ellen Glasgow
Prohibition party	Orville Wright	Ernest Hemingway
Carrie Chapman Catt	Wilbur Wright	Langston Hughes
Alice Paul	Charles Lindbergh	James Weldon
Jeannette Rankin	Amelia Earhart	Johnson
James Cox	Edna St.	Sinclair Lewis
Franklin Roosevelt	Vincent Millay	Amy Lowell
Calvin Coolidge	Sherwood Anderson	Claude McKay
Albert Fall	Countee Cullen	Eugene O'Neill
Marcus Garvey	Jessie Fauset	Ezra Pound
Ku Klux Klan	F. Scott Fitzgerald	Edith Wharton

Words and Terms

Roaring Twenties	League of Women	National Origins
Women's Christian	Voters	Plan
Temperance Union	Teapot Dome	Model T
18th Amendment	scandal	Harlem
bootlegging	Red Scare	Renaissance
speakeasies	Emergency Quota Act	jazz
21st Amendment	Immigration Act	lost generation
19th Amendment	of 1924	

This magazine cover illustration is titled "Nothing to Nothing." What do you think the artist is saying about college students in the 1920s?

The 1920s, called the Roaring Twenties by some, was a time of great technological and artistic growth. Automobiles, airplanes, radio, movies, jazz, and black culture flourished. Constitutional amendments brought the right to vote for women and a ban on alcohol. In their first presidential election, women voted overwhelmingly for Warren G. Harding and "a return to normalcy." People were eager to put aside the horrors of World War I. But there was a dark side to the glittering decade. The U.S. experienced labor unrest, fear of foreigners, and violent reactions against minorities.

PROHIBITION

In the unit Life at Mid-Century, you read about the temperance movement. During the years after the Civil War, the movement grew steadily. In 1872, the Prohibition party nominated its first presidential candidate. **Prohibition** is the act of banning or forbidding something, in this case, alcohol. The Woman's Christian Temperance Union was founded two years later.

Prohibition continued to gain support during the early 1900s. By 1908, 18 states had laws calling for statewide prohibition. The prohibitionists had gained enough power by 1919 to have the 18th Amendment passed and ratified. It went into effect in 1920. The amendment called for a ban on the "manufacture, sale, or transportation" of alcohol within the U.S. It also banned its import.

Although there was enough support to make prohibition law, there was not enough support to make it a success. From the beginning, many people opposed the law, and officials found it difficult to enforce. People made their own "bathtub gin" and "home brew" beer. Most did this for their own use, but some sold it to friends and neighbors. The real profits were in bootlegging, the illegal manufacture or sale of alcohol. Gangsters controlled this business, and wars broke out between opposing gangs. Illegal bars, called speakeasies, began to appear in alleys and side streets. Customers usually had to know a password to be admitted. Speakeasies were raided occasionally, but bribes and payoffs to city officials usually kept them open. In 1933, support for an end to prohibition led to ratification of the 21st Amendment.

WOMAN SUFFRAGE

As you may recall from the unit Industrialism and the West, much of the groundwork for woman suffrage had been laid in the late 1800s. By 1913, nine western states allowed women to vote. But suffragists wanted voting rights nationwide. A **suffragist** is a supporter of voting rights for women. Only a constitutional amendment could accomplish this goal quickly.

The final successful drive for woman suffrage was led by women such as Carrie Chapman Catt and Alice Paul. However, they used different means to win their goal. Paul harrassed public officials by

picketing, blocking sidewalks, and if arrested, going on hunger strikes in jail. In 1913, Paul led more than 5,000 women in a demonstration at Wilson's inaugural.

Other suffragists preferred less drastic means. Catt, for example, organized groups across the country to work for woman suffrage through political pressure. An amendment to give women the vote had been introduced at every session of Congress since 1878. In 1918, it was finally passed, in part because of the contribution that women were making to the war effort. The 19th Amendment was ratified in time for women to vote in the 1920 elections.

Women at the National American Woman Suffrage Association, of which Catt was president, cheered the new amendment. The association disbanded and formed the League of Women Voters. Catt became its first president. The purpose of the group was to provide nonpartisan information about candidates and issues. Meanwhile, women were beginning to be recognized in politics. In 1917, Jeanette Rankin had become the first woman to be elected to the House of Representatives. She served as a Republican Representative from Montana.

nonpartisan
(nahn-PAHR-tuh-zuhn):
not connected with
a political party

RETURN TO NORMALCY

In the 1920 presidential election, the Democrats nominated Governor James Cox of Ohio for President and Franklin Roosevelt, Wilson's Assistant Secretary of the Navy, for Vice-President. The Democratic platform called for ratification of the Treaty of Versailles and U.S. membership in the League of Nations. The Republicans turned to Ohio Senator Warren G. Harding and Governor Calvin Coolidge of Massachusetts as their candidates for President and Vice-President. The Republicans opposed the treaty as well as membership in the League. In his campaign speeches, Harding called for a "return to nor-

The cover of *Life* for March 6, 1924, featured Teapot Dome. Notice the man swimming for his life. Who do you think he might be?

foodstuff: food

malcy." He wanted to see an end to drastic reform movements at home and U.S. involvement abroad. Evidently others did, too, and Harding won the election overwhelmingly.

Harding's presidency was marred by a series of scandals involving friends to whom he had given jobs. One of the biggest scandals involved a cabinet member and government oil lands at Teapot Dome, Wyoming. The Secretary of the Interior, Albert Fall, had leased the lands to private oil companies in 1921. The Senate discovered that Fall had accepted a $100,000 bribe in return for awarding the leases. Fall became the first cabinet member to be convicted of a crime while in office. The scandals began to affect Harding's health and he died while visiting Alaska in 1923.

Vice-President Coolidge completed Harding's term. During Coolidge's presidency, Congress increased the tariffs on foreign goods. Half the war debt was paid off, and restrictions were placed on immigration. The U.S. seemed to be prospering. Under Harding and later Coolidge little reform or regulatory legislation for business was passed. Both Presidents opposed what they saw as government interference in economic affairs. Coolidge was easily elected to a full term in 1924. At the end of his term, Coolidge announced that he would not seek reelection.

NATIONWIDE UNREST

For some Americans, the "return to normalcy" was marked not by prosperity but by a struggle to survive. By 1920, much of Europe had recovered from World War I. Europeans were again able to grow enough foodstuffs to feed themselves. As a result, U.S. farm exports dropped off and farm prices fell. Declining prices meant declining profits for farmers. However, the prices of supplies and equipment kept increasing. Tenant farmers were especially hard hit and went even deeper into debt. The 1920s were also a difficult time for coal miners. Many lost their jobs as coal production declined. Oil began to compete with coal as a fuel. As more and more businesses switched from coal to oil, coal prices dropped. Coal mine owners either decreased production or closed their mines.

During the war, labor and management worked well together. The government needed goods delivered on time and employers were willing to meet workers' demands for wages and working conditions. As demand decreased after the war, factories slowed down. There were fewer jobs. In addition, many women, blacks, and immigrants lost their jobs to returning veterans.

For all American workers, the cost of living had doubled during the war. The **cost of living** is the average cost of buying necessary goods and services. Even those who had jobs had trouble supporting their families. During 1919, there was a series of strikes for pay increases and the right to form unions. Many people felt the strikes were started by Communists.

Communism (KAHM-yuh-niz-uhm) is an economic system in which the community or government owns all the means of production, such as farmlands and factories. The right of individuals to own the means of production is partly or entirely denied. Many Americans were afraid that the striking workers shared the Communist view of ownership. Two years earlier, Communists had seized control of the government of Russia. Some Americans feared Communists wanted to do the same in the U.S. This fear of a Communist takeover is known as the Red Scare. Very few of the strikers were interested in communism but the fear of the Red Scare helped to break the 1919 strikes.

Several acts of violence fueled the Red Scare. In 1919 and 1920, packages containing bombs were mailed to important business leaders and public officials. One bomb exploded in New York City killing 38 people. The Attorney General of the U.S. launched an investigation of Communists. Thousands of aliens, many of whom were not Communists, were arrested. Of these, about 250 were eventually judged to be Communists and deported.

Immigration Quotas

World War I and the Red Scare affected American attitudes toward immigration. In the 1920s, the U.S. passed several laws limiting immigration and setting up a quota system. A **quota** (KWOH-tuh) **system** is a plan that limits on a country-by-country basis the number of immigrants that are allowed to enter the U.S.

The quota acts used earlier census information to determine the number of Europeans that could enter the U.S. each year. The 1921 Emergency Quota Act limited European immigrants to 3 percent of those from a particular nation living in the U.S. in 1910. The Immigration Act of 1924 lowered the number to 2 percent and used an earlier

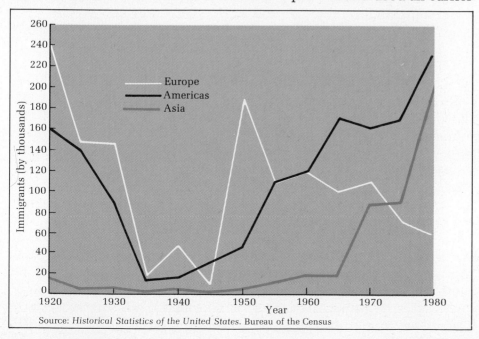

Source: *Historical Statistics of the United States.* Bureau of the Census

Immigration
from 1920 to 1980

595

census, that of 1890. As you may recall from the unit Industrialism and the West, immigrants from southern and central Europe did not begin arriving in any great numbers until after 1890. The 1924 law was intended to reduce immigration from this group. The law also banned all immigrants from Asia. In 1929, the National Origins Plan stated that no more than 150,000 imigrants from beyond the Western Hemisphere could enter the U.S. each year.

Ku Klux Klan

In the 1920s Americans' fear of outsiders was not limited to Communists and immigrants. Anyone who was different became an object of fear to some people. The Ku Klux Klan was especially active. The original KKK had been formed to deny black their rights. The society eventually died out, but a new KKK was formed in 1915. Besides blacks, the KKK turned its violence on Jews and Catholics.

Some blacks believed that they would never have a chance for equality in the U.S. One such black, Marcus Garvey, preached a message of black pride and separation from whites. Garvey started a "back to Africa" movement to build a homeland for blacks in Africa. At the height of his power in the early 1920s, he had over half a million followers.

TECHNOLOGY AND THE ARTS

The Roaring Twenties were a time of rapid growth in both technology and the arts. Though some areas of the economy, such as farming and mining, were depressed, many people had money to spend. Technological developments and increased production made it possible to own automobiles and radios and a wide variety of new goods.

Automobiles and Airplanes

In 1896, Henry Ford tested his first automobile. The early Ford cars were very expensive, and few people could afford them. In 1908, however, Ford began producing the inexpensive Model T. He had found a way to make cars quickly and efficiently to keep down the price. Ford put the cars on moving tracks called assembly lines. In an **assembly line,** each worker performs a different step in the production of an item as it moves in a direct line from start to finish. By 1925, Ford was making 9,000 cars a day and selling them for $250 each.

The automobile changed American life. Workers could now live farther from their jobs and drive to work. **Suburbs** (SUHB-uhrbs), or residential areas on the outskirts of cities, developed. The Model T also supplied a new form of recreation—the Sunday drive. By 1930, there were over 23 million automobiles in the U.S.

While Henry Ford was working on his Model T, Orville and Wilbur Wright were building an airplane. In 1903, at Kitty Hawk, North

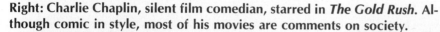

Top: Golf, like many sports, grew in popularity during the 1920s. Glenna Collett and other women athletes began competing in sports events during that period. Why did sports become so popular?

Right: Charlie Chaplin, silent film comedian, starred in *The Gold Rush*. Although comic in style, most of his movies are comments on society.

Top, left: The first sound cartoon was Walt Disney's *Steamboat Willie*. What made sound possible?

Top right: Babe Ruth made baseball popular by making it exciting. His career record of 714 home runs stood until Henry Aaron broke it in 1974.

Bottom: Duke Ellington, far right, and his band gained fame playing in Harlem. He was the first musician to write major jazz compositions.

Along with the production of cars on assembly lines, came the corner service station. This photograph was taken in New York City in 1923. What was the price of gasoline?

renaissance
(ren-uh-SAHNS): reawakening of ideas, interest

Carolina, they became the first people to fly a heavier-than-air machine. Although airplanes were used during World War I, they were not widely used for passenger service until the 1920s. In 1927, the first regularly scheduled passenger service began between Boston and New York City. Aviation opened up new careers for women. Airlines began hiring nurses to take care of passengers during flights. Charles Lindbergh's (LIND-berg) nonstop flight alone from New York to Paris on May 20-21, 1927, in the *Spirit of St. Louis* went far to popularize the use of airplanes. In 1932, Amelia Earhart (AIR-hahrt) became the first woman to fly solo across the Atlantic.

Electric Wonders

Electricity brought many changes in the way Americans lived and worked in the 1920s. As people began to put electricity in their homes and businesses, they bought such electric wonders as fans, clocks, vacuum cleaners, refrigerators, and washing machines. But nothing grew in popularity as rapidly as the radio. In 1920, the first U.S radio station, KDKA in Pittsburgh, broadcast its first program, the results of the presidential election. By 1924, there were more than 580 stations in operation and three million radios in use. Electricity contributed to the growth of the motion picture industry, too. By the mid-1920s, electricity made possible the addition of sound to movies.

HARLEM RENAISSANCE

By 1920, Harlem, a part of New York City, was the black cultural center of the U.S. Many gifted writers and entertainers made it their home. Wealthy and middle-class blacks lived there. It was also the home of two important journals. One was the *Crisis*, the publication of the NAACP. The other was *Opportunity*, the bulletin of the National Urban League. Both printed poems, stories, and nonfiction works by black writers.

The artistic output of black writers and artists during this time is known as the Harlem Renaissance. It marks a turning point in black creativity because of a change in the attitudes of the artists themselves. Their works began to reflect the vital part that black culture plays in America's heritage. Some black writers and artists also wanted to show black middle class life in their works. Others began to use their works to point out the discrimination and abuse that blacks were receiving.

JAZZ AGE

During the 1920s, American music, theater, and literature blossomed. The ragtime tunes of the late 1800s and early 1900s blended with black spirituals and blues to form jazz. Louis Armstrong, Fats Waller, Bessie Smith, and Duke Ellington became well known performers. Jazz became so popular that the 1920s are often called the Jazz Age.

SOME REPRESENTATIVE WRITERS OF THE 1920s

Writer	Work	Themes and/or Style
Sherwood Anderson	*Winesburg, Ohio; A Storyteller's Story*	Describes frustrations of small-town life in the Midwest; challenges traditional values
Countee Cullen	*Color; Copper Sun*	Describes living conditions of poor blacks
Jessie Fauset	*There Is Confusion; Plum Buns*	Explores black home life and discrimination in small towns
F. Scott Fitzgerald	*Tales of the Jazz Age; The Great Gatsby*	Records the Jazz Age; uses moral lessons
Ellen Glasgow	*Barren Ground; The Romantic Comedian*	Writes of upper-class life in the South
Ernest Hemingway	*The Sun Also Rises*	Records the "lost generation"
Langston Hughes	*The Weary Blues*	Describes economic and social conditions of poor blacks
James Weldon Johnson	*God's Trombones*	Combines Biblical material and black folklore
Sinclair Lewis	*Main Street; Babbitt*	Criticizes middle-class Americans
Amy Lowell	*What's O'Clock; Ballads For Sale*	Creates poems without rhyme or rhythm; use of images important
Claude McKay	*Harlem Shadows; Home to Harlem*	Describes discrimination and injustice against blacks
Edna St. Vincent Millay	*A Few Figs from Thistles; The Ballad of the Harp Weaver*	Writes romantic poems about love and death
Eugene O'Neill	*Strange Interlude*	Writes of family ties; uses various new techniques
Ezra Pound	*Cantos*	Shows corruption of values in the U.S.
Edith Wharton	*The Age of Innocence; Here and Beyond*	Writes of upper-class life

Ben Shahn, a noted realist painter of the 20th century, painted *Speakeasy Interior* c. 1934.

Other forms of entertainment were also popular. In 1927 alone, 250 shows were playing in New York City theaters. These included musicals such as *Showboat* and the dramas of Eugene O'Neill, Robert Sherwood, and George S. Kaufman. The large musical revues of Florenz Ziegfeld (ZIG-feld), starred such performers as Fannie Brice, Al Jolson, and Will Rogers. These shows were usually a series of musical acts featuring dancing, singing, and comedy.

Many authors of the period were part of a group of Americans called the "lost generation." They lived abroad and wrote about characters who led meaningless lives or whose lives were taken up with the search for pleasure. Other writers stayed in America and wrote about the hypocrisy and materialism of small town life. **Materialism** (muh-TIR-ee-uhl-iz-uhm) is the belief that the greatest happiness can be found in getting material things. Poets used similar themes.

LOOKING BACK

1. **a.** What conditions led to national prohibition?   **b.** List four reasons for its failure.
2. **a.** List two ways women worked to obtain suffrage in the early 1900s.   **b.** How was nationwide woman suffrage finally brought about?
3. What events marred the Harding presidency?
4. What caused unrest in the following groups during the 1920s: **a.** farmers?   **b.** coal miners?   **c.** factory workers?
5. **a.** Biases against which groups of immigrants are shown in the immigration laws of the 1920s?   **b.** Why did a new KKK form?
6. Identify and explain the effects of the following on American life: **a.** automobile.   **b.** electricity.
7. What were the themes of writers in the 1920s?

Chapter 2   The Crash and the Depression

LOOKING AHEAD

This chapter is about the end of the Jazz Age. It describes the presidential election of 1928, the stock market crash of 1929, the resulting depression, and the election of 1932. After you study this chapter, you will be able to:

- identify the assumption behind some Democrats' opposition to Alfred E. Smith.
- explain the stock market crash of 1929.
- identify the cause of widespread unemployment during the depression.
- state the policies of Herbert Hoover.
- describe Americans' feelings about the 1932 presidential election.

People

Herbert Hoover   Alfred E. Smith   Franklin D. Roosevelt

Words and Terms

stock market crash   Home Loan Bank Act   Smoot-Hawley
stock speculation   Reconstruction Finance   Tariff Act
on margin   Corporation   20th Amendment

As 1928 approached, more Americans had more of the good things than at any other time in the nation's past. Many thought the good times would never end. But 1929 saw the stock market collapse. The country was thrown into a depression far worse than any if had ever known.

ELECTION OF 1928

The presidential convention of 1928 was the first to be broadcast over radio. Across the country, Americans listened as the political parties nominated their candidates. The Republicans selected Herbert Hoover, Secretary of Commerce for both Harding and Coolidge and the director of the Food Administration during World War I.

The Democrats nominated Alfred E. Smith, Governor of New York and a Roman Catholic. Smith had a good record for reform legislation, but he was from a big city in the Northeast rather than from a farming state. This kept many western and southern Democrats from supporting him. Some members also felt that prejudice against Roman

Catholics would keep some people from voting for Smith. Hoover ran on the Republican record of prosperity and won easily.

THE CRASH

Throughout the 1920s, most Americans had been earning a good living. As the decade wore on, people were spending more and saving less. Easy credit helped people buy cars, homes, and household goods. Businesses were only too willing to sell an item for "a dollar down and a dollar a week." Soon many Americans were deep in debt. During the 1920s, there was also much stock speculation. People bought stocks and bonds hoping to sell them later at a higher price. Many of these people bought stocks on margin. That is, they put down only a small part of the price in cash and borrowed the rest.

During the first six months of Hoover's presidency, the economy was at its peak. In mid-October, however, stock prices began to fall. Industry was producing more goods than there were buyers. Unemployment was on the rise. Many people feared that the value of their stocks would not increase again. They started to sell while prices were still high enough to make a profit. On October 24, 1929, almost 13 million shares of stock were sold. This was more than double the amount that had been sold three days earlier.

The following Tuesday, October 29, was the worst day in the history of the stock market. It was the day of the stock market crash. Stock prices dropped so sharply that thousands of people lost all their money. The U.S. entered a depression that spread to Europe and the rest of the world. The depression lasted a decade—until World War II brought full production in factories and full employment.

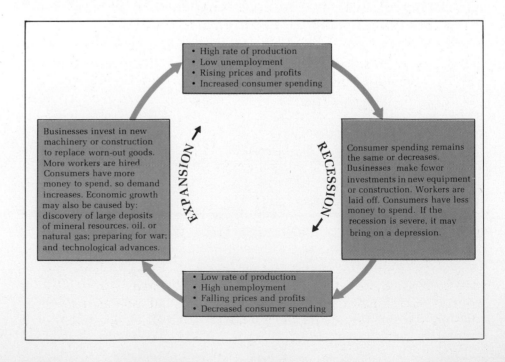

Employment Agency was painted by Isaac Soyer. As the depression grew worse in the 1930s, large numbers of people lost their jobs. What emotions does the artist show on the faces of these unemployed?

THE DEPRESSION

After the stock market crash, many people who had bought stocks on margin lost their entire investment. Many also lost their homes and cars because they could not repay their loans. One person describes what it was like after the crash:

> I saw men's hair literally turn white. I saw a woman faint dead away; they carried her out cold. I heard a middle aged doctor say: "There goes my son's college education." Terrible sights. Terrible sounds. Sitting there hour after hour, watching my own "investments" shrink and shrivel, my heart ached for the poor people around me.

literally (LIT-uhr-uhl-ee): true; without exaggerating

When people could not repay their loans, many banks had to close. They did not have enough money to cover their depositors' accounts. By 1932, many stocks were worthless and once-profitable businesses had gone bankrupt. At the same time, average working-class Americans stopped buying everything but the necessities of life. Goods began to pile up in factories and warehouses. Because they had large supplies of goods on hand, many businesses cut back on production. Workers were fired. The unemployed did not have money to buy goods, so production was cut back more. As more people lost their jobs, the depression deepened.

cover (KUHV-uhr): to take care of

Hoover's Policies

President Hoover did not think the depression would last long nor did he believe the federal government should provide for the unemployed. He thought that federal aid would extend federal control and destroy the self-respect of those who accepted the money. Although

Hoover gave no relief to the unemployed, he did approve some aid to homeowners and businesses. The Home Loan Bank Act helped homeowners pay their mortgages. Federal loans were also made available to financially troubled businesses through the Reconstruction Finance Corporation. The Smoot-Hawley (SMOOT HAW-lee) Tariff Act of 1930 was passed to help struggling farmers and manufacturers by raising the tariffs on imported foodstuffs and other goods. Unfortunately, the tariff raised the price of many goods that farmers used. Although they were earning more, they were paying out more.

Life in the Depression

By 1933, more than 12 million people, or about 25 percent of the labor force, were out of work. Others were working only a few hours a week. Many cities set up free soup kitchens and bread lines to keep people from starving. People sold apples and shined shoes to earn a few pennies. Some who could not pay their rent were forced out on the street. They slept on park benches and in alleys. Some families lived in abandoned buildings or in their cars. "Hoovervilles," small groups of cardboard and tin houses, grew up on the outskirts of cities.

ELECTION OF 1932

reassure (ree-uh-SHUR): to give confidence to

A popular slogan of the early depression years was, "Prosperity is just around the corner." The slogan was meant to reassure Americans that a return to good times was near. By the 1932 election, however, many Americans had grown tired of talk. They wanted a president who would lead the nation out of the depression.

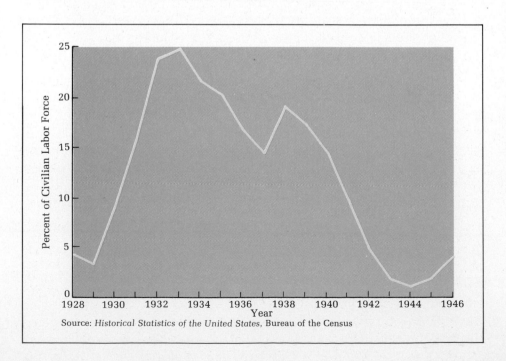

Source: *Historical Statistics of the United States*, Bureau of the Census

Unemployment from 1928 to 1946

BONUS BRIGADE

The Republicans renominated Hoover for President. The Democrats turned to the popular Governor of New York, Franklin D. Roosevelt, as their candidate. During the campaign, Hoover blamed the depression on World War I and the economic problems that grew out of it. Roosevelt said the depression was caused by problems within the U.S. economy itself and that Hoover's policies had made the problems worse. Roosevelt promised to end the depression but was vague about how. In November, Americans elected Roosevelt overwhelmingly.

He became the last President to be inaugurated on March 4. The 20th Amendment changed the presidential inauguration day to January 20.

Congress passed a law in 1924 giving a bonus to veterans of World War I to be paid in 1945. By 1932, many veterans were demanding the bonus be paid immediately. For two months, 15,000 veterans gathered in Washington. Hoover ordered first the police and then the army to break up the marchers' tent city. Two veterans were killed in the fighting that resulted.

LOOKING BACK

1. **a.** What were two reasons for some Democrats' opposition to Alfred Smith as President? **b.** What were the assumptions behind those reasons?
2. What caused the stock market to crash in 1929?
3. Why did many people lose their jobs in the depression?
4. **A.** How did Hoover feel about federal relief for the unemployed? **b.** What three laws were passed by the Hoover Administration to aid victims of the depression?
5. During the 1932 presidential election, what conditions were blamed for causing the depression according to: **a.** Hoover? **b.** Roosevelt?

Chapter 3 **The New Deal**

LOOKING AHEAD

This chapter is about the New Deal—President Roosevelt's program for rebuilding the economy. You will read about New Deal legislation, union activities, and the effect of the New Deal on minorities. After you study this chapter, you will be able to:

- read a table to explain who benefited from New Deal programs.
- explain Roosevelt's reason for wanting to expand the Supreme Court.
- describe the effect of New Deal programs on minorities.
- identify opinions for and against the New Deal.

Social Studies Vocabulary

bureaucracy

People

Franklin D. Roosevelt	Sidney Hillman	Eleanor Roosevelt
Frances Perkins	Mary McLeod	
John L. Lewis	Bethune	

Words and Terms

National Industrial Recovery Act	sit-down strike	Tennessee Valley Authority
National Recovery Administration	Agricultural Adjustment Administration	Social Security Act
Wagner Act	Soil Conservation Service	Indian Reorganization Act
National Labor Relations Board	Dust Bowl	
Congress of Industrial Organizations	Civilian Conservation Corps	
	Works Progress Administration	

Buttons such as this one as well as posters and other kinds of advertising were part of a campaign to make the National Recovery Administration popular.

President Roosevelt's program for economic recovery has come to be known as the New Deal. The term comes from Roosevelt's acceptance speech to the Democratic Convention in 1932. There, the presidential nominee promised "a new deal for the American people."

ROOSEVELT'S FIRST TERM

Roosevelt was an excellent public speaker and his words often stirred the hopes of Americans. In his 1933 inauguration speech, he told

Americans that "the only thing we have to fear is fear itself." But more than bold speeches were needed to turn the economy around. In his first 100 days in office, Roosevelt used all his powers to have 15 emergency bills passed. The first came after only two days in office.

Bank Holiday

After the stock market crashed, some people lost faith in banks, too, and began withdrawing their savings. The banks that had lent so much money they could not cover their depositors' accounts closed. This frightened other depositors who began withdrawing their money, thus forcing more banks to close.

Within two days of his inauguration, Roosevelt ordered all the nation's banks to close for four days. He called a special session of Congress to pass the Emergency Banking Act. This act required that records of all banks be examined and those banks found to be sound could reopen at the end of the bank holiday. In the first of many "fireside chats," President Roosevelt went on radio to tell the American people what was happening. He encouraged them to put their money back into the banks once the banks reopened. His action was successful. Over $1 billion was redeposited within three weeks.

sound: dependable

Industrial Recovery

The National Industrial Recovery Act (NIRA) was an attempt to set up fair competition in industry. This act provided for the National Recovery Administration (NRA). Under the NRA, industry would write its own codes, or laws. These codes would be studied by the NRA and submitted to the President for approval. The codes provided for such things as a minimum wage, a 40-hour work week, and an end to child

MINIMUM WAGE, 1938-81	
1938	$0.25
1945	0.40
1950	0.75
1956	1.00
1961	1.15
1963	1.25
1967	1.40
1968	1.60
1974	2.00
1975	2.10
1976	2.30
1978	2.65
1979	2.90
1980	3.10
1981	3.35

Source: U.S. Fair Labor Standards Act and Amendments

labor in factories. In 1935, the NRA was declared unconstitutional because the NRA had given law-making powers to the President. Congress had had no part in passing the codes. Also, the NRA had given the federal government control over commerce within states, which violated the rights of the states.

NRA was replaced by the Wagner Act. This gave workers the right to form unions and bargain collectively. It also established a National Labor Relations Board to prevent unfair labor practices. Many of the labor reforms came about through the efforts of the Secretary of Labor, Frances Perkins. She was the first woman to be appointed to a Cabinet post.

New Deal laws such as the Wagner Act encouraged industrial workers to organize. As you may recall from the unit Industrialism and the West, the AFL did not organize industrial unions or unskilled workers. In the 1930s, John L. Lewis, president of the AFL-United Mine Workers, and Sidney Hillman, president of the AFL-Amalgamated Clothing Workers formed the Committee for Industrial Organization (CIO), which was changed in 1938 to the Congress of Industrial Organizations.

In 1936, the CIO began to use a new strategy — the sit-down strike. Workers remained in their factories so that employers could not replace them with strikebreakers. In 1939, the Supreme Court declared the sit-down strike illegal. In the meantime, the CIO was growing.

Help for Farmers

While the New Deal was helping factory workers, it was also passing laws to aid farmers. The Agricultural Adjustment Administration

Russell Lee took this photograph of a farm family leaving the Dust Bowl. When the soil became so badly eroded they could no longer farm, many families packed their belongings in cars or trucks and moved to California. There they found jobs as farm laborers. By 1939, more than half the farmers in the Dust Bowl had left.

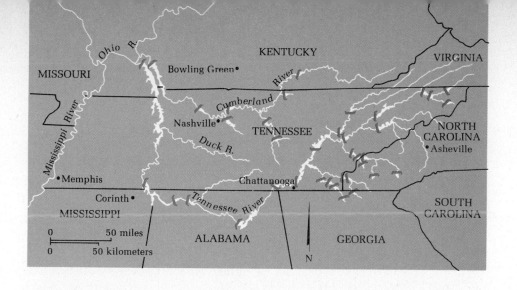

(AAA) paid farmers to cut back on production and destroy surplus livestock. This kept supply down while raising prices and profits. The AAA helped farmers who owned land but hurt tenant farmers and sharecroppers. They depended on producing as much as possible in order to survive.

The AAA was declared unconstitutional in 1936 because it had established a tax as a way to cut back on farm production. A new Agricultural Adjustment Administration act was passed in 1938. It permitted the federal government with a two-thirds approval of all farmers to set crop production quotas as a way to limit production.

Another New Deal agency, the Soil Conservation Service, came to the aid of thousands of farm families in an area that became known as the Dust Bowl. Between 1933 and 1939, parts of Kansas, Colorado, Oklahoma, Texas, and New Mexico suffered a severe drought. Winds sweeping across the dry fields created dust storms that blew away the topsoil. The Soil Conservation Service set up projects to show farmers how to control the winds by planting grass fields and rows of trees. The agency also showed farmers how to use dry farming and small irrigation systems. By 1939, over two million hectares (five million acres) of eroded Dust Bowl was again valuable farmland.

Conservation and Public Works

Among other major relief programs were the Civilian Conservation Corps (CCC) and the Works Progress Administration (WPA). Instead of just handing over checks or food to the needy, these two programs provided jobs. The CCC was open to young men between the ages of 18 and 25. Through the WPA, roads, bridges, schools, dams, and airports were built. Other WPA workers taught crafts, ran day nurseries, and taught naturalization classes for future citizens. The WPA also provided jobs for writers, artists, and musicians.

The Tennessee Valley Authority (TVA) used federal money to build 16 dams on the Tennessee River and its tributaries. By 1940, four of the dams were generating low-cost electricity to Tennessee Valley residents. The TVA also planned flood control and reforestation projects in the area.

The Works Progress Administration employed thousands of people to build roads, bridges, and other needed public projects. Do you think from the photograph that all the people hired by the WPA were used to this kind of work?

609

Social Security

The Roosevelt administration also passed social legislation. In 1935, the Social Security Act took effect. The law set up an old-age pension and provided for unemployment and disability insurance. It also helped care for people who were disabled and children whose parents had died. The money to fund the program was taken out of workers' paychecks. Still, millions of people such as farm workers and house servants, many of whom were black, were not covered by Social Security benefits.

MINORITIES AND THE NEW DEAL

Blacks were badly hurt by the depression. They were often the first to lose their jobs. But they found some help in such New Deal programs as the WPA and the CCC. Roosevelt was opposed to discrimination and included many black advisors and aides in his policymaking programs. Mary McLeod Bethune, for example, was appointed director of the National Youth Administration. Eleanor Roosevelt, the President's wife, worked tirelessly for fair treatment of blacks. However, when New Deal programs were handled at the local level, blacks sometimes received unequal treatment. The first AAA, by cutting back the amount of land that could be farmed, hurt a number of blacks. Many black tenant farmers and field hands lost their means of earning a living. The second AAA corrected some of the problems by making loans available to tenant farmers to buy their own land.

In the 1930s, most Native Americans lived in extreme poverty. Some benefitted from the CCC, NYA, and WPA, but many did not. In 1934, Congress passed the Wheeler-Howard Act to improve conditions and correct some of the problems that had been created by the Dawes Act. The 1934 act, also known as the Indian Reorganization Act, reestablished Native American nations and promoted ways to restore their traditions. Nations were allowed to buy land and were given some self-government and protection for their customs.

ROOSEVELT'S SECOND TERM

As the presidential election of 1936 approached, Republicans knew that trying to defeat Roosevelt would be a struggle. The nation's economy was slowly improving because of the New Deal and Roosevelt was popular with many Americans. However, the Republicans nominated Governor Alfred Landon (LAN-duhn) of Kansas. Their platform attacked Roosevelt's New Deal policies as extravagant and reckless. The Democratic platform promised a continuation of the New Deal, and Roosevelt won the election by a landslide.

Soon after his inauguration, Roosevelt requested authority to appoint additional justices to the Supreme Court. He wanted to increase

Native American Reservations

the number from 9 to 15. This would allow him to appoint justices who supported his New Deal programs. The Supreme Court had found several of Roosevelt's more important programs unconstitutional. Congress denied Roosevelt's request for what came to be called the "court-packing" plan. In the next three years, however, five justices retired and Roosevelt was able to appoint his New Deal court. However, many Americans began to think Roosevelt was power-hungry. His attempt to pack the Supreme Court and the declining economy in 1937 weakened his support.

END OF THE NEW DEAL

No major New Deal laws were passed in the last two years of Roosevelt's second term. Republicans and some Democrats in Congress opposed any more programs. The economy had improved some, and people in 1939 were not as interested in reform as they had been in 1933. Events in other parts of the world were causing them great concern. In September 1939, Europe became involved in what would become World War II. You will read more about this in the unit World War II and Its Aftermath.

ROOSEVELT'S NEW DEAL, 1933-38

Act or Agency	Some Provisions
Emergency Banking Act, 1933	Allowed government inspection of bank records; financially stable banks reopened
Glass-Steagall Banking Act, 1933	Placed limits on use of deposits for speculation; established FDIC
Federal Deposit Insurance Corporation (FDIC), 1933	Insured bank deposits for $2,500 (by 1981, each account insured for $100,000)
Federal Securities Act, 1933	Required firms issuing stocks to give investors full and accurate financial information
National Industrial Recovery Act (NIRA), 1933	Created National Recovery Administration and Public Works Administration
National Recovery Administration (NRA), 1933	Established minimum wage, maximum hours, right to join unions, and child labor laws; allowed firms to set standards of quality and minimum prices; found unconstitutional in 1935
Public Works Administration (PWA), 1933	Provided employment during depression: built public buildings, dams, bridges, schools, parks, sidewalks, and sewers
Civilian Conservation Corps (CCC), 1933	Provided employment during depression: jobs related to conservation
Civil Works Administration (CWA), 1933	Provided employment during depression: built roads, parks, schools, and airports
Agricultural Adjustment Act (AAA), 1933	Limited farm production to raise prices; found unconstitutional in 1936
Farm Credit Administration (FCA), 1933	Provided funds for farm mortgages
Federal Emergency Relief Administration (FERA), 1933	Provided employment during depression: built sewers, parks, schools, playgrounds, and airports
Home Owners Loan Corporation (HOLC), 1933	Provided $3 billion in home mortgage loans to one million people over three years
Tennessee Valley Authority (TVA), 1933	Built series of gates and dams to produce electric power, control floods, and enrich farmlands in Tennessee Valley

ROOSEVELT'S NEW DEAL, 1933-38

Act or Agency	Some Provisions
Securities and Exchange Commission (SEC), 1934	Protected public from investing in unsafe stocks and bonds; regulated stock market practices
Federal Communications Commission (FCC), 1934	Regulated radio, telephone, and telegraph systems
Federal Housing Administration (FHA), 1934	Provided funds for home repairs and construction of new houses
Reciprocal Trade Agreements Act, 1934	Provided new markets for American goods by lowering tariffs for nations that agreed to do the same for U.S.-made goods
Works Progress Administration (WPA), 1935	Provided employment during depression: built highways, dredged rivers, and completed conservation projects; created work for artists, writers, actors, and musicians
National Youth Administration (NYA), 1935	Provided employment for students to help them stay in school
Social Security Act, 1935	Established old-age pensions and aid for the physically disabled and homeless children
National Labor Relations Act (NLRA), 1935	Guaranteed workers right to form unions and bargain collectively; established National Labor Relations Board to correct or prevent unfair labor practices
Soil Conservation and Domestic Allotment Act, 1936	Paid farmers who worked to restore soil and prevent erosion
Rural Electrification Administration, 1936	Provided electricity to farms and homes in rural areas
U.S. Housing Authority (USHA), 1937	Established to develop adequate housing
Agricultural Adjustment Act (AAA), 1938	Permitted Department of Agriculture to set crop production quotas with approval of two thirds of farmers
Food, Drug, and Cosmetic Act, 1938	Required manufacturers to list ingredients of a product on its label
Fair Labor Standards Act, 1938	Established maximum work week of 40 hours; established minimum wage of $0.25 per hour

THE INGENIOUS QUARTERBACK!

Roosevelt wanted to increase the number of Supreme Court justices from 9 to 15. Congress refused to accept his plan, which came to be called "court-packing." Why did Roosevelt want to change the system? What is the cartoonist's point of view?

Opponents of the New Deal felt that many of the programs were wasteful or gave the government too much power. They did not like the idea of the government giving direct aid to the poor. Some charged that the New Deal had created a huge bureaucracy that was wasteful. A **bureaucracy** (byu-RAHK-ruh-see) is the name for the departments or bureaus that manage government. People who favored the New Deal felt that it helped the economy recover from the depression. It lowered unemployment and helped those who were still without jobs. It introduced reform laws such as Social Security that have had lasting effects. Perhaps the most important benefit was the feeling of hope the New Deal gave to people in their time of greatest need.

LOOKING BACK

1. Read the table and list the programs that benefited: **a.** homeowners. **b.** banks. **c.** farmers. **d.** students.
2. **a.** Why did Roosevelt want to expand the size of the Supreme Court? **b.** Why was he not successful?
3. What effect did New Deal programs have on: **a.** blacks? **b.** Native Americans?
4. Compare and contrast opinions on the New Deal.

PRACTICING YOUR SKILLS

What If . . .

The worst year of the depression was 1933. **What if** you had been Roosevelt's advisor? Which of his programs would you have supported? Which programs would you not have supported? What additional programs would you have drawn up?

Building Communication Skills

In your textbook, you have learned about the history of the U.S. by reading and looking at maps, paintings, photographs, and cartoons. Another source of historical information is an interview. An **interview** is a meeting in which one person asks another person questions to obtain information. The information will be based on a person's memory, opinions, and biases. You will not always be hearing facts, but you will be sharing in a first-hand experience. Here are a few tips to help you with an interview.

- Make an appointment at the convenience of the person you are planning to interview.
- Prepare a list of specific questions. For example, do not ask, "What were the 1930s like?" Instead, ask questions such as, "Did any banks in your town close?"
- Do not ask personal questions or press a person to answer a question that makes him or her uncomfortable.
- If you wish to take notes, first ask the person's permission. It is less distracting to listen and then write your notes at the end of the interview.
- Be a good listener. Do not interrupt the person.
- Do not make the interview too long. When it is over, thank the person.

Activity: Interview someone who lived during the depression and get their views of what it was like. Summarize your interview to use as the basis for a class discussion.

Reading, Researching, Writing, Reading a Graph

1. Read a biography of one of the artists, writers, or personalities in Chapter 1. Prepare a book report.
2. The 20th Amendment was also called the "lame duck" Amendment. Using reference materials in the library, research how this amendment got the name "lame duck". Write a paragraph to summarize your research.
3. Use the graph on page 604 and library resources to discover why unemployment dropped in 1937. Why was unemployment so low in 1943? Why did unemployment peak in 1933?

Exploring

Find out if any of the public buildings, parks, and so on, in your city were built under New Deal programs. The cornerstone of the building will have this information on it. Look for murals and mosaics inside schools, libraries, and post offices to see if WPA artists did them. There will usually be a plaque to identify this. Make a map showing how to find each building, road, airport, bridge, and so on.

Reading

Allen, Frederick. *Only Yesterday: An Informal History of the Nineteen-Twenties.* New York: Harper & Row. Paperback. Social history.

Bontemps, Arna, ed. *Harlem Renaissance Remembered.* New York: Dodd, Mead.

East, Dennis. *CIO and the Labor Movement.* New York: Viking, 1977.

Goldston, Robert. *The Road Between Wars: 1918-1941.* New York: Dial Press, 1978. From the Armistice to Pearl Harbor.

Lawson, Don. *FDR's New Deal.* New York: Crowell, 1979.

Ullman, Michael. *Jazz Lives: Portraits in Words & Pictures.* Washington, District of Columbia: New Republic, 1980.

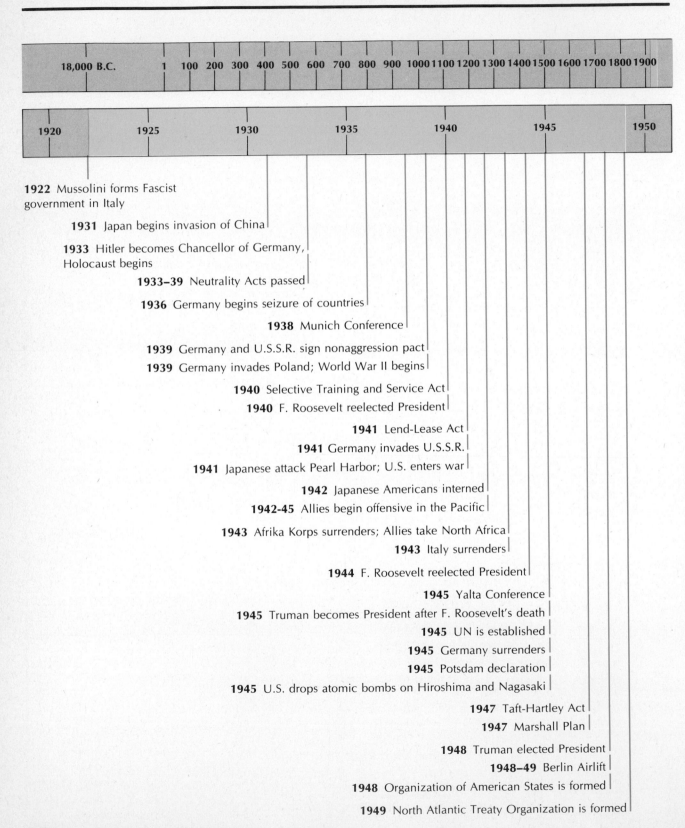

18,000 B.C.   1   100   200   300   400   500   600   700   800   900   1000 1100 1200 1300 1400 1500 1600 1700 1800 1900

1920   1925   1930   1935   1940   1945   1950

1922 Mussolini forms Fascist government in Italy

1931 Japan begins invasion of China

1933 Hitler becomes Chancellor of Germany, Holocaust begins

1933–39 Neutrality Acts passed

1936 Germany begins seizure of countries

1938 Munich Conference

1939 Germany and U.S.S.R. sign nonaggression pact

1939 Germany invades Poland; World War II begins

1940 Selective Training and Service Act

1940 F. Roosevelt reelected President

1941 Lend-Lease Act

1941 Germany invades U.S.S.R.

1941 Japanese attack Pearl Harbor; U.S. enters war

1942 Japanese Americans interned

1942-45 Allies begin offensive in the Pacific

1943 Afrika Korps surrenders; Allies take North Africa

1943 Italy surrenders

1944 F. Roosevelt reelected President

1945 Yalta Conference

1945 Truman becomes President after F. Roosevelt's death

1945 UN is established

1945 Germany surrenders

1945 Potsdam declaration

1945 U.S. drops atomic bombs on Hiroshima and Nagasaki

1947 Taft-Hartley Act

1947 Marshall Plan

1948 Truman elected President

1948–49 Berlin Airlift

1948 Organization of American States is formed

1949 North Atlantic Treaty Organization is formed

Chapter 1

The Coming of War

LOOKING AHEAD

In this chapter, you will read about the growing world tensions of the 1930s that were caused by Japanese, German, and Italian expansion. You will also read about U.S. foreign policy in the 1930s and the events that led to U.S. involvement in World War II. After you study this chapter, you will be able to:

- describe Japanese and Italian expansion in the 1930s.
- read a map to see how the division of land after World War I led to German expansion.
- list the events that led to German seizure of countries.
- identify the reasons Americans wanted to stay out of war.
- list the sequence of events that led to the Battle of Britain.
- identify the main points of the Atlantic Charter.
- explain why the U.S. entered the war.

Social Studies Vocabulary

mobilization	demilitarize	isolationism
totalitarian state	appeasement	

People

Adolf Hitler	Fascist party	Wendell Willkie
Nazi party	Neville Chamberlain	Winston Churchill
Benito Mussolini	Edouard Daladier	Hideki Tojo

Places

Manchuria	Rhineland	Pearl Harbor
Ethiopia	Sudetenland	

Events

Munich Conference	Buenos Aires Convention	Battle of Britain

Words and Terms

concentration camp	Neutrality Acts	Luftwaffe
Axis nations	Good Neighbor policy	Selective Training and Service Act
Siegfried Line	blitzkrieg	Lend-Lease Act
Maginot Line	Tripartite Pact	Atlantic Charter

During the 1930s, as conflicts developed overseas, many Americans feared the U.S. would be drawn into war. Some believed the U.S. should remain neutral as this poster shows.

The depression that you read about in the unit Between the Wars did not end with the New Deal. Roosevelt's programs improved the U.S. economy, but total recovery did not come until 1941. The U.S.

economy gained strength as the U.S. began arming for war. The events that led to U.S. mobilization took place in Europe and Asia. **Mobilization** (moh-buhl-uh-ZAY-shuhn) is bringing troops and equipment into active military service.

MORE TERRITORY AND MORE POWER

Many Americans believed that World War I was "the war to end all wars." But in little more than 20 years, the U.S. was again involved in a world conflict. As you may recall from the unit Reform and Expansion, one cause of World War I was competition for power and colonies. This same greed also led to World War II.

Japan on the March

In 1931, Japan seized a part of northern China known as Manchuria (man-CHOOR-ee-uh). The League of Nations condemned the attack. Japan replied by withdrawing from the League. A year later, the Japanese took the port of Shanghai (shang-HY). By the end of 1938, Japan controlled most of China's major ports and industrial and rail centers.

Rise of Hitler

In Europe, events were also taking place in Germany that were leading to war. In the early 1930s, Germany was caught in the worldwide depression. By 1932, one third of the German labor force was unemployed. Adolf Hitler promised Germans a better life under his Na-

Nazi persecution of Jews led to scenes like this, in which whole families were taken from their homes at gunpoint and sent to concentration camps. How did Hitler use propaganda in this campaign of terror?

tional Socialist German Workers party, known as the Nazi (NAH-tsee) party. In 1933 Hitler became Chancellor, or chief minister of Germany. Within a short time, he ended the German republic and set up a totalitarian state under his Nazi party. A **totalitarian state** (toh-tal-uh-TAIR-ee-uhn) is one in which every part of life—economic, religious, social, and educational—is controlled by the government. To ensure Nazi control of Germany, Hitler had his political enemies killed or placed in concentration camps. Hitler claimed that labor union members, Communists, democrats, and Jews had lost World War I for Germany. This became an excuse for removing these people from Germany. His persecution was aimed especially at Jews.

Italian Expansion

Meanwhile, Italy, under the leadership of dictator Benito Mussolini (moos-soh-LEE-nee), was also gaining strength. After World War I ended, Italy suffered serious economic problems. There were strikes and riots. Some people feared that Communists would take over in Italy as they had in Russia, which became the Union of Soviet Socialist Republics (U.S.S.R.). In 1919, Mussolini formed the Fascist (FASH-ist) party to lead Italy out of the chaos of the war. The Fascists believed in an all-powerful central government. They took control of Italy in 1922 and did much to restore order to Italy's economy. By 1935, Italy was strong enough to invade and take control of Ethiopia (ee-thee-OH-pee-uh), in Africa. In the same year, Germany and Italy signed an alliance and became known as the Axis (AK-sis) nations.

chaos (KAY-ahs): great confusion; complete disorder

GERMANY ON THE MOVE

Soon after coming to power, Hitler began rearming Germany. This was in violation of the Treaty of Versailles. Hitler increased the size of the German armed forces and stockpiled weapons. In 1936, German soldiers occupied the Rhineland (RYN-land), a region of western Germany that had been demilitarized after World War I. To **demilitarize** (dee-MIL-uh-tuh-ryz) is to prohibit an area from being used for military purposes. Hitler began to build a defense line of concrete and steel known as the Siegfried (SEEG-freed) Line. It faced the similar Maginot (MAZH-ih-noh) Line built by France after World War I to protect its border with Germany.

stockpile (STAHK-pyl): to store up in advance

In 1938, Hitler annexed Austria. The Austrians offered little resistance. Many Austrians viewed themselves as German because of the common language and culture. Hitler then turned his attention to a region of Czechoslovakia known as Sudetenland (soo-DAY-tuhn-land) where many German-speaking people lived. He used nationalism as a an excuse to take over the area.

In order to prevent another Austria, British and French representatives met with German and Italian leaders in Munich (MYOO-nik), Germany, in 1938 to discuss Czechoslovakia's future. British Prime

Nazi flags hang from buildings in Berlin as Hitler (in the car, left) inspects his personal guard. Most Nazi actions, including this parade, were meant as propaganda to show that the Nazi war machine was superior to the rest of the world and could not be beaten.

Minister Neville Chamberlain (CHAYM-ber-lin) and French Premier Edouard Daladier (dah-lah-DYAY) tried a policy of appeasement. **Appeasement** (uh-PEEZ-muhnt) is giving in to an enemy's demands to prevent war. Hitler could have the Sudetenland if he would leave the rest of Czechoslovakia alone. The Czechs, who had been given no voice in the Munich Conference, were forced to agree. The following March, Hitler broke the agreement and took all of Czechoslovakia.

U.S. REACTION

aggression
(uh-GRESH-uhn):
policy of attacking
other nations

Americans watched the aggression of Japan, Italy, and Germany with concern. As you may recall from the unit Between the Wars, the U.S. in the 1930s was in the worst economic depression in its history. The country was not prepared to go to war, and most people were determined that the nation remain neutral. Some Americans, known as isolationists, claimed that a war in Europe or Asia did not necessarily mean that the security of the U.S. was threatened. **Isolationism** (eye-suh-LAY-shuhn-iz-uhm) is the belief that a nation should not involve itself in foreign affairs.

In an attempt to keep the U.S. out of war, Congress passed Neutrality Acts in 1933, 1936, and 1937. The first act called for an embargo on the sale or shipment of arms, ammunition, and other war supplies to belligerent nations. In 1936, the act was amended to forbid loans as well. The 1937 act forbade civilian travel on ships of belligerent nations. It also required nations at war to pay cash for nonmilitary goods bought in the U.S. and to transport them in their own ships.

belligerent
(buh-LIJ-uhr-uhnt):
involved in war

In late 1939, Roosevelt urged Congress to repeal the arms embargo. After several weeks of debate, Congress agreed and passed the Neutrality Act of 1939. Great Britain and France could buy weapons if they paid for them in cash and transported them in their own ships.

While matters in the rest of the world worsened, Roosevelt worked at strengthening the ties between the U.S. and Latin America through the Good Neighbor policy. He recognized that U.S. security was tied to the security of these nations. At the Buenos Aires (BWAY-nohs EYE-rays) Convention in 1936, the nations of the Western Hemisphere promised to consult one another if the peace of their part of the world was threatened by an outside nation.

THE FALL OF EUROPE

In August 1939, Germany and the U.S.S.R. signed a nonaggression pact. They agreed not to wage war against each other. On September 1, Hitler's armies invaded Poland. They met determined resistance, but German tanks rolled over the nation. Honoring a pledge to aid Poland, France and Great Britain declared war against Germany on September 3. Fourteen days later, the U.S.S.R. sent soldiers into Poland and divided the country with Germany.

In 1940, the Soviets also took Finland, Latvia (LAT-vee-uh), Lithuania (lith-u-AY-nee-uh), and Estonia (es-TOH-nee-uh), after heroic resistance. In spring, Hitler's armies attacked and defeated Norway, Denmark, Belgium, the Netherlands, and Luxembourg. German troops advanced so quickly that it was called a blitzkrieg (BLITS-kreeg) or lightning war. The Germans penetrated the Maginot Line and France surrendered in June 1940. Within a few months, Hitler had taken all of continental western Europe except Sweden and Switzerland. They remained neutral throughout the war. In September, 1940, Italy, Germany, and Japan signed the Tripartite (try-PAHR-tyt) Pact, forming the Rome-Berlin-Tokyo Axis.

With the fall of France, the Battle of Britain began. Germany's air force, the Luftwaffe (LOOFT-vahf-uh), launched an all-out bombing attack on Great Britain. The U.S. watched the events of 1940 with growing alarm. Stockpiles of weapons were built up. The Selective Training and Service Act, the first peacetime draft in U.S. history, was passed in September. All men between 21 and 35 were ordered to register. War clouds hung over the presidential election. Republican candidate Wendell Willkie attacked Roosevelt's domestic policies, but most Americans were more concerned with foreign affairs. Although Willkie won 45 percent of the popular vote, Roosevelt was reelected. He became the first President to serve a third term.

In Great Britain, the new Prime Minister, Winston Churchill, turned to the U.S. for help. He asked for destroyers, arms, and aircraft. Roosevelt transferred 50 U.S. destroyers to Great Britain in exchange for several naval bases on British possessions. The U.S. gave further aid to Britain through the Lend-Lease Act. According to the act, the President could lend or lease such articles as destroyers to countries whose defense was vital to U.S. security. In June 1941, the Germans invaded the U.S.S.R. The Soviets and British entered into an alliance and the U.S. extended its lend-lease policy to the U.S.S.R.

In August 1941, Roosevelt and Churchill met for a series of talks. The result was the Atlantic Charter, an eight-point declaration of the

September 1, 1939: World War II begins with the Nazi invasion of Poland. Before its end, Europe, North America, Asia, parts of Africa, the islands of the Pacific, and Australia would be involved.

Across the nation, lines of draftees crowded draft board offices as the U.S. began to mobilize for war. These draftees are in Chinatown.

aims of the war. The charter stated that no nation could keep any territory that was gained during the war. It also guaranteed the right of all nations to form their own governments after the war.

U.S. ENTERS THE WAR

In 1940, the U.S. had ended its trade treaty with Japan to show disapproval of Japanese aggression. The U.S. had also put an embargo on the shipment of scrap metal and gasoline to Japan. By late 1941, tension between the two nations had increased. Roosevelt appealed to Japanese Premier Hideki Tojo (toh-joh) to restore peace in Asia. On December 7, 1941, Japanese planes attacked the U.S. naval base at Pearl Harbor, Hawaii. Much of the U.S. Pacific fleet was destroyed. The next day the U.S. and Great Britain declared war on Japan. The following week, Germany and Italy declared war on the U.S. The U.S. had entered World War II.

LOOKING BACK

1. In what regions did the following expand in the 1930s: **a.** Japan? **b.** Italy?
2. Study the map on page 586. What areas that had belonged to Germany before 1918 did the Germans retake by 1940?
3. Beginning with 1936, list the sequence of German seizures of European nations.
4. **a.** Why did U.S. isolationists want to stay out of war? **b.** What were the terms of the Neutrality Acts passed by Congress during the 1930s?
5. List the sequence of events in Europe during 1939 and 1940 that led to the Battle of Britain.
6. **a.** What was the purpose of the Atlantic Charter? **b.** How did the U.S. react to Japanese expansion in 1940 and 1941?
7. Why did the U.S. finally enter World War II?

Chapter 2   The Home Front

LOOKING AHEAD

This chapter describes how the nation mobilized people and supplies for war production and about the sacrifices Americans made for the war effort. You will also read about discrimination against minorities during the war. The chapter also identifies the issues in the presidential election of 1944. After you study this chapter, you will be able to:

- explain how the U.S. handled the draft during the war.
- describe the effects of wartime industry on Americans.
- identify the problems minorities faced during the war.
- compare the issues in the 1944 presidential election with those of the 1940 election.

Social Studies Vocabulary

integration	consumer goods	minority group

People

Nisei	A. Philip Randolph	Thomas Dewey

Words and Terms

draftees	internment camp
War Production Board	Japanese American Claims Act
Office of Price Administration	Fair Employment Practices Commission
rationing	

On December 8, 1941, the U.S. was at war, and Americans were faced with the huge job of preparing for combat. Before the war was over, most Americans were involved in the war effort—either on the home front or on the battlefield. As they entered the war, Americans were filled with uncertainty. President Roosevelt recognized this and called for a national day of prayer on New Year's Day 1942.

MOBILIZATION

As the war began, the government was faced with the job of calling up all those who had registered for the draft under the Selective Training and Service Act. Over 6,000 draft boards were established to sign up draftees. The boards were staffed by more than 200,000 people, most of whom were volunteer workers.

By 1945, about 12.5 million people had served in uniform. Over one million of these were black. All branches of the armed forces enlisted blacks. However, as in earlier wars, blacks served in segregated units. Some black units had black officers, and the number of black officers increased during the war. Black leaders and the black press called for equal treatment of blacks by integrating units. **Integration** (in-tuh-GRAY-shuhn) means to unify different groups into one group. However, it was not until 1945 that any government action was taken. In that year, some units in Germany were integrated. But it was not until Truman issued an executive order in 1948 forbidding discrimination that any real progress was made.

About 25,000 Native Americans served in World War II. A group of Navajo worked in a special communications unit. They used the Navajo language to broadcast secret messages. In this way, they confused the enemy who were never able to break their supposed code. About 300,000 Mexican Americans also served.

Over 200,000 women enlisted during World War II. Many of the jobs they did released men for combat. Women worked as nurses, drivers, clerks, cooks, and mechanics. The Army, Navy, Coast Guard, and Marines had branches for women. Women pilots ferried new planes to military units in war zones.

As in World War I, women took men's places at work. This woman is welding part of the USS *George Washington Carver* that was launched in1943. The 1,000 women who worked on the ship were just a small percentage of the six million women who worked in war industries.

War Production

During the years between the wars, when the armed forces were small, the nation had no trouble producing enough military supplies. To aid the Allies in 1940 and 1941, production was stepped up some. But when the U.S. entered World War II, war production had to increase dramatically. To accomplish this, the President created the War Production Board in January 1942. It supervised the production of war goods and divided raw materials between military and civilian needs. Many civilian industries were switched to war production. Plants that had made vacuum cleaners in 1941 were making machine guns in 1942. Production was stopped on all nonessential items, such as toasters, that used materials needed for the war effort.

Because of the increase in jobs, many Americans moved from the farms and small towns of the Midwest and South to the industrial centers of the Northeast. Shipyards and aircraft factories attracted large numbers of people to California, Texas, and Washington. As in World War I, women took men's places in the labor force. More than six million women were employed in war industries in 1942. Over 12 percent of shipyard and 40 percent of aircraft workers were women.

Price Controls and Rationing

Unemployment almost disappeared during the war. Because more people were working, they had more money to spend. But there were fewer things to buy. The great demand for scarce **consumer goods**—goods bought by people for their own use—made prices rise drastically. To control inflation, the government created the Office of Price Administration (OPA) in 1941. This agency tried to keep the cost of living from rising too high or too quickly.

In March 1942, the OPA announced the first wartime rationing. Rationing (RASH-uhn-ing) is a means of limiting the amount and distribution of goods. The government began rationing because the war created shortages of certain items—sugar, coffee, tea, meat, butter, and canned foods, among other goods. A rubber shortage led to the rationing of tires. Nationwide gas rationing began in May 1942. By January 1943, all nonessential, or pleasure driving, was banned.

Most people learned to manage with the shortages. Some people raised their own food in victory gardens and canned or preserved food they grew. Scrap drives were held, and Americans were asked to give newspapers and items of rubber or metal that could be recycled for the war effort. People patched tires with artificial rubber and wore cardboard in their worn-out shoes.

CIVIL RIGHTS

Abuses of civil rights occurred against various minority groups during the war. A **minority group** is a group that differs from the general population in some way. As you have just read, many people migrated to cities in search of jobs in war-related industries. The cities were not prepared for such large numbers of new residents—white and minorities. All groups faced difficulties in locating housing and jobs and, generally, adjusting to lives in a new environment. Minorities, however, had the worst problems and met the most discrimination, especially in being hired. Sometimes blacks applying for jobs were ignored or, once hired, were not considered for promotions. In 1941, A. Philip Randolph, president of the Brotherhood of Sleeping Car Porters, planned a peaceful march on Washington, D.C., to protest unfair hiring practices. The march was called off when President Roosevelt issued an executive order forbidding any racial discrimination in defense industries. This order resulted in the creation of the Fair Employment Practices Commission.

As you may recall from the unit The U.S. in World War I, German Americans were treated badly by other Americans during World War I. Although the U.S. was at war with Germany and Italy, people of German and Italian descent were not widely mistreated during World War II. This was not true for Japanese Americans, however.

In early 1942, over 100,000 Japanese Americans were removed from their homes in California and moved to internment camps in Utah, Wyoming, Arizona, and Colorado. They were moved away from the coast and away from strategic areas—powerlines, airfields, defense plants. More than 70,000 of these people were Nisei (nee-say)—Japanese Americans born in the U.S. The Japanese Americans were

These schoolchildren from San Juan Bautista, California, were part of the nationwide drive to save scrap metal during World War II. Why would the government encourage such a campaign?

Left: A sign in the window of a drugstore owned by Japanese Americans tells its own story of personal loss caused by internment. Right: Soldiers stand guard as a group of Japanese Americans, carrying only a few personal belongings, boards a bus for an internment camp.

forcibly removed because the government thought they were a threat to the security of the U.S. In 1948, Congress passed the Japanese American Claims Act. This provided repayment for some property losses. However, it did not repair the humiliation felt by thousands of Japanese Americans nor did it help them regain their jobs.

ELECTION OF 1944

The nation may have been at war, but this did not stop the process of electing a President. Because of wartime prosperity, many people had forgotten how bad the depression had been. This helped the Republicans who nominated Governor Thomas Dewey of New York. They campaigned against the tired, old administration. Their hopes were fueled by discontent over wartime shortages and rationing. President Roosevelt campaigned on the idea that it was wrong to change leaders during wartime. Americans seemed to believe this, and Roosevelt was elected to a fourth term as President.

LOOKING BACK

1. How did the U.S. handle the draft during the war?
2. **a.** What changes occurred in industry because of the war? **b.** How did war industries affect the migration of Americans within the U.S.? **c.** How were women affected by the changes in U.S. industry? **d.** Why was rationing introduced?
3. **a.** Why were Japanese Americans placed in camps during World War II? **b.** What problems did some U.S. cities face during the war? **c.** What were some problems that blacks faced on the home front?
4. Compare the issues of the 1940 and 1944 presidential elections. Why do you think the issues were so different?

Chapter 3

The Battlefront

LOOKING AHEAD

In this chapter, you will read about the fighting in Europe, North Africa, and the Pacific that led to the defeat of the Axis powers. You will also read about Allied plans for war and peace, the establishment of the United Nations, and the start of the cold war. After you study this chapter, you will be able to:

- list the sequence of events that led to Allied victory in Europe.
- describe Allied strategy for the war in the Pacific.
- identify the results of the Yalta and Potsdam conferences.
- read a strategy map to determine the Allies' objectives for D-Day.
- describe the structure of the UN.
- describe the causes of the cold war.

Social Studies Vocabulary

anti-Semitism   satellite   cold war

People

Erwin Rommel   George Patton   Josef Stalin
Bernard Montgomery   Douglas MacArthur   Chiang Kai-shek
Dwight D. Eisenhower   Chester Nimitz
Walter Model   Harry S Truman

Places

Suez Canal   the Philippines   Iwo Jima
El Alamein   Coral Sea   Okinawa
North Africa   Midway Island   Hiroshima
Sicily   Guadalcanal   Nagasaki
Normandy   Leyte Gulf

Events

D-Day   Dumbarton Oaks   Potsdam
Battle of the Bulge   conference   conference
Yalta conference

Words and Terms

Allies   Operation Overlord   leapfrogging
Afrika Korps   Holocaust   United Nations

World War II was fought on two major fronts—Europe/North Africa and the Pacific. Allied military strategy was to end the war in Europe and North Africa first. The Allies—all the countries who joined to fight the Axis—believed that if the Soviet Union surrendered and the

D-Day, June 6, 1944

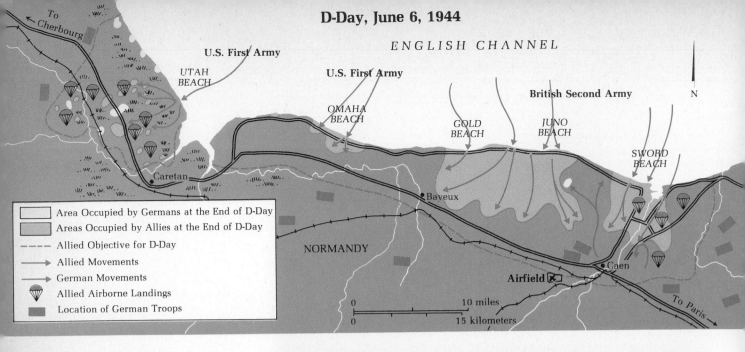

ENGLISH CHANNEL

To Cherbourg

U.S. First Army

UTAH BEACH

U.S. First Army

OMAHA BEACH

British Second Army

GOLD BEACH

JUNO BEACH

SWORD BEACH

N

Caretan

Bayeux

NORMANDY

Airfield

Caen

To Paris

Area Occupied by Germans at the End of D-Day
Areas Occupied by Allies at the End of D-Day
Allied Objective for D-Day
Allied Movements
German Movements
Allied Airborne Landings
Location of German Troops

0   10 miles
0   15 kilometers

628

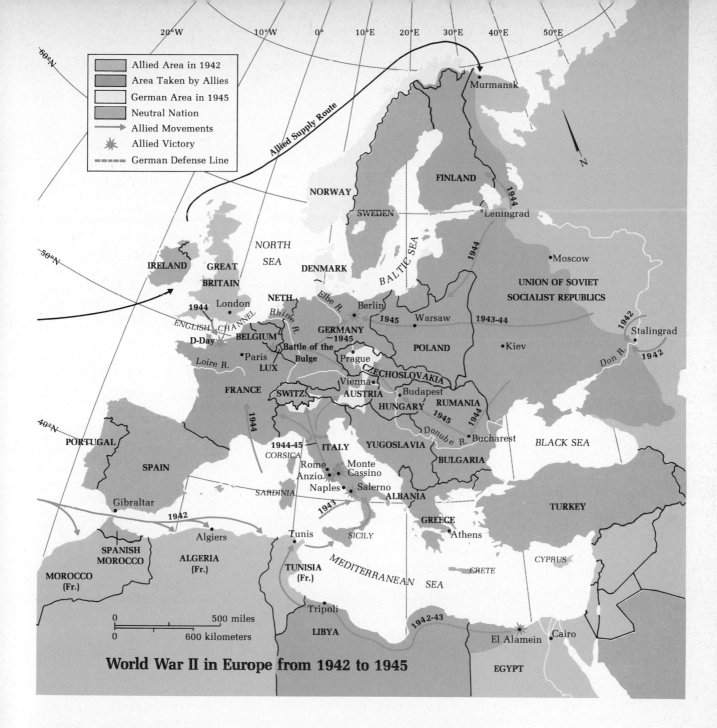

Map Legend

- Allied Area in 1942
- Area Taken by Allies
- German Area in 1945
- Neutral Nation
- → Allied Movements
- ✳ Allied Victory
- - - - German Defense Line

World War II in Europe from 1942 to 1945

Map labels: Murmansk, FINLAND, NORWAY, SWEDEN, Leningrad, BALTIC SEA, Moscow, UNION OF SOVIET SOCIALIST REPUBLICS, IRELAND, GREAT BRITAIN, NORTH SEA, DENMARK, NETH., Elbe R., Berlin, Warsaw, 1943–44, Stalingrad, 1942, 1944, London, Rhine R., GERMANY –1945, 1945, Kiev, Don R., ENGLISH CHANNEL, BELGIUM, Battle of the Bulge, Prague, D-Day, 1944, LUX., Paris, Loire R., CZECHOSLOVAKIA, Vienna, AUSTRIA, Budapest, HUNGARY, RUMANIA, 1945, 1944, FRANCE, SWITZ., YUGOSLAVIA, Danube R., Bucharest, BLACK SEA, PORTUGAL, 1944, 1944–45, ITALY, CORSICA, Rome, Monte Cassino, Anzio, BULGARIA, TURKEY, SPAIN, Naples, Salerno, ALBANIA, 1943, GREECE, Gibraltar, 1942, SARDINIA, SICILY, Athens, CYPRUS, SPANISH MOROCCO, Algiers, Tunis, MEDITERRANEAN SEA, CRETE, ALGERIA (Fr.), TUNISIA (Fr.), MOROCCO (Fr.), Tripoli, 1942–43, El Alamein, Cairo, LIBYA, EGYPT, Allied Supply Route

Scale: 0 — 500 miles; 0 — 600 kilometers

Opposite, top left: During the war, women operated heavy equipment, worked in aircraft and weapons factories, and unloaded ships. Some pilots ferried planes to war zones.

Opposite, top right: A field artillery unit sets up a new position. Compare and contrast the uniforms and equipment with the pictures of World War I. How do you account for the changes that occurred in less than thirty years?

Opposite, bottom: On D-Day, over 150,000 Allied troops landed on the Normandy coast. Many died, but the invasion was successful. According to the map, what obstacles other than German forces did these soldiers have to overcome?

Suez (soo-EZ) Canal was lost to the Axis, Great Britain might also fall. Throughout 1941, the Germans were slowly advancing into Soviet territory. In 1941, Hitler also sent his Afrika Korps under General Erwin Rommel (RAHM-uhl) to aid the Italians in driving the British from North Africa.

FIGHTING IN EUROPE AND NORTH AFRICA

In July 1942, the British stopped German advances toward the Suez Canal at El Alamein (el ahl-uh-MAYN), Egypt. By October, British forces under General Sir Bernard Montgomery were moving west across North Africa. In November, an Allied invasion of Algeria and Morocco (muh-RAHK-oh) led by U.S. General Dwight D. Eisenhower (EYE-zuhn-how-er) caught the Germans by surprise. By May 1943, the Afrika Korps was forced to surrender.

offensive (uh-FEN-siv): military attack

The Soviets were able to halt German advances inside the USSR by winter 1941-42. The Soviets then began an offensive and moved steadily westward. In July 1943, Allied soldiers landed in Sicily (SIS-uh-lee), and Mussolini fled. On September 8, a new Italian government surrendered to the Allies, but the Germans continued to occupy the country. In September 1943, the Allies began a drive to conquer Italy. They landed on the southern beaches and slowly fought their way northward through Italy. Fighting in Italy was at a standstill around Rome by 1945.

On June 6, 1944, known as D-Day, Allied forces began their major offensive in Europe—Operation Overlord. Led by Eisenhower, the Allies landed more than two million troops on the beaches of Normandy, in northwestern France. German forces fought bitterly but were gradually forced to retreat. In August 1944, Paris was liberated. In September, the first U.S. troops entered Germany. In December, the Germans under Field Marshall Walter Model (MOH-duhl) made a brief offensive in northern France, known as the Battle of the Bulge. By January 1945, the offensive had been crushed by troops commanded by U.S. General George Patton. At the same time, the Soviets continued to advance into Germany from the east. On April 25, U.S. and Soviet soldiers met at the Elbe (EL-buh) River, 112 kilometers (70 miles) south of Berlin. On April 30, Hitler committed suicide in Berlin. German leaders surrendered on May 7, 1945, ending the war.

The Holocaust

liberate (LIB-uh-rayt): to set free

Toward the end of World War II, the world learned the extent of Hitler's anti-Semitism. **Anti-Semitism** (an-tee-SEM-uh-tiz-uhm) is hostility and discrimination against Jews. When the Allies liberated Nazi concentration camps in such places as Auschwitz (OWSH-vits), Dachau (DAHK-ow), Buchenwald (BOO-kuhn-vahlt), and Bergen-Belsen (BAIR-guhn BEL-zuhn), they found unburied corpses, gas chambers, and crematories. From skeleton-like prisoners they learned that in many camps, the inmates worked as slaves on construction

WORLD WAR II: ADVANTAGES AND DISADVANTAGES OF EACH SIDE

	Advantages		Disadvantages	
	Allies	**Axis**	**Allies**	**Axis**
Military	Had large quantity of troops, ships, weapons, and other supplies Developed and used atomic bomb on Japan	Had large quantity of troops, ships, weapons, and other supplies Developed and used rockets for attacks on Great Britain	Had to transport U.S. troops and supplies across two oceans	Germany, the major Axis power, fighting a war on two of its borders
Economic	U.S. and British industry and farming able to supply Allied troops with food and supplies	Germany and Japan able to supply Axis troops with food and supplies by themselves or with the aid of occupied nations		
Political	Had strong governments with popular support	Had strong governments with popular support until last years of war	France, a major ally, defeated early in war	Italy switched from Axis to Allies later in war
Population	War supported by most citizens in all nations	War supported by most citizens in all nations		

projects. The disabled and sick were killed. Many people starved to death. Jews were put to death because they were Jewish. In some camps, medical experiments often ended in painful deaths for the victims. The total number of people who died in the Holocaust (HAHL-uh-cawst), as this period is called, may never be known. It is estimated, however, that as many as six million Jews died.

FIGHTING IN THE PACIFIC

Soon after attacking Pearl Harbor, the Japanese occupied Guam and Wake Island. Early in 1942, Burma and the Philippines fell to Japan.

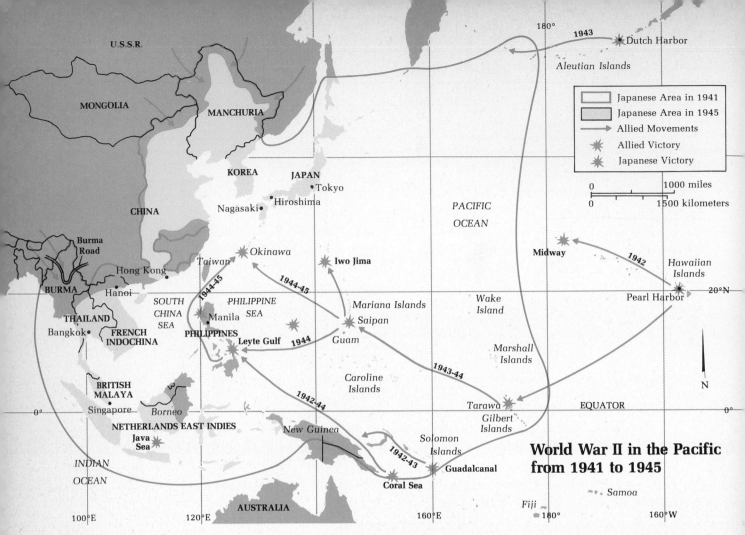

World War II in the Pacific
from 1941 to 1945

Japanese Area in 1941
Japanese Area in 1945
Allied Movements
Allied Victory
Japanese Victory

Above: Cartoonist Bill Mauldin viewed a soldier's hard lot with a sense of humor.

Right: Marines raise the flag on Iwo Jima, February 23, 1945.

Bombers return from a raid on Japanese positions. Why were aircraft important to the war in the Pacific?

Right: People pick their way through the ruins of Nagasaki after the atomic bomb was dropped.

Below: Why was the strategy of "leapfrogging" from island to island successful? After fierce naval battles, such as this one off Santa Cruz, Allied forces captured the Philippines in fall, 1944. Why were the Philippines an important goal?

After these quick victories, the Japanese expected the Allies to ask for peace. Instead, they fought back.

In May 1942, a Japanese fleet headed for New Guinea (GIN-ee) was intercepted by a U.S. fleet in the Coral Sea. The U.S. had broken the Japanese military code and so knew of Japanese plans in advance. In a four-day battle, fought only by aircraft, the Japanese were forced to turn back. The following month, a three-day battle near Midway Island marked the turning point of the Pacific war. Japan lost four aircraft carriers and many of its planes. Japan's conquest of the Pacific had ended, and the Allied offensive had begun.

To conquer Japan, the Allies developed a two-pronged strategy. Ground forces, under the command of U.S. General Douglas MacArthur, would drive from New Guinea to the Philippines. Instead of taking every island along the way, MacArthur's forces would "leapfrog" islands — attacking key islands and going around others. Naval forces, under the command of Admiral Chester Nimitz (NIM-its), would cut through the Central Pacific toward Japan.

In August 1942, a series of land and sea battles began near Guadalcanal (gwahd-uhl-kuh-NAHL) in the Solomon Islands. By February 1943, Guadalcanal, the first stepping-stone to Japan, had been taken. In fall 1943, the navy began its Central Pacific drive. By summer 1944, the navy had bases in the Gilbert, Marshall, and Mariana (MAIR-ee-ah-nuh) Islands.

Meanwhile, MacArthur's forces were leapfrogging toward the Philippines. In October 1944, one of the most important battles of the Pacific war was fought at Leyte (LAY-tee) Gulf, and the Japanese suffered an overwhelming defeat. In spring 1945, Iwo Jima (ee-woh jee-mah) and Okinawa (oh-kee-nah-wah) fell to the Allies. By this time, Allied planes based in the Marianas were bombing Japanese cities. The Japanese, however, refused to admit defeat.

Military experts predicted that another year of fighting would be needed to conquer Japan. To avoid this, the U.S. made a fateful decision. Vice-President Harry S Truman had become President in April 1945 upon the death of Roosevelt. To end the war, Truman ordered the atomic bomb used.

On August 6, 1945, an air force plane dropped an atomic bomb on the Japanese city of Hiroshima (hee-roh-SHEE-muh). About 75,000 people were killed and another 100,00 were injured. The city was leveled. When the Japanese government still refused to surrender, a second atomic bomb was dropped on Nagasaki (nah-gah-sah-kee). On August 15, Japan surrendered and World War II was over.

PLANNING FOR WAR AND PEACE

During World War II, Allied leaders had met several times to discuss war strategy and ways to keep peace after the war. The most important and perhaps the most controversial wartime conference was held at Yalta (YAWL-tuh) in the U.S.S.R. in February 1945.

intercept
(in-tuhr-SEPT):
to catch; to stop

controversial
(kahn-truh-VER-shuhl):
open to argument

634

At Yalta, President Roosevelt, Prime Minister Churchill, and Soviet leader Josef Stalin met. Roosevelt and Churchill wanted the Soviets to enter the war against Japan and to support a postwar international organization. As a result, Stalin was able to get the two to agree to several of his demands. He insisted that Polish Communists control Poland's government until free elections could be held. Since Soviet troops were already in Poland, little could be gained by refusing Stalin's demand. The U.S.S.R. was also granted control of Outer Mongolia (mahn-GOHL-yuh) and other Chinese lands. Chiang Kai-shek (jeeahng ky-shek), the leader of China, was forced by the U.S. and Great Britain to agree to Stalin's terms. In return, Stalin agreed to enter the war against Japan. The Soviet leader also agreed to hold free elections after the war in those eastern and central European nations occupied by Soviet troops.

Shortly after the Yalta conference, the war in Europe ended and the friendship among the Allies began to weaken. Stalin was actively encouraging the development of Communist governments in central and eastern Europe.

Allied leaders — left to right, Winston Churchill, Franklin D. Roosevelt, and Josef Stalin — hold a meeting at Yalta. They discussed issues related to the war in the Pacific and peace in Europe. What were some agreements they reached? Were all the agreements kept?

Results of the War

As they had agreed at the Potsdam (POHTS-dahm) Conference in Potsdam, Germany, the Allies divided Germany into four zones in 1945. The U.S.S.R. controlled the eastern zone. The western zones were divided among France, Great Britain, and the U.S. Berlin fell within the Soviet zone and was divided into four sectors. Germany gave up land to Poland, Belgium, and Czechoslovakia. Germany was disarmed and industrial equipment that was not essential to rebuilding the German economy was sent to the U.S.S.R.

Europe After World War II

Before the country could be reunited, the Allies had to agree on the kind of government Germany should have. The Soviets wanted a Communist government, an idea the other Allies opposed. Since they could not agree, the Allies continued to occupy separate zones.

Japan, too, was occupied by Allied forces. They remained there until 1952. The Allies required Japan to give up all its former possessions. The Japanese were allowed to rearm only for defense. In addition, the U.S.S.R. and the U.S. set up occupation zones in Korea (koh-REE-uh), a former Japanese territory.

The United Nations

One of the outcomes of the wartime conferences was the United Nations (UN). The UN had its beginnings in June 1941 when the nations fighting the Axis powers agreed to work together to establish a world free of aggression. Six months later, 26 nations enlarged that agreement. The term *United Nations* was used for the first time.

In August 1944, at the Dumbarton (DUHM-bahr-tuhn) Oaks conference outside Washington D.C., the general structure of the UN was agreed on. It would be similar to the League of Nations in that there would be a General Assembly made up of representatives of all member nations. There would also be a Security Council. It would be made up of the strongest nations who had a special responsibility to maintain world peace.

The final stage of UN planning came in April 1945, when 50 nations attended a conference in San Francisco. On June 25, the nations unanimously approved the charter for the UN. The charter called for the creation of six major groups. In addition to the General Assembly and Security Council, there would be the Secretariat (sek-ruh-TAIR-ee-it), the Economic and Social Council, the International Court of Justice, and the Trusteeship Council. The charter also created a number of special agencies such as the World Health Organization.

THE COLD WAR BEGINS

In the late 1940s, all the nations along the USSR's western border fell to communism. With the help of Soviet occupation troops, Poland, Czechoslovakia, Hungary, Bulgaria, Rumania, and Yugoslavia set up Communist governments. The free elections promised by Stalin were never held. These eastern European nations became Soviet satellites. A **satellite** (SAT-uh-lyt) is a country that follows a more powerful nation in matters of policy.

U.S. leaders became concerned over this expansion of Soviet influence. They viewed Soviet actions as an attempt to spread communism throughout Europe. The **cold war** is the name used to describe the conflict in the years after World War II between the non-Communist nations led by the U.S. and the Communist nations led by the U.S.S.R. The weapons were political, psychological, and economic rather than military. The U.S.S.R. exploded its first atomic bomb in 1949, and both the U.S. and the Soviet Union recognized that any military conflict could mean the destruction of both nations. As a result, they developed ways of avoiding armed conflict while still pursuing their goals.

pursue (puhr-SYOO): to try to get; to seek

LOOKING BACK

1. **a.** Why did the Allies plan to defeat Germany first? **b.** List the events in Europe that led to the defeat of Italy and Germany.
2. **a.** Describe the importance of the battles of the Coral Sea and Midway Island in the Pacific. **b.** Describe the Allies two-pronged strategy to defeat Japan. **c.** Why did President Truman decide to use the atomic bomb against Japan?
3. **a.** What were the two purposes behind Allied wartime conferences? **b.** What were the results of the Yalta conference? **c.** What were the results of the Potsdam conference?
4. **a.** What were the Allies' objectives for D-Day? **b.** What disadvantages did they overcome?
5. List the parts of the UN.
6. **a.** Why were the Allies divided over the question of Germany after World War II? **b.** What happened to the governments of eastern European nations after the war? **c.** How did the U.S. view Soviet actions in eastern Europe? **d.** What weapons were used to fight the cold war?

Chapter 4

After the War

LOOKING AHEAD

This chapter describes the problems facing the U.S. after World War II. You will read about how the nation demobilized and reconverted from a wartime to a peacetime economy. You will also read about U.S. domestic and foreign policy under President Truman. After you study this chapter, you will be able to:

- identify U.S. labor problems after World War II.
- explain the problems blacks faced after the war.
- identify ways in which the U.S. worked to prevent Communist expansion after the war.

Social Studies Vocabulary

closed shop	bloc	containment
ghetto	foreign aid	

People

George Meany	Strom Thurmond	Chiang Kai-shek
Walter Reuther	Thomas Dewey	Mao Tse-tung
Dixiecrat party	George C. Marshall	

Places

Greece	China	German Democratic
Turkey	Federal Republic	Republic
Berlin	of Germany	Taiwan

Events

Berlin Airlift

Words and Terms

G.I. Bill of Rights	Marshall Plan
demobilization	Nationalist Chinese
baby boom	Organization of American States
Taft-Hartley Act	Point Four Program
AFL-CIO	North Atlantic Treaty Organization
National Housing Act	

domestic (duh-MES-tik): of one's own country

The U.S. faced domestic and foreign challenges after World War II. The return to peacetime meant that many Americans had to change the way they had been living and working for the previous four years. Industry switched from wartime production to the making of consumer goods. In foreign affairs, the U.S. did not turn to isolationism as it had after World War I. The nation assumed a role as a world leader.

DEMOBILIZATION AND RECONVERSION

Even before the war ended, the U.S. made plans to help returning veterans. Congress passed the Servicemen's Readjustment Act, or G.I. Bill of Rights. The bill provided for new veterans hospitals and for physical and mental rehabilitation programs for veterans. It also set up a placement agency to help veterans find jobs and provided unemployment compensation to those who could not find work. The bill provided for low-interest housing, business loans, and up to four years of education.

The U.S. also began the **demobilization** (dee-moh-buhl-eye-ZAY-shuhn)—returning to peacetime activity—and reconversion of industry. Factories went from turning out airplanes to making cars again. A major problem that the country faced was how to absorb into the labor force the 12.5 million men and women returning to civilian life. Six million women had taken jobs in defense industries during the war. After the war, many needed or wanted to continue working outside the home. However, they often lost their jobs to returning veterans. Soon after the war in Asia ended, 800,000 people, mostly women, were unemployed in the aircraft industry alone. As families were reunited, there was a baby boom. Many women continued to work, however, and by 1950, 28 percent of the labor force was women.

Labor Problems

As industry returned to the production of consumer goods, people began to spend the money they had saved during the war. There was a great demand for automobiles, refrigerators, vacuum cleaners, and other household goods. The demand was greater than the supply, and prices began to rise. As prices rose, workers demanded higher wages. When management did not meet their demands, workers in various industries went on strike.

In 1945 and 1946, more than one million workers went out on strike in the steel and automobile industries. In 1946, the United Mine Workers struck coal mines but returned to work after President Truman put the mines under government control. In May 1946, Truman warned that striking rail workers would be drafted, and the government would take over the railroads if the strike did not end.

In 1947, Congress passed the Taft-Hartley Act. It gave the President the power to prevent strikes, such as railroad strikes, that threatened the nation's health and safety. The act also forbade **closed shops**—those that required workers to join whatever union had organized a particular company. Most labor leaders opposed the Taft-Hartley Act because of the restrictions it placed on unions.

Civil Rights

Blacks made some gains in the late 1940s and early 1950s. Job opportunities for blacks increased in the fast-growing automobile, elec-

In 1955, under a banner stating the unity and equality of all workers, Walter Reuther (right) of the CIO and George Meany (left) of the AFL symbolically join hands and form the AFL-CIO. Meany was elected president of the new organization, which recognized craft as well as industrial workers.

639

A smiling President Truman holds up a newspaper with headlines announcing the election of Dewey. The error occurred because opinion polls stopped sampling voters early and missed a shift in their views.

tronics, and chemical industries. The number of black teachers, college professors, lawyers, medical doctors, and business owners also increased. As they had during the war, however, blacks faced discrimination in hiring, promotion, and wage practices.

Blacks were also discriminated against in housing and education. Because whites often would not sell houses or rent apartments to blacks, blacks were forced to live in segregated communities. Often these were in the oldest, most rundown sections of cities and towns. Large black ghettoes grew in Boston's Roxbury section, Harlem in New York City, and Watts in Los Angeles. A **ghetto** (GET-oh) is a section of a city in which only one ethnic group lives. Because of where the people lived, the schools in these areas were usually all black. Blacks often felt that their schools received less money and attention than schools with white students.

To improve their situation, blacks began to organize in order to vote as a **bloc**—a group supporting the same political issues. They hoped that the use of their political strength would gain them the support of white politicians. Blacks also found white allies in the civil rights struggle. Political leaders, such as Hubert Humphrey, and labor leaders, such as Walter Reuther (ROO-thuhr) of the United Automobile Workers, believed that whites should work to end discrimination. President Truman set up government committees to investigate discrimination in labor practices and higher education.

TRUMAN'S ELECTION

Because President Truman was a strong supporter of civil rights, the Democrats were divided over nominating him for President in 1948. Southern Democrats, who did not agree with the President, formed the States' Rights or Dixiecrat party. They selected Strom Thurmond, the Governor of South Carolina. The Republicans renominated Thomas Dewey, the Governor of New York. Many Americans believed that Dewey would beat Truman. The President was blamed for rising inflation and for allowing the Soviets to dominate eastern Europe. Truman won, however. He had gained the support of organized labor, blacks, and farmers. He had vetoed the Taft-Hartley Act and supported civil rights and programs to aid farmers.

In 1949, Truman succeeded in getting Congress to increase Social Security benefits. The minimum wage was increased to $0.75 an hour. Congress passed the National Housing Act in the same year. This act provided money to build 800,000 housing units. It also helped low-income families to pay their rent. The 22nd Amendment became law during Truman's presidency. It stated that no person could be elected to the presidency more than twice. Anyone who had completed more than two years of another President's term could be elected to only one his or her own.

FOREIGN POLICY

To prevent additional Soviet expansion, President Truman proposed to help Western Europe recover from the war. He called for $400 million in foreign aid for Greece and Turkey. **Foreign aid** is help in the form of money, goods, advisors, or services that one nation gives to another. In asking Congress for this aid in 1947, Truman outlined the policy of **containment** (kuhn-TAYN-muhnt). This means the keeping of another nation within its existing boundaries. It became America's foreign policy throughout the cold war.

Marshall Plan

Truman's Secretary of State George C. Marshall proposed the European Recovery Plan. Through the plan, also known as the Marshall Plan, the U.S. gave money, supplies, and technical advice to Western European nations to help their economic recovery. The Marshall Plan resulted in the growth of industrial production and an increase in the standard of living for Western Europeans. This greatly reduced the threat of Communist takeovers in Western Europe.

Berlin and China

The U.S., France, and Great Britain united their sectors in 1948. Angered by this move, Stalin tried to force the Allies into giving up Berlin. He had all ground and water routes into the city blockaded beginning in June 1948. The Allies responded with the Berlin Airlift which continued until May 1949 when Stalin ended his blockade. In September, the Allies united their zones of Germany and set up the Federal Republic of Germany, usually referred to as West Germany. The Soviet Union established the German Democratic Republican, or East Germany, a month later.

China also presented a problem to President Truman. During World War II, the Nationalist Chinese government of Chiang Kai-shek fought alongside the Chinese Communists against the Japanese. After the

Residents of the bombed city of Berlin watch the arrival of a transport. The airlift brought food, clothing, fuel, and other supplies to the blockaded city for almost a year. What was the reason for the blockade?

war, a civil war broke out between the two groups. The U.S. supported the Nationalists. However, the Communist Chinese, led by Mao Tse-Tung (MOW dzuh-dung), defeated the Nationalist in 1949. Chiang and his supporters fled to Taiwan and set up a Nationalist Chinese government there. In 1950, President Truman announced that the U.S. would not recognize or trade with Communist China.

OAS AND NATO

The U.S. helped to form the Organization of American States (OAS) in 1948. The 25 member nations agreed that an act of aggression against one nation in the Americas would be an act of aggression against all nations. President Truman issued his Point Four Program. It provided scientific and technical assistance to African, Asian, and Latin American countries. The plan worked to improve health care, farming methods, and transportation systems. In July 1949, the U.S. became one of the founding nations of the North Atlantic Treaty Organization (NATO). Its purpose was to settle disputes and establish a system of military defense in the North Atlantic regions.

LOOKING BACK

1. **a.** How did the U.S. labor force change after World War II?
   b. What problems did labor face?
2. **a.** What problems did blacks face after the war? **b.** What method did blacks use to work for their civil rights?
3. **a.** How did the U.S. work to prevent Communist takeovers in Greece and Turkey? **b.** What was the purpose of the Marshall Plan? **c.** How did the U.S. react to the Soviet blockade of Berlin? **d.** How did the U.S. react to the Communist takeover in China? **e.** Why was the OAS formed? **f.** What was the purpose of NATO?

PRACTICING YOUR SKILLS

What If . . .

In Chapter 1 of this unit, you read about the nonaggression pact signed by Germany and the U.S.S.R. **What if** Germany had kept its promise not to invade the U.S.S.R.? How would fighting a war only on its one front have affected Germany's war effort?

Researching, Drawing a Map, Writing, Reading

1. Prepare an illustrated report on one of the campaigns or battles of World War II. Use maps to show the fighting. Add pictures, drawings, or models to show the kinds of weapons used.
2. Read a biography of one of the people in this unit and write a book report.
3. Select a European city that was damaged during the war. Find pictures for a bulletin board display to compare the postwar city to the present-day city.
4. In the music section of the library, locate some of the songs that were popular during World War II. Write a two-page report on what the songs were about.
5. Using reference books in the library, choose one of the UN agencies and describe its functions in a two-page report.

Exploring

Interview someone who remembers what World War II was like on the home front. Ask what he or she recalls about shortages, rationing, air raid drills and so on. Write a report to share with the class.

Building Communication Skills

A **public opinion poll** is a survey to find out attitudes, beliefs, or opinions of a large number of people. A small group of people, called the sample, is questioned about a certain topic. If members of this group have been selected carefully, their opinions will accurately reflect those of a much larger group, or population, even an entire nation. Here are some tips to help you conduct a successful poll:

- Define your goals. What do you want to find out?
- Select a representative sample. Make sure you select a wide variety of people. Otherwise, the results of your poll will reflect only the opinions of your sample and not a larger group.
- Design a questionnaire. Ask only questions that concern your goals. Make the questions short and easy to answer.
- Interview your sample.
- Analyze your results. Look for generalizations. What are the results?

1. Using 10 percent of the people in your class as a sample, follow the above tips and conduct a poll on a national issue. **2.** Test the reliability of your poll by surveying the entire class. If you get the same results you received from the poll, then your survey was reliable. If you do not get the same results, try to discover why your poll was inaccurate.

Reading

Barry, James P. *Berlin Olympics, Nineteen Thirty-Six: Black American Athletes Counter Nazi Propaganda.* New York: Watts, 1975.

Deighton, Len. *Blitzkrieg: From the Rise of Hitler to the Fall of Dunkirk.* New York: Knopf, 1980.

Foreman, James. *Code Name Valkyrie.* New York: Dell, 1975. Paperback. Count von Stauffenberg and the plot to kill Hitler.

Ganin, Zvi. *Truman, American Jewry, and Israel 1945-1948.* New York: Holmes and Meier, 1979.

Jackson, Robert. *Fighter!* New York: St. Martin's, 1980. Air combat, 1936-1945.

Uchida, Yoshiko. *Journey Home.* New York: Atheneum, 1978. Fiction. Paperback. Japanese American family after release from internment.

UNIT III WAR, PEACE, AND CIVIL RIGHTS

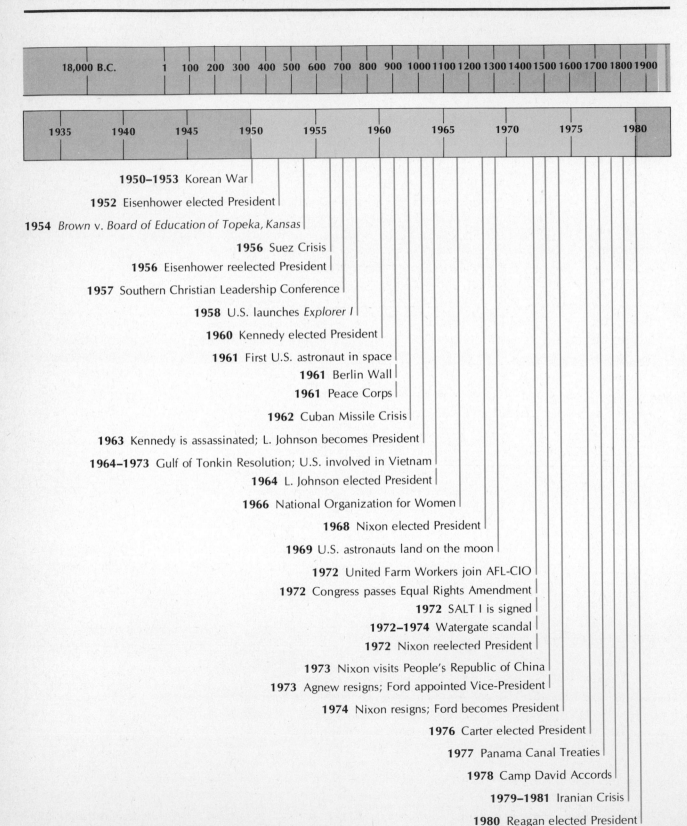

| 18,000 B.C. | 1 | 100 | 200 | 300 | 400 | 500 | 600 | 700 | 800 | 900 | 1000 | 1100 | 1200 | 1300 | 1400 | 1500 | 1600 | 1700 | 1800 | 1900 |

| 1935 | 1940 | 1945 | 1950 | 1955 | 1960 | 1965 | 1970 | 1975 | 1980 |

1950–1953 Korean War

1952 Eisenhower elected President

1954 *Brown v. Board of Education of Topeka, Kansas*

1956 Suez Crisis

1956 Eisenhower reelected President

1957 Southern Christian Leadership Conference

1958 U.S. launches *Explorer I*

1960 Kennedy elected President

1961 First U.S. astronaut in space

1961 Berlin Wall

1961 Peace Corps

1962 Cuban Missile Crisis

1963 Kennedy is assassinated; L. Johnson becomes President

1964–1973 Gulf of Tonkin Resolution; U.S. involved in Vietnam

1964 L. Johnson elected President

1966 National Organization for Women

1968 Nixon elected President

1969 U.S. astronauts land on the moon

1972 United Farm Workers join AFL-CIO

1972 Congress passes Equal Rights Amendment

1972 SALT I is signed

1972–1974 Watergate scandal

1972 Nixon reelected President

1973 Nixon visits People's Republic of China

1973 Agnew resigns; Ford appointed Vice-President

1974 Nixon resigns; Ford becomes President

1976 Carter elected President

1977 Panama Canal Treaties

1978 Camp David Accords

1979–1981 Iranian Crisis

1980 Reagan elected President

Chapter 1   The Eisenhower Years

LOOKING AHEAD

This chapter is about the U.S. during the 1950s. You will read about the Korean War, foreign and domestic affairs under President Eisenhower, and changes in American life. After you study this chapter, you will be able to:

- state the cause of the Korean War and its outcome.
- describe U.S.-Soviet relations during the 1950s.
- explain some of the causes of tension in the Middle East in the 1950s.
- summarize the domestic achievements of Eisenhower.
- explain the 1954 Supreme Court decision involving desegregation.
- explain the growth of suburbs and its effect on cities.
- ★ read a graph to identify a trend in the automobile industry.

Social Studies Vocabulary

arms race	censure	nonviolence
peaceful coexistence	*de jure* segregation	trend
truce	*de facto* segregation	

People

Dwight D. Eisenhower	Nikita Khrushchev	Martin Luther
Adlai E. Stevenson	Rosa Parks	King, Jr.

Places

Palestine	Little Rock, Arkansas
Israel	Montgomery, Alabama

Events

Korean War	Geneva Conference	Suez Crisis

Words and Terms

Eisenhower Doctrine
Department of Health, Education, and Welfare
Federal Highway Act
Soil Bank Bill
Sputnik I
Explorer I
National Aeronautics and Space Administration

National Defense Education Act
McCarthyism
Brown v. Board of Education of Topeka, Kansas
Southern Christian Leadership Conference
tract houses

I LIKE IKE

Campaign buttons and other souvenirs are as much a part of U.S. politics as the two-party system. This button supporting Dwight D. Eisenhower is from 1952.

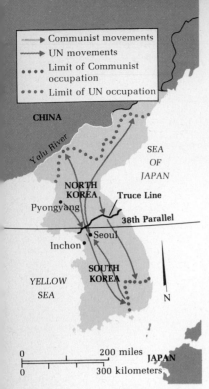

Legend:
→ Communist movements
→ UN movements
•••• Limit of Communist occupation
•••• Limit of UN occupation

CHINA
Yalu River
SEA OF JAPAN
NORTH KOREA
Truce Line
Pyongyang
38th Parallel
Seoul
Inchon
YELLOW SEA
SOUTH KOREA
N
JAPAN

0   200 miles
0   300 kilometers

Korean War

The cold war of the 1940s continued into the 1950s. President Truman had pledged to keep communism from spreading. In 1950, his determination was tested as the Chinese Communists and North Koreans used force in an effort to take over South Korea. Many Americans, however, were more interested in their own lives than in the events in Korea. Technology was making life easier and giving people more leisure time.

KOREA

Korea was divided into two parts at the end of World War II. In 1948, U.S. forces were withdrawn from South Korea after elections were held. That same year, the Soviets put a Communist government into power in North Korea and withdrew their forces. In June 1950, North Korean soldiers crossed the 38th parallel—the dividing line between North and South Korea—and invaded South Korea. The North Koreans were receiving supplies from the U.S.S.R.

The UN voted to send soldiers to aid South Korea. Although 16 nations sent soldiers, 90 percent of the UN force was American. By September, the North Koreans had advanced through South Korea until they formed a circle around Pusan (poo-sahn). On September 15, UN troops landed at Inchon (in-chahn) on the western coast of Korea and began an invasion of North Korea. On November 26, the Chinese joined the North Koreans and drove the UN troops south. The fighting shifted back and forth until summer 1951. By then, the fighting had centered around the 38th parallel. In July 1951, peace talks began while the war continued.

ELECTION OF 1952

Halfway around the world, Americans turned to the business of electing a President. The Republicans nominated General Dwight D. Eisenhower, commander of the Allied troops in Europe in World War II. In selecting Eisenhower, the Republicans were continuing a long tradition of nominating military heroes for the presidency. In his campaign, Eisenhower criticized Truman's handling of the Korean War. Eisenhower also said he would cut taxes and end the excessive spending of the Truman administration. The Democrats nominated Governor Adlai E. Stevenson of Illinois. Their platform promised to continue the programs of Roosevelt and Truman. Eisenhower defeated Stevenson in November 1952—and again in the 1956 election.

FOREIGN AFFAIRS

The Koreans signed an armistice on July 27, 1953, and the Communist takeover of South Korea was halted. The country remained divided at the 38th parallel. Because of tensions in the area, U.S. troops were permanently based in South Korea.

646

The Arms Race

The buildup of arms by both the U.S. and the U.S.S.R. was an area of concern for Americans in the 1950s. The two nations were increasing their stockpiles of rockets and guided missiles. In 1952, the U.S. exploded its first hydrogen bomb. A hydrogen bomb is more destructive than an atomic bomb. A year later the Soviets, too, had developed a hydrogen bomb.

In July 1955, Eisenhower and Soviet leader Nikita Khrushchev (kroosh-CHAWF) met in Geneva, Switzerland, to discuss a reduction in the arms race. An **arms race** is the competition among countries to develop more and better weapons. Eisenhower proposed that the U.S. and the U.S.S.R. allow aerial inspection of each other's missile bases. Khrushchev refused. The Geneva conference did not solve any problems, but it did bring about **peaceful coexistence**—living together without conflict—between the two nations.

aerial (AIR-ee-uhl): in the air

Middle East Tensions

There were conflicts in other parts of the world, however, that involved the two countries. One area of tension was in the Middle East.

During World War I, Great Britain and France had agreed that after the war Great Britain would control the area of Palestine (PAL-uhs-tyn). The British declared their support for a Jewish homeland in Palestine. During the 1920s and 1930s, Jews from all over the world began migrating there. Many were fleeing Hitler's persecutions. Arabs in Palestine saw the Jewish immigrants as economic and social

This cartoon from the 1950s expresses one point of view about the arms race. What would be another viewpoint?

threats. The Arabs feared they would be outnumbered by the immigrants and turned to violence against the Jews.

After World War II, the British asked the UN to consider the future of Palestine. In 1947, the UN recommended that Palestine be divided into three areas of government: Jewish, Arab, and the city of Jerusalem. The Arabs refused. In 1948, the state of Israel was declared. The day after independence, soldiers from the Arab states of Egypt, Iraq, Lebanon, Syria, and Transjordan (now Jordan) attacked Israel. After a year of fighting, the UN arranged a **truce**—a temporary stop in fighting. The Arab nations, however, refused to recognize Israel. To them, the land belonged to Arabs. Over 700,000 Arabs fled Israel to neighboring nations. These Palestinian refugees became a source of tension between Israel and its Arab neighbors.

Raids between Israel and Egypt continued in the early 1950s. Another war broke out in 1956. In the summer of that year, Egypt seized control of the Suez Canal from Great Britain and France. In October, Israeli troops invaded Egypt and, two days later, British and French troops joined the invasion. In the UN Security Council, the U.S. voted with the U.S.S.R. to order the three nations to withdraw from Egypt. The UN sent in a peace-keeping force. However, the Suez Crisis left the alliance of Great Britain, France, and the U.S. badly shaken.

With trouble in the Middle East, the Soviets began increasing their aid to Communists in the area. To keep their efforts from working, President Eisenhower announced the Eisenhower Doctrine in January 1957. Under this doctrine, Congress appropriated $200 million in economic and military aid to help Middle Eastern nations fight communism. The U.S. sent troops into Lebanon in 1958 to help keep in power a government friendly to the U.S.

DOMESTIC AFFAIRS

During his presidency, Eisenhower increased and expanded Social Security benefits to an additional ten million people, raised the minimum wage to $1.00 an hour, and established the Department of Health, Education, and Welfare. Eisenhower also signed the Federal Highway Act, calling for the construction of a national highway system. To solve the problem of farm surpluses, the Soil Bank Bill was passed in 1956. Farmers were paid to take land out of production and, thereby, reduce surpluses.

Besides competing in an arms race, the U.S. and the U.S.S.R. each tried to be the first in space. In 1957, the Soviets launched their satellite *Sputnik I*. Three months later, in January 1958, the U.S. launched its own satellite *Explorer I*. That same year the National Aeronautics and Space Administration (NASA) was established to guide the development of the U.S. space program. As a result of the lead the Soviets had taken in space technology, Americans began to reevaluate U.S. education. In 1958, the National Defense Education Act was passed to provide financial aid for students.

recognize: to admit the existence or independence of

reevaluate (ree-ih-VAL-yoo-ayt): to rethink importance of

648

Joseph McCarthy, Senator from Wisconsin, bangs the witness table while making a point during the Army-McCarthy hearings. What does the term *McCarthyism* mean?

McCarthyism

One of the most controversial events of the 1950s involved Senator Joseph McCarthy of Wisconsin. He took advantage of the anti-Communist mood of the country to build a large public following. He charged that Communists and Communist sympathizers were working at all levels of the federal government. He hoped that publicity from his charges would help his reelection in 1952. Because of his popularity, many Senators and Representatives would not accuse him of lying or demand to see the proof of his charges.

sympathizer (SIM-puh-thyz-uhr): one who shares a belief or feeling

When McCarthy accused the U.S. Army of having Communists in its ranks, the Senate held the Army-McCarthy hearings. During the televised hearings in 1954, McCarthy's charges were found to be unsupported by fact. The Senate later censured McCarthy for his tactics. **Censure** (SEN-shuhr) means to criticize someone for incorrect behavior. The Senate censure caused McCarthy to lose most of his support. The term *McCarthyism* has come to be used to describe any public attack on a person's loyalty that is based on unproven charges.

Civil Rights

As you may recall from the unit Industrialism and the West, the Supreme Court approved separate but equal facilities for blacks and whites in 1896. In 1954, in *Brown* v. *Board of Education of Topeka, Kansas,* the Supreme Court reversed this decision. Linda Brown traveled a mile to and from her black school each day, yet there was a white school a few blocks from her home. The Court declared that separate was not equal. It ordered the desegregation of public schools "with all deliberate speed."

But desegregation did not come easily. Many schools had *de jure* (dee-JOOR-ee) **segregation**—segregation by law. Outside the South, especially in cities of the North and West, there was *de facto* (dee-FAC-toh) **segregation** — separation that resulted not from law but from circumstances. For example, because blacks were forced to live in the same neighborhoods, they created all-black enrollments in schools. De facto segregation would remain unchanged until court-ordered busing in the 1970s.

In areas where there was *de jure* segregation, public schools were immediately affected by the *Brown* decision. Many school districts obeyed the Court ruling, but others refused. In Little Rock, Arkansas, a federal court ordered a high school to admit nine black students in September 1957. The Governor of Arkansas ordered the National Guard to surround the school to keep the students out. The federal court ordered the Governor to remove the guards and he did so. After the black students were admitted, rioting broke out. President Eisenhower sent army troops to restore order.

Besides education, blacks worked to end segregation in other areas. Rosa Parks was arrested in December 1955 in Montgomery, Alabama, when she refused to give her seat in a bus to a white passenger. The seats in the back of the buses were for blacks, but there was no empty seat for Parks. The Reverend Martin Luther King, Jr., organized a boycott of the Montgomery bus system after Parks's arrest. Because most of the bus riders were black, the boycott was successful. After 80 days, the system was almost bankrupt, and the owners agreed to integrate the buses. In 1957, Dr. King and others formed the Southern Christian Leadership Conference (SCLC) to encourage blacks to end discrimination through **nonviolence.** This is a plan of action that uses peaceful means, such as boycotts, to achieve a goal.

CHANGES IN AMERICAN LIFE

Many changes occurred in the lives of Americans during the 1950s. The U.S. led the world in the production of goods and services. New labor-saving devices such as automatic washers, dryers, and dishwashers made housework easier. In the 1950s, more women were working outside the home than at any time except for the war years.

During the 1950s, the population rose by 28 million. Two factors contributed to this. First was the baby boom. Second, people were living longer because of better health care. The greatest population growth occurred in the West. The Southeast and Southwest also saw increases, especially with the migration of large numbers of retired people. The movement of people away from farms that had begun before World War II continued through the 1950s. In 1940, 33 percent of Americans held farm-related jobs. By 1960, the figure had dropped to 7 percent.

Helping the movement of people was the automobile. Car ownership doubled between 1940 and 1960. Americans did not hesitate to pack up and move — across the country, if necessary — to find better jobs or a good life after retirement.

The automobile also contributed to the growth of suburbs. After World War II, there was a severe housing shortage. Developers bought large areas of land called tracts and put up inexpensive homes. Veterans literally stood in line to buy these houses with G.I. loans. Because of the distance from the city, families began buying two cars—one for the husband to drive to work and another for the wife's use.

As millions of Americans moved to the suburbs, the cities suffered. The people who were left behind were often low-income families who could not afford better housing. As a result, the taxes that cities collected and used for such services as police and fire protection decreased. With the decrease in revenues, cities had to find other sources of income. City wage and sales taxes, higher transportation costs, and increases in property taxes were passed.

For blacks it was different. Even those who could afford better housing were kept out of suburbs and limited to certain areas in most urban areas. Blacks usually gained housing opportunities through federally-funded housing projects. Such projects were usually segregated and helped develop racial imbalance in urban areas.

Because of the population explosion after World War II, more children entered school in the 1950s than at any time in U.S. history, and more children stayed in school. Elementary school enrollments rose from 19.4 million in 1950 to 34.3 million in 1960. The postwar baby boom did not affect high school enrollments until the 1960s. Because more jobs and better-paying jobs required a high school diploma, education became important as a means of getting a job.

Tract houses such as these in Levittown, New York, sprang up quickly after World War II. The houses in a development were very similar and developments often had their own schools and shopping center. Why was there a growing need for housing after the war?

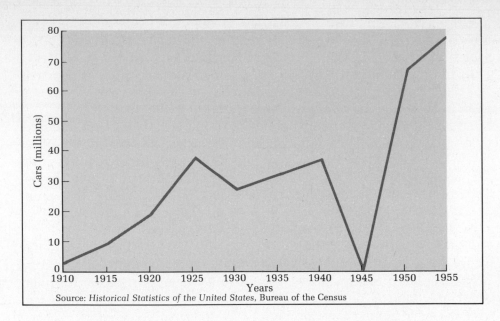

Passenger Car Sales between 1910 and 1955

Source: *Historical Statistics of the United States,* Bureau of the Census

BUILDING GRAPH SKILLS

In earlier units, you read graphs just for the information on them. But you can also read a graph to find a trend. A **trend** is the general way something is going. The figures in a graph show a trend by going up, down, or remaining the same. By studying trends representing the past and present, you can sometimes predict what future figures will be. This graph shows factory sales of cars from 1910 to 1950. **1.** Are the figures on the graph increasing, decreasing, or staying the same? **2.** Why do you think there was a decrease in sales in 1945? **3.** Judging by the trend of the graph, would the figure for 1960 be higher, lower, or the same as the 1950 figure? **4.** What factors would influence this trend?

LOOKING BACK

1. **a.** How did the division of Korea after World War II lead to the Korean War?   **b.** What was the outcome of the Korean War?
2. **a.** Why was the 1955 meeting in Geneva important?   **b.** With what nation did the U.S. side in the Suez Crisis?
3. **a.** List the sequence of events that led to the creation of Israel.   **b.** Why did Arabs refuse to recognize the state of Israel?
4. List four achievements of Eisenhower's domestic policy.
5. Describe the Supreme Court case *Brown* v. *Board of Education of Topeka, Kansas* and its results.
6. **a.** What two factors led to the growth of suburbs?   **b.** Why did cities suffer as suburbs grew?
7. **a.** How does a graph indicate a trend?   **b.** Can you always predict the future of a trend?   **c.** What factors influenced automobile production in 1945?   **d.** What factors influenced it in 1960?   **e.** Full-sized automobiles were big sellers in 1960. Why were their sales down by the 1980s?

Chapter 2   Kennedy-Johnson Era

LOOKING AHEAD

This chapter is about the administrations of Presidents Kennedy and Johnson. You will read about their programs for improving life in America, their foreign policies, and the continuing struggle of minorities for equal rights. The chapter also describes the growing involvement of the U.S. in Vietnam. After you study this chapter, you will be able to:

- describe Kennedy's plans for a U.S. space program.
- describe various methods minorities used in the 1960s to gain their civil rights.
- state the purpose of the Alliance for Progress.
- list the chronology that led to the Berlin Crisis and its end.
- describe U.S.-Cuba relations.
- list the major programs of the Great Society.
- list the sequence of events leading up to and covering U.S. involvement in Vietnam.

Social Studies Vocabulary

civil disobedience   urban renewal
developing nation   guerrilla warfare

People

John F. Kennedy   Malcolm X   Lyndon B. Johnson
Richard Nixon   Cesar Chavez   Barry Goldwater
Alan Shepard   Nikita Khrushchev   Robert Weaver
Martin Luther King, Jr. Fidel Castro   Thurgood Marshall

Events

Bay of Pigs invasion   Cuban Missile Crisis   Vietnam War

Words and Terms

New Frontier   23rd Amendment
Congress of Racial Equality   Medicaid
Student Nonviolent   Medicare
   Coordinating Committee   Food Stamps Act
Black Panthers   Voting Rights Act
Black Muslims   Department of Housing and
Chicano   Urban Development
Peace Corps   Department of Transportation
Alliance for Progress   Volunteers in Service to
Civil Rights Act   America
Economic Opportunity Act   Gulf of Tonkin Resolution
Great Society

Thousands marched to the Washington Monument in August 1963 to protest the lack of civil rights for blacks. Millions more watched the demonstration on television. Among the speakers was Martin Luther King, Jr., who made his "I Have a Dream" speech. What was his dream?

turbulent
(TER-byuh-luhnt):
violent;
greatly disturbed

image (IM-ij):
the impression
given of oneself

The 1960s were a turbulent decade. A President was assassinated. Americans were again fighting a war. Antiwar protests, riots, and demands by minorities for their civil rights filled newspaper headlines and television newscasts. The decade began by showing the important effect that television could have on history.

KENNEDY AND THE NEW FRONTIER

Since 1952, television had become increasingly important in presidential elections. National conventions were televised, and candidates paid huge sums of money for television advertisements. By 1960, the image that a candidate projected onto home screens weighed heavily in deciding who won.

That year, 70 million people watched four televised debates between the Democratic candidate for President, John F. Kennedy, and the Republican nominee, Richard Nixon. Kennedy was a young Senator from Massachusetts. Nixon had been Eisenhower's Vice-President for eight years. Kennedy won by a little more than 100,000 votes. He became the first Roman Catholic to be elected President. Many people believed that Kennedy owed his victory to the calm, knowledgeable image he showed during the televised debates.

Kennedy had great hopes for the future and called his legislative program the New Frontier. He hoped to pass a civil rights bill and health care bills for the poor and aged. He wanted to increase Social Security benefits and provide more money for education. Kennedy was deeply committed to the U.S. space program and announced that the U.S. would put a man on the moon before the end of the decade. The first step toward such a landing came in 1961. Alan Shepard became the first American to be rocketed into space. He traveled 185 kilometers (115 miles) away from the earth and back. In 1962, the first of many communication satellites was launched. This satellite system eventually made it possible to broadcast live-television coverage around the world.

Civil Rights

During the Kennedy years, the campaign for black civil rights continued. In 1962, the Governor of Mississippi tried to keep James Meredith from enrolling in the all-white University of Mississippi. President Kennedy called in federal troops to restore order after riots broke out on campus. Meredith was then allowed to attend classes, and the troops were withdrawn.

In August 1963, more than 200,000 people, protesting discrimination against blacks took part in a march on Washington, D.C. Martin Luther King, Jr., made a stirring speech asking that people be judged by their character and not by the color of their skin.

> I say to you today, my friends, that in spite of the difficulties and frustrations of the moment I still have a dream. It is a dream deeply rooted in the American dream. I have a dream that one day this nation will rise up and live out the true meaning of its creed: "We hold these truths to be self-evident; that all men are created equal."

In the early 1960s, the Congress of Racial Equality (CORE) encouraged **civil disobedience.** This is a form of protest against government in which people use nonviolent means to resist authority. CORE organized sit-ins and freedom marches to protest segregated restaurants, bus and train waiting rooms, and theaters.

The Student Nonviolent Coordinating Committee (SNCC) was formed in 1960 to organize peaceful demonstrations to end segregation. The group dropped nonviolence from its program and changed its name to Student National Coordinating Committee. The Black Panthers, formed in 1966, favored violent revolution, if necessary, to achieve desegregation. Black Muslims, on the other hand, were against integration. They wanted separation of the races and community control of separate facilities. One of their major spokesmen, Malcolm X, later broke with the group and called for integration.

Cesar Chavez leads a group of union members of the National Farm Workers of America. Chavez formed the union in the early 1960s to gain better wages and working conditions for migrant farm workers, many of whom in the Southwest and California are Mexican Americans.

A Navy plane flies low as a U.S. destroyer pulls alongside a Soviet freighter leaving Cuba. The canvas-covered objects on the deck of the freighter are thought to be Soviet missiles being taken back to the U.S.S.R. after the Cuban Missile Crisis.

In addition to blacks, Chicanos pushed for an end to discrimination in the 1960s. Chicano (chi-KAH-noh), is the name many Mexican Americans use for themselves. Many Chicanos who live in the Southwest and California are farm workers. In 1962, Cesar Chavez (CHAH-vays) organized California grape pickers into a union. The union later added other Chicano fruit and vegetable pickers and extended membership to migrant workers in Florida. Using marches, fasts, boycotts, and strikes, Chavez was able to gain contracts with many growers by 1970. In 1972, as the United Farm Workers (UFW), the union joined the AFL-CIO.

Foreign Aid

Early in his presidency, Kennedy established the Peace Corps. This agency sent women and men overseas to work in developing nations that asked for U.S. aid. **Developing nations** are those that have not reached an economic level high enough to ensure an adequate standard of living for all their citizens. The purpose of the Peace Corps was to provide engineering, medical, and farming assistance.

At Kennedy's urging, the U.S. and 19 Latin American countries formed the Alliance for Progress in 1961. The U.S. sent large sums of money for education, housing, and health care to Alliance members. The program was mildly successful in improving U.S.-Latin American relations. However, much of the money was spent by military governments for weapons rather than for social reforms.

Crisis in Berlin

As it had since the late 1940s, Berlin continued to be a source of tensions in the 1960s. In early 1961, Khrushchev declared that if the other nations did not withdraw from Berlin, the U.S.S.R. would sign a separate peace treaty with East Germany. All routes into West Berlin, which the Soviets then controlled, would belong to East Germany. The Allies would have to negotiate with East Germany for entrance into the city. Khrushchev knew the Allies did not recognize the Communist government of East Germany.

The situation grew worse when the East Germans began to build a wall to divide East and West Berlin. More than 4,000 people were escaping each week from East to West Germany through Berlin. The East Germans believed that the Berlin Wall would reduce the number of escapees.

To show the Western powers' determination to keep West Berlin free of Communist control, Kennedy sent soldiers and armored vehicles overland to Berlin. They passed through East Germany without interference. Faced with U.S. determination, Khrushchev, in October, announced he would not insist on a treaty. The Berlin Crisis passed.

Cuba

In the late 1950s, the U.S. had aided Fidel Castro in overthrowing the Cuban dictatorship of Fulgencio Batista (bah-TEES-tah). Castro had promised that he would restore democracy to Cuba. However, in 1960, Castro allied Cuba with the Soviet Union and took over all American-owned businesses. Thousands of Cubans fled to the U.S. rather than live in a Communist country. The U.S. broke diplomatic relations with Cuba.

Many of the anti-Castro Cubans in the U.S. wanted to invade and retake their homeland. President Kennedy refused U.S. military support but agreed to supply weapons and ships. On April 17, 1961, some 1,400 anti-Castro Cubans landed in Cuba at the Bay of Pigs. They hoped to be joined by Cubans who would take up arms against Castro. This did not happen, and the invaders were easily crushed by Castro's army.

Another crisis developed in October 1962. At that time, the U.S. discovered that the Soviets had secretly built missile bases in Cuba. President Kennedy ordered a naval blockade to prevent Soviet ships from delivering the missiles. After a very tense week, Khrushchev ordered the Soviet ships to return home without delivering the missiles.

Assassination

Late in 1963, President Kennedy was making plans for the presidential election the following year. In November, he and his wife Jacqueline flew to Texas for a political appearance. While riding in a motorcade through Dallas on November 22, the President was fatally shot. The nation was stunned. Vice-President Lyndon B. Johnson, who had been riding in another car, took the oath of office before returning to Washington. The government held an investigation and found that the assassin, Lee Harvey Oswald, had acted alone. However, some still question the findings and believe there was a conspiracy.

Jacqueline Kennedy, wife of the slain President, and their children, John and Caroline, wait for the funeral procession to begin. The tragedy for the young family added to the shock and sorrow that the nation felt over the assassination of John F. Kennedy.

JOHNSON'S PRESIDENCY

Americans looked to the new President to fulfill many of Kennedy's New Frontier promises. In the year of Kennedy's term that Johnson completed, he was able to have the Civil Rights Act passed. This law prohibited racial discrimination in any facilities or places of public use such as restaurants, hotels, and theaters. Employers could no longer discriminate when hiring employees, and unions could not restrict membership because of race.

The Great Society

Early in 1964, Johnson proposed the Economic Opportunity Act to fight a "war on poverty." This act provided $1 billion to help young people continue their education or learn new skills through on-the-job training. With such laws as the Economic Opportunity Act, Johnson promised to build a Great Society. This promise was the basis of the Democrats' platform in the 1964 election. Johnson's opponent was Senator Barry Goldwater of Arizona, a conservative Republican. Johnson won easily.

This election was the first in which residents of Washington, D.C., were able to vote for President. This right was given them by the 23rd Amendment, ratified in 1961. This amendment will be replaced by the District of Columbia representation amendment if ratified by 1985.

After his election, Johnson pressed for programs that gave medical care to the poor and the elderly—Medicaid and Medicare—and federal aid to students. The Food Stamps Act provided funds for low-income families to buy more and better food. The Voting Rights Act

The Medicare and Medicaid programs of Lyndon Johnson's Great Society helped the old and/or poor to afford good health care services.

658

did away with literacy tests. Johnson also created the Department of Housing and Urban Development (HUD) and the Department of Transportation. Robert Weaver, who headed HUD, was the first black to be appointed to a Cabinet post. In 1967, Johnson appointed the first black Justice to the Supreme Court, Thurgood Marshall.

Great Society laws also concerned such areas as the environment, traffic safety, urban renewal, and crime control. **Urban renewal** is the replacement of slum areas in cities with businesses and better housing. Johnson also set up Volunteers in Service to America (VISTA). VISTA was similar to the Peace Corps, but volunteers worked in the U.S. rather than in foreign countries. Two amendments were ratified during Johnson's administration. In 1964, the 24th Amendment abolished poll taxes. Ratified in 1965, the 25th Amendment provided for presidential succession.

Frustration and Protest

The Kennedy-Johnson years were years of prosperity for many Americans. Unemployment was low — 3.8 percent in 1966 — and wages were good. But often, the unemployed were blacks. Black frustration over discrimination in employment, housing, and education sometimes turned to violence. Between 1964 and 1968, riots broke out in the Watts section of Los Angeles, in Cleveland, Chicago, Detroit, and Newark. The violence reached a climax in April 1968 when Martin Luther King, Jr., was assassinated.

Johnson appointed a commission to investigate the causes of the rioting. The Kerner Commission's report, issued in March 1968, identified many causes including hiring practices that denied good jobs to blacks. Because they were not able to find good-paying jobs, many blacks were forced to live in poverty. The report recommended creating 2 million jobs, on-the-job training programs, low- and moderate-income housing, and federal laws covering the sale and rental of housing. Soon after Dr. King's assassination, Congress passed a civil rights act. It banned discrimination in renting or selling of most housing.

The antiwar movement of the 1960s drew people from all ages and classes of society. Many entertainers joined the movement. Here Peter, Paul, and Mary sing at an antiwar rally. What were the opposing views on U.S. involvement in Vietnam?

VIETNAM WAR

In the 1960s, the U.S. became involved in a conflict in Southeast Asia. After World War II, fighting had broken out between French and Vietnamese in French-controlled Vietnam. Some of the Vietnamese were Communists, called Vietminh (vee-ET-MIN), under the leadership of Ho Chi Minh (HO CHEE MIN). In 1954, a settlement was reached that divided the country in two. The French withdrew. The Communists were allowed to occupy North Vietnam above the 17th parallel. South Vietnam was to be controlled by non-Communists.

In 1957, Communist forces in South Vietnam began a guerrilla war against the government. **Guerrilla** (guh-RIL-uh) **warfare** is fought by

Vietnam War

small groups who attack the enemy with ambushes and raids. The guerrillas, called Viet Cong, were supplied mostly from North Vietnam along the Ho Chi Minh Trail.

In September 1961, at the request of the President of South Vietnam, President Kennedy sent about 700 military advisors to South Vietnam. By 1963, the number had grown to 16,000. The U.S. was also sending military supplies. In July 1964, the North Vietnamese attacked two U.S. destroyers in the Gulf of Tonkin (TAHN-KIN), off the Vietnamese coast. President Johnson ordered the bombing of North Vietnam. At his request, Congress passed the Gulf of Tonkin Resolution. It gave the President the power to use whatever means necessary to fight attacks against U.S. forces. By the end of 1967, the U.S. had more than 500,000 soldiers in South Vietnam. North Vietnamese soldiers had invaded the South and were fighting alongside the Viet Cong. The fighting reached a peak in early 1968.

In the early 1960s, few people opposed U.S. intervention in Vietnam. By the late 1960s, however, as U.S. bombing raids and the number of U.S. troops in Vietnam increased, opposition grew. Antiwar protests attracted Americans of all age groups. But antiwar activity seemed to draw most of its support from college students.

Early antiwar protests were peaceful, but violence became more common as the war continued. Protestors burned American flags and draft cards and took over buildings on some college campuses. Many men eligible for the draft fled to Canada rather than serve. People opposed the Vietnam War because they felt U.S. involvement was immoral. They were outraged that a superpower would send its military to kill people who posed no threat to U.S. security. Supporters of the war felt that the conflict was not simply a civil war involving Communists and non-Communists. It was another case of Communists trying to take over an independent government.

LOOKING BACK

1. **a.** What were two achievements of the U.S. space program under President Kennedy? **b.** What was Kennedy's long-range goal for the space program?
2. **a.** Why did Kennedy send federal troops to Mississippi in 1962? **b.** What was the purpose of the march on Washington? **c.** How did Mexican American farm workers fight job discrimination?
3. What was the purpose of the Alliance for Progress?
4. Describe in chronological order the events that made up the Berlin Crisis.
5. **a.** Why did the U.S. support Castro in the 1950s? **b.** Why did the U.S. withdraw support? **c.** State the purpose of the Bay of Pigs invasion. **d.** Why did the Cuban Missile Crisis occur?
6. Describe three programs of President Johnson's Great Society.
7. Make a time line from 1960 to 1967 showing the events that led to U.S. involvement in Vietnam.

Chapter 3   Nixon-Ford Administrations

LOOKING AHEAD

This chapter describes the presidencies of Richard M. Nixon and Gerald R. Ford. You will read about the end of the Vietnam War and the foreign and domestic policies of these administrations. You will also learn about a scandal that caused President Nixon to resign. After you study this chapter, you will be able to:

- list the sequence of events that brought a conclusion to the Vietnam War.
- describe changes in U.S. relations with the Soviet Union during the Nixon administration.
- explain the changes in U.S. policy toward China.
- identify three achievements of Nixon's domestic policy.
- list the sequence of events in the Watergate scandal.
- explain how Ford became President without being elected.

Social Studies Vocabulary

detente   recession

People

Eugene McCarthy	Leonid Brezhnev	Leon Jaworski
Robert Kennedy	Henry Kissinger	Spiro T. Agnew
Lyndon Johnson	Neil Armstrong	Gerald R. Ford
Hubert H. Humphrey	Edwin Aldrin	Nelson Rockefeller
Richard Nixon	George McGovern	
George Wallace	John Sirica	

Places

Cambodia   People's Republic of China

Events

Paris peace talks   Watergate scandal

Words and Terms

Vietnamization   26th Amendment
Strategic Arms Limitation   Environmental Protection
    Treaty   Agency
Consumer Protection Agency

The year 1968 was marked by turbulence and violence. As you read in Chapter 2, the U.S. was torn by urban riots and antiwar protests. The election of a new president calmed some of the conflicts.

ELECTION OF 1968

Two Democrats, Senators Eugene McCarthy of Wisconsin and Robert Kennedy of New York, the late President's brother, challenged Johnson for the presidential nomination. Both opposed U.S. policy in Vietnam. Because of these challenges and the demonstrations against his policy, Johnson announced he would not seek reelection. He gave his support to his Vice-President, Hubert H. Humphrey. In June, while campaigning in Los Angeles, Robert Kennedy was shot and fatally wounded. In August, the Democrats nominated Humphrey. While they were meeting inside the convention hall in Chicago, antiwar demonstrators and police clashed in the streets outside.

fatally
(FAY-tuhl-ee):
in a manner
causing death

That same month, the Republicans had again nominated Richard Nixon. In the election, Nixon defeated Humphrey in a very close race. The major issues were the crime rate, rioting, and the Vietnam War. Nixon promised to return law and order to the nation. He also promised to bring about an honorable peace in the Vietnam War. Former Alabama Governor George Wallace ran as a third-party candidate and received almost 14 percent of the vote.

NIXON'S FOREIGN POLICY

Soon after taking office in 1969, Nixon sent a team of negotiators to Paris for peace talks with the North Vietnamese. While the peace talks went on, Nixon announced his policy of Vietnamization (vee-et-nuh-muh-ZAY-shuhn). U.S. troops would gradually be withdrawn and replaced by South Vietnamese soldiers. By the end of the year, one fourth of the U.S. troops in South Vietnam had returned home. In spring 1970, U.S. and South Vietnamese soldiers attacked North Vietnamese troops and supplies in neighboring Cambodia (kam-BOH-dee-uh). The Cambodian raids touched off new protests in the U.S. In May, four people were killed by National Guard at a demonstration at Kent State University in Ohio.

Throughout 1971, the Paris peace talks went on as Nixon continued to withdraw U.S. troops from Vietnam. In late 1972, the U.S. resumed bombing North Vietnam. Fighting continued off and on until January 27, 1973. On that day a cease-fire agreement was signed between North and South Vietnam and the U.S. By the end of March, the last U.S. troops were withdrawn. In 1975, the South Vietnamese government collapsed, and the North Vietnamese took control.

Besides the Vietnam War, other foreign affairs problems received Nixon's attention. In 1969, the U.S. and the Soviet Union met in the first of a series of talks on a Strategic Arms Limitation Treaty (SALT). The purpose of the talks was to bring about an end to the arms race without threatening the security of either nation. Because the subject of arms limitation is very complex, the talks were lengthy and cautious. After three years of discussion, the first agreements were drawn up in 1973. SALT I, as it was called, was signed by President Nixon and

Soviet President Leonid Brezhnev (BREZH-nyuhf) in 1972. Talks had already begun on SALT II, which would deal with newer weapons and ways to monitor a nation's carrying out of the agreement.

The 1970s began a period of **detente** (DAY-tahnt), the relaxing of tensions, between the U.S. and the Soviet Union. The cold war seemed to be thawing as President Nixon visited Moscow in 1972. He and Brezhnev announced that their nations would work together on health research, space exploration, science, and trade.

People's Republic of China

As you may recall from the unit World War II and Its Aftermath, Communists under Mao Tse Tung took over the government of China after the war. For many years, the People's Republic of China, as it was renamed, was closed to Westerners. Opponents of the government were persecuted and there was little economic growth. By the early 1970s, however, the situation was more stable. In 1971, the UN General Assembly voted to admit the People's Republic as a member and recognize it as the only China. Nationalist China was expelled.

In 1972, President Nixon who had been a strong supporter of Nationalist China surprised the world by visiting the People's Republic. The U.S. had had no diplomatic or trade ties with mainland China since 1949. As a result of his visit, the U.S. and the People's Republic accepted a policy of peaceful coexistence. Trade agreements were worked out, and Nixon agreed that Taiwan was a part of China. U.S. troops would be withdrawn from Taiwan, but the U.S. would continue diplomatic and trade relations with the Nationalist Chinese.

The Middle East

President Nixon also worked to ease tensions in the Middle East. In 1967 the Israelis had driven back an Arab attack and seized lands they considered Israeli. In 1973, the Arabs again attacked Israel. The war ended with a cease-fire in 1974. To bring peace to the region, Nixon supported a settlement in which the Arab nations would recognize Israel's right to exist. In 1974, U.S. Secretary of State Henry Kissinger began a series of talks in the Middle East. One of the major issues was the future of the Palestinian refugees who had fled Israel. Arabs supported a separate state for them made from Israeli territory. The U.S. and Israel refused.

DOMESTIC AFFAIRS

When Nixon took office in 1969, the U.S. was experiencing serious inflation. The following year the U.S. experienced a recession. A **recession** (rih-SESH-uhn) is a decrease in employment, sales, and so on. It is shorter and less severe than a depression. Stock prices declined while unemployment increased. Prices and wages, however, kept rising. In 1971, Nixon put a freeze on wages and prices. By 1972, inflation and unemployment were down and the recession was over.

A number of programs were passed during Nixon's presidency. To help protect Americans against fraud when buying goods, the Consumer Protection Agency was established. The 26th Amendment giving 18 year olds the right to vote was ratified in 1971. In 1970, the Environmental Protection Agency (EPA) was established. Its purpose was to monitor and prevent air, water, and land pollution. Open dumps were cleaned up. Factories were fined or closed down if they polluted the air or the water. Regulations to limit automobile pollution of the air were passed.

freeze: to hold at a definite amount

fraud (FRAWD): cheating; dishonesty

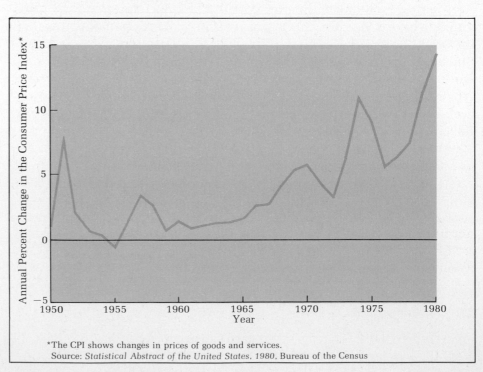

Rate of Inflation from 1950 to 1980

*The CPI shows changes in prices of goods and services.
Source: *Statistical Abstract of the United States, 1980,* Bureau of the Census

One of the most dramatic events of the Nixon years centered on the space program. In July 1969, President Kennedy's goal of an American on the moon by the end of the 1960s was realized. Astronauts Neil Armstrong and Edwin Aldrin landed on the moon. They took pictures of the moon's surface, performed experiments, and brought back samples of the moon's surface.

WATERGATE

In the presidential election of 1972, Nixon won by a landslide. He overwhelmingly defeated his Democratic opponent Senator George McGovern of South Dakota. Nixon's successful trip to China and an announcement that "peace is at hand" in Vietnam convinced many people to vote for Nixon. Unfortunately, a political scandal emerged from the election campaign that would cause Nixon's disgrace.

The Watergate scandal began in June 1972 with a burglary attempt on the Democratic party's offices in the Watergate Hotel in Washington, D.C. During their trial, it was discovered that the burglars had been employed by Nixon's campaign committee. In March 1973, one of the convicted burglars wrote the judge in the case, John Sirica (suh-RI-kuh). In this letter, he said the facts had been covered up and the defendants pressured into pleading guilty. In April, the President denied involvement and said he had begun his own investigation. Several top Nixon aides resigned shortly after and were later found guilty of conspiracy in the attempt to cover up the Watergate crime.

Congress had already named a special Senate committee to determine if all the people involved had been discovered. In May 1973, the Senate Watergate hearings began. During the televised hearings, it was learned that Nixon had secretly taped all conversations in his office beginning in 1971. Special Prosecutor Leon Jaworski (juh-WOR-skee), who had been appointed by the President, requested several of the tapes. The Special Prosecutor was acting on testimony by a Nixon aide that the President himself was involved in the coverup. Nixon refused to give up the tapes.

Meanwhile, another discovery rocked the administration. In October 1973, Vice-President Spiro T. Agnew was forced to resign. Evidence showed he had accepted bribes while Governor of Maryland and after becoming Vice-President. Nixon, using the 25th Amendment, appointed Representative Gerald R. Ford of Michigan to replace Agnew.

In fall 1973, the House Judiciary Committee began hearings to determine if there was enough evidence to impeach Nixon. In April 1974, Nixon released typewritten copies of some of the tapes but withheld others claiming "executive privilege." On August 5, obeying a Supreme Court order, Nixon released more tapes. These showed he had been involved in the coverup. Many people had been urging the President to resign to spare the nation the agony of an impeachment. On August 9, 1974, Nixon became the first U.S. President to resign.

President Kennedy's goal of a man on the moon by the end of the 1960s came true as Neil Armstrong on July 20, 1969, became the first human to walk on the moon. As he stepped onto the moon, he said, "One small step for a man, one giant leap for mankind." What do you think he meant?

The House Judiciary Committee listens to a witness during the Nixon impeachment hearings. What was the sequence of events that led to the committee's vote to recommend Nixon's impeachment? What does impeachment mean? What other President faced impeachment?

FORD AS PRESIDENT

With Nixon's resignation, Gerald Ford became President. He chose Nelson Rockefeller, the former Governor of New York, as Vice-President. Americans looked forward to a new beginning under a new President, free of involvement in Watergate. Many Americans were angered, however, when Ford granted a pardon to Nixon for any federal crimes Nixon may have committed while President.

The U.S. was experiencing both inflation and unemployment. By 1975, it was clear that the U.S. had sunk into another recession. Automobile factories laid off workers because many people were not spending money for new cars. Those who had cars had to wait in long lines to buy gas. Arab oil-producing states had ordered an embargo against nations who supported Israel. The price of the little gas available increased dramatically. By 1976, there was little improvement in the economy. Unemployment was rising steadily.

In foreign affairs, Ford worked for peace in the Middle East. Secretary of State Kissinger continued his talks with Arab states and Israel. In relations with the Soviet Union, Ford continued the policy of detente.

LOOKING BACK

1. **a.** Describe the sequence of events that led to a conclusion of the Vietnam War. **b.** What later happened to South Vietnam?
2. How did relations between the U.S. and the U.S.S.R. improve under President Nixon?
3. What changes came about in U.S. policy toward the People's Republic of China under Nixon?
4. List and explain three domestic achievements of the Nixon administration.
5. List the sequence of events in the Watergate scandal. Begin with the 1972 break-in attempt and end with Nixon's resignation.
6. How did Gerald Ford become President without being elected?

Chapter 4 — The Recent Past

LOOKING AHEAD

This chapter describes the problems that Jimmy Carter faced as President: the Iranian crisis, a worsening economy, and environmental dangers. The chapter also describes the continuing struggle of women, the disabled, the old, and minorities to gain their rights. You will read about the issues and outcome of the 1980 presidential election and President Reagan's policies. After you study this chapter, you will be able to:

- identify the main idea behind Carter's policies.
- state two achievements of Carter's foreign policy.
- list the sequence of events in the Iranian crisis.
- state two causes for the worsening economy in the late 1970s.
- identify the goals in terms of rights of women, the disabled, the old, and minorities.
- compare and contrast the major candidates' views of the issues in the 1980 election.
- describe the policies of President Reagan.

This was a familiar sign in 1974 and again in 1979. When gas became plentiful again in 1979, the price slowly edged up over a dollar as the Organization of Petroleum Exporting Countries raised their price for crude oil from which gasoline is made.

Social Studies Vocabulary

human rights	militancy	primary
energy crisis	reverse discrimination	

People

Jimmy Carter	Ruhollah Khomeini	George Bush
Menahem Begin	Betty Friedan	John Anderson
Anwar Sadat	Edward M. Kennedy	
Mohammed Reza Pahlavi	Walter Mondale	
	Ronald Reagan	

Places

Panama	Afghanistan

Events

Iranian crisis	Three Mile Island accident

Words and Terms

Camp David Accords	feminist movement
SALT II	Equal Rights Amendment
Organization of Petroleum Exporting Countries	American Indian Movement
	La Raza Unida
Department of Energy	bilingual education
National Organization for Women	Brown Berets

As the nation faced its two-hundredth birthday, it also faced a presidential election. The voters seemed to want to put the divisions caused by Vietnam and the tragedy of Watergate behind them. Unfortunately, the problems only seemed to grow worse.

ELECTION OF 1976

Ford faced strong competition for the Republican presidential nomination from former Governor of California, Ronald Reagan. However, Ford was able to gain enough support at the convention to win the nomination. Jimmy Carter, former Governor of Georgia, was the Democratic nominee. The League of Women Voters sponsored a series of televised debates between the two candidates. These were the first such debates between presidential candidates since 1960. The major campaign issue was Ford's handling of the economy. Carter won the election in one of the closest races of this century.

THE CARTER ADMINISTRATION

Carter began his administration by announcing that human rights would be the guiding factor in both his foreign and domestic affairs. **Human rights** are those rights that belong to people because they are human—the right to life, liberty, and the pursuit of happiness. These are the principles on which the U.S. was founded. Carter's policy angered a number of nations, among them the Soviet Union. Carter spoke out for Soviet dissidents who were being jailed or exiled for protesting their government's policies. The U.S.S.R. said that this was an internal matter and of no concern to the U.S.

dissident (DIS-uh-duhnt): one who disagrees

Foreign Policy

In other areas, Carter's foreign policy was more successful. In 1977, the U.S. and Panama agreed that the U.S. would turn over control of the Panama Canal to Panama by the end of the century.

President Carter also played a major role in the Middle East. In 1978, he set up talks between Menahem Begin (BAY-gin) of Israel and Anwar Sadat (suh-DAT) of Egypt at Camp David, Maryland. At the end of the talks, the three signed the Camp David Accords. The accords called for a peace treaty and the establishment of diplomatic relations. Certain territories were to be returned to Egypt and self-rule for other areas was to be negotiated. Talks broke down over this. Israel refused to agree to a Palestinian state.

accord (uh-CORD): an agreement between nations

Despite Carter's human rights policy, relations with the Soviet Union went well for a time. In 1979, President Carter and Soviet President Brezhnev signed the SALT II agreement. Carter delayed Senate consideration of the agreement, however, after the U.S.S.R. invaded Afghanistan (af-GAN-uh-stan) in December 1979. The U.S. stopped

Left to right: Anwar Sadat of Egypt, President Carter, and Menahem Begin of Israel sign the Camp David Accords. The territories in question were won by the Israelis in the Six-Day War in 1967 when they beat back an Arab attack.

all grain shipments to the U.S.S.R. and boycotted the 1980 summer Olympics in Moscow.

U.S. relations with China continued to improve in the late 1970s. In January 1979, President Carter announced that the U.S. and the People's Republic would establish diplomatic relations. In March, the two countries exchanged ambassadors and opened embassies. U.S. companies signed trade agreements with China. At the same time, the U.S. cut its diplomatic relations with Nationalist China. The U.S. did keep unofficial relations with Taiwan and promised military support if needed.

Problems in Iran also affected the U.S. In 1979, the Shah, or ruler of Iran, Mohammed Reza Pahlavi (PAHL-uh-vee), fled his country after a year of violent antigovernment demonstrations. Ayatollah Ruhollah Khomeini (khoh-MAY-nee), a religious leader, returned to Iran from 15 years of exile. Khomeini, who had overwhelming popular support, took control of the government.

On November 4, 1979, about 400 so-called students seized the American embassy in Tehran, Iran, and took 63 Americans as hostages. Three other Americans were held at the Iranian Foreign Ministry. The students charged that the Americans were spies and would be released only after the Shah and his wealth were returned to Iran. The Shah, who was ill, was in a U.S. hospital at the time.

hostage (HAHS-tij): person held as a guarantee

Carter responded by suspending oil imports from Iran and freezing Iranian assets in the U.S. He also hinted at possible military action while negotiating through the UN and other channels. Nothing seemed to work. In April 1980, Carter ordered a top-secret rescue attempt. Because of equipment failure, the mission was called off. However, eight U.S. military personnel died in the attempt.

Negotiations finally worked and on January 19, 1981, the U.S. agreed to transfer to Iran some $8 billion in Iranian assets that were in the U.S. In return, Iran would release the hostages. One half hour after Carter left office on January 20, 1981, the hostages were flown out of Iran.

669

Domestic Affairs

Carter's biggest domestic problem, and one which he could not solve, was the nation's economy. Unemployment remained near 8 percent throughout his term while the inflation rate soared. Unfortunately, inflation was so high—18 percent by mid-1980—that wages for most Americans did not keep up with price increases.

Carter blamed the inflation on rising oil prices and unlimited buying on credit. The price of oil charged by the Organization of Petroleum Exporting Countries (OPEC) had risen throughout the 1970s. Also, Americans kept buying on credit. They feared that if they waited, inflation would push the costs of goods even higher. By spring 1980, the U.S. had fallen into a recession. Some businesses had partially shutdown, and many Americans were thrown out of work. Unemployment was rising and so were prices.

A few months after he took office, Carter called attention to the nation's **energy crisis**—a critical shortage of the means to produce energy, Carter urged all citizens to conserve as much energy as possible. He asked for an increase in coal production and for greater use of solar energy. In 1977, Carter created the Department of Energy. The U.S. began exploring new methods of producing energy. Nuclear power was one alternative but it was opposed by people who believed it was unsafe. An accident at a nuclear power plant in 1979 helped to reinforce their opinion. In March, a pump at the nuclear power plant at Three Mile Island, near Harrisburg, Pennsylvania, broke down and threatened the area with a nuclear disaster. The TMI accident caused some Americans to reevaluate nuclear energy as a solution to the energy crisis. Many Americans urged the government to abandon the development of nuclear power plants.

alternative
(ahl-TER-nuh-tiv):
a choice from two
or more things

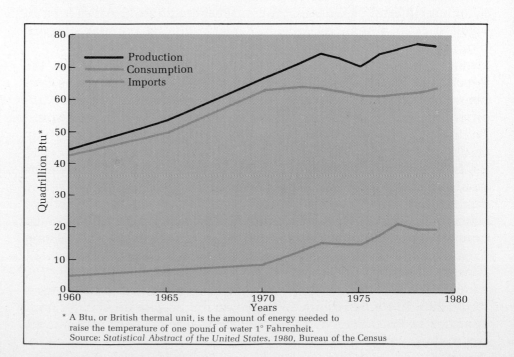

**Energy Production,
Consumption,
and Imports
from 1960 to 1979**

In the 1970s, much of the attention of women was focused on the workplace. By the early 1980s, 30 million women had full-time jobs outside the home. Here a woman speaks to a group of businesspeople on the importance of fair and effective job interviews. Why do you think this topic would be important to women and minorities?

MINORITIES IN THE 1970s

The decade of the 1970s was a time of much action on the part of the disabled, the old, women, and minorities in their attempts to gain their rights. Although the means were most often peaceful, more people were involved in the struggles. The old protested society's narrow view of their abilities and needs. The disabled worked to make society aware of how well they can function. They were able to have laws passed to have ramps and other aids added to public buildings.

Woman's Rights

World War II helped remove some job barriers for women. Between 1940 and 1960, women entered the labor force in larger numbers than ever before. But some people felt that a woman's place was in the home. In 1963, Betty Friedan (FREE-dan) explained her view of the difference between society's idea of women and their real position in *The Feminine Mystique.* She wrote that women had been trained to accept less pay than men for the same work. In 1966, Freidan formed the National Organization for Women (NOW) to work for laws that would make women's place equal to that of men. With this began the feminist movement—a movement to support women's rights.

In 1972, Congress passed the Equal Rights Amendment (ERA) to the Constitution. The amendment reads: "Equality of rights under law shall not be denied or abridged by the United States or by any State on account of sex." Some Americans opposed ERA because they felt women would lose some protections under the law. Other Americans thought ERA would give women the equality in jobs and wages they had been seeking for many years. As the 1979 deadline for ratification approached, only 35 of the needed 38 states had ratified ERA. After much debate, Congress voted to extend the ratification deadline to June 30, 1982.

Blacks

For black Americans, the 1970s saw a return to nonviolence as a means of gaining their rights. Black Muslims began to accept white members in 1975. Black Panthers set up free food programs, health clinics, and schools in poorer areas. Black studies, which many colleges introduced in the 1960s, continued to expand in the 1970s. Black men and women were hired for jobs previously denied them in such areas as entertainment and big business. The number of blacks in Congress increased and more cities had black officials.

Despite gains, some blacks felt that the civil rights movement was being forgotten. With the worsening economy of the 1970s, many political leaders began calling for relief for the middle-class majority of Americans. Although middle-class blacks benefitted, poorer blacks did not and resented the cutbacks in government programs.

Native Americans

In 1973, the American Indian Movement (AIM) took over the town of Wounded Knee, South Dakota. As you may recall from the unit Industrialism and the West, the last major battle between Native Americans and government forces had taken place there. AIM leaders demanded the return of all lands taken from Native Americans in violation of treaty agreements. After 73 days, AIM leaders agreed to surrender.

More Native American groups began to publicize their problems with business and government by peaceful means in the 1970s. Here representatives meet at an international conference on the rights of Native Americans to the natural resources on their reservations.

While some Native Americans used **militancy**—aggressive, sometimes violent, behavior—to publicize their demands, others turned to the courts. In June 1975, the Supreme Court ruled that the Sioux should be paid $105 million for lands in the Black Hills of South Dakota taken illegally when gold was discovered there in the 1870s. The decision was appealed. This was only one of several court suits, demanding either the return of land or payment.

There was another major goal that Native Americans achieved in the 1970s. They were able to make others aware that the view of Native Americans portrayed in the movies and on television was stereotyped. People began to see that there were many and varied Native American groups other than the Plains Indians. They also began to realize that even their view of the Plains Indians was false in many ways. The use of the term *Native American* rather than *Indian* is just one symbol of this new awareness.

portray (por-TRAY): to show

Hispanic Americans

Approximately 15 million Hispanic Americans live in the U.S. They include descendants of Spanish settlers; Chicanos, or Mexican Americans; Puerto Ricans; Cubans; and people from Central and South America. By the 1990s, Hispanic Americans will replace blacks as the largest minority in the U.S. The concerns of Hispanic Americans are as varied as their backgrounds and the areas in which they live.

A number of Hispanic Americans in the Southwest and California are descended from Spanish land-grant families. Many of these people are now fighting to regain the lands taken from their families by the government.

Since the early 1900s, Mexicans in increasing numbers have crossed the border into the U.S. looking for work. Many of them come for a short time to earn money and then return home. Others choose to stay. Today, there are about 9 million Americans of Mexican descent in the U.S. Most of them live in California and the Southwest.

On the East Coast, thousands of Puerto Ricans each year are flown to the mainland to plant and harvest crops. After the harvest, they are flown back to Puerto Rico. Some, however, choose to stay, take permanent jobs, and bring their families to the mainland.

Many of the Cubans who fled Castro's government in the 1960s were wealthy business owners and professional people. Many settled in Florida and set up banks and other businesses. Some people from Central and South America come to find jobs, and some come to find political freedom.

Many Hispanic Americans are poor. Because some do not speak English, they often have trouble getting jobs. They also face discrimination in housing and education. For years, school districts were unsympathetic to the demands of Hispanic Americans for bilingual education—instruction in Spanish as well as English. Hispanics protested that students who speak Spanish as their first language fall hopelessly behind their classmates when given all teaching and as-

This mural, or wall painting, shows California from prehistoric times to the present. Minority students under the direction of artist Judy Bacca began the community project in 1976 in the San Fernando valley.

signments in English. Frustrated by their lack of progress, these students drop out of school. Beginning in the late 1960s, groups such as La Raza Unida (luh RAH-suh oo-NEE-duh) were able to force school districts with large Hispanic populations to provide bilingual education. Even with an education, Hispanics often find themselves discriminated against by employers.

Organizations such as the United Farm Workers and Brown Berets (buh-RAYZ), a group similar to the Black Panthers, have helped some Hispanics. But more groups are beginning to see the value of political action. As blacks did earlier, Hispanic Americans are organizing drives to register Hispanics to vote. By voting as a bloc, Hispanic Americans hope to elect lawmakers sympathetic to their concern. In 1981, for example, voters elected a Hispanic as mayor of San Antonio, Texas—the first Hispanic mayor of a major U.S. city.

Reverse Discrimination

According to the idea of **reverse discrimination,** policies meant to help women or minorities may, in truth, discriminate against all men and/or white men. For example, in 1977 the Supreme Court ruled a section of the Social Security Act unconstitutional because it discriminated against men. The section allowed women to collect the Social Security benefits of their deceased husbands. Men, however, were not permitted to collect the benefits of their deceased wives. The Court ruled that men could collect benefits if the spouse had provided at least half the income.

The following year the Court seemed to strike down certain policies meant to give minorities a chance for higher education. Alan Bakke

deceased (di-SEEST): dead

(BAK-ee), a white male, had twice been denied admission to the University of California's medical school. In a suit brought before the Supreme Court, Bakke charged that his civil rights had been denied. Sixteen percent of the places in the medical school had been set aside for minorities. Agreeing with Bakke, the Court declared unconstitutional college admissions plans based on racial or ethnic quotas. At the same time, the Court ruled that race could be one factor used for college admissions.

ELECTION OF 1980

Many Democrats were displeased with Carter's handling of the economy and of the Iranian crisis. During 1980, Senator Edward M. Kennedy of Massachusetts, brother of the slain President, challenged Carter for the Democratic nomination. Although Kennedy did well in a number of primaries, Carter was able to gain enough support to win the nomination. A **primary** is an election in which party members choose their party's candidates for office. Walter Mondale was renominated for Vice-President.

The Republicans chose Ronald Reagan who, as you may recall from the last chapter, was a candidate for the nomination in 1976. George Bush, who had opposed Reagan during the 1980 primaries, received the vice-presidential nomination. John Anderson, a former Republican, ran as a third-party candidate.

During the campaign, Carter claimed that the U.S. had made progress both at home and in foreign affairs. He attacked Reagan's proposals as damaging to the economy and threatening to world peace. Reagan, however, reflected the conservative mood of the country. He believed that the federal government had grown too large. He called for a reduction in the number of federal jobs and federal spending, a tax cut, and a tougher stand against communism.

Reagan defeated Carter in a landslide. He won 489 of the 538 electoral votes. Americans seemed to be voting for a change. They were tired of high inflation, high unemployment, and a foreign policy that seemed to show a weakness on the part of the U.S.

REAGAN

Soon after becoming President, Reagan placed a hiring freeze on federal jobs. In February 1981, he announced his plans for cutting federal spending and reducing taxes. Although Reagan found much support for his economic plans, he also found some strong opposition. Some Americans claimed that Reagan's spending cuts would hurt the poor and the middle class. The tax cuts would benefit only the wealthy.

In foreign affairs, the Reagan administration warned the Soviet Union that it would not permit Soviet interference in other parts of

Ronald Reagan won 489 electoral votes to Carter's 49. However, he won only 51 percent of the total vote and only 53 percent of those eligible voted. Since 1960 there has been a steady decline in the number of people who vote. In the not-too-distant future, less than half the voters might vote in presidential elections.

the world. Reagan soon translated his tough anti-Communist talk into action. He announced in March that the U.S. would increase its aid to the military government of El Salvador and send advisors to train Salvadoran government troops. The government was fighting Communist-supplied guerrillas. Remembering U.S. involvement in Vietnam, some Americans urged President Reagan to use caution.

The early days of Reagan's presidency were marred when he was wounded in an assassination attempt. He and three others were shot as he left a Washington hotel after making a speech. The suspected assassin was caught at the scene. He appeared to be mentally disturbed.

LOOKING BACK

1. **a.** Define human rights as President Carter used the term. **b.** How did human rights affect U.S. foreign and domestic policies?
2. **a.** Which earlier President's policy was overturned by the Panama Canal treaties? **Hint:** Use the index to find the correct page. **b.** Why were the Camp David Accords important?
3. List in chronological order the events of the Iranian crisis.
4. According to President Carter, what were two causes of the worsening economy in the late 1970s?
5. What gains were made by each of the following groups in the 1970s: **a.** the old? **b.** the disabled? **c.** women? **d.** blacks? **e.** Native Americans? **f.** Hispanic Americans?
6. What were the issues in the 1980 election according to: **a.** Jimmy Carter? **b.** Ronald Reagan?
7. **a.** What were President Reagan's plans to bring about economic recovery? **b.** What reasons did critics give for opposing them? **c.** What was Reagan's policy toward the Soviet Union?

676

Chapter 5   Technology and Culture

LOOKING AHEAD

This chapter describes the influence that science and technology have had on American culture since World War II. You will read about how television changed people's leisure habits and how women, the disabled, the aged, and minorities have won a more realistic portrayal of their lives on television and in the movies. The chapter also describes changes in people's reading habits, the art of the period, the youth culture of the 1960s and its effects on music. You will also read about computers and space explorations. After you study this chapter, you will be able to:

- describe television's effect on Americans' leisure habits.
- explain why the portrayal of women, the disabled, the old, and minorities on television and in the movies has changed.
- state two causes for changes in Americans' reading habits.
- read pictures to describe different styles of art.
- describe the influence of the baby boom generation on American society.
- identify the importance of computers in American life.
- list four achievements of the U.S. space program since 1970.

People

Isaac Asimov	Robert Lowell	Louise Nevelson
Saul Bellow	Arthur Miller	Alexander Calder
Gwendolyn Brooks	Joyce Carol Oates	Romare Bearden
Pearl Buck	Theodore Roethke	Andrew Wyeth
Ralph Ellison	John Steinbeck	Jasper Johns
William Faulkner	Piri Thomas	Jackson Pollock
Robert Frost	Eudora Welty	Elvis Presley
Nikki Giovanni	E. B. White	the Beatles
Lorraine Hansberry	Tennessee Williams	Jonas Salk
Lillian Hellman	Richard Wright	Albert Sabin

Words and Terms

public television	rock and roll	*Columbia*
spectator sport	counterculture	laser
paperback books	data processing	recombinant DNA
youth culture	space probe	

Throughout this text, you have been reading about and examining the culture of American society as that society has grown and changed. Over the past hundred years or so, new ways of expressing culture have developed: magazines, paperback books, radio, movies, televi-

One of the most popular television shows of the 1950s and early 1960s was I Love Lucy. At that time, television shows tried to keep costs low so the major set for the show was the apartment of Lucy and Ricky Riccardo, on the right. Fred and Ethel Mertz, on the left, were their landlords.

choreographer
(koh-ree-AHG-ruh-fuhr): one who designs dance

sion, cassettes, video discs, and so on. These have made it possible for the works of artists, writers, musicians, choreographers, and other artists reach an ever-widening audience. Without advances in science and technology, however, none of this could have happened.

TELEVISION

During the 1920s and 1930s, Americans gathered around the radio. But in 1941, television arrived. Although World War II interrupted its growth, television by the 1950s had changed the leisure habits of millions of Americans. Movie theaters across the country closed as people stayed home to watch TV. Sometimes popular radio programs moved to television. Such stars as Jack Benny, George Burns, and Gracie Allen soon became familiar faces as well as voices to their audiences. Radio stations turned increasingly to news, music, sports, or talk shows where listeners could call in their comments.

By the mid-1960s, 93 percent of all households had one or more TV sets. Political conventions, congressional hearings, news programs, and documentaries brought people closer to current events. Newscasts gained large audiences as people realized how much events in other parts of the world affected them. In the 1960s, programs devoted to investigative reporting began to appear. Often these covered a problem or important political issue. Other types of popular programming were situation comedies, police shows, and Westerns.

Beginning in the late 1960s, various research studies showed that excessive violence in television programs had harmful effects on children. Groups began to demand an end to the brutality and senseless killing on television. Minorities and women also began to protest their stereotyped portrayals. The television industry tried to regulate

documentary
(dahk-yuh-MEN-tuh-ree): presentation of factual information

678

By the 1970s, one week's episode of a television show could cost several hundred thousand dollars. Movies cost millions. This is just one of the sets for a science fiction movie of the 1970s. Note the camera crew and equipment on the right.

itself. Efforts were made to reduce the amount of violence in Saturday morning cartoons and in television programming in general. The casts of many weekly series were integrated. Several weekly series were created based on minority experiences, and women and minorities were shown in positions of authority. More realistic portrayals of the old were shown, and dramas about the disabled began to appear.

Because of dissatisfaction with commercial television, public television gained popularity in the late 1960s. Supported by contributions, public television presents educational and cultural programming. *Sesame Street* and *The Electric Company* were designed especially to help young children do well in school. Public television also gives people who would never have a chance to attend an opera or a ballet the opportunity to see them on television.

One area that was greatly affected by television was sports. During the 1930s and 1940s, baseball was the most popular spectator sport. People listened to professional baseball games on the radio. Or if they lived in a city with a team, they could go to the ball park. But with the arrival of television, millions of people could watch baseball and also football, basketball, ice hockey, and, in the 1970s, professional soccer. Even golf and tennis became popular spectator sports. By the 1970s, businesses were willing to spend hundreds of thousands of dollars to advertise on *Monday Night Football*, the Olympic coverage, or the World Series. As a result, networks were willing to pay team owners huge sums to broadcast the games. Top athletes then began demanding hundreds of thousands of dollars a year to play.

MOVIES

Although television reduced the number of people who went to the movies, moviemakers quickly adapted. Some began to make lavish

lavish (LAV-ish): very abundant

679

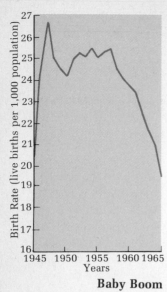

Baby Boom

Source: *Historical Statistics of the United States*, Bureau of the Census

spectaculars with casts of thousands and big name stars. Other producers made low-budget horror films about natural and human-made disasters. The more serious producers, directors, and actors continued to make movies about life as they saw it. Growing up in America, religious subjects, aging, disabilities, racial discrimination, and politics were just some of the themes portrayed. Movies made from Broadway musicals were always popular. In the 1970s, after the nation's success with its space program, the number of movies about space increased and played to record-breaking crowds.

Along with changes in other parts of American society, the movie industry began to change. It worked out a rating system to help parents guide their children's selection of movies. Increasing numbers of women found jobs behind the camera as well as in front of it. As television took steps to integrate its programming, so films were integrated. A number of movies appeared that were based on the experiences of various minority groups. Minorities also found jobs in the technical side of the movie industry.

LITERATURE

accessible
(ak-SES-uh-buhl):
easy to reach

After World War II, paperback books appeared. They were cheaper to produce than hardback books and easier to carry. Books became more accessible as racks of paperbacks appeared in drugstores and supermarkets. More people began reading for pleasure. Along with novels, nonfiction works, especially about environmental or consumer problems, became popular in the 1960s.

With the arrival of the 40-hour work week after World War II, people had more time for hobbies. Self-help books that told people how to be better golfers, gardeners, photographers, and so on, sold millions of copies. Physical fitness books and diet books appeared on the nonfiction best-seller lists in the 1970s. People were becoming aware of the importance of being physically fit.

In serious literature, war was the topic of many novels and short stories in the late 1940s and 1950s. By the 1960s, people were writing of a search for values. In the late 1960s and 1970s, there were books about the Vietnam war, pollution, discrimination, and poverty. However, literature was as varied as its readers. Historical and romantic novels were as much in demand as books on spies and outer space.

THE YOUTH CULTURE

adolescence
(ad-uh-LES-uhns): period
between childhood
and adulthood

The baby boom generation reached adolescence in the late 1950s. There were 13 million teenagers by 1960. Because they were such a large group, their interests and tastes affected the entire society.

Like their parents, teenagers enjoyed the prosperity of the times. They had more money to spend on entertainment, clothes, cars, and so on, than the youth of any earlier generation. Manufacturers made

SOME REPRESENTATIVE WRITERS OF THE 1930s-1980s

Writer	Work	Theme
Isaac Asimov	*Foundation and Empire*	Science Fiction
Saul Bellow	*Mr. Sammler's Planet*	Urban Jewish American Life
Gwendolyn Brooks	*A Street in Bronzeville*	Poems on the problems of urban blacks
Pearl Buck	*The Good Earth*	Life in prewar China
Ralph Ellison	*Invisible Man*	A black man's loss of identity
William Faulkner	*A Fable*	Experiences of a soldier in World War I
Robert Frost	*West-Running Brook*	Poems set in New England
Nikki Giovanni	*My House*	Poems about experiences of urban blacks
Lorraine Hansberry	*A Raisin in the Sun*	Play about a black family in Chicago who wants to move into a better home
Lillian Hellmann	*Watch on the Rhine*	Play about refugee from Nazi Germany who alerts the U.S. to threat of Nazism
Robert Lowell	*Life Studies*	Poems about the writer's life in New England.
Arthur Miller	*Death of a Salesman*	Play about a man destroyed by materialism
Joyce Carol Oates	*Crossing the Border*	Lives of American travelers and immigrants in Canada
Theodore Roethke	*The Far Field*	Poems drawn from childhood and nature
John Steinbeck	*The Grapes of Wrath*	Hardships of migrant farm workers in the 1930s
Piri Thomas	*Down These Mean Streets*	Puerto Rican life
Eudora Welty	*A Curtain of Green*	Short stories about southern life
E. B. White	*The Second Tree from the Corner*	Humorous views of American life
Tennessee Williams	*The Glass Menagerie*	Play about the fantasy world of a disabled young woman
Richard Wright	*Native Son*	Effects of racism on a black man

Unlike realists and impressionists, abstract artists do not try to show actual images a person might see. Above: What common objects did Louise Nevelson include in her sculpture *Royal Tide II?* Below: Romare Bearden's *One Night Stand* stresses the musicians' expressions and instruments, not actual figures.

Among other works, Alexander Calder created large mobiles such as this one, *Red Flags*. How does a mobile differ from other sculptures you have seen?

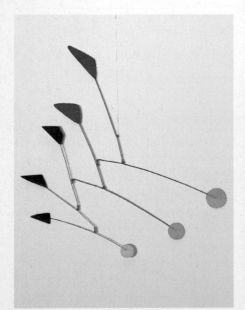

Top: In spite of many artistic movements in the 1960s and 1970s, realists such as Andrew Wyeth were popular. His *Drumlin* shows close attention to detail.

Right: Some artists wished to blend the world of everyday things with the world of art. Jasper Johns created *Fool's House* in 1962. How has he combined painting with common household items?

Below: Jackson Pollock's paintings, such as *Number 27,* are full of action. He created them by placing the canvas on the floor and dripping paint on it. In this way he felt he became part of his work.

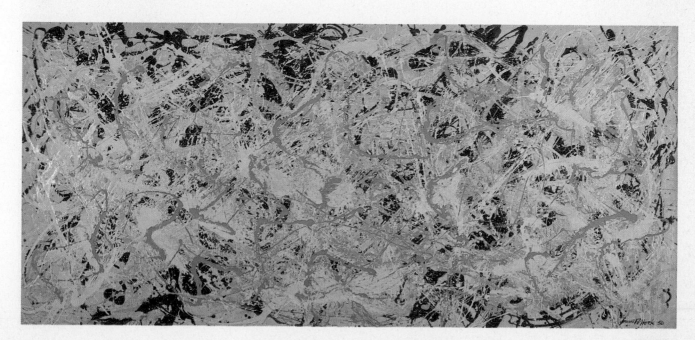

Beatles' records were popular in the U.S. before they made their first U.S. tour in 1964, but television brought them instant fame and mobs of screaming teenaged fans. What other effects did television have on the nation? What effects did the youth culture have on the nation?

commune (KAHM-yoon): community

special efforts to attract this new group of consumers. They created products such as cosmetics and clothes that appealed to teenagers' interests. Advertising influenced and reflected the nation's obsession with the "youth culture," as it was called. To sell their products, businesses emphasized the need to look and act young. One carry-over to adults was the interest in physical fitness.

One industry that grew dramatically because of teenage consumers was the record industry. During the early 1950s, people of all ages listened to the same kind of music. But by the end of the decade, teenagers were listening and dancing to rock and roll. The basis of rock and roll was in black music, but it was Elvis Presley who introduced it to white Americans. By the early 1960s, there were a dozen or so big-name rock and roll stars, among them Presley, Chuck Berry, Chubby Checker, and Bill Haley and the Comets. By the mid-1960s, fans had discovered the Beatles.

By the late 1960s, the baby boom generation was old enough to vote, and the males were old enough to be drafted. Many of them were disturbed by the domestic and foreign policies made by people of their parents' generation. A popular saying of the period was "Never trust anyone over 30." Many, who were the children of middle- and upper-class families, rejected the values of earlier generations. Some wanted to create a counterculture of a simpler life. In many cases, young people went back to the land to farm. Some started communes. In some ways, these communes were similar to the utopian communities of the 1800s.

By the end of the Vietnam era and the Nixon years, the counterculture had begun to fade. Many of those who had belonged to it were in their 30s themselves. They had jobs and families. Although still concerned with such issues as minority rights and the environment, their younger brothers and sisters were not so eager to join protest groups. It seemed more practical to spend their time on their education.

SCIENCE AND TECHNOLOGY

Technological advances since World War II have greatly changed the way people live and work. Television, newspapers, magazines, and paperbacks have made information about these advances available in language the average person can understand.

Computers

Electronic computers came into general use in the late 1950s. Since that time, each new computer is more complex and brings with it greater possibilities for changing the way people live. Computers have taken over many jobs that humans once did and perform them with lightning speed. Without computers, humans would not have been able to journey into space.

Data processing, or handling information, is the computer's major function. Many businesses do their bookkeeping and accounting by computer. Ticketing and scheduling for airlines and rail lines are done by computer. Data processing can also be used to make predictions about the future. A computer can determine a trend and then make predictions based on it. Major television networks use computers to predict the winners on election night from trends computers determine. With data processing have come new jobs.

Space Exploration

After the space explorations of the early 1970s, NASA began to send out computer-piloted space probes. Space probes are spacecraft used to explore deep into space. In 1976, *Viking I* landed on Mars and sent back pictures of the red planet. Instruments on the spacecraft analyzed the atmosphere and soil for signs of life. *Pioneer Venus I* reached Venus in 1978 and photographed the surface and atmosphere of the planet. In 1979, *Voyager I* and *II* reached Jupiter and revealed unexpected data about the planet and its many moons. Both spacecraft continued farther into space toward Saturn. *Voyager I* reached it in 1980. Photographs sent back to Earth showed that Saturn had at least 1,000 rings instead of the six scientists had originally estimated. In 1981, NASA launched the first space shuttle, *Columbia*.

Other Discoveries

One of the most important scientific discoveries since World War II has been the laser (LAY-zuhr). Developed in 1958, it has a light beam that is so strong that it can penetrate the hardest and most heat-resistant material. The laser has many uses in industry. For example, it can be used in drilling tunnels and laying pipelines. Laser beams are also used in surgery and in photography.

The development of polio vaccines by Jonas Salk (SAWK) and Albert Sabin (SAY-bin) were important medical breakthroughs of the

The space shuttle *Columbia* rises through the early morning sky on its first flight. The space shuttle will allow travelers to leave and return to Earth in a reusable space vehicle.

A scientist works with recombinant DNA. The scientific advances that have made possible the U.S. successes in space are also being used to help provide a better life for Americans.

virus (VY-ruhs): disease causing life form

organism (OR-guhn-iz-uhm): any living thing

1950s and 1960s. The development of a vaccine for German measles also freed millions of children from the dangers of that disease.

In the early 1970s, scientists found that some forms of cancer are caused by viruses. Interferon (in-tuhr-FEER-ahn), a natural virus fighter, was being tested as a possible cure for virus-caused cancers. The discovery of the technique of gene splicing, or recombinant DNA (deoxyribonucleic acid), made possible the production of large quantities of synthetic interferon. The technology involving recombinant DNA allows biologists to take genes from one organism and plant them in another to grow new cells. Scientists may eventually be able to cure cancer because of the techniques of recombinant DNA.

LOOKING BACK

1. What was the effect of television on: **a.** movies? **b.** radio? **c.** professional sports?
2. **a.** Why did women and minorities protest the way television and movies portrayed them? **b.** How were women and minorities now portrayed?
3. What two factors caused changes in Americans' reading habits?
4. **a.** Name the abstract artists whose works appear on pp. 682-83. **b.** How does their work differ from realist or impressionist art?
5. How did the baby boom generation influence: **a.** business? **b.** advertising? **c.** music? **d.** What are the differences between the youth of the counterculture and the youth of the 1970s?
6. List three uses for computers.
7. **a.** List four achievements of the U.S. space program since 1970. **b.** Why is space exploration important?

PRACTICING YOUR SKILLS

What If . . .

In Chapter 5, you read about the changes technology has made in American life. **What if** television had not been invented? Would radios, movies, professional sports, and reading habits have changed? Would people play more sports? Would movies be less expensive? Television brought home to millions the stereotyped treatment of women, minorities, and the disabled. Would these groups have been able to bring about changes in the attitudes of Americans without the added publicity television gave their causes?

Researching, Graphing, Writing, Making a Table, Making a Time Line

1. Using reference materials, find the unemployment rate for the years 1970 to 1980. Make a line graph showing this data.
2. Write a three-page research paper comparing and contrasting U.S.–Soviet relations under Presidents Eisenhower and Nixon.
3. Using reference materials make a table of President Johnson's Great Society programs. Headings for the table should include: Law, Year Passed, Purpose.
4. Reread the section on the Carter administration in Chapter 4. Draw a line down the center of a blank piece of paper. On one side list what you feel were his accomplishments and on the other what you feel were his disappointments. What accomplishments should have helped him win the 1980 election? Which disappointments do you feel helped him lose the election?
5. Make a time line listing the accomplishments of the U.S. space program since 1958.

Exploring

Use back issues of local newspapers from the library for 1974 and 1979 to see if your city experienced long gas lines during the oil shortage. If so, how long did the gas lines last? Compare the price of gasoline before and after each shortage.

Reading

Carter, Jimmy. *Why Not the Best?* New York:' Bantam, 1976. Paperback. Autobiography.

Collier, Zena. *Seven for the People: Public Interest Groups at Work.* New York: Messner, 1979.

Goldman, Alex J. *John Fitzgerald Kennedy: The World Remembers.* New York: Fleet, 1968.

Goldston, Robert. *The American Nightmare.* Indianapolis: Bobbs-Merrill, 1973. Paperback. McCarthyism.

Leuchtenberg, William E. *The Age of Change, from 1945.* Morristown, New Jersey: Silver Burdett, 1974. Social, political, and military history.

Lindop, Edmund. *An Album of the Fifties.* New York: Watts, 1978.

McKown, Robin. *The Resignation of Nixon: A Discredited President Gives Up the Highest Office.* New York: Watts, 1975.

Newlon, Clarke C. *L.B.J. The Man from Johnson City.* New York: Dodd, Mead, 1976.

Noble, Iris. *Contemporary Women Scientists of America.* New York: Messner, 1979.

Paterson, Thomas G. *On Every Front: The Making of the Cold War.* New York: Norton, 1979. Paperback.

Polenberg, Richard. *One Nation Divisible: Class, Race, and Ethnicity in the United States Since 1938.* New York: Penguin, 1980. Paperback.

Radding, Charles. *The Modern Presidency.* New York: Watts, 1979.

Reagan, Ronald, and Charles Hobbs. *Ronald Reagan's Call to Action.* New York: Warner, 1976. Paperback.

Wilson, Beth P. *Giants for Justice: Bethune, Randolph, & King.* New York: Harcourt, Brace, Jovanovich, 1978.

LIFE IN AMERICA

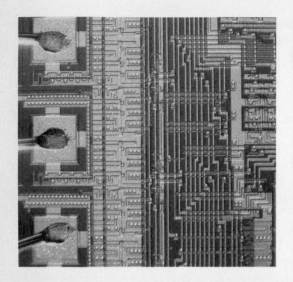

Top left: Tiny circuits, often called computer chips, have made it possible to build computers that handle more data more quickly. They have also led to the development of pocket calculators and digital watches. You could fit several such chips on the end of your finger. The detail shown here can only be seen under a microscope.

Top right: The space probe *Voyager 1* sent back photographs and other data of Saturn in 1980. It found new information on the number and shape of Saturn's rings. Why do people continue to explore space?

Bottom: The first skyscrapers were built in the late 1800s as large numbers of people began living and working in cities. Architects still look for attractive and efficient uses of limited city property. Special glass used in this building helps control the temperature inside.

The Future

LOOKING AHEAD

This last part of *Faces of America* is about the U.S. of the future—your future. The text describes what futurists expect the population, life-style, and work of Americans to be in the future. After you read this section, you will be able to:

★ use data from graphs, a table, and a map to infer changes in the age and location of the U.S. population in 2000.
★ read graphs for trends in energy use and transportation.
● infer the effects of technology on daily life.
★ use information from graphs, a table, and a map to predict what life might be like in the year 2000.

So far in *Faces of America*, you have learned about the past and the present of the United States. This last part of the book describes what you might expect to find in the nation's future. Discussing the future is important because you, today's student, will spend more than half your life in the next century. Although no one can accurately predict the future, one thing about it is certain—change. The future will be different than today. How different is up to those who live in it and shape it. To live in the future, we will all have to learn to adapt to the changes around us and to learn to make changes ourselves.

To help plan for the years ahead, scientists called futurists make hypotheses about the future. They analyze trends from the past and present and extrapolate their data into the future. Their predictions can help government—local, state, and federal—plan their policies to deal with changes in the future. You may recall reading about futurists and the skill of predicting alternative futures on page 93. All the **What If** activities you have been doing can be considered practice for the future.

extrapolate (ik-STRAP-uh-layt): to use known data to arrive at a conclusion about the unknown

CHANGES IN POPULATION

Futurists predict that by the year 2000 the population of the U.S. will number more than 260 million. That is about 34 million more than the current population. In addition, the population, on the average, will be older. People between 25 and 65 will make up half the population by the end of this century.

The population is also expected to shift from one area of the country to another. The movement to the Sun Belt that began after

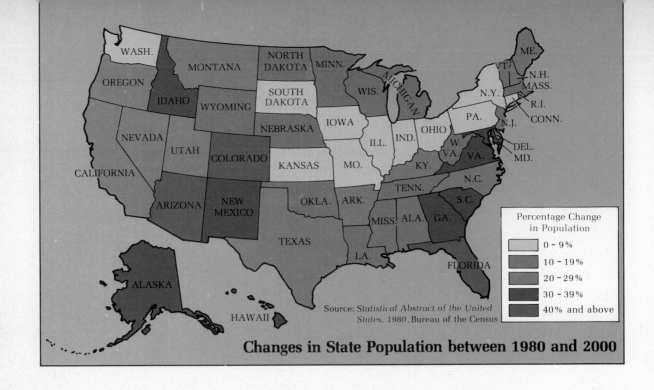

Changes in State Population between 1980 and 2000

Source: *Statistical Abstract of the United States, 1980,* Bureau of the Census

Percentage Change in Population
- 0 – 9%
- 10 – 19%
- 20 – 29%
- 30 – 39%
- 40% and above

SOME EXAMPLES OF NEW TECHNOLOGY THAT MAY AFFECT YOU

Technology	Application
Computers	Faster, cheaper, able to communicate with other models of computers; decreased paper use. Business use for filing, typing, sending and receiving messages and pictures; financial transactions among banks and merchants without paper money or checks; control of home lighting and heating; sending and receiving messages at home; shopping at home; may make it possible to work at home
Robots	Already introduced into industry; can perform monotonous* tasks quickly and efficiently; can work in unsafe or unpleasant conditions
Satellites	More communications satellites, especially for business use; collect solar energy and beam it back for use on earth
Space shuttle	Will permit industrial plants to operate in space; used to repair satellites; improve national defense
Gene splicing (recombinant DNA)	Artificial production of new vaccines, drugs, and so on; will make scarce and expensive products cheaper and more available
Synthetic blood	Liquid that can carry oxygen the way real blood does; has already been used to save lives. Other medical improvements: nuclear powered hearts; better artificial organs; synthetic skin
Synthetic fuels	Will ease growing demand for oil, especially for transportation use

*monotonous (muh-NAHT-uh-nuhs): unchanging; repeated over and over

690

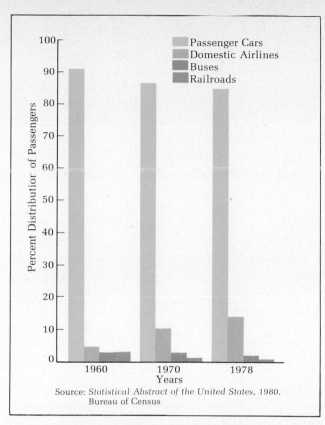

Source: *Statistical Abstract of the United States, 1980,*
Bureau of Census

**Changes in Passenger Traffic
between 1960 and 1978**

Use the graphs, table, and map on these pages to predict how both the nation and your life may change by the year 2000. You may have to combine data from more than one source. **1.** What age groups will increase in size by 2000? **2.** How might they influence: **a.** school enrollment? **b.** health care programs? **3.** What trends are developing in the labor force? **4.** Why might large numbers of people move to the Sun Belt in the next 20 years? (Consider the reasons why people moved west in the past.) **5.** Why will Florida's population grow so much? **6. a.** What trend do you see in travel between cities in the future? **b.** What will influence this trend?

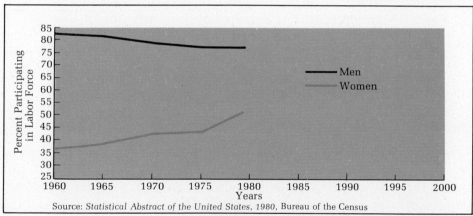

Source: *Statistical Abstract of the United States, 1980,* Bureau of the Census

**Changes in
the Labor Force**

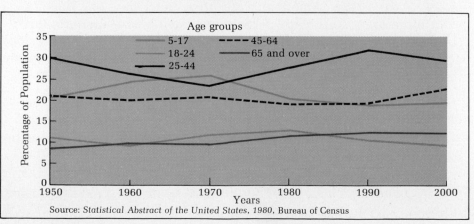

Source: *Statistical Abstract of the United States, 1980,* Bureau of Census

**Changes in the
Age of the Population
between 1950 and 2000**

World War II will continue. As a result, states in the southern third of the U.S. will have a greater share of the population. People moving to this area will include those looking for jobs in new industries such as synthetic fuel production. Others will be retired people seeking a milder climate. Population growth in the older industrial centers of the Northeast and Midwest will slow. Manufacturing industries will continue to build factories outside of cities to avoid high taxes. Cities will not grow as rapidly as in the past. But towns and suburbs will attract more people because of improved transportation, better schools, and more jobs.

synthetic
(sin-THET-ik):
artificial

CHANGES IN LIFE-STYLE

Based on current trends, it appears that new inventions and improved technology will affect how, and even where, we live and work in the future. At the same time, Americans will have to adjust to shrinking supplies of nonrenewable natural resources.

Life at Home

Some Americans are already taking advantage of computer technology by buying home computer systems. Although these are still expensive, by the end of the century, a home computer system may be no more expensive than a stereo system. Technology will also bring changes to communications systems and entertainment. Instead of reading the newspaper, people may read the news on the home computer screen. If cable television, videotape, and video discs become more common, they may affect television programming as television influenced radio programming.

Energy

The country's demand for oil will increase as the population increases. Much of that demand will be satisfied by imported oil. At the same time, however, synthetic fuels, such as oil and gas extracted from coal, tar sands, and oil shale, will become important. Other energy sources that Americans are now using but will depend on even more are nuclear and solar power. All these alternate energy sources are expensive today. But improved production technology and the rising cost of foreign oil may make these energy sources seem inexpensive in the future.

Transportation

Although oil is becoming more expensive and is a nonrenewable resource, futurists predict that Americans will not give up their cars. But, cars will be more fuel efficient. Because of the need to conserve energy, more people will use public transportation where available. More cities will build or improve their transportation systems. For long distance trips, Americans will depend more on air travel.

Health

Americans are living longer today than they did a hundred years ago and this trend is expected to continue. Health and safety conditions will continue to improve. Disease prevention and health care will be emphasized even more than in the 1970s. Medical researchers will continue to look for cures to such diseases as cancer.

Patients with less serious problems will be treated at home rather than in hospitals. New scientific discoveries and the use of new medical technology will give doctors better approaches to diagnosing and treating diseases. Technological breakthroughs such as computers to print out phone messages for the deaf will give the disabled more access to all areas of daily life.

diagnose
(DY-uhg-nohs):
to recognize a disease
by its symptoms

Jobs

Because of the changes in the population and in technology, jobs of the future will be different. A growing population will demand more goods and services, which will create new jobs. In some occupations, however, there will be fewer job openings. For instance, the need for farm workers will decline as farming becomes even more dependent on labor-saving machinery. But new technology will create new jobs.

Working hours will be more flexible. Already, many businesses are using flextime, or flexible schedules. In some companies, two people share the same job so each person only works half the time. Today, half of all women over age 16 are part of the labor force. This number is expected to increase. Women with young children may be helped by flexible schedules, job-sharing, and technology that allows them to work at home.

After the baby boom ended, the birth rate declined sharply. Therefore, futurists are predicting that today's junior and senior high school students may find less competition for jobs than there is now. More jobs will be created and today's older people will begin to retire.

LOOKING BACK

★ 1. **a.** What age group is expected to make up the largest percentage of the population in the year 2000? **b.** Which areas of the country will see the greatest increase in population by the year 2000?

★ 2. **a.** What kinds of businesses might suffer from fuel shortages? **b.** How will Americans change transportation habits to save energy?

3. How do you think changing technology will affect: **a.** entertainment? **b.** health care? **c.** mail and telephone service? **d.** your educational needs?

★ 4. Imagine it is 2000. Using what you have learned from the past and present, write a paragraph describing how you will be living. Include: **a.** where you live, **b.** your job, **c.** how you travel to work. **d.** what you do in your free time.

PRESIDENTIAL SUCCESSION

Year of Election	President/ Vice-President	Electoral vote	Popular vote	Percentage of Total Popular Vote
1789	George Washington/John Adams	69	—[1]	—
1792	George Washington/John Adams	132	—	—
1796	John Adams/Thomas Jefferson	71	—	—
1800	Thomas Jefferson/Aaron Burr	73	—	—
1804	Thomas Jefferson/George Clinton	162	—	—
1808	James Madison/George Clinton	122	—	—
1812	James Madison/Elbridge Gerry	128	—	—
1816	James Monroe/Daniel D. Tompkins	183	—	—
1820	James Monroe/Daniel D. Tompkins	231	—	—
1824	John Q. Adams/John C. Calhoun	84	108,740	30%
1828	Andrew Jackson/John C. Calhoun	83	647,286	56%
1832	Andrew Jackson/Martin Van Buren	219	687,502	56%
1836	Martin Van Buren/Richard M. Johnson	170	765,483	51%
1840	William H. Harrison/John Tyler*	234	1,274,624	53%
1844	James K. Polk/George M. Dallas	170	1,338,464	50%
1848	Zachary Taylor/Millard Fillmore*	163	1,360,967	47%
1852	Franklin Pierce/William R. King	254	1,601,117	51%
1856	James Buchanan/John C. Breckinridge	174	1,832,955	45%
1860	Abraham Lincoln/Hannibal Hamlin	180	1,865,593	40%
1864	Abraham Lincoln/Andrew Johnson*	212	2,206,938	55%
1868	Ulysses S. Grant/Schuyler Colfax	214	3,013,421	53%
1872	Ulysses S. Grant/Henry Wilson	286	3,596,745	56%
1876	Rutherford B. Hayes/William A. Wheeler	185	4,036,572	48%
1880	James A. Garfield/Chester A. Arthur*	214	4,453,295	49%
1884	Grover Cleveland/Thomas A. Hendricks	219	4,879,507	49%

[1] In the earliest elections, the electors were chosen by the state legislatures.
*Succeeded to the presidency upon the President's death.

PRESIDENTIAL SUCCESSION

Year of Election	President/ Vice-President	Electoral vote	Popular vote	Percentage of Total Popular Vote
1888	Benjamin Harrison/Levi P. Morton	233	5,447,129	48%
1892	Grover Cleveland/Adlai E. Stevenson	277	5,555,426	46%
1896	William McKinley/Garret A. Hobart	271	7,102,246	51%
1900	William McKinley/Theodore Roosevelt*	292	7,218,491	51%
1904	Theodore Roosevelt/Charles W. Fairbanks	336	7,628,461	56%
1908	William H. Taft/James S. Sherman	321	7,675,320	52%
1912	Woodrow Wilson/Thomas R. Marshall	435	6,296,547	42%
1916	Woodrow Wilson/Thomas R. Marshall	277	9,127,695	49%
1920	Warren G. Harding/Calvin Coolidge*	404	16,143,407	60%
1924	Calvin Coolidge/Charles G. Dawes	382	15,718,211	54%
1928	Herbert C. Hoover/Charles Curtis	444	21,391,993	58%
1932	Franklin D. Roosevelt/John N. Garner	472	22,809,638	57%
1936	Franklin D. Roosevelt/John N. Garner	523	27,752,869	61%
1940	Franklin D. Roosevelt/Henry A. Wallace	449	27,307,819	55%
1944	Franklin D. Roosevelt/Harry S Truman*	432	25,606,585	53%
1948	Harry S Truman/Alben W. Barkley	303	24,105,812	50%
1952	Dwight D. Eisenhower/Richard M. Nixon	442	33,936,234	55%
1956	Dwight D. Eisenhower/Richard M. Nixon	457	35,590,472	57%
1960	John F. Kennedy/Lyndon B. Johnson*	303	34,227,000	50%
1964	Lyndon B. Johnson/Hubert H. Humphrey	486	43,129,000	61%
1968	Richard M. Nixon/Spiro T. Agnew	301	31,770,237	43%
1972	Richard M. Nixon/Spiro T. Agnew†	520	47,169,911	61%
1976	Jimmy Carter/Walter F. Mondale	297	40,830,763	51%
1980	Ronald Reagan/George Bush	489	43,899,248	51%

† Spiro T. Agnew resigned and Gerald Ford was appointed Vice-President; Nixon resigned and Ford became President; Nelson A. Rockefeller became Vice-President.
*Succeeded to the presidency upon the President's death.

STATES: DATE OF ENTRY, AND CAPITAL

State	Date of Entry	Capital	State	Date of Entry	Capital
Delaware	1787	Dover	Florida	1845	Tallahassee
Pennsylvania	1787	Harrisburg	Texas	1845	Austin
New Jersey	1787	Trenton	Iowa	1846	Des Moines
Georgia	1788	Atlanta	Wisconsin	1848	Madison
Connecticut	1788	Hartford	California	1850	Sacramento
Massachusetts	1788	Boston	Minnesota	1858	St. Paul
Maryland	1788	Annapolis	Oregon	1859	Salem
South Carolina	1788	Columbia	Kansas	1861	Topeka
New Hampshire	1788	Concord	West Virginia	1863	Charleston
Virginia	1788	Richmond	Nevada	1864	Carson City
New York	1788	Albany	Nebraska	1867	Lincoln
North Carolina	1789	Raleigh	Colorado	1876	Denver
Rhode Island	1790	Providence	North Dakota	1889	Bismarck
Vermont	1791	Montpelier	South Dakota	1889	Pierre
Kentucky	1792	Frankfort	Montana	1889	Helena
Tennessee	1796	Nashville	Washington	1889	Olympia
Ohio	1803	Columbus	Idaho	1890	Boise
Louisiana	1812	Baton Rouge	Wyoming	1890	Cheyenne
Indiana	1816	Indianapolis	Utah	1896	Salt Lake City
Mississippi	1817	Jackson	Oklahoma	1907	Oklahoma City
Illinois	1818	Springfield	New Mexico	1912	Sante Fe
Alabama	1819	Montgomery	Arizona	1912	Phoenix
Maine	1820	Augusta	Alaska	1959	Juneau
Missouri	1821	Jefferson City	Hawaii	1959	Honolulu
Arkansas	1836	Little Rock	District of Columbia	(1791)	
Michigan	1837	Lansing			

Social Studies Vocabulary/Glossary

abolitionist (ab-uh-LISH-uhn-ist) **movement**: movement to end slavery.

acculturation (uh-kuhl-chuh-RAY-shuhn): a culture's taking of some traits from another culture with which it has contact over a long period.

A.D.: after Christ.

alliance (uh-LY-uhns): a joining of groups by formal agreement to promote their common interests.

ally (AL-eye): person, group, or country united with another for their common benefit.

amendment: change in or an addition to a document.

amnesty (AM-nis-tee): general pardon, especially for offenses against the federal government.

annexation (an-ek-SAY-shuhn): addition of territory to a nation.

anti-Semitism (an-tee-SEM-uh-tiz-uhm): hostility and discrimination against Jews.

appeasement (uh-PEEZ-muhnt): giving in to an enemy's demands to prevent war.

archaeologist (ahr-kee-AHL-uh-jist): scientist who studies past cultures.

armistice (AHR-muh-stis): agreement to end a war.

arms race: competition among countries to develop more and better weapons.

artifact (AHR-tuh-fakt): any object made by people.

arts, the: painting, literature, drama, music, and so on.

assembly line: line of machines and workers; each performs a different step in the production of an item as it moves in a direct line from start to finish.

assumption: what a person thinks or takes for granted to be true.

autonomy (aw-TAHN-uh-mee): right of self-government.

balance of trade: difference in money value between exports and imports.

bar graph: graph showing by bars of varying lengths the sizes of different things at the same time.

basin: bowl-shaped hollow in the land.

B.C.: before Christ.

bias (BY-uhs): strong feeling for or against a person or thing without any facts to support that feeling.

bill of rights: statement of basic rights of individuals.

bloc: group supporting same political issues.

blockade (blahk-AYD): to prevent passage in or out; the act of preventing passage in or out.

bond: note from government or a corporation promising repayment of the selling price with interest within a certain period of time.

boycott: refusal, usually organized, to buy or sell a product, or deal with a certain group, company, or nation; form of protest or punishment.

bureaucracy (byoo-RAHK-ruh-see): departments, or bureaus, that manage government.

c., circa (SER-kuh): around, with dates.

cash crop: crop raised for profit rather than for farmer's own use.

caucus (KAW-kuhs): meeting of party leaders to decide on candidates, policies, and political strategy.

cause and effect: relationship between events; one event produces the other.

censure (SEN-shuhr): to criticize someone for incorrect behavior.

census (SEN-suhs): official count of population; includes information on age, sex, jobs, and so on.

central government: government that acts for all states in matters of common concern.

charter: grant by government of permission to organize or of rights and privileges.

chief executive: head of state.

chronology (kruh-NAHL-uh-jee): order in which events occur; sequence of events.

civil disobedience: form of protest against the government in which nonviolent means are used to resist authority.

civil rights: rights that citizens are guaranteed by law.

civil service system: system that handles regulations governing the hiring and firing of government employees.

civil war: war between parts of the same state or nation.

clan: group of people who claim to be descended from the same person.

class: grouping of people according to social and economic rank.

classify: to arrange data into a system according to topics.

climate: general weather conditions of a region.

closed shop: company where employer agrees to hire only union members.

cold war: conflict between nations that uses diplomatic, psychological, or economic means rather than military force.

collective bargaining: negotiation between workers and management to settle the terms of a contract for wages, hours, and working conditions.

colonization (kahl-uh-nuh-ZAY-shuhn): the building of permanent settlements in another country; settlers remain citizens of parent country.

colony: group of people sent to another land to set up permanent settlements, while remaining citizens of parent country.

commerce: buying, selling, or trading.

commissioner (kuh-MISH-uhn-er): government representative.

communism (KAHM-yuh-niz-uhm): economic system in which a community or a government owns all means of production such as factories; right of individuals to own means of production is partly or entirely denied.

compare and contrast: to look for ways two or more things are the same as well as different.

competition (kahm-puh-TISH-uhn): effort of producers or sellers of similar goods to win more business by offering lowest prices or best conditions.

compromise (KAHM-pruh-myz): the settlement of conflict by having all parties agree to give up some of their demands; to settle a conflict in this manner.

confederation (kuhn-fed-uhr-AY-shuhn): government system resulting from loose joining of states into a union; states give up some but not most of their government powers.

conservation (kahn-suhr-VAY-shuhn): protection of natural resources.

conservative (kuhn-SER-vuh-tiv): one who wants to keep things the way they are; one who resists quick change.

constitution (kahn-stuh-TOO-shuhn): set of basic laws and a plan of government.

constitutional government: system of government in which law limits government's power.

consumer goods: goods bought by people for their own use.

containment (kuhn-TAYN-muhnt): policy of keeping another nation within existing boundaries.

context clue: clues in the text that suggest a word's meaning.

continuity (kahn-tuh-NOO-uh-tee) **and change:** related events happening one after another that lead to change.

convention: meeting held for a special purpose.

corporation (kor-puh-RAY-shuhn): group acting legally as an individual for business purposes.

cost of living: average cost of buying necessary goods and services (necessities).

council (KOWN-suhl): group of people who make laws or advise a ruler.

craft: work that requires skill with the hands.

craft union: organization of skilled workers who work at the same job but in different industries.

credit: the promise of payment in the future for goods or borrowed money.

creole (KREE-ohl): American-born descendant of colonists from Spain.

cultural diffusion (dih-FYOO-zhuhn): spread of culture traits from one group to another.

culture: all tools and objects people make and use, their ways of eating and dressing, their everyday activities, their language, religious beliefs, customs, values, folklore.

culture region: area in which people of different groups have adapted to their surroundings in similar ways.

culture trait: characteristic shared by members of the same culture.

custom: usual way of doing something or of acting.

customs duties: taxes on goods brought into a colony or country.

data (DAY-tuh): information.

debate: formal argument of two sides of a problem.

de facto (dee-FAK-toh) **segregation:** separation of groups that exists because of circumstances rather than by law.

de jure (dee-JOOR-ee) **segregation:** separation of groups by law.

demilitarize (dee-MIL-uh-tuh-ryz): to take away military control or to prohibit an area from being used for military purposes.

democracy (dih-MAHK-ruh-see): a form of government in which citizens rule either directly or through elected representatives.

dendrochronology (den-droh-kruh-NAHL-uh-jee): tree-ring dating.

depression (dih-PRESH-uhn): time of little business activity; low prices, few profits, high unemployment, little demand for goods, many business and bank failures.

detente (DAY-tahnt): relaxing of international tensions through negotiation.

developing nation: nation that is not at high enough economic level to ensure adequate standard of living for all citizens.

dictatorship (DIK-tay-ter-ship): government system in which one person exercises complete authority.

discrimination (dis-krim-uh-NAY-shuhn): unequal treatment.

discussion: talking about something.

division of labor: giving of certain jobs or parts of jobs to certain people to do.

doctrine (DAHK-truhn): statement of policy.

domesticate (duh-MES-tih-kayt): to change wild plants into ones that can be planted and harvested as crops.

domestic system: system in which work is done at home and then collected and sold by merchants.

draft: government's call on its citizens to serve in the military.

economy (ih-KAHN-uh-mee): system for making, distributing, and using goods and providing services.

emancipation (ih-man-suh-PAY-shuhn): act of setting free, especially slaves.

embargo (em-BAHR-goh): a government's refusal to allow trade with other countries.

emigrate (EM-uh-grayt): to leave one's homeland to live somewhere else.

empire: large territory or group of states ruled by a single government.

energy crisis: critical shortage of the means to produce energy.

ethnic group: group of people who share social and political ties, a common culture, and/or come from the same geographic region.

excise tax (EK-syz): tax on goods made or sold within a country.

executive branch: government branch that runs nation's affairs and carries out policies.

expansionism (eks-PAN-shuhn-iz-uhm): belief in the right of a country to increase its territory, often at the expense of others.

export: item sent to another country to sell; to send goods to another country to sell.

extended family: family that includes father, mother, unmarried and married children and their families, grandparents, uncles, aunts, and cousins.

factory system: method in which workers and machines produce goods in a factory.

federal government: system of government in which separate states unite under central organization that controls matters of common interest; each state keeps power over affairs within its own borders.

federalism (FED-uhr-uhl-iz-uhm): government system which divides power among national, state, and local authorities.

flow chart: shows, by pictures or words, order of steps in a process.

folk art: art made by ordinary people rather than by professional artists.

folk song: song passed down from generation to generation.

foreign (FOR-uhn) **aid:** help in the form of money, goods, advisors, or services that one nation gives to another.

foreign (FOR-uhn) **policy:** government's plans for dealing with other countries.

frontier: undeveloped land; boundary between settled lands and wilderness.

futurist (FYOO-chuhr-ist): person who studies the future.

generalization (jen-uhr-uhl-uh-ZAY-shuhn): conclusion reached after gathering and analyzing data; pulls together common themes or ideas behind a number of examples and specific facts.

geography: study of the earth's physical features, political and natural divisions, natural resources, climate, peoples, land use, industries, and products.

ghetto (GET-oh): section of a city in which only one ethnic group lives.

goods and services: things made and activities done for others for a price.

government: formal way of exercising power over others.

guerrilla warfare (guh-RIL-uh): fighting by small groups who use ambushes and raids.

heritage (HER-uh-tij): something that is passed from one generation to the next, such as religion or traditions.

historical map: map showing historical data.

historical time period: time span marked by work of an important person or by particular event; it can be any length of time, that is, it has no time limit and may overlap other historical time periods.

human rights: rights that belong to people because they are human—right to life, liberty, the pursuit of happiness.

hypothesis (hy-PAHTH-uh-sis): an educated guess; prediction of reasonable possible answer.

immigrant (IM-uh-gruhnt): person who comes to a country from another country to live.

impeach: to charge a government official with wrongdoing in office.

imperialism (im-PIR-ee-uhl-iz-uhm): extending economic or political control over other nations, sometimes by force.

import: item brought into a country for sale; to bring goods into a country to sell.

income tax: direct tax on a person's income.

indentured servant (in-DEN-chuhrd): person who agrees to work without pay for a certain period in exchange for passage.

industrialization (in-duhs-tree-uhl-uh-ZAY-shuhn): change of economy from one based on farming to one based on industry.

industrial (in-DUHS-tree-uhl) **revolution:** the rapid change from a farming to an industrial economy that began in England in the 1700s.

industrial union: a union of skilled and unskilled workers in the same industry.

inference (IN-fuhr-uhns): statement that interprets or explains the meaning of data; it is not fact but is based on facts.

inflation (in-FLAY-shuhn): rapid increase in price of goods and services.

initiative (in-NISH-uh-tiv): right of citizens to propose laws to legislatures.

injunction (in-JUHNGK-shuhn): court order commanding a person or group to do, or stop doing, something.

integration (in-tuh-GRAY-shuhn): the unifying of different groups into one group.

interest: fee or price for borrowing money.

interstate commerce: trade between two or more states.

interview: meeting in which one person asks another questions to obtain information.

isolationism (eye-suh-LAY-shuhn-iz-uhm): belief that a nation should not involve itself in foreign affairs.

isthmus (IS-muhs): narrow strip of land that joins two larger areas.

joint-stock company: company organized to raise money to finance an activity by selling shares in the company.

judicial branch (joo-DISH-uhl): government branch that tries court cases.

kickback: money given by a business to a politician in return for government contracts.

labor force: number of people employed or able and willing to work.

labor union: organization of workers formed to deal with employers.

land grant: land given by a government.

land use map: map showing use of land in an area.

latitude: distance measured in degrees north and south of the equator.

law of supply and demand: principle that the price of goods rises as demand for them increases; price falls as supply increases.

league (LEEG): union of two or more peoples, groups, or nations to promote common interests.

legend: on a map, the list that explains the map's symbols; story, that may or may not be true, that is passed from one generation to the next.

legislative branch (LEJ-is-lay-tiv): government branch that makes laws.

legislature (LEJ-is-lay-chuhr): group in government with the duty and power to make laws.

life-style: way of life.

line graph: graph showing by lines sizes of similar items at different times.

longitude (LAHN-juh-tood): distance measured in degrees east or west of Greenwich, England.

loose constructionist: one who believes in an interpretation of the U.S. Constitution that supports expansion of federal government's powers.

main idea: key point of a paragraph, section, or chapter.

manifest destiny (MAN-uh-fest DES-tuh-nee): belief in the right of the U.S. to spread its power across the continent.

market: demand for a particular item.

materialism (muh-TIR-ee-uhl-iz-uhm): belief that the greatest happiness can be found in getting material things.

material remains: artifacts, bones, plants, rocks, and soil that show people were in a particular place at a particular time.

mean: average.

mercantilism (MER-kuhn-til-iz-uhm): economic theory or belief that colonies exist only to make governing country richer.

mestizo (mes-TEE-zoh): a person of part Spanish and part Native American ancestry.

militancy (MIL-uh-tuhn-see): aggressive sometimes violent behavior.

minister (MIN-is-tuhr): person who represents his or her government to the government of a foreign nation.

minority group (muh-NOR-uh-tee): group that differs from the general population in some way.

mixed farming: system in which several different crops as well as livestock are raised.

mobilization (moh-buhl-uh-ZAY-shuhn): the bringing of troops and equipment into active military service.

monopoly (muh-NAHP-uhl-ee): complete control of the manufacturing and/or selling of a product or service.

myth (MITH): story which often explains a group's beliefs.

nation: group of people with a similar culture; Native American grouping.

nationalism (NASH-uhn-uhl-iz-uhm): loyal or patriotic feeling for one's nation.

nativist (NAYT-iv-uhst): one who believes that native-born people should be favored over immigrants.

natural environment: natural influences and conditions that affect group's development.

natural region: area in which at least one single physical feature exists throughout.

natural regions map: map showing natural regions of an area.

natural resource: something found naturally on or in land and water such as fish, animals, soil, forests, minerals, and so on; also air and water.

natural resources map: map showing natural resources of an area.

negotiate (nih-GOH-shee-ayt): to discuss a problem in order to work out a solution.

neutrality (noo-TRAL-uh-tee): refusal to take sides or become involved.

nonrenewable resource (nahn-rih-NOO-uh-buhl): natural resource that cannot be replaced, such as fossil fuels.

nonviolence (nahn-VY-uh-luhns): plan of action using peaceful means to achieve a goal.

nuclear family (NOO-klee-uhr): family that includes only parent(s) and children.

opinion (uh-PIN-yuhn): belief that is based on what a person thinks rather than on proven fact.

outlining: way to organize ideas; it has a special form to arrange topics, and so on.

panic: financial crisis in which people lose confidence in the economy.

parallel (PAR-uh-lel): imaginary line that represents a degree of latitude.

paraphrase (PAR-uh-frayz): writing another's words into your own.

peaceful coexistence (koh-eg-ZIS-tuhns): living together without conflict.

people, a: all the persons who belong to the same culture.

petition (puh-TISH-uhn): request.

physical feature: part of earth's surface such as valley, mountain, river, lake, and so on.

pie graph: circle graph showing parts of a whole.

plain: flat land.

plateau: large area of raised, flat land; a plain on a mountain.

platform: political party's statement of goals and policies.

point of view: what a person thinks about a situation, event, or another person.

political map: map showing states or countries and their capitals.

political (puh-LIT-uh-kuhl) **party:** group of people with similar views who unite to promote their goals.

political patronage (PAY-truhn-ij): giving of government jobs to supporters of the party in power whether a person is qualified or not; spoils system.

politics (PAHL-uh-tiks): activities and organizations through which people and groups seek power or the control of government.

popular sovereignty (SAHV-ruhn-tee): allowing people to vote on questions for themselves.

population density: average number of people living in a given area.

predicting alternative futures: changing one's way of looking at a situation to come up with a different possible solution.

prehistoric (pree-his-TOR-ik): belonging to the time before history was recorded.

prejudice (PREJ-uh-dis): dislike for or intolerance of others without knowledge to support or disprove one's opinion.

primary: election in which party members choose their party's candidates for office.

primary source: first-hand or eyewitness account of an event; it may be a letter, journal, document, photograph, or other material remain.

proclamation (prahk-luh-MAY-shuhn): official declaration or announcement.

professional art: art created by specially trained artists.

profit: money remaining to a business after all its expenses are paid.

progressive (pruh-GRES-iv): one who favors reform, improvement, and progress through government action.

prohibition (proh-uh-BISH-uhn): act of banning or forbidding something; the period in U.S. history when alcohol was forbidden.

propaganda (prahp-uh-GAN-duh): spreading of information, beliefs, and ideas to influence opinions and beliefs of others.

proprietary (pruh-PRY-uh-ter-ee) **colony:** a colony whose charter grants the ownership of its land to one person or group.

protective tariff (TAR-if): tax on foreign goods to raise their prices and protect the producers of the same goods in the taxing country.

public opinion poll: survey to find out attitudes, beliefs, or opinions of large numbers of people.

quota system (KWOH-tuh): plan that limits number of immigrants from any one country allowed to enter another country.

radiocarbon dating: method of determining age of wood, bone, and other once-living things by measuring carbon-14 left in them.

ratification (rat-uh-fuh-KAY-shuhn): approval or formal agreement.

raw material: material such as coal used in the manufacture of other goods.

rebate (REE-bayt): refund or part of a payment.

recall (ri-KAWL): to remember information.

recall (REE-kawl): voters' right to remove elected officials from office.

recession (rih-SESH-uhn): decrease in business activity with a decrease in employment, sales, and so on; shorter and less severe than a depression.

referendum (ref-uhr-EN-duhm): submission by the legislature of an issue to the vote of citizens.

repeal (rih-PEEL): to cancel a law.

representative (rep-rih-ZEN-tuh-tiv) **assembly:** group of people elected by their fellow citizens to make laws.

representative government: government in which lawmaking power is given by the people to those they elect.

republic: government in which officials and representatives are elected by the people to whom certain rights are guaranteed.

reverse discrimination: occurs when policies meant to help women or minorities cause discrimination against all men and/or white men.

revolution (rev-uh-LOO-shuhn): basic change in or complete overthrow of a government, political system, or society.

role: part a person has in a group.

royal colony: colony whose government and council were appointed by the monarch.

satellite (SAT-uhl-yte): country that follows a more powerful one in matters of policy.

scale: key to the size of areas shown on a map.

scan: to look over a piece of reading matter very quickly to find particular information.

secede (sih-SEED): withdraw from membership.

secondary source: second-hand information about an event, including comments, from one who was not involved.

sectionalism (SEK-shuhn-uhl-iz-uhm): division of a country or political group into sections whose objectives and interests are different; loyalty to one's own section's interests.

segregation (seg-ruh-GAY-shuhn): keeping groups separated by law or custom.

self-government: government of, by, and for the people.

sequence of events: arrangement of events in the order in which they occur; chronology.

skilled worker: person whose work demands special ability or training.

slavery (SLAYV-uhr-ee): owning of people.

social mobility (moh-BIL-uh-tee): moving from one class to another.

society (suh-SY-uh-tee): any group of people who have shared interests or shared culture and identity.

states' rights: rights and powers belonging to the states rather than to the federal government; belief that these include all powers that the U.S. Constitution does not actually give to the federal government or deny the states.

statistical (stuh-TIS-tuh-kuhl): having to do with numerical facts.

status (STAY-tuhs): social position.

stereotype (STER-ee-uh-typ): idea about person or thing based on oversimplified view.

strict constructionist: one who believes in an interpretation of the U.S. Constitution that does not support the expansion of the federal government's power.

strike: refusal to work until an employer agrees to certain worker demands.

subsidy (SUHB-suh-dee): money granted by the government to aid nongovernment organizations.

suburbs (SUHB-uhrbs): residential areas on the outskirts of cities.

suffrage (SUHF-rij): right to vote.

suffragist (SUHF-ruh-jist): supporter of voting rights for women.

summarize: to state what you have read in more general terms and with fewer details than in the original material.

supporting detail: fact that backs up a main idea.

surplus (SER-pluhs): more than is needed.

table: arrangement of data into rows and columns according to topics.

tariff (TAR-if): tax on imports.

third party: party made up of dissatisfied members of the major political parties; it usually focuses on only a few issues.

time line: arrangement of events with their dates in the order in which they occurred.

time zone: region in which same time is used.

topic sentence: statement of what a paragraph is about.

totalitarian state (toh-tal-uh-TAIR-ee-uhn): state in which every part of life — economic, religious, social, educational — is controlled by government.

trade: buying, selling, or exchanging of goods and service.

tradition (truh-DISH-uhn): custom, practice, or way of doing something that is handed down from one generation to the next.

treason: betrayal of one's own government by trying to overthrow it or by helping a foreign government in working against it.

treaty: agreement between nations.

trend: general way something is going.

truce (TROOS): agreement to a temporary stop in fighting.

trust: a corporation made from several corporations whose stock is controlled by a single board of managers.

unskilled worker: person whose work does not demand a special skill or craft.

urbanization (er-buhn-uh-ZAY-shuhn): the changing of an area from rural to city.

urban renewal: replacement of slum areas in the city with better housing and new businesses.

values: qualities a person or group considers important.

veto (VEE-toh): to reject or forbid a proposed law; such a rejection.

war bond: bond issued by the government to raise money for fighting a war.

ACKNOWLEDGMENTS

Page 4 Adaptation of "Steps in the SQ3R Method" from *Effective Study*, 4th edition, by Francis P. Robinson. Copyright 1941, 1946 by Harper & Row, Publishers, Inc. Copyright © 1961, 1970 by Francis P. Robinson. By permission of Harper & Row, Publishers, Inc.

Page 41 "To the Great Council of the Thirteen Fires. The Speech of Corn Plant, Half Town, and Big Tree, Chiefs and Counsellors of the Seneca Nation." Adapted from *Documents Relative to Indian Affairs*, (n.d.).

Page 45 "Sister, I Bring You a Horse." From *Smithsonian Institution Bureau of American Ethnology*, Bulletin 61, page 411: "Teton Sioux Music," Frances Densmore. Washington, D.C.: Government Printing Office, 1918. Reprinted by permission of the Smithsonian Institution Press.

Page 49 Adaptation of "Banda Noqai" from "Plains Indian Age-Societies: Historical and Comparative Summary," by Robert H. Lowie in *Anthropological Papers of the American Museum of Natural History*, Vol. XI, #XIII, pp. 818-19, New York, 1916. Reprinted by permission of the American Museum of Natural History.

Page 50 Adapted from *The Nez Percés: Tribesmen of the Columbia Plateau*, pp. 116-17, by Francis Haines. Copyright 1955 by the University of Oklahoma Press, Publishing Division of the University at Norman, Oklahoma. By permission of the publisher.

Page 54 "When Spring Comes." Adapted from "Introduction to Zuni Ceremonialism," Ruth L. Bunzel: page 484 in *Smithsonian Institution Bureau of American Ethnology, Forty-Seventh Annual Report, 1929-1930*. Washington, D.C.: Government Printing Office, 1932. By permission of the Smithsonian Institution Press.

Page 58 Adaptation of "Pomo Myths" by S. A. Barrett from the *Bulletin of the Public Museum of the City of Milwaukee*, Vol. 15, Nov. 6, 1933, p. 86. By permission of the Milwaukee Public Museum.

Page 73 Adapted from "The Voyages of Columbus and of John Cabot," p. 294. Edited by Edward Gaylord Bourne. In *Original Narratives of American History*. New York: Charles Scribner's Sons, 1906.

Page 83 Adapted from *Cabeza de Vaca's Adventures in the Unknown Interior of America*, translated and edited by Cyclone Covey; copyright © 1961 by Macmillan Publishing Co., Inc. By permission of the publisher.

Page 98 Adapted from *Don Juan de Onate: Colonizer of New Mexico, 1595-1628*, pp. 692-3. Albuquerque, N.M.: University of New Mexico Press, 1953.

Page 110: Adapted from the *Mayflower Compact*.

Page 113 Adapted from the *Body of Liberties*.

Page 118 Adapted from the *Charter for Connecticut*.

Page 125 Adapted from the *Toleration Act*.

Page 135 Adaptation of William Penn's Letter to the Inhabitants of Pennsylvania, 8 April, 1681, from *The Papers of William Penn*. Courtesy of the Historical Society of Pennsylvania.

Page 142 Adapted from *The Mission Era: The Missions at Work, 1731-1761* by Carlos E. Castaneda. In *Our Catholic Heritage in Texas, 1519-1936*, Vol. III, pp. 111-12. Austin, Tex.: Von Boeckman-Jones Co., 1938. By permission of the Texas State Council Knights of Columbus.

Page 152 Adapted from *The Life of Olaudah Equiano, or Gustavus Vassa the African*, by Gustavus Vassa, pp. 43-47. New York: Negro Universities Press, Greenwood Press, 1969. By permission of Greenwood Press, Westport, Conn.

Page 157 Adapted from *William Fitzhugh and His Chesapeake World*, edited by Richard Beale Davis. Copyright 1963 by the University of North Carolina Press. Published for the Virginia Historical Society. By permission of the publisher.

Page 172 Excerpted from *American History: A Survey*, Vol. 1: To 1877, 5th Edition, by Richard N. Current, T. Harry Williams, and Frank Friedel. Copyright © 1978 by the authors. Reprinted by permission of Alfred A. Knopf, Inc.

Page 179 From "Meat Out of the Eater," by Michael Wigglesworth. In *The Cyclopaedia of American Literature from the Earliest Period to the Present Day*, Vol. 1, p. 62, by Evert A. & George L. Duyckinck. Philadelphia: T. Ellwood Zell, 1875.

Page 179 "To the University of Cambridge, in New England," Phillis Wheatley, from *Memoir and Poems of Phillis Wheatley, a Native African and a Slave*. Boston: George W. Light, 1834.

Page 186 Adapted from "Observations on the Trade and Revenue of North America," in *The Livingston-Redmond Collection*; copyright © Roland Redmond. At Franklin D. Roosevelt Library, Hyde Park, N.Y.

Page 206 Adapted from *Letters from a Farmer in Pennsylvania to the Inhabitants of the British Colonies*. Philadelphia and London: London University, 1774.

Page 218 Adapted from *Peter Oliver's Origin and Progress of the American Rebellion: A Tory View*, p. 121. Edited by Douglass Adair and John A. Schutz, Stanford, Cal.: Stanford University Press, 1967. By permission of the Henry E. Huntington Library and Art Gallery.

Page 223 From the letter of Abigail Adams to John Adams, March 31, 1776. In *Adams Family Correspondence*, edited by L. H. Butterfield, Cambridge, Mass.: Harvard University Press, 1963. Reprinted by permission of the publisher.

Page 238 Reproduced from *Music in America, An Anthology from the Landing of the Pilgrims to the Close of the Civil War, 1620–1865*, compiled and edited by W. Thomas Marrocco and Harold Gleason, with the permission of W. W. Norton & Company, Inc. Copyright © 1964 by W. W. Norton & Company, Inc.

Page 239 Adapted from "The Articles of Capitulation," in *The Writings of George Washington*, page 533. Edited by Jared Sparks. Boston: Russell, Odiorne, and Metcalf, and Hilliard, Gray and Co., 1835.

Page 243 Adapted from *How to Study in College* by Walter Pauk, Boston: Houghton Mifflin Company, 1974.

Page 247 Adapted from the *Articles of Confederation*.

Page 255 Adapted from *The Papers of James Madison: His Reports of Debates in the Federal Convention*, Vol. III, p. 1390. Edited by Henry D. Gilpin. Washington, D.C.: Langtree and O'Sullivan, 1840.

Page 256 Adapted from *The Framing of the Constitution of the United States* by Max Farrand, p. 110-11. New Haven, Conn.: Yale University Press, 1913. By permission of the publisher.

Page 267 Adapted from the *Constitution of the United States.*

Page 305 Adapted from *The Works of Alexander Hamilton*, Vol. III, p. 192. Edited by Henry Cabot Lodge. New York: G. P. Putnam's Sons, 1885.

Page 306 From *Letters and Addresses of Thomas Jefferson*, edited by William Parker and Jonas Viles. The National Jefferson Society, 1903.

Page 316 Adapted from George Washington's *Farewell Address to the People of the United States.*

Page 323 Adapted from *History of the Expedition Under the Command of Captains Lewis and Clark*, Vol. II, pp. 164-5 by Paul Allen. Philadelphia: Bradford and Inskeep, 1814.

Page 342 Adapted from "The Development of the Monroe Doctrine as Monroe Stated It" in *American History Told by Contemporaries*, Vol. III, edited by Albert Bushnell Hart. New York: Macmillan Publishing Co., Inc., 1901.

Page 345 Adapted from *The Republic of the United States of America*, by Alexis deTocqueville, translated by Henry Reeves. New York: A. S. Barnes and Co., 1858.

Page 353 Adapted from *Worcester vs. Georgia* in *Peters' Reports of Cases Argued and Adjudged in the Supreme Court of the United States January Term 1832*, Vol. VI, 3rd edition, p. 556. Edited by Frederick C. Brightly. New York: Banks and Brothers, 1884.

Page 371 Adapted from *The Diary of George Templeton Strong: Young Man in New York, 1835-1849*, p. 108. Edited by Alan Nevins and Milton Halsey Thomas. Copyright 1952 by Macmillan Publishing Co., Inc., renewed 1980 by Milton Halsey Thomas. By permission of the publisher.

Page 378 Adapted from *The Welsh in America*, pp. 101-2, edited by Alan Conway. Copyright © 1961 by the University of Minnesota. Reprinted by permission of University of Minnesota Press, Minneapolis.

Page 387 Adapted from *The Lowell Offering*, pp. 52-3, edited by Benita Eisler. Philadelphia: J. B. Lippincott Company, 1977.

Page 390 Adapted from *Twelve Years a Slave* by Solomon Northrup. Baton Rouge: Louisiana State University Press, 1968. Original 1854 edition published by Miller, Orton and Mulligan, Auburn, N.Y.

Page 398 Adapted from *The Works of Orestes A. Brownson*, Vol. XVIII, pp. 388-9. Edited by Henry F. Brownson. Detroit: Thorndike Nourse, Publisher, 1885.

Page 425 Adapted from *Exploring Expedition to Oregon: Reverend Gustavus Hines*, p. 317, by Darby and Miller. Buffalo, N.Y.: Derby, 1851.

Page 428 Adapted from *Three Years in California*, pp. 246-7, by Rev. Walter Colton, U.S.N. New York: A. S. Barnes and Company, 1850.

Page 436 Adapted from *Congressional Globe*, Vol. 21, pt. 1, pp. 451, 455. U.S. Senate, 31st Congress, 1st session, 1850.

Page 442 From *The Penguin Book of American Folk Songs*, page 82, compiled and edited by Alan Lomax. Baltimore: Penguin Books, 1964. Reprinted by permission of Alan Lomax.

Page 444 Adapted from *A Defence of Negro Slavery As It Exists in the United States*, pp. 96, 153-57, by Matthew Estes. Montgomery, Ala.: Press of the *Alabama Journal*, 1846.

Page 444 Adapted from *The Impending Crisis of the South: How to Meet It*, pp. 21, 25, by Hinton Rowan Helper. New York: A. B. Burdick, 1860.

Page 447 Adapted from *Uncle Tom's Cabin: Or, Life Among the Lowly*, pp. 124-5, by Harriet Beecher Stowe. Boston: Houghton Mifflin Company, 1896.

Page 457 Adapted from *The Life and Writings of Frederick Douglass*, Vol. III, *The Civil War, 1861-1865*,. pp. 64-5, by Philip S. Foner. New York: International Publishers Co., Inc., 1952. By permission of the publisher.

Page 459 Adapted from *A Constitutional View of the Late War Between the States*, Vol. I, p. 10, by Alexander H. Stephens. Philadelphia: National Publishing Co., 1868. Chicago: Zeigler, McCordy & Co (n.d.).

Page 495 Adapted from *Been In the Storm So Long*, p. 447-8, by Leon F. Litwack. New York: Alfred A. Knopf, Inc., 1979. By permission of the publisher.

Page 510 Adaptation of "An Indian's View of Indian Affairs," by Joseph, Chief of the Nez Percés. From *North American Review*, Vol. 128, No. 269, pp. 432-3, April, 1879.

Page 511 Adapted from *A Century of Dishonor*, pp. 339-41, by Helen Hunt Jackson. New York: Harper & Row, Publishers, Inc., 1881.

Page 547 Adapted from *The First Battle: A Story of the Campaign of 1896*, Vol. I, pp. 205-6, by William J. Bryan. Port Washington, N.Y.: Kennikat Press Corporation, 1971. Reprint of the original published in 1896.

Page 603 From *The Great Boom & Panic*, p. 172, by Robert T. Patterson. Chicago: Regnery/Gateway Publishers, Inc., Book Publishers, 1965. By permission of the publisher.

Page 655 Adapted from *The Days of Martin Luther King, Jr.*, pp. 327-8, by Jim Bishop. Copyright 1971 by Jim Bishop. New York: G. P. Putnam's Sons, 1971.

PICTURE CREDITS

Courtesy Southeby Parke-Bernet **225**/ GC **212,216**/ HSP **215**/ MMA **237**(b)/ MCNY **236**(t)/ NYHS **241**(c)/ NYPL PC **211**/ Private Collection **233**/ The U.S. Naval Academy Museum **240**(b)/ Valley Forge Historical Society **239**/ Yale University Art Gallery **221,236**(b),**241**(t,b).

Section II, Unit 4
BB **260**/ Independence National Historical Collection **255**/ NYHS **249**/ NYPL: I.N. Phelps Stokes Collection, Print Collection, Art, Prints and Photographs Division **263**/ Peabody Museum of Salem, MA: Mark Sexton **251**.

Section III, Unit 1
ANS **301**/ BMC **331**(t)/ BA **312**/ CHS **322**/ CP **315**/ Issac Delgado Museum of Art; Gift of Edgar William and Bernice Chrysler Garbish **330**(b)/ HPS **314**/ LOC **304,328**/ The Mariner's Museum of Newport News, VA **331**(b)/ MHS **330**(tr)/ Missouri Historical Society **317**/ NGA: Gift of Edgar William and Bernice Chrysler Garbish **302**/ NYHS **313,324**/ NYPL: I.N. Phelps Stokes Collection, Print Collection, Art, Prints and Photographs Division **316**; Rare Books and Manuscripts Division **323**/ NYPL PC **319**/ ROM **331**(c)/ SI: National Collection of Fine Arts **308,309,332**.

Section III, Unit 2
Boston Art Commission, Faneuil Hall **350**/ Cincinnati Art Museum: Gift of Mrs. T.E. Houston **356**/ Corcoran Gallery of Art: American Collection **347**/ CP **340**/ LOC **353**/ MHS **348**/ Museum of History, Mexico City **342**/ NYHS **349**/ NYPL: Rare Books and Manuscripts Division **352**/ NYPL PC **337**/ The St. Louis Art Museum **344**.

Section III, Unit 3
GC **372**/ LOC **366,371**/ Merrimack Valley Textile Museum **360,361**/ NYPL: I.N. Phelps Stokes Collection, Print Collection, Art, Prints and Photographs Division **367**/ NYPL PC **359,362**.

Section IV, Unit 1
BA **379,391,397**(r),**400,404**/ BB **378**/ CHS **397**(l)/ Cincinnati Art Museum **407**(b)/ Cincinnati Historical Society **392**/ Bruce Coleman, Inc.: Harry Hartman **407**(tr)/ LOC **384,395**/ MHS **407**(tl)/ MMA: Morris K. Jessup Fund, 1933 **406**(t)/ MCNY **409**/ Museum of Early Southern Decorative Arts, Winston-Salem, NC **402**/ NGA: Index of American Design **381**/ NYHS **399**/ NYPL: General Research Division **410**; Rare Books and Manuscripts Division **394,406**(bl)/ NYPL PC **385**/ New York State Historical Association, Cooperstown **403**/ Courtesy of Shaker Community, Inc., Hancock Shaker Village, Pittsfield, MA **406**(br)/ Vassar College **405**/ The Whaling Museum, New Bedford, MA **386**/ Yale University Art Gallery: Mabel Brady Garvan Collection **387**.

Section IV, Unit 2
California State Library **426,427**/ Life Magazine: Herb Orth **421**(c,t)/ Los Angeles County Museum of Natural History **423**/ Museum of New Mexico **415**/ NYPL: I.N. Phelps Stokes Collection, Print Collection, Art, Prints and Photographs Division **420**(b),**421**(b),**429**/ Oregon Historical Society **424**/ Courtesy of the San Antonio Museum Association, San Antonio, TX. On loan from Bexar County **416**.

Section IV, Unit 3
BBC Hulton Picture Library **444**/ BA **440,434,446,450,451,455**/ BB **445**/ GC **433,460**/ LOC **442**(tl),**435**/ NYHS **452**/ NYPL: General Research Division **457**/ Pennsylvania Academy of the Fine Arts, Lambert Fund Purchase **456**/ Philbrook Art Center, Tulsa, OK **441**.

Section IV, Unit 4
BA **463,467,469**(bl),**484,499**/ CHS **468**(br)/ CP **473**(b)/ GC **465, 470,487,490,496**/ Harper's Weekly **477**/ The Historic New Orleans Collection **479**/ HPS **495**/ LOC **468**(br),**469**(bl),**474,482, 489,492**/ The Museum of the Confederacy **500**/ New Hampshire Historical Society **472**(b)/ NYPL: Music Division **473**(tr)/ Rutherford B. Hayes Library **497**/ South Carolina Historical Society **480**/ The Union League of Philadelphia **469**(t).

Section V, Unit 1
AMNH **511**/ BA **542,552,559**/ BB **526,540**/ CP **534,546**/ The Gilcrest Museum, Tulsa, OK **517**/ GC **541**/ HPS **528**/ International Museum at George Eastman House: Lewis Hine **537**(l,r)/ LOC **545,549,550**(br)/ Los Angeles County Museum of Natural History: History division **523**/ MMA: 1934, gift of the Alfred N. Punnett Fund and gift of George D. Pratt **556**(b); 1896, gift of H.O. Havermeyer and 1951, gift of the Louis Comfort Tiffany Foundation **556**(t)/ Museum of African Art, Washington, D.C. **555,557**(b)/ MCNY **560**/ MFA: gift of the daughters of Edward Darley Boit **557**(tl)/ National Archives **567**/ Nebraska State Historical Society: Solomon D. Butcher Collection **519**/ NYHS **525**/ NYPL: The Research Libraries **550**(l)/ NYPL PC **531,553**/ Southwest Museum **506**/ University of Illinois Library at Chicago Circle: Jane Addams Memorial Collection **520**/ Wells Fargo Bank History Dept., San Francisco **514**/ Wichita Art Museum: The Roland P. Murdock Collection **557**(tr).

Section V, Unit 2
Air Force Art Collection **583**(b)/ BA **568,573**(c,b),**579**/ BMC **581**(b)/ MCNY **578**/ CP **566,571,577,582**(br),**583**(t)/ GC **570**/ LOC **575**/ National Archives **567,581**(t),**582**(bl)/ NYPL PC **569**/ West Point Museum Collections, U.S. Military Academy **582**(tl).

Section VI, Unit 1
BB **593,598,607**/ CP **591,594,597**(tr,tl,cr,cl,bl),**605,606**/ LOC **608,614**/ MCNY **600**/ NYPL PC **609**/ Whitney Museum of American Art: Geoffrey Clements **603**.

Section VI, Unit 2
Courtesy of the AFL-CIO **639**/ BA **620,621,628**(cr,br),**633**(t),**640**/ CP **617,622,626**(tr)/ HPS **642**/ LOC **625,626**(tl),**628**(cl),**633**(b), **635**/ © Bill Mauldin, courtesy of Wil-Jo Associates **632**(bl)/ NYPL: Schomburg Center for Research and Black Culture **624**/ Wide World Photos **632**(br)/ Yivo Institute for Jewish Research **618**.

Section VI, Unit 3
George Ballis **655**/ Black Star: Owen **669**; Fred Ward **654,657**/ Courtesy of Leo Castelli Gallery, New York **683**(tr)/ Courtesy of Coe-Kerr Gallery: Private Collection **683**(tl)/ Contact Press Images: Douglas Kirkland **674,686**; NASA **685**/ Courtesy of Cortier Ekstrom Gallery: Private Collection **682**(br)/ CP **645,678**/ HPS **649**/ Courtesy of the Estate of Alexander Calder, M. Knoedler & Company Inc., N.Y. **682**(bl)/ © Messner—Rochester Times-Union **647**/ NASA **665**/ Photo Researchers: Russ Kinne **651**; Catherine Ursillo **671**/ Sygma: Barbier **679**; Brucelle **672**; Alain Dejean **666**(b); Owen Franken **676**; J.P. Laffont **666**(t); Whitney Museum of American Art: gift of the artist **682**(t); Collection **683**(b)/ Woodfin Camp & Associates: Sylvia Johnson **658**; Wally McNamee **663**; Martin Weaver **660**.

Epilogue
Image Bank: Philip Harrington **688**(tl)/ NASA **688**(tr)/ Photo Researchers: Earl Scott **688**(b).

INDEX

Drake, Francis, 87, 91
Dred Scott decision, 454
Dreiser (DRY-suhr), Theodore, 554
Du Bois (doo-BOYS), W. E. B., *550-51*
due process of law, 287
Dumbarton (DUHM-bahr-tuhn) Oaks Conference, 636
Dunbar, Paul Laurence, 553
Duncanson, Robert S., 405, *407*
Dunmore, Lord, 222
Durand, Asher B., 405
Dust Bowl, *608-09*
Dutch: colonies, 89, *131-33*, 147, 171; explorers, 89; immigrants, *382-83*
Dutch East India Company, 88
Dutch West India Company, 89, 131, 159

Eakins (AY-kinz), Thomas, 555, *556*
Earhart (AIR-hahrt), Amelia, 598
earthworks, 38
Eastern Orthodox Church, 528
Economic Opportunity Act, 658
economy (ih-KAHN-uh-mee), 23; and American System, 336-38; and Carter, 670; of colonies, 144, 155, *156, 157, 158*-63, 202; in Confederation period, 248-51; and depression, 602-03, 605; and embargo, 326; in 1840s, 413; and immigration, 378; and industry; 532; and New Deal, 617-18; of new nation, 304-05; 1920s, 594; and sectional differences, 385-93; of South, 350, 389-92, 494-95; and transportation, 366-67, 370-72; in World War II, 624
Edison, Thomas, 558
education: bilingual, 673-74; of blacks, *395*, 396, 484, *487*, 499, 550, 555, 649-50; changes in, 400-01, 555, 557; in colonies, 145-46, 169, *170*-71; federal aid to, 648; formal, 145; higher, 408; and Northwest Ordinance, 401; public, 171, 253, 345-46, *400-01, 487*, 499, 649-50; after World War II, 651
Edwards, Jonathan, 171
Eggleston, Edward, 554
Egypt, 648, 668-*69*
Eighteenth Amendment, 292, 592
Eighth Amendment, 287
Eisenhower (EYE-zuhn-how-er), Dwight D., 630, 646-50
Eisenhower Doctrine, 648
El Alamein (el ahl-uh-MAYN), 630
elastic clause, 266, 275
El Caney (el ka-NE-uh), Cuba, 572
election: (1796), 318; (1800), 320; (1804), 324; (1808), 327; (1812),
336; (1816), 336; (1820), 336; (1824), 346-*47*; (1828), 347; (1832), 355; (1836), 356; (1840), 356; (1844), 417; (1848), 434-35; (1852), 448; (1856), 451-*52*; (1860), 456-57; (1864), 476, 482; (1868), 492, 497; (1872), 497; (1876), 498-99, *541, 543*; (1880), 543; (1884), 545; (1888), 544; (1892), 547; (1896), *546*-48; (1900), 548; (1904), 565; (1908), 566; (1912), 567; (1916), 580; (1920), 593; (1924), 594; (1928), 601-02; (1932), 604-05; (1936), 610; (1940), 621; (1944), 626; (1948), *640*; (1952), *645, 646*; (1956), 646; (1960), 654; (1964), 658; (1968), 661-62; (1972), 665; (1976), 668; (1980), 675
Election Day, 279
electoral college, 278, 301, 320
electricity, *16*, 19, 23, 180, 408, 598, 613
Eleventh Amendment, 288
Eliot, John, 113-*14*, 121
Elizabeth I, Queen of England, 92, 148
Ellington, Duke, *597, 598*
Ellis Island, *526*
Ellison, Ralph, 681
El Salvador (el SAL-vuh-dor), 79, 676
emancipation (ih-man-suh-PAY-shuhn), 481
Emancipation Proclamation, 481-*82*
embargo (em-BAHR-goh), 326; oil, 666; World War II, 620
Embargo Act, 326-27
Emergency Banking Act, 607, 612
Emergency Quota Act, 595
Emerson, Ralph Waldo, 403
emigrate (EM-uh-grayt), 381
empire, 80
energy: crisis, *670*; and industry, 361; sources, 23, 532, 692
Energy, Department of, 670
English colonies: cultural life, 173-80; economy, 155-63; family life, 167-69; goverment, 107, 110, 112, 120-22, 128-29, 135-36; immigrants, 147-50; Jamestown and Virginia, 102-07; Middle colonies, 131-36, 158-59; and Native Americans, 104, 107, 110-11, 113-14, 118, 121, 127-28, 139, 193; New England, 108-22; reasons for settling, 103, 108-09; religion, 116, 123-25, 134-35, 171-72; Roanoke, 92; slavery in, 125, 151; social classes, 165-67; Southern, 123-29, 160-61; towns and cities, 162-63. *See also* British colonies
enumerated (ih-NOO-muhr-ayt-uhd) goods, 185
enumerated powers, 263, 272-75
Environmental Protection Agency, 665
equal protection of the laws, 290
Equal Rights Amendment, 671-72
Era of Good Feelings, 336
Ericson (ER-ik-suhn), Leif (LAYV), 71
Erie Canal, *368, 369-70*
Espionage (ES-pee-uh-nahzh) Act, 581
Estevanico (es-tay-vahn-EE-koh), *81*, 83
ethnic group, 524, 528
Europe: changes in, 65-69; explorations, 70-76; Monroe Doctrine, 342-43; World War I, 578-86; World War II, 617-22, 627-31, 641
evangelists (ih-VAN-juh-lists), 171
excise (EK-syz) tax, 272-73, 307, 320
executive branch, 247, 259, 264-65, 277-80
expansionism (eks-PAN-shuhn-iz-uhm), 414, 446
Explorer I, 648
explorers, 66-67, 77-87, 91
exports, 160-61, 184, 213, 250, 326, *390*, 547, 596
ex post facto law, 275
extended family, 48, 145
extradition (eks-truh-DISH-shuhn), 283

factory system, 360-61
Fair Employment Practices Commission, 626
Fair Labor Standards Act, 613
Fall, Albert, *594*
fall line, 14, *16*
Fallen Timbers, Battle of, 309-10
Farm Credit Administration, 612
farmers: alliances, 545-46; cooperatives, 545; and greenbacks, 544; and New Deal, 608, 610; pioneer, *308-09, 392-93*; Southern, 389-92; and tariff, 604; tenant, 105, 149, 159
farming, 19-22; in colonies, 99, 111, 143-44, 155, *156, 157, 158*-59, 167; decline in, 650; earliest, 31, 36-38; of future, 693; hard times for, 594; machinery, 363, 393; mid-1800s, 385; in Midwest, 393; Native American, 31, *33*-34, 37-40, 42-45, 51-54, 512; in South, 494-95; surpluses, 648
Farragut (FAR-uh-guht), David, 471
Fascist (FASH-ist) party, 619
Faulkner (FAWK-nuhr), William, 681
Fauset, Jessie, 599
Federal Communications Commission, 613
Federal Deposit Insurance Corporation, 612
Federal Emergency Relief Administration, 612

government (continued): 44-45, 49, 80; representative, 112; republican, 283. *See also* colonial government; federal government; local government; state government

grand jury, 287

grange movement, *545*-46

Grant, Ulysses S.: in Civil War, 464, 471-75; President, 492, 497, 536

Gray, Robert, 424

Great American Desert, 423, 506

Great Awakening, 171-*72*

Great Basin culture region, 34-*35*, 47-50

Great Britain: and Canada, 340; during Civil War, 481; colonial territories, *198-99, 242*; in Confederation period, 250; control of American colonies, *183*-90; and Florida, 341; and France, 193-94; French and Indian War, 194-99; immigrants from, 382-83, 526, 529; industrial revolution in, 359-60; Jay's Treaty, 314-15; name changed to, 127; and Oregon, 424, 426; and U.S. sea rights, 325-27; World War I, 579-85, World War II, 619, 630, 635. *See also* British colonies; Revolutionary War; War of 1812

Great Compromise, 258

Great Lakes, 88-89, 91, 194, 393

Great Plains, *13*-15, 19, 423, 428, 448, 517

Great Potato Famine, 380

Great Salt Lake Valley, 429

Great Sioux Reservation, 507

Great Society, *658*

Great Valley, 154

Great Wagon Road, *152, 154,* 161, 367-*68*

Greece, 641; immigrants from, 529

Greeley (GREE-lee), Horace, 497

Green, Anne Catherine Hoof, 168

Green, George F., 558

Greenback party, 498, 543

Greenback-Labor party, 543-44

greenbacks, 478, 544

Greene, Catherine, 362

Green Mountain Boys, 220

Greenville, Treaty of, 310

Grenville, George, 200, 202-05

Grimke, Angelina and Sarah, 404, 440-41

Guadalcanal (gwahd-uhl-kuh-NAHL), *632, 634*

Guadalupe Hidalgo (gwahd-uh-LOO-pay ee-DAHL-goh), Treaty of, 419, 427, 516

Guam (GWAHM), 574, 631

guerrilla (guh-RIL-uh) warfare, 659-60, 676

Gulf Coastal Plain, *13*-14, 19

Gulf of Tonkin (TAHN-kin) Resolution, 660

Gutenberg (GOOT-uhn-berg), Johann, 67

Guthrie (GUHTH-ree), Oklahoma, 513

haciendas (hah-see-EN-duhs), 101, 144

Haiti (HAY-tee), 75, 322, 576

Half-Breeds, 543

Halleck, Henry W., 471

Hamilton, Alexander: and Burr, 324; Constitutional Convention, 255; Federalist, 261; Secretary of the Treasury, 303-06; view of America, 359

Hampton Institute, 488

Hancock, Winfield Scott, 543

Hansberry, Lorraine, 681

Harding, Warren G., 592-94

Harlem Renaissance (ren-uh-SAHNS), *597,* 598

Harper, Frances, 404

Harrison, Benjamin, 537, 544-45

Harrison, William Henry, 326-27, 356, 544

Harte, Bret, 554

Hartford Convention, 329, 332

Harvard College, 170

Hat Act, 186

Hawaii: 14-15, *17,* 22, 571, 622

Hawthorne, Nathaniel, 403-04

Hay, John, 575

Hayes, Rutherford B., 498, 542-43

Haymarket Riots, 538-39

Health, Education, and Welfare, Department of, 648

Hearst, William Randolph, 553-54

Hellman, Lillian, 681

Hemingway, Ernest, 599

Henry, Joseph, 408

Henry, Patrick, *203*-4, 215, 255 261

Henry Street Settlement House, 524

Henry the Navigator, 72-73, 75

Henry VIII, King of England, 69, 109

Hepburn Act, 565

heritage (HER-uh-tij), 380

Herulfsson (HAR-yuhlf-suhn), Bjarni (bee-YAR-nee), 71

Hesselius (he-SEE-lih-uhs), Gustavus, *175*

Hillman, Sidney, 608

Hine, Lewis, *537*

Hiroshima (hee-roh-SHEE-muh), 634

Hispanic Americans, 673-74. *See also* Chicanos; Cuba; land grants; Mexican Americans; Puerto Rico; Spain

historical map, 76

historical time period, 336

Hitler, Adolf, 618-21

Ho Chi Minh (HO CHEE MIN), 659

Hohokam (hoh-HOH-kuhm), *52, 53*

Holocaust (HAHL-uh-cawst), *618,* 630-31

Holy Experiment, 135

Holy Land, 66, 72

Home Loan Bank Act, 604

Home Owners Loan Corporation, 612

Homer, Winslow, 555

Homestead Act, 515

Homestead Steel Strike, 539

Honduras (hahn-DUR-uhs), 74-75, 79

Hooker, Joseph, 474

Hooker, Thomas, *117*

Hoover, Herbert, 580, 601-05

Hopewell culture, *39*

Hopi (HOH-pee), *35,* 54-*55, 512,* 611

House of Burgesses (BER-jih-sez), 107, 109, 204

House of Representatives: *347;* apportionment, 267-68; and Constitution, 264; defined, 258; election of, 267; free v. slave states (1800-1850), *438;* officers, 268; qualifications, 267; vacancies, 268

Housing and Urban Development, Department of (HUD), 659

housing development, *651*

Howard University, 555

Howe, Elias, *359,* 363

Howe, Julia Ward, 548

Howe, Samuel Gridley, 401

Howe, William, 220, 224

Howells, William Dean, 554

Hudson, Henry, 88-91

Hudson River School, 405

Huerta (oo-ER-tuh), Victoriano, 576

Hughes, Charles Evans, 580

Hughes, Langston, 599

Huguenots (HYOO-guh-nahts), 150

Hull House, *520,* 524

human rights, 668

Humphrey, Hubert H., 640, 662

Hungary, 637; immigrants from, 527, 529

Hunkpapa Sioux, 509

Hurons (HYUR-uhns), 86, 193

Hutchinson, Anne, *116*-17

Hutchinson, Thomas, 212-13

hypothesis (hy-PAHTH-uh-sis), 459

Idaho, 49, 506-07, 509, 515

Ife (EE-fay), Kingdom of, *151*

ILGWU, 538

Illinois, 24, 193, 253, 363, 381, 454, 477, 532; statehood, 344

immigrants (IM-uh-gruhnts), 7, *378;* adapting to new life, *528*-30; Asians, *530, 590;* and cities, 378, 521; in colonies, 147-53, 159-60,

representative government, 112, 189
republic, 311, 427
Republican party, 496, *541-44*, 547-48, 566-67, 580, 593-94, 601, 605, 610, 640, 654, 658, 668, 675; creation of, 451
reservations (reh-zer-VAY-shuhns), 351, 429, 507-08, *611*
Reuther (ROO-thuhr), Walter, *639-40*
Revels, Hiram R., *496-97*
Revere, Paul, *174, 202, 207, 217*
reverse discrimination, 674-75
revolution (rev-uh-LOO-shuhn), 208, 213, 311, 320, 391
Revolutionary War: advantages and disadvantages, 235; background, 211-25; blacks in, *221,* 232-33; building an army, *231,* 232-34; Declaration of Independence, 224-30; fighting, 231-42; financing, 234; foreign support, 220, 234; Native Americans and, 233-34; peace treaty, 242; results, 242, *251;* women in, *233*
"revolution of 1800," 320
Revolution of 1830, 381
Revolution of 1848, 381
Rhineland (RYN-land), 619
Rhode Island, 116-17, 122, 171, 188-89, 222, 255, 261
Richmond, Virginia, 372, 471, 494, 521-22
right of deposit, 315, 321
Riis (REES), Jacob, 524, 565
Rillieux (rihl-YOO), Norbert, 363
Rio Grande (REE-oh GRAND), 54, 97, 414, 418, *421*
riots, urban, 659
Roaring Twenties, 592
rock and roll, 684
Rockefeller, John D., 535, 565
Rockefeller, Nelson, 666
Rocky Mountains, *13*-14, 323, 419, 423-24, 428, 506
Roethke, Theodore, 681
role, 40
Rolfe, John, 105
Roman Catholic Church, 65-66, 69, 109, 123-25, 171, 178, 189, 192, 214; immigrants and, 380, 383-84, 528
romanticism (roh-MAN-tuh-siz-uhm), 403, 405
Rommel (RAHM-uhl), Erwin, 630
Roosevelt (ROH-zuh-velt), Eleanor, 610
Roosevelt, Franklin D., 294, 593, 605, *635;* New Deal, 606-10; World War II, 621, 634
Roosevelt, Theodore, 548, 564-67, 572, 575-76
Roosevelt Corollary, 576
Rough Riders, 572
Royal African Company, 125, 151

royal colony, 107, 122, 128-29, 133, 188-89
Ruggles, David, 440
Rumania, 637; immigrants from, 527, 529
Rural Electrification Administration, 613
Rush, Benjamin, 405
Rush-Bagot (BAG-uht) Agreement, 340
Russia, *242;* immigrants from, 527, 529; and Oregon, 424; World War I, 579. *See also* Soviet Union
Ruth, Babe, *597*

Sabin (SAY-bin), Albert, 685
sabotage (SAB-uh-tahzh), 282
Sacajawea (sak-uh-juh-WEE-uh), 322-23
Sacramento, California, 428, 532
Sadat (suh-DAT), Anwar, 668-69
sagas (SAH-guhs), 71
St. Augustine (AW-guhs-teen), 96, *142*
Saint-Gaudens (saynt-GOH-duhnz), August, 555
St. Lawrence River and Valley, 86, 88, 91, 191-94
St. Louis, 322, 381, *522*
Saint Mihiel (SAHN mee-YEL), 585
Salem, Peter, *221*
Salish (SAY-lish), *62*
Salk (SAWK), Jonas, 685
SALT: I, 662; II, 663, 666, 668
Samoset (SAM-oh-set), 110-11
San Antonio (sahn ahn-TOH-nyoh), 100, *142, 416,* 674
Sand Creek Massacre, 508
San Diego (san dee-AY-goh), 86, 101, *142,* 419
San Francisco, 87, 91, 101, *142,* 428-29, 521; population growth, *522*
San Jacinto (san juh-SIN-toh), Battle of, 417, *420*
San Juan Hill, 572, *573*
San Salvador (san Sal-vuh-dor), 74
Santa Anna (SAHN-tah AH-nah), Antonio Lopez de, 416-17
Santa Fe, 97, 99, *100, 142, 415*
Santa Fe Ring, 516
Santa Fe Trail, *414*-15
Santee Sioux, *35,* 508, 512
Santiago (sahn-TYAH-goh), Cuba, 572, *573*
santos (SAN-tohs), 175
Sarajevo (SAH-rah-ye-voh), 579
Saratoga, New York, *237,* 238
Sargent, John Singer, 555, *557*
satellite (SAT-uh-lyt): political, 637; space, 654, 690
Sauk (SAWK), *35,* 309-*10, 352, 611*
Savannah, Georgia, *128,* 150, 156, 160, 166, 391
scalawag (SKAL-uh-wag), 496

scale (map), 11
Scandinavia (skan-duh-NAY-vee-uh), 70; immigrants from, 383, 526, 529
science, 179-80, 405-06, 558, 685
Scotch-Irish, 148-49
Scott, Dred, 454
Scott, Winfield, 419-20, 448
seasoning (slavery), 153
secede (sih-SEED), 332, 433, 443, 457, 483-84
Second Amendment, 286
secondary source, 143, *202-03, 225, 249,* 256, *420, 575*
Second Bank of the U.S., 337-38, 354-55
Second Continental Congress, 219-24, 231-32, 234, 242, 246
Second Seminole War, 354
sectionalism (SEK-shuhn-uhl-iz-uhm), 252-53, 328, 335, 338, 433-38
Securities and Exchange Commission, 613
Sedition (suh-DISH-uhn), Act, *319;* World War I, 581
segregation (seg-ruh-GAY-shuhn), 449, 450, 499, 640, 649-50, 655
Selective Service Act, 581
Selective Training and Service Act, 621, 623
self-government, 110-11, 113, 117, 135, 192, 214, 574, 610
Seminole (SEM-uh-nohl), *35,* 309, *310, 340,* 341, 352, 354, 470, 513, *611*
Senate, 258; and Constitution, 264, 268-69; election, 268; impeachment trials, 269; officers, 269; President of, 269; qualifications, 269; term of service, 268-69
Seneca (SEN-uh-kuh), *35,* 40, 470, *611*
Seneca Falls Convention, 398
"separate but equal," 549-50, 649
sequence of events, 34
Sequoyah (sih-KWOY-uh), *353*
Serbia, 579; immigrants from, 529
Serra (SER-uh), Fray Junipero, 101
Seven Cities of Cibola (SEE-boh-luh), 54, 83
Seventeenth Amendment, 291, 566
Seventh Amendment, 287
Seward (SOO-erd), William, 570
Seymour (SEE-mor), Horatio, 492
Shakers, *407*
sharecropper, 494-95, 609
Shawnee (shaw-NEE), *35,* 309-*10, 327-28, 354*
Shays's Rebellion, 248-*49*
Shepard, Alan, 654
Sherman, Roger, 225, 255
Sherman, William T., 475
Sherman Antitrust Act, 535, 537, *566*

Supreme Court, 264, 279-82, 321, 353, 659; *Brown* ruling, 649-50; Dred Scott case, 454; Nixon tapes, 665; "packing" plan, 611; *Plessy* v. *Ferguson*, 549-50; and Sioux, 673; and sit-down strike, 608; and trusts, 564

surplus (SER-pluhs), 60

Sutter's Mill, 427

Sweden, 383; colonies, 130, 133, 147

Swiss immigrants, 148, 383

Sylvis, William, 538

Taft, William Howard, 566

Taft-Hartley Act, 639

Taiwan, 642, 663, 669

Tanner, Henry Ossawa, 555, *557*

Tarbell, Ida M., 565

tariff (TAR-if), 304; of Abominations, 350-51; Coolidge and, 594; protective, 336-37, 350; Payne-Aldrich, 566; reform, 543-45; Smoot-Hawley, 604; Underwood, 567

taxation: and cities, 651; colonial, 122, 132, 184-86, 188, 190, 202-04, 216; and Constitution, 275-76

taxation without representation, *203-04*

Taylor, Zachary, 418, *433*, 435-36

Tea Act, 213

technology, 389-93, 596-98, 646, 685-86, 690-93

Tecumseh (tih-KUHM-suh), 327-38

television, 654, 659, 672, *678-79*, 685, 692

temperance (TEM-puhr-uhns) movement, 399, 404, 592

tenement, 522-23

Tennessee, 40, 83, 308, 367, 395; Reconstruction, 484; secession, 458

Tennessee Valley Authority (TVA), *609*, 612

Tenskwatawa (ten-SKWAH-tah-wah), the Prophet, 327

Tenth Amendment, 264, 288

Teton (TEE-tuhn) Sioux, *35*, 45, *321*, 508-09, *512*

Texas, 82-84, 97, 100-01, 142, 414, *422*, 436, 506, 509, 517, 532; Reconstruction, 493; as republic, 416-17; secession, 458; statehood, 417

Thames (TEMZ), Battle of the, 328

Thayendanegea (thuh-yen-duh-NAY-gih-uh), 233

theater, 180, 203, 408, 559

Third Amendment, 286

third party, 542, 662, 675

Thirteenth Amendment, 289, 485, 550

Thomas, Piri, 681

Thoreau (THOR-oh), Henry David, 403

three-fifths clause, 259, 267-68

Three Mile Island accident, 670

Thurmond, Strom, 640

Tidewater, 153-54

Tiffany, Louis Comfort, *556*

Tilden (TIL-duhn), Samuel J., 498, 525

time line, 34, 55

time zone, *533*

Timucua (tim-uh-KOO-uh), 97

Tippecanoe (tip-ih-kuh-NOO), Battle of, 327-*28*

Tlingit, *35*, 61-62

Tocqueville (tawk-VEEL), Alexis de, 344-45

Tojo (toh-joh), Hideki, 622

Toleration (tahl-uhr-AY-shuhn) Act, 125

Tompkins, Sally Louisa, 467

Tordesillas (tord-uh-SEE-yuhs), Treaty of, 78

Tories, *216*, 218, 222, 224, 232-33, 242, 314

totalitarian (toh-tal-uh-TAIR-ee-uhn) state, 619

totem (TOH-tuhm) poles, *59*, 61, *183*

Tourgee (toor-ZHAY), Albion, 549-50

Toussaint L'Ouverture (TOO-san loo-ver-TYOOR), Pierre, 322

Townshend (TOWN-zuhnd) Acts, 205-08, *211*, 212-13, 229

tract houses, *651*

trade, 36; balance of, 184; colonial, 99-100, 122, 159-62, 183-86; in Confederation period, 249-51; European, 66-67; foreign, *326*; laws, 184-86; Native American, 39, 43-44, 49-51, 61-62

trade routes: *67, 161*

tradition (truh-DISH-uhn), 10, 40, 79, 164, 221, 380, 383, 610

Trail of Tears, 354

transportation, 413, 692; and growth of Midwest, 392-93; and industry, 24; revolution in, 365-72, 378

Transportation, Department of, 659

treason, 282

treaty, 78; and Constitution, 259, 264. *See also* names of treaties

trench warfare, 584

trends, 652, 689

Trenton, New Jersey, *237*, 238

trial by jury, 282, 287

Triangular Trade, 151, 160-*61*, 203

Tripartite (try-PAHR-tyt) Pact, 621

Triple Alliance, 579

Triple Entente (ahn-TAHNT), 579

Truman, Harry S, 624, 634, *640-42*, 646

Trumbull, John, *221*, 405

trust, 535, 564

Truth, Sojourner, 398, 404, 440

Tubman, Harriet, *442*

Turkey, 641; immigrants from, 529

Turner, Nat, 443

turnpike, 368

Tuscarora (tuhs-kuh-ROR-uh), *35, 40*, 127-28, 233, *611*

Tuscarora War, 127-28

Tuskegee (tuhs-KEE-gee) Institute, *550, 555*

Tweed, William, "Boss," *525*

Twelfth Amendment, 288-89, 320, 344, *347*

Twentieth Amendment, 292-93, 605

Twenty-fifth Amendment, 295-96, 665

Twenty-first Amendment, 293-94, 592

Twenty-fourth Amendment, 294-95

Twenty-second Amendment, 294

Twenty-sixth Amendment, 296, 664

Twenty-third Amendment, 294, 658

Tyler, John, 356, 417

Tyler, Royall, 408

tyranny (TIR-uh-nee), 204

U-boat, 580

unalienable rights, 227

Uncle Tom's Cabin, 446-47

underground railroad, *441-42*

Underwood Tariff, 567

unemployment, 361, *404*, 410, 414, *603-04, 624, 639, 659, 664, 666*, 670, 675

Union, the, 311; in Civil War, 463-75; in 1861, *458*; reconstructed, 493; and sectionalism, 433

Union Pacific Railroad, 532, 536

United Automobile Workers, 640

United Farm Workers, 674

United Mine Workers, 639

United Nations, 636-37, 646, 648

U.S. Steel Corporation, 536, 565-66

universities, 146, 170-71, 401, 408

unskilled worker, 151, 162, 165, 389, 396, 487, 529, 608

urbanization (er-buhn-uh-ZAY-shuhn), 520-21

urban renewal, 659

U.S.S.R. *See* Soviet Union

Utah, 53, 419, 429-30, 436, 506-08, 548; statehood, 515

Utah Territory, 430, 437-38

Ute, *35, 509*

utopian (yoo-TOH-pee-uhn) community, 399-400

Valley Forge, Pennsylvania, *237, 238*

values, 58

Van Buren, Martin, 353, 355-56, 434

van Rensellaer (vahn REN-suh-lahr), Maria, 132

vaudeville (VAW-duh-vil), 559-60